Things Unattempted Yet in Prose or Rhyme

First Edition

Ian Blake Newhem, Editor

SUNY Rockland Community College

Copyright © 2012 University Readers, Inc. All rights reserved. No part of this publication may be reprinted, reproduced, transmitted, or utilized in any form or by any electronic, mechanical, or other means, now known or hereafter invented, including photocopying, microfilming, and recording, or in any information retrieval system without the written permission of University Readers, Inc.

Copyedits by Barbara Benitez, Mount Holyoke College, and Roxy Moskowitz, SUNY Rockland.

First published in the United States of America in 2012 by University Readers, Inc.

Trademark Notice: Product or corporate names may be trademarks or registered trademarks, and are used only for identification and explanation without intent to infringe.

16 15 14 13 12   1 2 3 4 5

Printed in the United States of America

ISBN: 978-1-60927-337-8

Contents

Introduction: Things Unattempted Yet in Prose or Rhyme	3
On Literary Criticism	7
Ian Blake Newhem	
On Writing the Literary Analysis Paper	19
Katherine E. Lynch	
On Critical Reading	23
Clifford L. Garner	
On the Use of Periods in the Analysis of Literature	27
Clifford L. Garner	

Poetry   31

General Prologue	33
Geoffrey Chaucer	
The Knight's Tale	56
Geoffrey Chaucer	
The Wife of Bath's Prologue and Tale	117
Geoffrey Chaucer	
Sonnet 18, Sonnet 116, and Sonnet 130	152
William Shakespeare	
The Canonization	152
John Donne	
A Valediction: Forbidding Mourning	153
John Donne	
Good Friday, 1613. Riding Westward	154
John Donne	
Lycidas	155
John Milton	
Paradise Lost, Books 1–5	158
John Milton	
To His Coy Mistress	260
Andrew Marvell	

A Modest Proposal Jonathan Swift	261
The Rape of the Lock Alexander Pope	266
An Essay on Criticism Alexander Pope	276
Elegy Written in a Country Churchyard Thomas Gray	285
The Lamb William Blake	287
The Tyger William Blake	287
London William Blake	288
Lines Composed a Few Miles Above Tintern Abbey William Wordsworth	289
The World is Too Much with Us William Wordsworth	292
London William Wordsworth	292
Composed upon Westminster Bridge William Wordsworth	293
Ode on a Grecian Urn John Keats	294
Dover Beach Matthew Arnold	296
Poems Emily Dickinson	297
God's Grandeur Gerard Manley Hopkins	304
The Windhover Gerard Manley Hopkins	304
The Second Coming William Butler Yeats	305
Sailing to Byzantium William Butler Yeats	306
Out, Out— Robert Frost	307
Stopping by Woods on a Snowy Evening Robert Frost	308
Home Burial Robert Frost	309

The Road Not Taken Robert Frost	311
The Love Song of J. Alfred Prufrock T. S. Eliot	312
The Waste Land T. S. Eliot	315
Dulce et Decorum Est Wilfred Owen	324
Musée des Beaux-Arts W. H. Auden	325
Skunk Hour Robert Lowell	326
Diving into the Wreck Adrienne Rich	327
Daddy Sylvia Plath	328
Lady Lazarus Sylvia Plath	330

FICTION 333

Young Goodman Brown Nathaniel Hawthorne	335
The Cask of Amontillado Edgar Allan Poe	342
The Black Cat Edgar Allan Poe	346
Bartleby the Scrivener Herman Melville	351
A Simple Heart Gustave Flaubert	371
The Necklace Guy De Maupassant	388
The Yellow Wallpaper Charlotte Perkins Gilman	393
The Open Boat Stephen Crane	402
The Second Choice Theodore Dreiser	415
The Metamorphosis Franz Kafka	426

Odour of Chrysanthemums D. H. Lawrence	451
A Rose for Emily William Faulkner	462
The Dead James Joyce	467
Araby James Joyce	489
A Painful Case James Joyce	492
The Lottery Shirley Jackson	497
A Conversation with My Father Grace Paley	502
Lost in the Funhouse John Barth	505
The Kugelmass Episode Woody Allen	518
What We Talk About When We Talk About Love Raymond Carver	524
Happy Endings Margaret Atwood	531
Rape Fantasies Margaret Atwood	533
The Crevasse Bernardo Atxaga	538

Introduction: Things Unattempted Yet in Prose or Rhyme

The more sophisticated among college Composition and Literature readers might find at first the assertion that "literature is life" sinks into the trite abyss. But for those students lacking confidence in their critical abilities, the statement might instead smack of the kind of dandified romantic notions to which English professors seem wont to resort—and to which the average student, not possessing the magic key to unlock the likes of Shakespeare, Milton, or Melville, will probably never succumb. Yet the idea that literature behaves more like a living organism than some inert contrivance provides a useful analogy for our purposes here.

For one thing, the art of literary criticism (looking into, evaluating, and writing about texts) shares the same basic tenets and techniques as many other forms of human interaction with the world. We meet new people with personalities and behaviors that we must figure out as we move on with our relationships. We visit new places with new topographies and cultures that we have to navigate, with one part thrill and one part trepidation. We embark on new academic courses and new jobs and new adventures, all of which require us to learn novel and increasingly complex tactics, and often whole new languages, in order to achieve something akin to mastery. So, too, do we encounter new authors, new texts, new forms of writing, and new methods of reading and criticizing.

Ultimately, our experience negotiating all these endeavors coalesces in subjective *judgment*. After learning all we could learn about the person, place, course, occupation, adventure, or text, what did we think? Thumbs up or thumbs down? Either way, can we articulate *why*? Did we consider the time we spent valuable? Did we learn something about the world, about art, about ourselves? Did we change somehow? And if so, how? Note that no two people will ever come up with the exact same answers to those critical questions. In many ways, the questions matter more than the answers. In other words, your professor will teach you *what to look for* as you read. What you *find* there is another matter entirely.

You might wonder, why bother criticizing literature at all? Why not just enjoy it—or even ignore it? And why do we have to *go so deep*? The easiest answer is: That's what we do in the study of English. We wouldn't ask a biochemist why she goes "so deep" in her study of her chosen subject, would we? In *Western Wind: An Introduction to Poetry*, poet and professor John Frederick Nims writes:

> There are people who think that knowledge destroys their spontaneous reaction to anything beautiful. They are seldom right; generally, the more we know, the more we see to appreciate. There are people who think that to analyze a poem or, as they like to say, to "tear it apart," is

to destroy it. But one no more destroys a poem by means of analysis than one destroys birds or flowers or anything else by means of a diagram.[1]

On the contrary, if you're interested in birds, that diagram helps you identify their components, helps you label them so you can use the language of an ornithologist, and helps you tell the difference between a Glaucous Gull and a Long-tailed Jaeger.

So, too, with an analysis of literature. The aim of literary criticism is, first and foremost, a deeper "understanding," and at least, a fuller *appreciation* of literature. You learn how to *see more*, to *get more* out of texts, to *uncover* and *create* richer, denser, more interesting "meanings."

To this end, your professor will open for you a new toolbox full of implements particularly effective for putting together (and sometimes taking apart) literature and your thoughts about it. Not the least of these tools will be a thoroughgoing review of the rhetorical modes (compare/contrast, persuasion, process analysis, etc.) you learned in your Composition 101 course, as well as more advanced training in research and essay writing, this time focused on literature. The director of the Sam Draper Mentor/Talented Students Honors Program at SUNY Rockland employs this analogy: In 101, we teach you how to make serviceable tables and chairs—the sort you might find in the cafeteria of a summer camp. But in 102, we teach you how to build the Taj Mahal. Similarly, while in 101 you merely scratched the surface of critical writing, in 102 you will catapult your critical skills exponentially further.

Along those lines, you will become familiar with a host of methods to help you tackle the texts you read. For example, your professor might concentrate on **period**. Because texts are situated historically, socially, and intellectually *during their time*, we might ask questions such as, What can we learn about this text from a knowledge of the sociopolitical, cultural, or religious events of the time during which the writer wrote the text? What, for example, are the salient characteristics of the Romantic movement manifest in its poetry—as opposed to, say, the Naturalist, Realist, or Modernist movements?

Instead, your professor might highlight **genre** and **form** as key places to begin a study of literature. Different forms and genres have diverse aims, conventions, and attributes. So we might ask, What are the forms and functions of sonnets in juxtaposition to elegies? What's the difference between the epic and the epistolary forms, and where might they converge? How are the elements of fiction—such as tone, characterization, point of view, and figurative language—similar to the building blocks of drama, and where do they diverge?

Finally, your professor might emphasize **critical theory**. What are the various lenses—deconstructionist, New Historical, Psychoanalytical, etc.—through which we might evaluate each text and author? A critical approach might focus exclusively on the constituent parts of the work itself, and how they hold together (such as in Formalist criticism). Or it might come to the work with a set of coherent, preconceived assumptions, values, or beliefs stated up front (as in Feminist or Marxist criticism).

More likely, your professor will teach you to synthesize all these approaches, as well as others, into a unified method you can employ to increase your experience of reading and writing about texts.

Just don't forget: You will find these texts firmly set in the human theater in which you already play at least a walk-on part. These characters—not to mention their authors—are grounded in the same anguish and elation of the human struggle that you already have begun to understand as you look critically at your own life and the lives of those around you. You will find all the existential quandaries that we share across the ages and the pages (despite major differences related to period): Who are we? Where did we come from? Where are we going? How should we think of ourselves? How should we treat others? Are we alone? Is the world just? Does evil exist? Why do so many suffer, yet some are spared? What happens after we die?

For this reason, and notwithstanding the many complexities you will encounter this semester, the

---

[1] Nims, John Frederick. *Western Wind: An Introduction to Poetry.* New York: Random House, 1983.

literature you read and analyze becomes inevitably about you, because it *informs* you, becoming part of you. So what moves you? What horrifies you? What angers you? What makes you laugh? What provides for you, as Robert Frost suggests of a good poem, "a momentary stay against confusion?"[2]

    Ian Blake Newhem
    The Sam Draper Mentor/Talented Students Honors Program
    SUNY Rockland Community College
    November 2010

---

[2] Frost, Robert. "The Figure a Poem Makes." 1939.

On Literary Criticism

By Ian Blake Newhem

In addition to our continuing study of Composition and the Rhetorical Modes, Literary Criticism will form the core of our exploration of English from this point forward. Let's define some key terms here. "Literature" is easy: That's just the fancy English teacher word for the piece of writing we have in front of us. Another word for that is the "text." It might be a poem, a short story, an essay, a play, a novel, a picture book, a film, or some other type of text. "Criticism" is a bit more complex. In this context, it doesn't necessarily mean "the finding of fault." It means *to look into and evaluate* something. So Literary Criticism means to look into and evaluate texts.

Let's break that down further. "Looking into" is the first thing we do in a Literature course. *Why* do we look into literature? In order to enjoy it more, but also in order to "*eval*uate" it. Note the root there, which shares a meaning with the word "value." We *look into* literature and then place a *value* on it. Do we like the text? Would we publish it? Anthologize it? Teach it? Share it with our children? Pay for it? Tattoo it on our skin? Stop reading it? Ignore it? Censor it? Ban it? Burn it? You get the idea.

The study of Literary Criticism is really the study of the approaches and methods we use to answer those questions, the lenses through which we look to find sensible, defensible answers. In short, Literary Criticism is about *what*, *why*, and *how* we read.[1] Let's look at the basic premises of Literary Criticism, as depicted in the following diagram—sometimes called the Discourse Triangle or the Rhetorical Triangle, which I call the Triangle of Literary Criticism:

The Triangle of Literary Criticism (TLC)

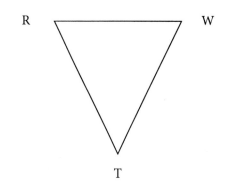

R=Reader / W=Writer / T=Text

In order to both look into and evaluate literature, we need to consider three distinct but interdependent aspects of the experience of literature. First, we need a Text. We need the poem itself. If it's yet unwritten, or just sitting in a poet's pocket, we can neither

---

1 Richter, David H. *Falling into Theory: Conflicting Views on Reading Literature.* Boston: Bedford/St. Martins, 1994.

look into it nor evaluate it. However, if we have a Text in front of us, we've got all kinds of things to look into. How is it put together? What words have been deployed and to what effect? How well do the beginning, middle, and end parts work together? All valid questions, but the questioning can't stop there. Texts don't simply "exist" in a vacuum. And magical leprechauns don't create Texts. Writers do. So we need to consider the Writer, too. What were her intentions in creating the text? Social commentary? Irony? Revenge? Hooking up? Who was she, and when, why, and how did she write? What else did she write? Lastly, all these questions we're asking remind us that there is an "us" in this equation: a Reader. A Writer writes a Text, but a Reader is required to look into and evaluate that Text. And at that point, we enter into the realm of individual interpretation. Why does one Reader put up his thumb and another put it down? How do Readers complete the triangle to make "meaning" out of mere squiggles on a page? The various forms of Literary Criticism fall closer or farther away from one or more of the three parts of the TLC. Perhaps the most useful and enduring ones are those that take into account all three aspects. In any case, when you as a student of Literature practice Literary Criticism, you should be clear about your location on the TLC.

Conceptualizing Critical Approaches

Just as there are various and often contradictory approaches to Politics—Republicanism, Libertarianism, Totalitarianism, etc.—so, too, can we approach a text with widely divergent attitudes. It's important to realize that none of the approaches to Literary Criticism is "right" or "wrong," and that they typically don't work in black and white ways, but usually in shades of grey. They fall in and out of vogue depending upon the temperament of scholars and critics, and as periods wax and wane, lending themselves to certain forms of criticism. They also tend to overlap each other, or at least incorporate features of each other, though they also often conflict, sometimes simultaneously. Finally, know that most individual critics don't remain pigeonholed for long. They tend to move from "school" to "school" of criticism throughout their careers.

Picture a filing cabinet called "Approaches to Literary Criticism." Now imagine for a moment that each critical approach comes as a set of more or less clear instructions for looking into and evaluating Texts. We find each approach in a separate file folder in that cabinet, labeled with its name, say "Post-Colonial Criticism." Remember, all of the folders are critical approaches. But if we remove one folder, we'll find directions for *that* form, instructions on what to do with a literary Text while employing that form of Literary Criticism. If we use those instructions for looking into a certain text, we're going to discover things about the text that we might not find were we to have used a different critical approach, another set of instructions. Our "evaluation," too, might be different, depending on the approach. This is important to realize. We know a person evaluating from a Democratic perspective will judge a political candidate quite differently from one employing a Republican perspective. So, too, will a Formalist critic evaluate, say, the *Harry Potter* novels, differently from a Christian critic. Note here that we need not *be* Democrats to attempt to evaluate a candidate or policy from a Democratic *perspective*. We need only understand the basic tenets of the Democratic philosophy. We can say, even if we're Communists, "According to the Democratic rulebook, that's a near perfect Democratic policy, except for that one feature, which violates a hallmark principle of the Democratic party." Same goes for looking into and evaluating Texts. We need not ourselves subscribe to a Feminist philosophy to criticize a Text using the rulebook of Feminist Criticism.

Here's another way of conceptualizing it. Think about each approach to Literary Criticism as a different-colored lens through which we might look into and evaluate a text. One set of lenses helps bring into focus certain facets or features of a given text (say, adherence to a Jewish moral code), whereas another set of lenses emphasizes what might be a wholly different aspect of the text (such as the relative power of rich characters over poor ones). We can mix and match the lenses the way an optometrist provides us many combinations of lenses until we see clearly the Text on the wall.

It's important to remember that two people employing the same critical approach will not necessarily find the same things while looking into a Text, nor will they necessarily evaluate a Text in the same way. So, for example, one Christian literary critic might like the *Harry Potter* novels because of their strong ethical implications, their concentration on a misunderstood and reluctant Messianic figure, and the triumph of good over evil. But another Christian critic might object to the supernatural elements of the story on the grounds that they're bordering on the Satanic.

The Mega 10 Forms of Literary Criticism

There are scores of forms of Literary Criticism—probably even more than that. Here we're going to discuss—in brief—some basic approaches we're going to encounter in the class lectures and the criticism we read, and with which we're going to need to become familiar in our own criticism of the Texts in this anthology. We're going to call these common forms "The Mega 10." Each represents a well-known, relatively distinct, and articulated approach to looking into and evaluating literature. Below are the very basic outlines for the Mega 10. They're much more complex and multifaceted than we have room for here. We'll discuss them in much more detail in class.

FORMALIST CRITICISM	
Locus on TLC	T
Mastery/Mystery	Easy to use; moderately hard to master
Other names / Related Forms	New Criticism
Genesis	1910
Heyday	1930s–50s and continuing to present
Bumper-Sticker Slogan	"It's right there in black and white!"
Progenitor	Joel Spingarn (Columbia University)
Principal proponents	T.S. Eliot, Ezra Pound, Cleanth Brooks, John Crowe Ransom, Wayne C. Booth
Associated Places	Britain, America ("The Chicago School"), Russia (Russian Formalism)
Outline	The clue is in the name: Formalism cherishes the *form* of the Text, meaning the internal structure, also known as "the arrangement of the parts." Formalist critics posit that Texts are independent and "autonomous" of any outside influences, including the Reader's idiosyncrasies and the "sovereignty of the author"[2] necessary for historical- and biographical-based forms of criticism. Scrupulous Readers should systematically look into each individual Text "in itself," aesthetically, without regard to period or other groupings. These critics argue that by conducting rigorous "close readings," Readers can "understand" Texts that are "unified wholes" embodying "universal values."
Formalist Criticism in Action	The Text, *Madame Bovary* might meet the "masterpiece" test of a Formalist critic because of its structure: the words deployed, the internal resonances, the interconnectedness of elements in the beginning, middle, and end.
Pros	It's all there right in black and white for you to discover. Everything you need to know is in the Text alone. If you can't find it there, it doesn't exist. And the "closer" you read, the more likely it is that you'll find stuff.
Cons	Your own (Reader's) response becomes irrelevant, as though the Reader is not a part of the process of "understanding." It also assumes that Texts exist in some kind of vacuum independent of the Writer and her intentions, which seems absurd to the foes of this form. Finally, the focus here is on the *means* of the Writer, and not the ends on the Reader and the world at large.
Trouble Spots	What if you're not a close reader? What if you just can't find stuff? Also, don't be confused by the "New" in New Criticism; it's old. Also remember that "close reading" is necessary for all forms of criticism.

---

[2] Foucault, Michel. "What is an Author?" Language, Counter-Memory, Practice. Transl. Donald F. Bouchard and Sherry Simon. Ithaca: Cornell UP, 1977. 113-38. Print.

ETHICAL CRITICISM	
Locus on TLC	R/W/T
Mastery/Mystery	Moderately hard to use, moderately hard to master (many forms)
Other names / Related Forms	"The Moral Approach," "Neo-Humanism," Religious Criticism, African-American Criticism, Gay and Lesbian Criticism, etc.
Genesis	Ancient Greece, with a great resurgence in the 1960s & 70s
Heyday	1960s–present
Bumper-Sticker Slogan	"Literature matters in the real world."
Progenitors	Plato, Aristotle, Horace
Principal proponents	Sir Phillip Sidney, Dr. Johnson, Matthew Arnold, F.R. Leavis, Wayne C. Booth, Toni Morrison (Af-Am Crit), Barbara Johnson (Af-Am Crit), T.S. Eliot (Christian Crit), Eve Kosofsky Sedgwick (Gay and Lesbian Crit), Michel Foucault
Associated Places	America, Europe
Outline	Here, the focus is on the *ends* of the Text, its effect on real people in the real world, and a Text's "moral implications to humanity."[2] Ethical/Moral Critics conduct a methodical examination of a Text based on any coherent set of articulated values, stated transparently up front. When we group together Reader-Response critics along political or philosophical ("ethical") lines, we find groups of more or less likeminded critics. For example, African-American critics will look into and evaluate Texts based on the Writer's treatment of African-American characters, themes, settings, and "values" associated with the African-American community. The idea is that there is such a thing as "black" aesthetic, a "gay" aesthetic, and so on, often based in marginalization and oppression, and reflected in the "sociological, political, ideological, and cultural situation" (Brock University) of the Writer and his Readers.
Ethical Criticism in Action	Religious critics might find a plethora of Christian symbols, themes, and settings in Hawthorne's short story, "Young Goodman Brown," e.g. Faith, prayer, Satan, the serpent, the Black Mass, redemption, heaven, and hell. They might find the Text supports the fundamental tenets of Christianity, including the eternal punishment for losing faith and succumbing to the devil.
Pros	It's less "academic" and more "real world." As with Reader-Response Criticism, you get to use who you are and what you believe as a lens through which to look into and evaluate texts. By practicing with other forms of Ethical Criticism, though, you get many more tools in your critical arsenal.
Cons	Strong Ethical critics—especially those very committed to specific beliefs – are sometimes blinded by their own politics, and fail to see other aspects of the Text. They also sometimes rush to judgment on some Writers who don't seem to immediately identify with the Reader's belief system. Also, the emphasis on content rather than the form sometime leads to an ignorance of the empirical quality of writing. We might reject a Writer for her beliefs, even if she's a master at her craft.
Trouble Spots	What if we haven't articulated our ethics in advance? What if we don't state them up front? What if we deliberately hide them? What shall we do (or urge our society to do) with Texts that are questionable or even "indefensible?"[4] Note that some critics categorize Gay and Lesbian Criticism with Gender Studies or "Queer Theory."

---

3 Scott, Wilbur. *Five Approaches to Literary Criticism*. New York: Collier Books, 1962. Print.

4 Booth, Wayne C. "Who is Responsible in Ethical Criticism, and for What?" *The Company We Keep: An Ethics of Fiction*. Berkeley: University of California Press, 1989. Print.

FEMINIST CRITICISM	
LOCUS ON TLC	R/W/T
MASTERY/MYSTERY	Easy to use, moderately difficult to master
OTHER NAMES / RELATED FORMS	Ethical Criticism
GENESIS	1700s
HEYDAY	1960s–present
BUMPER-STICKER SLOGAN	"A woman needs a man like a fish needs a bicycle!"
PROGENITOR	Mary Wollstonecraft
PRINCIPAL PROPONENTS	Simone de Beauvoir, Elaine Showalter, Alice Walker, Cammile Paglia
ASSOCIATED PLACES	Europe, America
OUTLINE	Feminist Criticism has its roots firmly in the larger Feminist movement. It focuses on the relative power of female and male characters, as well as Writers. Its basic premise is that women and men should be equal, but it also seeks to explore the singular experience of women through the ages. It's also concerned with the less obvious form of marginalization of women that must have occurred to allow for the vast majority of works in the canon to be written by men (Tyson).[5]
FEMINIST CRITICISM IN ACTION	A Feminist critic might explore the struggles of the character Jane in Gilman's short story, "The Yellow Wallpaper," as she seeks to escape the patronizing authority of her husband, John, ultimately succumbing to madness as her only means of liberation. Another Feminist critic might examine Groening's character Lisa Simpson, or Fern in White's novel, *Charlotte's Web* as powerful female forces fighting male domination with wile, intelligence, and inner strength far beyond their male co-characters.
PROS	Nearly every Text ever written is rife with possibilities for a Mars-Venus criticism.
CONS	As with any orthodoxy, strict adherence to this form of criticism can blind a Reader to other aspects of the text.
TROUBLE SPOTS	Should we reject out of hand Writers who ostensibly demean – or ignore – female characters, themes, and settings?

---

5 Tyson, Lois. *Critical Theory Today: A User-Friendly Guide*. Second Ed. London: Routledge, 2006. Print.

PSYCHOANALYTICAL CRITICISM	
Locus on TLC	R/W/T
Mastery/Mystery	Moderately difficult to use, moderately difficult to master
Other names / Related Forms	Freudian Criticism
Genesis	1880s
Heyday	1930s–present
Bumper-Sticker Slogan	"Tell me about your mother."
Progenitor	Sigmund Freud
Principal proponents	Carl Jung, Jacques Lacan, Bruno Bettelheim, Harold Bloom
Associated Places	Austria, Europe, Britain, America
Outline	Where Psychology meets Lit. Sigmund Freud forever changed our concept of the way the human mind works, and the way that humans develop either healthily or variously neurotically into adults. So revolutionary were Freud's theories, that they affected nearly every other realm of study, including Literary Criticism. Here we look into and evaluate Texts based on Freud's theories of the Subconscious, the tripartite mind (Id, Ego, and Superego), and the several childhood "issues" children experience during their development—most of them related to emerging sexuality and associated shame, coveting, projection, transference, and sublimation. We can psychoanalyze Writers, characters and symbols in Texts, and ourselves as Readers based on Freud's theories.
Psychoanalytical Criticism in Action	A Psychoanalytical critic might look at the character Montressor in Poe's short story, "The Cask of Amontillado" as a man deeply disturbed by an Id that's overpowering his Ego. She might see the various "masks," "cloaks," "rapiers," "swords," "torches," "catacombs," and "niches" employed by Montressor as classic Freudian (psychosexual) symbols.
Pros	Many Texts, from Milton's *Paradise Lost* to Milne's *Winnie the Pooh* burst at the seams with archetypal "Freudian" symbols, such as the manifold phallic symbols in much literature by male Writers. Childhood, parents, sex, guilt—these are the bases for so much literature that you can usually find some entree into most Texts from the Freudian angle. Note that one can use Psychoanalytical Criticism retroactively, looking into and evaluating Texts written well before Freud's seminal discoveries.
Cons	"Sometimes a cigar is just a cigar," as Freud purportedly said (Try telling that to Monica Lewinsky).
Trouble Spots	What if a Text is like a Rorschach Test, and what emerges out of the inkblots for you says a lot more about you than the Writer or the Text itself? What if Freud was just a "witch doctor," as Nabokov insists? Also note that technically, Jungian Criticism is its own category.

MARXIST CRITICISM	
Locus on TLC	W/T
Mastery/Mystery	Moderately difficult to use, difficult to master
Other names / Related Forms	N/A
Genesis	1840s–70s
Heyday	1930s–present
Bumper-Sticker Slogan	"Whom does it benefit?"
Progenitor	Karl Marx
Principal proponents	Georg Wilhelm Friedrich Hegel, Friedrich Engels, Leon Trotsky, Walter Benjamin, Terry Eagleton
Associated Places	Germany, Russia, Northern England
Outline	Like Freud did for the mind, Marx fundamentally changed the nature of our discourse about class and socioeconomic status. He clarified a framework for investigating and promoting the basic, age-old striving of the nearly impotent working "masses" against a seemingly all-powerful elite. The bosses and the upper class control the peons and the poor, and try, relatively effortlessly, to maintain their power through money, propaganda, materialistic stuff, brainwashing, and force. Meantime, the great, unwashed majority plot, usually unsuccessfully, to overthrow their overlords and take over.
Marxist Criticism in Action	A Marxist critic might look at the characters in the Melville short story, "Bartleby the Scrivener" as classic symbols of an epic struggle between the bosses and the workers, those controlling the means of production versus those all but enslaved by a system that abuses and dopes the masses. Despite the narrator's insistence, Bartleby "prefers not to" act well his part as a cog in an increasingly dehumanizing machine. They might conclude that Bartleby ultimately triumphs in a private revolution, albeit a fatal one, against the status quo.
Pros	Always seems timely (The "Occupy Wall Street" movement, the concept of the "99 Percent.") Tends to appeal to the average (typically liberal) English professor, especially those who came of age in the 1960s.
Cons	Marx is a complex character, and while it's easy to scratch the surface of his theories, you can get yourself into trouble the deeper you delve.
Trouble Spots	What if Marxism is just a Molotov cocktail's throw from Communism? What if The Who's song, "Won't Get Fooled Again" is right: *Meet the new boss / Same as the old boss?*"

NEW HISTORICAL CRITICISM	
LOCUS ON TLC	R/W/T
MASTERY/MYSTERY	Moderately difficult to use, moderately difficult to master (many time periods)
OTHER NAMES / RELATED FORMS	"Cultural Studies"
GENESIS	1930s
HEYDAY	1980s–present
BUMPER-STICKER SLOGAN	"It's all relative." (Purdue U.)[6]
PROGENITOR	N/A
PRINCIPAL PROPONENTS	Pierre Bourieu, Michel Foucault, Hayden White
ASSOCIATED PLACES	America, Europe, Britain
OUTLINE	The basic idea is that Texts are situated in the times in which they are written. Historical periods and their associated themes and zeitgeists are the *con*-texts for Texts. Furthermore, we continue to reinterpret and largely re-write the first, rough drafts of history, which says a lot more about us as Readers than the "facts" of the past. In any case, we can use New Historical Criticism in three key ways. 1. We can use a Text to discover things about the time during which the Text was written and the culture out of which it came; and 2. We can use our knowledge of the time when a Text was written (and the culture in which it was written) to better our understanding of the Text. Finally, 3. We can learn about our own time and culture by the ways in which we subjectively interpret Texts of the past.
NEW HISTORICAL CRITICISM IN ACTION	A New Historical critic might look at Milton's *Paradise Lost* as a poem uniquely situated in its time (Christ's College).[7] They might look into politics of the plot—perhaps especially the speeches Milton offers his main character, Satan—and find a not-so-subtle allegory about the English Civil War, the tyrannical reign and eventual execution of King Charles, the Restoration (and the ultimate failure thereof), and the other social, political, and military conflicts of the mid-17th Century.
PROS	Allows us to situate Texts in time. We're less likely to suggest censoring or banning Twain's *Tom Sawyer* for use of the "N-word" because of its resonance during the antebellum era in the South.
CONS	We can seldom use the form of criticism in isolation—with Milton, for example, we'd be remiss if we ignored the Religious and Psychoanalytical aspects, not to mention if we eschewed a Formalist approach. Also, using New Historical Criticism requires significant investment in studying the social, political, and cultural milieu in which the Writer lived and during which he wrote.
TROUBLE SPOTS	What if a future critic looked into just one Text of today (say, an episode of "Jersey Shore"), and made sweeping assumptions about our time? Also, don't be confused by the "New" part of "New Historical." Just focus on the word "History." But note it's *his* story. Whose story is absent from this record?

---

[6] The Writing Lab, The OWL at Purdue, the English Department, Purdue University. http://owl.english.purdue.edu

[7] Roberts, Gabriel. "Politics in Paradise Lost." *Darkness Visible: A Resource for Studying Milton's Paradise Lost.* Christ's College, Cambridge University. www.christs.cam.ac.uk/darknessvisible

POST-COLONIAL CRITICISM	
LOCUS ON TLC	W/T
MASTERY/MYSTERY	Easy to use, moderately difficult to master
OTHER NAMES / RELATED FORMS	New Historical Criticism / Cultural Studies
GENESIS	Early 20th-Century
HEYDAY	1990s–present
BUMPER-STICKER SLOGAN	"To the victors go the spoils."
PROGENITOR	N/A
PRINCIPAL PROPONENTS	Kamau Braithwaite, Dominick LaCapra, Edward Said
ASSOCIATED PLACES	America, Africa, India, Australia
OUTLINE	Post-Colonial Criticism is like New Historical Criticism / Cultural Studies, except that it focuses on Texts written by Writers who belong to colonial powers and/or colonized areas. It looks at "issues of power, economics, politics, religion, and culture and how these elements work in relation to colonial hegemony" (Purdue U.).[8] It also looks into the process of canonization, and asks the question, which Texts do we value, and why?
POST-COLONIAL CRITICISM IN ACTION	A Post-Colonial critic might look at Jean de Brunhof's *Babar* stories as a propagandistic indoctrination of a young "savage" "colonized" by the rich, white power elite of the West, and into the lavish excesses and shallow morals of the European Empire at the expense of his true nature and his own cultural heritage.
PROS	Offers a balm against the repeated glorification of the West's dominance over the oppressed.
CONS	Because the focus is on the content, as adjudged through a distinctly political lens, we might tend to reject certain Writers or Texts, despite their Formalistic success.
TROUBLE SPOTS	What Texts are we criticizing and why have they made it into the canon—and what happened to all the others that didn't make the cut?

STRUCTURALISM	
LOCUS ON TLC	T
MASTERY/MYSTERY	Very difficult to use, extremely difficult to master
OTHER NAMES / RELATED FORMS	Semiotics
GENESIS	1910s
HEYDAY	1960s–present
BUMPER-STICKER SLOGAN	"Read the signs."

---

[8] The Writing Lab, The OWL at Purdue, the English Department, Purdue University. http://owl.english.purdue.edu

Progenitors	Ferdinand de Sausssure, Charles Sanders Peirce
Principal proponents	Claude Lévi-Strauss, Noam Chomsky, Northrop Frye, Roland Barthes, Umberto Eco, Roman Jakobson, Jacques Lacan, Jacques Derrida, Louis Althusser, Heinrich Plett, Christine Brooke-Rose
Associated Places	France, Europe (Prague, Moscow, Poland), America
Outline	Structuralism is also known as "semiotics," or "semiology," the study of "signs" and how they work together in every field into "syntaxes," "grammars," and "languages." One principal proponent argued, "semiology aims to take in any system of signs, whatever their substance and limits; images, gestures, musical sounds, objects, and the complex associations of all of these, which form the content of ritual, convention or public entertainment: these constitute, if not *languages*, at least systems of signification" (Barthes).[9] Arising out of Formalism, this form of criticism – perhaps the most complex and difficult to master – proposes that looking into multiple Texts for such signs, critics can develop and articulate a formal analysis or "morphology" describing how narratives and other genres operate across the board. This would create a kind of "literary mathematics," essentially a series of logical equations about plot, themes, and characters that reveal a "deep structure" beneath all Texts that repeats, inverts, and varies in predictable ways. In this way, we might study literature the way we study architecture or music—looking at the differences, but mainly the similarities, between structural elements of Texts, or like the way we categorize taxonomically living things in biological sciences based on structural elements, such as the presence or absence of canine teeth. Ultimately, the key here is how we as Readers *make meaning* out of the signs – words, images, symbols, techniques, conventions of genre – we find in Texts. "A semiotic analysis of a literary text deals, instead of themes and general meaning, with the way in which meaning is produced by the structures of independent signs, by codes and conventions" (Surdulescu).[10]
Structuralist Criticism in Action	A Structuralist critic might perform a close-reading of the devices present in a single long, emblematic sentence in the Faulkner short story, "The Bear," and produce the following exhaustive catalogue:[11] The long sentence, with colons, semicolons, dashes, and parentheses The vocabulary that evokes an older morality and a realm of high romance The allusions to romantic episodes in history and in literature The sentence that employs a negative or a series of negatives followed by a positive The use of synonyms for the purpose of repetition A symbolist or poetic extension of the meaning of words The reaching out for a metaphor or simile the "vehicle" of which is foreign to the subject being discussed Breaking with standard grammatical forms; sometimes solecisms The use of paradox The piling up of adjectives The merging of two words into one word The use of hyphenated words While on first blush this effort seems consistent with a mere Formalist approach, the Structuralist critic goes on to investigate what each of those enumerated "signs" might mean in the rhetoric of the South.
Pros	Prepares you for much more advanced literary analysis such as you will encounter on the Master's level and beyond. A very cursory familiarity is necessary in order to engage in the much more common Deconstructionist Criticism.

---

9 Barthes, Roland. *Elements of Semiology*. New York: Hill and Wang, 1968. Print.

10 Surdulescu, Radu. *Form, Structure, and Structurality in Critical Theory*. Bucharest: Editura Univesitatii din Bucuresti, 2000. Print.

11 O'Connor, William Van. "Rhetoric in Southern Writing: Faulkner." *The Georgia Review*, XII:1 (Spring, 1958), 83-86. Print.

CONS	Very difficult to just "dip into," and nearly impossible to master.
TROUBLE SPOTS	What's the exact difference between "structuralism," "semiotics," "semantics," "semiosis," "syntagmatics," etc.?

DECONSTRUCTIONIST CRITICISM	
LOCUS ON TLC	R/W/T
MASTERY/MYSTERY	Moderately difficult to use, very difficult to master
OTHER NAMES / RELATED FORMS	Post-structuralism
GENESIS	1960s
HEYDAY	1960's–present
BUMPER-STICKER SLOGAN	"Meaning is meaningless."
PROGENITOR	Jacques Derrida
PRINCIPAL PROPONENTS	Immanuel Kant, Friedrich Nietzsche, Roland Barthes, Michel Foucault, Jacques Lacan
ASSOCIATED PLACES	France, Europe, Britain, America (Yale U.)
OUTLINE	Growing naturally out of (and in opposition to) Structuralism, Deconstruction argues that the systems of signs for literature – language – is shifty, unstable, ambiguous, contradictory, and irreconcilable (Abcarian and Klotz).[12] This results from the fact that "signifiers slide" (the "meaning" of a words is vague at best, and certainly not fixed). As a result, Readers cannot legitimately make "meaning" out of Texts, and the concept of "understanding" is moot.
DECONSTRUCTIONIST CRITICISM IN ACTION	A Deconstructionist critic might begin with this simple sentence[13]: *Time flies like an arrow*. Now, to deconstruct this sentence, we realize several utterly divergent possible "meanings," depending upon the various options for what the signs (words) "signify" (refer to in the "real world"): Time (noun) flies (verb) like an arrow (adverb clause) = Time passes quickly. Time (verb) flies (object) like an arrow (adverb clause) = Get out your stopwatch and time the speed of flies as you would time an arrow's flight. Time flies (compound noun) like (verb) an arrow (object) = Time flies are fond of arrows (or at least of one particular arrow). How can we determine the "truth" and "meaning" of mere squiggles on a page, especially when we consider the Writer's intent and the Reader's interpretation?
PROS	This form of criticism allows the close-reader to develop multiple interpretations of the Text. It covers all three sides of the TLC.
CONS	Requires extensive knowledge of Structuralism, semiotics, and history to master. Also, you're always in danger of deconstructing Texts into an abyss.
TROUBLE SPOTS	Can you tell where Structuralism ends and Deconstructionism begins?

---

12 Abcarian, Richard and Marvin Klotz. *Literature: The Human Experience*. Tenth Ed. New York: Bedford/St. Martins Press, 2009. Print.

13 Tyson, Lois. *Critical Theory Today: A User-Friendly Guide*. Second Ed. London: Routledge, 2006. Print.

On Writing the Literary Analysis Paper

By Katherine E. Lynch, Ph. D

So, you, English 102 student, have been charged to write a "literary analysis" paper. Perhaps you have some experience with this genre, or perhaps this will be your first foray into the process of writing such an essay. The pages that follow will offer you a brief explanation of the historical context of literary analysis as a methodology, as well as some pragmatic advice about how to undertake the writing task. But before I discuss the genre of literary analysis, I want to talk more generally about how to begin the process of writing a college-level paper. As you contemplate your writing assignments, keep two commandments in mind: 1. Know thy assignment; and 2. Know thy audience.

To know your assignment means to understand exactly what your professor is asking you to do in your essay. How long must it be? Does your paper require an argumentative thesis? Is there a certain structure your professor requires? Are you allowed or encouraged to use outside sources? Should you be writing in a scholarly tone, or are you meant to write in a more informal style? These are only a few of the questions to which you will want to know the answers before beginning your essay. If you feel uncertain about the assignment at any point, you'll want to visit your professor's office hours with specific, clarifying questions.

Understanding the audience to whom you are writing can be more difficult. We writers make choices every day based on our understanding of our readers. Consider, for example, how you would phrase an e-mail asking a teacher for an extension on a paper, versus how you would phrase an e-mail to your best friend requesting a personal favor. These two audiences exist in very different relationships to you; your teacher is an authority figure, while your best friend is a peer whom you know well. An e-mail to one's teacher generally requires a formal and perhaps even slightly deferential tone, phrased in grammatically complete and properly punctuated sentences. An e-mail to one's best friend, however, will likely employ colloquial language, incomplete sentences, and an informal tone.

It is equally important to consider your audience while you write papers for your college courses. Does your professor want you to write the paper with only her in mind? Or have you been asked to write to a more general audience? In the latter case, the writer must include more explanation about her topic and the texts to which she is referring than she otherwise might were she writing only with her professor in mind. I, like most professors, ask my students to write to *the audience of the classroom*—that is, both to their peers within the class and to me, the professor. As a result, my students can make certain assumptions about their audience—that they have all read the texts we've discussed in class, for example. But they must also thoroughly explain any text or concept with which they believe their peers, or I, might be unfamiliar.

Having stressed the importance of knowing thy assignment and knowing thy audience, let's turn to a discussion of the kind of essay you'll be composing in English 102: *literary analysis* papers. Contemporary theories of how best to analyze literature have their genesis in the philosophy of the early twentieth century, when a literary movement called "New Criticism" developed in response to the rise of the scientific method in the Academy (see a companion piece here, "On Literary Criticism"). As the scientific method revolutionized the ways in which people discovered truths about the universe, scholars of literature asked themselves how literary truths could be conceptualized in this new world order. Art Berman, in his 1988 book *From the New Criticism to Deconstruction: The Reception of Structuralism and Post-structuralism,* summarizes the central tenets of New Criticism as follows: "That poetry has an important meaning but not a meaning with the truth values of science, while at the same time critical method is itself a scientific-like endeavor, is an essential assumption of New Criticism" (Berman 29).[2] In other words: literature offers its audience a kind of "truth" that is different from scientific "truth," but critics must apply the scientific method to literary texts in order to make convincing arguments about these texts.

How does this methodology work? First, it is crucial to understand the text – the story, novel, play, or poem that you are reading – to be its own universe with its own rules, definitions, and set of meanings:

The New Critics assumed that the poem itself is a self-contained and self-sustaining entity. The relationships among the words of the poem construct a linguistic milieu that contains a meaning defined by that milieu. Meaning is not derived by evoking direct factual correspondences between the poem and facts of the matter otherwise ascertainable, although the critics are obliged to ask how the poem does relate to the external world. The poem is an object, open to an analysis that can be confined (more in theory than in practice) to the poem itself (30).

The cornerstone of this methodology is called *close reading*, which is a technique for uncovering the meaning of a text through a kind of literary dissection. If your teacher asks you to do a strict "close reading" of a text, then it is likely that he wants you to focus *only* on that text and how you create meaning within it. Details about the author's life and historical context are not relevant to strict close-reading: "Designating the poem as an autonomous object to be studied entails rejecting critical methods that would understand the poem through history, biography, sociology, or other non-literary disciplines" (30). Nowadays, literary scholars combine close reading with these other kinds of criticism in order to make arguments about texts. However, your teacher might wish you to undertake strict close reading in your assignments as you learn this important skill.

How does one learn to become a good close-reader of texts? First, it is important to understand that close reading always involves *reading the text multiple times*. On your first read-through, stay relaxed. Allow yourself to experience the text as a human being; immerse yourself in the plot of a story or the imagery and language of a poem. Embrace your emotional reactions to the text: Do you like it? Do you hate it? Does it speak to you? Is it challenging? How? Why? If you encounter any moments in the text that you find particularly intriguing or confusing, you might want to take note of them by inserting flags in the text or jotting down a few words in your notebook. This is called "dialectical reading." (See the companion piece here called "On Critical Reading".)

When you are ready to begin developing a literary argument, you must first go back and reread part or all of the text. Now is the time to be vigilant. You are on the lookout for *patterns*. Repeated words and repeated images – "textual echoes" – are usually indicators that the word, phrase, or image in question is important in some way. Taking stock of these words and images will help you to identify the *ideas*

---

2 Berman, Art. *From the New Criticism to Deconstruction: The Reception of Structuralism and Post-structuralism.* Champaign, IL: U of Illinois Press, 1988. Print.

that recur throughout a text. We call these recurring ideas *themes*.

In addition to watching for repetition, keep an eye out for when changes occur. In a story, does the point of view shift between characters? If so, does the author use different styles, tones, diction, or imagery when she is writing from different characters' perspectives? In a poem, does the rhyme scheme change? In a play, does a given character's speech patterns change or remain consistent? These are only some of the questions you might ask yourself as you reread your text.

Consider also how your author makes use of figurative language. Does he use metaphors, similes, analogies, and the like? If so, when does the author tend to employ these devices? Are these figures of speech related to the themes of the text? What conclusions can you draw about the text by examining the author's rhetorical choices?

Depending on the nature of your assignment, you will either want to cast a wide or a narrow net as you engage in the process of close reading. If your assignment is very focused on one particular aspect of the text (e.g. the use of metaphor in one short story), then you will want to reread the text with only that aspect in mind. However, if your assignment grants you the freedom to choose your own focus, then you will want to investigate any aspect of the text that strikes you as noteworthy, until you have fixed upon your specific topic.

When you are finished with your rereading and note-taking process, it's time to begin organizing your thoughts. Do this in whatever manner best complements your learning style. Some visual and tactile learners might wish to write down each of their insights on the front of an index card. On the back of the card, these writers will indicate where proof for each specific claim can be found in the text. Then, they piece together the index cards like a puzzle, arranging and rearranging as necessary during the writing process. Other writers will prefer to create a more conventional outline with letters and numbers to indicate various layers of thought. Still others may want to "talk out" their ideas into a recorder (or smart phone).

As you organize your ideas, you'll want to start considering your *thesis*. The thesis of a literary analysis paper is a distillation of its central argument, usually in one or two sentences. Your thesis should appear near the beginning of the paper (consult your teacher for more specific instructions), and it must always be *debatable*. So, for example, "Jeffrey Eugenides makes frequent references to Greek mythology in *Middlesex*" is not an acceptable thesis because it is an *observation* rather than an *argument*. A thesis must always answer *how* or *why*. A more acceptable thesis would be: "Jeffrey Eugenides makes frequent use of Greek mythology in *Middlesex* in order to cast his novel as an epic in the Homeric tradition." This thesis is an argument; one could disagree with my claim about the reason for Eugenides' use of Greek myth.

Once you have a working thesis, you'll want to set about proving it, step by step. Go back to your original outline and rearrange any of the pieces as needed in order to create a logical argument that flows from point to point. Each paragraph should start with a topic sentence that makes a promise to the reader about the particular focus of that paragraph. Then, you must offer evidence (mostly *textual* evidence, in the case of a literary analysis paper) in support of your main point. Each piece of evidence must then be analyzed; in other words, you must explain *how* and *why* the evidence proves the claim articulated by your topic sentence. Finally, it is wise to end your paragraph either by connecting your analysis back to the thesis of the essay, by transitioning into the main point of the next paragraph (which serves to move your analysis forward). For example: if I were proving my thesis about *Middlesex*, I would include the following paragraphs in the first draft of my essay: 1. a paragraph about Eugenides' references to Homer within *Middlesex*; 2. a paragraph about his use of the rhetorical device known as the "invocation to the Muse;" 3. a paragraph about his choice to name his narrator "Calliope" after the Muse of epic poetry; and 4. a paragraph about Calliope's transformation within the plot of the novel. Some professors might want you to incorporate those various "points of proof" into your thesis, providing a complete blueprint for the body of the paper to come.

As you work to prove your thesis, consider the kinds of rhetorical modes that will best allow you to argue your point. *Argumentation* is itself a rhetorical mode that is inherent in the process of literary analysis. When writing your paper, be sure to avoid excessive plot summary, as this will detract from the claims you're making about your text. Other rhetorical modes that are particularly useful in literary analysis include *definition* (in which you explain how the text defines and makes use of a certain concept or term); *exemplification* (in which you provide examples from the text in order to support your claims); and *comparison/contrast* (in which you demonstrate how two or more aspects of the text are alike, different, or both). Your teacher might introduce you to other rhetorical modes, such as *process analysis* and *cause and effect*, but no matter which one(s) you use in your paper, always use them in the service of *proving your thesis*. Doing so requires that you make frequent use of evidence from the text (either in the form of quotes or paraphrases) and that you *properly cite* this evidence within your paragraphs.

Once you have written a first draft, you'll want to give yourself some time away from your paper. If possible, let it sit for several days. Then, return to it with a fresh eye and begin the revision process. Remember: *revision* does not mean simply *editing* for grammar, spelling, and punctuation. Revision means *re-imagining* your paper. Do you need to reorganize paragraphs? Do you need to rewrite certain sections? Do you need to change your thesis now that you've written the rest of your argument? At this point in the process, visiting the Reading and Writing Center for a fresh perspective will be very useful to you.

As you develop the mental muscles required for literary analysis, you will find that you begin to see all texts differently, whether their medium is writing, music, visual art, or film and television. By engaging in literary analysis, you will develop a more nuanced and critical perspective on the world around you, especially in this text-heavy digital age. So have fun, and enjoy delving deeply into the infinitely-signifying realm of the literary!

On Critical Reading

By Clifford L. Garner, Ph. D

Analyzing literature isn't what some people call "tearing apart" someone's writing. Instead it is a clear recognition that poems and stories are constructed things, and as such, have a kind of architecture that we might examine to decide how it makes meaning happen, and what we think that meaning could be. All reading is in some sense interpretation, and critical reading involves us in presenting and defending a particular interpretation.

Why Do It? To understand and appreciate more clearly a work of art. To see how the architect of a work of art has made her artifice: what design elements are present, what tools were used to build it, and ultimately how it comments or glosses on human life in some way. The remainder of this essay will discuss how to apply critical reading methodologies to the major genres of literature: poetry and fiction.

POETRY

What are some things to look for when reading?

In general, when reading a poem critically, you should look for the following things:

1. The title is either literally or figuratively the first line of the poem, and often can tell you a lot about the poem. Sometimes it presents us with a reading direction for the whole poem. The Frost poem, "Out, Out—" is a good example, with its title alluding to Macbeth's funereal conception of life after the death of his queen.
2. Read the entire poem a few times and ask yourself about setting, voice, topic, and how those things are present to you.
3. Look at the ending and ask yourself how you got there and how the ending makes sense in relation to the whole poem.
4. Ask yourself about the organization and structure of the poem—why is it set up the way it is, and how does each part logically follow the next? Does that forward meaning? If so, how? If not, why not?
5. What's the tone of the poem? Is it happy, angry, sarcastic, scolding? How is the tone present to you and how does it impact the meaning you see there?
6. Because poetry has its origins in the spoken word, poetry is a very aural medium. So, read it aloud! See if the poem can yield the meaning you impute to it by verbal stresses. See if the imagery comes to life for you as you read it aloud. Look for cues about how the Writer intends for the poem to sound, e.g. line-breaks ("end-stops" or "ejambments"), punctuation (e.g. dashes or full-stops), and built-in pauses ("caesuras").

ELEMENTS

Look for the following elements as you analyze the poem and figure out their place in the construction of meaning in the poem:

Genre

What kind of poem is it? Poetry types include elegy, epic, epistle, lyric, monologue, narrative, and sonnet, etc. Each has particular conventions and purposes. For example, an elegy such as Milton's "Lycidas," is going to have a different focus and emphasis than a satire such as Pope's "The Rape of the Lock." If we know this, it makes our analysis more apt to be appropriate.

Voice

The speaker or "persona" of the poem is often very important, especially in narrative poetry. The persona is almost *never* the poet himself—with some notable exceptions (e.g. Whitman). The key questions about voice include whether it's a dramatized voice, such as the speaker in Eliot's "The Love Song of J. Alfred Prufrock," or an un-dramatized, and therefore, unidentified voice, such as in Hopkins' poetry. In either case, your analysis should involve an understanding of the point of view of that voice and what impact that voice has upon the poem and its meaning.

Structure

Thematic structure is the way in which the Writer presents the "argument" to the reader. Sonnets, such as those of Shakespeare, provide a good example of thematic structure, with the first eight lines presenting a problem, and the final six "resolving" the problem. Formal structure is the way in which the stanzas or sections of the poem relate to the entire poem. Eliot's "The Wasteland," for example, has a number of sections formally presenting different views and dramatic presentations of the decline of Western culture into a moral and cultural wasteland.

Setting

The poem can use setting in any number of ways: It might be a real, concrete setting (by the banks of the River Wye in Wordsworth's "Tintern Abbey"). It might be setting used to evoke a mood, such as looking through a frosty window in Coleridge's "Frost at Midnight." The setting might provide a symbol or the start of allegory necessary for an understanding of the poem's argument. The reader needs to ask *why* the Writer chose that particular setting, and to what effect. Could Blake's poem "London" have been set in Dublin or Dubuque?

Use of Language and Imagery

What kind of language use is evident to the Reader, and what might that particular lexicon connote? In Chaucer's language, for example, we see certain animals and birds mentioned—a careful Reader should ask *why* those particular animals and birds appear? Might *The Canterbury Tales* have begun with an invocation of magisterial eagles trumpeting, instead of the "smale foweles" that "maken melodye"? How do the words and the images that are presented lend themselves to the forwarding of meaning as intended by the Writer and interpreted by the Reader?

Sound and Repetitions

What mood is evoked by the sounds of the poem, especially when it's read aloud? Is it gloomy? Bellicose? Erotic? When a poet repeats herself, it doesn't indicate a lack of vocabulary. So what role do repeated motifs and words play? This is a good question for the careful reader. Answer it. Sometimes, as in the "sprung rhythm" of Hopkins, the sound and metrics of the poem are crucial to understanding it. Reading a poem aloud will often bring out the relation between sound and sense.

Reader's Distance from Poem

This isn't just a question about temporal and historical distance. In many ways, you are closer to the

Romantic poets than you are to the poetry of Pound or Eliot. You share with the Romantics a worldview and a sensibility that those more "modern" poets did not—we'll explore this paradox more in class. But this is an important question. When you read Chaucer or Milton, you are far enough away temporally and philosophically that it behooves you to understand the historical and cultural context of *The Canterbury Tales* or *Paradise Lost* so that you don't read into those Texts ideas or interpretations that would never have been propounded in that time. This implies that while there are often infinite possible "readings" of Texts, those that account for the historical and biographical contexts often lead to more "informed" readings.

Ideology

What ideas – philosophical, cultural, religious, etc. – are presented in the poem, and how are they representative or not representative of common human experience? Are they relevant to you now? Do the WWI poets Owen, Brooke, and Sasson glorify life in the trenches—or decry it? Seeing what is depicted directly and placed in the foreground is important. However, seeing what is left out or "suppressed" is often equally important to understanding the poem. What's ostensibly "missing" from Lawrence's "Snake?" Asking the question about the poem's ideology may lead to some surprising answers!

FICTION

Analysis of a work of fiction is very similar to, and has very similar aims as, reading a poem. Key differences include the attempted verisimilitude of fiction, which makes it more – or so the claim goes – *representative* of the world in some ways. Fiction is almost also always in narrative form, whereas a poem isn't always narrative in presentation (e.g. it might be lyrical).

Plot

In her short story, "Happy Endings," Atwood refers to plot as "a what and a what and a what." By that she means that plot is an arrangement of occurrences that have some interrelationship. Figuring out that interrelationship can lead the Reader to an understanding of the piece of fiction and its thesis.

Setting

Writers use setting to establish a place and time for the plot to occur. However, the artistic writer can use it to extend meaning. For example, Kafka uses the setting (and several changes in the setting) of "The Metamorphosis" as an analogue to the changing relations between family members in the story. In the process, the Reader learns much about what Kafka has to say about human emotion, utility, and the function of the family in a capitalistic culture.

Character

Fiction is almost always about character. The characters are often representative of – or at least they present aspects of – human nature. In Flaubert's "Madame Bovary," Charles Bovary is an "oaf" in many ways, yet he represents human goodness, desire, and emotion in a profound, if pathetic, way. Meanwhile, the character Rodolphe, while sophisticated and intelligent, represents human selfishness and banality. It is the contrast between the two characters that helps drive our understanding of human nature in the fiction.

Narrator/P.O.V.

The "teller" of the story (the person through whose point of view the narrative unfolds), the narrator might be inside or outside the action of the piece. There are a number of kinds of narrative. First person ("I" voice) narrators pull us close to the story because of subjectivity. Third person narrators place us in a position outside the action and give us a sense of objectivity. There's also a rare but effective second person narrative style, characterized by the pronoun "you," whose intent is similar to first person, i.e.

bringing the Reader into the action as much as possible. There are reliable narrators who tell us the "truth," and unreliable narrators who give us information we have to doubt (one of Poe's favorite devices). In any case, the decoding of the narrator and the narrator's function by the Reader can help us in our understanding of the fiction.

Reality

Nabokov said that "reality" is the only word that must always be used with quotation marks. That being said, it's important to analyze what "reality" the fiction is presenting. The narrative might present a world that seems to adhere to rules of space and time we recognize, or it might present a more psychological or "experimental" world that presents little or no parallel with a "reality" we recognize (think of "The Metamorphosis" here, or much Post-Modernist fiction). However, the reality presented by the text is important to our understanding of the world view of the Text, and therefore its ideological commitments and rejections. Figuring this out is very complex work because it's not only the inclusions that matter here; we also need to explore what the Writer has excluded as well, as that, too, is a matter for contemplation and analysis.

Tradition and Form

Different genres use character, narrator, setting, plot, and the like in different ways, and for different intent. So, one must ask oneself, what sort of writing is this? Is it a novel of manners, a romance, a comedy, a satire, or some other form? Does it conform (i.e. in form and content) to the genre you've identified, or does it play with the form for some reason you need to determine? Meaning can adhere in both conformity and non-conformity to a genre.

All the above is by way of suggesting to you that there's much more to reading a Text than reading a text. You need to read it critically, caress its details in which inheres its uniqueness. You read critically to deal with what the poem or prose says to you and understand how it says it to you. You read critically to rub your mind up against the greatest minds of each age and what they have written.

On the Use of Periods in the Analysis of Literature

By Clifford L. Garner, Ph. D

In order to lend some external authority to the analysis of literature, scholars have historically tried, to some extent, to place the work of art in context. This context is an agglomeration of time, historical occurrences, philosophy, aesthetics, ideas, and movements that are the background influencing the composition of the work of art. Philologist and comparative literature expert René Wellek describes literary periods as providing "systems of norms,"[3] and as such they place the analyst of literature on common ground with other Readers and provide an appropriate philosophical and historical framework to lend that authority to their criticism.

In broad outlines—and by no means not comprehensive or exact ones—the Texts in this book corresponds to the following periods in the English language:

- Medieval (500 - 1500 A.D.), roughly corresponding with the fall of Rome and ending with the Renaissance. Ex.: Chaucer.
- Renaissance (1500 - 1660), culminating in the Restoration of Charles II. Ex.: Milton.
- Neo-Classical/Augustan (1660 - 1800), from the aforementioned Restoration through the "Age of Enlightenment." Ex.: Pope.
- Romantic (1800 - 1865), starting at the end of the 18th century and going through to the middle of the 19th century. Ex.: Wordsworth.
- Realist (1840 - 1914), starting with the coronation of Queen Victoria (or around the Civil War in America) and continuing to the First World War. Ex. Crane.
- Modern (1900 – 1945), beginning with the 20th century and continuing to the end of the Second World War. Ex.: Joyce.
- Post-Modern (1935 – present). Ex.: Barth

In trying to pin-down literary periods, one immediately notices that there are no precise end dates and beginning dates. The overlaps between periods are obvious. Governing ideas, techniques, and the like often begin to germinate long before the period flourishes, as occurred in the Modernist and Post-Modernist periods. A Writer like Melville foreshadowed later periods. Similarly, the philosophical and technical underpinnings of periods and movements often proceed far into succeeding periods. For example, there are clearly discernable elements of Romantic ideas and imagery in writers from later periods as diverse as Flaubert, Crane, James, and Nabokov.

There are also often sub-groups or periods-within-periods that scholars have identified. For example, Elizabethan literature is a sub-grouping that would include William Shakespeare, but not

---

[3] Wellek, René and Austin Warren. *Theory of Literature*. Third Ed. New York: Mariner Books, 1984. Print.

Jonson or Donne, though all these figures are considered Renaissance writers. Further, inside periods, there are huge differences of approach and style. For example, the Realism of Dickens is far different in style and intent from the Realism of Flaubert.

Despite these challenges, you can use the fundamental tenets of literary periods to help you prepare yourself to enter into a dialogue with an historical Text with information about the culture and time that produced that Text. Use that information to inform your interaction with, and analysis of, the work of art as it most likely has a different set of assumptions and a different world view than you do. But use the periods with the *caveat* that it is often the case that a great work of art at once represents and transcends its period.

Finding information and discussion of periods is pretty easy, because you are all adept at cyber- research. Here are a few starting places that are not meant to be in any way limiting:

For all periods, the Norton Anthologies have good summaries of all the periods and are available online.

- For Medieval, Renaissance/Restoration literature and 18th century/Augustan literature: www.luminarium.org
- For Romantic literature: www.rc.umd.edu
- For Realism: www.online-literature.com/periods/realism.php
- For Modernism: start with www.online-literature.com/periods/modernism.php then move to a link-rich environment http://faculty.gvsu.edu/websterm/modlitlinks.html
- For Post-Modernism: www.artandpopularculture.com/postmodernism

Section I
Poetry

Canterbury Tales:

General Prologue

Geoffrey Chaucer

Here bygynneth the Book of the Tales of Caunterbury

1 **Whan that Aprille with his shoures sote**
    When April with its sweet-smelling showers
2 **The droghte of Marche hath perced to the rote,**
    Has pierced the drought of March to the root,
3 **And bathed every veyne in swich licour,**
    And bathed every vein (of the plants) in such liquid
4 **Of which vertu engendred is the flour;**
    By which power the flower is created;
5 **Whan Zephirus eek with his swete breeth**
    When the West Wind also with its sweet breath,
6 **Inspired hath in every holt and heeth**
    In every wood and field has breathed life into
7 **The tendre croppes, and the yonge sonne**
    The tender new leaves, and the young sun
8 **Hath in the Ram his halfe cours y-ronne,**
    Has run half its course in Aries,
9 **And smale fowles maken melodye,**
    And small fowls make melody,
10 **That slepen al the night with open yë,**
    Those that sleep all the night with open eyes
11 **(So priketh hem nature in hir corages):**
    (So Nature incites them in their hearts),
12 **Than longen folk to goon on pilgrimages**
    Then folk long to go on pilgrimages,
13 **(And palmers for to seken straunge strondes)**
    And professional pilgrims to seek foreign shores,
14 **To ferne halwes, couthe in sondry londes;**
    To distant shrines, known in various lands;
15 **And specially, from every shires ende**
    And specially from every shire's end
16 **Of Engelond to Caunterbury they wende,**
    Of England to Canterbury they travel,
17 **The holy blisful martir for to seke,**
    To seek the holy blessed martyr,
18 **That hem hath holpen, whan that they were seke.**
    Who helped them when they were sick.
19 **Bifel that, in that seson on a day,**
    It happened that in that season on one day,
20 **In Southwerk at the Tabard as I lay**
    In Southwark at the Tabard Inn as I lay
21 **Redy to wenden on my pilgrimage**
    Ready to go on my pilgrimage
22 **To Caunterbury with ful devout corage,**
    To Canterbury with a very devout spirit,
23 **At night was come in-to that hostelrye**
    At night had come into that hostelry
24 **Wel nyne and twenty in a companye,**
    Well nine and twenty in a company
25 **Of sondry folk, by aventure y-falle**
    Of various sorts of people, by chance fallen
26 **In felawshipe, and pilgrims were they alle,**
    In fellowship, and they were all pilgrims,
27 **That toward Caunterbury wolden ryde;**
    Who intended to ride toward Canterbury.
28 **The chambres and the stables weren wyde,**
    The bedrooms and the stables were spacious,

Geoffrey Chaucer; Walter W. Skeat, ed., "The General Prologue," *The Complete Works of Geoffrey Chaucer*, vol. 4. Copyright in the Public Domain.

Geoffrey Chaucer; Larry D. Benson, trans., *The General Prologue: An Interlinear Translation*, from http://www.courses.fas.harvard.edu/~chaucer/teachslf/gp-par.htm,. Copyright © 2008 by The President and Fellows of Harvard College. Permission to reprint granted by the publisher.

29	**And wel we weren esed atte beste.**
	And we were well accommodated in the best way.
30	**And shortly, whan the sonne was to reste,**
	And in brief, when the sun was (gone) to rest,
31	**So hadde I spoken with hem everichon,**
	I had so spoken with everyone of them
32	**That I was of hir felawshipe anon,**
	That I was of their fellowship straightway,
33	**And made forward erly for to ryse,**
	And made agreement to rise early,
34	**To take our wey, ther as I yow devyse.**
	To take our way where I (will) tell you.
35	**But natheles, whyl I have tyme and space,**
	But nonetheless, while I have time and opportunity,
36	**Er that I ferther in this tale pace,**
	Before I proceed further in this tale,
37	**Me thinketh it acordaunt to resoun**
	It seems to me in accord with reason
38	**To telle yow al the condicioun**
	To tell you all the circumstances
39	**Of ech of hem, so as it semed me,**
	Of each of them, as it seemed to me,
40	**And whiche they weren, and of what degree,**
	And who they were, and of what social rank,
41	**And eek in what array that they were inne;**
	And also what clothing that they were in;
42	**And at a knight than wol I first biginne.**
	And at a knight then will I first begin.
43	**A KNIGHT ther was, and that a worthy man,**
	A KNIGHT there was, and that (one was) a worthy man,
44	**That fro the tyme that he first bigan**
	Who from the time that he first began
45	**To ryden out, he loved chivalrye,**
	To ride out, he loved chivalry,
46	**Trouthe and honour, fredom and curteisye.**
	Fidelity and good reputation, generosity and courtesy.
47	**Ful worthy was he in his lordes werre,**
	He was very worthy in his lord's war,
48	**And therto hadde he riden, no man ferre,**
	And for that he had ridden, no man farther,
49	**As wel in Cristendom as in hethenesse,**
	As well in Christendom as in heathen lands,
50	**And ever honoured for his worthinesse;**
	And (was) ever honored for his worthiness;
51	**At Alisaundre he was, whan it was wonne.**
	He was at Alexandria when it was won.
52	**Ful ofte tyme he hadde the bord bigonne**
	He had sat very many times in the place of honor,
53	**Aboven alle naciouns in Pruce.**
	Above (knights of) all nations in Prussia;
54	**In Lettow hadde he reysed and in Ruce,**
	He had campaigned in Lithuania and in Russia,
55	**No Cristen man so ofte of his degree.**
	No Christian man of his rank so often.
56	**In Gernade at the sege eek hadde he be**
	Also he had been in Grenada at the siege
57	**Of Algezir, and riden in Belmarye.**
	Of Algeciras, and had ridden in Morocco.
58	**At Lyeys was he and at Satalye,**
	He was at Ayash and at Atalia,
59	**Whan they were wonne, and in the Grete See**
	When they were won, and in the Mediterranean
60	**At many a noble aryve hadde he be.**
	He had been at many a noble expedition.
61	**At mortal batailles hadde he been fiftene,**
	He had been at fifteen mortal battles,
62	**And foughten for our feith at Tramissene**
	And fought for our faith at Tlemcen
63	**In listes thryes, and ay slayn his foo.**
	Three times in formal duels, and each time slain his foe.
64	**This ilke worthy knight had been also**
	This same worthy knight had also been
65	**Somtyme with the lord of Palatye**
	At one time with the lord of Balat
66	**Agayn another hethen in Turkye;**
	Against another heathen in Turkey;
67	**And everemoore he hadde a sovereyn prys.**
	And evermore he had an outstanding reputation
68	**And though that he were worthy, he was wys,**
	And although he was brave, he was prudent,
69	**And of his port as meke as is a mayde.**
	And of his deportment as meek as is a maid.
70	**He nevere yet no vileinye ne sayde**
	He never yet said any rude word

71	**In al his lyf un-to no maner wight.**	92	**He was as fresh as is the month of May.**
	In all his life unto any sort of person.		He was as fresh as is the month of May.
72	**He was a verray parfit gentil knight.**	93	**Short was his goune, with sleves longe and wyde.**
	He was a truly perfect, noble knight.		His gown was short, with long and wide sleeves.
73	**But for to tellen yow of his array,**	94	**Wel coude he sitte on hors and faire ryde.**
	But to tell you of his clothing,		He well knew how to sit on horse and handsomely ride.
74	**His hors were gode, but he was nat gay.**	95	**He coude songes make and wel endyte,**
	His horses were good, but he was not gaily dressed.		He knew how to make songs and well compose (the words),
75	**Of fustian he wered a gipoun**	96	**Juste and eek daunce, and wel purtreye and wryte.**
	He wore a tunic of coarse cloth		Joust and also dance, and well draw and write.
76	**Al bismotered with his habergeoun,**	97	**So hote he lovede that by nightertale**
	All stained (with rust) by his coat of mail,		He loved so passionately that at nighttime
77	**For he was late y-come from his viage,**	98	**He sleep namoore than dooth a nightingale.**
	For he was recently come (back) from his expedition,		He slept no more than does a nightingale.
78	**And wente for to doon his pilgrymage.**	99	**Curteys he was, lowly, and servysable,**
	And went to do his pilgrimage.		Courteous he was, humble, and willing to serve,
79	**With hym ther was his sone, a yong SQUYER,**	100	**And carf biforn his fader at the table.**
	With him there was his son, a young SQUIRE,		And carved before his father at the table.
80	**A lovyere, and a lusty bacheler,**	101	**A YEMAN hadde he and servaunts namo**
	A lover and a lively bachelor,		He (the Knight) had A YEOMAN and no more servants
81	**With lokkes crulle as they were leyd in presse.**	102	**At that tyme, for hym liste ride so,**
	With locks curled as if they had been laid in a curler.		At that time, for it pleased him so to travel,
82	**Of twenty yeer of age he was, I gesse.**	103	**And he was clad in cote and hood of grene.**
	He was twenty years of age, I guess.		And he (the yeoman) was clad in coat and hood of green.
83	**Of his stature he was of evene lengthe,**	104	**A sheef of pecok-arwes, brighte and kene,**
	Of his stature he was of moderate height,		A sheaf of peacock arrows, bright and keen,
84	**And wonderly deliver, and greet of strengthe.**	105	**Under his belt he bar ful thriftily**
	And wonderfully agile, and of great strength.		He carried under his belt very properly
85	**And he hadde been somtyme in chivachye**	106	**(Wel coude he dresse his takel yemanly;**
	And he had been for a time on a cavalry expedition		(He well knew how to care for his equipment as a yeoman should;
86	**In Flaundres, in Artoys, and Pycardie,**	107	**His arwes drouped noght with fetheres lowe),**
	In Flanders, in Artois, and Picardy,		His arrows did not fall short because of drooping feathers),
87	**And born him weel, as of so litel space,**	108	**And in his hand he bar a myghty bowe.**
	And conducted himself wel, for so little a space of time,		And in his hand he carried a mighty bow.
88	**In hope to stonden in his lady grace.**		
	In hope to stand in his lady's good graces.		
89	**Embrouded was he, as it were a mede**		
	He was embroidered, as if it were a mead		
90	**Al ful of fresshe floures, whyte and rede.**		
	All full of fresh flowers, white and red.		
91	**Singinge he was, or floytinge, al the day;**		
	Singing he was, or fluting, all the day;		

109	**A not-heed hadde he, with a broun visage.**	129	**Ne wette hir fingres in hir sauce depe;**
	He had a close-cropped head, with a brown face.		Nor wet her fingers deep in her sauce;
110	**Of wode-craft wel coude he al the usage.**	130	**Wel coude she carie a morsel and wel kepe,**
	He well knew all the practice of woodcraft.		She well knew how to carry a morsel (to her mouth) and take good care
111	**Upon his arm he bar a gay bracer,**	131	**That no drope ne fille up-on hir brest.**
	He wore an elegant archer's wrist-guard upon his arm,		That no drop fell upon her breast.
112	**And by his syde a swerd and a bokeler,**	132	**In curteisye was set ful muche hir lest.**
	And by his side a sword and a small shield,		Her greatest pleasure was in good manners.
113	**And on that other syde a gay daggere**	133	**Hir over lippe wyped she so clene,**
	And on that other side an elegant dagger		She wiped her upper lip so clean
114	**Harneised wel, and sharp as point of spere;**	134	**That in hir coppe ther was no ferthing sene**
	Well ornamented and sharp as the point of a spear;		That in her cup there was seen no tiny bit
115	**A Cristofre on his brest of silver shene.**	135	**Of grece, whan she dronken hadde hir draughte.**
	A Christopher-medal of bright silver on his breast.		Of grease, when she had drunk her drink.
116	**An horn he bar, the bawdrik was of grene;**	136	**Ful semely after hir mete she raughte.**
	He carried a horn, the shoulder strap was green;		She reached for her food in a very seemly manner.
117	**A forster was he, soothly, as I gesse.**	137	**And sikerly she was of greet desport,**
	He was a forester, truly, as I guess.		And surely she was of excellent deportment,
118	**Ther was also a Nonne, a PRIORESSE,**	138	**And ful plesaunt, and amiable of port,**
	There was also a Nun, a PRIORESS,		And very pleasant, and amiable in demeanor,
119	**That of hir smyling was ful simple and coy;**	139	**And peyned hir to countrefete chere**
	Who was very simple and modest in her smiling;		And she took pains to imitate the manners
120	**Hire gretteste ooth was but by Seinte Loy;**	140	**Of court, and been estatlich of manere,**
	Her greatest oath was but by sëynt Loy;		Of court, and to be dignified in behavior,
121	**And she was cleped madame Eglentyne.**	141	**And to ben holden digne of reverence.**
	And she was called Madam Eglantine.		And to be considered worthy of reverence.
122	**Ful wel she song the service divyne,**	142	**But for to speken of hir conscience,**
	She sang the divine service very well,		But to speak of her moral sense,
123	**Entuned in hir nose ful semely;**	143	**She was so charitable and so pitous**
	Intoned in her nose in a very polite manner;		She was so charitable and so compassionate
124	**And Frensh she spak ful faire and fetisly,**	144	**She wolde wepe, if that she sawe a mous**
	And she spoke French very well and elegantly,		She would weep, if she saw a mouse
125	**After the scole of Stratford atte Bowe,**	145	**Caught in a trappe, if it were deed or bledde.**
	In the manner of Stratford at the Bow,		Caught in a trap, if it were dead or bled.
126	**For Frensh of Parys was to hir unknowe.**	146	**Of smale houndes had she, that she fedde**
	For French of Paris was to her unknown.		She had some small hounds that she fed
127	**At mete wel y-taught was she with-alle;**	147	**With rosted flesh, or milk and wastel-breed.**
	At meals she was well taught indeed;		With roasted meat, or milk and fine white bread.
128	**She leet no morsel from hir lippes falle,**	148	**But soore weep she if oon of hem were deed,**
	She let no morsel fall from her lips,		But sorely she wept if one of them were dead,

149 **Or if men smoot it with a yerde smerte;**
Or if someone smote it smartly with a stick;
150 **And al was conscience and tendre herte.**
And all was feeling and tender heart.
151 **Ful semely hir wimpul pinched was,**
Her wimple was pleated in a very seemly manner,
152 **Hir nose tretys; hir eyen greye as glas,**
Her nose well formed, her eyes gray as glass,
153 **Hir mouth ful smal, and ther-to softe and reed;**
Her mouth very small, and moreover soft and red.
154 **But sikerly she hadde a fair forheed;**
But surely she had a fair forehead;
155 **It was almost a spanne brood, I trowe;**
It was almost nine inches broad, I believe;
156 **For, hardily, she was nat undergrowe.**
For, certainly, she was not undergrown.
157 **Ful fetis was hir cloke, as I was war.**
Her cloak was very well made, as I was aware.
158 **Of smal coral aboute hir arm she bar**
About her arm she bore of small coral
159 **A peire of bedes, gauded al with grene,**
A set of beads, adorned with large green beads,
160 **And ther-on heng a broche of gold ful shene,**
And thereon hung a brooch of very bright gold,
161 **On which ther was first write a crowned A,**
On which there was first written an A with a crown,
162 **And after *Amor vincit omnia*.**
And after "Love conquers all."

163 **Another NONNE with hir hadde she,**
She had another NUN with her,
164 **That was hir chapeleyne, and PREESTES thre.**
Who was her secretary, and three priests.

165 **A MONK ther was, a fair for the maistrye,**
There was a MONK, an extremely fine one,
166 **An out-rydere, that lovede venerye;**
An outrider (a monk with business outside the monastery), who loved hunting,
167 **A manly man, to been an abbot able.**
A virile man, qualified to be an abbot.
168 **Ful many a deyntee hors hadde he in stable,**
He had very many fine horses in his stable,
169 **And, when he rood, men mighte his brydel here**
And when he rode, one could hear his bridle
170 **Ginglen in a whistling wynd als clere**
Jingle in a whistling wind as clear
171 **And eek as loude as dooth the chapel-belle**
And also as loud as does the chapel belle
172 **Ther as this lord was keper of the celle.**
Where this lord was prior of the subordinate monastery.
173 **The reule of seint Maure or of seint Beneit—**
The rule of Saint Maurus or of Saint Benedict—
174 **By-cause that it was old and som-del streit**
Because it was old and somewhat strict
175 **This ilke monk leet olde thinges pace,**
This same Monk let old things pass away,
176 **And held after the newe world the space.**
And followed the broader customs of modern times.
177 **He yaf nat of that text a pulled hen,**
He gave not a plucked hen for that text
178 **That seith, that hunters been nat holy men,**
That says that hunters are not holy men,
179 **Ne that a monk, whan he is cloisterlees,**
Nor that a monk, when he is heedless of rules,
180 **Is lykned til a fish that is waterlees—**
Is like a fish that is out of water—
181 **This is to seyn, a monk out of his cloistre.**
This is to say, a monk out of his cloister.
182 **But thilke text held he nat worth an oistre;**
But he considered that same text not worth an oyster;
183 **And I seyde his opinioun was good.**
And I said his opinion was good.
184 **What sholde he studie, and make himselven wood,**
Why should he study and make himself crazy,
185 **Upon a book in cloistre alwey to poure,**
Always to pore upon a book in the cloister,
186 **Or swinken with his handes, and laboure,**
Or work with his hands, and labor,
187 **As Austin bit? How shal the world be served?**
As Augustine commands? How shall the world be served?

188	**Lat Austyn have his swink to him reserved.**	206	**A fat swan loved he best of any roost.**
	Let Augustine have his work reserved to him!		A fat swan loved he best of any roast.
189	**Therfore he was a pricasour aright:**	207	**His palfrey was as broun as is a berye.**
	Therefore he was indeed a vigorous horseman:		His saddle horse was as brown as is a berry.
190	**Grehoundes he hadde, as swift as fowel in flight;**	208	**A FRERE ther was, a wantown and a merye,**
	He had greyhounds as swift as fowl in flight;		There was a FRIAR, a pleasure-loving and merry one,
191	**Of prikyig and of huntyng for the hare**	209	**A limitour, a ful solempne man.**
	Of tracking and of hunting for the hare		A limiter (with an assigned territory), a very solemn man.
192	**Was al his lust, for no cost wolde he spare.**	210	**In alle the ordres foure is noon that can**
	Was all his pleasure, by no means would he refrain from it.		In all the four orders of friars is no one that knows
193	**I seigh his sleves purfiled at the hond**	211	**So muche of daliaunce and fair langage.**
	I saw his sleeves lined at the hand		So much of sociability and elegant speech.
194	**With grys, and that the fyneste of a lond;**	212	**He hadde maad ful many a mariage**
	With squirrel fur, and that the finest in the land;		He had made very many a marriage
195	**And, for to festne his hood under his chin,**	213	**Of yonge wommen at his owne cost.**
	And to fasten his hood under his chin,		Of young women at his own cost.
196	**He hadde of gold y-wroght a curious pyn;**	214	**Un-to his ordre he was a noble post.**
	He had a very skillfully made pin of gold;		He was a noble supporter of his order.
197	**A love-knotte in the gretter ende ther was.**	215	**Ful wel biloved and famulier was he**
	There was an elaborate knot in the larger end.		Very well beloved and familiar was he
198	**His heed was balled, that shoon as any glas,**	216	**With frankeleyns over-al in his contree,**
	His head was bald, which shone like any glass,		With landowners every where in his country,
199	**And eek his face, as he had been enoynt.**	217	**And eek with worthy wommen of the toun:**
	And his face did too, as if he had been rubbed with oil.		And also with worthy women of the town;
200	**He was a lord ful fat and in good point;**	218	**For he hadde power of confessioun,**
	He was a very plump lord and in good condition;		For he had power of confession,
201	**His eyen stepe, and rollinge in his heed,**	219	**As seyde him-self, more than a curat,**
	His eyes were prominent, and rolling in his head,		As he said himself, more than a parish priest,
202	**That stemed as a forneys of a leed;**	220	**For of his ordre he was licentiat.**
	Which gleamed like a furnace under a cauldron;		For he was licensed by his order.
203	**His botes souple, his hors in greet estat.**	221	**Ful swetely herde he confessioun,**
	His boots supple, his horse in excellent condition.		He heard confession very sweetly,
204	**Now certeinly he was a fair prelat;**	222	**And plesaunt was his absolucioun:**
	Now certainly he was a handsome ecclesiastical dignitary;		And his absolution was pleasant:
205	**He was nat pale as a for-pyned goost.**	223	**He was an esy man to yeve penaunce,**
	He was not pale as a tormented spirit.		He was a lenient man in giving penance,
		224	**Ther as he wiste to han a good pitaunce.**
			Where he knew he would have a good gift.
		225	**For unto a povre ordre for to yive**
			For to give to a poor order (of friars)
		226	**Is signe that a man is wel y-shrive;**
			Is a sign that a man is well confessed;

227	**For if he yaf, he dorste make avaunt,**	248	**But al with riche and selleres of vitaille.**
	For if he gave, he (the friar) dared to assert,		But all with rich people and sellers of victuals.
228	**He wiste that a man was repentaunt;**	249	**And over-al, ther as profit sholde aryse,**
	He knew that a man was repentant;		And every where, where profit should arise,
229	**For many a man so hard is of his herte,**	250	**Curteys he was and lowely of servyse.**
	For many a man is so hard in his heart,		He was courteous and graciously humble;
230	**He may nat wepe al-thogh him sore smerte.**	251	**Ther nas no man no-wher so vertuous.**
	He can not weep, although he painfully suffers.		There was no man anywhere so capable (of such work).
231	**Therfore in stede of weping and preyeres**	252	**He was the beste beggere in his hous;**
	Therefore instead of weeping and prayers		He was the best beggar in his house;
232	**Men moot yeve silver to the povre freres.**	252a	**[And yaf a certeyn ferme for the graunt;**
	One may give silver to the poor friars.		[And he gave a certain fee for his grant (of begging rights);
233	**His tipet was ay farsed ful of knyves**	252b	**Noon of his bretheren cam ther in his haunt;]**
	His hood was always stuffed full of knives		None of his brethren came there in his territory;]
234	**And pinnes, for to yeven faire wyves.**	253	**For thogh a widwe hadde noght a sho,**
	And pins, to give to fair wives.		For though a widow had not a shoe,
235	**And certeinly he hadde a mery note:**	254	**So plesaunt was his "In principio,"**
	And certainly he had a merry voice:		So pleasant was his "In the beginning,"
236	**Wel coude he singe and pleyen on a rote;**	255	**Yet wolde he have a ferthyng, er he wente.**
	He well knew how to sing and play on a rote (string instrument);		Yet he would have a farthing, before he went away.
237	**Of yeddinges he bar utterly the prys.**	256	**His purchas was wel bettre than his rente.**
	He absolutely took the prize for reciting ballads.		His total profit was much more than his proper income.
238	**His nekke whyt was as the flour-de-lys;**	257	**And rage he coude, as it were right a whelpe.**
	His neck was white as a lily flower;		And he knew how to frolic, as if he were indeed a pup.
239	**Ther-to he strong was as a champioun.**	258	**In love-dayes ther coude he muchel helpe,**
	Furthermore he was strong as a champion fighter.		He knew how to be much help on days for resolving disputes,
240	**He knew the tavernes wel in every toun**	259	**For there he was nat lyk a cloisterer**
	He knew the taverns well in every town		For there he was not like a cloistered monk
241	**And everich hostiler and tappestere**	260	**With a thredbar cope, as is a povre scoler,**
	And every innkeeper and barmaid		With a threadbare cope, like a poor scholar,
242	**Bet than a lazar or a beggestere,**	261	**But he was lyk a maister or a pope.**
	Better than a leper or a beggar-woman,		But he was like a master of arts or a pope.
243	**For un-to swich a worthy man as he**	262	**Of double worsted was his semi-cope,**
	For unto such a worthy man as he		Of wide (expensive) cloth was his short cloak,
244	**Acorded nat, as by his facultee,**	263	**That rounded as a belle out of the presse.**
	It was not suitable, in view of his official position,		Which was round as a bell fresh from the clothespress.
245	**To have with seke lazars aqueyntaunce.**		
	To have acquaintance with sick lepers.		
246	**It is nat honest; it may nat avaunce,**		
	It is not respectable; it can not be profitable,		
247	**For to delen with no swich poraille,**		
	To deal with any such poor people,		

264 **Somwhat he lipsed, for his wantownesse,**
  Somewhat he lisped, for his affectation,
265 **To make his English sweete up-on his tonge;**
  To make his English sweet upon his tongue;
266 **And in his harping, whan that he had songe,**
  And in his harping, when he had sung,
267 **His eyen twinkled in his heed aright**
  His eyes twinkled in his head exactly
268 **As doon the sterres in the frosty night.**
  As do the stars in the frosty night.
269 **This worthy limitour was cleped Huberd.**
  This worthy friar was called Huberd.

270 **A MARCHANT was ther with a forked berd,**
  There was a MERCHANT with a forked beard,
271 **In mottelee, and hye on horse he sat;**
  Wearing parti-colored cloth, and proudly he sat on his horse;
272 **Up-on his heed a Flaundrish bever hat,**
  Upon his head (he wore a) Flemish beaver hat,
273 **His botes clasped faire and fetisly.**
  His boots were buckled handsomely and elegantly.
274 **His resons he spak ful solempnely,**
  His opinions he spoke very solemnly,
275 **Souninge alwey thencrees of his wynnyng.**
  Concerning always the increase of his profits.
276 **He wolde the see were kept for any thing**
  He wanted the sea to be guarded at all costs
277 **Bitwixe Middelburgh and Orewelle.**
  Between Middelburgh (Holland) and Orwell (England).
278 **Wel coude he in eschaunge sheeldes selle.**
  He well knew how to deal in foreign currencies.
279 **This worthy man ful wel his wit bisette:**
  This worthy man employed his wit very well:
280 **Ther wiste no wight that he was in dette,**
  There was no one who knew that he was in debt,
281 **So estatly was he of his governaunce**
  He was so dignified in managing his affairs
282 **With his bargaynes and with his chevisaunce.**
  With his buying and selling and with his financial deals.
283 **For sothe he was a worthy man with-alle,**
  Truly, he was a worthy man indeed,
284 **But, sooth to seyn, I noot how men him calle.**
  But, to say the truth, I do not know what men call him.

285 **A CLERK ther was of Oxenford also,**
  There was also a CLERK (scholar) from Oxford,
286 **That un-to logik hadde longe y-go.**
  Who long before had begun the study of logic.
287 **As lene was his hors as is a rake,**
  His horse was as lean as is a rake,
288 **And he nas nat right fat, I undertake,**
  And he was not very fat, I affirm,
289 **But loked holwe, and ther-to sobrely.**
  But looked emaciated, and moreover abstemious.
290 **Ful thredbar was his overest courtepy,**
  His short overcoat was very threadbare,
291 **For he had geten him yet no benefyce,**
  For he had not yet obtained an ecclesiastical living,
292 **Ne was so worldly for to have offyce.**
  Nor was he worldly enough to take secular employment.
293 **For him was lever have at his beddes heed**
  For he would rather have at the head of his bed
294 **Twenty bokes, clad in blak or reed,**
  Twenty books, bound in black or red,
295 **Of Aristotle and his philosophye**
  Of Aristotle and his philosophy
296 **Than robes riche, or fithele, or gay sautrye.**
  Than rich robes, or a fiddle, or an elegant psaltery.
297 **But al be that he was a philosophre,**
  But even though he was a philosopher,
298 **Yet hadde he but litel gold in cofre;**
  Nevertheless he had but little gold in his strongbox;
299 **But al that he mighte of his freendes hente,**
  But all that he could get from his friends,

300 **On bokes and on lerninge he it spente,**
　　He spent on books and on learning,
301 **And bisily gan for the soules preye**
　　And diligently did pray for the souls
302 **Of hem that yaf him wher-with to scoleye.**
　　Of those who gave him the wherewithal to attend the schools.
303 **Of studie took he most cure and most hede.**
　　He took most care and paid most heed to study.
304 **Noght o word spak he more than was nede,**
　　He spoke not one word more than was needed,
305 **And that was seyd in forme and reverence,**
　　And that was said with due formality and respect,
306 **And short and quik, and ful of hy sentence;**
　　And short and lively and full of elevated content;
307 **Souninge in moral vertu was his speche,**
　　His speech was consonant with moral virtue,
308 **And gladly wolde he lerne, and gladly teche.**
　　And gladly would he learn and gladly teach.

309 **A SERGEANT OF THE LAWE, war and wys,**
　　A SERGEANT OF THE LAW (high-ranking attorney), prudent and wise,
310 **That often hadde been at the parvys,**
　　Who often had been at the Porch of St. Paul's (where lawyers gather)
311 **Ther was also, ful riche of excellence.**
　　Was also there, very rich in superior qualities.
312 **Discreet he was, and of greet reverence—**
　　He was judicious and of great dignity—
313 **He semed swich, his wordes weren so wise.**
　　He seemed such, his words were so wise.
314 **Iustice he was ful often in assyse,**
　　He was very often a judge in the court of assizes,
315 **By patente and by pleyn commissioun.**
　　By royal appointment and with full jurisdiction.
316 **For his science and for his heigh renoun,**
　　For his knowledge and for his excellent reputation,
317 **Of fees and robes hadde he many oon.**
　　He had many grants of yearly income.
318 **So greet a purchasour was no-wher noon:**
　　There was nowhere so great a land-buyer:
319 **Al was fee simple to hym in effect;**
　　In fact, all was unrestricted possession to him;
320 **His purchasing mighte nat been infect.**
　　His purchasing could not be invalidated.
321 **No-wher so bisy a man as he ther nas,**
　　There was nowhere so busy a man as he,
322 **And yet he semed bisier than he was.**
　　And yet he seemed busier than he was.
323 **In termes hadde he caas and doomes alle**
　　He had in Year Books all the cases and decisions
324 **That from the tyme of king William were falle.**
　　That from the time of king William have occurred.
325 **Therto he coude endyte and make a thing,**
　　Furthermore, he knew how to compose and draw up a legal document,
326 **Ther coude no wight pinche at his wryting;**
　　So that no one could find a flaw in his writing;
327 **And every statut coude he pleyn by rote.**
　　And he knew every statute completely by heart.
328 **He rood but hoomly in a medlee cote,**
　　He rode but simply in a parti-colored coat,
329 **Girt with a ceint of silk, with barres smale;**
　　Girded with a belt of silk, with small stripes;
330 **Of his array telle I no lenger tale.**
　　I tell no longer tale of his clothing.

331 **A FRANKELEYN was in his companye.**
　　A FRANKLIN was in his company.
332 **Whyt was his berd as is the dayesye;**
　　His beard was white as a daisy;
333 **Of his complexioun he was sangwyn.**
　　As to his temperament, he was dominated by the humor blood.
334 **Wel loved he by the morwe a sop in wyn;**
　　He well loved a bit of bread dipped in wine in the morning;

335	**To liven in delyt was evere his wone,**
	His custom was always to live in delight,
336	**For he was Epicurus owne sone,**
	For he was Epicurus' own son,
337	**That heeld opinioun that pleyn delyt**
	Who held the opinion that pure pleasure
338	**Was verraily felicitee parfyt.**
	Was truly perfect happiness.
339	**An housholdere, and that a greet, was he;**
	He was a householder, and a great one at that;
340	**Seint Iulian he was in his contree.**
	He was Saint Julian (patron of hospitality) in his country.
341	**His breed, his ale, was alwey after oon;**
	His bread, his ale, was always of the same (good) quality;
342	**A bettre envyned man was no-wher noon.**
	Nowhere was there any man better stocked with wine.
343	**With-oute bake mete was never his hous,**
	His house was never without baked pies
344	**Of fish and flesh, and that so plentevous,**
	Of fish and meat, and that so plentiful
345	**It snewed in his hous of mete and drinke,**
	That in his house it snowed with food and drink;
346	**Of alle deyntees that men coude thinke.**
	Of all the dainties that men could imagine,
347	**After the sondry sesons of the yeer,**
	In accord with the various seasons of the year,
348	**So chaunged he his mete and his soper.**
	So he varied his midday meal and his supper.
349	**Ful many a fat partrich hadde he in mewe,**
	He had very many fat partridges in pens,
350	**And many a breem and many a luce in stewe.**
	And many a bream and many a pike in his fish pond.
351	**Wo was his cook, but-if his sauce were**
	Woe was his cook unless his sauce was
352	**Poynaunt and sharp, and redy al his gere.**
	Hotly spiced and sharp, and ready all his cooking equipment.
353	**His table dormant in his halle alway**
	In his hall his dining table always
354	**Stood redy covered al the longe day.**
	Stood covered (with table cloth) and ready all the long day.
355	**At sessiouns ther was he lord and sire;**
	He presided as lord and sire at court sessions;
356	**Ful ofte tyme he was knight of the shire.**
	He was a member of parliament many times.
357	**An anlas and a gipser al of silk**
	A dagger and a purse all of silk
358	**Heng at his girdel, whyt as morne milk.**
	Hung at his belt, white as morning milk.
359	**A shirreve hadde he been, and a countour;**
	He had been a sheriff, and an auditor of taxes.
360	**Was no-wher such a worthy vavasour.**
	There was nowhere such a worthy landowner.
361	**AN HABERDASSHERE and a CARPENTER,**
	A HABERDASHER and a CARPENTER,
362	**A WEBBE, a DYERE, and a TAPICER—**
	A WEAVER, a DYER, and a TAPESTRY-MAKER—
363	**Were with us eek, clothed in o liveree,**
	And they were all clothed in one livery
364	**Of a solempne and a greet fraternitee.**
	Of a solempne and greet fraternitee.
365	**Ful fresh and newe hir gere apyked was;**
	Their equipment was adorned all freshly and new;
366	**Hir knyves were y-chaped noght with bras,**
	Their knives were not mounted with brass
367	**But al with silver, wroght ful clene and weel,**
	But entirely with silver, wrought very neatly and well,
368	**Hir girdles and hir pouches every-deel.**
	Their belts and their purses every bit.
369	**Wel semed ech of hem a fair burgeys,**
	Each of them well seemed a solid citizen
370	**To sitten in a yeldhalle on a deys.**
	To sit on a dais in a city hall.
371	**Everich, for the wisdom that he can,**
	Every one of them, for the wisdom that he knows,
372	**Was shaply for to been an alderman.**
	Was suitable to be an alderman.

373	**For catel hadde they y-nogh and rente,**	390	**He rood up-on a rouncy, as he couthe,**
	For they had enough possessions and income,		He rode upon a cart horse, insofar as he knew how,
374	**And eek hir wyves wolde it wel assente;**	391	**In a gowne of falding to the knee.**
	And also their wives would well assent to it;		In a gown of woolen cloth (that reached) to the knee.
375	**And elles certein were they to blame.**	392	**A daggere hanging on a laas hadde he**
	And otherwise certainly they would be to blame.		He had a dagger hanging on a cord
376	**It is ful fair to been y-clept "ma dame,"**	393	**Aboute his nekke under his arm adoun.**
	It is very fine to be called "my lady,"		About his neck, down under his arm.
377	**And goon to vigilyës al bifore,**	394	**The hote somer had maad his hewe al broun;**
	And go to feasts on holiday eves heading the procession,		The hot summer had made his hue all brown;
378	**And have a mantel royalliche y-bore.**	395	**And, certeinly, he was a good felawe.**
	And have a gown with a train royally carried.		And certainly he was a boon companion.
379	**A COOK they hadde with hem for the nones**	396	**Ful many a draughte of wyn had he y-drawe**
	A COOK they had with them for the occasion		He had drawn very many a draft of wine
380	**To boille the chiknes with the mary-bones,**	397	**From Burdeux-ward, whyl that the chapman sleep.**
	To boil the chickens with the marrow bones,		While coming from Bordeaux, while the merchant slept.
381	**And poudre-marchant tart, and galingale.**	398	**Of nyce conscience took he no keep.**
	And tart poudre-marchant and galingale (spices).		He had no concern for a scrupulous conscience.
382	**Wel coude he knowe a draughte of London ale.**	399	**If that he faught, and hadde the hyer hond,**
	He well knew how to judge a draft of London ale.		If he fought and had the upper hand,
383	**He coude roste, and sethe, and broille, and frye,**	400	**By water he sente hem hoom to every lond.**
	He knew how to roast, and boil, and broil, and fry,		He sent them home by water to every land (they walked the plank).
384	**Maken mortreux, and wel bake a pye.**	401	**But of his craft to rekene wel his tydes,**
	Make stews, and well bake a pie.		But of his skill to reckon well his tides,
385	**But greet harm was it, as it thoughte me,**	402	**His stremes and his daungers him bisydes,**
	But it was a great harm, as it seemed to me,		His currents, and his perils near at hand,
386	**That on his shine a mormal hadde he;**	403	**His herberwe and his mone, his lodemenage,**
	That he had an open sore on his shin.		His harbors, and positions of his moon, his navigation,
387	**For blankmanger, that made he with the beste.**	404	**Ther nas noon swich from Hulle to Cartage.**
	As for white pudding, he made that of the best quality.		There was none other such from Hull to Cartagena (Spain).
388	**A SHIPMAN was ther, woning fer by weste:**	405	**Hardy he was, and wys to undertake;**
	A SHIPMAN was there, dwelling far in the west;		He was bold and prudent in his undertakings;
389	**For aught I woot, he was of Dertemouthe.**	406	**With many a tempest hadde his berd been shake.**
	For all I know, he was from Dartmouth.		His beard had been shaken by many a tempest.

407	**He knew wel alle the havenes, as they were,**	427	**For ech of hem made other for to winne;**
	He knew all the harbors, how they were,		For each of them made the other to profit;
408	**From Gootlond to the cape of Finistere,**	428	**Hir frendschipe nas nat newe to biginne.**
	From Gotland to the Cape of Finisterre,		Their friendship was not recently begun.
409	**And every cryke in Britayne and in Spayne;**	429	**Wel knew he the olde Esculapius,**
	And every inlet in Brittany and in Spain.		He well knew the old Aesculapius,
410	**His barge y-cleped was the Maudelayne.**	430	**And Deiscorides, and eek Rufus,**
	His ship was called the Maudelayne.		And Dioscorides, and also Rufus,
411	**With us ther was a DOCTOUR OF PHISYK;**	431	**Old Ypocras, Haly, and Galien;**
	With us there was a DOCTOR OF MEDICINE		Old Hippocrates, Haly, and Galen,
412	**In al this world ne was ther noon him lyk**	432	**Serapion, Razis, and Avicen;**
	In all this world there was no one like him,		Serapion, Rhazes, and Avicenna,
413	**To speke of phisik and of surgerye;**	433	**Averrois, Damascien, and Constantyn;**
	To speak of medicine and of surgery,		Averroes, John the Damascan, and Constantine,
414	**For he was grounded in astronomye.**	434	**Bernard, and Gatesden, and Gilbertyn.**
	For he was instructed in astronomy.		Bernard, and Gaddesden, and Gilbertus.
415	**He kepte his pacient a ful greet del**	435	**Of his diete mesurable was he,**
	He took care of his patient very many times		He was moderate in his diet,
416	**In houres, by his magik naturel.**	436	**For it was of no superfluitee,**
	In (astronomically suitable) hours by (use of) his natural science.		For it was of no excess,
417	**Wel coude he fortunen the ascendent**	437	**But of greet norissing and digestible.**
	He well knew how to calculate the planetary position		But greatly nourishing and digestible.
418	**Of his images for his pacient.**	438	**His studie was but litel on the Bible.**
	Of his astronomical talismans for his patient.		His study was but little on the Bible.
419	**He knew the cause of everich maladye,**	439	**In sangwyn and in pers he clad was al,**
	He knew the cause of every malady,		He was clad all in red and in blue,
420	**Were it of hoot or cold, or moiste, or drye,**	440	**Lyned with taffata and with sendal.**
	Were it of hot, or cold, or moist, or dry elements,		Lined with taffeta and with silk.
421	**And where they engendred, and of what humour:**	441	**And yet he was but esy of dispence;**
	And where they were engendered, and by what bodily fluid.		And yet he was moderate in spending;
422	**He was a verrey parfit practisour.**	442	**He kepte that he wan in pestilence.**
	He was a truly, perfect practitioner:		He kept what he earned in (times of) plague.
423	**The cause y-knowe, and of his harm the rote,**	443	**For gold in phisik is a cordial,**
	The cause known, and the source of his (patient's) harm,		Since in medicine gold is a restorative for the heart,
424	**Anon he yaf the seke man his bote.**	444	**Therefore he lovede gold in special.**
	Straightway he gave the sick man his remedy.		Therefore he loved gold in particular.
425	**Ful redy hadde he his apothecaries,**	445	**A good WYF was ther of bisyde BATHE,**
	He had his apothecaries all ready		There was a good WIFE OF beside BATH,
426	**TTo sende him drogges and his letuaries,**	446	**But she was som-del deef, and that was scathe.**
	To send him drugs and his electuaries,		But she was somewhat deaf, and that was a pity.
		447	**Of clooth-making she hadde swich an haunt**
			She had such a skill in cloth-making
		448	**She passed hem of Ypres and of Gaunt.**
			She surpassed them of Ypres and of Ghent.
		449	**In al the parisshe wyf ne was ther noon**
			In all the parish there was no wife

450	**That to the offring bifore hir sholde goon;**	470	**Y-wimpled wel, and on hir heed an hat**
	Who should go to the Offering before her;		Wearing a large wimple, and on her head a hat
451	**And if ther dide, certeyn so wrooth was she**	471	**As brood as is a bokeler or a targe;**
	And if there did, certainly she was so angry		As broad as a buckler or a shield;
452	**That she was out of alle charitee.**	472	**A foot-mantel aboute hir hipes large,**
	That she was out of all charity (love for her neighbor).		An overskirt about her large hips,
453	**Hir coverchiefs ful fyne were of ground;**	473	**And on hir feet a paire of spores sharpe.**
	Her kerchiefs were very fine in texture;		And on her feet a pair of sharp spurs.
454	**I dorste swere they weyeden ten pound**	474	**In felawschip wel coude she laughe and carpe.**
	I dare swear they weighed ten pound		In fellowship she well knew how to laugh and chatter.
455	**That on a Sonday were upon hir heed.**	475	**Of remedyes of love she knew per-chaunce,**
	That on a Sunday were upon her head.		She knew, as it happened, about remedies for love
456	**Hir hosen weren of fyn scarlet reed,**	476	**For she coude of that art the olde daunce.**
	Her stockings were of fine scarlet red,		For she knew the old dance (tricks of the trade) of that art.
457	**Ful streite y-teyd, and shoes ful moiste and newe.**		
	Very closely laced, and shoes very supple and new.	477	**A good man was ther of religioun,**
458	**Bold was hir face, and fair, and reed of hewe.**		A good man was there of religion,
	Bold was her face, and fair, and red of hue.	478	**And was a povre PERSOUN of a toun,**
459	**She was a worthy womman al hir lyve:**		And (he) was a poor PARSON of a town,
	She was a worthy woman all her life:	479	**But riche he was of holy thoght and werk.**
460	**Housbondes at chirche-dore she hadde fyve,**		But he was rich in holy thought and work.
	She had (married) five husbands at the church door,	480	**He was also a lerned man, a clerk,**
461	**Withouten oother companye in youthe;**		He was also a learned man, a scholar,
	Not counting other company in youth;	481	**That Cristes gospel trewely wolde preche;**
462	**But thereof nedeth nat to speke as nouthe.**		Who would preach Christ's gospel truly;
	But there is no need to speak of that right now.	482	**His parisshens devoutly wolde he teche.**
463	**And thryes hadde she been at Ierusalem;**		He would devoutly teach his parishioners.
	And she had been three times at Jerusalem;	483	**Benigne he was, and wonder diligent,**
464	**She hadde passed many a straunge streem;**		He was gracious, and wonderfully diligent,
	She had passed many a foreign sea;	484	**And in adversitee ful pacient,**
465	**At Rome she hadde been, and at Boloigne,**		And very patient in adversity,
	She had been at Rome, and at Boulogne,	485	**And swich he was y-preved ofte sythes.**
466	**In Galice at seint Iame, and at Coloigne.**		And such he was proven many times.
	In Galicia at Saint-James (of Compostella), and at Cologne.	486	**Ful looth were him to cursen for his tythes,**
467	**She coude muche of wandring by the weye..**		He was very reluctant to excommunicate for (nonpayment of) his tithes,
	She knew much about wandering by the way.	487	**But rather wolde he yeven, out of doute,**
468	**Gat-tothed was she, soothly for to seye.**		But rather would he give, there is no doubt,
	She had teeth widely set apart, truly to say.	488	**Un-to his povre parisshens aboute**
469	**Up-on an amblere esily she sat,**		Unto his poor parishioners about
	She sat easily upon a pacing horse,	489	**Of his offring, and eek of his substaunce.**
			Some of his offering (received at mass), and also some of his income.

490	**He coude in litel thing han suffisaunce.**	510	**To seken him a chaunterie for soules,**
	He knew how to have sufficiency in few possessions.		To seek an appointment as a chantry priest (praying for a patron)
491	**Wyd was his parisshe, and houses fer a-sonder,**	511	**Or with a bretherhed to been withholde;**
	His parish was wide, and houses far apart,		Or to be hired (as a chaplain) by a guild;
492	**But he ne lafte nat, for reyn ne thonder,**	512	**But dwelte at hoom, and kepte wel his folde,**
	But he did not omit, for rain nor thunder,		But dwelt at home, and kept well his sheep fold (parish),
493	**In siknes nor in meschief to visyte**	513	**So that the wolf ne made it nat miscarie;**
	In sickness or in trouble to visit		So that the wolf did not make it go wrong;
494	**The ferreste in his parisshe, muche and lyte,**	514	**He was a shepherde and no mercenarie.**
	Those living farthest away in his parish, high-ranking and low,		He was a shepherd and not a hireling.
495	**Up-on his feet, and in his hand a staf.**	515	**And though he holy were and vertuous,**
	Going by foot, and in his hand a staff.		And though he was holy and virtuous,
496	**This noble ensample to his sheep he yaf,**	516	**He was to sinful man nat despitous,**
	He gave this noble example to his sheep,		He was not scornful to sinful men,
497	**That first he wroghte, and afterward he taughte;**	517	**Ne of his speche daungerous ne digne,**
	That first he wrought, and afterward he taught;		Nor domineering nor haughty in his speech,
498	**Out of the gospel he tho wordes caughte,**	518	**But in his techyng discreet and benigne.**
	He took those words out of the gospel,		But in his teaching courteous and kind.
499	**And this figure he added eek ther-to,**	519	**To drawen folk to heven by fairnesse,**
	And this metaphor he added also to that,		To draw folk to heaven by gentleness,
500	**That if gold ruste, what shal iren do?**	520	**By good ensample, this was his bisynesse.**
	That if gold rust, what must iron do?		By good example, this was his business.
501	**For if a preest be foul, on whom we truste,**	521	**But it were any persone obstinat,**
	For if a priest, on whom we trust, should be foul		Unless it were an obstinate person,
502	**No wonder is a lewed man to ruste;**	522	**What-so he were, of heigh or lowe estat,**
	It is no wonder for a layman to go bad;		Whoever he was, of high or low rank,
503	**And shame it is, if a preest take keep,**	523	**Him wolde he snibben sharply for the nones.**
	And it is a shame, if a priest is concerned:		He would rebuke him sharply at that time.
504	**A shiten shepherde and a clene sheep.**	524	**A bettre preest, I trowe that nowher noon is.**
	A shit-stained shepherd and a clean sheep.		I believe that nowhere is there a better priest.
505	**Wel oghte a preest ensample for to yive,**	525	**He wayted after no pompe and reverence,**
	Well ought a priest to give an example,		He expected no pomp and ceremony,
506	**By his clennesse, how that his sheep shold live.**	526	**Ne maked him a spyced conscience,**
	By his purity, how his sheep should live.		Nor made himself an overly fastidious conscience,
507	**He sette nat his benefice to hyre**	527	**But Cristes lore and his apostles twelve**
	He did not rent out his benefice (ecclesiastical living)		But Christ's teaching and His twelve apostles
508	**And leet his sheep encombred in the myre**	528	**He taughte; and first he folwed it him-selve.**
	And leave his sheep encumbered in the mire		He taught; but first he followed it himself.
509	**And ran to London, un-to sëynt Poules**		
	And run to London unto Saint Paul's		

529	**With hym ther was a PLOWMAN, was his brother,**	546	**Ful big he was of brawn, and eek of bones.**
	With him there was a PLOWMAN, who was his brother,		He was very strong of muscle, and also of bones.
530	**That hadde y-lad of dong ful many a fother;**	547	**That proved wel, for over-al ther he cam,**
	Who had hauled very many a cartload of dung;		That was well proven, for wherever he came,
531	**A trewe swinker and a good was he,**	548	**At wrastling he wolde have alwey the ram.**
	He was a true and good worker,		At wrestling he would always take the the prize.
532	**Livinge in pees and parfit charitee.**	549	**He was short-sholdred, brood, a thikke knarre,**
	Living in peace and perfect love.		He was stoutly built, broad, a large-framed fellow;
533	**God loved he best with al his hole herte**	550	**Ther nas no dore that he nolde heve of harre,**
	He loved God best with all his whole heart		There was no door that he would not heave off its hinges,
534	**At alle tymes, thogh him gamed or smerte,**	551	**Or breke it, at a renning, with his heed.**
	At all times, whether it pleased or pained him,		Or break it by running at it with his head.
535	**And thanne his neighebour right as him-selve.**	552	**His berd as any sowe or fox was reed,**
	And then (he loved) his neighbor exactly as himself.		His beard was red as any sow or fox,
536	**He wolde thresshe, and ther-to dyke and delve,**	553	**And ther-to brood, as though it were a spade.**
	He would thresh, and moreover make ditches and dig,		And moreover broad, as though it were a spade.
537	**For Cristes sake, for every povre wight,**	554	**Up-on the cop right of his nose he hade**
	For Christ's sake, for every poor person,		Upon the exact top of his nose he had
538	**Withouten hire, if it lay in his myght.**	555	**A werte, and ther-on stood a tuft of heres,**
	Without payment, if it lay in his power.		A wart, and thereon stood a tuft of hairs,
539	**His tythes payed he ful faire and wel,**	556	**Reed as the brustles of a sowes erys;**
	He paid his tithes completely and well,		Red as the bristles of a sow's ears;
540	**Bothe of his propre swink and his catel.**	557	**His nose-thirles blake were and wyde.**
	Both of his own labor and of his possessions.		His nostrils were black and wide.
541	**In a tabard he rood upon a mere.**	558	**A swerd and bokeler bar he by his syde;**
	He rode in a tabard (sleeveless jacket) upon a mare.		He wore a sword and a buckler by his side.
542	**Ther was also a REVE, and a MILLERE,**	559	**His mouth as greet was as a greet forneys.**
	There was also a REEVE, and a MILLER,		His mouth was as large as a large furnace.
543	**A SOMNOUR, and a PARDONER also,**	560	**He was a Ianglere and a goliardeys,**
	A SUMMONER, and a PARDONER also,		He was a loudmouth and a buffoon,
544	**A MAUNCIPLE, and my-self—ther were namo.**	561	**And that was most of sinne and harlotryes.**
	A MANCIPLE, and myself—there were no more.		And that was mostly of sin and deeds of harlotry.
545	**The MILLERE was a stout carl, for the nones;**	562	**Wel coude he stelen corn, and tollen thryes;**
	The MILLER was a stout fellow indeed;		He well knew how to steal corn and take payment three times;
		563	**And yet he hadde a thombe of gold, pardee.**
			And yet he had a thumb of gold, indeed.
		564	**A whyt cote and a blew hood wered he.**
			He wore a white coat and a blue hood.

565	**A baggepype wel coude he blowe and sowne,**	584	**And able for to helpen al a shire**
	He well knew how to blow and play a bag-pipe,		And (they would be) able to help all a shire
566	**And ther-with-al he broghte us out of towne.**	585	**In any cas that mighte falle or happe;**
	And with that he brought us out of town.		In any emergency that might occur or happen;
567	**A gentil MAUNCIPLE was ther of a temple,**	586	**And yet this maunciple sette hir aller cappe.**
	There was a fine MANCIPLE of a temple (law school),		And yit this Manciple fooled them all.
568	**Of which achatours mighte take exemple**	587	**The REVE was a sclendre colerik man.**
	Of whom buyers of provisions might take example		The REEVE was a slender choleric man.
569	**For to be wyse in bying of vitaille.**	588	**His berd was shave as ny as ever he can.**
	For how to be wise in buying of victuals;		His beard was shaved as close as ever he can;
570	**For whether that he payde, or took by taille,**	589	**His heer was by his eres round y-shorn.**
	For whether he paid (cash) or took (goods) on credit,		His hair was closely cropped by his ears;
571	**Algate he wayted so in his achat,**	590	**His top was dokked lyk a preest biforn.**
	Always he watched so (carefully for his opportunity) in his purchases		The top of his head in front was cut short like a priest's.
572	**That he was ay biforn and in good stat.**	591	**Ful longe were his legges, and ful lene,**
	That he was always ahead and in good state.		His legs were very long and very lean,
573	**Now is nat that of God a ful fair grace,**	592	**Y-lyk a staf, ther was no calf y-sene.**
	Now is not that a very fair grace of God,		Like a stick; there was no calf to be seen.
574	**That swich a lewed mannes wit shal pace**	593	**Wel coude he kepe a gerner and a binne;**
	That such an unlearned man's wit shall surpass		He well knew how to keep a granary and a storage bin;
575	**The wisdom of an heep of lerned men?**	594	**Ther was noon auditour coude on him winne.**
	The wisdom of a heap of learned men?		There was no auditor who could earn anything (by catching him).
576	**Of maistres hadde he mo than thryes ten,**	595	**Wel wiste he, by the droghte, and by the reyn,**
	He had more than three times ten masters,		He well knew by the drought and by the rain
577	**That were of lawe expert and curious;**	596	**The yelding of his seed, and of his greyn.**
	Who were expert and skillful in law;		(What would be) the yield of his seed and of his grain.
578	**Of which ther were a doseyn in that hous,**	597	**His lordes sheep, his neet, his dayerye,**
	Of whom there were a dozen in that house		His lord's sheep, his cattle, his herd of dairy cows,
579	**Worthy to been stiwardes of rente and lond**	598	**His swyn, his hors, his stoor, and his pultrye,**
	Worthy to be stewards of rent and land		His swine, his horses, his livestock, and his poultry
580	**Of any lord that is in Engelond,**	599	**Was hoolly in this reves governing,**
	Of any lord that is in England,		Was wholly in this Reeve's control,
581	**To make him live by his propre good,**	600	**And by his covenaunt yaf the rekening,**
	To make him live by his own wealth		And in accord with his contract he gave the reckoning,
582	**In honour dettelees, but he were wood,**		
	In honor and debtless (unless he were crazy),		
583	**Or live as scarsly as him list desire;**		
	Or live as economically as it pleased him to desire;		

601	**Sin that his lord was twenty yeer of age;**	
	Since his lord was twenty years of age.	
602	**Ther coude no man bringe him in arrerage.**	
	There was no man who could find him in arrears.	
603	**Ther nas baillif, ne herde, ne other hyne,**	
	There was no farm manager, nor herdsman, nor other servant,	
604	**That he ne knew his sleighte and his covyne;**	
	Whose trickery and treachery he did not know;	
605	**They were adrad of him, as of the deeth.**	
	They were afraid of him as of the plague.	
606	**His woning was ful fair up-on an heeth,**	
	His dwelling was very nicely situated upon an heath;	
607	**With grene treës shadwed was his place.**	
	His place was shaded by green trees.	
608	**He coude bettre than his lord purchace.**	
	He could buy property better than his lord could.	
609	**Ful riche he was astored prively,**	
	He was secretly very richly provided,	
610	**His lord wel coude he plesen subtilly,**	
	He well knew how to please his lord subtly,	
611	**To yeve and lene him of his owne good,**	
	By giving and lending him some of his lord's own possessions,	
612	**And have a thank, and yet a cote and hood.**	
	And have thanks, and also a coat and hood (as a reward).	
613	**In youthe he lerned hadde a good mister;**	
	In youth he had learned a good craft:	
614	**He was a wel good wrighte, a carpenter.**	
	He was a very good craftsman, a carpenter.	
615	**This reve sat up-on a ful good stot,**	
	This Reeve sat upon a very good horse	
616	**That was al pomely grey, and highte Scot.**	
	That was all dapple gray and was called Scot.	
617	**A long surcote of pers up-on he hade,**	
	He had on a long outer coat of dark blue,	
618	**And by his syde he bar a rusty blade.**	
	And by his side he wore a rusty sword.	
619	**Of Northfolk was this reve, of which I telle,**	
	Of Northfolk was this Reeve of whom I tell,	
620	**Bisyde a toun men clepen Baldeswelle.**	
	Near to a town men call Bawdeswelle.	

621 **Tukked he was, as is a frere, aboute,**
He had his coat hitched up and belted, like a friar,

622 **And ever he rood the hindreste of our route.**
And ever he rode as the last of our company.

623 **A SOMONOUR was ther with us in that place,**
There was a SUMMONER with us in that place,

624 **That hadde a fyr-reed cherubinnes face,**
Who had a fire-red cherubim's face,

625 **For sawcefleem he was, with eyen narwe.**
For it was pimpled and discolored, with swollen eyelids.

626 **As hoot he was, and lecherous, as a sparwe;**
He was as hot and lecherous as a sparrow,

627 **With scalled browes blake, and piled berd;**
With black, scabby brows and a beard with hair fallen out.

628 **Of his visage children were aferd.**
Children were afraid of his face.

629 **Ther nas quik-silver, litarge, ne brimstoon,**
There was no mercury, lead monoxide, nor sulphur,

630 **Boras, ceruce, ne oille of tartre noon,**
Borax, white lead, nor any oil of tarter,

631 **Ne oynement that wolde clense and byte,**
Nor ointment that would cleanse and burn,

632 **That him mighte helpen of his whelkes whyte,**
That could cure him of his white pustules,

633 **Nor of the knobbes sitting on his chekes.**
Nor of the knobs sitting on his cheeks.

634 **Wel loved he garleek, oynons, and eek lekes,**
He well loved garlic, onions, and also leeks,

635 **And for to drinken strong wyn, reed as blood.**
And to drink strong wine, red as blood;

636 **Thanne wolde he speke, and crye as he were wood.**
Then he would speak and cry out as if he were crazy.

637 **And whan that he wel dronken hadde the wyn,**
And when he had drunk deeply of the wine,

638	**Than wolde he speke no word but Latyn.** Then he would speak no word but Latin.		658	**'Purs is the erchedeknes helle,' seyde he.** "Purse is the archdeacon's hell," he said.
639	**A fewe termes hadde he, two or three,** He had a few legal terms, two or three,		659	**But wel I woot he lyed right in dede;** But well I know he lied right certainly;
640	**That he had lerned out of som decree;** That he had learned out of some text of ecclesiastical law;		660	**Of cursing oghte ech gilty man him drede—** Each guilty man ought to be afraid of excommunication—
641	**No wonder is, he herde it al the day;** That is no wonder, he heard it all the day;		661	**For curs wol slee, right as assoilling saveth—** For excommunication will slay just as forgiveness saves—
642	**And eek ye knowen wel, how that a Iay** And also you know well how a jay		662	**And also war him of a significavit.** And let him also beware of a Significavit (order for imprisonment).
643	**Can clepen 'Watte,' as well as can the pope.** Can call out "Walter" as well as the pope can.		663	**In daunger hadde he at his owne gyse** In his control he had as he pleased
644	**But who-so coude in other thing him grope,** But whoever knew how to examine him in other matters,		664	**The yonge girles of the diocyse,** The young people of the diocese,
645	**Thanne hadde he spent al his philosophye;** (Would find that) he had used up all his learning;		665	**And knew hir counseil, and was al hir reed.** And knew their secrets, and was the adviser of them all.
646	**Ay 'Questio quid iuris' wolde he crye.** Always "The question is, what point of the law applies?" he would cry.		666	**A gerland hadde he set up-on his heed,** He had set a garland upon his heed,
647	**He was a gentil harlot and a kinde;** He was a fine rascal and a kind one;		667	**As greet as it were for an ale-stake;** As large as if it were for the sign of a tavern
648	**A bettre felawe sholde men noght finde.** One could not find a better fellow.		668	**A bokeler hadde he maad him of a cake.** He had made himself a shield of a cake.
649	**He wolde suffre, for a quart of wyn,** For a quart of wine he would allow		669	**With him ther rood a gentil Pardoner** With him there rode a fine PARDONER
650	**A good felawe to have his concubyn** A good fellow to have his concubine		670	**Of Rouncival, his freend and his compeer,** Of Rouncivale, his friend and his companion,
651	**A twelf-month, and excuse him atte fulle:** For twelve months, and excuse him completely;		671	**That streight was comen fro the court of Rome.** Who had come straight from the court of Rome.
652	**Ful prively a finch eek coude he pulle.** Secretly he also knew how to pull off a clever trick.		672	**Ful loude he song, 'Com hider, love, to me.'** Very loud he sang "Come hither, love, to me!"
653	**And if he fond o-wher a good felawe,** And if he found anywhere a good fellow,		673	**This somnour bar to him a stif burdoun,** This Summoner harmonized with him in a strong bass;
654	**He wolde techen him to have non awe,** He would teach him to have no awe		674	**Was never trompe of half so greet a soun.** There was never a trumpet of half so great a sound.
655	**In swich cas, of the erchedeknes curs,** Of the archdeacon's curse (of excommunication) in such a case,		675	**This pardoner hadde heer as yelow as wex,** This pardoner had hair as yellow as wax,
656	**But-if a mannes soule were in his purs;** Unless a man's soul were in his purse;			
657	**For in his purs he sholde y-punisshed be.** For in his purse he would be punished.			

50 ⁓ Things Unattempted Yet in Prose or Rhyme

676	**But smothe it heng, as dooth a strike of flex;**	697	**That sëynt Peter hadde, whan that he wente**
	But smooth it hung as does a clump of flax;		That Saint Peter had, when he went
677	**By ounces henge his lokkes that he hadde,**	698	**Up-on the see, til Iesu Crist him hente.**
	By small strands hung such locks as he had,		Upon the sea, until Jesus Christ took him.
678	**And ther-with he his shuldres overspradde;**	699	**He hadde a croys of latoun, ful of stones,**
	And he spread them over his shoulders;		He had a cross of latten (brass-like alloy) covered with stones,
679	**But thinne it lay, by colpons oon and oon;**	700	**And in a glas he hadde pigges bones.**
	But thin it lay, by strands one by one;		And in a glass container he had pigs' bones.
680	**But hood, for Iolitee, ne wered he noon,**	701	**But with thise relikes, whan that he fond**
	But to make an attractive appearance, he wore no hood,		But with these relics, when he found
681	**For it was trussed up in his walet.**	702	**A povre person dwelling up-on lond,**
	For it was trussed up in his knapsack.		A poor parson dwelling in the countryside,
682	**Him thoughte, he rood al of the newe Iet;**	703	**Up-on a day he gat him more moneye**
	It seemed to him that he rode in the very latest style;		In one day he got himself more money
683	**Dischevele, save his cappe, he rood al bare.**	704	**Than that the person gat in monthes tweye.**
	With hair unbound, save for his cap, he rode all bare-headed.		Than the parson got in two months;
684	**Swiche glaringe eyen hadde he as an hare.**	705	**And thus, with feyned flaterye and Iapes,**
	He had glaring eyes such as has a hare.		And thus, with feigned flattery and tricks,
685	**A vernicle hadde he sowed on his cappe.**	706	**He made the person and the peple his apes.**
	He had sewn a Veronica upon his cap.		He made fools of the parson and the people.
686	**His walet lay biforn him in his lappe,**	707	**But trewely to tellen, atte laste,**
	Before him in his lap, (he had) his knapsack,		But truly to tell at the last,
687	**Bret-ful of pardoun come from Rome al hoot.**	708	**He was in chirche a noble ecclesiaste.**
	Brimful of pardons come all fresh from Rome.		He was in church a noble ecclesiast.
688	**A voys he hadde as smal as hath a goot.**	709	**Wel coude he rede a lessoun or a storie,**
	He had a voice as small as a goat has.		He well knew how to read a lesson or a story,
689	**No berd hadde he, ne never sholde have,**	710	**But alderbest he song an offertorie;**
	He had no beard, nor never would have;		But best of all he sang an Offertory;
690	**As smothe it was as it were late y-shave;**	711	**For wel he wiste, whan that song was songe,**
	It (his face) was as smooth as if it were recently shaven.		For he knew well, when that song was sung,
691	**I trowe he were a gelding or a mare.**	712	**He moste preche, and wel affyle his tonge,**
	I believe he was a eunuch or a homosexual.		He must preach and well smooth his speech
692	**But of his craft, fro Berwik into Ware,**	713	**To winne silver, as he ful wel coude;**
	But as to his craft, from Berwick to Ware		To win silver, as he very well knew how;
693	**Ne was ther swich another pardoner.**	714	**Therefore he song so meriely and loude.**
	There was no other pardoner like him.		Therefore he sang the more merrily and loud.
694	**For in his male he hadde a pilwe-beer,**		
	For in his pouch he had a pillow-case,	715	**Now have I told you shortly, in a clause,**
695	**Which that, he seyde, was our lady veyl:**		Now have I told you truly, briefly,
	Which he said was Our Lady's veil;	716	**Thestat, tharray, the nombre, and eek the cause**
696	**He seyde, he hadde a gobet of the seyl**		The rank, the dress, the number, and also the cause
	He said he had a piece of the sail		

717	**Why that assembled was this companye**
	Why this company was assembled
718	**In Southwerk, at this gentil hostelrye,**
	In Southwark at this fine hostelry
719	**That highte the Tabard, faste by the Belle.**
	That is called the Tabard, close by the Bell.
720	**But now is tyme to yow for to telle**
	But now it is time to tell to you
721	**How that we baren us that ilke night,**
	How we conducted ourselves that same night,
722	**Whan we were in that hostelrye alight.**
	When we had arrived in that hostelry;
723	**And after wol I telle of our viage,**
	And after that I will tell of our journey
724	**And al the remenaunt of our pilgrimage.**
	And all the rest of our pilgrimage.
725	**But first I pray yow, of your curteisye,**
	But first I pray yow, of your courtesy,
726	**That ye narette it nat my vileinye,**
	That you do not attribute it to my rudeness,
727	**Thogh that I pleynly speke in this matere,**
	Though I speak plainly in this matter,
728	**To telle yow hir wordes and hir chere;**
	To tell you their words and their behavior,
729	**Ne thogh I speke hir wordes properly.**
	Nor though I speak their words accurately.
730	**For this ye knowen al-so wel as I,**
	For this you know as well as I,
731	**Who-so shal telle a tale after a man,**
	Whoever must repeat a story after someone,
732	**He moot reherce, as ny as ever he can,**
	He must repeat as closely as ever he knows how
733	**Everich a word, if it be in his charge,**
	Every single word, if it be in his power,
734	**Al speke he never so rudeliche and large;**
	Although he may speak ever so rudely and freely,
735	**Or elles he moot telle his tale untrewe,**
	Or else he must tell his tale inaccurately,
736	**Or feyne thing, or finde wordes newe.**
	Or make up things, or find new words.
737	**He may nat spare, al-thogh he were his brother;**
	He may not refrain from (telling the truth), although he were his brother;
738	**He moot as wel seye o word as another.**
	He must as well say one word as another.
739	**Crist spak him-self ful brode in holy writ,**
	Christ himself spoke very plainly in holy writ,
740	**And wel ye woot, no vileinye is it.**
	And you know well it is no rudeness.
741	**Eek Plato seith, who-so that can him rede,**
	Also Plato says, whosoever knows how to read him,
742	**The wordes mote be cosin to the dede.**
	The words must be closely related to the deed.
743	**Also I prey yow to foryeve it me,**
	Also I pray you to forgive it to me,
744	**Al have I nat set folk in hir degree**
	Although I have not set folk in order of their rank
745	**Here in this tale, as that they sholde stonde;**
	Here in this tale, as they should stand.
746	**My wit is short, ye may wel understonde.**
	My wit is short, you can well understand.
747	**Greet chere made our hoste us everichon,**
	Our Host made great hospitality to everyone of us,
748	**And to the soper sette he us anon;**
	And to the supper he set us straightway.
749	**And served us with vitaille at the beste.**
	He served us with victuals of the best sort;
750	**Strong was the wyn, and wel to drinke us leste.**
	The wine was strong, and it well pleased us to drink.
751	**A semely man our hoste was with-alle**
	Our host was an impressive man indeed
752	**For to han been a marshal in an halle;**
	(Qualified) to be a master of ceremonies in a hall.
753	**A large man he was with eyen stepe,**
	He was a large man with prominent eyes,
754	**A fairer burgeys is ther noon in Chepe:**
	There was no better business man in Cheapside:
755	**Bold of his speche, and wys, and wel y-taught,**
	Bold of his speech, and wise, and well mannered,

756	**And of manhod him lakkede right naught.**	775	**And therfore wol I maken yow disport,**
	And he lacked nothing at all of the qualities proper to a man.		And therefore I will make a game for you,
757	**Eek therto he was right a mery man,**	776	**As I seyde erst, and doon yow som confort.**
	Also moreover he was a right merry man;		As I said before, and provide you some pleasure.
758	**And after soper pleyen he bigan,**	777	**And if yow lyketh alle, by oon assent,**
	And after supper he began to be merry,		And if pleases you all unanimously
759	**And spak of mirthe amonges othere thinges,**	778	**Now for to stonden at my Iugement,**
	And spoke of mirth among other things,		To be subject to my judgment,
760	**Whan that we hadde maad our rekeninges;**	779	**And for to werken as I shal yow seye,**
	When we had paid our bills,		And to do as I shall tell you,
761	**And seyde thus: 'Now, lordinges, trewely,**	780	**To-morwe, whan ye ryden by the weye,**
	And said thus: "Now, gentlemen, truly,		Tomorrow, when you ride by the way,
762	**Ye been to me right welcome hertely:**	781	**Now, by my fader soule, that is deed,**
	You are right heartily welcome to me;		Now, by the soul of my father who is dead,
763	**For by my trouthe, if that I shal nat lye,**	782	**But ye be merye, I wol yeve yow myn heed.**
	For by my word, if I shall not lie (I must say),		Unless you be merry, I will give you my head!
764	**I ne saugh this yeer so mery a companye**	783	**Hold up your hond, withouten more speche.'**
	I saw not this year so merry a company		Hold up your hands, without more speech."
765	**At ones in this herberwe as is now.**		
	At one time in this lodging as is (here) now.	784	**Our counseil was nat longe for to seche;**
766	**Fayn wolde I doon yow mirthe, wiste I how.**		Our decision was not long to seek out;
	I would gladly make you happy, if I knew how.	785	**Us thoughte it was noght worth to make it wys,**
767	**And of a mirthe I am right now bithoght,**		It seemed to us it was not worthwhile to deliberate on it,
	And I have just now thought of an amusement,	786	**And graunted him withouten more avys,**
768	**To doon yow ese, and it shal coste noght.**		And (we) granted his request without more discussion,
	To give you pleasure, and it shall cost nothing.	787	**And bad him seye his verdit, as him leste.**
			And asked him to say his decision as it pleased him.
769	**'Ye goon to Caunterbury; God yow spede,**		
	You go to Canterbury—God give you success,	788	**'Lordinges,' quod he, 'now herkneth for the beste;**
770	**The blisful martir quyte yow your mede.**		'Gentlemen,' said he, 'now listen for the best course of action;
	May the blessed martyr give you your reward.	789	**But tak it not, I prey yow, in desdeyn;**
771	**And wel I woot, as ye goon by the weye,**		But, I pray yow, do not take it in disdain (scorn it).
	And well I know, as you go by the way,	790	**This is the poynt, to speken short and pleyn,**
772	**Ye shapen yow to talen and to pleye;**		This is the point, to speak briefly and clearly,
	You intend to tell tales and to amuse yourselves;	791	**That ech of yow, to shorte with your weye,**
773	**For trewely, confort ne mirthe is noon**		That each of yow, to make our way seem short by this means,
	For truly, it is no comfort nor mirth		
774	**To ryde by the weye doumb as a stoon;**		
	To ride by the way dumb as a stone;		

792	**In this viage, shal telle tales tweye,**
	Must tell two tales in this journey
793	**To Caunterbury-ward, I mene it so,**
	On the way to Canterbury, that is what I mean,
794	**And hom-ward he shal tellen othere two,**
	And on the homeward trip he shall tell two others,
795	**Of aventures that whylom han bifalle.**
	About adventures that in old times have happened.
796	**And which of yow that bereth him best of alle,**
	And whoever of you who does best of all,
797	**That is to seyn, that telleth in this cas**
	That is to say, who tells in this case
798	**Tales of best sentence and most solas,**
	Tales of best moral meaning and most pleasure,
799	**Shal have a soper at our aller cost**
	Shall have a supper at the cost of us all
800	**Here in this place, sitting by this post,**
	Here in this place, sitting by this post,
801	**Whan that we come agayn fro Caunterbury.**
	When we come back from Canterbury.
802	**And for to make yow the more mery,**
	And to make you the more merry,
803	**I wol my-selven gladly with yow ryde,**
	I will myself gladly ride with you,
804	**Right at myn owne cost, and be your gyde.**
	Entirely at my own cost, and be your guide;
805	**And who-so wol my Iugement withseye**
	And whosoever will not accept my judgment
806	**Shal paye al that we spenden by the weye.**
	Shall pay all that we spend by the way.
807	**And if ye vouche-sauf that it be so,**
	And if you grant that it be so,
808	**Tel me anon, with-outen wordes mo,**
	Tell me straightway, without more words,
809	**And I wol erly shape me therfore.'**
	And I will get ready early for this.'
810	**This thing was graunted, and our othes swore**
	This thing was granted, and our oaths sworn
811	**With ful glad herte, and preyden him also**
	With very glad hearts, and (we) prayed him also
812	**That he wold vouche-sauf for to do so,**
	That he would consent to do so,
813	**And that he wolde been our governour,**
	And that he would be our governor,
814	**And of our tales Iuge and reportour,**
	And judge and score keeper of our tales,
815	**And sette a soper at a certeyn prys;**
	And set a supper at a certain price,
816	**And we wold reuled been at his devys,**
	And we will be ruled as he wishes
817	**In heigh and lowe; and thus, by oon assent,**
	In every respect; and thus unanimously,
818	**We been acorded to his Iugement.**
	We are accorded to his judgment.
819	**And ther-up-on the wyn was fet anon;**
	And thereupon the wine was fetched immediately;
820	**We dronken, and to reste wente echon,**
	We drank, and each one went to rest,
821	**With-outen any lenger taryinge.**
	Without any longer tarrying.
822	**A-morwe, whan that day bigan to springe,**
	In the morning, when day began to spring,
823	**Up roos our host, and was our aller cok,**
	Our host arose, and was the rooster of us all (awakened us).
824	**And gadrede us togidre, alle in a flok,**
	And gathered us together all in a flock,
825	**And forth we riden, a litel more than pas,**
	And forth we rode at little more than a walk
826	**Un-to the watering of seint Thomas.**
	Unto the watering of Saint Thomas;
827	**And there our host bigan his hors areste,**
	And there our Host stopped his horse
828	**And seyde; 'Lordinges, herkneth, if yow leste.**
	And said, 'Gentlemen, listen, if you please.
829	**Ye woot your forward, and I it yow recorde.**
	You know your agreement, and I remind you of it.
830	**If even-song and morwe-song acorde,**
	If what you said last night agrees with what you say this morning,

831	**Lat se now who shal telle the firste tale.**	846	**Of which ful blythe and glad was every wight;**
	Let's see now who shall tell the first tale.		For which everyone was very happy and glad,
832	**As ever mote I drinke wyn or ale,**	847	**And telle he moste his tale, as was resoun,**
	As ever I may drink wine or ale,		And he must tell his tale, as was reasonable,
833	**Who-so be rebel to my Iugement**	848	**By forward and by composicioun,**
	Whosoever may be rebel to my judgment		By our previous promise and by formal agreement,
834	**Shal paye for al that by the weye is spent.**	849	**As ye han herd; what nedeth wordes mo?**
	Shall pay for all that is spent by the way.		As you have heard; what more words are needed?
835	**Now draweth cut, er that we ferrer twinne;**	850	**And whan this gode man saugh it was so,**
	Now draw straws, before we depart further (from London);		And when this good man saw that it was so,
836	**He which that hath the shortest shal biginne.**	851	**As he that wys was and obedient**
	He who has the shortest shall begin.		Like one who was wise and obedient
837	**Sire knight,' quod he, 'my maister and my lord,**	852	**To kepe his forward by his free assent,**
	Sir Knight," said he, "my master and my lord,		To keep his agreement by his free assent,
838	**Now draweth cut, for that is myn acord.**	853	**He seyde: 'Sin I shal biginne the game,**
	Now draw a straw, for that is my decision.		He said, 'Since I must begin the game,
839	**Cometh neer,' quod he, 'my lady prioresse;**	854	**What, welcome be the cut, a Goddes name!**
	Come nearer," he said, 'my lady prioress.		What! Welcome be the draw, in God's name!
840	**And ye, sir clerk, lat be your shamfastnesse,**	855	**Now lat us ryde, and herkneth what I seye.'**
	And you, sir clerk, let be your modesty,		Now let us ride, and listen to what I say.'
841	**Ne studieth noght; ley hond to, every man.'**		
	And study not; lay hand to (draw a straw), every man!'		
842	**Anon to drawen every wight bigan,**	856	**And with that word we riden forth our weye;**
	Every person began straightway to draw,		And with that word we rode forth on our way,
843	**And shortly for to tellen, as it was,**	857	**And he bigan with right a mery chere**
	And shortly to tell as it was,		And he began with a truly merry demeanor
844	**Were it by aventure, or sort, or cas,**	858	**His tale anon, and seyde in this manere.**
	Were it by chance, or destiny, or luck,		To tell his tale straightway, and said as you may hear.
845	**The sothe is this, the cut fil to the knight,**		
	The truth is this: the draw fell to the Knight,		

Canterbury Tales:

The Knight's Tale, Part I

Geoffrey Chaucer

Heere bigynneth the Knyghtes Tale.

Iamque domos patrias, Sithice post aspera gentis prelia, laurigero, etc.

And now (Theseus drawing nigh his) native land in laurelled car after battling with the Scithian folk, etc.

859 **Whylom, as olde stories tellen us,**
    Once, as old histories tell us,
860 **Ther was a duk that highte Theseus;**
    There was a duke who was called Theseus;
861 **Of Athenes he was lord and governour,**
    He was lord and governor of Athens,
862 **And in his tyme swich a conquerour,**
    And in his time such a conqueror
863 **That gretter was ther noon under the sonne.**
    That there was no one greater under the sun.
864 **Ful many a riche contree hadde he wonne;**
    Very many a powerful country had he won;
865 **What with his wisdom and his chivalrye,**
    What with his wisdom and his chivalry,
866 **He conquered al the regne of Femenye,**
    He conquered all the land of the Amazons,
867 **That whylom was y-cleped Scithia;**
    That once was called Scithia,
868 **And weddede the quene Ipolita,**
    And wedded the queen Ypolita,
869 **And broghte hir hoom with him in his contree**
    And brought her home with him into his country
870 **With muchel glorie and greet solempnitee,**
    With much glory and great ceremony,
871 **And eek hir yonge suster Emelye.**
    And also her young sister Emelye.
872 **And thus with victorie and with melodye**
    And thus with victory and with festivity
873 **Lete I this noble duk to Athenes ryde,**
    I leave this noble duke riding to Athens,
874 **And al his hoost, in armes, him bisyde.**
    And all his host in arms beside him.
875 **And certes, if it nere to long to here,**
    And certainly, if it were not too long to hear,
876 **I wolde han told yow fully the manere,**
    I would have told you fully the manner
877 **How wonnen was the regne of Femenye**
    How the reign of Femenye was won
878 **By Theseus, and by his chivalrye;**
    By Theseus and by his chivalry;
879 **And of the grete bataille for the nones**
    And of the great battle at that time
880 **Bitwixen Athenës and Amazones;**
    Between Athenians and Amazons;
881 **And how asseged was Ipolita,**
    And how Ypolita was besieged,
882 **The faire hardy quene of Scithia;**
    The fair, bold queen of Scithia;
883 **And of the feste that was at hir weddinge,**
    And of the festivity that was at their wedding,
884 **And of the tempest at hir hoom-cominge;**
    And of the storm at her home-coming;

Geoffrey Chaucer; Walter W. Skeat, ed., "The Knight's Tale," *The Complete Works of Geoffrey Chaucer*, vol. 4. Copyright in the Public Domain.

Geoffrey Chaucer; Larry D. Benson, trans., *The Knight's Tale, Part I: An Interlinear Translation (Lines 859–1354)*, from http://www.courses.fas.harvard.edu/chaucer/granted by the publisher.

885	**But al that thing I moot as now forbere.**
	But all that matter I must now forgo.
886	**I have, God woot, a large feeld to ere,**
	I have, God knows, a large field to till,
887	**And wayke been the oxen in my plough.**
	And the oxen in my plow are weak.
888	**The remenant of the tale is long y-nough.**
	The remnant of the tale is long enough.
889	**I wol nat letten eek noon of this route;**
	Also I will not hinder any one of this company;
890	**Lat every felawe telle his tale aboute,**
	Let every fellow tell his tale in turn,
891	**And lat see now who shal the soper winne;**
	And let's see now who shall win the supper;
892	**And ther I lefte, I wol ageyn biginne.**
	And where I left off, I will again begin.
893	**This duk, of whom I make mencioun,**
	This duke, of whom I make mention,
894	**When he was come almost unto the toun,**
	When he was come almost unto the town,
895	**In al his wele and in his moste pryde,**
	In all his prosperity and in his most pride,
896	**He was war, as he caste his eye asyde,**
	He was aware, as he cast his eye aside,
897	**Wher that ther kneled in the hye weye**
	Where there kneeled in the high way
898	**A companye of ladies, tweye and tweye,**
	A company of ladies, two by two,
899	**Ech after other, clad in clothes blake;**
	Each after another, clad in black clothes;
900	**But swich a cry and swich a wo they make,**
	But such a cry and such a woeful (lament) they make
901	**That in this world nis creature livinge,**
	That in this world is no living creature
902	**That herde swich another weymentinge;**
	That (ever) heard lamentation such as this;
903	**And of this cry they nolde never stenten,**
	And of this cry they would not ever stop
904	**Til they the reynes of his brydel henten.**
	Until they seized the reins of his bridle.
905	**'What folk ben ye, that at myn hoom-cominge**
	'What folk are you, who at my homecoming
906	**Perturben so my feste with crynge?'**
	So disturb my festival with crying?'
907	**Quod Theseus, 'have ye so greet envye**
	Said Theseus, 'have you such great envy
908	**Of myn honour, that thus compleyne and crye?**
	Of my honor, (you) who thus lament and cry?
909	**Or who hath yow misboden, or offended?**
	Or who has injured or offended you?
910	**And telleth me if it may been amended;**
	And tell me if it may be remedied,
911	**And why that ye ben clothed thus in blak?'**
	And why you are clothed thus in black?'
912	**The eldest lady of hem alle spak,**
	The eldest lady of them all spoke,
913	**When she hadde swowned with a deedly chere,**
	After she had swooned with (so) deadly a countenance,
914	**That it was routhe for to seen and here,**
	That it was pitiful to see and hear,
915	**And seyde: 'Lord, to whom Fortune hath yiven**
	She said, "Lord, to whom Fortune has given
916	**Victorie, and as a conquerour to liven,**
	Victory, and (allowed) to live as a conqueror,
917	**Noght greveth us your glorie and your honour;**
	Your glory and your honor does not grieve us,
918	**But we biseken mercy and socour.**
	But we beseech (you for) mercy and succor.
919	**Have mercy on our wo and our distresse.**
	Have mercy on our woe and our distress!
920	**Som drope of pitee, thurgh thy gentillesse,**
	Some drop of pity, because of thy nobility,
921	**Up-on us wrecched wommen lat thou falle.**
	Let thou fall upon us wretched women,
922	**For certes, lord, ther nis noon of us alle,**
	For, certainly, lord, there is not one of us all
923	**That she nath been a duchesse or a quene;**
	Who has not been a duchess or a queen;

924	**Now be we caitifs, as it is wel sene:**	945	**And wol nat suffren hem, by noon assent,**
	Now we are miserable wretches, as it is easily seen:		And will not allow them, not at all,
925	**Thanked be Fortune, and hir false wheel,**	946	**Neither to been y-buried nor y-brent,**
	Thanks be to Fortune and her false wheel,		Neither to be buried nor burned,
926	**That noon estat assureth to be weel.**	947	**But maketh houndes ete hem in despyt.'**
	Who assures no estate (will continue) to be well.		But makes hounds eat them as an insult.'
927	**And certes, lord, to abyden your presence,**	948	**And with that word, with-outen more respyt,**
	And certainly, lord, to await your presence,		And with that word, without more delay,
928	**Here in the temple of the goddesse Clemence**	949	**They fillen gruf, and cryden pitously,**
	Here in this temple of the goddess Clemency		They fell face down and cried piteously,
929	**We han ben waytinge al this fourtenight;**	950	**'Have on us wrecched wommen som mercy,**
	We have been waiting all this fortnight.		"Have some mercy on us wretched women,
930	**Now help us, lord, sith it is in thy might.**	951	**And lat our sorwe sinken in thyn herte.'**
	Now help us, lord, since it is in thy power.		And let our sorrow sink in thy heart.'
931	**I wrecche, which that wepe and waille thus,**	952	**This gentil duk doun from his courser sterte**
	I, wretch, who weep and wail thus,		This gentle duke leaped down from his war horse
932	**Was whylom wyf to king Capaneus,**	953	**With herte pitous, whan he herde hem speke.**
	Was once wife to king Cappaneus,		With compassionate heart, when he heard them speak.
933	**That starf at Thebes, cursed be that day!**	954	**Him thoughte that his herte wolde breke,**
	Who died at Thebescursed be that day!		It seemed to him that his heart would break,
934	**And alle we, that been in this array,**	955	**Whan he saugh hem so pitous and so mat,**
	And all of us who are in this condition		When he saw them so pitiful and so dejected,
935	**And maken al this lamentacioun,**	956	**That whylom weren of so greet estat.**
	And make all this lamentation,		That once were of such high rank;
936	**We losten alle our housbondes at that toun,**	957	**And in his armes he hem alle up hente,**
	We lost all our husbands at that town,		And in his arms he caught up them all,
937	**Whyl that the sege ther-aboute lay.**	958	**And hem conforteth in ful good entente;**
	While the siege lay around it.		And comforts them with very good will,
938	**And yet now the olde Creon, weylaway!**	959	**And swoor his ooth, as he was trewe knight,**
	And yet now the old Creon, woe oh woe!		And swore his oath, as he was true knight,
939	**That lord is now of Thebes the citee,**	960	**He wolde doon so ferforthly his might**
	Who is now lord of the city of Thebes,		(That) he would do his might so completely
940	**Fulfild of ire and of iniquitee,**	961	**Up-on the tyraunt Creon hem to wreke,**
	Filled with anger and with iniquity,		To avenge them upon the tyrant Creon
941	**He, for despyt, and for his tirannye,**	962	**That al the peple of Grece sholde speke**
	He, for spite and for his tyranny,		That all the people of Greece should speak (about)
942	**To do the dede bodyes vileinye,**		
	To do dishonor to the dead bodies		
943	**Of alle our lordes, whiche that ben slawe,**		
	Of all our lords who are slain,		
944	**Hath alle the bodyes on an heep y-drawe,**		
	Has dragged all the bodies in a heap,		

963	**How Creon was of Theseus y-served,**
	How Creon was treated by Theseus
964	**As he that hadde his deeth ful wel deserved.**
	As one who had very well deserved his death.
965	**And right anoon, with-outen more abood,**
	And right away, without more delay,
966	**His baner he desplayeth, and forth rood**
	He displays his banner, and rode forth
967	**To Thebes-ward, and al his host bisyde;**
	Toward Thebes, and all his army beside (him).
968	**No neer Athenës wolde he go ne ryde,**
	He would not walk nor ride any nearer to Athens,
969	**Ne take his ese fully half a day,**
	Nor take his ease fully half a day,
970	**But onward on his wey that night he lay;**
	But that night he lay (camped) on his way,
971	**And sente anoon Ipolita the quene,**
	And sent straightway Ypolita the queen,
972	**And Emelye hir yonge suster shene,**
	And Emelye, her beautiful young sister,
973	**Un-to the toun of Athenës to dwelle;**
	Unto the town of Athens to dwell,
974	**And forth he rit; ther nis namore to telle.**
	And forth he rides; there is no more to tell.
975	**The rede statue of Mars, with spere and targe,**
	The red statue of Mars, with spear and shield,
976	**So shyneth in his whyte baner large,**
	So shines in his large white banner
977	**That alle the feeldes gliteren up and doun;**
	That all the fields glitter all around;
978	**And by his baner born is his penoun**
	And by his banner is carried his pennon
979	**Of gold ful riche, in which ther was y-bete**
	Of very rich gold, in which there was embroidered
980	**The Minotaur, which that he slough in Crete.**
	The Minotaur, which he defeated in Crete.
981	**Thus rit this duk, thus rit this conquerour,**
	Thus rides this duke, thus rides this conqueror,
982	**And in his host of chivalrye the flour,**
	And in his army the flower of chivalry,
983	**Til that he cam to Thebes, and alighte**
	Until he came to Thebes and dismounted
984	**Faire in a feeld, ther as he thoghte fighte.**
	Graciously in a field, where he intended to fight.
985	**But shortly for to speken of this thing,**
	But briefly to speak of this thing,
986	**With Creon, which that was of Thebes king,**
	With Creon, who was king of Thebes,
987	**He faughte, and slough him manly as a knight**
	He fought, and slew him boldly as a knight
988	**In pleyn bataille, and putte the folk to flight;**
	In open battle, and put the army to flight;
989	**And by assaut he wan the citee after,**
	And by assault he won the city afterwards,
990	**And rente adoun bothe wal, and sparre, and rafter;**
	And tore down both wall and beam and rafter;
991	**And to the ladyes he restored agayn**
	And he gave back to the ladies
992	**The bones of hir housbondes that were slayn,**
	The bones of their husbands who were slain,
993	**To doon obsequies, as was tho the gyse.**
	To do obsequies, as was then the custom.
994	**But it were al to long for to devyse**
	But it would be all too long to describe
995	**The grete clamour and the waymentinge**
	The great clamor and the lamentation
996	**That the ladyes made at the brenninge**
	That the ladies made at the burning
997	**Of the bodyes, and the grete honour**
	Of the bodies, and the great honor
998	**That Theseus, the noble conquerour,**
	That Theseus, the noble conqueror,
999	**Doth to the ladyes, whan they from him wente;**
	Does to the ladies, when they went from him;
1000	**But shortly for to telle is myn entente.**
	But briefly to tell is my intent.
1001	**Whan that this worthy duc, this Theseus,**
	When this worthy duke, this Theseus,

1002	**Hath Creon slayn, and wonne Thebes thus,**		1021	**And han hem caried softe un-to the tente**
	Has slain Creon and thus won Thebes,			And have carried them softy unto the tent
1003	**Stille in that feeld he took al night his reste,**		1022	**Of Theseus, and he ful sone hem sente**
	Still in that field he took all night his rest,			Of Theseus; and he very soon sent them
1004	**And dide with al the contree as him leste.**		1023	**To Athenës, to dwellen in prisoun**
	And did with all the country as he pleased.			To Athens, to dwell in prison
			1024	**Perpetuelly, he nolde no raunsoun.**
1005	**To ransake in the tas of bodyes dede,**			Perpetually—he would not (accept) any ransom.
	To search in the heap of dead bodies,		1025	**And whan this worthy duk hath thus y-don,**
1006	**Hem for to strepe of harneys and of wede,**			And when this worthy duke has thus done, t
	To strip them of armor and of clothing,		1026	**He took his host, and hoom he rood anon**
1007	**The pilours diden bisinesse and cure,**			He took his army, and home he rides straightway
	The scavengers took great pains and worked hard,		1027	**With laurer crowned as a conquerour;**
1008	**After the bataille and disconfiture.**			As a conqueror crowned with laurel;
	After the battle and defeat.		1028	**And there he liveth, in Ioye and in honour,**
1009	**And so bifel, that in the tas they founde,**			And there he lives in joy and in honor
	And (it) so befell that in the heap they found,		1029	**Terme of his lyf; what nedeth wordes mo?**
1010	**Thurgh-girt with many a grevous blody wounde,**			For the duration of his life; what more words are needed?
	Pierced through with many a grievous bloody wound,		1030	**And in a tour, in angwish and in wo,**
1011	**Two yonge knightes ligging by and by,**			And in a tower, in anguish and in woe,
	Two young knights lying side by side,		1031	**Dwellen this Palamoun and eek Arcite,**
1012	**Bothe in oon armes, wroght ful richely,**			This Palamon and his fellow Arcite
	Both with the same coat of arms, very richly wrought,		1032	**For evermore, ther may no gold hem quyte.**
1013	**Of whiche two, Arcita hight that oon,**			For evermore (remain); no gold can ransom them.
	Of which two one was called Arcite,			
1014	**And that other knight hight Palamon.**		1033	**This passeth yeer by yeer, and day by day,**
	And that other knight was called Palamon.			This passes year by year and day by day,
1015	**Nat fully quike, ne fully dede they were,**		1034	**Til it fil ones, in a morwe of May,**
	They were not fully alive, nor fully dead,			Until it befell once, in a morning of May,
1016	**But by hir cote-armures, and by hir gere,**		1035	**That Emelye, that fairer was to sene**
	But by their coats of arms and by their equipment			That Emelye, who was fairer to be seen
1017	**The heraudes knewe hem best in special,**		1036	**Than is the lilie upon his stalke grene,**
	The heralds best knew them in particular			Than is the lily upon its green stalk,
1018	**As they that weren of the blood royal**		1037	**And fressher than the May with floures newe—**
	As they that were of the royal blood			And fresher than the May with new flowers—
1019	**Of Thebes, and of sustren two y-born.**		1038	**For with the rose colour stroof hir hewe,**
	Of Thebes, and born of two sisters.			For her hue vied with color of the rose,
1020	**Out of the tas the pilours han hem torn,**		1039	**I noot which was the fairer of hem two—**
	The scavengers have pulled them out of the heap,			I do not know which was the finer of them two—

1040	**Er it were day, as was hir wone to do,**
	Before it was day, as was her custom to do,
1041	**She was arisen, and al redy dight;**
	She was arisen and all ready prepared,
1042	**For May wol have no slogardye a-night.**
	For May will have no laziness at night.
1043	**The sesoun priketh every gentil herte,**
	The season urges on every gentle heart,
1044	**And maketh him out of his sleep to sterte,**
	And makes it out of its sleep to awake suddenly,
1045	**And seith, 'Arys, and do thyn observaunce.'**
	And says 'Arise, and do thy observance.'
1046	**This maked Emelye have remembraunce**
	This made Emelye remember
1047	**To doon honour to May, and for to ryse.**
	To do honor to May, and to rise.
1048	**Y-clothed was she fresh, for to devyse;**
	She was gaily clothed, so to say:
1049	**Hir yelow heer was broyded in a tresse,**
	Her yellow hair was braided in a tress
1050	**Bihinde hir bak, a yerde long, I gesse.**
	Behind her back, a yard long, I guess.
1051	**And in the gardin, at the sonne up-riste,**
	And in the garden, at the rising of the sun,
1052	**She walketh up and doun, and as hir liste**
	She walks up and down, and as she pleases
1053	**She gadereth floures, party whyte and rede,**
	She gathers flowers, mixed white and red,
1054	**To make a sotil gerland for hir hede,**
	To make an intricate garland for her head;
1055	**And as an aungel hevenly she song.**
	And she sang (as) heavenly as an angel.
1056	**The grete tour, that was so thikke and strong,**
	The great tower, that was so thick and strong,
1057	**Which of the castel was the chief don-geoun,**
	Which was the main fortification of the castle
1058	**(Ther-as the knightes weren in prisoun,**
	(Where the knights were in prison
1059	**Of whiche I tolde yow, and tellen shal)**
	Of which I told yow and shall tell)
1060	**Was evene Ioynant to the gardin-wal,**
	Was just next to the garden wall
1061	**Ther as this Emelye hadde hir pleyinge.**
	Where this Emelye took her pleasure.
1062	**Bright was the sonne, and cleer that morweninge,**
	The sun was bright and clear that morning,
1063	**And Palamon, this woful prisoner,**
	And Palamon, this woeful prisoner,
1064	**As was his wone, by leve of his gayler,**
	As was his custom, by permission of his jailer,
1065	**Was risen, and romed in a chambre on heigh,**
	Had risen and roamed in a chamber on high,
1066	**In which he al the noble citee seigh,**
	In which he saw all the noble city,
1067	**And eek the gardin, ful of braunches grene,**
	And also the garden, full of green branches,
1068	**Ther-as this fresshe Emelye the shene**
	Where this fresh Emelye the bright
1069	**Was in hir walk, and romed up and doun.**
	Was in her walk, and roamed up and down.
1070	**This sorweful prisoner, this Palamoun,**
	This sorrowful prisoner, this Palamon,
1071	**Goth in the chambre, roming to and fro,**
	Goes in the chamber roaming to and fro
1072	**And to him-self compleyning of his wo;**
	And to himself lamenting his woe.
1073	**That he was born, ful ofte he seyde, 'alas!'**
	That he was born, full often he said, 'alas!'
1074	**And so bifel, by aventure or cas,**
	And so it happened, by chance or accident,
1075	**That thurgh a window, thikke of many a barre**
	That through a window, thickly set with many a bar
1076	**Of yren greet, and square as any sparre,**
	Of iron, great and square as any beam,
1077	**He caste his eye upon Emelya,**
	He cast his eye upon Emelye,
1078	**And ther-with-al he bleynte, and cryde 'a!'**
	And with that he turned pale and cried, 'A!'

1079	**As though he stongen were un-to the herte.**	1096	**But I was hurt right now thurgh-out myn yë**
	As though he were stabbed unto the heart.		But I was hurt right now through my eye
1080	**And with that cry Arcite anon up-sterte,**	1097	**In-to myn herte, that wol my bane be.**
	And with that cry Arcite immediately leaped up		Into my heart, so that it will be the death of me.
1081	**And seyde, 'Cosin myn, what eyleth thee,**	1098	**The fairnesse of that lady that I see**
	And said, "My cousin, what ails thee,		The fairness of that lady whom I see
1082	**That art so pale and deedly on to see?**	1099	**Yond in the gardin romen to and fro,**
	Who art so pale and deadly to look upon?		Yonder in the garden roaming to and fro
1083	**Why crydestow? who hath thee doon offence?**	1100	**Is cause of al my crying and my wo.**
	Why didst thou cry out? Who has done thee offence?		Is cause of all my crying and my woe.
1084	**For Goddes love, tak al in pacience**	1101	**I noot wher she be womman or goddesse;**
	For the love of God, take all in patience		I know not whether she is woman or goddess,
1085	**Our prisoun, for it may non other be;**	1102	**But Venus is it, soothly, as I gesse.'**
	Our imprisonment, for it may not be otherwise;		But truly it is Venus, as I suppose.'
1086	**Fortune hath yeven us this adversitee.**	1103	**And ther-with-al on kneës doun he fil,**
	Fortune has given us this adversity.		And with that he fell down on his knees,
1087	**Som wikke aspect or disposicioun**	1104	**And seyde: 'Venus, if it be thy wil**
	Some wicked aspect or disposition		And said, 'Venus, if it be thy will
1088	**Of Saturne, by sum constellacioun,**	1105	**Yow in this gardin thus to transfigure**
	Of Saturn, by some arrangement of the heavenly bodies,		Thus to transfigure yourself in this garden
1089	**Hath yeven us this, al-though we hadde it sworn;**	1106	**Bifore me, sorweful wrecche creature,**
	Has given us this, although we had sworn it would not be;		Before me, sorrowful, wretched creature,
1090	**So stood the heven whan that we were born;**	1107	**Out of this prisoun help that we may scapen.**
	So stood the heavens when we were born.		Help that we may escape out of this prison.
1091	**We moste endure it: this is the short and pleyn.'**	1108	**And if so be my destinee be shapen**
	We must endure it; this is the short and plain.'		And if it be so that my destiny is shaped
		1109	**By eterne word to dyen in prisoun,**
			By eternal decree to die in prison,
		1110	**Of our linage have som compassioun,**
			Have some compassion on our (noble) lineage
1092	**This Palamon answerde, and seyde ageyn,**	1111	**That is so lowe y-broght by tirannye.'**
	This Palamon answered and said in reply,		Which is brought so low by tyranny.'
1093	**'Cosyn, for sothe, of this opinioun**	1112	**And with that word Arcite gan espye**
	'Cousin, truly, concerning this opinion		And with that word Arcite did see
1094	**Thou hast a veyn imaginacioun.**	1113	**Wher-as this lady romed to and fro.**
	Thou hast a foolish conception.		Where this lady roamed to and fro,
1095	**This prison caused me nat for to crye.**	1114	**And with that sighte hir beautee hurte him so,**
	This prison did not cause me to cry out,		And with that sight her beauty hurt him so,
		1115	**That, if that Palamon was wounded sore,**
			That, if Palamon was sorely wounded,
		1116	**Arcite is hurt as muche as he, or more.**
			Arcite is hurt as much as he, or more.

Line		Line	
1117	**And with a sigh he seyde pitously:**	1137	**But that thou sholdest trewely forthren me**
	And with a sigh he said piteously,		But rather thou shouldest truly help me
1118	**'The fresshe beautee sleeth me sodeynly**	1138	**In every cas, and I shal forthren thee.**
	'The fresh beauty slays me suddenly		In every case, as I shall help thee.
1119	**Of hir that rometh in the yonder place;**	1139	**This was thyn ooth, and myn also, certeyn;**
	Of her who roams in the yonder place;		This was thy oath, and mine also, certainly;
1120	**And, but I have hir mercy and hir grace,**	1140	**I wot right wel, thou darst it nat withseyn.**
	And unless I have her mercy and her grace,		I know right well, thou darest not deny it.
1121	**That I may seen hir atte leeste weye,**	1141	**Thus artow of my counseil, out of doute.**
	So that I can at least see her,		Thus thou art my trusted confidant, without doubt,
1122	**I nam but deed; ther nis namore to seye.'**	1142	**And now thou woldest falsly been aboute**
	I am as good as dead; there is no more to say.'		And now thou wouldest falsely be busy preparing
1123	**This Palamon, whan he tho wordes herde,**	1143	**To love my lady, whom I love and serve,**
	This Palamon, when he heard those words,		To love my lady, whom I love and serve,
1124	**Dispitously he loked, and answerde:**	1144	**And ever shal, til that myn herte sterve.**
	Angrily he looked and answered,		And ever shall until my heart dies.
1125	**'Whether seistow this in ernest or in pley?'**	1145	**Now certes, fals Arcite, thou shalt nat so.**
	'Sayest thou this in earnest or in play?'		Nay, certainly, false Arcite, thou shalt not (do) so.
1126	**'Nay,' quod Arcite, 'in ernest, by my fey!**	1146	**I loved hir first, and tolde thee my wo**
	'Nay,' said Arcite, 'in earnest, by my faith!		I loved hire first, and told thee my woe
1127	**God help me so, me list ful yvele pleye.'**	1147	**As to my counseil, and my brother sworn**
	So help me God, I have no desire to play.'		As to my confidant and my sworn brother
1128	**This Palamon gan knitte his browes tweye:**	1148	**To forthre me, as I have told biforn.**
	This Palamon did knit his two brows.		To further me, as I have told before.
1129	**'It nere,' quod he, 'to thee no greet honour**	1149	**For which thou art y-bounden as a knight**
	'It would not be,' said he, 'any great honor to thee		For which thou art bound as a knight
1130	**For to be fals, ne for to be traytour**	1150	**To helpen me, if it lay in thy might,**
	To be false, nor to be traitor		To help me, if it lay in thy power,
1131	**To me, that am thy cosin and thy brother**	1151	**Or elles artow fals, I dar wel seyn.'**
	To me, who am thy cousin and thy brother		Or else thou art false, I dare well say.'
1132	**Y-sworn ful depe, and ech of us til other,**	1152	**This Arcitë ful proudly spak ageyn,**
	Sworn very sincerely, and each of us to the other,		This Arcite full proudly spoke in return:
1133	**That never, for to dyen in the peyne,**	1153	**'Thou shalt,' quod he, 'be rather fals than I;**
	That never, though we had to die by torture,		'Thou shalt,' said he, 'be rather false than I;
1134	**Til that the deeth departe shal us tweyne,**	1154	**But thou art fals, I telle thee utterly;,**
	Until death shall part us two,		But thou art false, I tell thee flatly,
1135	**Neither of us in love to hindren other,**	1155	**For *par amour* I loved hir first er thow.**
	Neither of us in love (is) to hinder the other,		As a mistress I loved her first before thou.
1136	**Ne in non other cas, my leve brother;**	1156	**What wiltow seyn? thou wistest nat yet now**
	Nor in any other case, my dear brother,		What wilt thou say? Thou knowest not yet now

1157	**Whether she be a womman or goddesse!**	1177	**We stryve as dide the houndes for the boon,**
	Whether she is a woman or goddess!		We strive as the hounds did for the bone;
1158	**Thyn is affeccioun of holinesse,**	1178	**They foughte al day, and yet hir part was noon;**
	Thine is a feeling of holiness,		They fought all day, and yet their share was nothing.
1159	**And myn is love, as to a creature;**	1179	**Ther cam a kyte, whyl that they were wrothe,**
	And mine is love as to a creature;		There came a kite, while they were so angry,
1160	**For which I tolde thee myn aventure**	1180	**And bar awey the boon bitwixe hem bothe.**
	For which I told thee my circumstance		And carried away the bone between them both.
1161	**As to my cosin, and my brother sworn.**	1181	**And therfore, at the kinges court, my brother,**
	As to my cousin and my sworn brother.		And therefore, at the king's court, my brother,
1162	**I pose, that thou lovedest hir biforn;**	1182	**Ech man for him-self, ther is non other.**
	I posit (this assumption): that thou lovedest her first;		Each man for himself, there is no other (way).
1163	**Wostow nat wel the olde clerkes sawe,**	1183	**Love if thee list; for I love and ay shal;**
	Knowest thou not well the old clerks' saying,		Love, if it please thee, for I love and always shall;
1164	**That 'who shal yeve a lover any lawe?'**	1184	**And soothly, leve brother, this is al.**
	That 'who shall give a lover any law?'		And truly, dear brother, this is all.
1165	**Love is a gretter lawe, by my pan,**	1185	**Here in this prisoun mote we endure,**
	Love is a greater law, by my skull,		Here in this prison we must endure,
1166	**Than may be yeve to any erthly man.**	1186	**And everich of us take his aventure.'**
	Than may be given to any earthly man.		And each one of us take his chance.'
1167	**And therefore positif lawe and swich decree**	1187	**Greet was the stryf and long bitwixe hem tweye,**
	And therefore positive (man-made) law and such decree		Great and long was the strife between them two,
1168	**Is broke al-day for love, in ech degree.**	1188	**If that I hadde leyser for to seye;**
	Is broken every day for love in every way.		If I had leisure to tell (it);
1169	**A man moot nedes love, maugree his heed.**	1189	**But to theffect. It happed on a day,**
	A man must of necessity love, in spite of all he can do;		But to the point. It happened on a day,
1170	**He may nat fleen it, thogh he sholde be deed,**	1190	**(To telle it yow as shortly as I may)**
	He can not flee (from) it, though he should be dead,		To tell it to you as briefly as I can,
1171	**Al be she mayde, or widwe, or elles wyf.**	1191	**A worthy duk that highte Perotheus,**
	Whether she be maid, or widow, or else wife.		A worthy duke that was called Perotheus,
1172	**And eek it is nat lykly, al thy lyf,**	1192	**That felawe was un-to duk Theseus**
	And also it is not likely all thy life		Who was a friend to duke Theseus
1173	**To stonden in hir grace; namore shal I;**	1193	**Sin thilke day that they were children lyte,**
	To stand in her good graces; no more shall I;		Since that same time that they were little children,
1174	**For wel thou woost thy-selven, verraily,**	1194	**Was come to Athenes, his felawe to visyte,**
	For well thou thyself knowest, truly,		Had come to Athens to visit his friend,
1175	**TThat thou and I be dampned to prisoun**		
	That thou and I are condemned to prison		
1176	**Perpetuelly; us gayneth no raunsoun.**		
	Perpetually; no ransom can help us.		

1195	**And for to pleye, as he was wont to do,**
	And to amuse himself as he was accustomed to do;
1196	**For in this world he loved no man so:**
	For in this world he loved no man so (much),
1197	**And he loved him as tendrely ageyn.**
	And he (Theseus) loved him as tenderly in turn.
1198	**So wel they loved, as olde bokes seyn,**
	So well they loved, as old books say,
1199	**That whan that oon was deed, sothly to telle,**
	That when one was dead, truly to tell,
1200	**His felawe wente and soghte him doun in helle;**
	His friend went and sought him down in hell;
1201	**But of that story list me nat to wryte.**
	But of that story I do not desire to write.
1202	**Duk Perotheus loved wel Arcite,**
	Duke Perotheus loved well Arcite,
1203	**And hadde him knowe at Thebes yeer by yere;**
	And had known him at Thebes year after year,
1204	**And fynally, at requeste and preyere**
	And finally at request and prayer
1205	**Of Perotheus, with-oute any raunsoun,**
	Of Perotheus, without any ransom,
1206	**Duk Theseus him leet out of prisoun,**
	Duke Theseus let him out of prison
1207	**Freely to goon, wher that him liste over-al,**
	Freely to go all over, wherever he wishes,
1208	**In swich a gyse, as I you tellen shal.**
	In such a manner as shall I tell you.
1209	**This was the forward, pleynly for tendyte,**
	This was the agreement, plainly to write,
1210	**Bitwixen Theseus and him Arcite:**
	Between Theseus and this Arcite:
1211	**That if so were, that Arcite were y-founde**
	That if it so were that Arcite were found
1212	**Ever in his lyf, by day or night or stounde**
	Ever in his life, by day or night, at any moment
1213	**In any contree of this Theseus,**
	In any country of this Theseus,
1214	**And he were caught, it was acorded thus,**
	And if he were caught, it was agreed thus,
1215	**That with a swerd he sholde lese his heed;**
	That with a sword he should lose his head.
1216	**Ther nas non other remedye ne reed,**
	There was no other remedy nor course of action;
1217	**But taketh his leve, and homward he him spedde;**
	But (he) takes his leave, and homeward he sped.
1218	**Let him be war, his nekke lyth to wedde!**
	Let him be ware! His neck lies as a pledge.
1219	**How greet a sorwe suffreth now Arcite!**
	How great a sorrow now suffers Arcite!
1220	**The deeth he feleth thurgh his herte smyte;**
	He feels the death smite through his heart;
1221	**He wepeth, wayleth, cryeth pitously;**
	He weeps, wails, cries piteously;
1222	**To sleen him-self he wayteth prively.**
	To slay himself he secretly awaits (an opportunity).
1223	**He seyde, 'Allas that day that I was born!**
	He said, "Alas that day that I was born!
1224	**Now is my prison worse than biforn;**
	Now my prison is worse than before;
1225	**Now is me shape eternally to dwelle**
	Now I am destined eternally to dwell
1226	**Noght in purgatorie, but in helle.**
	Not in purgatory, but in hell.
1227	**Allas! that ever knew I Perotheus!**
	Alas, that ever I knew Perotheus!
1228	**For elles hadde I dwelled with Theseus**
	For else I would have remained with Theseus,
1229	**Y-fetered in his prisoun ever-mo.**
	Fettered in his prison evermore.
1230	**Than hadde I been in blisse, and nat in wo.**
	Then would I have been in bliss and not in woe.
1231	**Only the sighte of hir, whom that I serve,**
	Only the sight of her whom I serve,
1232	**Though that I never hir grace may deserve,**
	Though I never can deserve her grace,

1233	**Wolde han suffised right y-nough for me.**	1252	**Of purveyaunce of God, or of fortune,**
	Would have sufficed right enough for me.		About the providence of God, or of Fortune,
1234	**O dere cosin Palamon,' quod he,**	1253	**That yeveth hem ful ofte in many a gyse**
	O dear cousin Palamon,' said he,		That gives them full often in many a manner
1235	**'Thyn is the victorie of this aventure,**	1254	**Wel bettre than they can hem-self devyse?**
	'The victory of this adventure is thine.		Much better than they can themselves imagine?
1236	**Ful blisfully in prison maistow dure;**	1255	**Som man desyreth for to han richesse,**
	Very blissfully in prison thou can remain;		One man desires to have riches,
1237	**In prison? certes nay, but in paradys!**	1256	**That cause is of his mordre or greet siknesse.**
	In prison? Certainly not, but in paradise!		Which is the cause of his murder or great sickness;
1238	**Wel hath fortune y-turned thee the dys,**	1257	**And som man wolde out of his prison fayn,**
	Well has Fortune turned the dice for thee,		And one man would happily (go) out of his prison,
1239	**That hast the sighte of hir, and I thabsence.**	1258	**That in his hous is of his meynee slayn.**
	That hast the sight of her, and I the absence.		Who is slain in his house by members of his household.
1240	**For possible is, sin thou hast hir presence,**	1259	**Infinite harmes been in this matere;**
	For it is possible, since thou hast her presence,		Infinite harms are in this matter.
1241	**And art a knight, a worthy and an able,**	1260	**We witen nat what thing we preyen here.**
	And art a knight, a worthy and an able (one),		We know not what thing we pray for here;
1242	**That by som cas, sin fortune is chaungeable,**	1261	**We faren as he that dronke is as a mous;**
	That by some chance, since Fortune is changeable,		We act like one who is drunk as a mouse.
1243	**Thou mayst to thy desyr som-tyme atteyne.**	1262	**A dronke man wot wel he hath an hous,**
	Thou mayest sometime attain thy desire.		A drunk man knows well he has a house,
1244	**But I, that am exyled, and bareyne**	1263	**But he noot which the righte wey is thider;**
	But I, who am exiled and barren		But he does not know which is the right way to it,
1245	**Of alle grace, and in so greet despeir,**	1264	**And to a dronke man the wey is slider.**
	Of all grace, and in so great despair		And to a drunk man the way is slippery.
1246	**That ther nis erthe, water, fyr, ne eir,**	1265	**And certes, in this world so faren we;**
	That there is not earth, water, fire, nor air,		And certainly, so we fare in this world;
1247	**Ne creature, that of hem maked is,**	1266	**We seken faste after felicitee,**
	Nor creature that is made of them,		We seek eagerly after felicity,
1248	**That may me helpe or doon confort in this.**	1267	**But we goon wrong ful often, trewely.**
	That can help me or do comfort (to me) in this.		But we go wrong very often, truly.
1249	**Wel oughte I sterve in wanhope and distresse;**	1268	**Thus may we seyen alle, and namely I,**
	Well ought I to die in despair and distress;		Thus can we all say, and especially I,
1250	**Farwel my lyf, my lust, and my gladnesse!**	1269	**That wende and hadde a greet opinioun,**
	Farwell my life, my desire, and my gladness!		Who supposed and had a firm belief
1251	**Allas, why pleynen folk so in commune**	1270	**That, if I mighte escapen from prisoun,**
	Alas, why do folk so commonly complain		That if I might escape from prison,

1271	**Than hadde I been in Ioye and perfit hele,**	1290	**For whom that I mot nedes lese my lyf.**
	Then I would have been in joy and perfect well-being,		For whom I must of necessity lose my life.
1272	**Ther now I am exyled fro my wele.**	1291	**For, as by wey of possibilitee,**
	Whereas now I am exiled from my source of happiness.		For, as by way of possibility,
1273	**Sin that I may nat seen yow, Emelye,**	1292	**Sith thou art at thy large, of prison free,**
	Since I can not see you, Emelye,		Since thou art at thy liberty, free of prison,
1274	**I nam but deed; ther nis no remedye.'**	1293	**And art a lord, greet is thyn avauntage,**
	I am as good as dead; there is not any remedy.'		And art a lord, thy advantage is great,
1275	**Up-on that other syde Palamon,**	1294	**More than is myn, that sterve here in a cage.**
	Upon that other side Palamon,		More than is mine, who die here in a cage.
1276	**Whan that he wiste Arcite was agon,**	1295	**For I mot wepe and wayle, whyl I live,**
	When he knew Arcite was gone,		For I must weep and wail, while I live,
1277	**Swich sorwe he maketh, that the grete tour**	1296	**With al the wo that prison may me yive,**
	He makes such sorrow that the great tour		With all the woe that prison may give me,
1278	**Resouneth of his youling and clamour.**	1297	**And eek with peyne that love me yiveth also,**
	Resounds with his yowling and clamor.		And also with pain that love gives me also,
1279	**The pure fettres on his shines grete**	1298	**That doubleth al my torment and my wo.'**
	The great fetters themselves on his shins		That doubles all my torment and my woe.'
1280	**Weren of his bittre salte teres wete.**	1299	**Ther-with the fyr of Ielousye up-sterte**
	Were wet from his bitter, salt tears.		With that the fire of jealousy started up
1281	**'Allas!' quod he, 'Arcita, cosin myn,**	1300	**With-inne his brest, and hente him by the herte**
	'Alas,' said he, 'Arcite, cousin mine,		Within his breast, and seized him by the heart
1282	**Of al our stryf, God woot, the fruyt is thyn.**	1301	**So woodly, that he lyk was to biholde**
	Of all our strife, God knows, the profit is thine.		So madly that he was to look upon like
1283	**Thow walkest now in Thebes at thy large,**	1302	**The box-tree, or the asshen dede and colde.**
	Thou walkest freely now in Thebes,		The box tree or the ash dead and cold.
1284	**And of my wo thou yevest litel charge.**	1303	**Tho seyde he; 'O cruel goddes, that governe**
	And thou care little about my woe.		Then said he, "O cruel gods that govern
1285	**Thou mayst, sin thou hast wisdom and manhede,**	1304	**This world with binding of your word eterne,**
	Thou mayest, since thou hast wisdom and manhood,		This world with binding of your eternal word,
1286	**Assemblen alle the folk of our kinrede,**	1305	**And wryten in the table of athamaunt**
	Assemble all the folk of our family,		And write in the table of adamant (hardest of stones)
1287	**And make a werre so sharp on this citee,**	1306	**Your parlement, and your eterne graunt,**
	And make a war so sharp on this city		Your decision and your eternal decree,
1288	**That by som aventure, or som tretee,**	1307	**What is mankinde more un-to yow holde**
	That by some chance or some treaty		Why is mankind more obligated unto you
1289	**Thou mayst have hir to lady and to wyf,**		
	Thou mayest have her as lady and as wife		

1308 **Than is the sheep, that rouketh in the folde?**
Than is the sheep that cowers in the sheepfold?

1309 **For slayn is man right as another beste,**
For man is slain exactly like another beast,

1310 **And dwelleth eek in prison and areste,**
And dwells also in prison and detention,

1311 **And hath siknesse, and greet adversitee,**
And has sickness and great adversity,

1312 **And ofte tymes giltelees, pardee!**
And often times guiltless, indeed!

1313 **What governaunce is in this prescience,**
What (sort of) governance is in this foreknowledge,

1314 **That giltelees tormenteth innocence?**
That torments guiltless innocence?

1315 **And yet encreseth this al my penaunce,**
And yet this increases all my suffering,

1316 **That man is bounden to his observaunce,**
That man is bound to his duty,

1317 **For Goddes sake, to letten of his wille,**
For God's sake, to refrain from his desire,

1318 **Ther as a beest may al his lust fulfille.**
Whereas a beast may fulfill all his desire.

1319 **And whan a beest is deed, he hath no peyne;**
And when a beast is dead he has no pain;

1320 **But man after his deeth moot wepe and pleyne,**
But man after his death must weep and lament,

1321 **Though in this world he have care and wo:**
Though in this world he may have (had) care and woe:

1322 **With-outen doute it may stonden so.**
Without doubt such is the case.

1323 **The answere of this I lete to divynis,**
The answer to this I leave to theologians,

1324 **But wel I woot, that in this world gret pyne is.**
But well I know that great pain is in this world.

1325 **Allas! I see a serpent or a theef,**
Alas, I see a serpent or a thief,

1326 **That many a trewe man hath doon mescheef,**
That has done mischief to many a true man,

1327 **Goon at his large, and wher him list may turne.**
Go at his liberty, and can go where he pleases.

1328 **But I mot been in prison thurgh Saturne,**
But I must be in prison because of Saturn,

1329 **And eek thurgh Iuno, Ialous and eek wood,**
And also because of Juno, jealous and also mad,

1330 **That hath destroyed wel ny al the blood**
Who has destroyed well nigh all the blood

1331 **Of Thebes, with his waste walles wyde.**
Of Thebes with its wide devastated walls;

1332 **And Venus sleeth me on that other syde**
And Venus slays me on that other side

1333 **For Ielousye, and fere of him Arcite.'**
For jealousy and fear of this Arcite.'

1334 **Now wol I stinte of Palamon a lyte,**
Now will I cease (speaking of) of Palamon for a little while,

1335 **And lete him in his prison stille dwelle,**
And leave him to dwell in his prison still,

1336 **And of Arcita forth I wol yow telle.**
And of Arcite forth I will tell you.

1337 **The somer passeth, and the nightes longe**
The summer passes, and the long nights

1338 **Encresen double wyse the peynes stronge**
Increase doubly the strong pains

1339 **Bothe of the lovere and the prisoner.**
Both of the lover and the prisoner.

1340 **I noot which hath the wofullere mester.**
I know not which has the more woeful task.

1341 **For shortly for to seyn, this Palamoun**
For, briefly to say (it), this Palamon

1342 **Perpetuelly is dampned to prisoun,**
Is damned perpetually to prison,

1343 **In cheynes and in fettres to ben deed;**
In chains and in fetters to be dead;

1344	**And Arcite is exyled upon his heed**		1350	**But in prison he moot dwelle alway.**
	And Arcite is exiled on threat of losing his head			But in prison he must always dwell;
1345	**For ever-mo as out of that contree,**		1351	**That other wher him list may ryde or go,**
	For evermore, out of that country,			That other where he pleases may ride or walk,
1346	**Ne never-mo he shal his lady see.**		1352	**But seen his lady shal he never-mo.**
	Nor nevermore shall see his lady.			But he shall see his lady nevermore.
1347	**Yow loveres axe I now this questioun:**		1353	**Now demeth as yow liste, ye that can,**
	Yow lovers now I ask this question:			Now judge as it pleases you, you who know (of such things),
1348	**Who hath the worse, Arcite or Palamoun?**		1354	**For I wol telle forth as I bigan.**
	Who has the worse, Arcite or Palamon?			For I will tell forth as I began.
1349	**That oon may seen his lady day by day,**			
	That one may see his lady every day,			

Explicit prima pars
The first part ends

The Canterbury Tales

The Knight's Tale, Part II

Geoffrey Chaucer

Sequitur pars secunda
The second part follows

1355	**Whan that Arcite to Thebes comen was,**		1361	**His sleep, his mete, his drink is him biraft,**
	When Arcite was come to Thebes,			He is bereft of his sleep, his food, his drink
1356	**Ful ofte a day he swelte and seyde 'allas,'**		1362	**That lene he wex, and drye as is a shaft.**
	Very often each day he grew faint and said 'alas,'			So that he became lean and dry as is a stick;
1357	**For seen his lady shal he never-mo.**		1363	**His eyen holwe, and grisly to biholde;**
	For he shall never more see his lady.			His eyes sunken and grisly to behold,
1358	**And shortly to concluden al his wo,**		1364	**His hewe falwe, and pale as asshen colde,**
	And shortly to conclude (telling) all his woe,			His hue sickly yellow and pale as cold ashes,
1359	**So muche sorwe had never creature**		1365	**And solitarie he was, and ever allone,**
	So much sorrow never had creature			And he was solitary and ever alone,
1360	**That is, or shal, whyl that the world may dure.**		1366	**And wailling al the night, making his mone.**
	That is, or shall (be), while the world may endure.			And wailing all the night, making his moan;
			1367	**And if he herde song or instrument,**
				And if he heard song or instrument,

Geoffrey Chaucer; Larry D. Benson, trans., *The Knight's Tale, Part II: An Interlinear Translation (lines 1355–1880)*, from http://www.courses.fas.harvard.edu/chaucer/teachslf/kt-par2.htm. Copyright © 2008 by The President and Fellows of Harvard College. Permission to reprint granted by the publisher.

1368	**Then wolde he wepe, he mighte nat be stent;**	1386	**Biforn him stood, and bad him to be murye.**
	Then would he weep, he could not be stopped.		Stood before him and commanded him to be merry.
1369	**So feble eek were his spirits, and so lowe,**	1387	**His slepy yerde in hond he bar uprighte;**
	So feeble also were his spirits, and so low,		His sleep-inducing staff he carried upright in his hand;
1370	**And chaunged so, that no man coude knowe**	1388	**An hat he werede up-on his heres brighte.**
	And changed so, that no man could know		He wore a hat upon his bright hair.
1371	**His speche nor his vois, though men it herde.**	1389	**Arrayed was this god (as he took keep)**
	His speech nor his voice, though men heard it.		This god was dressed, as he (Arcite) noticed,
1372	**And in his gere, for al the world he ferde**	1390	**As he was whan that Argus took his sleep;**
	And in his behavior for all the world he fared		As he was when he put Argus to sleep;
1373	**Nat oonly lyk the loveres maladye**	1391	**And seyde him thus: 'To Athenes shaltou wende;**
	Not only like the lover's malady		And said to him thus: "To Athens shalt thou go,
1374	**Of Hereos, but rather lyk manye**	1392	**Ther is thee shapen of thy wo an ende.'**
	Of Hereos, but rather like mania,		Where an end of thy woe is destined for thee."
1375	**Engendred of humour malencolyk,**	1393	**And with that word Arcite wook and sterte.**
	Engendered by the melancholic humor		And with that word Arcite awoke and leaped up.
1376	**Biforen, in his celle fantastyk.**	1394	**'Now trewely, how sore that me smerte,'**
	In the front lobe, in his imagination.		'Now truly, however sorely it may pain me,'
1377	**And shortly, turned was al up-so-doun**	1395	**Quod he, 'to Athenes right now wol I fare;**
	And shortly, all was turned topsy-turvy		Said he, "I will go to Athens right now,
1378	**Bothe habit and eek disposicioun**	1396	**Ne for the drede of deeth shal I nat spare**
	Both the physical condition and also the mental disposition		Nor shall I refrain for the dread of death
1379	**Of him, this woful lovere daun Arcite.**	1397	**To see my lady, that I love and serve;**
	Of him, this woeful lover dan Arcite.		From seeing my lady, whom I love and serve.
1380	**What sholde I al-day of his wo endyte?**	1398	**In hir presence I recche nat to sterve.'**
	Why should I all daylong write of his woe?		In her presence I care not if I die.'
1381	**Whan he endured hadde a yeer or two**	1399	**And with that word he caughte a greet mirour,**
	When he had endured a year or two		And with that word he picked up a large mirror,
1382	**This cruel torment, and this peyne and wo,**	1400	**And saugh that chaunged was al his colour,**
	This cruel torment and this pain and woe,		And saw that all his color was changed,
1383	**At Thebes, in his contree, as I seyde,**	1401	**And saugh his visage al in another kinde.**
	At Thebes, in his country, as I said,		And saw his visage all (changed) to another sort.
1384	**Up-on a night, in sleep as he him leyde,**	1402	**And right anoon it ran him in his minde,**
	Upon one night as he laid himself in sleep,		And right away it ran to him in his mind,
1385	**Him thoughte how that the winged god Mercurie**		
	It seemed to him that the winged god Mercury		

1403	**That, sith his face was so disfigured**	1424	**And ther-to be was strong and big of bones**
	That, since his face was so disfigured		And moreover he was tall and strong of bones
1404	**Of maladye, the which he hadde endured,**	1425	**To doon that any wight can him devyse.**
	By the malady which he had endured,		To do what any one can command him.
1405	**He mighte wel, if that he bar him lowe,**	1426	**A yeer or two he was in this servyse,**
	He might well, if he conducted himself humbly,		A year or two he was in this service,
1406	**Live in Athenes ever-more unknowe,**	1427	**Page of the chambre of Emelye the brighte;**
	Live in Athens evermore unknown,		Page of the chamber of Emelye the bright,
1407	**And seen his lady wel ny day by day.**	1428	**And 'Philostrate' he seide that he highte.**
	And see his lady almost every day.		And he said that he was called Philostrate.
1408	**And right anon he chaunged his array,**	1429	**But half so wel biloved a man as he**
	And right away he changed his clothing,		But half so well beloved a man as he
1409	**And cladde him as a povre laborer,**	1430	**Ne was ther never in court, of his degree;**
	And clad himself as a poor laborer,		Was never in court (anyone) of his rank;
1410	**And al allone, save oonly a squyer,**	1431	**He was so gentil of condicioun,**
	And all alone, except only a squire		He was so noble in manner
1411	**That knew his privetee and al his cas,**	1432	**That thurghout al the court was his renoun.**
	Who knew his private affairs and all his situation,		That his fame was (spread) throughout all the court.
1412	**Which was disgysed povrely, as he was,**	1433	**They seyden, that it were a charitee**
	Who was disguised as poorly as he was,		They said that it would be a act of charity
1413	**To Athenes is he goon the nexte way.**	1434	**That Theseus wolde enhauncen his degree,**
	To Athens he is gone the nearest way.		If Theseus would advance his rank,
1414	**And to the court he wente up-on a day,**	1435	**And putten him in worshipful servyse,**
	And to the court he went upon a day,		And put him in noble employment,
1415	**And at the gate he profreth his servyse,**	1436	**Ther as he mighte his vertu excercyse.**
	And at the gate he offers his service		Where he could exercise his abilities.
1416	**To drugge and drawe, what so men wol devyse.**	1437	**And thus, with-inne a whyle, his name is spronge**
	To drudge and draw water, whatever men will command.		And thus within a short time his fame is sprung,
1417	**And shortly of this matere for to seyn,**	1438	**Bothe of his dedes, and his goode tonge,**
	And shortly to speak of this matter,		Both for his deeds and his good speech,
1418	**He fil in office with a chamberleyn,**	1439	**That Theseus hath taken him so neer**
	He was given employment by a household attendant		That Theseus has taken him so near
1419	**The which that dwelling was with Emelye.**	1440	**That of his chambre he made him a squyer,**
	Who was dwelling with Emelye,		That he has made him a squire of his chamber,
1420	**For he was wys, and coude soon aspye**	1441	**And yaf him gold to mayntene his degree;**
	For he was wise and could soon take the measure		And gave him gold to maintain (a life style suitable to) his rank.
1421	**Of every servaunt, which that serveth here.**	1442	**And eek men broghte him out of his contree**
	Of every servant, who serves here.		And also men brought him out of his country,
1422	**Wel coude he hewen wode, and water bere,**		
	He could well hew wood, and carry water,		
1423	**For he was yong and mighty for the nones,**		
	For he was young and mighty indeed,		

1443	**From yeer to yeer, ful prively, his rente;**
	From year to year, very secretly, his income;
1444	**But honestly and slyly he it spente,**
	But properly and slyly he spent it,
1445	**That no man wondred how that he it hadde.**
	So that no man wondered how he acquired it.
1446	**And three yeer in this wyse his lyf he ladde,**
	And three years in this manner he led his life,
1447	**And bar him so in pees and eek in werre,**
	And conducted himself so that, in peace and also in war,
1448	**Ther nas no man that Theseus hath derre.**
	There was no man whom Theseus holds dearer.
1449	**And in this blisse lete I now Arcite,**
	And in this bliss I now leave Arcite,
1450	**And speke I wol of Palamon a lyte.**
	And I will speak of Palamon a little.
1451	**In derknesse and horrible and strong prisoun**
	In darkness and horrible and strong imprisonment
1452	**This seven yeer hath seten Palamoun,**
	These seven years Palamon has sat
1453	**Forpyned, what for wo and for distresse;**
	Wasted by suffering, what for woe and for distress.
1454	**Who feleth double soor and hevinesse**
	Who feels double pain and sadness
1455	**But Palamon? that love destreyneth so,**
	But Palamon, whom love so afflicts
1456	**That wood out of his wit he gooth for wo;**
	That he goes mad, out of his wits because of woe?
1457	**And eek therto he is a prisoner**
	And also moreover he is a prisoner
1458	**Perpetuelly, noght oonly for a yeer.**
	Perpetually, not just for a year.
1459	**Who coude ryme in English proprely**
	Who could rime in English properly
1460	**His martirdom? for sothe, it am nat I;**
	His martyrdom? In truth it is not I;
1461	**Therefore I passe as lightly as I may.**
	Therefore I pass on as quickly as I can.
1462	**It fel that in the seventhe yeer, in May,**
	It happened that in the seventh year, of May
1463	**The thridde night, (as olde bokes seyn,**
	The third night (as old books say,
1464	**That al this storie tellen more pleyn,)**
	That tell all this story more fully),
1465	**Were it by aventure or destinee,**
	Whether it was by chance or fate,
1466	**(As, whan a thing is shapen, it shal be,)**
	(As, when a thing is pre-ordained, it must be,)
1467	**That, sone after the midnight, Palamoun,**
	That soon after midnight Palamon,
1468	**By helping of a freend, brak his prisoun,**
	With the help of a friend, broke out of his prison
1469	**And fleeth the citee, faste as he may go;**
	And flees the city as fast as he can go.
1470	**For he had yive his gayler drinke so**
	For he had so given his jailer drink
1471	**Of a clarree, maad of a certeyn wyn,**
	Of a spiced and sweetened drink made of a certain wine,
1472	**With nercotikes and opie of Thebes fyn,**
	With narcotics and pure opium of Thebes,
1473	**That al that night, thogh that men wolde him shake,**
	That all that night, though men would shake him,
1474	**The gayler sleep, he mighte nat awake;**
	The jailer slept; he could not awake.
1475	**And thus he fleeth as faste as ever he may.**
	And thus he flees as fast as ever he can.
1476	**The night was short, and faste by the day,**
	The night was short and very close to the day
1477	**That nedes-cost he moste him-selven hyde,**
	So that by necessity he must hide himself,
1478	**And til a grove, faste ther besyde,**
	And to a grove close by
1479	**With dredful foot than stalketh Palamoun.**
	With fearful foot then stalks Palamon.

1480	**For shortly, this was his opinioun,**
	For, shortly, this was his idea,
1481	**That in that grove he wolde him hyde al day,**
	That in that grove he would hide himself all day,
1482	**And in the night than wolde he take his way**
	And in the night then he would take his way
1483	**To Thebes-ward, his freendes for to preye**
	Toward Thebes, to pray his friends
1484	**On Theseus to helpe him to werreye;**
	To help him to wage war on Theseus;
1485	**And shortly, outher he wolde lese his lyf,**
	And shortly, he would either lose his life
1486	**Or winnen Emelye un-to his wyf;**
	Or win Emelye to be his wife.
1487	**This is theffect and his entente pleyn.**
	This is the purpose and his full intent.
1488	**Now wol I torne un-to Arcite ageyn,**
	Now I will turn again to Arcite,
1489	**Saluëth in hir song the morwe gray;**
	That little knew how near his trouble was,
1490	**Til that Fortune had broght him in the snare.**
	To which Fortune had brought him in the snare.
1491	**The bisy larke, messager of day,**
	The busy lark, messenger of day,
1492	**Saluëth in hir song the morwe gray;**
	Salutes the morning gray in her song,
1493	**And fyry Phebus ryseth up so brighte,**
	And fiery Phoebus rises up so bright
1494	**That al the orient laugheth of the lighte,**
	That all the orient laughs because of the light,
1495	**And with his stremes dryeth in the greves**
	And with his rays dries in the groves
1496	**The silver dropes, hanging on the leves.**
	The silver drops hanging on the leaves.
1497	**And Arcite, that is in the court royal**
	And Arcite, who in the royal court
1498	**With Theseus, his squyer principal,**
	With Theseus is chief squire,
1499	**Is risen, and loketh on the myrie day.**
	Is risen and looks on the merry day.
1500	**And, for to doon his observaunce to May,**
	And to do his observance to May,
1501	**Remembring on the poynt of his desyr,**
	Meditating on the object of his desire,
1502	**He on a courser, sterting as the fyr,**
	He on a war horse, leaping about like the fire,
1503	**Is riden in-to the feeldes, him to pleye,**
	Has ridden into the fields to amuse himself,
1504	**Out of the court, were it a myle or tweye;**
	Out of the court, about a mile or two.
1505	**And to the grove, of which that I yow tolde,**
	And to the grove of which I told you
1506	**By aventure, his wey he gan to holde,**
	By chance he began to hold his way
1507	**To maken him a gerland of the greves,**
	To make himself a garland of the branches,
1508	**Were it of wodebinde or hawethorn-leves,**
	Were it of woodbine or hawthorn leaves,
1509	**And loude he song ageyn the sonne shene:**
	And loud he sang in the bright sun:
1510	**'May, with alle thy floures and thy grene,**
	'May, with all thy flowers and thy greenery,
1511	**Wel-come be thou, faire fresshe May,**
	Welcome be thou, fair, fresh May,
1512	**I hope that I som grene gete may.'**
	In hope that I can get something green.'
1513	**And from his courser, with a lusty herte,**
	And from his war horse, with an eager heart,
1514	**In-to the grove ful hastily he sterte,**
	He rushed into the grove hastily,
1515	**And in a path he rometh up and doun,**
	And in a path he roams up and down,
1516	**Ther-as, by aventure, this Palamoun**
	Where by chance this Palamon
1517	**Was in a bush, that no man mighte him see,**
	Was in a thicket, so that no man could see him,
1518	**For sore afered of his deeth was he.**
	For he was sorely afraid of his death.
1519	**No-thing ne knew he that it was Arcite:**
	In no way did he know that it was Arcite;

1520	**God wot he wolde have trowed it ful lyte.**	1539	**Selde is the Friday al the wyke y-lyke.**
	God knows he would scarcely have believed it		Friday is seldom like all the rest of the week.
1521	**But sooth is seyd, gon sithen many yeres,**	1540	**Whan that Arcite had songe, he gan to syke,**
	But truly it is said, since many years ago,		When Arcite had sung, he began to sigh
1522	**That 'feeld hath eyen, and the wode hath eres.'**	1541	**And sette him doun with-outen any more:**
	That 'field has eyes and the wood has ears.'		And sat himself down without any more.
1523	**It is ful fair a man to bere him evene,**	1542	**'Alas!' quod he, 'that day that I was bore!**
	It is very good for a man to act calmly,		'Alas,' he said, "that day that I was born!
1524	**For al-day meteth men at unset stevene.**	1543	**How longe, Iuno, thurgh thy crueltee,**
	For every day people meet at unexpected times.		How long, Juno, through thy cruelty,
1525	**Ful litel woot Arcite of his felawe,**	1544	**Woltow werreyen Thebes the citee?**
	Arcite knows full little of his fellow,		Wilt thou make war on the city of Thebes?
1526	**That was so ny to herknen al his sawe,**	1545	**Allas! y-broght is to confusioun**
	Who was near enough to hear all his speech,		Alas, to ruin is brought
1527	**For in the bush he sitteth now ful stille.**	1546	**The blood royal of Cadme and Amphioun;—**
	For in the thicket he sits now very still.		The royal blood of Cadmus and Amphion—
1528	**Whan that Arcite had romed al his fille,**	1547	**Of Cadmus, which that was the firste man**
	When Arcite had roamed all his fill,		Of Cadmus, who was the first man
1529	**And songen al the roundel lustily,**	1548	**That Thebes bulte, or first the toun bigan,**
	And sung all the rondel cheerfully,		Who built Thebes, before the town first began,
1530	**In-to a studie he fil sodeynly,**	1549	**And of the citee first was crouned king,**
	He fell suddenly into a state of anxiety,		And first was crowned king of the city.
1531	**As doon thise loveres in hir queynte geres,**	1550	**Of his linage am I, and his of-spring**
	As these lovers do in their strange manners,		I am of his lineage and his offspring
1532	**Now in the croppe, now doun in the breres,**	1551	**By verray ligne, as of the stok royal:**
	Now in the tree top, now down in the briars,		By true lineage, of the royal family,
1533	**Now up, now doun, as boket in a welle.**	1552	**And now I am so caitif and so thral,**
	Now up, now down, like a bucket in a well.		And now I am so wretched and so enslaved,
1534	**Right as the Friday, soothly for to telle,**	1553	**That he, that is my mortal enemy,**
	Exactly like the Friday, truly for to tell,		That he who is my mortal enemy,
1535	**Now it shyneth, now it reyneth faste,**	1554	**I serve him as his squyer povrely.**
	Now it shines, now it rains hard,		I meekly serve him as his squire.
1536	**Right so can gery Venus overcaste**	1555	**And yet doth Iuno me wel more shame,**
	Just so can fickle Venus sadden		And yet Juno does me much more shame,
1537	**The hertes of hir folk; right as hir day**	1556	**For I dar noght biknowe myn owne name;**
	The hearts of her folk; just as her day		For I dare not acknowledge my own name;
1538	**Is gerful, right so chaungeth she array.**	1557	**But ther-as I was wont to highte Arcite,**
	Is changeable, just so she changes her array.		But whereas I was accustomed to be called Arcite,
		1558	**Now highte I Philostrate, noght worth a myte.**
			Now I am called Philostrate, not worth a penny.

1559	**Allas! thou felle Mars, allas! Iuno,**
	Alas! thou fierce Mars, alas! Juno,
1560	**Thus hath your ire our kinrede al fordo,**
	Thus has your anger destroyed all our lineage,
1561	**Save only me, and wrecched Palamoun,**
	Save only me and wretched Palamon,
1562	**That Theseus martyreth in prisoun.**
	Whom Theseus torments in prison.
1563	**And over al this, to sleen me utterly,**
	And in addition to all this, to slay me utterly
1564	**Love hath his fyry dart so brenningly**
	Love has his fiery dart so ardently
1565	**Y-stiked thurgh my trewe careful herte,**
	Stabbed through my faithful, sorrowful heart
1566	**That shapen was my deeth erst than my sherte.**
	That my death was destined before my first garment was made.
1567	**Ye sleen me with your eyen, Emelye;**
	You slay me with your eyes, Emelye!
1568	**Ye been the cause wherfor that I dye.**
	You are the cause by which I die.
1569	**Of al the remenant of myn other care**
	Of all the rest of my other troubles
1570	**Ne sette I nat the mountaunce of a tare,**
	I do not reckon at the value of a weed,
1571	**So that I coude don aught to your plesaunce!'**
	Provided that I could do anything to please you.'
1572	**And with that word he fil doun in a traunce**
	And with that word he fell down in a trance
1573	**A longe tyme; and after he up-sterte.**
	A long time, and afterwards he leaped up.
1574	**This Palamoun, that thoughte that thurgh his herte**
	This Palamon, that thought that through his heart
1575	**He felte a cold swerd sodeynliche glyde,**
	He felt a cold sword suddenly glide,
1576	**For ire he quook, no lenger wolde he byde.**
	For anger he trembled; no longer would he wait.
1577	**And whan that he had herd Arcites tale,**
	And when he had heard Arcite's tale,
1578	**As he were wood, with face deed and pale,**
	As if he were mad, with face dead and pale,
1579	**He sterte him up out of the buskes thikke,**
	He leaped up out of the thick bushes
1580	**And seyde: 'Arcite, false traitour wikke,**
	And said: 'Arcite, false, wicked traitor,
1581	**Now artow hent, that lovest my lady so,**
	Now art thou taken, who lovest my lady so,
1582	**For whom that I have al this peyne and wo,**
	For whom that I have all this pain and woe,
1583	**And art my blood, and to my counseil sworn,**
	And art of my blood, and sworn to be in my confidence,
1584	**As I ful ofte have told thee heer-biforn,**
	As I full often have told thee before now,
1585	**And hast by-iaped here duk Theseus,**
	And hast tricked here duke Theseus,
1586	**And falsly chaunged hast thy name thus;**
	And thus hast falsely changed thy name;
1587	**I wol be deed, or elles thou shalt dye.**
	I will be dead, or else thou shalt die.
1588	**Thou shalt nat love my lady Emelye,**
	Thou shalt not love my lady Emelye,
1589	**But I wol love hir only, and namo;**
	But I will love her only and no other;
1590	**For I am Palamoun, thy mortal fo.**
	For I am Palamon, thy mortal foe.
1591	**And though that I no wepne have in this place,**
	And though I have no weapon in this place,
1592	**But out of prison am astert by grace,**
	But out of prison am escaped by good luck,
1593	**I drede noght that outher thou shalt dye,**
	I doubt not that either thou shalt dye,
1594	**Or thou ne shalt nat loven Emelye.**
	Either thou shalt not love Emelye,
1595	**Chees which thou wilt, for thou shalt nat asterte.'**
	Choose which thou wish, or thou shalt not escape!'

1596	**This Arcitë, with ful despitous herte,**
	This Arcite, with full spiteful heart,
1597	**Whan he him knew, and hadde his tale herd,**
	When he knew him, and had heard his tale,
1598	**As fiers as leoun, pulled out a swerd,**
	As fierce as a lion pulled out his sword,
1599	**And seyde thus: 'by God that sit above,**
	And said thus: 'by God who sits above,
1600	**Nere it that thou art sik, and wood for love,**
	Were it not that thou art sick and mad for love,
1601	**And eek that thou no wepne hast in this place,**
	And also because thou hast no weapon in this place,
1602	**Thou sholdest never out of this grove pace,**
	Thou shouldest never walk out of this grove,
1603	**That thou ne sholdest dyen of myn hond.**
	Rather thou shouldest die of my hand.
1604	**For I defye the seurtee and the bond**
	For I repudiate the pledge and the bond
1605	**Which that thou seyst that I have maad to thee.**
	Which thou sayest that I have made to thee.
1606	**What, verray fool, think wel that love is free,**
	Lo! True fool, think well that love is free,
1607	**And I wol love hir, maugre al thy might!**
	And I will love her in spite of all thy might!
1608	**But, for as muche thou art a worthy knight,**
	But for as much as thou art a worthy knight
1609	**And wilnest to darreyne hir by batayle,**
	And desire to decide the right to her by battle,
1610	**Have heer my trouthe, to-morwe I wol nat fayle,**
	Have here my pledge; tomorrow I will not fail,
1611	**With-outen witing of any other wight,**
	Without the knowledge of any other person,
1612	**That here I wol be founden as a knight,**
	But here I will be found as a knight,
1613	**And bringen harneys right y-nough for thee;**
	And bring armor right enough for thee;
1614	**And chees the beste, and leve the worste for me.**
	And choose the best, and leave the worst for me.
1615	**And mete and drinke this night wol I bringe**
	And food and drink this night will I bring
1616	**Y-nough for thee, and clothes for thy beddinge.**
	Enough for thee, and bed-clothes for thy bedding.
1617	**And, if so be that thou my lady winne,**
	And if it so be that thou win my lady,
1618	**And slee me in this wode ther I am inne,**
	And slay me in this wood where I am in,
1619	**Thou mayst wel have thy lady, as for me.'**
	Thou mayest well have thy lady as far as I am concerned.'
1620	**This Palamon answerde: 'I graunte it thee.'**
	This Palamon answered, 'I agree.'
1621	**And thus they been departed til a-morwe,**
	And thus they are departed until morning,
1622	**When ech of hem had leyd his feith to borwe.**
	When each of them had laid his faith as a pledge.
1623	**O Cupide, out of alle charitee!**
	O Cupid, devoid of all kindness to others!
1624	**O regne, that wolt no felawe have with thee!**
	O reign, that will have no partner with thee!
1625	**Ful sooth is seyd, that love ne lordshipe**
	Full truly it is said that love nor lordship
1626	**Wol noght, his thankes, have no felawe-shipe;**
	Will not, willingly, have any partnership.
1627	**Wel finden that Arcite and Palamoun.**
	Arcite and Palamon well find that (to be true).

1628	**Arcite is riden anon un-to the toun,**	1647	**So ferden they, in chaungyng of hir hewe,**
	Arcite has ridden immediately into the town,		So fared they in changing colors of their faces,
1629	**And on the morwe, er it were dayes light,**	1648	**As fer as everich of hem other knewe.**
	And on the morning, before it was day's light,		When each of them knew the other.
1630	**Ful prively two harneys hath he dight,**	1649	**Ther nas no good day, ne no saluing;**
	Very secretly he has prepared two sets of armor,		There was no 'good day,' nor no salutations,
1631	**Bothe suffisaunt and mete to darreyne**	1650	**But streight, with-outen word or rehersing,**
	Both sufficient and suitable to decide		But straightway, without word or conversing,
1632	**The bataille in the feeld bitwix hem tweyne.**	1651	**Everich of hem halp for to armen other,**
	The battle in the field between them two;		Each one of them helped to arm the other
1633	**And on his hors, allone as he was born,**	1652	**As freendly as he were his owne brother;**
	And on his horse, alone as he was born,		As friendly as if he were his own brother;
1634	**He carieth al this harneys him biforn;**	1653	**And after that, with sharpe speres stronge**
	He carries all the armor before him.		And after that, with sharp strong spears
1635	**And in the grove, at tyme and place y-set,**	1654	**They foynen ech at other wonder longe.**
	And in the grove, at time and place set,		They thrust at each other a wonderfully long time.
1636	**This Arcite and this Palamon ben met.**	1655	**Thou mightest wene that this Palamoun**
	This Arcite and this Palamon are met.		Thou mightest suppose that this Palamon
1637	**Tho chaungen gan the colour in hir face;**	1656	**In his fighting were a wood leoun,**
	The color in their faces began to change;		In his fighting was a mad lion,
1638	**Right as the hunter in the regne of Trace,**	1657	**And as a cruel tygre was Arcite:**
	Just as the hunters in the reign of Thrace,		And Arcite was like a cruel tiger;
1639	**That stondeth at the gappe with a spere,**	1658	**As wilde bores gonne they to smyte,**
	He who stands at the gap in the forrest with a spear,		They began to smite like wild boars,
1640	**Whan hunted is the leoun or the bere,**	1659	**That frothen whyte as foom for ire wood.**
	When the lion or the bear is hunted,		That froth at the mouth white as foam for mad anger.
1641	**And hereth him come russhing in the greves,**	1660	**Up to the ancle foghte they in hir blood.**
	And hears him come rushing in the bushes,		They fought up to the ankle in their blood.
1642	**And breketh bothe bowes and the leves,**	1661	**And in this wyse I lete hem fighting dwelle;**
	And breaks both boughs and the leaves,		And in this manner I leave them to remain fighting,
1643	**And thinketh, 'heer cometh my mortel enemy,**	1662	**And forth I wol of Theseus yow telle.**
	And thinks, "Here comes my mortal enemy!		And forth I will tell you of Theseus.
1644	**With-oute faile, he moot be deed, or I;**	1663	**The destinee, ministre general,**
	Without fail, he must be dead, or I,		The destiny, general minister,
1645	**For outher I mot sleen him at the gappe,**	1664	**That executeth in the world over-al**
	For either I must slay him at the gap,		That executes in the world everywhere
1646	**Or he mot sleen me, if that me mishappe:'**		
	Or he must slay me, if I suffer misfortune.'		

1665	The purveyaunce, that God hath seyn biforn,
	The providence that God has foreseen,
1666	So strong it is, that, though the world had sworn
	So strong it is that, though the world had sworn
1667	The contrarie of a thing, by ye or nay,
	The contrary of a thing by yes or no,
1668	Yet somtyme it shal fallen on a day
	Yet sometimes it shall happen on one day
1669	That falleth nat eft with-inne a thousand yere.
	That happens not again in a thousand years.
1670	For certeinly, our appetytes here,
	For certainly, our desires here,
1671	Be it of werre, or pees, or hate, or love,
	Be it of war, or peace, or hate, or love,
1672	Al is this reuled by the sighte above.
	All this is ruled by the foresight above.
1673	This mene I now by mighty Theseus,
	I mean this now in regard to mighty Theseus,
1674	That for to honten is so desirous,
	Who is so desirous to hunt,
1675	And namely at the grete hert in May,
	And especially at the large hart in May,
1676	That in his bed ther daweth him no day,
	That in his bed there dawns for him no day
1677	That he nis clad, and redy for to ryde
	That he is not clad, and ready to ride
1678	With hunte and horn, and houndes him bisyde.
	With huntsman and horn and hounds beside him.
1679	For in his hunting hath he swich delyt,
	For in his hunting he has such delight
1680	That it is al his Ioye and appetyt
	That it is all his joy and desire
1681	To been him-self the grete hertes bane;
	To be himself the large hart's slayer,
1682	For after Mars he serveth now Diane.
	For next to Mars he now serves Diana.
1683	Cleer was the day, as I have told er this,
	The day was clear, as I have told before this,
1684	And Theseus, with alle Ioye and blis,
	And Theseus with all joy and bliss,
1685	With his Ipolita, the fayre quene,
	With his Ypolita, the faire queen,
1686	And Emelye, clothed al in grene,
	And Emelye, clothed all in green,
1687	On hunting be they riden royally.
	On hunting they are ridden royally.
1688	And to the grove, that stood ful faste by,
	And to the grove that stood very close by,
1689	In which ther was an hert, as men him tolde,
	In which there was a hart, so people told him,
1690	Duk Theseus the streighte wey hath holde.
	Duke Theseus has held the straight way.
1691	And to the launde he rydeth him ful right,
	And directly to the glade he rides,
1692	For thider was the hert wont have his flight,
	For through there the hart was accustomed to take his escape,
1693	And over a brook, and so forth on his weye.
	And (flee) over a brook, and so forth on his way.
1694	This duk wol han a cours at him, or tweye,
	This duke will have a run or two at him
1695	With houndes, swiche as that him list comaunde.
	With such hounds as he pleases to command.
1696	And whan this duk was come un-to the launde,
	And when this duke was come unto the glade,
1697	Under the sonne he loketh, and anon
	He looks toward the sun, and immediately
1698	He was war of Arcite and Palamon,
	He was aware of Arcite and Palamon,
1699	That foughten breme, as it were bores two;
	Who fought as fiercely as if it were two wild boars.
1700	The brighte swerdes wenten to and fro
	The bright swords went to and fro
1701	So hidously, that with the leeste strook
	So hideously that with the weakest stroke

1702	**It seemed as it wolde felle an ook;** It seemed as if it would fell an oak.	1721	**But slee me first, for seynte charitee;** But slay me first, by holy charity!
1703	**But what they were, no-thing he ne woot.** But who they were, he knew nothing.	1722	**But slee my felawe eek as wel as me.** But slay my fellow also as well as me;
1704	**This duk his courser with his spores smoot,** This duke smote his warhorse with his spurs,	1723	**Or slee him first; for, though thou knowe it lyte,** Or slay him first, for though thou little knowest it,
1705	**And at a stert he was bitwix hem two,** And with a sudden leap he was between them two,	1724	**This is thy mortal fo, this is Arcite,** This is thy mortal foe, this is Arcite,
1706	**And pulled out a swerd and cryed, 'ho!** And pulled out a sword and cried, 'Stop!	1725	**That fro thy lond is banished on his heed,** Who is banished from thy land on (pain of losing) his head,
1707	**Namore, up peyne of lesing of your heed.** No more, on the penalty of the loss of your head!	1726	**For which he hath deserved to be deed.** For which he has deserved to be dead.
1708	**By mighty Mars, he shal anon be deed,** By mighty Mars, he shall at once be dead	1727	**For this is he that cam un-to thy gate,** For this is he that came unto thy gate
1709	**That smyteth any strook, that I may seen!** Who smites any stroke that I can see!	1728	**And seyde, that he highte Philostrate.** And said that he was called Philostrate.
1710	**But telleth me what mister men ye been,** But tell me what sort of men you are,	1729	**Thus hath he Iaped thee ful many a yeer,** Thus has he tricked thee for many years,
1711	**That been so hardy for to fighten here** Who are so bold as to fight here	1730	**And thou has maked him thy chief squyer;** And thou hast made him thy chief squire;
1712	**With-outen Iuge or other officere,** Without judge or other officer,	1731	**And this is he that loveth Emelye.** And this is he that loves Emelye.
1713	**As it were in a listes royally?'** As it would be in a properly conducted duel?'	1732	**For sith the day is come that I shal dye,** For since the day is come that I must dye,
1714	**This Palamon answerde hastily,** This Palamon answered hastily	1733	**I make pleynly my confessioun,** I make plainly my confession
1715	**And seyde: 'sire, what nedeth wordes mo?** And said, 'sire, what more words are needed?	1734	**That I am thilke woful Palamoun,** That I am that same woeful Palamon
1716	**We have the deeth deserved bothe two.** We have deserved the death, both of us two.	1735	**That hath thy prison broken wikkedly.** That wickedly has broken (out of) thy prison.
1717	**Two woful wrecches been we, two caytyves,** Two woeful wretches are we, two miserable people,	1736	**I am thy mortal fo, and it am I** I am thy mortal foe, and it is I
1718	**That been encombred of our owne lyves;** Who are burdened down by our own lives;	1737	**That loveth so hote Emelye the brighte,** Who loves the beautiful Emelye so passionately
1719	**And as thou art a rightful lord and Iuge,** And as thou art a rightful lord and judge,	1738	**That I wol dye present in hir sighte.** That I will die at this moment in her sight.
1720	**Ne yeve us neither mercy ne refuge,** Give us neither mercy nor refuge,	1739	**Therfore I axe deeth and my Iuwyse;** Therefore I ask death and my judicial sentence;
		1740	**But slee my felawe in the same wyse,** But slay my fellow in the same way,
		1741	**For bothe han we deserved to be slayn.'** For we have both deserved to be slain.'

1742	**This worthy duk answerde anon agayn,**
	This worthy duke answered at once in reply,
1743	**And seyde, 'This is a short conclusioun:**
	And said, 'This is a brief (easy) decision.
1744	**Youre owne mouth, by your confessioun,**
	Your own mouth, by your confession,
1745	**Hath dampned you, and I wol it recorde,**
	Has condemned you, and I will pronounce it;
1746	**It nedeth noght to pyne yow with the corde.**
	There is no deed to torture you with the cord.
1747	**Ye shul be deed, by mighty Mars the rede!'**
	You shall be dead, by mighty Mars the red!'
1748	**The quene anon, for verray wommanhede,**
	The queen at once, for true womanliness,
1749	**Gan for to wepe, and so dide Emelye,**
	Began to weep, and so did Emelye,
1750	**And alle the ladies in the companye.**
	And all the ladies in the company.
1751	**Gret pitee was it, as it thoughte hem alle,**
	Great pity was it, as it seemed to them all,
1752	**That ever swich a chaunce sholde falle;**
	That ever such a misfortune should occur,
1753	**For gentil men they were, of greet estat,**
	For they were gentle men of high rank,
1754	**And no-thing but for love was this debat;**
	And this debate was for nothing but love;
1755	**And sawe hir blody woundes wyde and sore;**
	And saw their bloody wounds wide and sore,
1756	**And alle cryden, bothe lasse and more,**
	And all cried, both low ranking and high,
1757	**'Have mercy, lord, up-on us wommen alle!'**
	'Have mercy, Lord, upon all of us women!'
1758	**And on hir bare knees adoun they falle,**
	And they fall down on their bare knees
1759	**And wolde have kist his feet ther-as he stood,**
	And would have kissed his feet there where he stood,
1760	**Til at the laste aslaked was his mood;**
	Until at the last his mood was calmed,
1761	**For pitee renneth sone in gentil herte.**
	For pity comes soon to a gentle heart.
1762	**And though he first for ire quook and sterte,**
	And though he first for anger shook and trembled,
1763	**He hath considered shortly, in a clause,**
	He has considered shortly, in brief,
1764	**The trespas of hem bothe, and eek the cause:**
	The trespass of them both, and also the cause,
1765	**And al-though that his ire hir gilt accused,**
	And although his anger reproached them for their guilt,
1766	**Yet in his reson he hem bothe excused;**
	Yet in his reason he excused them both,
1767	**As thus: he thoghte wel, that every man**
	As thus: he thought well that every man
1768	**Wol helpe him-self in love, if that he can,**
	Will help himself in love, if he can,
1769	**And eek delivere him-self out of prisoun;**
	And also deliver himself out of prison.
1770	**And eek his herte had compassioun**
	And also his heart had compassion
1771	**Of wommen, for they wepen ever in oon;**
	Of women, for they weep continually,
1772	**And in his gentil herte he thoghte anoon,**
	And in his gentle heart he thought straightway,
1773	**And softe un-to himself he seyde: 'fy**
	And softly to himself he said, 'fie
1774	**Up-on a lord that wol have no mercy,**
	Upon a lord that will have no mercy,
1775	**But been a leoun, bothe in word and dede,**
	But be a lion, both in word and deed,
1776	**To hem that been in repentaunce and drede**
	To those who are in repentance and fear,
1777	**As wel as to a proud despitous man**
	As well as to a proud, spiteful man
1778	**That wol maynteyne that he first bigan!**
	Who will persist in what he first began.
1779	**That lord hath litel of discrecioun,**
	That lord has little sound judgment,
1780	**That in swich cas can no divisioun,**
	That in such cases knows no distinctions,

1781	**But weyeth pryde and humblesse after oon.'**	1801	**Se how they blede! be they noght wel arrayed?**
	But considers pride and humility equal.'		See how they bleed! Are they not in fine condition?
1782	**And shortly, whan his ire is thus agoon,**	1802	**Thus hath hir lord, the god of love, y-payed**
	And shortly, when his anger is thus gone,		Thus has their lord, the god of love, paid
1783	**He gan to loken up with eyen lighte,**	1803	**Hir wages and hir fees for hir servyse!**
	He began to look up with bright eyes		Their wages and their fees for their service!
1784	**And spak thise same wordes al on highte:—**	1804	**And yet they wenen for to been ful wyse**
	And spoke these same words all aloud:—		And yet they consider themselves very wise,
1785	**The god of love, a!** *benedicite,*	1805	**That serven love, for aught that may bifalle!**
	The god of love, ah, bless my soul!		Those who serve love, whatever may happen.
1786	**How mighty and how greet a lord is he!**	1806	**But this is yet the beste game of alle,**
	How mighty and how great a lord is he!		But this is yet the best joke of all,
1787	**Ayeins his might ther gayneth none obstacles,**	1807	**That she, for whom they han this Iolitee,**
	Against his power there avail no obstacles.		That she for whom they have this sport
1788	**He may be cleped a god for his miracles;**	1808	**Can hem ther-for as muche thank as me;**
	He may be called a god for his miracles,		Owes them as much gratitude for this as she owes me.
1789	**For he can maken at his owne gyse**	1809	**She woot namore of al this hote fare,**
	For he can make, as he pleases,		She knows no more of all this passionate business,
1790	**Of everich herte, as that him list devyse.**	1810	**By God, than woot a cokkow or an hare!**
	Of every heart whatever he wants to devise.		By God, than knows a cuckoo or a hare!
1791	**Lo heer, this Arcite and this Palamoun,**	1811	**But al mot been assayed, hoot and cold;**
	Lo here this Arcite and this Palamon,		But all must be tried, hot or cold;
1792	**That quitly weren out of my prisoun,**	1812	**A man mot been a fool, or yong or old;**
	Who freely were out of my prison,		A man must be a fool, either young or old;
1793	**And mighte han lived in Thebes royally,**	1813	**I woot it by my-self ful yore agoon:**
	And could have lived royally in Thebes,		I know it by my own experience very long ago:
1794	**And witen I am hir mortal enemy,**	1814	**For in my tyme a servant was I oon.**
	And know I am their mortal enemy,		For in my time I was a servant (of love).
1795	**And that hir deeth lyth in my might also,**	1815	**And therfore, sin I knowe of loves peyne,**
	And that their death lies in my power also,		And therefore, since I know of love's pain
1796	**And yet hath love, maugree hir eyen two,**	1816	**And woot how sore it can a man distreyne,**
	And yet has Love, despite anything they could do,		And know how sorely it can afflict a man,
1797	**Y-broght hem hider bothe for to dye!**	1817	**As he that hath ben caught ofte in his las,**
	Brought them both hither to die!		As one who has been often caught in its snare,
1798	**Now loketh, is nat that an heigh folye?**	1818	**I yow foryeve al hoolly this trespas,**
	Now look, is that not a great folly?		I wholly forgive you this trespass,
1799	**Who may been a fool, but-if he love?**	1819	**At requeste of the quene that kneleth here,**
	Who can be a fool unless he is in love?		At the request of the queen, who kneels here,
1800	**Bihold, for Goddes sake that sit above,**		
	Behold, for the sake of God who sits above,		

1820	**And eek of Emelye, my suster dere.**	1839	**This is to seyn, she may nat now han bothe,**
	And also of Emelye, my dear sister.		This is to say, she can not now have both,
1821	**And ye shul bothe anon un-to me swere,**	1840	**Al be ye never so Ielous, ne so wrothe.**
	And you must both immediately swear unto me		Although you be never so jealous nor so angry.
1822	**That never-mo ye shul my contree dere,**	1841	**And for-thy I yow putte in this degree,**
	That you shall never more harm my country,		And therefore I put you in this situation,
1823	**Ne make werre up-on me night ne day,**	1842	**That ech of yow shal have his destinee**
	Nor make war upon me at any time,		That each of you shall have his destiny
1824	**But been my freendes in al that ye may;**	1843	**As him is shape; and herkneth in what wyse;**
	But be my friends in all that you can;		As is ordained for him, and listen in what way;
1825	**I yow foryeve this trespas every del.'**	1844	**Lo, heer your ende of that I shal devyse.**
	I forgive you this trespass completely.'		Lo, hear what I shall arrange for your fate.
1826	**And they him swore his axing fayre and wel,**	1845	**My wil is this, for plat conclusioun,**
	And they fairly and well swore to him (to do) his request,		My will is this, for flat conclusion,
1827	**And him of lordshipe and of mercy preyde,**	1846	**With-outen any replicacioun,**
	And prayed him to be their lord and to have mercy,		Without any arguing,
1828	**And he hem graunteth grace, and thus he seyde:**	1847	**If that yow lyketh, tak it for the beste,**
	And he grants them his favor, and thus he said:		If this pleases you, take it for the best,
1829	**'To speke of royal linage and richesse,**	1848	**That everich of yow shal gon wher him leste**
	'To speak of royal lineage and riches,		That each one of you shall go where he pleases
1830	**Though that she were a quene or a princesse,**	1849	**Frely, with-outen raunson or daunger;**
	Though she were a queen or a princess,		Freely, without ransom or resistance,
1831	**Ech of yow bothe is worthy, doutelees,**	1850	**And this day fifty wykes, fer ne ner,**
	Each of you both is worthy, doubtless,		And fifty weeks from this day, more or less,
1832	**To wedden whan tyme is, but nathelees**	1851	**Everich of yow shal bringe an hundred knightes,**
	To wed when it is time; but none the less		Each one of you shall bring a hundred knights,
1833	**I speke as for my suster Emelye,**	1852	**Armed for listes up at alle rightes,**
	I speak for my sister Emelye,		Armed up for the lists in all respects,
1834	**For whom ye have this stryf and Ielousye;**	1853	**Al redy to darreyne hir by bataille.**
	For whom you have this strife and jealousy;		All ready to decide the right to her by battle.
1835	**Ye woot your-self, she may not wedden two**	1854	**And this bihote I yow, with-outen faille,**
	You know yourself she can not wed two		And this I promise you without fail,
1836	**At ones, though ye fighten ever-mo:**	1855	**Up-on my trouthe, and as I am a knight,**
	At once, though you were to fight for evermore,		Upon my word, and as I am a knight,
1837	**That oon of yow, al be him looth or leef,**	1856	**That whether of yow bothe that hath might,**
	That one of you, whether he likes it or not,		That whichever of you both who has the power,
1838	**He moot go pypen in an ivy-leef;**		
	He must go whistle in an ivy leaf;		

1857	**This is to seyn, that whether he or thou**	1870	**Who loketh lightly now but Palamoun?**
	This is to say, that whether he or thou		Who but Palamon looks happy now?
1858	**May with his hundred, as I spak of now,**	1871	**Who springeth up for Ioye but Arcite?**
	Can with his hundred, as I spoke of now,		Who springs up for joy but Arcite?
1859	**Sleen his contrarie, or out of listes dryve,**	1872	**Who couthe telle, or who couthe it endyte,**
	Slay his opponent, or drive him out of the lists,		Who could tell, or who could describe in writing,
1860	**Him shal I yeve Emelya to wyve,**	1873	**The Ioye that is maked in the place**
	Then I shall give Emelye as wife		The joy that is made in the place
1861	**To whom that fortune yeveth so fair a grace.**	1874	**Whan Theseus hath doon so fair a grace?**
	To whom Fortune gives so good a gift (to win the battle).		When Theseus has behaved so graciously?
1862	**The listes shal I maken in this place,**	1875	**But doun on knees wente every maner wight,**
	I shall make the lists in this place,		But down on knees went every sort of person,
1863	**And God so wisly on my soule rewe,**	1876	**And thanked him with al her herte and might,**
	And as God may surely have pity on my soul		And thanked him with all their heart and might,
1864	**As I shal even Iuge been and trewe.**	1877	**And namely the Thebans ofte sythe.**
	I shall be an impartial and true judge.		And especially the Thebans many times.
1865	**Ye shul non other ende with me maken,**	1878	**And thus with good hope and with herte blythe**
	You shall make no other agreement with me,		And thus with good hope and with happy heart
1866	**That oon of yow ne shal be deed or taken.**	1879	**They take hir leve, and hom-ward gonne they ryde**
	(Save this:) that one of you must be dead or taken.		They take their leave, and homeward did they ride
1867	**And if yow thinketh this is wel y-sayd,**	1880	**To Thebes, with his olde walles wyde.**
	And if it seems to you that this is well said,		To Thebes with his old wide walls.
1868	**Seyeth your avys, and holdeth yow apayd.**		
	Say your opinion, and consider yourself satisfied.		
1869	**This is your ende and your conclusioun.'**		
	This is your (destined) end and your conclusion.'		

Explicit secunda pars
The second part ends

Canterbury Tales:

The Knight's Tale, Part III

Geoffrey Chaucer

Geoffrey Chaucer; Larry D. Benson, trans., *The Knight's Tale, Part III: An Interlinear Translation (lines 1881–2482)*, from http://www.courses.fas.harvard.edu/~chaucer/teachslf/kt-par3.ht,. Copyright © 2008 by The President and Fellows of Harvard College. Permission to reprint granted by the publisher.

Sequitur pars tercia
The third part follows

1881	**I trowe men wolde deme it necligence,**
	I suppose men would consider it negligence,
1882	**If I foryete to tellen the dispence**
	If I forget to tell the expenditure
1883	**Of Theseus, that goth so bisily**
	Of Theseus, who goes (about) so busily
1884	**To maken up the listes royally;**
	To build the lists royally,
1885	**That swich a noble theatre as it was,**
	That such a noble theatre as it was
1886	**I dar wel seyn that in this world ther nas.**
	I dare well say there was not (another such) in this world.
1887	**The circuit a myle was aboute,**
	The circumference was a mile around,
1888	**Walled of stoon, and diched al with-oute.**
	Walled with stone, and surrounded by a ditch.
1889	**Round was the shap, in maner of compas,**
	Round was the shape, in the manner of a circle,
1890	**Ful of degrees, the heighte of sixty pas,**
	Full of tiers of seats, the height of sixty paces,
1891	**That, whan a man was set on o degree,**
	That when a man was set on one tier of seats,
1892	**He letted nat his felawe for to see.**
	He did not hinder his fellow from seeing.
1893	**Est-ward ther stood a gate of marbel whyt,**
	Eastward there stood a gate of white marble,
1894	**West-ward, right swich another in the opposit.**
	Westward just such another on the opposite (side).
1895	**And shortly to concluden, swich a place**
	And shortly to conclude, such a place
1896	**Was noon in erthe, as in so litel space;**
	Was none in earth, (constructed) in so little time;
1897	**For in the lond ther nas no crafty man,**
	For in the land there was no skilled man,
1898	**That geometrie or ars-metrik can,**
	Who knows geometry or arithmetic,
1899	**Ne purtreyour, ne kerver of images,**
	Nor painter, nor carver of images,
1900	**That Theseus ne yaf him mete and wages**
	That Theseus did not give him food and wages
1901	**The theatre for to maken and devyse.**
	To make and devise the theatre.
1902	**And for to doon his ryte and sacrifyse,**
	And to do his rite and sacrifice,
1903	**He est-ward hath, up-on the gate above,**
	He has eastward, upon the gate above,
1904	**In worship of Venus, goddesse of love,**
	In worship of Venus, goddess of love,
1905	**Don make an auter and an oratorie;**
	Had made an altar and a chapel;
1906	**And west-ward, in the minde and in memorie**
	And on the westward gate, in memory
1907	**Of Mars, he maked hath right swich another,**
	Of Mars, he has made just such another,
1908	**That coste largely of gold a fother.**
	That cost fully a cartload of gold.
1909	**And north-ward, in a touret on the wal,**
	And northward, in a turret on the wall,
1910	**Of alabastre whyt and reed coral**
	Of white alabaster and red coral,
1911	**An oratorie riche for to see,**
	A chapel, rich to look upon,
1912	**In worship of Dyane of chastitee,**
	In worship of Diana of chastity,
1913	**Hath Theseus don wroght in noble wyse.**
	Has Theseus had made in noble style.
1914	**But yet hadde I foryeten to devyse**
	But yet had I forgotten to describe
1915	**The noble kerving, and the portreitures,**
	The noble sculpture and the portraits,
1916	**The shap, the countenaunce, and the figures,**
	The shape, the appearance, and the figures
1917	**That weren in thise oratories three.**
	That were in these three chapels.
1918	**First in the temple of Venus maystow see**
	First in the temple of Venus canst thou see

1919	**Wroght on the wal, ful pitous to biholde,**	
	Wrought on the wall, full piteous to behold,	
1920	**The broken slepes, and the sykes colde;**	
	The broken sleeps, and the cold sighs;	
1921	**The sacred teres, and the waymentinge;**	
	The sacred tears, and the lamenting;	
1922	**The fyry strokes of the desiring,**	
	The fiery strokes of the desiring,	
1923	**That loves servaunts in this lyf enduren;**	
	That love's servants endure in this life;	
1924	**The othes, that hir covenants assuren;**	
	The oaths that assure their covenants;	
1925	**Plesaunce and hope, desyr, fool-hardinesse,**	
	Pleasure and hope, desire, foolhardiness,	
1926	**Beautee and youthe, bauderie, richesse,**	
	Beauty and youth, mirth, riches,	
1927	**Charmes and force, lesinges, flaterye,**	
	Charms and force, lies, flattery,	
1928	**Dispense, bisynesse, and Ielousye,**	
	Expenditures, attentiveness, and jealousy,	
1929	**That wered of yelwe goldes a gerland,**	
	Who wore a garland of yellow marigolds,	
1930	**And a cokkow sitting on hir hand;**	
	And a cuckoo sitting on her hand;	
1931	**Festes, instruments, caroles, daunces,**	
	Feasts, musical instruments, dance-songs, dances,	
1932	**Lust and array, and alle the circumstaunces**	
	Desire and festivity, and all the details	
1933	**Of love, whiche that I rekne and rekne shal,**	
	Of love, which I recounted and shall recount,	
1934	**By ordre weren peynted on the wal,**	
	Were painted in sequence on the wall,	
1935	**And mo than I can make of mencioun.**	
	And more than I can make mention of.	
1936	**For soothly, al the mount of Citheroun,**	
	For truly all the mount of Cithaeron,	
1937	**Ther Venus hath hir principal dwelling,**	
	Where Venus has her principal dwelling,	
1938	**Was shewed on the wal in portreying,**	
	Was shown on the wall in portraits,	
1939	**With al the gardin, and the lustinesse.**	
	With all the garden (of Love) and the pleasure.	
1940	**Nat was foryeten the porter Ydelnesse,**	
	The porter, Idleness, was not forgotten,	
1941	**Ne Narcisus the faire of yore agon,**	
	Nor the handsome Narcissus of many years ago,	
1942	**Ne yet the folye of king Salamon,**	
	Nor yet the folly of king Solomon,	
1943	**Ne yet the grete strengthe of Hercules—**	
	Nor yet the great strength of Hercules—	
1944	**Thenchauntements of Medea and Circes—**	
	The enchantments of Medea and Circes—	
1945	**Ne of Turnus, with the hardy fiers corage,**	
	Nor of Turnus, with the hardy fierce courage,	
1946	**The riche Cresus, caytif in servage.**	
	The riche Cresus, wretched in servitude.	
1947	**Thus may ye seen that wisdom ne richesse,**	
	Thus can you see that wisdom nor riches,	
1948	**Beautee ne sleighte, strengthe, ne hardinesse,**	
	Beauty nor trickery, strength nor bravery,	
1949	**Ne may with Venus holde champartye;**	
	Can not share power with Venus,	
1950	**For as hir list the world than may she gye.**	
	For she may rule the world as she pleases.	
1951	**Lo, alle thise folk so caught were in hir las,**	
	Lo, all these folk were so caught in her snare,	
1952	**Til they for wo ful ofte seyde 'allas!'**	
	Until for woe they very often said 'alas!'	
1953	**Suffyceth heer ensamples oon or two,**	
	One or two examples here suffice,	
1954	**And though I coude rekne a thousand mo.**	
	Even though I could recount a thousand more.	
1955	**The statue of Venus, glorious for to see,**	
	The statue of Venus, glorious to look upon,	
1956	**Was naked fleting in the large see,**	
	Was naked, floating in the large sea,	
1957	**And fro the navele doun all covered was**	
	And from the navel down all was covered	
1958	**With wawes grene, and brighte as any glas.**	
	With waves green and bright as any glass.	
1959	**A citole in hir right hand hadde she,**	
	She had a citole (zither-like instrument) in her right hand,

1960	**And on hir heed, ful semely for to see,**	1978	**Of stubbes sharpe and hidous to biholde;**
	And on her head, very elegant to look upon,		Of stumps sharp and hideous to behold,
1961	**A rose gerland, fresh and wel smellinge;**	1979	**In which ther ran a rumbel and a swough,**
	A rose garland, fresh and fragrant;		Through which there ran a rumbling in a moaning of wind,
1962	**Above hir heed hir dowves flikeringe.**	1980	**As though a storm sholde bresten every bough:**
	Above her head her doves fluttering.		As though a storm should burst every bough.
1963	**Biforn hir stood hir sone Cupido,**	1981	**And downward from an hille, under a bente,**
	Before her stood her son Cupid,		And downward from a hill, close to a grassy slope,
1964	**Up-on his shuldres winges hadde he two;**	1982	**Ther stood the temple of Mars armipotente,**
	He had two wings upon his shoulders;		There stood the temple of Mars, powerful in arms,
1965	**And blind he was, as it is ofte sene;**	1983	**Wroght al of burned steel, of which thentree**
	And he was blind, as it is often seen;		Wrought all of burnished steel, of which the entry
1966	**A bowe he bar and arwes brighte and kene.**	1984	**Was long and streit, and gastly for to see.**
	He carried a bow and arrows bright and keen.		Was long and narrow, and frightening to look upon.
1967	**Why sholde I noght as wel eek telle yow al**	1985	**And ther-out cam a rage and such a vese,**
	Why should I not as well also tell you all		And out of there came a rush of wind and such a blast,
1968	**The portreiture, that was up-on the wal**	1986	**That it made al the gates for to rese.**
	The portraiture that was upon the wall		That it made all the gate to shake.
1969	**With-inne the temple of mighty Mars the rede?**	1987	**The northren light in at the dores shoon,**
	Within the temple of mighty Mars the red?		The northern light shone in at the doors,
1970	**Al peynted was the wal, in lengthe and brede,**	1988	**For windowe on the wal ne was ther noon,**
	All painted was the wall, in length and breadth,		For there was no window on the wall,
1971	**Lyk to the estres of the grisly place,**	1989	**Thurgh which men mighten any light discerne.**
	Like to the interior of the grisly place,		Through which men might discern any light.
1972	**That highte the grete temple of Mars in Trace,**	1990	**The dores were alle of adamant eterne,**
	That is called the Great Temple of Mars in Thrace,		The door was all of eternal adamant (hardest of stones),
1973	**In thilke colde frosty regioun,**	1991	**Y-clenched overthwart and endelong**
	In that same cold, frosty region,		Bound crosswise and lengthwise
1974	**Ther-as Mars hath his sovereyn mansioun.**	1992	**With iren tough; and, for to make it strong,**
	Where Mars has his most excellent mansion.		With tough iron; and to make it strong,
1975	**First on the wal was peynted a foreste,**	1993	**Every piler, the temple to sustene,**
	First a forest was painted on the wall,		Every pillar, to support the temple,
1976	**In which ther dwelleth neither man ne beste,**	1994	**Was tonne-greet, of iren bright and shene.**
	In which there dwells neither man nor beast,		Was big as a large barrel, (made) of iron bright and shining.
1977	**With knotty knarry bareyn treës olde**		
	With knotty, gnarled, barren old trees,		

1995	Ther saugh I first the derke imagining	2014	A thousand slayn, and nat of qualm y-storve;
	There I saw first the malicious plotting		A thousand slain, and not killed by the plague;
1996	Of felonye, and al the compassing;	2015	The tiraunt, with the prey by force y-raft;
	Of Felony, and all the scheming;		The tyrant, with his prey taken by force;
1997	The cruel ire, reed as any glede;	2016	The toun destroyed, ther was no-thing laft.
	The cruel Anger, red as any glowing coal;		The town destroyed, there was nothing left.
1998	The pykepurs, and eek the pale drede;	2017	Yet saugh I brent the shippes hoppesteres;
	The pick-purse, and also the pale fear;		Yet I saw burned the ships dancing (on the waves);
1999	The smyler with the knyf under the cloke;	2018	The hunte strangled with the wilde beres:
	The smiler with the knife under the cloak;		The hunter killed by the wild bears:
2000	The shepne brenning with the blake smoke;	2019	The sowe freten the child right in the cradel;
	The stable burning with the black smoke;		The sow devouring the child right in the cradle;
2001	The treson of the mordring in the bedde;	2020	The cook y-scalded, for al his longe ladel.
	The treason of the murdering in the bed;		The cook scalded, despite his long-handled spoon.
2002	The open werre, with woundes al bi-bledde;	2021	Noght was foryeten by the infortune of Marte;
	The open war, all covered with blood from wounds;		Nothing concerning the evil influence of Mars was forgotten.
2003	Contek, with blody knyf and sharp manace;	2022	The carter over-riden with his carte,
	Strife, with bloody knife and sharp menacing;		The wagon driver run over by his wagon,
2004	Al ful of chirking was that sory place.	2023	Under the wheel ful lowe he lay adoun.
	All full of creaking was that sorry place.		He lay down full low under the wheel.
2005	The sleere of him-self yet saugh I ther,	2024	Ther were also, of Martes divisioun,
	There yet I saw slayer of himself there,		There were also, of those influenced by Mars,
2006	His herte-blood hath bathed al his heer;	2025	The barbour, and the bocher, and the smith
	His heart-blood has bathed all his hair;		The barber, and the butcher, and the smith
2007	The nayl y-driven in the shode a-night;	2026	That forgeth sharpe swerdes on his stith.
	The nail driven in the top of the head at night;		Who forges sharp swords on his anvil.
2008	The colde deeth, with mouth gaping up-right.	2027	And al above, depeynted in a tour,
	The cold death, with mouth gaping upwards.		And all above, painted in a tower,
2009	Amiddes of the temple sat meschaunce,	2028	Saw I conquest sittinge in greet honour,
	Amidst the temple sat misfortune,		I saw conquest, sitting in great honor,
2010	With disconfort and sory contenaunce.	2029	With the sharpe swerd over his heed
	With grief and sorry countenance.		With the sharp sword over his head
2011	Yet saugh I woodnesse laughing in his rage;	2030	Hanginge by a sotil twynes threed.
	Yet I saw Madness, laughing in his rage;		Hanging by a thin thread of twine.
2012	Armed compleint, out-hees, and fiers outrage.	2031	Depeynted was the slaughtre of Iulius,
	Armed Discontent, Alarm, and fierce Violence;		Depicted was the slaughter of Julius,
2013	The careyne in the bush, with throte y-corve:		
	The corpse in the woods, with (its) throat cut:		

2032	**Of grete Nero, and of Antonius;**	2053	**To telle yow al the descripcioun.**
	Of great Nero, and of Antonius;		To tell you all the description.
2033	**Al be that thilke tyme they were unborn,**	2054	**Depeynted been the walles up and doun**
	Although at that same time they were unborn,		The walls are painted all over
2034	**Yet was hir deeth depeynted ther-biforn,**	2055	**Of hunting and of shamfast chastitee.**
	Yet was their death depicted before then,		(With scenes) of hunting and of modest chastity.
2035	**By manasinge of Mars, right by figure;**	2056	**Ther saugh I how woful Calistopee,**
	By menacing of Mars, according to the horoscope;		There I saw how woeful Callisto,
2036	**So was it shewed in that portreiture**	2057	**Whan that Diane agreved was with here,**
	So was it shown in that portraiture,		When Diana was angry with her,
2037	**As is depeynted in the sterres above,**	2058	**Was turned from a womman til a bere,**
	As is depicted in the stars above		Was turned from a woman into a bear,
2038	**Who shal be slayn or elles deed for love.**	2059	**And after was she maad the lode-sterre;**
	Who shall be slain or else dead for love.		And after she was made the North Star;
2039	**Suffyceth oon ensample in stories olde,**	2060	**Thus was it peynt, I can say yow no ferre;**
	Suffices one illustrative tale in old histories;		Thus was it painted; I can tell you no more;
2040	**I may not rekne hem alle, thogh I wolde.**	2061	**Hir sone is eek a sterre, as men may see.**
	I can not recount them all even if I desired to.		Her son is also a star, as one can see.
2041	**The statue of Mars up-on a carte stood,**	2062	**Ther saugh I Dane, y-turned til a tree,**
	The statue of Mars stood upon a chariot,		There I saw Daphne, turned into a tree,
2042	**Armed, and loked grim as he were wood;**	2063	**I mene nat the goddesse Diane,**
	Armed, and looked as grim as if he were mad;		I mean not the goddess Diana,
2043	**And over his he'ed ther shynen two figures**	2064	**But Penneus doughter, which that highte Dane.**
	And over his head there shine two figures		But Penneus' daughter, who is called Daphne.
2044	**Of sterres, that been cleped in scriptures,**	2065	**Ther saugh I Attheon an hert y-maked,**
	Of stars, that are called in books,		There I saw Actaeon changed into a hart,
2045	**That oon Puella, that other Rubeus.**	2066	**For vengeaunce that he saugh Diane al naked;**
	That one Puella, that other Rubeus.		For vengeance that he saw Diana all naked;
2046	**This god of armes was arrayed thus:—**	2067	**I saugh how that his houndes have him caught,**
	This god of arms was arrayed thus.		I saw how his hounds have caught him,
2047	**A wolf ther stood biforn him at his feet**	2068	**And freten him, for that they knewe him naught.**
	A wolf stood there before him at his feet		And devoured him, because they did not know him.
2048	**With eyen rede, and of a man he eet;**	2069	**Yet peynted was a litel forther-moor,**
	With red eyes, and he ate of a man;		Yet was painted a little further on,
2049	**With sotil pencel was depeynt this storie,**	2070	**How Atthalante hunted the wilde boor,**
	With subtle brush was depicted this story		How Atalanta hunted the wild boar,
2050	**In redoutinge of Mars and of his glorie.**	2071	**And Meleagre, and many another mo,**
	In reverence of Mars and of his glory.		And Meleager, and many more others,
2051	**Now to the temple of Diane the chaste**	2072	**For which Diane wroghte him care and wo.**
	Now to the temple of Diana the chaste		For which Diana wrought him care and woe.
2052	**As shortly as I can I wol me haste,**		
	As briefly as I can, I will hasten myself,		

Line	Middle English	Modern English
2073	**Ther saugh I many another wonder storie,**	There I saw many another wonderful story,
2074	**The whiche me list nat drawen to memorie.**	The which I do not desire to call to mind.
2075	**This goddesse on an hert ful hye seet,**	This goddess sat full high on a hart,
2076	**With smale houndes al aboute hir feet;**	With small hounds all about her feet,
2077	**And undernethe hir feet she hadde a mone,**	And underneath her feet she had a moon,
2078	**Wexing it was, and sholde wanie sone.**	Waxing it was and should wane soon.
2079	**In gaude grene hir statue clothed was,**	Her statue was clothed in yellowish green,
2080	**With bowe in honde, and arwes in a cas.**	With bow in hand and arrows in a quiver.
2081	**Hir eyen caste she ful lowe adoun,**	She cast her eyes down full low
2082	**Ther Pluto hath his derke regioun.**	Where Pluto has his dark region.
2083	**A womman travailinge was hir biforn,**	A woman in childbirth was before her,
2084	**But, for hir child so longe was unborn,**	But because her child was so long unborn,
2085	**Ful pitously Lucyna gan she calle,**	Very piteously did she call on Lucina,
2086	**And seyde, 'help, for thou mayst best of alle.'**	And said, 'help, for thou canst (do so) best of all!'
2087	**Wel couthe he peynten lyfly that it wroghte,**	He who made it well knew how to paint in a life-like manner,
2088	**With many a florin he the hewes boghte.**	With many a florin he bought the paints.
2089	**Now been thise listes maad, and Theseus,**	Now these lists are made, and Theseus,
2090	**That at his grete cost arrayed thus**	Who at his great cost thus prepared
2091	**The temples and the theatre every del,**	The temples and the theatre in all respects,
2092	**Whan it was doon, him lyked wonder wel.**	When it was done, it greatly pleased him.
2093	**But stinte I wol of Theseus a lyte,**	But I will stop speaking of Theseus a little while,
2094	**And speke of Palamon and of Arcite.**	And speak of Palamon and of Arcite.
2095	**The day approcheth of hir retourninge,**	The day of their return approaches,
2096	**That everich sholde an hundred knightes bringe,**	When each one should bring a hundred knights,
2097	**The bataille to darreyne, as I yow tolde;**	To decide the battle, as I told you;
2098	**And til Athenes, hir covenant for to holde,**	And to Athens, to keep their agreement,
2099	**Hath everich of hem broght an hundred knightes**	Each one of them has brought a hundred knights
2100	**Wel armed for the werre at alle rightes.**	Well armed for the battle in all respects.
2101	**And sikerly, ther trowed many a man**	And surely many a man there believed
2102	**That never, sithen that the world bigan,**	That never, since the world began,
2103	**As for to speke of knighthod of hir hond,**	To speak of knighthood of (the deeds of) their hand,
2104	**As fer as God hath maked see or lond,**	As far as God has made sea or land,
2105	**Nas, of so fewe, so noble a companye.**	Was not of so few so noble a company.
2106	**For every wight that lovede chivalrye,**	For every person that loved chivalry,
2107	**And wolde, his thankes, han a passant name,**	And would, willingly, have an outstanding reputation
2108	**Hath preyed that he mighte ben of that game;**	Has prayed that he might participate in that game;
2109	**And wel was him, that ther-to chosen was.**	And well it was for him who was chosen to be there.

Line		Line	
2110	**For if ther fille to-morwe swich a cas,**	2127	**Everich after his opinioun.**
	For if there fell tomorrow such a situation,		Every one according to his preference.
2111	**Ye knowen wel, that every lusty knight,**	2128	**Ther maistow seen coming with Palamoun**
	You know well that every vigorous knight,		There mayst thou seen, coming with Palamon
2112	**That loveth paramours, and hath his might,**	2129	**Ligurge him-self, the grete king of Trace;**
	Who loves passionately and has his might,		Lycurgus himself, the great king of Thrace.
2113	**Were it in Engelond, or elles-where,**	2130	**Blak was his berd, and manly was his face.**
	Were it in England or elsewhere,		Black was his beard, and manly was his face.
2114	**They wolde, hir thankes, wilnen to be there.**	2131	**The cercles of his eyen in his heed,**
	They would, willingly, desire to be there.		The circles of his eyes in his head,
2115	**To fighte for a lady, *benedicite*!**	2132	**They gloweden bitwixe yelow and reed;**
	To fight for a lady, bless me!		They glowed between yellow and red;
2116	**It were a lusty sighte for to see.**	2133	**And lyk a griffon loked he aboute,**
	It would be a pleasing sight to see.		And he looked about like a griffin (with an eagle's head),
2117	**And right so ferden they with Palamon.**	2134	**With kempe heres on his browes stoute;**
	And right so fared those with Palamon.		With shaggy hairs on his stout brows;
2118	**With him ther wenten knightes many oon;**	2135	**His limes grete, his braunes harde and stronge,**
	With him there went knights many a one;		His limbs large, his muscles hard and strong,
2119	**Som wol ben armed in an habergeoun,**	2136	**His shuldres brode, his armes rounde and longe.**
	One of them will be armed in a coat of mail,		His shoulders broad, his arms round and long;
2120	**In a brest-plat and in a light gipoun;**	2137	**And as the gyse was in his contree,**
	And in a breastplate and a light tunic;		And as was the fashion in his country,
2121	**And somme woln have a peyre plates large;**	2138	**Ful hye up-on a char of gold stood he,**
	And one of them will have a set of plate armor;		He stood full high upon a chariot of gold,
2122	**And somme woln have a Pruce shield, or a targe;**	2139	**With foure whyte boles in the trays.**
	And one of them will have a Prussian shield or a buckler;		With four white bulls in the traces.
2123	**Somme woln ben armed on hir legges weel,**	2140	**In-stede of cote-armure over his harnays,**
	One of them will be well armed on his legs,		Instead of a tunic with his coat of arms over his armor,
2124	**And have an ax, and somme a mace of steel.**	2141	**With nayles yelwe and brighte as any gold,**
	And have an axe, and one a mace of steel.		With claws yellow and bright as any gold,
2125	**Ther nis no newe gyse, that it nas old.**	2142	**He hadde a beres skin, col-blak, for-old.**
	There is no new fashion that has not been old.		He had a bear's skin, coal-black because of age.
2126	**Armed were they, as I have you told,**	2143	**His longe heer was kembd bihinde his bak,**
	They were armed, as I have told you,		His long hair was combed behind his back;
		2144	**As any ravenes fether it shoon for-blak:**
			Like any raven's feather it shone because of its blackness;

2145	**A wrethe of gold arm-greet, of huge wighte,**
	A wreath of gold, thick as an arm, of huge weight,
2146	**Upon his heed, set ful of stones brighte,**
	Upon his head, set full of bright stones,
2147	**Of fyne rubies and of dyamaunts.**
	Of fine rubies and of diamonds.
2148	**Aboute his char ther wenten whyte alaunts,**
	About his chariot there went white wolfhounds,
2149	**Twenty and mo, as grete as any steer,**
	Twenty and more, as big as any steer,
2150	**To hunten at the leoun or the deer,**
	To hunt for the lion or the deer,
2151	**And folwed him, with mosel faste y-bounde,**
	And followed him with muzzles securely bound,
2152	**Colers of gold, and torets fyled rounde.**
	Wearing collars of gold, and rings for leashes filed round.
2153	**An hundred lordes hadde he in his route**
	He had a hundred lords in his company
2154	**Armed ful wel, with hertes sterne and stoute.**
	Very well armed, with stern and stout hearts.
2155	**With Arcita, in stories as men finde,**
	With Arcite, as people find in histories,
2156	**The grete Emetreus, the king of Inde,**
	The great Emetreus, the king of India,
2157	**Up-on a stede bay, trapped in steel,**
	Upon a reddish-brown steed with trappings of steel,
2158	**Covered in cloth of gold diapred weel,**
	Covered in cloth of gold, well decorated (with geometric patterns),
2159	**Cam ryding lyk the god of armes, Mars.**
	Came riding like the god of arms, Mars.
2160	**His cote-armure was of cloth of Tars,**
	His tunic with his coat of arms was of cloth of Tarsia (in Turkestan),
2161	**Couched with perles whyte and rounde and grete.**
	Adorned with pearls white and round and big.
2162	**His sadel was of brend gold newe y-bete;**
	His saddle was newly adorned with pure gold;
2163	**A mantelet upon his shuldre honginge,**
	A short cloak hanging upon his shoulder,
2164	**Bret-ful of rubies rede, as fyr sparklinge.**
	Brimful of rubies red as sparkling fire.
2165	**His crispe heer lyk ringes was y-ronne,**
	His curly hair like rings was run (fashioned),
2166	**And that was yelow, and glitered as the sonne.**
	And that was yellow, and glittered like the sun.
2167	**His nose was heigh, his eyen bright citryn,**
	His nose was high, his eyes bright lemon yellow,
2168	**His lippes rounde, his colour was sangwyn,**
	His lips round, his color was ruddy,
2169	**A fewe fraknes in his face y-spreynd,**
	A few freckles were sprinkled in his face,
2170	**Betwixen yelow and somdel blak y-meynd,**
	Between yellow and somewhat mingled with black;
2171	**And as a leoun he his loking caste.**
	And as a lion he cast about his look.
2172	**Of fyve and twenty yeer his age I caste.**
	I reckon his age at five and twenty years.
2173	**His berd was wel bigonne for to springe;**
	His beard had well begun to spring;
2174	**His voys was as a trompe thunderinge.**
	His voice was like a trumpet thundering.
2175	**Up-on his heed he wered of laurer grene**
	Upon his head he wore of green laurel
2176	**A gerland fresh and lusty for to sene.**
	A garland, fresh and pleasing to look upon.
2177	**Up-on his hand he bar, for his deduyt,**
	Upon his hand he carried for his delight,
2178	**An egle tame, as eny lilie whyt.**
	A tame eagle, white as any lily.
2179	**An hundred lordes hadde he with him there,**
	He had a hundred lords with him there,
2180	**Al armed, sauf hir heddes, in al hir gere,**
	All armed, except for their heads, in all their equipment,
2181	**Ful richely in alle maner thinges.**
	Very richly in every detail.

2182	**For trusteth wel, that dukes, erles, kinges,**	2202	**Or which of hem can dauncen best and singe,**
	For trust well that dukes, earls, kings,		Or which of them can dance best and sing,
2183	**Were gadered in this noble companye,**	2203	**Ne who most felingly speketh of love:**
	Were gathered in this noble company,		Nor who speaks most feelingly of love:
2184	**For love and for encrees of chivalrye.**	2204	**What haukes sitten on the perche above,**
	For love and for the benefit of chivalry.		What hawks sit on the perch above,
2185	**Aboute this king ther ran on every part**	2205	**What houndes liggen on the floor adoun:**
	About this king there ran on all sides		What hounds lie down on the floor:
2186	**Ful many a tame leoun and lepart.**	2206	**Of al this make I now no mencioun;**
	Full many a tame lion and leopard.		I now make no mention of all this:
2187	**And in this wyse thise lordes, alle and some,**	2207	**But al theffect, that thinketh me the beste;**
	And in this manner these lords, one and all,		But (speak only) of the substance; that seems to me the best;
2188	**Ben on the Sonday to the citee come**	2208	**Now comth the poynt, and herkneth if yow leste.**
	Are come to the city on the Sunday		Now comes the point, and listen if you please.
2189	**Aboute pryme, and in the toun alight.**		
	About nine a.m., and in the town dismounted.	2209	**The Sonday night, er day bigan to springe,**
			The Sunday night, before day began to spring,
2190	**This Theseus, this duk, this worthy knight,**	2210	**When Palamon the larke herde singe,**
	This Theseus, this duke, this worthy knight,		When Palamon heard the lark sing,
2191	**Whan he had broght hem in-to his citee,**	2211	**Although it nere nat day by houres two,**
	When he had brought them into his city,		Although it was not day by two hours,
2192	**And inned hem, everich in his degree,**	2212	**Yet song the larke, and Palamon also.**
	And provided them lodging, each one according to his rank,		Yet sang the lark, and Palamon also.
2193	**He festeth hem, and dooth so greet labour**	2213	**With holy herte, and with an heigh corage**
	He feasts them, and does such great labor		With pious heart and with a noble disposition
2194	**To esen hem, and doon hem al honour,**	2214	**He roos, to wenden on his pilgrimage**
	To entertain them and do them all honor		He rose to go on his pilgrimage
2195	**That yet men weneth that no mannes wit**	2215	**Un-to the blisful Citherea benigne,**
	That people still believe that the wit of no man		To the blessed gracious Citherea,
2196	**Of noon estat ne coude amenden it.**	2216	**I mene Venus, honurable and digne.**
	Of any rank could do better.		I mean Venus, honorable and worshipful.
2197	**The minstralcye, the service at the feste,**	2217	**And in hir houre he walketh forth a pas**
	The music, the service at the feast,		And in her (planetary) hour he walks forth slowly
2198	**The grete yiftes to the moste and leste,**	2218	**Un-to the listes, ther hir temple was,**
	The great gifts to every one,		Unto the lists where her temple was,
2199	**The riche array of Theseus paleys,**	2219	**And doun he kneleth, and with humble chere**
	The rich adornment of Theseus' palace,		And down he kneels, and with humble expression
2200	**Ne who sat first ne last up-on the deys,**		
	Nor who sat first nor last upon the dais,		
2201	**What ladies fairest been or best daunsinge,**		
	What ladies are fairest or best in dancing,		

2220 **And herte soor, he seyde as ye shul here.**
And painful heart he said as you shall hear.

2221 **'Faireste of faire, o lady myn, Venus,**
'Fairest of the fair, o lady mine, Venus,

2222 **Doughter to Iove and spouse of Vulcanus,**
Daughter to Jove and spouse of Vulcan,

2223 **Thou glader of the mount of Citheroun,**
Thou maker of joy of the mount of Citheron,

2224 **For thilke love thou haddest to Adoun,**
For that same love thou haddest to Adonis,

2225 **Have pitee of my bittre teres smerte,**
Have pity on my bitter, smarting tears,

2226 **And tak myn humble preyer at thyn herte.**
And take my humble prayer to thy heart.

2227 **Allas! I ne have no langage to telle**
Alas! I do not have any language to tell

2228 **Theffectes ne the torments of myn helle;**
The effects nor the torments of my hell;

2229 **Myn herte may myne harmes nat biwreye;**
My heart can not reveal my harms;

2230 **I am so confus, that I can noght seye.**
I am so befuddled that I can not say (anything).

2231 **But mercy, lady bright, that knowest weel**
But mercy, lady bright, who knowest well

2232 **My thought, and seest what harmes that I feel,**
My thought and seest what harms I feel,

2233 **Considere al this, and rewe up-on my sore,**
Consider all this and have pity upon my pain,

2234 **As wisly as I shal for evermore,**
As surely as I shall for evermore,

2235 **Emforth my might, thy trewe servant be,**
According to my power (as much as I can), be thy true servant,

2236 **And holden werre alwey with chastitee;**
And make war always against chastity;

2237 **That make I myn avow, so ye me helpe.**
I make that my vow, providing you help me!

2238 **I kepe noght of armes for to yelpe,**
I care not to boast of arms,

2239 **Ne I ne axe nat to-morwe to have victorie,**
Nor do I ask to have victory tomorrow,

2240 **Ne renoun in this cas, ne veyne glorie**
Nor renown in this case, nor vain glory

2241 **Of pris of armes blowen up and doun,**
Nor fame for deeds of arms proclaimed everywhere,

2242 **But I wolde have fully possessioun**
But I would have fully possession

2243 **Of Emelye, and dye in thy servyse;**
Of Emelye, and die in thy service;

2244 **Find thou the maner how, and in what wyse.**
Find thou the manner how and in what way.

2245 **I recche nat, but it may bettre be,**
I care not if it may better be,

2246 **To have victorie of hem, or they of me,**
To have victory over them, or they over me,

2247 **So that I have my lady in myne armes.**
So that I have my lady in my arms.

2248 **For though so be that Mars is god of armes,**
For though it be true that Mars is god of arms,

2249 **Your vertu is so greet in hevene above,**
Your power is so great in heaven above,

2250 **That, if yow list, I shal wel have my love,**
That if you please, I shall well have my love,

2251 **Thy temple wol I worshipe evermo,**
I will worship thy temple evermore,

2252 **And on thyn auter, wher I ryde or go,**
And on thy altar, whether I ride or walk (whatever I do),

2253 **I wol don sacrifice, and fyres bete.**
I will do sacrifice and kindle fires.

2254 **And if ye wol nat so, my lady swete,**
And if you will not (do) so, my lady sweet,

2255 **Than preye I thee, to-morwe with a spere**
Then I pray thee, tomorrow with a spear

2256 **That Arcita me thurgh the herte bere.**
That Arcite stab me through the heart.

2257 **Thanne rekke I noght, whan I have lost my lyf,**
Then I care not, when I have lost my life,

2258 **Though that Arcita winne hir to his wyf.**
Though Arcite win her to be his wife.

2259	This is theffect and ende of my preyere,		2279	The hornes fulle of meth, as was the gyse;
	This is the substance and goal of my prayer,			The horns full of mead, as was the custom;
2260	Yif me my love, thou blisful lady dere.'		2280	Ther lakked noght to doon hir sacrifyse.
	Give me my love, thou blessed dear lady.'			There lacked nothing (needed) to do her sacrifice.
2261	Whan thorisoun was doon of Palamon,		2281	Smoking the temple, ful of clothes faire,
	When the prayer of Palamon was done,			The temple smoking (with incense), full of fair cloths,
2262	His sacrifice he dide, and that anon		2282	This Emelye, with herte debonaire,
	He did his sacrifice, and that quickly			This Emelye, with gentle heart,
2263	Ful pitously, with alle circumstaunces,		2283	Hir body wessh with water of a welle;
	Full piteously, with all due ceremony,			Washed her body with water of a well.
2264	Al telle I noght as now his observaunces.		2284	But how she dide hir ryte I dar nat telle,
	Although I tell not now his observances;			But how she did her rite I dare not tell,
2265	But atte laste the statue of Venus shook,		2285	But it be any thing in general;
	But at the last the statue of Venus shook,			Unless it be some thing in general;
2266	And made a signe, wher-by that he took		2286	And yet it were a game to heren al;
	And made a sign, whereby he understood			And yet it would be a pleasure to hear all;
2267	That his preyere accepted was that day.		2287	To him that meneth wel, it were no charge:
	That his prayer was accepted that day.			To one who means well it would be no matter of concern;
2268	For thogh the signe shewed a delay,		2288	But it is good a man ben at his large.
	For though the sign showed a delay,			But it is good for a man to be without restriction (speak freely).
2269	Yet wiste he wel that graunted was his bone;		2289	Hir brighte heer was kempt, untressed al;
	Yet he knew well that his request was granted;			Her bright hair was combed, all loose;
2270	And with glad herte he wente him hoom ful sone.		2290	A coroune of a grene ook cerial
	And with glad heart he went home very soon.			A crown of an evergreen oak
			2291	Up-on hir heed was set ful fair and mete.
				Was set upon her head full fair and suitable.
2271	The thridde houre inequal that Palamon		2292	Two fyres on the auter gan she bete,
	The third planetary hour after Palamon			Two fires on the altar did she kindle,
2272	Bigan to Venus temple for to goon,		2293	And dide hir thinges, as men may biholde
	Began to go to Venus' temple,			And did her duties, as men can behold
2273	Up roos the sonne, and up roos Emelye,		2294	In Stace of Thebes, and thise bokes olde.
	Up rose the sun, and up rose Emelye,			In Statius' *Thebaid* and such old books.
2274	And to the temple of Diane gan hye.		2295	Whan kindled was the fyr, with pitous chere
	And to the temple of Diana did hasten.			When the fire was kindled, with a pitiful expression
2275	Hir maydens, that she thider with hir ladde,		2296	Un-to Diane she spak, as ye may here.
	Her maidens, whom she led thither with her,			Unto Diana she spoke as you may hear.
2276	Ful redily with hem the fyr they hadde,			
	They had the fire full readily with them,		2297	'O chaste goddesse of the wodes grene,
2277	Thencens, the clothes, and the remenant al			'O chaste goddess of the green woods,
	The incense, the cloths, and all the rest			
2278	That to the sacrifyce longen shal;			
	That is needed for the sacrifice;			

2298	To whom bothe hevene and erthe and see is sene,	2317	As sende love and pees bitwixe hem two;
	To whom both heaven and earth and sea is visible,		Send love and peace between them two;
2299	Quene of the regne of Pluto derk and lowe,	2318	And fro me turne awey hir hertes so,
	Queen of the dark and low reign of Pluto,		And turn away their hearts from me so,
2300	Goddesse of maydens, that myn herte hast knowe	2319	That al hir hote love, and hir desyr,
	Goddess of maidens, whom my heart hast known		That all their hot love and their desire,
2301	FFul many a yeer, and woost what I desire,	2320	And al hir bisy torment, and hir fyr
	Full many a year, and knowest what I desire,		And all their intense torment, and their fire
2302	As keep me fro thy vengeaunce and thyn ire,	2321	Be queynt, or turned in another place;
	Keep me from thy vengeance and thy ire,		Will be quenched, or turned to another place;
2303	That Attheon aboughte cruelly.	2322	And if so be thou wolt not do me grace,
	Which Acteon paid for cruelly.		And if it so be thou wilt not do me grace,
2304	Chaste goddesse, wel wostow that I	2323	Or if my destinee be shapen so,
	Chaste goddess, well knowest thou that I		Or if my destiny is shaped so
2305	Desire to been a mayden al my lyf,	2324	That I shal nedes have oon of hem two,
	Desire to be a maiden all my life,		That I must by necessity have one of them two,
2306	Ne never wol I be no love ne wyf.	2325	As sende me him that most desireth me.
	Nor never will I be no lover nor wife.		Send me him who most desires me.
2307	I am, thou woost, yet of thy companye,	2326	Bihold, goddesse of clene chastitee,
	I am, thou knowest, yet of thy company,		Behold, goddess of clean chastity,
2308	A mayde, and love hunting and venerye,	2327	The bittre teres that on my chekes falle.
	A maiden, and love hunting and the chase,		The bitter tears that fall on my cheeks.
2309	And for to walken in the wodes wilde,	2328	Sin thou are mayde, and keper of us alle,
	And to walk in the wild woods,		Since thou art maiden and guardian of us all,
2310	And noght to been a wyf, and be with childe.	2329	My maydenhede thou kepe and wel conserve,
	And not to be a wife and be with child.		Thou care for and well conserve my maidenhood,
2311	Noght wol I knowe companye of man.	2330	And whyl I live a mayde, I wol thee serve.'
	I do not desire to know company of man.		And while I live, as a maiden I will serve thee.'
2312	Now help me, lady, sith ye may and can,		
	Now help me, lady, since you can and know how,	2331	The fyres brenne up-on the auter clere,
2313	For tho thre formes that thou hast in thee.		The fires burn brightly upon the altar,
	For those three forms that thou hast in thee.	2332	Whyl Emelye was thus in hir preyere;
2314	And Palamon, that hath swich love to me,		While Emelye was thus in her prayer.
	And Palamon, that has such love to me,	2333	But sodeinly she saugh a sighte queynte,
2315	And eek Arcite, that loveth me so sore,		But suddenly she saw a curious sight,
	And also Arcite, who loves me so painfully,	2334	For right anon oon of the fyres queynte,
2316	This grace I preye thee with-oute more,		For right away one of the fires quenched
	This grace I pray thee and ask no more,	2335	And quiked agayn, and after that anon
			And rekindled again, and after that straightway
		2336	That other fyr was queynt, and al agon;
			That other fire was quenched and all gone;

2337	**And as it queynte, it made a whistelinge,**	2358	**And with that word, the arwes in the cas**
	And as it quenched it made a roaring sound,		And with that word, the arrows in the quiver
2338	**As doon thise wete brondes in hir brenninge,**	2359	**Of the goddesse clateren faste and ringe,**
	As these wet brands do in their burning,		Of the goddess clatter fast and ring,
2339	**And at the brondes ende out-ran anoon**	2360	**And forth she wente, and made a vanisshinge;**
	And at the brand's end (the fire) ran out straightway		And forth she went and vanished;
2340	**As it were blody dropes many oon;**	2361	**For which this Emelye astoned was,**
	As if it were many bloody drops;		For which this Emelye was astonished,
2341	**For which so sore agast was Emelye,**	2362	**And seyde, 'What amounteth this, allas!**
	For which so sorely frightened was Emelye,		And said, 'What does this mean, alas?
2342	**That she was wel ny mad, and gan to crye,**	2363	**I putte me in thy proteccioun,**
	That she was well nigh mad and began to cry,		I put me in thy protection,
2343	**For she ne wiste what it signifyed;**	2364	**Diane, and in thy disposicioun.'**
	For she did not know what it signified;		Diana, and in thy power."
2344	**But only for the fere thus hath she cryed,**	2365	**And hoom she gooth anon the nexte weye.**
	But simply for fear has she cried thus,		And home she goes at once the nearest way.
2345	**And weep, that it was pitee for to here.**	2366	**This is theffect, ther is namore to seye.**
	And wept that it was a pity to hear.		This is the substance; there is no more to say.
2346	**And ther-with-al Diane gan appere,**	2367	**The nexte houre of Mars folwinge this,**
	And right then Diana did appear,		The next (planetary) hour of Mars following this,
2347	**With bowe in hond, right as an hunteresse,**	2368	**Arcite un-to the temple walked is**
	With bow in hand, just like a huntress,		Arcite has walked unto the temple
2348	**And seyde: 'Doghter, stint thyn hevinesse.**	2369	**Of fierse Mars, to doon his sacrifyse,**
	And said, 'Daughter, cease thy sadness.		Of fierce Mars to do his sacrifice,
2349	**Among the goddes hye it is affermed,**	2370	**With alle the rytes of his payen wyse.**
	Among the high gods it is affirmed,		With all the rites of his pagan manner (of worship).
2350	**And by eterne word write and confermed,**	2371	**With pitous herte and heigh devocioun,**
	And by eternal word written and confirmed,		With sorrowful heart and intense devotion,
2351	**Thou shalt ben wedded un-to oon of tho**	2372	**Right thus to Mars he seyde his orisoun:**
	Thou shalt be wedded unto one of those		Right thus to Mars he said his prayer:
2352	**That han for thee so muchel care and wo;**		
	Who have for thee so much care and woe;	2373	**'O strong god, that in the regnes colde**
2353	**But un-to which of hem I may nat telle.**		'O strong god, who in the cold reigns
	But unto which of them I may not tell.	2374	**Of Trace honoured art, and lord y-holde,**
2354	**Farwel, for I ne may no lenger dwelle.**		Of Thrace art honored and considered lord,
	Farwell, for I can stay no longer.	2375	**And hast in every regne and every lond**
2355	**The fyres which that on myn auter brenne**		And hast in every reign and every land
	The fires which burn on my altar	2376	**Of armes al the brydel in thyn hond,**
2356	**Shul thee declaren, er that thou go henne,**		All the control of arms in thy hand,
	Shall declare to thee, before thou go hence,		
2357	**Thyn aventure of love, as in this cas.'**		
	Thy destiny concerning love, as in this situation.'		

2377	**And hem fortunest as thee list devyse,**	2397	**Ne reccheth never wher I sinke or flete.**
	And grants them fortune as it pleases thee to command.		Nor cares never whether I sink or swim.
2378	**Accept of me my pitous sacrifyse.**	2398	**And wel I woot, er she me mercy hete,**
	Accept of me my sorrowful sacrifice.		And well I know, before she may promise me mercy,
2379	**If so be that my youthe may deserve,**	2399	**I moot with strengthe winne hir in the place;**
	If it so be that my youth may deserve,		I must win her with strength in the lists;
2380	**And that my might be worthy for to serve**	2400	**And wel I woot, withouten help or grace**
	And that my power be worthy to serve		And well I know, without help or grace
2381	**Thy godhede, that I may been oon of thyne,**	2401	**Of thee, ne may my strengthe noght availle.**
	Thy godhead, so that I may be one of thine,		Of thee my strength can not avail.
2382	**Than preye I thee to rewe up-on my pyne.**	2402	**Than help me, lord, to-morwe in my bataille,**
	Then pray I thee to have pity upon my pain.		Then help me, lord, tomorrow in my battle,
2383	**For thilke peyne, and thilke hote fyr,**	2403	**For thilke fyr that whylom brente thee,**
	For that same pain and that same hot fire,		For that same fire that once burned thee,
2384	**In which thou whylom brendest for desyr,**	2404	**As wel as thilke fyr now brenneth me;**
	In which thou once burned for desire,		As well as that same fire now burns me,
2385	**Whan that thou usedest the grete beautee**	2405	**And do that I to-morwe have victorie.**
	When that thou enjoyed the beauty		And bring it about so that I have victory tomorrow.
2386	**Of fayre yonge fresshe Venus free,**	2406	**Myn be the travaille, and thyn be the glorie!**
	Of fair, young, fresh Venus the noble,		Mine be the labor, and thine be the glory!
2387	**And haddest hir in armes at thy wille,**	2407	**Thy soverein temple wol I most honouren**
	And haddest her in arms as you wished,		I will most honor thy most excellent temple
2388	**Al-though thee ones on a tyme misfille**	2408	**Of any place, and alwey most labouren**
	Although once things went wrong for you		Over any place, and always most labor
2389	**Whan Vulcanus had caught thee in his las,**	2409	**In thy plesaunce and in thy craftes stronge,**
	When Vulcan had caught thee in his snare,		In thy pleasure and in thy strong crafts,
2390	**And fond thee ligging by his wyf, allas!**	2410	**And in thy temple I wol my baner honge,**
	And found thee lying by his wife, alas!		And in thy temple I will hang my banner,
2391	**For thilke sorwe that was in thyn herte,**	2411	**And alle the armes of my companye;**
	For that same sorrow that was in thy heart,		And all the arms of my company,
2392	**Have routhe as wel up-on my peynes smerte.**	2412	**And evere-mo, un-to that day I dye,**
	Have pity as well upon my painful sufferings.		And evermore, until that day I die,
2393	**I am yong and unkonning, as thou wost,**	2413	**Eterne fyr I wol biforn thee finde.**
	I am young and ignorant, as thou knowest,		Eternal fire I will provide before thee (on your altar).
2394	**And, as I trowe, with love offended most,**	2414	**And eek to this avow I wol me binde:**
	And, as I suppose, injured most by love		And also I will bind myself to this vow:
2395	**That ever was any lyves creature;**	2415	**My berd, myn heer that hongeth long adoun,**
	Than ever was any living creature,		My beard, my hair, that hangs long down,
2396	**For she, that dooth me al this wo endure,**	2416	**That never yet ne felte offensioun**
	For she that causes me to endure all this woe		That never yet felt injury

2417	**Of rasour nor of shere, I wol thee yive,**	2435	**And thus with Ioye, and hope wel to fare,**
	Of razor nor of shears, I will give thee,		And thus with joy and hope to fare well
2418	**And ben thy trewe servant whyl I live.**	2436	**Arcite anon un-to his inne is fare,**
	And be thy true servant while I live.		Arcite at once is gone unto his lodging,
2419	**Now lord, have routhe up-on my sorwes sore,**	2437	**As fayn as fowel is of the brighte sonne.**
	Now, lord, have pity upon my painful sorrows,		As happy as a fowl is for the bright sun.
2420	**Yif me victorie, I aske thee namore.'**	2438	**And right anon swich stryf ther is bigonne**
	Give me victory; I ask of thee no more.'		And right away such strife there is begun,
2421	**The preyere stinte of Arcita the stronge,**	2439	**For thilke graunting, in the hevene above,**
	The prayer of Arcite the strong stopped,		Because of that same grant, in the heaven above,
2422	**The ringes on the temple-dore that honge,**	2440	**Bitwixe Venus, the goddesse of love,**
	The rings that hung on the temple door,		Between Venus, the goddess of love,
2423	**And eek the dores, clatereden ful faste,**	2441	**And Mars, the sterne god armipotente,**
	And also the doors, clattered very fast,		And Mars, the stern god powerful in arms,
2424	**Of which Arcita som-what him agaste.**	2442	**That Iupiter was bisy it to stente;**
	Of which Arcite was somewhat afraid.		That Jupiter was hard put to stop it,
2425	**The fyres brende up-on the auter brighte,**	2443	**Til that the pale Saturnus the colde,**
	The fires upon the altar burned (so) brightly		Until the pale Saturn the hostile,
2426	**That it gan al the temple for to lighte;**	2444	**That knew so manye of aventures olde,**
	That it began to illuminate all the temple;		Who knew so many of old adventures,
2427	**And swete smel the ground anon up-yaf,**	2445	**Fond in his olde experience an art,**
	A sweet smell the ground at once yielded up,		Found in his old experience a plan
2428	**And Arcita anon his hand up-haf,**	2446	**That he ful sone hath plesed every part.**
	And Arcita immediately raised up his hand,		That he full soon has pleased every side.
2429	**And moore encens into the fyr he caste,**	2447	**As sooth is sayd, elde hath greet avantage;**
	And he cast more incense into the fire,		As is truly said, old age has a great advantage;
2430	**With othere rytes mo; and atte laste**	2448	**In elde is bothe wisdom and usage;**
	With more other rites; and at the last		In old age is both wisdom and experience;
2431	**The statue of Mars bigan his hauberk ringe.**	2449	**Men may the olde at-renne, and noght at-rede.**
	The statue of Mars began to ring its coat of mail.		One can outrun the old but not outwit them.
2432	**And with that soun he herde a murmuringe**	2450	**Saturne anon, to stinten stryf and drede,**
	And with that sound he heard a murmuring		Saturn anon, to stop strife and fear,
2433	**Ful lowe and dim, that sayde thus, 'Victorie:'**	2451	**Al be it that it is agayn his kynde,**
	Very low and faint, that said thus, 'Victory:'		Although it is against his natural disposition,
2434	**For which he yaf to Mars honour and glorie.**	2452	**Of al this stryf he gan remedie fynde.**
	For which he (Arcite) gave to Mars honor and glory.		He found a remedy for all this strife.
		2453	**'My dere doghter Venus,' quod Saturne,**
			'My dear daughter Venus,' said Saturn,
		2454	**'My cours, that hath so wyde for to turne,**
			'My orbit, that has so wide (a course) to turn,

2455	**Hath more power than wot any man.**	2471	**That Palamon, that is thyn owene knyght,**
	Has more power than any man knows.		So that Palamon, who is thine own knight,
2456	**Myn is the drenching in the see so wan;**	2472	**Shal have his lady, as thou hast him hight.**
	Mine is the drowning in the sea so dark;		Shall have his lady, as thou hast promised him.
2457	**Myn is the prison in the derke cote;**	2473	**Though Mars shal helpe his knight, yet nathelees**
	Mine is the imprisonment in the dark cell;		Though Mars shall help his knight, yet nonetheless
2458	**Myn is the strangling and hanging by the throte;**	2474	**Bitwixe yow ther moot be som tyme pees,**
	Mine is the killing and hanging by the throat,		Between you there must be peace sometime,
2459	**The murmure, and the cherles rebelling,**	2475	**Al be ye noght of o complexioun,**
	The murmur (of discontent) and the churls' rebelling,		Although you are not of one (the same) temperament,
2460	**The groyning, and the pryvee empoysoning:**	2476	**That causeth al day swich divisioun.**
	The grumbling, and the secret poisoning;		Which daily causes such dissension.
2461	**I do vengeance and pleyn correccioun**	2477	**I am thin ayel, redy at thy wille;**
	I exact vengeance and do full punishment,		I am thy grandfather, ready (to do) as you wish;
2462	**Whyl I dwelle in the signe of the leoun.**	2478	**Weep thou namore, I wol thy lust fulfille.'**
	While I dwell in the (zodiacal) sign of the lion.		Weep now no more; I will fulfill thy desire.'
2463	**Myn is the ruine of the hye halles,**		
	Mine is the ruin of the high halls,	2479	**Now wol I stinten of the goddes above,**
2464	**The falling of the toures and of the walles**		Now I will stop (speaking) of the gods above,
	The falling of the towers and of the walls	2480	**Of Mars, and of Venus, goddesse of love,**
2465	**Up-on the mynour or the carpenter.**		Of Mars, and of Venus, goddess of love,
	Upon the miner or the carpenter.	2481	**And telle yow, as pleynly as I can,**
2466	**I slow Sampsoun in shaking the piler;**		And tell you as plainly as I can
	I slew Sampson, shaking the pillar;	2482	**The grete effect, for which that I bigan.**
2467	**And myne be the maladyes colde,**		The essential part, for which I began.
	And mine are the cold maladies,		
2468	**The derke tresons, and the castes olde;**		*Explicit tercia pars*
	The dark treasons, and the old plots;		The third part ends
2469	**My loking is the fader of pestilence.**		
	My (astrological) aspect is the father of pestilence.		
2470	**Now weep namore, I shal doon diligence**		
	Now weep no more; I shall do my diligence		

Canterbury Tales:

The Knight's Tale, Part IV

Geoffrey Chaucer

Sequitur pars quarta
The fourth part follows

2483 **Greet was the feste in Athenes that day,**
Great was the feast in Athens that day,
2484 **And eek the lusty seson of that May**
And also the pleasing season of that May
2485 **Made every wight to been in swich plesaunce,**
Made every person to be in such delight
2486 **That al that Monday Iusten they and daunce,**
That all that Monday they joust and dance,
2487 **And spenden it in Venus heigh servyse.**
And spend that day in Venus's noble service.
2488 **But by the cause that they sholde ryse**
But because they must rise
2489 **Erly, for to seen the grete fight,**
Early, to see the great fight,
2490 **Unto hir reste wente they at night.**
Unto their rest they went at nightfall.
2491 **And on the morwe, whan that day gan springe,**
And in the morning, when day did spring,
2492 **Of hors and harneys, noyse and clateringe**
Noise and clattering of horses and armor
2493 **Ther was in hostelryes al aboute;**
There was in hostelries all about;
2494 **And to the paleys rood ther many a route**
And to the palace there rode many a company
2495 **Of lordes, up-on stedes and palfreys.**
Of lords upon steeds and palfreys.
2496 **Ther maystow seen devysing of herneys**
There canst thou see preparation of armor
2497 **So uncouth and so riche, and wroght so weel**
So exotic and so rich, and wrought so well
2498 **Of goldsmithrie, of browding, and of steel;**
Of goldsmiths' works, of embroidery, and of steel;
2499 **The sheeldes brighte, testers, and trappures;**
The bright shields, horses' head-armor, and horse-armor,
2500 **Gold-hewen helmes, hauberks, cote-armures;**
Gold-colored helms, coats of mail, tunics with heraldic devices;
2501 **Lordes in paraments on hir courseres,**
Lords in richly decorated robes on their coursers,
2502 **Knightes of retenue, and eek squyeres**
Knights of (their) retinues, and also squires
2503 **Nailinge the speres, and helmes bokelinge,**
Nailing heads to the spear-shafts, and buckling helms,
2504 **Gigginge of sheeldes, with layneres lacinge;**
Fitting the shields with straps, fastening with laces;

Geoffrey Chaucer; Larry D. Benson, trans., *The Knight's Tale, Part IV: An Interlinear Translation* (lines 2483–3108), from http://www.courses.fas.harvard.edu/~chaucer/teachslf/kt-par4.htm,. Copyright © 2008 by The President and Fellows of Harvard College . Permission to reprint granted by the publisher.

2505	**Ther as need is, they weren no-thing ydel;**	2522	**Longe after that the sonne gan to springe.**
	Where it is needed they were not at all idle;		Long after the sun began to rise.
2506	**The fomy stedes on the golden brydel**	2523	**The grete Theseus, that of his sleep awaked**
	The steeds frothing on the golden bridles		The great Theseus, who was awakened of his sleep
2507	**Gnawinge, and faste the armurers also**	2524	**With minstralcye and noyse that was maked,**
	Gnawing, and fast the armorers also		By the music and noise that was made,
2508	**With fyle and hamer prikinge to and fro;**	2525	**Held yet the chambre of his paleys riche,**
	With file and hammer are spurring to and fro;		Remained yet in the chamber of his rich palace
2509	**Yemen on fote, and communes many oon**	2526	**Til that the Thebane knightes, bothe y-liche**
	Yeomen on foot, and foot soldiers many a one		Until the Theban knights, both equally
2510	**With shorte staves, thikke as they may goon;**	2527	**Honoured, were into the paleys fet.**
	With short staves, thick as they can go;		Honored, were fetched into the palace.
2511	**Pypes, trompes, nakers, clariounes,**	2528	**Duk Theseus was at a window set,**
	Pipes, trumpets, kettle drums, bugles,		Duke Theseus was set at a window,
2512	**That in the bataille blowen blody sounes;**	2529	**Arrayed right as he were a god in trone.**
	That blow bloody sounds in the battle;		Arrayed exactly as if he were a god on a throne.
2513	**The paleys ful of peples up and doun,**	2530	**The peple preesseth thider-ward ful sone**
	The palace full of people everywhere,		The people press thither full soon
2514	**Heer three, ther ten, holding hir questioun,**	2531	**Him for to seen, and doon heigh reverence,**
	Here three, there ten, debating,		In order to see him, and to do great reverence,
2515	**Divyninge of thise Thebane knightes two.**	2532	**And eek to herkne his hest and his sentence.**
	Conjecturing about these two Theban knights.		And also to hear his command and his decision.
2516	**Somme seyden thus, somme seyde it shal be so;**	2533	**An heraud on a scaffold made an ho,**
	Some said thus, some said it shall be so;		A herald on a scaffold made a ho,
2517	**Somme helden with him with the blake berd,**	2534	**Til al the noyse of the peple was y-do;**
	Some held with him with the black beard,		Until all the noise of people was done,
2518	**Somme with the balled, somme with the thikke-herd;**	2535	**And whan he saugh the peple of noyse al stille,**
	Some with the bald, some with the thickly haired;		And when he saw the people all still of noise,
2519	**Somme sayde, he loked grim and he wolde fighte;**	2536	**Tho showed he the mighty dukes wille.**
	Some said he looked grim, and he would fight:		Then showed he the mighty duke's will:
2520	**He hath a sparth of twenty pound of wighte.**	2537	**'The lord hath of his heigh discrecioun**
	He has a battle-ax of twenty pounds of weight.		'The lord has of his great sound judgment
		2538	**Considered, that it were destruccioun**
			Considered that it would be destruction
2521	**Thus was the halle ful of divyninge,**	2539	**To gentil blood, to fighten in the gyse**
	Thus was the hall full of conjecturing,		To gentle blood to fight in the manner

2540	**Of mortal bataille now in this empryse;**	2557	**No lenger shal the turneyinge laste.**
	Of mortal battle now in this undertaking.		The tournament shall last no longer.
2541	**Wherfore, to shapen that they shul not dye,**	2558	**God spede yow; goth forth, and ley on faste.**
	Wherefore, to arrange matters so that they shall not die,		God give you success! Go forth and lay on fast!
2542	**He wol his firste purpos modifye.**	2559	**With long swerd and with maces fight your fille.**
	He will modify his previous plan.		With long sword and with mace fight your fill.
2543	**No man therfor, up peyne of los of lyf,**	2560	**Goth now your wey; this is the lordes wille.'**
	No man therefore, upon punishment of loss of life,		Go now on your way; this is the lord's will.'
2544	**No maner shot, ne pollax, ne short knyf**	2561	**The voys of peple touchede the hevene,**
	No sort of arrow, nor battle-axe, nor short knife		The voice of people touched the heaven,
2545	**Into the listes sende, or thider bringe;**	2562	**So loude cryden they with mery stevene:**
	Send into the lists or bring there;		So loudly they cried with merry voices,
2546	**Ne short swerd for to stoke, with poynt bytinge,**	2563	**'God save swich a lord, that is so good,**
	Nor short sword, to stab with piercing point,		'God save such a lord, that is so good
2547	**No man ne drawe, ne bere it by his syde.**	2564	**He wilneth no destruccioun of blood!'**
	May no man neither draw, nor bear it by his side.		He desires no destruction of blood!'
2548	**Ne no man shal un-to his felawe ryde**	2565	**Up goon the trompes and the melodye.**
	And no man shall ride at his opponent		Up go the trumpets and the melody,
2549	**But o cours, with a sharp y-grounde spere;**	2566	**And to the listes rit the companye**
	More than one course with a sharply honed spear;		And to the lists rides the company,
2550	**Foyne, if him list, on fote, him-self to were.**	2567	**By ordinaunce, thurgh-out the citee large,**
	Let him thrust, if he wishes, on foot, to defend himself.		In battle array, throughout all the city,
2551	**And he that is at meschief, shal be take,**	2568	**Hanged with cloth of gold, and nat with sarge.**
	And he who is at a disadvantage shall be taken		Hung with cloth of gold, and not with serge.
2552	**And noght slayn, but be broght un-to the stake**	2569	**Ful lyk a lord this noble duk gan ryde,**
	And not slain, but be brought unto the stake		Fully like a lord this noble duke did ride,
2553	**That shal ben ordeyned on either syde;**	2570	**Thise two Thebanes up-on either syde;**
	That shall be placed on either side;		These two Thebans upon either side,
2554	**But thider he shal by force, and ther abyde.**	2571	**And after rood the quene, and Emelye,**
	But thither he must (go) by force, and remain there.		And after rode the queen and Emelye,
2555	**And if so falle, the chieftayn be take**	2572	**And after that another companye**
	And if so happen that the chieftain be taken		And after that another company
2556	**On either syde, or elles slee his make,**	2573	**Of oon and other, after hir degree.**
	On either side, or else should slay his opponent,		One after another, according to their rank.
		2574	**And thus they passen thurgh-out the citee,**
			And thus they pass throughout the city,
		2575	**And to the listes come they by tyme.**
			And they come to the lists in good time.

2576	**It nas not of the day yet fully pryme,**	2595	**Whan that hir names rad were everichoon,**
	It was not yet fully prime (nine a.m.) of the day		When every one of their names were read,
2577	**Whan set was Theseus ful riche and hye,**	2596	**That in hir nombre gyle were ther noon,**
	When Theseus was set very splendidly and nobly,		So that in their total number there would be no deception,
2578	**Ipolita the quene and Emelye,**	2597	**Tho were the gates shet, and cryed was loude:**
	Ypolita the queen, and Emelye,		Then the gates were shut, and cried was aloud:
2579	**And other ladies in degrees aboute.**	2598	**'Do now your devoir, yonge knightes proude!'**
	And other ladies about in tiers.		'Do now your duty, proud young knights!'
2580	**Un-to the seetes preesseth al the route.**	2599	**The heraudes lefte hir priking up and doun;**
	Unto the seats press all the crowd.		The heralds left their spurring up and down;
2581	**And west-ward, thurgh the gates under Marte,**	2600	**Now ringen trompes loude and clarioun;**
	And westward, through the gates under Mars,		Now trumpets and bugles ring loud.
2582	**Arcite, and eek the hundred of his parte,**	2601	**Ther is namore to seyn, but west and est**
	Arcite, and also the hundred of his party,		There is no more to say, but from west and east
2583	**With baner reed is entred right anon;**	2602	**In goon the speres ful sadly in arest;**
	With red banner is entered right away;		In go the spears very firmly in the lance-rests;
2584	**And in that selve moment Palamon**	2603	**In goth the sharpe spore in-to the syde.**
	And in that same moment Palamon		In goes the sharp spur into the flank.
2585	**Is under Venus, est-ward in the place,**	2604	**Ther seen men who can Iuste, and who can ryde;**
	Is under Venus, eastward in the place,		There people see who can joust and who can ride;
2586	**With baner whyt, and hardy chere and face.**	2605	**Ther shiveren shaftes up-on sheeldes thikke;**
	With white banner and hardy countenance and face.		There splinter spears upon thick shields;
2587	**In al the world, to seken up and doun,**	2606	**He feleth thurgh the herte-spoon the prikke.**
	In all the world, to seek up and down,		He feels the stabbing through the breast-bone.
2588	**So even with-outen variacioun,**	2607	**Up springen speres twenty foot on highte;**
	So evenly, without variation,		Up spring spears twenty foot on height;
2589	**Ther nere swiche companyes tweye.**	2608	**Out goon the swerdes as the silver brighte.**
	There were not two such companies,		Out go the swords bright as silver;
2590	**For ther nas noon so wys that coude seye,**	2609	**The helmes they to-hewen and to-shrede;**
	For there was no one so wise that could say		The helms they hew to pieces and cut into shreds
2591	**That any hadde of other avauntage**	2610	**Out brest the blood, with sterne stremes rede.**
	That any one had advantage over the other		Out burst the blood in strong red streams.
2592	**Of worthinesse, ne of estaat, ne age,**		
	In worthiness, nor in status, nor age,		
2593	**So even were they chosen, for to gesse.**		
	So evenly were they chosen, as I estimate.		
2594	**And in two renges faire they hem dresse.**		
	And in two fair ranks they arrange themselves.		

2611	**With mighty maces the bones they to-breste.**	2626	**Ther nas no tygre in the vale of Galgopheye,**
	With mighty maces they break the bones to pieces.		There was not any tiger in the vale of Gargaphia,
2612	**He thurgh the thikkeste of the throng gan threste.**	2627	**Whan that hir whelp is stole, whan it is lyte,**
	He did thrust through the thickest of the throng;		When her whelp is stolen when it is little,
2613	**Ther stomblen stedes stronge, and doun goth al.**	2628	**So cruel on the hunte, as is Arcite**
	There strong steeds stumble, and down goes all,		So cruel on the hunt as is Arcite
2614	**He rolleth under foot as dooth a bal.**	2629	**For Ielous herte upon this Palamoun:**
	He rolls under foot as does a ball;		For jealous heart upon this Palamon:
2615	**He foyneth on his feet with his tronchoun,**	2630	**Ne in Belmarye ther nis so fel leoun,**
	On his feet he stabs with the broken shaft of his spear,		Nor in Benmarin there is not so fierce a lion,
2616	**And he him hurtleth with his hors adoun.**	2631	**That hunted is, or for his hunger wood,**
	And he hurtles him down with his horse;		That is hunted, or maddened by his hunger,
2617	**He thurgh the body is hurt, and sithen y-take,**	2632	**Ne of his praye desireth so the blood,**
	He is hurt through the body and then taken,		Nor of his prey desires so the blood,
2618	**Maugree his heed, and broght un-to the stake,**	2633	**As Palamon to sleen his fo Arcite.**
	Despite all he can do, and brought unto the stake;		As Palamon to slay his foe Arcite.
2619	**As forward was, right ther he moste abyde;**	2634	**The Ielous strokes on hir helmes byte;**
	As was the agreement, right there he must abide.		The fervent strokes bite on their helms;
2620	**Another lad is on that other syde.**	2635	**Out renneth blood on bothe hir sydes rede.**
	Another on that other side is led away.		Out runs red blood on both their sides.
2621	**And som tyme dooth hem Theseus to reste,**	2636	**Som tyme an ende ther is of every dede;**
	And for a while Theseus makes them rest,		Some time there is an end of every deed;
2622	**Hem to refresshe, and drinken if hem leste.**	2637	**For er the sonne un-to the reste wente,**
	To refresh themselves and drink, if they wish.		For before the sun went unto its rest,
2623	**Ful ofte a-day han thise Thebanes two**	2638	**The stronge king Emetreus gan hente**
	Many times these two Thebans have		The strong king Emetreus did seize
2624	**Togidre y-met, and wroght his felawe wo;**	2639	**This Palamon, as he faught with Arcite,**
	Met together, and (each) wrought woe to his opponent;		This Palamon, as he fought with Arcite,
2625	**Unhorsed hath ech other of hem tweye.**	2640	**And made his swerd depe in his flesh to byte;**
	Each has unhorsed the other of them two.		And made his sword deep in his flesh to bite,
		2641	**And by the force of twenty is he take**
			And by the force of twenty he (Palamon) is taken
		2642	**Unyolden, and y-drawe unto the stake.**
			Without having surrendered, and dragged to the stake.
		2643	**And in the rescous of this Palamoun**
			And in the rescue of this Palamon
		2644	**The stronge king Ligurge is born adoun;**
			The strong king Lygurge is born down;

2645	**And king Emetreus, for al his strengthe,**	2664	**What seith she now? what dooth this quene of love?**
	And king Emetreus, despite all his strength,		What says she now? What does this queen of love,
2646	**Is born out of his sadel a swerdes lengthe,**	2665	**But wepeth so, for wanting of hir wille,**
	Is carried out of his saddle a sword's length,		But weeps so, for lack of (having) her will,
2647	**So hitte him Palamon er he were take;**	2666	**Til that hir teres in the listes fille;**
	So hit him Palamon before he was taken.		Until her tears fell in the lists?
2648	**But al for noght, he was broght to the stake.**	2667	**She seyde: 'I am ashamed, doutelees.'**
	But all for naught; he was brought to the stake.		She said, 'I am disgraced, doubtless.'
2649	**His hardy herte mighte him helpe naught;**	2668	**Saturnus seyde: 'Doghter, hold thy pees.**
	His hardy heart could not help him;		Saturn said, 'Daughter, hold thy peace!
2650	**He moste abyde, whan that he was caught**	2669	**Mars hath his wille, his knight hath al his bone,**
	He must abide, when he was caught,		Mars has his will, his knight has all his request,
2651	**By force, and eek by composicioun.**	2670	**And, by myn heed, thou shalt ben esed sone.'**
	By force and also by the agreed terms of battle.		And, by my head, thou shalt be relieved soon.'
2652	**Who sorweth now but woful Palamoun,**	2671	**The trompes, with the loude minstralcye,**
	Who sorrows now but woeful Palamon,		The trumpeters, with the loud music,
2653	**That moot namore goon agayn to fighte?**	2672	**The heraudes, that ful loude yolle and crye,**
	That must no more go again to fight?		The heralds, who full loudly yell and cry,
2654	**And whan that Theseus had seyn this sighte,**	2673	**Been in hir wele for Ioye of daun Arcite.**
	And when Theseus had seen this sight,		Are in their happiest state for joy of dan Arcite.
2655	**Un-to the folk that foghten thus echoon**	2674	**But herkneth me, and stinteth now a lyte,**
	Unto each one of the folk that fought thus		But listen to me, and stop the noise for a little,
2656	**He cryde, 'Ho! namore, for it is doon!**	2675	**Which a miracle ther bifel anon.**
	He cried, 'Stop! no more, for it is done!		(Hear) what a miracle at once befell there.
2657	**I wol be trewe Iuge, and no partye.**	2676	**This fierse Arcite hath of his helm y-don,**
	I will be true judge, and no partisan.		This fierce Arcite has taken off his helm,
2658	**Arcite of Thebes shal have Emelye,**	2677	**And on a courser, for to shewe his face,**
	Arcite of Thebes shall have Emelye,		And on a war horse, to show his face,
2659	**That by his fortune hath hir faire y-wonne.'**	2678	**He priketh endelong the large place,**
	Who by his fortune has won her fairly.'		He spurs from one end to the other of the large open space,
2660	**Anon ther is a noyse of peple bigonne**	2679	**Loking upward up-on this Emelye;**
	Immediately there is a noise of people begun		Looking upward upon this Emelye;
2661	**For Ioye of this, so loude and heigh with-alle,**	2680	**And she agayn him caste a freendlich yë,**
	For joy of this, so loud and clamorous indeed		And she to him cast a friendly eye
2662	**It semed that the listes sholde falle.**	2681	**(For wommen, as to speken in comune,**
	It seemed that the lists should fall.		(For women, so to speak in general,
2663	**What can now faire Venus doon above?**		
	What now can fair Venus do above?		

2682	They folwen al the favour of fortune),	2702	With alle blisse and greet solempnitee.
	They all follow the favor of Fortune),		With all bliss and great solemnity.
2683	And she was al his chere, as in his herte.	2703	Al be it that this aventure was falle,
	And was all his source of pleasure, in his heart.		Although this accident had happened,
2684	Out of the ground a furie infernal sterte,	2704	He nolde noght disconforten hem alle.
	Out of the ground leaped an infernal fury,		He would not distress them all.
2685	From Pluto sent, at requeste of Saturne,	2705	Men seyde eek, that Arcite shal nat dye;
	Sent from Pluto at the request of Saturn,		People said also that Arcite shall not dye;
2686	For which his hors for fere gan to turne,	2706	He shal ben heled of his maladye.
	For which his horse for fear began to turn,		He shall be healed of his injuries.
2687	And leep asyde, and foundred as he leep;	2707	And of another thing they were as fayn,
	And leaped aside, and stumbled as he leaped;		And of another thing they were as happy,
2688	And, er that Arcite may taken keep,	2708	That of hem alle was ther noon y-slayn,
	And before Arcite can take heed,		That of them all there was no one slain,
2689	He pighte him on the pomel of his heed,	2709	Al were they sore y-hurt, and namely oon,
	He hit himself on the top of his head,		Although they (were) sorely hurt, and especially one,
2690	That in the place he lay as he were deed,	2710	That with a spere was thirled his brest-boon.
	That in the place he lay as if he were dead,		Whose breastbone was pierced by a spear.
2691	His brest to-brosten with his sadel-bowe.	2711	To othere woundes, and to broken armes,
	His breast shattered by his saddlebow.		To other wounds and to broken arms
2692	As blak he lay as any cole or crowe,	2712	Some hadden salves, and some hadden charmes;
	He lay as black as any coal or crow,		Some had salves, and some had charms;
2693	So was the blood y-ronnen in his face.	2713	Fermacies of herbes, and eek save
	The blood was so run in his face.		Medicines made of herbs, and also of sage
2694	Anon he was y-born out of the place	2714	They dronken, for they wolde hir limes have.
	Immediately he was carried out of the place,		They drank, for they wanted to have their limbs cured.
2695	With herte soor, to Theseus paleys.	2715	For which this noble duk, as he wel can,
	With painful heart, to Theseus's palace.		For which this noble duke, as he well knows how,
2696	Tho was he corven out of his harneys,	2716	Conforteth and honoureth every man,
	Then was he cut out of his armor,		Comforts and honors every man,
2697	And in a bed y-brought ful faire and blyve,	2717	And made revel al the longe night,
	And brought in a bed very gently and quickly,		And made revel all the long night
2698	For he was yet in memorie and alyve,	2718	Un-to the straunge lordes, as was right.
	For he was yet conscious and alive,		For the foreign lords, as was right.
2699	And alway crying after Emelye.	2719	Ne ther was holden no disconfitinge,
	And always crying for Emelye.		Nor was it considered any defeat (in battle)
2700	Duk Theseus, with al his companye,	2720	But as a Iustes or a tourneyinge;
	Duke Theseus, with all his company,		But (only) as a joust or a tournament;
2701	Is comen hoom to Athenes his citee,	2721	For soothly ther was no disconfiture,
	Is come home to Athens, his city,		For truly there was no defeat.

2722	*For falling nis nat but an aventure;*	2740	**Ther was namore, but 'far wel, have good day!'**
	For falling is nothing but an accident,		There was no more but 'Fare well, have good day!'
2723	**Ne to be lad with fors un-to the stake**	2741	**Of this bataille I wol namore endyte,**
	Nor to be led by force unto the stake		Of this battle I will write no more,
2724	**Unyolden, and with twenty knightes take,**	2742	**But speke of Palamon and of Arcite.**
	Without having surrendered, and taken by twenty knights,		But speak of Palamon and of Arcite.
2725	**O persone allone, with-outen mo,**	2743	**Swelleth the brest of Arcite, and the sore**
	One person alone, without others,		The breast of Arcite swells, and the pain
2726	**And haried forth by arme, foot, and to,**	2744	**Encreesseth at his herte more and more.**
	And dragged forth by arm, foot, and toe,		At his heart increases more and more.
2727	**And eek his stede driven forth with staves,**	2745	**The clothered blood, for any lechecraft,**
	And also his steed driven forth with staves		The clotted blood, despite any medical treatment,
2728	**With footmen, bothe yemen and eek knaves,**	2746	**Corrupteth, and is in his bouk y-laft,**
	By men on foot, both yeomen and also foot soldiers,		Corrupts, and is left in the trunk of his body,
2729	**It nas aretted him no vileinye,**	2747	**That neither veyne-blood, ne ventusinge,**
	He incurred no shameful blame for it;		That neither blood letting at a vein, nor applying suction cups,
2730	**Ther may no man clepen it cowardye.**	2748	**Ne drinke of herbes may ben his helpinge.**
	No man there may call it cowardice.		Nor drink of herbs can be any help to him.
2731	**For which anon duk Theseus leet crye,**	2749	**The vertu expulsif, or animal,**
	For which anon duke Theseus had proclaimed,		The power expulsive (to expel fluids), or animal,
2732	**To stinten alle rancour and envye,**	2750	**Fro thilke vertu cleped natural**
	To put a stop to all rancor and ill-will,		From that power called natural
2733	**The gree as wel of o syde as of other,**	2751	**Ne may the venim voyden, ne expelle.**
	The victory (is given) as well to one side as to the other,		Can not remove nor expel the poison.
2734	**And either syde y-lyk, as otheres brother;**	2752	**The pypes of his longes gonne to swelle,**
	And either side equal as the other's brother;		The pipes of his lungs began to swell,
2735	**And yaf hem yiftes after hir degree,**	2753	**And every lacerte in his brest adoun**
	And gave them gifts in accordance with their ranks,		And every muscle down in his breast
2736	**And fully heeld a feste dayes three;**	2754	**Is shent with venim and corrupcioun.**
	And held a feast for fully three days,		Is destroyed by poison and corrupted matter.
2737	**And conveyed the kinges worthily**	2755	**Him gayneth neither, for to gete his lyf,**
	And honorably escorted the kings		Avails him neither, to preserve his life,
2738	**Out of his toun a Iournee largely.**	2756	**Vomyt upward, ne dounward laxatif;**
	Out of his town a full day's journey.		Vomit upward, nor downward laxative.
2739	**And hoom wente every man the righte way.**	2757	**Al is to-brosten thilke regioun,**
	And home went every man the direct way.		All is shattered in that region;
		2758	**Nature hath now no dominacioun.**
			Nature now has no power to control.

Things Unattempted Yet in Prose or Rhyme

2759	**And certeinly, ther nature wol nat wirche,**		2779	**Allone, with-outen any companye.**
	And certainly, where Nature will not work,			Alone, without any company.
2760	**Far-wel, phisyk! go ber the man to chirche!**		2780	**Far-wel, my swete fo! myn Emelye!**
	Fare well medicine! Go bear the man to church!			Fare well, my sweet foe, my Emelye!
2761	**This al and som, that Arcita mot dye,**		2781	**And softe tak me in your armes tweye,**
	This is the whole of it, that Arcite must die,			And softly take me in your two arms,
2762	**For which he sendeth after Emelye,**		2782	**For love of God, and herkneth what I seye.**
	For which he sends after Emelye,			For love of God, and listen to what I say.
2763	**And Palamon, that was his cosin dere;**		2783	**'I have heer with my cosin Palamon**
	And Palamon, who was his dear cousin.			'I have here with my cousin Palamon
2764	**Than seyde he thus, as ye shul after here.**		2784	**Had stryf and rancour, many a day a-gon,**
	Then said he thus, as you shall after hear.			Had strife and rancor many a day ago
2765	**'Naught may the woful spirit in myn herte**		2785	**For love of yow, and for my Ielousye.**
	'The woeful spirit in my heart can not			For love of you, and for my jealousy.
2766	**Declare o poynt of alle my sorwes smerte**		2786	**And Iupiter so wis my soule gye,**
	Declare one small part of all my painful sorrows			And as Jupiter may guide my soul,
2767	**To yow, my lady, that I love most;**		2787	**To speken of a servant proprely,**
	To you, my lady, whom I love most;			To speak specifically of a servant (of love),
2768	**But I biquethe the service of my gost**		2788	**With alle circumstaunces trewely,**
	But I bequeath the service of my ghost			With all the attendant attributes truly,
2769	**To yow aboven every creature,**		2789	**That is to seyn, trouthe, honour, and knighthede,**
	To you above every creature,			That is to say, truth, honor, knighthood,
2770	**Sin that my lyf may no lenger dure.**		2790	**Wisdom, humblesse, estaat, and heigh kinrede,**
	Since my life can no longer endure.			Wisdom, humbleness, rank, and noble ancestry,
2771	**Allas, the wo! allas, the peynes stronge,**		2791	**Fredom, and al that longeth to that art,**
	Alas, the woe! Alas, the strong pains,			Nobility of character, and all that belongs to that art,
2772	**That I for yow have suffred, and so longe!**		2792	**So Iupiter have of my soule part,**
	That I have suffered for you, and so long!			As Jupiter may have concern for my soul,
2773	**Allas, the deeth! allas, myn Emelye!**		2793	**As in this world right now ne knowe I non**
	Alas, the death! Alas, my Emelye!			In this world right now I know no one
2774	**Allas, departing of our companye!**		2794	**So worthy to ben loved as Palamon,**
	Alas, separation of our company!			So worthy to be loved as Palamon,
2775	**Allas, myn hertes quene! allas, my wyf!**		2795	**That serveth yow, and wol don al his lyf.**
	Alas, my heart's queen! Alas, my wife,			Who serves you, and will do so all his life.
2776	**Myn hertes lady, endere of my lyf!**		2796	**And if that ever ye shul been a wyf,**
	My heart's lady, ender of my life!			And if ever you shall be a wife,
2777	**What is this world? what asketh men to have?**		2797	**Foryet nat Palamon, the gentil man.'**
	What is this world? What do people ask to have?			Forget not Palamon, the gentle man.'
2778	**Now with his love, now in his colde grave**		2798	**And with that word his speche faille gan,**
	Now with his love, now in his cold grave			And with that word his speech began to fail,

2799	**For from his feet up to his brest was come**	2819	**Swowninge, and bar hir fro the corps away.**
	For from his feet up to his breast had come		Swooning, and carried her away from the corpse.
2800	**The cold of deeth, that hadde him overcome.**	2820	**What helpeth it to tarien forth the day,**
	The cold of death, which had overcome him.		What helps it to waste the whole day
2801	**And yet more-over, in his armes two**	2821	**To tellen how she weep, bothe eve and morwe?**
	And yet moreover, for in his two arms		To tell how she wept both evening and morning?
2802	**The vital strengthe is lost, and al ago.**	2822	**For in swich cas wommen have swich sorwe,**
	The vital strength is lost and all gone.		For in such cases women have such sorrow,
2803	**Only the intellect, with-outen more,**	2823	**Whan that hir housbonds been from hem ago,**
	Only the intellect, nothing else,		When their husbands are gone from them,
2804	**That dwelled in his herte syk and sore,**	2824	**That for the more part they sorwen so,**
	That dwelled in his heart sick and sore,		That for the most part they so sorrow,
2805	**Gan faillen, when the herte felte deeth,**	2825	**Or elles fallen in swich maladye,**
	Began to fail when the heart felt death.		Or else fall in such illness
2806	**Dusked his eyen two, and failled breeth.**	2826	**That at the laste certeinly they dye.**
	His two eyes grew dark, and his breath failed,		That at the last certainly they die.
2807	**But on his lady yet caste he his yë;**		
	But on his lady yet he cast his eye;	2827	**Infinite been the sorwes and the teres**
2808	**His laste word was, 'mercy, Emelye!'**		Infinite are the sorrows and the tears
	His last word was, 'Mercy, Emelye!'	2828	**Of olde folk, and folk of tendre yeres,**
2809	**His spirit chaunged hous, and wente ther,**		Of old folk and folk of tender years
	His spirit changed house and went where,	2829	**In al the toun, for deeth of this Theban;**
2810	**As I cam never, I can nat tellen wher.**		In all the town for the death of this Theban.
	Since I came never (there), I can not tell where.	2830	**For him ther wepeth bothe child and man;**
2811	**Therfor I stinte, I nam no divinistre;**		For him there weep both child and man;
	Therefore I stop; I am no theologian;	2831	**So greet a weping was ther noon, certayn,**
2812	**Of soules finde I nat in this registre,**		There was no such great weeping, certainly,
	I find nothing about souls in this register,	2832	**Whan Ector was y-broght, al fresh y-slayn,**
2813	**Ne me ne list thilke opiniouns to telle**		When Hector was brought, just recently slain,
	Nor do I wish to tell such beliefs	2833	**To Troye; allas! the pitee that was ther,**
2814	**Of hem, though that they wryten wher they dwelle.**		To Troy; alas! The lamentation that was there,
	Of them, though they write of where they (the souls) dwell.	2834	**Cracching of chekes, rending eek of heer.**
2815	**Arcite is cold, ther Mars his soule gye;**		Scratching of cheeks, also tearing of hair.
	Arcite is cold, may Mars guide his soul!	2835	**'Why woldestow be deed,' thise wommen crye,**
2816	**Now wol I speken forth of Emelye.**		'Why wouldst thou be dead,' these women cry,
	Now will I speak forth of Emelye.	2836	**'And haddest gold y-nough, and Emelye?'**
2817	**Shrighte Emelye, and howleth Palamon,**		'Since thou haddest gold enough, and Emelye?'
	Emelye shrieked, and Palamon howls,		
2818	**And Theseus his suster took anon**		
	And Theseus immediately took his sister		

2837	**No man mighte gladen Theseus,**
	No man might comfort Theseus,
2838	**Savinge his olde fader Egeus,**
	Except for his old father Egeus,
2839	**That knew this worldes transmutacioun,**
	Who knew the changes of this world,
2840	**As he had seyn it chaungen up and doun,**
	As he had seen it change both up and down,
2841	**Ioye after wo, and wo after gladnesse:**
	Joy after woe, and woe after gladness,
2842	**And shewed hem ensamples and lyknesse.**
	And showed them examples and comparisons.

2843	**'Right as ther deyed never man,' quod he,**
	'Right as there died never a man,' said he,
2844	**'That he ne livede in erthe in som degree,**
	'Who did not live in earth to some extent
2845	**Right so ther livede never man,' he seyde,**
	Just so there lived never a man,' he said,
2846	**'In al this world, that som tyme he ne deyde.**
	'In all this world, who some time did not die.
2847	**This world nis but a thurghfare ful of wo,**
	This world is nothing but a thoroughfare full of woe,
2848	**And we ben pilgrimes, passinge to and fro;**
	And we are pilgrims, passing to and fro;
2849	**Deeth is an ende of every worldly sore.'**
	Death is an end of every worldly pain.'
2850	**And over al this yet seyde he muchel more**
	And beyond all this yet he said much more
2851	**To this effect, ful wysly to enhorte**
	To this effect, full wisely to exhort
2852	**The peple, that they sholde hem reconforte.**
	The people that they should comfort themselves.

2853	**Duk Theseus, with al his bisy cure,**
	Duke Theseus, with all his careful attention,
2854	**Caste now wher that the sepulture**
	Considered now where the tomb
2855	**Of good Arcite may best y-maked be,**
	Of good Arcite may best be made,
2856	**And eek most honurable in his degree.**
	And also most honorable in (regard to) his rank.
2857	**And at the laste he took conclusioun,**
	And at the last he concluded
2858	**That ther as first Arcite and Palamoun**
	That there where first Arcite and Palamon
2859	**Hadden for love the bataille hem bitwene,**
	Had the battle between them for love,
2860	**That in that selve grove, swote and grene,**
	That in that same grove, sweet-smelling and green,
2861	**Ther as he hadde his amorous desires,**
	Where he had his amorous desires,
2862	**His compleynt, and for love his hote fires,**
	His lament, and for love his hot fires,
2863	**He wolde make a fyr, in which thoffice**
	He would make a fire in which the rite
2864	**Funeral he mighte al accomplice;**
	Of a funeral he might fully perform;
2865	**And leet comaunde anon to hakke and hewe**
	And he ordered immediately to hack and hew
2866	**The okes olde, and leye hem on a rewe**
	The old oaks, and lay them in a row
2867	**In colpons wel arrayed for to brenne;**
	In piles arranged to burn well;
2868	**His officers with swifte feet they renne**
	His officers with swift feet they run
2869	**And ryde anon at his comaundement.**
	And ride quickly at his commandment.
2870	**And after this, Theseus hath y-sent**
	And after this, Theseus has sent
2871	**After a bere, and it al over-spradde**
	For a bier, and it all overspread
2872	**With cloth of gold, the richest that he hadde.**
	With cloth of gold, the richest that he had.
2873	**And of the same suyte he cladde Arcite;**
	And of the same material he clad Arcite;
2874	**Upon his hondes hadde he gloves whyte;**
	Upon his hands he had white gloves;
2875	**Eek on his heed a croune of laurer grene,**
	Also on his head a crown of green laurel,

2876	**And in his hond a swerd ful bright and kene.**	2892	**Up-on thise stedes, that weren grete and whyte,**
	And in his hand a sword full bright and keen.		Upon these steeds, that were large and white,
2877	**He leyde him bare the visage on the bere,**	2893	**Ther seten folk, of which oon bar his sheeld,**
	He laid him, with the face bare, on the bier;		There sat folk, of which one carried his (Arcite's) shield,
2878	**Therwith he weep that pitee was to here.**	2894	**Another his spere up in his hondes heeld;**
	Therewith he wept that it was a pity to hear.		Another held his spear upright in his hands,
2879	**And for the peple sholde seen him alle,**	2895	**The thridde bar with him his bowe Turkeys,**
	And in order that all the people should see him,		The third carried with him his Turkish bow,
2880	**Whan it was day, he broghte him to the halle,**	2896	**Of brend gold was the cas, and eek the harneys;**
	When it was day, he brought him to the hall,		Of pure gold was the quiver and also the fittings;
2881	**That roreth of the crying and the soun.**	2897	**And riden forth a pas with sorweful chere**
	That resounds with the crying and the sound.		And they rode forth slowly with sorrowful demeanor
		2898	**Toward the grove, as ye shul after here.**
			Toward the grove, as you shall later hear.
2882	**Tho cam this woful Theban Palamoun,**	2899	**The nobleste of the Grekes that ther were**
	Then came this woeful Theban Palamon,		The noblest of the Greeks that were there
2883	**With flotery berd, and ruggy asshy heres,**	2900	**Upon hir shuldres carieden the bere,**
	With waving beard and rough hair sprinkled with ashes,		Carried the bier upon their shoulders,
2884	**In clothes blake, y-dropped al with teres;**	2901	**With slakke pas, and eyen rede and wete,**
	In black clothes, all sprinkled with tears;		With slow pace and eyes red and wet,
2885	**And, passing othere of weping, Emelye,**	2902	**Thurgh-out the citee, by the maister-strete,**
	And, excelling others in weeping, Emelye,		Throughout the city by the main street,
2886	**The rewfulleste of al the companye.**	2903	**That sprad was al with blak, and wonder hye**
	The most pitiful of all the company.		Which was all spread with black, and wonderfully high
2887	**In as muche as the service sholde be**	2904	**Right of the same is al the strete y-wrye.**
	In order that the ritual should be		The street is covered with exactly the same.
2888	**The more noble and riche in his degree,**	2905	**Up-on the right hond wente old Egeus,**
	The more noble and rich in its degree,		Upon the right hand went old Egeus,
2889	**Duk Theseus leet forth three stedes bringe,**	2906	**And on that other syde duk Theseus,**
	Duke Theseus had three steeds brought forth,		And on that other side duke Theseus,
2890	**That trapped were in steel al gliteringe,**	2907	**With vessels in hir hand of gold ful fyn,**
	That were equipped with trappings of steel all glittering,		With vessels of pure gold in their hands,
2891	**And covered with the armes of daun Arcite.**	2908	**Al ful of hony, milk, and blood, and wyn;**
	And covered with the coat of arms of Don Arcite.		All full of honey, milk, and blood, and wine;
		2909	**Eek Palamon, with ful greet companye;**
			Also Palamon, with a very large company;

2910	**And after that cam woful Emelye,**
	And after that came woeful Emelye,
2911	**With fyr in honde, as was that tyme the gyse,**
	With fire in hand, as was at that time the custom,
2912	**To do thoffice of funeral servyse.**
	To do the office of funeral service.
2913	**Heigh labour, and ful greet apparaillinge**
	Much labor and full great preparation
2914	**Was at the service and the fyr-makinge,**
	Was at the service and the fire-making,
2915	**That with his grene top the heven raughte,**
	Which with its green top reached the heaven,
2916	**And twenty fadme of brede the armes straughte;**
	And twenty fathom of breadth the sides stretched;
2917	**This is to seyn, the bowes were so brode.**
	This is to say, the boughs were so broad.
2918	**Of stree first ther was leyd ful many a lode.**
	There was first laid very many a load of straw.
2919	**But how the fyr was maked up on highte,**
	But how the fire was made on high,
2920	**And eek the names how the treës highte,**
	Nor also the names that the trees are called,
2921	**As ook, firre, birch, asp, alder, holm, popler,**
	Such as oak, fir, birch, aspen, alder, holm oak, poplar,
2922	**Wilow, elm, plane, ash, box, chasteyn, lind, laurer,**
	Willow, elm, plane, ash, box, chestnut, linden, laurel,
2923	**Mapul, thorn, beech, hasel, ew, whippeltree,**
	Maple, thorn, beech, hazel, yew, dogwood,
2924	**How they weren feld, shal nat be told for me;**
	How they were cut down shall not be told by me;
2925	**Ne how the goddes ronnen up and doun,**
	Nor how the gods ran up and down,
2926	**Disherited of hir habitacioun,**
	Disinherited of their habitation,
2927	**In which they woneden in reste and pees,**
	In which they dwelt in rest and peace,
2928	**Nymphes, Faunes, and Amadrides;**
	Nymphs, fawns and hamadryades (wood nymphs);
2929	**Ne how the bestes and the briddes alle**
	Nor how the beasts and the birds all
2930	**Fledden for fere, whan the wode was falle;**
	Fled for fear, when the wood was cut down;
2931	**Ne how the ground agast was of the light,**
	Nor how frightened by the light was the ground,
2932	**That was nat wont to seen the sonne bright;**
	Which was not accustomed to see the bright sun;
2933	**Ne how the fyr was couched first with stree,**
	Nor how the fire was laid first with straw,
2934	**And than with drye stokkes cloven a three,**
	And then with dry branches cut in thirds,
2935	**And than with grene wode and spycerye,**
	And then with green wood and mixtures of spices,
2936	**And than with cloth of gold and with perrye,**
	And then with cloth of gold and with precious stones
2937	**And gerlandes hanging with ful many a flour,**
	And garlands, hanging with full many a flower;
2938	**The mirre, thencens, with al so greet odour;**
	The myrrh, the incense, with such great fragrance;
2939	**Ne how Arcite lay among al this,**
	Nor how Arcite lay among all this,
2940	**Ne what richesse aboute his body is;**
	Nor what richness about his body is;
2941	**Ne how that Emelye, as was the gyse,**
	Nor how Emelye, as was the custom,
2942	**Putte in the fyr of funeral servyse;**
	Lighted the fire of funeral service;

2943	**Ne how she swowned whan men made the fyr,**
	Nor how she swooned when men made the fire,
2944	**Ne what she spak, ne what was hir desyr;**
	Nor what she spoke, nor what was her desire;
2945	**Ne what Ieweles men in the fyr tho caste,**
	Nor what jewels men threw in the fire,
2946	**Whan that the fyr was greet and brente faste;**
	When the fire was great and burned fast;
2947	**Ne how som caste hir sheeld, and som hir spere,**
	Nor how some threw their shields, and some their spears,
2948	**And of hir vestiments, whiche that they were,**
	And of their vestments, which they wore,
2949	**And cuppes ful of wyn, and milk, and blood,**
	And cups full of wine, and milk, and blood,
2950	**Into the fyr, that brente as it were wood;**
	Into the fire, that burned as if it were mad;
2951	**Ne how the Grekes with an huge route**
	Nor how the Greeks, with a huge company,
2952	**Thryës riden al the fyr aboute**
	Thrice ride all the fire about
2953	**Up-on the left hand, with a loud shoutinge,**
	Upon the left hand, with a loud shouting,
2954	**And thryës with hir speres clateringe;**
	And thrice with their spears clattering;
2955	**And thryës how the ladies gonne crye;**
	And thrice how the ladies did cry;
2956	**Ne how that lad was hom-ward Emelye;**
	And how Emelye was led homeward;
2957	**Ne how Arcite is brent to asshen colde;**
	Nor how Arcite is burned to cold ashes;
2958	**Ne how that liche-wake was y-holde**
	Nor how that wake was held
2959	**Al thilke night, ne how the Grekes pleye**
	All that same night; nor how the Greeks play
2960	**The wake-pleyes, ne kepe I nat to seye;**
	The funeral games I care not to say
2961	**Who wrastleth best naked, with oille enoynt,**
	Who wrestles best, naked with oil anointed,
2962	**Ne who that bar him best, in no disioynt.**
	Nor who bore him best, in any difficulty.
2963	**I wol nat tellen eek how that they goon**
	I will not tell also how they go
2964	**Hoom til Athenes, whan the pley is doon;**
	Home to Athens, when the games are done;
2965	**But shortly to the poynt than wol I wende,**
	But shortly to the point then I will go,
2966	**And maken of my longe tale an ende.**
	And make an end of my long tale.
2967	**By processe and by lengthe of certeyn yeres**
	By the course of events and by length of a certain number of years
2968	**Al stinted is the moorning and the teres**
	All stopped is the mourning and the tears
2969	**Of Grekes, by oon general assent.**
	Of the Greeks, by one general assent.
2970	**Than semed me ther was a parlement**
	Then it seemed to me there was a parliament
2971	**At Athenes, up-on certeyn poynts and cas;**
	At Athens, upon certain topics and cases;
2972	**Among the whiche poynts y-spoken was**
	Among which topics was discussed (a proposal)
2973	**To have with certeyn contrees alliaunce,**
	To have alliance with certain countries,
2974	**And have fully of Thebans obeisaunce.**
	And have fully the submission of the Thebans.
2975	**For which this noble Theseus anon**
	For which this noble Theseus immediately
2976	**Leet senden after gentil Palamon,**
	Ordered (someone) to send for gentle Palamon,
2977	**Unwist of him what was the cause and why;**
	Unknown by him (Palamon) what was the cause and why;
2978	**But in his blake clothes sorwefully**
	But in his black clothes sorrowfully

Things Unattempted Yet in Prose or Rhyme 113

2979	**He cam at his comaundement in hye.**	2995	**'Hath stablissed, in this wrecched world adoun,**
	He came at his (Theseus's) commandment in haste.		'Has established in this wretched world below
2980	**Tho sente Theseus for Emelye.**	2996	**Certeyne dayes and duracioun**
	Then Theseus sent for Emelye.		Specific (numbers of) days and (term of) duration
2981	**Whan they were set, and hust was al the place,**	2997	**To al that is engendred in this place,**
	When they were set, and all the place was hushed,		To all that is engendered in this place,
2982	**And Theseus abiden hadde a space**	2998	**Over the whiche day they may nat pace,**
	And Theseus had waited for a while		Beyond the which day they can not pass,
2983	**Er any word cam from his wyse brest,**	2999	**Al mowe they yet tho dayes wel abregge;**
	Before any word came from his wise breast,		Although they may yet well shorten those days;
2984	**His eyen sette he ther as was his lest,**	3000	**Ther needeth non auctoritee allegge,**
	He set his eyes where his object of desire was,		There is no need to cite any written authority,
2985	**And with a sad visage he syked stille,**	3001	**For it is preved by experience,**
	And with a sad face he sighed softly,		For it is proven by experience,
2986	**And after that right thus he seyde his wille.**	3002	**But that me list declaren my sentence.**
	And after that exactly thus he pronounced his decision.		Unless I wish to make my meaning more clear.
2987	**'The firste moevere of the cause above,**	3003	**Than may men by this ordre wel discerne,**
	'The first mover of the first cause above,		Then one can by this order well discern,
2988	**Whan he first made the faire cheyne of love,**	3004	**That thilke moevere stable is and eterne.**
	When he first made the faire chain of love,		That that same mover is stable and eternal.
2989	**Greet was theffect, and heigh was his entente;**	3005	**Wel may men knowe, but it be a fool,**
	Great was the effect, and noble was his plan;		Well may one know, unless it be a fool,
2990	**Wel wiste he why, and what ther-of he mente;**	3006	**That every part deryveth from his hool.**
	Well knew he why, and what thereof he meant;		That every part derives from its whole,
2991	**For with that faire cheyne of love he bond**	3007	**For nature hath nat take his beginning**
	For with that faire chain of love he bound		For nature has not taken its beginning
2992	**The fyr, the eyr, the water, and the lond**	3008	**Of no partye ne cantel of a thing,**
	The fire, the air, the water, and the land		Of no part or portion of a thing,
2993	**In certeyn boundes, that they may nat flee;**	3009	**But of a thing that parfit is and stable,**
	In definite bounds, from which they may not flee;		But of a thing that is complete and stable,
		3010	**Descending so, til it be corrumpable.**
			Descending (from that) until it becomes corruptible.
2994	**That same prince and that moevere,' quod he,**	3011	**And therfore, of his wyse purveyaunce,**
	That same prince and that mover,' said he,		And therefore, by his wise foresight,
		3012	**He hath so wel biset his ordinaunce,**
			He has so well established his plan,
		3013	**That speces of thinges and progressiouns**
			That types of being and natural processes
		3014	**Shullen enduren by successiouns,**
			Shall endure (for a set time) one after another,

3015	**And nat eterne be, with-oute lye:**	3033	**Ther helpeth noght, al goth that ilke weye.**
	And not eternally, without any lie:		Nothing helps there; all goes that same way.
3016	**This maistow understonde and seen at eye.**	3034	**Thanne may I seyn that al this thing moot deye.**
	This thou canst understand and plainly see.		Then may I say that all things must die.
3017	**'Lo the ook, that hath so long a norisshinge**	3035	**What maketh this but Iupiter the king?**
	'Lo the oak, that is so slow to mature,		What causes this but Jupiter, the king,
3018	**From tyme that it first biginneth springe,**	3036	**The which is prince and cause of alle thing,**
	From the time that it first begins to spring,		Who is prince and cause of all things,
3019	**And hath so long a lyf, as we may see,**	3037	**Converting al un-to his propre welle,**
	And has so long a life, as we may see,		Causing all to return to its own origin
3020	**Yet at the laste wasted is the tree.**	3038	**From which it is deryved, sooth to telle.**
	Yet at the last the tree is wasted away.		From which it is derived, to tell the truth?
		3039	**And here-agayns no creature on lyve**
3021	**'Considereth eek, how that the harde stoon**		And against this no living creature,
	'Consider also how the hard stone	3040	**Of no degree availleth for to stryve.**
3022	**Under our feet, on which we trede and goon,**		Of any rank, is helped by striving.
	Under our feet, on which we tread and go,	3041	**'Thanne is it wisdom, as it thinketh me,**
3023	**Yit wasteth it, as it lyth by the weye.**		'Then is it wisdom, as it seems to me,
	Eventually it is worn away as it lies by the way.	3042	**To maken vertu of necessitee,**
3024	**The brode river somtyme wexeth dreye.**		To make virtue of necessity,
	The broad river sometimes grows dry;	3043	**And take it wel, that we may nat eschue,**
3025	**The grete tounes see we wane and wende.**		And take it well what we may not escape,
	We see the great cities grow weak and pass away.	3044	**And namely that to us alle is due.**
3026	**Than may ye see that al this thing hath ende.**		And namely that which is due to us all.
	Then you can see that all things have an end.	3045	**And who-so gruccheth ought, he dooth folye,**
			And whoever complains in any way, he does folly,
3027	**'Of man and womman seen we wel also,**	3046	**And rebel is to him that al may gye.**
	'Of man and woman also we see well,		And is rebel to Him that can rule all.
3028	**That nedeth, in oon of thise termes two,**	3047	**And certeinly a man hath most honour**
	That by necessity, in one of these two periods of time,		And certainly a man has most honor
3029	**This is to seyn, in youthe or elles age,**	3048	**To dyen in his excellence and flour,**
	This is to say, in youth or else in age,		To die in his (time of) excellence and flower,
3030	**He moot ben deed, the king as shal a page;**	3049	**Whan he is siker of his gode name;**
	He must be dead, the king as must a servant boy;		When he is sure of his good name;
3031	**Som in his bed, som in the depe see,**	3050	**Than hath he doon his freend, ne him, no shame.**
	One in his bed, one in the deep sea,		Then he has not done his friend, nor himself, any shame.
3032	**Som in the large feeld, as men may se;**	3051	**And gladder oghte his freend ben of his deeth,**
	One in the large field, as people can see;		And his friend ought to be more pleased with his death,

3052	**Whan with honour up-yolden is his breeth,**	3071	**I rede that we make, of sorwes two,**
	When his breath is yielded up with honor,		I advise that we make of two sorrows
3053	**Than whan his name apalled is for age;**	3072	**O parfyt Ioye, lasting ever-mo;**
	Than when his name is faded because of age;		One perfect joy, lasting evermore.
3054	**For al forgeten is his vasselage.**	3073	**And loketh now, wher most sorwe is her-inne,**
	For all forgotten is his knightly prowess.		And look now, where most sorrow is herein,
3055	**Than is it best, as for a worthy fame,**	3074	**Ther wol we first amenden and biginne.**
	Then is it best, for a worthy fame,		There will we first amend and begin.
3056	**To dyen whan that he is best of name.**		
	To die when he has the most fame.	3075	**'Suster,' quod he, 'this is my fulle assent,**
3057	**The contrarie of al this is wilfulnesse.**		'Sister,' said he, 'this is my full intention,
	The contrary of all this is willfulness.	3076	**With al thavys heer of my parlement,**
3058	**Why grucchen we? why have we hevinesse,**		With all the advice of my parliament here,
	Why do we complain, why do we have sadness,	3077	**That gentil Palamon, your owne knight,**
3059	**That good Arcite, of chivalrye flour**		That gentle Palamon, your own knight,
	That good Arcite, flower of chivalry	3078	**That serveth yow with wille, herte, and might,**
3060	**Departed is, with duetee and honour,**		Who serves you with will, heart, and might,
	Is departed with all due honor,	3079	**And ever hath doon, sin that ye first him knewe,**
3061	**Out of this foule prison of this lyf?**		And ever has done so since you first knew him,
	Out of this foul prison of this life?	3080	**That ye shul, of your grace, up-on him rewe,**
3062	**Why grucchen heer his cosin and his wyf**		That you shall of your grace have pity upon him,
	Why do his cousin and his wife complain here	3081	**And taken him for housbonde and for lord:**
3063	**Of his wel-fare that loved hem so weel?**		And take him for husband and for lord.
	Of the welfare of him, who loved them so well?	3082	**Leen me your hond, for this is our acord.**
3064	**Can he hem thank? nay, God wot, never a deel,**		Lend me your hand, for this is our decision.
	Can he show them his gratitude? Nay, God knows, not a bit;	3083	**Lat see now of your wommanly pitee.**
3065	**That bothe his soule and eek hem-self offende,**		Let your womanly pity now be seen.
	They offend both his soul and themselves as well,	3084	**He is a kinges brother sone, pardee;**
3066	**And yet they mowe hir lustes nat amende.**		He is a king's brother's son, indeed;
	And as yet they may not change their desires.	3085	**And, though he were a povre bacheler,**
			And even if he were a poor young knight,
3067	**'What may I conclude of this longe serie,**	3086	**Sin he hath served yow so many a yeer,**
	'What can I conclude of this long argument,		Since he has served you so many a year,
3068	**But, after wo, I rede us to be merie,**	3087	**And had for yow so greet adversitee,**
	But after woe I advise us to be merry		And has had for you such great adversity,
3069	**And thanken Iupiter of al his grace?**	3088	**It moste been considered, leveth me;**
	And thank Jupiter for all his grace?		It must be taken in account, believe me,
3070	**And, er that we departen from this place,**	3089	**For gentil mercy oghte to passen right.'**
	And before we depart from this place,		For gentle mercy ought to prevail over justice.'

3090 **Than seyde he thus to Palamon ful right;**
Then said he thus to Palamon the knight:

3091 **'I trowe ther nedeth litel sermoning**
'I suppose little preaching is needed here

3092 **To make yow assente to this thing.**
To make you assent to this thing.

3093 **Com neer, and tak your lady by the hond.'**
Come near, and take your lady by the hand.'

3094 **Bitwixen hem was maad anon the bond,**
Between them was made right away the bond

3095 **That highte matrimoine or mariage,**
That is called matrimony or marriage,

3096 **By al the counseil and the baronage.**
By all the council and the baronage.

3097 **And thus with alle blisse and melodye**
And thus with all bliss and festivity

3098 **Hath Palamon y-wedded Emelye.**
Palamon has wedded Emelye.

3099 **And God, that al this wyde world hath wroght,**
And God, who has made all this wide world,

3100 **Sende him his love, that hath it dere a-boght.**
Send him his love who has dearly paid for it;

3101 **For now is Palamon in alle wele,**
For now is Palamon in complete happiness,

3102 **Living in blisse, in richesse, and in hele;**
Living in bliss, in riches, and in health,

3103 **And Emelye him loveth so tendrely,**
And Emelye loves him so tenderly,

3104 **And he hir serveth al-so gentilly,**
And he serves her so gently,

3105 **That never was ther no word hem bitwene**
That never was there any word between them

3106 **Of Ielousye, or any other tene.**
Of jealousy or any other vexation.

3107 **Thus endeth Palamon and Emelye;**
Thus ends Palamon and Emelye;

3108 **And God save al this faire compaignye! Amen.**
And God save all this fair company! Amen.

Heere is ended the Knightes Tale

Canterbury Tales:
The Wife of Bath Prologue

Geoffrey Chaucer

The Prologe of the Wyves Tale of Bathe

1 **'Experience, though noon auctoritee**
'Experience, though no written authority

2 **Were in this world, were right y-nough to me**
Were in this world, is good enough for me

3 **To speke of wo that is in mariage;**
To speak of the woe that is in marriage;

4 **For, lordinges, sith I twelf yeer was of age,**
For, gentlemen, since I was twelve years of age,

5 **Thonked be god that is eterne on lyve,**
Thanked be God who is eternally alive,

6 **Housbondes at chirche-dore I have had fyve;**
I have had five husbands at the church door;

Geoffrey Chaucer; Walter W. Skeat, ed., "The Wife of Bath's Prologue & Tale," *The Complete Works of Geoffrey Chaucer*, vol. 4. Copyright in the Public Domain.

Geoffrey Chaucer; Larry D. Benson, trans., *The Wife of Bath's Prologue & Tale: An Interlinear Translation,* from http://www.courses.fas.harvard.edu/~chaucer/teachslf/wbt-par.htm,. Copyright © 2008 by The President and Fellows of Harvard College. Permission to reprint granted by the publisher.

7	**For I so ofte have y-wedded be;**	28	**God bad us for to wexe and multiplye;**
	If I so often might have been wedded;		God commanded us to grow fruitful and multiply;
8	**And alle were worthy men in hir degree.**	29	**That gentil text can I wel understonde.**
	And all were worthy men in their way.		That gentle text I can well understand.
9	**But me was told certeyn, nat longe agon is,**	30	**Eek wel I woot he seyde, myn housbonde**
	But to me it was told, certainly, it is not long ago,		Also I know well, he said my husband
10	**That sith that Crist ne wente never but onis**	31	**Sholde lete fader and moder, and take me;**
	That since Christ went never but once		Should leave father and mother and take to me.
11	**To wedding in the Cane of Galilee,**	32	**But of no nombre mencioun made he,**
	To a wedding, in the Cana of Galilee,		But he made no mention of number,
12	**That by the same ensample taughte he me**	33	**Of bigamye or of octogamye;**
	That by that same example he taught me		Of marrying two, or of marrying eight;
13	**That I ne sholde wedded be but ones.**	34	**Why sholde men speke of it vileinye?**
	That I should be wedded but once.		Why should men then speak evil of it?
14	**Herke eek, lo! which a sharp word for the nones**	35	**Lo, here the wyse king, dan Salomon;**
	Listen also, lo, what a sharp word for this purpose		Lo, (consider) here the wise king, dan Salomon;
15	**Besyde a welle Iesus, god and man,**	36	**I trowe he hadde wyves mo than oon;**
	Beside a well, Jesus, God and man,		I believe he had wives more than one.
16	**Spak in repreve of the Samaritan:**	37	**As, wolde god, it leveful were to me**
	Spoke in reproof of the Samaritan:		As would God it were lawful unto me
17	**"Thou hast y-had fyve housbondes," quod he,**	38	**To be refresshed half so ofte as he!**
	"Thou hast had five husbands," he said,		To be refreshed half so often as he!
18	**"And thilke man, the which that hath now thee,**	39	**Which yifte of god hadde he for alle his wyvis!**
	"And that same man that now has thee		What a gift of God he had because of all his wives!
19	**Is noght thyn housbond;" thus seyde he certeyn;**	40	**No man hath swich, that in this world alyve is.**
	Is not thy husband;" thus he said certainly		No man that in this world is alive has such (a gift).
20	**What that he mente ther-by, I can nat seyn;**	41	**God woot, this noble king, as to my wit,**
	What he meant by this, I can not say;		God knows, this noble king, according to my judgment,
21	**But that I axe, why that the fifthe man**	42	**The firste night had many a mery fit**
	But I ask, why the fifth man		The first night had many a merry fit
22	**Was noon housbond to the Samaritan?**	43	**With ech of hem, so wel was him on lyve!**
	Was no husband to the Samaritan?		With each of them, so well things went for him in his lifetime.
23	**How manye mighte she have in mariage?**	44	**Blessed be god that I have wedded fyve!**
	How many might she have in marriage?		Blessed be God that I have wedded five!
24	**Yet herde I never tellen in myn age**	44a	**[Of whiche I have pyked out the beste,**
	I never yet heard tell in my lifetime		[Of which I have picked out the best,
25	**Upon this nombre diffinicioun;**	44b	**Bothe of here nether purs and of here cheste.**
	A definition of this number.		Both of their lower purse (scrotum) and of their strongbox.
26	**Men may devyne and glosen up and doun.**		
	Men may conjecture and interpret in every way,		
27	**But wel I woot expres, with-oute lye,**		
	But well I know, expressly, without lie,		

44c	Diverse scoles maken parfyt clerkes,	62	Or wher comanded he virginitee?
	Differing schools make perfect clerks,		Or where commanded he virginity?
44d	And diverse practyk in many sondry werkes	63	I woot as wel as ye, it is no drede,
	And differing practice in many various works		I know as well as you, it is no doubt,
44e	Maketh the werkman parfyt sekirly;	64	Thapostel, whan he speketh of maydenhede;
	Makes the workman truly perfect;		The apostle, when he speaks of maidenhood;
44f	Of fyve husbondes scoleiyng am I.]	65	He seyde, that precept ther-of hadde he noon.
	Of five husbands' schooling am I.]		He said that he had no precept concerning it.
45	Welcome the sixte, whan that evere he shal.	66	Men may conseille a womman to been oon,
	Welcome the sixte, whan that ever he shal.		Men may advise a woman to be one,
46	For sothe, I wol nat kepe me chast in al;	67	But conseilling is no comandement;
	For truly, I will not keep myself chaste in everything;		But advice is no commandment;
47	Whan myn housbond is fro the world y-gon,	68	He putte it in our owene Iugement.
	When my husband is gone from the world,		He left it to our own judgment.
48	Som Cristen man shal wedde me anon;	69	For hadde god comanded maydenhede,
	Some Christian man shall wed me straightway;		For had God commanded maidenhood,
49	For thanne thapostle seith, that I am free	70	Thanne hadde he dampned wedding with the dede;
	For then the apostle says that I am free		Then had he damned marriage along with the act (of procreation);
50	To wedde, a goddes half, wher it lyketh me.	71	And certes, if ther were no seed y-sowe,
	To wed, by God's side (I swear), wherever it pleases me.		And certainly, if there were no seed sown,
51	He seith that to be wedded is no sinne;	72	Virginitee, wher-of than sholde it growe?
	He says that to be wedded is no sin;		Then from what should virginity grow?
52	Bet is to be wedded than to brinne.	73	Poul dorste nat comanden atte leste
	It is better to be wedded than to burn.		In any case, Paul dared not command
53	What rekketh me, thogh folk seye vileinye	74	A thing of which his maister yaf noon heste.
	What do I care, though folk speak evil		A thing of which his master gave no command.
54	Of shrewed Lameth and his bigamye?	75	The dart is set up for virginitee;
	Of cursed Lamech and his bigamy?		The prize is set up for virginity;
55	I woot wel Abraham was an holy man,	76	Cacche who so may, who renneth best lat see.
	I know well Abraham was a holy man,		Catch it whoever can, let's see who runs best.
56	And Iacob eek, as ferforth as I can;		
	And Jacob also, insofar as I know;	77	But this word is nat take of every wight,
57	And ech of hem hadde wyves mo than two;		But this word does not apply to every person,
	And each of them had more than two wives,	78	But ther as god list give it of his might.
58	And many another holy man also.		But where God desires to give it by his power.
	And many another holy man also.	79	I woot wel, that thapostel was a mayde;
59	Whan saugh ye ever, in any maner age,		I know well that the apostle was a virgin;
	Where can you find, in any historical period,	80	But natheless, thogh that he wroot and sayde,
60	That hye god defended mariage		But nonetheless, though he wrote and said
	That high God forbad marriage		
61	By expres word? I pray you, telleth me;		
	By express word? I pray you, tell me.		

81	**He wolde that every wight were swich as he,**	101	**Somme been of tree, and doon hir lord servyse.**
	He would that every person were such as he,		Some are of wood, and do their lord service.
82	**Al nis but conseil to virginitee;**	102	**God clepeth folk to him in sondry wyse,**
	All is nothing but advice to (adopt) virginity.		God calls folk to him in various ways,
83	**And for to been a wyf, he yaf me leve**	103	**And everich hath of god a propre yifte,**
	And he gave me leave to be a wife		And each one has of God an individual gift,
84	**Of indulgence; so it is no repreve**	104	**Som this, som that,—as him lyketh shifte.**
	By explicit permission; so it is not blameful		Some this, some that, as it pleases Him to provide.
85	**To wedde me, if that my make dye,**	105	**Virginitee is greet perfeccioun,**
	To wed me, if my mate should die,		Virginity is great perfection,
86	**With-oute excepcioun of bigamye.**	106	**And continence eek with devocioun.**
	Without objection on the grounds of bigamy.		And continence also with devotion,
87	**Al were it good no womman for to touche,**	107	**But Crist, that of perfeccioun is welle,**
	Although it would be good to touch no woman,		But Christ, who is the source of perfection,
88	**He mente as in his bed or in his couche;**	108	**Bad nat every wight he shold go selle**
	He meant in his bed or in his couch;		Did not command that every one should go sell
89	**For peril is bothe fyr and tow tassemble;**	109	**All that he hadde, and give it to the pore,**
	For it is perilous to assemble both fire and flax;		All that he had, and give it to the poor,
90	**Ye knowe what this ensample may resemble.**	110	**And in swich wyse folwe hime and his fore.**
	You know what this example may apply to.		And in such wise follow him and his footsteps.
91	**This is al and som, he heeld virginitee**	111	**He spak to hem that wolde live parfitly;**
	This is the sum of it: he held virginity		He spoke to those who would live perfectly;
92	**More parfit than wedding in freletee.**	112	**And lordinges, by your leve, that am nat I.**
	More perfect than wedding in weakness.		And gentlemen, by your leave, I am not that.
93	**Freeltee clepe I, but-if that he and she**	113	**I wol bistowe the flour of al myn age**
	Weakness I call it, unless he and she		I will bestow the flower of all my age
94	**Wolde leden al hir lyf in chastitee.**	114	**In the actes and in fruit of mariage.**
	Would lead all their life in chastity.		In the acts and in fruit of marriage.
95	**I graunte it wel, I have noon envye,**	115	**Telle me also, to what conclusioun**
	I grant it well; I have no envy,		Tell me also, to what purpose
96	**Thogh maydenhede preferre bigamye;**	116	**Were membres maad of generacioun,**
	Though maidenhood may have precedence over a second marriage;		Were members of generation made,
97	**Hem lyketh to be clene, body and goost,**	117	**And for what profit was a wight y-wroght?**
	It pleases them to be clean, body and spirit;		And by so perfectly wise a Workman wrought?
98	**Of myn estaat I nil nat make no boost.**	118	**Trusteth right wel, they wer nat maad for noght.**
	Of my state I will make no boast,		Trust right well, they were not made for nothing.
99	**For wel ye knowe, a lord in his houshold,**		
	For well you know, a lord in his household,		
100	**He hath nat every vessel al of gold;**		
	He has not every utensil all of gold;		

119	**Glose who-so wole, and seye bothe up and doun,**	139	**Crist was a mayde, and shapen as a man,**
	Interpret whoever will, and say both up and down,		Christ was a virgin and shaped like a man,
120	**That they were maked for purgacioun**	140	**And many a seint, sith that the world bigan,**
	That they were made for purgation		And many a saint, since the world began;
121	**Of urine, and our bothe thinges smale**	141	**Yet lived they ever in parfit chastitee.**
	Of urine, and both our small things		Yet lived they ever in perfect chastity.
122	**Were eek to knowe a femele from a male,**	142	**I nil envye no virginitee;**
	Were also to know a female from a male,		I will envy no virginity;
123	**And for noone other cause: sey ye no?**	143	**Lat hem be breed of pured whete-seed,**
	And for no other cause: do you say no?		Let them be bread of pure wheat-seed,
124	**The experience woot wel it is noght so;**	144	**And lat us wyves hoten barly-breed;**
	The experience knows well it is not so;		And let us wives be called barley-bread;
125	**So that the clerkes be nat with me wrothe,**	145	**And yet with barly-breed, Mark telle can,**
	Provided that the clerks be not angry with me,		And yet with barley-bread, Mark can tell it,
126	**I sey this, that they maked been for bothe,**	146	**Our lord Iesu refresshed many a man.**
	I say this: that they are made for both;		Our Lord Jesus refreshed many a man.
127	**This is to seye, for office, and for ese**	147	**In swich estaat as god hath cleped us**
	That is to say, for urination and for ease		In such estate as God has called us
128	**Of engendrure, ther we nat god displese.**	148	**I wol persevere, I nam nat precious.**
	Of procreation, in which we do not displease God.		I will persevere; I am not fussy.
129	**Why sholde men elles in hir bokes sette,**	149	**In wyfhode I wol use myn instrument**
	Why else should men set in their books,		In wifehood I will use my instrument
130	**That man shal yelde to his wyf hir dette?**	150	**As frely as my maker hath it sent.**
	That man shall pay to his wife her debt?		As freely as my Maker has it sent.
131	**Now wher-with sholde he make his payement,**	151	**If I be daungerous, god yeve me sorwe!**
	Now with what should he make his payment,		If I be niggardly, God give me sorrow!
132	**If he ne used his sely instrument?**	152	**Myn housbond shal it have bothe eve and morwe,**
	If he did not use his blessed instrument?		My husband shall have it both evenings and mornings,
133	**Than were they maad up-on a creature,**	153	**Whan that him list com forth and paye his dette.**
	Then were they made upon a creature,		When it pleases him to come forth and pay his debt.
134	**To purge uryne, and eek for engendrure.**	154	**An housbonde I wol have, I nil nat lette,**
	To purge urine, and also for procreation.		A husband I will have, I will not desist,
135	**But I seye noght that every wight is holde,**	155	**Which shal be bothe my dettour and my thral,**
	But I say not that every person is required,		Who shall be both my debtor and my slave,
136	**That hath swich harneys as I to yow tolde,**	156	**And have his tribulacioun with-al**
	That has such equipment as I to you told,		And have his suffering also
137	**To goon and usen hem in engendrure;**	157	**Up-on his flessh, whyl that I am his wyf.**
	To go and use them in procreation.		Upon his flesh, while I am his wife.
138	**Than sholde men take of chastitee no cure.**	158	**I have the power duringe al my lyf**
	Then should men have no regard for chastity.		I have the power during all my life
		159	**Up-on his propre body, and noght he.**
			Over his own body, and not he.

160 **Right thus the apostel tolde it un-to me;**
Right thus the Apostle told it unto me,

161 **And bad our housbondes for to love us weel.**
And commanded our husbands to love us well.

162 **Al this sentence me lyketh every-deel'—**
All this sentence pleases me every bit"—

163 **Up sterte the Pardoner, and that anon,**
Up sprang the Pardoner, and that at once;

164 **'Now dame,' quod he, 'by god and by seint Iohn,**
'Now, madam,' he said, 'by God and by Saint John!

165 **Ye been a noble prechour in this cas!**
You are a noble preacher in this case.

166 **I was aboute to wedde a wyf; allas!**
I was about to wed a wife; alas!

167 **What sholde I bye it on my flesh so dere?**
Why should I pay for it so dearly on my flesh?

168 **Yet hadde I lever wedde no wyf to-yere!'**
Yet would I rather wed no wife this year!'

169 **'Abyde!' quod she, 'my tale is nat bigonne;**
'Wait!' she said, 'my tale is not begun.

170 **Nay, thou shalt drinken of another tonne**
Nay, thou shalt drink from another barrel,

171 **Er that I go, shal savoure wors than ale.**
Before I go, which shall taste worse than ale.

172 **And whan that I have told thee forth my tale**
And when I have told thee forth my tale

173 **Of tribulacioun in mariage,**
Of suffering in marriage,

174 **Of which I am expert in al myn age,**
Of which I am expert in all my life,

175 **This to seyn, my-self have been the whippe;—**
This is to say, myself have been the whip;—

176 **Than maystow chese whether thou wolt sippe**
Than may thou choose whether thou will sip

177 **Of thilke tonne that I shal abroche.**
Of that same barrel that I shall open.

178 **Be war of it, er thou to ny approche;**
Beware of it, before thou too near approach;

179 **For I shal telle ensamples mo than ten.**
For I shall tell examples more than ten.

180 **Who-so that nil be war by othere men,**
Whoever will not be warned by (the examples of) other men,

181 **By him shul othere men corrected be.**
Shall be an example by which other men shall be corrected.

182 **The same wordes wryteth Ptholomee;**
The same words writes Ptholomy;

183 **Rede in his Almageste, and take it there.'**
Read in his Almagest, and take it there.'

184 **'Dame, I wolde praye yow, if your wil it were,'**
'Madam, I would pray you, if it were your will,'

185 **Seyde this Pardoner, 'as ye bigan,**
Said this Pardoner, 'as you began,

186 **Telle forth your tale, spareth for no man,**
Tell forth your tale, refrain for no man,

187 **And teche us yonge men of your praktike.'**
And teach us young men of your practice.'

188 **'Gladly,' quod she, 'sith it may yow lyke.**
'Gladly,' she said, 'since it may please you;

189 **But yet I praye to al this companye,**
But yet I pray to all this company,

190 **If that I speke after my fantasye,**
If I speak according to my fancy,

191 **As taketh not a-grief of that I seye;**
Do not be annoyed by what I say,

192 **For myn entente nis but for to pleye.**
For my intention is only to amuse.

193 **Now sires, now wol I telle forth my tale.—**
Now, sir, now will I tell forth my tale.—

194 **As ever mote I drinken wyn or ale,**
As ever may I drink wine or ale,

195 **I shal seye sooth, tho housbondes that I hadde,**
I shall speak the truth; those husbands that I had,

196	**As three of hem were gode and two were badde.**	216	**That many a night they songen 'weilawey!'**
	Three of them were good, and two were bad.		That many a night they sang 'Woe is me!'
197	**The three men were gode, and riche, and olde;**	217	**The bacoun was nat fet for hem, I trowe,**
	The three were good men, and rich, and old;		The bacon was not fetched for them, I believe,
198	**Unnethe mighte they the statut holde**	218	**That som men han in Essex at Dunmowe.**
	Hardly might they the statute hold (pay the debt)		That some men have in Essex at Dunmowe.
199	**In which that they were bounden un-to me.**	219	**I governed hem so wel, after my lawe,**
	In which they were bound unto me.		I governed them so well, according to my law,
200	**Ye woot wel what I mene of this, pardee!**	220	**That ech of hem ful blisful was and fawe**
	You know well what I mean of this, by God!		That each of them was very blissful and eager
201	**As help me God, I laughe whan I thinke**	221	**To bringe me gaye thinges fro the fayre.**
	So help me God, I laugh when I think		To bring me gay things from the fair.
202	**How pitously a-night I made hem swinke;**	222	**They were ful glad whan I spak to hem fayre;**
	How pitifully at night I made them work!		They were very glad when I spoke to them pleasantly,
203	**And by my fey, I tolde of it no stoor.**	223	**For God it woot, I chidde hem spitously.**
	And, by my faith, I set no store by it.		For, God knows it, I cruelly scolded them.
204	**They had me yeven hir gold and hir tresoor;**		
	They had given me their land and their treasure;	224	**Now herkneth, how I bar me proprely,**
205	**Me neded nat do lenger diligence**		Now listen how well I conducted myself,
	I needed not work hard any longer	225	**Ye wyse wyves, that can understonde.**
206	**To winne hir love, or doon hem reverence.**		You wise wives, that can understand.
	To win their love, or do them reverence.		
207	**They loved me so wel, by god above,**	226	**Thus shul ye speke and bere hem wrong on honde;**
	They loved me so well, by God above,		Thus should you speak and accuse them wrongfully;
208	**That I ne tolde no deyntee of hir love!**	227	**For half so boldely can ther no man**
	That I reckoned little of their love!		For half so boldly can there no man
209	**A wys womman wol sette hir ever in oon**	228	**Swere and lyen as a womman can.**
	A wise woman will be constantly busy		Swear and lie, as a woman can.
210	**To gete hir love, ther as she hath noon.**	229	**I sey nat this by wyves that ben wyse,**
	To get their love, yes, when she has none.		I do not say this concerning wives that are wise,
211	**But sith I hadde hem hoolly in myn hond,**	230	**But-if it be whan they hem misavyse.**
	But since I had them wholly in my hand,		Unless it be when they are ill advised.
212	**And sith they hadde me yeven all hir lond,**	231	**A wys wyf, if that she can hir good,**
	And since they had me given all their land,		A wise wife, if she knows what is good for her,
213	**What sholde I taken hede hem for to plese,**	232	**Shal beren him on hond the cow is wood,**
	Why should I take care to please them,		Shall deceive him by swearing the bird is crazy,
214	**But it were for my profit and myn ese?**		
	Unless it were for my profit and my pleasure?		
215	**I sette hem so a-werke, by my fey,**		
	I set them so to work, by my faith,		

233	**And take witnesse of hir owene mayde**	254	**Thou seyst that every holour wol hir have;**
	And prove it by taking witness of her own maid		Thou sayest that every lecher wants to have her;
234	**Of hir assent; but herkneth how I sayde.**	255	**She may no whyle in chastitee abyde,**
	Who is in league with her. But listen how I spoke:		She can not remain chaste for any length of time,
		256	**That is assailled up-on ech a syde.**
235	**'Sir olde kaynard, is this thyn array?**		Who is assailed on every side.
	'Sir old doddering fool, is this thy doing?		
236	**Why is my neighebores wyf so gay?**	257	**Thou seyst, som folk desyre us for richesse,**
	Why is my neighbor's wife so gay?		Thou sayest some folk desire us for riches,
237	**She is honoured over-al ther she goth;**	258	**Somme for our shap, and somme for our fairnesse;**
	She is honored everywhere she goes;		Some for our shape, and some for our fairness;
238	**I sitte at hoom, I have no thrifty cloth.**	259	**And som, for she can outher singe or daunce,**
	I sit at home; I have no decent clothing.		And one because she can either sing or dance,
239	**What dostow at my neighebores hous?**	260	**And som, for gentillesse and daliaunce;**
	What dost thou at my neighbor's house?		And some because of noble descent and flirtatious talk;
240	**Is she so fair? artow so amorous?**	261	**Som, for hir handes and hir armes smale;**
	Is she so fair? Art thou so amorous?		Some because of their hands and their slender arms;
241	**What rowne ye with our mayde?** *benedicite!*	262	**Thus goth al to the devel by thy tale.**
	What do you whisper with our maid? Bless me!		Thus goes all to the devil, according to you.
242	**Sir olde lechour, lat thy Iapes be!**	263	**Thou seyst, men may nat kepe a castel-wal;**
	Sir old lecher, let thy tricks be!		Thou sayest men may not defend a castle wall,
243	**And if I have a gossib or a freend,**	264	**It may so longe assailled been over-al.**
	And if I have a close friend or an acquaintance,		It may so long be assailed on all sides.
244	**With-outen gilt, thou chydest as a feend,**		
	Innocently, thou scold like a fiend,	265	**And if that she be foul, thou seist that she**
245	**If that I walke or pleye un-to his hous!**		And if she be ugly, thou sayest that she
	If I walk or go unto his house to amuse myself!	266	**Coveiteth every man that she may se;**
246	**Thou comest hoom as dronken as a mous,**		Covets every man that she may see;
	Thou comest home as drunk as a mouse,	267	**For as a spaynel she wol on him lepe,**
247	**And prechest on thy bench, with yvel preef!**		For like a spaniel she will on him leap,
	And preach on thy bench, bad luck to you!	268	**Til that she finde som man hir to chepe;**
248	**Thou seist to me, it is a greet meschief**		Until she find some man to buy (take) her;
	Thou sayest to me it is a great misfortune	269	**Ne noon so grey goos goth ther in the lake,**
249	**To wedde a povre womman, for costage;**		Nor does any goose go there in the lake, no matter how drab,
	To wed a poor woman, because of expense;	270	**As, seistow, that wol been with-oute make.**
250	**And if that she be riche, of heigh parage,**		That, thou sayest, will be without a mate.
	And if she be rich, of high birth,		
251	**Than seistow that it is a tormentrye**		
	Then thou sayest that it is a torment		
252	**To suffre hir pryde and hir malencolye.**		
	To put up with her pride and her angry moods.		
253	**And if that she be fair, thou verray knave,**		
	And if she be fair, thou utter knave,		

271 **And seyst, it is an hard thing for to welde**
And thou sayest it is a hard thing to control

272 **A thing that no man wol, his thankes, helde.**
A thing that no man will, willingly, hold.

273 **Thus seistow, lorel, whan thow goost to bedde;**
Thus sayest thou, scoundrel, when thou goest to bed;

274 **And that no wys man nedeth for to wedde,**
And that no wise man needs to wed,

275 **Ne no man that entendeth un-to hevene.**
Nor any man that hopes (to go) to heaven.

276 **With wilde thonder-dint and firy levene**
With wild thunder-bolt and fiery lightning

277 **Mote thy welked nekke be to-broke!**
May thy wrinkled neck be broken in pieces!

278 **Thow seyst that dropping houses, and eek smoke,**
Thou sayest that leaky houses, and also smoke,

279 **And chyding wyves, maken men to flee**
And scolding wives make men to flee

280 **Out of hir owene hous; a! *benedicite*!**
Out of their own houses; ah, bless me!

281 **What eyleth swich an old man for to chyde?**
What ails such an old man to chide like that?

282 **Thow seyst, we wyves wol our vyces hyde**
Thou sayest we wives will hide our vices

283 **Til we be fast, and than we wol hem shewe;**
Until we be securely tied (in marriage), and then we will them show;

284 **Wel may that be a proverbe of a shrewe!**
Well may that be a proverb of a scoundrel!

285 **Thou seist, that oxen, asses, hors, and houndes,**
Thou sayest that oxen, asses, horses, and hounds,

286 **They been assayed at diverse stoundes;**
They are tried out a number of times;

287 **Bacins, lavours, er that men hem bye,**
Basins, wash bowls, before men them buy,

288 **Spones and stoles, and al swich housbondrye,**
Spoons and stools, and all such household items,

289 **And so been pottes, clothes, and array;**
And so are pots, clothes, and adornments;

290 **But folk of wyves maken noon assay**
But folk of wives make no trial

291 **Til they be wedded; olde dotard shrewe!**
Until they are wedded; old doddering scoundrel!

292 **And than, seistow, we wol oure vices shewe.**
And then, sayest thou, we will show our vices.

293 **Thou seist also, that it displeseth me**
Thou sayest also that it displeases me

294 **But-if that thou wolt preyse my beautee,**
Unless thou will praise my beauty,

295 **And but thou poure alwey up-on my face,**
And unless thou peer always upon my face,

296 **And clepe me "faire dame" in every place;**
And call me "dear lady" in every place.

297 **And but thou make a feste on thilke day**
And unless thou make a feast on that same day

298 **That I was born, and make me fresh and gay,**
That I was born, and make me happy and gay,

299 **And but thou do to my norice honour,**
And unless thou do honor to my nurse,

300 **And to my chamberere with-inne my bour,**
And to my chambermaid within my bedchamber,

301 **And to my fadres folk and his allyes;—**
And to my father's folk and his allies;—

302 **Thus seistow, olde barel ful of lyes!**
Thus sayest thou, old barrelful of lies!

303 **And yet of our apprentice Ianekyn,**
And yet of our apprentice Janekin,

304 **For his crisp heer, shyninge as gold so fyn,**
Because of his curly hair, shining like gold so fine,

305 **And for he squiereth me bothe up and doun,**
And because he familiarly attends me everywhere,

306	**Yet hastow caught a fals suspecioun;**	322	**Wher that we goon, we wol ben at our large.**
	Yet hast thou caught a false suspicion;		Where we go; we will be free (to do as we wish).
307	**I wol hym noght, thogh thou were deed to-morwe.**	323	**Of alle men y-blessed moot he be,**
	I do not want him, though thou were dead tomorrow.		Of all men blessed may he be,
308	**But tel me this, why hydestow, with sorwe,**	324	**The wyse astrologien Dan Ptholome,**
	But tell me this, why hidest thou, bad luck to you,		The wise astrologer, Dan Ptolemy,
309	**The keyes of thy cheste awey fro me?**	325	**That seith this proverbe in his Almageste,**
	The keys of thy strongbox away from me?		Who says this proverb in his Almagest,
310	**It is my good as wel as thyn, pardee.**	326	**"Of alle men his wisdom is the hyeste,**
	It is my property as well as thine, by God!		"Of all men his wisdom is the highest
311	**What wenestow make an idiot of our dame?**	327	**That rekketh never who hath the world in honde."**
	What, think thou to make a fool of the lady of the house?		Who never cares who has the world in his control."
312	**Now by that lord, that called is seint Iame,**	328	**By this proverbe thou shalt understonde,**
	Now by that lord that is called Saint James,		By this proverb thou shalt understand,
313	**Thou shalt nat bothe, thogh that thou were wood,**	329	**Have thou y-nogh, what thar thee recche or care**
	Thou shalt not both, though thou were crazy with anger,		If thou have enough, why should thou take note or care
314	**Be maister of my body and of my good;**	330	**How merily that othere folkes fare?**
	Be master of my body and of my property;		How merrily other folks fare?
315	**That oon thou shalt forgo, maugree thyne yën;**	331	**For certeyn, olde dotard, by your leve,**
	One of them thou must give up, despite anything you can do;		For, certainly, old senile fool, by your leave,
316	**What nedeth thee of me to enquere or spyën?**	332	**Ye shul have queynte right y-nough at eve.**
	What helps it to inquire about me or spy?		You shall have pudendum right enough at eve.
317	**I trowe, thou woldest loke me in thy chiste!**	333	**He is to greet a nigard that wol werne**
	I believe thou would lock me in thy strongbox!		He is too great a miser that would refuse
318	**Thou sholdest seye, "wyf, go wher thee liste,**	334	**A man to lighte his candle at his lanterne;**
	Thou should say, "Wife, go where you please,		A man to light a candle at his lantern;
319	**Tak your disport, I wol nat leve no talis;**	335	**He shal have never the lasse light, pardee;**
	Enjoy yourself; I will not believe any gossip;		He shall have never the less light, by God.
320	**I knowe yow for a trewe wyf, dame Alis."**	336	**Have thou y-nough, thee thar nat pleyne thee.**
	I know you for a true wife, dame Alys."		If thou have enough, thou need not complain.
321	**We love no man that taketh kepe or charge**	337	**Thou seyst also, that if we make us gay**
	We love no man who takes notice or concern about		Thou sayest also, that if we make ourselves gay
		338	**With clothing and with precious array,**
			With clothing, and with precious adornments,

339	That it is peril of our chastitee;		
	That it is dangerous to our chastity;		
340	And yet, with sorwe, thou most enforce thee,		
	And yet—bad luck to thee!—thou must reinforce thy argument,		
341	And seye thise wordes in the apostles name,		
	And say these words in the Apostle's name:		

339 That it is peril of our chastitee;
   That it is dangerous to our chastity;
340 And yet, with sorwe, thou most enforce thee,
   And yet—bad luck to thee!—thou must reinforce thy argument,
341 And seye thise wordes in the apostles name,
   And say these words in the Apostle's name:
342 "In habit, maad with chastitee and shame,
   "In clothing made with chastity and shame
343 Ye wommen shul apparaille yow," quod he,
   You women shall apparel yourselves," he said,
344 "And noght in tressed heer and gay perree,
   "And not in carefully arranged hair and gay precious stones,
345 As perles, ne with gold, ne clothes riche;"
   Such as pearls, nor with gold, nor rich cloth;"
346 After thy text, ne after thy rubriche
   In accordance with thy text, nor in accord with thy interpretation,
347 I wol nat wirche as muchel as a gnat.
   I will not do as much as a gnat.

348 Thou seydest this, that I was lyk a cat;
   Thou said this, that I was like a cat;
349 For who-so wolde senge a cattes skin,
   For if anyone would singe a cat's skin,
350 Thanne wolde the cat wel dwellen in his in;
   Then would the cat well stay in his dwelling;
351 And if the cattes skin be slyk and gay,
   And if the cat's skin be sleek and gay,
352 She wol nat dwelle in house half a day,
   She will not stay in house half a day,
353 But forth she wole, er any day be dawed,
   But forth she will (go), before any day be dawned,
354 To shewe hir skin, and goon a-caterwawed;
   To show her skin and go yowling like a cat in heat.
355 This is to seye, if I be gay, sir shrewe,
   This is to say, if I be well dressed, sir scoundrel,
356 I wol renne out, my borel for to shewe.
   I will run out to show my poor clothes.

357 Sire olde fool, what eyleth thee to spyën?
   Sir old fool, what help is it for thee to spy?
358 Thogh thou preye Argus, with his hundred yën,
   Though thou pray Argus with his hundred eyes,
359 To be my warde-cors, as he can best,
   To be my bodyguard, as he best knows how,
360 In feith, he shal nat kepe me but me lest;
   In faith, he shall not keep me but as I please;
361 Yet coude I make his berd, so moot I thee.
   Yet could I deceive him, as I may prosper!

362 Thou seydest eek, that ther ben thinges three,
   Thou said also that there are three things,
363 The whiche thinges troublen al this erthe,
   The which things trouble all this earth,
364 And that no wight ne may endure the ferthe;
   And that no one can endure the fourth.
365 O leve sir shrewe, Iesu shorte thy lyf!
   O dear sir scoundrel, Jesus shorten thy life!
366 Yet prechestow, and seyst, an hateful wyf
   Yet thou preachest and sayest a hateful wife
367 Y-rekened is for oon of thise meschances.
   Is reckoned as one of these misfortunes.
368 Been ther none othere maner resemblances
   Are there no other sorts of comparisons
369 That ye may lykne your parables to,
   That you can use in your sayings,
370 But-if a sely wyf be oon of tho?
   Without a poor wife's being one of them?

371 Thou lykenest wommanes love to helle,
   Thou also compare women's love to hell,
372 To bareyne lond, ther water may not dwelle.
   To barren land, where water may not remain.
373 Thou lyknest it also to wilde fyr;
   Thou compare it also to Greek (inextinguishable) fire;
374 The more it brenneth, the more it hath desyr
   The more it burns, the more it has desire

375	**To consume every thing that brent wol be.**	394	**Whan that for syk unnethes mighte he stonde.**
	To consume every thing that will be burned.		When for sickness they could hardly stand.
376	**Thou seyst, that right as wormes shende a tree,**	395	**Yet tikled it his herte, for that he**
	Thou sayest, just as worms destroy a tree,		Yet I tickled his heart, for he
377	**Right so a wyf destroyeth hir housbonde;**	396	**Wende that I hadde of him so greet chiertee.**
	Right so a wife destroys her husband;		Believed that I had of him so great affection!
378	**This knowe they that been to wyves bonde.'**	397	**I swoor that al my walkinge out by nighte**
	This know they who are bound to wives.'		I swore that all my walking out by night
379	**Lordinges, right thus, as ye have understonde,**	398	**Was for tespye wenches that he dighte;**
	Gentlemen, right thus, as you have heard,		Was to spy out wenches with whom he had intercourse;
380	**Bar I stifly myne olde housbondes on honde,**	399	**Under that colour hadde I many a mirthe.**
	I firmly swore to my old husbands		Under that pretense I had many a mirth.
381	**That thus they seyden in hir dronkenesse;**	400	**For al swich wit is yeven us in our birthe;**
	That thus they said in their drunkenness;		For all such wit is given us in our birth;
382	**And al was fals, but that I took witnesse**	401	**Deceite, weping, spinning god hath yive**
	And all was false, but I took witness		Deceit, weeping, spinning God has given
383	**On Ianekin and on my nece also.**	402	**To wommen kindely, whyl they may live.**
	On Janekin, and on my niece also.		To women naturally, while they may live.
384	**O lord, the peyne I dide hem and the wo,**	403	**And thus of o thing I avaunte me,**
	O Lord! The pain I did them and the woe,		And thus of one thing I boast:
385	**Ful giltelees, by goddes swete pyne!**	404	**Atte ende I hadde the bettre in ech degree,**
	Entirely guiltless (they were), by God's sweet pain!		At the end I had the better in every way,
386	**For as an hors I coude byte and whyne.**	405	**By sleighte, or force, or by som maner thing,**
	For like a horse I could bite and whinny.		By trickery, or force, or by some such thing,
387	**I coude pleyne, thogh I were in the gilt,**	406	**As by continuel murmur or grucching;**
	I could complain, and yet was in the wrong,		As by continual grumbling or grouching.
388	**Or elles often tyme hadde I ben spilt.**	407	**Namely a bedde hadden they meschaunce,**
	Or else many times had I been ruined.		Especially in bed they had misfortune:
389	**Who-so that first to mille comth, first grint;**	408	**Ther wolde I chyde and do hem no plesaunce;**
	Whoever first comes to the mill, first grinds;		There would I scold and do them no pleasure;
390	**I pleyned first, so was our werre y-stint.**	409	**I wolde no lenger in the bed abyde,**
	I complained first, so was our war ended.		I would no longer in the bed abide,
391	**They were ful glad to excusen hem ful blyve**	410	**If that I felte his arm over my syde,**
	They were very glad to excuse themselves quickly		If I felt his arm over my side,
392	**Of thing of which they never agilte hir lyve.**	411	**Til he had maad his raunson un-to me;**
	Of things of which they were never guilty in their lives.		Until he had paid his penalty to me;
393	**Of wenches wolde I beren him on honde,**	412	**Than wolde I suffre him do his nycetee.**
	Of wenches would I falsely accuse them,		Then would I allow him to do his foolishness.

413	**And ther-fore every man this tale I telle,**	432	**How mekely loketh Wilkin oure sheep;**
	And therefore this tale I tell to every man,		How meekly looks Willy, our sheep!
414	**Winne who-so may, for al is for to selle.**	433	**Com neer, my spouse, lat me ba thy cheke!**
	Anyone can profit, for everything is for sale.		Come near, my spouse, let me kiss thy cheek!
415	**With empty hand men may none haukes lure;**	434	**Ye sholde been al pacient and meke,**
	One can lure no hawks with an empty hand;		You should be all patient and meek,
416	**For winning wolde I al his lust endure,**	435	**And han a swete spyced conscience,**
	For profit I would endure all his lust,		And have a sweet tender disposition,
417	**And make me a feyned appetyt;**	436	**Sith ye so preche of Iobes pacience.**
	And make me a feigned appetite;		Since you so preach of Job's patience.
418	**And yet in bacon hadde I never delyt;**	437	**Suffreth alwey, sin ye so wel can preche;**
	And yet in bacon (old meat) I never had delight.		Suffer always, since you so well can preach;
419	**That made me that ever I wolde hem chyde.**	438	**And but ye do, certain we shal yow teche**
	That made me so that I would always scold them,		And unless you do, certainly we shall teach you
420	**For thogh the pope had seten hem biside,**	439	**That it is fair to have a wyf in pees.**
	For though the pope had sat beside them,		That it is fair to have a wife in peace.
421	**I wolde nat spare hem at hir owene bord.**	440	**Oon of us two moste bowen, doutelees;**
	I would not spare them at their own table,		One of us two must bow, doubtless,
422	**For by my trouthe, I quitte hem word for word.**	441	**And sith a man is more resonable**
	For, by my troth, I paid them back word for word.		And since a man is more reasonable
423	**As help me verray god omnipotent,**	442	**Than womman is, ye moste been suffrable.**
	As help me true God omnipotent,		Than a woman is, you must be able to bear suffering.
424	**Thogh I right now sholde make my testament,**	443	**What eyleth yow to grucche thus and grone?**
	Though I right now should make my will,		What ails you to grouch thus and groan?
425	**I ne owe hem nat a word that it nis quit.**	444	**Is it for ye wolde have my queynte allone?**
	I owe them not one word that has not been avenged.		Is it because you want to have my pudendum all to yourself?
426	**I broghte it so aboute by my wit,**	445	**Why taak it al, lo, have it every-deel;**
	I brought it so about by my wit		Why, take it all! Lo, have it every bit!
427	**That they moste yeve it up, as for the beste;**	446	**Peter! I shrewe yow but ye love it weel!**
	That they had to give it up, as the best they could do,		By Saint Peter! I would curse you, if you did not love it well;
428	**Or elles hadde we never been in reste.**	447	**For if I wolde selle my *bele chose*,**
	Or else had we never been at peace;		For if I would sell my 'pretty thing,'
429	**For thogh he loked as a wood leoun,**	448	**I coude walke as fresh as is a rose;**
	For though he looked like a furious lion,		I could walk as fresh (newly clothed) as is a rose;
430	**Yet sholde he faille of his conclusioun.**	449	**But I wol kepe it for your owene tooth.**
	Yet should he fail to attain his goal.		But I will keep it for your own pleasure.
		450	**Ye be to blame, by god, I sey yow sooth.'**
			You are to blame, by God! I tell you the truth.'
431	**Thanne wolde I seye, 'gode lief, tak keep**	451	**Swiche maner wordes hadde we on honde.**
	Then I would say, 'Sweetheart, see		Such sorts of words we had in hand.

452 **Now wol I speken of my fourthe housbonde.**
   Now will I speak of my fourth husband.

453 **My fourthe housbonde was a revelour,**
   My fourth husband was a reveller,

454 **This is to seyn, he hadde a paramour;**
   This is to say, he had a mistress;

455 **And I was yong and ful of ragerye,**
   And I was young and full of playfulness,

456 **Stiborn and strong, and Ioly as a pye.**
   Stubborn and strong, and jolly as a magpie.

457 **Wel coude I daunce to an harpe smale,**
   How well I could dance to a small harp,

458 **And singe, y-wis, as any nightingale,**
   And sing, indeed, like any nightingale,

459 **Whan I had dronke a draughte of swete wyn.**
   When I had drunk a draft of sweet wine.

460 **Metellius, the foule cherl, the swyn,**
   Metellius, the foul churl, the swine,

461 **That with a staf birafte his wyf hir lyf,**
   Who with a staff deprived his wife of her life,

462 **For she drank wyn, thogh I hadde been his wyf,**
   Because she drank wine, if I had been his wife,

463 **He sholde nat han daunted me fro drinke;**
   He should not have frightened me away from drink;

464 **And, after wyn, on Venus moste I thinke:**
   And after wine on Venus must I think:

465 **For al so siker as cold engendreth hayl,**
   For as surely as cold engenders hail,

466 **A likerous mouth moste han a likerous tayl.**
   A gluttonous mouth must have a lecherous tail.

467 **In womman vinolent is no defence,**
   In drunken women there is no defense,

468 **TThis knowen lechours by experience.**
   This lechers know by experience.

469 **But, lord Crist! whan that it remembreth me**
   But, Lord Christ! When I remember

470 **Up-on my yowthe, and on my Iolitee,**
   My youth, and my gaiety,

471 **It tikleth me aboute myn herte rote.**
   It tickles me to the bottom of my heart.

472 **Unto this day it dooth myn herte bote**
   Unto this day it does my heart good

473 **That I have had my world as in my tyme.**
   That I have had my world in my time.

474 **But age, allas! that al wol envenyme,**
   But age, alas, that all will poison,

475 **Hath me biraft my beautee and my pith;**
   Has deprived me of my beauty and my vigor;

476 **Lat go, fare-wel, the devel go therwith!**
   Let it go, farewell, the devil go with it!

477 **The flour is goon, ther is na-more to telle,**
   The flour is gone; there is no more to tell;

478 **The bren, as I best can, now moste I selle;**
   The bran, as I best can, now I must sell;

479 **But yet to be right mery wol I fonde.**
   But yet I will try to be right merry.

480 **Now wol I tellen of my fourthe housbonde.**
   Now will I tell of my fourth husband.

481 **I seye, I hadde in herte greet despyt**
   I say, I had in heart great anger

482 **That he of any other had delyt.**
   That he had delight in any other.

483 **But he was quit, by god and by seint Ioce!**
   But he was paid back, by God and by Saint Joce!

484 **I made him of the same wode a croce;**
   I made him a cross of the same wood;

485 **Nat of my body in no foul manere,**
   Not of my body, in no foul manner,

486 **But certeinly, I made folk swich chere,**
   But certainly, I treated folk in such a way,

487 **That in his owene grece I made him frye**
   That I made him fry in his own grease

488 **For angre, and for verray Ialousye.**
   For anger, and for pure jealousy.

489 **By god, in erthe I was his purgatorie,**
   By God, in earth I was his purgatory,

490 **For which I hope his soule be in glorie.**
   For which I hope his soul may be in glory.

491 **For god it woot, he sat ful ofte and song**
   For, God knows it, he sat very often and cried out in pain

492 **Whan that his shoo ful bitterly him wrong.**
   When his shoe very bitterly pinched him.

493	**Ther was no wight, save god and he, that wiste,**
	There was no person who knew it, save God and he,
494	**In many wyse, how sore I him twiste.**
	In many a way, how painfully I tortured him.
495	**He deyde whan I cam fro Ierusalem,**
	He died when I came from Jerusalem,
496	**And lyth y-grave under the rode-beem,**
	And lies buried under the rood beam,
497	**Al is his tombe noght so curious**
	Although his tomb is not so elaborate
498	**As was the sepulcre of him, Darius,**
	As was the sepulcher of that Darius,
499	**Which that Appelles wroghte subtilly;**
	Which Appelles wrought skillfully;
500	**It nis but wast to burie him preciously.**
	It is nothing but waste to bury him expensively.
501	**Lat him fare-wel, god yeve his soule reste,**
	Let him fare well; God give his soul rest,
502	**He is now in the grave and in his cheste.**
	He is now in his grave and in his casket.

503	**Now of my fifthe housbond wol I telle.**
	Now of my fifth husband I will tell.
504	**God lete his soule never come in helle!**
	God let his soul never come in hell!
505	**And yet was he to me the moste shrewe;**
	And yet he was to me the greatest scoundrel;
506	**That fele I on my ribbes al by rewe,**
	That feel I on my ribs one after another,
507	**And ever shal, un-to myn ending-day.**
	And ever shall unto my final day.
508	**But in our bed he was so fresh and gay,**
	But in our bed he was so lively and gay,
509	**And ther-with-al so wel coude he me glose,**
	And moreover he so well could deceive me,
510	**Whan that he wolde han my *bele chose*,**
	When he would have my 'pretty thing',
511	**That thogh he hadde me bet on every boon,**
	That though he had beat me on every bone,
512	**He coude winne agayn my love anoon.**
	He could win back my love straightway.
513	**I trowe I loved him beste, for that he**
	I believe I loved him best, because he
514	**Was of his love daungerous to me.**
	Was of his love standoffish to me.
515	**We wommen han, if that I shal nat lye,**
	We women have, if I shall not lie,
516	**In this matere a queynte fantasye;**
	In this matter a curious fantasy;
517	**Wayte what thing we may nat lightly have,**
	Note that whatever thing we may not easily have,
518	**Ther-after wol we crye al-day and crave.**
	We will cry all day and crave for it.
519	**Forbede us thing, and that desyren we;**
	Forbid us a thing, and we desire it;
520	**Prees on us faste, and thanne wol we flee.**
	Press on us fast, and then will we flee.
521	**With daunger oute we al our chaffare;**
	With niggardliness we spread out all our merchandise;
522	**Greet prees at market maketh dere ware,**
	A great crowd at the market makes wares expensive,
523	**And to greet cheep is holde at litel prys;**
	And too great a supply makes them of little value;
524	**This knoweth every womman that is wys.**
	Every woman that is wise knows this.

525	**My fifthe housbonde, god his soule blesse!**
	My fifth husband, God bless his soul!
526	**Which that I took for love and no richesse,**
	Whom I took for love, and no riches,
527	**He som-tyme was a clerk of Oxenford,**
	He was formerly a clerk of Oxford,
528	**And had left scole, and wente at hoom to bord**
	And had left school, and came home to board
529	**With my gossib, dwellinge in oure toun,**
	With my close friend, dwelling in our town;
530	**God have hir soule! hir name was Alisoun.**
	God have her soul! Her name was Alisoun.
531	**She knew myn herte and eek my privetee**
	She knew my heart, and also my secrets
532	**Bet than our parisshe-preest, so moot I thee!**
	Better than our parish priest, as I may prosper!

533	**To hir biwreyed I my conseil al.**	551	**I hadde the bettre leyser for to pleye,**
	To her I revealed all my secrets.		I had the better opportunity to amuse myself,
534	**For had myn housbonde pissed on a wal,**	552	**And for to see, and eek for to be seye**
	For had my husband pissed on a wall,		And to see, and also to be seen
535	**Or doon a thing that sholde han cost his lyf,**	553	**Of lusty folk; what wiste I wher my grace**
	Or done a thing that should have cost his life,		By amorous folk; what did I know about where my good fortune
536	**To hir, and to another worthy wyf,**	554	**Was shapen for to be, or in what place?**
	To her, and to another worthy wife,		Was destined to be, or in what place?
537	**And to my nece, which that I loved weel,**	555	**Therefore I made my visitaciouns,**
	And to my niece, whom I loved well,		Therefore I made my visitations
538	**I wolde han told his conseil every-deel.**	556	**To vigilies and to processiouns,**
	I would have told every one of his secrets.		To religious feasts and to processions,
539	**And so I dide ful often, god it woot,**	557	**To preching eek and to thise pilgrimages,**
	And so I did very often, God knows it,		To preaching also, and to these pilgrimages,
540	**That made his face ful often reed and hoot**	558	**To pleyes of miracles and mariages,**
	That made his face often red and hot		To plays about miracles, and to marriages,
541	**For verray shame, and blamed him-self for he**	559	**And wered upon my gaye scarlet gytes.**
	For true shame, and blamed himself because he		And wore my gay scarlet robes.
542	**Had told to me so greet a privetee.**	560	**Thise wormes, ne thise motthes, ne thise mytes,**
	Had told to me so great a secret.		These worms, nor these moths, nor these mites,
543	**And so bifel that ones, in a Lente,**	561	**Upon my peril, frete hem never a deel;**
	And so it happened that once in a Springtime,		Upon my peril (I swear), chewed on them never a bit;
544	**(So often tymes I to my gossib wente,**	562	**And wostow why? for they were used weel.**
	(Since frequently I went to visit my close friend,		And know thou why? Because they were well used.
545	**For ever yet I lovede to be gay,**		
	For I always loved to be gay,		
546	**And for to walke, in March, Averille, and May,**	563	**Now wol I tellen forth what happed me.**
	And to walk in March, April, and May,		Now will I tell forth what happened to me.
547	**Fro hous to hous, to here sondry talis),**	564	**I seye, that in the feeldes walked we,**
	From house to house, to hear various bits of gossip),		I say that in the fields we walked,
548	**That Iankin clerk, and my gossib dame Alis,**	565	**Til trewely we hadde swich daliance,**
	That Jankin the clerk, and my close friend dame Alys,		Until truly we had such flirtation,
549	**And I my-self, in-to the feldes wente.**	566	**This clerk and I, that of my purveyance**
	And I myself, into the fields went.		This clerk and I, that for my provision for the future
550	**Myn housbond was at London al that Lente;**	567	**I spak to him, and seyde him, how that he,**
	My husband was at London all that Spring;		I spoke to him and said to him how he,
		568	**If I were widwe, sholde wedde me.**
			If I were a widow, should wed me.
		569	**For certeinly, I sey for no bobance,**
			For certainly, I say this for no boast,

570	**Yet was I never with-outen purveyance**	591	**But for that I was purveyed of a make,**
	I was never yet without providing beforehand		But because I was provided with a mate,
571	**Of mariage, nof othere thinges eek.**	592	**I weep but smal, and that I undertake.**
	For marriage, nor for other things also.		I wept but little, and that I affirm.
572	**I holde a mouses herte nat worth a leek,**	593	**To chirche was myn housbond born a-morwe**
	I hold a mouse's heart not worth a leek,		To church was my husband carried in the morning
573	**That hath but oon hole for to sterte to,**	594	**With neighebores, that for him maden sorwe;**
	That has but one hole to flee to,		By neighbors, who for him made sorrow;
574	**And if that faille, thanne is al y-do.**	595	**And Iankin oure clerk was oon of tho.**
	If that should fail, then all is lost.		And Jankin, our clerk, was one of those.
575	**I bar him on honde, he hadde enchanted me;**	596	**As help me god, whan that I saugh him go**
	I falsely swore that he had enchanted me;		As help me God, when I saw him go
576	**My dame taughte me that soutiltee.**	597	**After the bere, me thoughte he hadde a paire**
	My mother taught me that trick.		After the bier, I thought he had a pair
577	**And eek I seyde, I mette of him al night;**	598	**Of legges and of feet so clene and faire,**
	And also I said I dreamed of him all night;		Of legs and of feet so neat and fair,
578	**He wolde han slayn me as I lay up-right,**	599	**That al myn herte I yaf un-to his hold.**
	He would have slain me as I lay on my back,		That all my heart I gave unto his keeping.
579	**And al my bed was ful of verray blood,**	600	**He was, I trowe, a twenty winter old,**
	And all my bed was full of real blood,		He was, I believe, twenty years old,
580	**But yet I hope that he shal do me good;**	601	**And I was fourty, if I shal seye sooth;**
	'But yet I hope that you shall do me good;		And I was forty, if I shall tell the truth;
581	**For blood bitokeneth gold, as me was taught.**	602	**But yet I hadde alwey a coltes tooth.**
	For blood symbolizes gold, as I was taught.		But yet I had always a colt's tooth.
582	**And al was fals, I dremed of it right naught,**	603	**Gat-tothed I was, and that bicam me weel;**
	And all was false; I dreamed of it not at all,		With teeth set wide apart I was, and that became me well;
583	**But as I folwed ay my dames lore,**	604	**I hadde the prente of sëynt Venus seel.**
	But I followed always my mother's teaching,		I had the print of Saint Venus's seal.
584	**As wel of this as of other thinges more.**	605	**As help me god, I was a lusty oon,**
	As well in this as in other things more.		As help me God, I was a lusty one,
585	**But now sir, lat me see, what I shal seyn?**	606	**And faire and riche, and yong, and wel bigoon;**
	But now, sir, let me see what I shall say.		And fair, and rich, and young, and well fixed;
586	**A! ha! by god, I have my tale ageyn.**	607	**And trewely, as myne housbondes tolde me,**
	A! Ha! By God, I have my tale again.		And truly, as my husbands told me,
587	**Whan that my fourthe housbond was on bere,**	608	**I had the beste *quoniam* mighte be.**
	When my fourth husband was on the funeral bier,		I had the best pudendum that might be.
588	**I weep algate, and made sory chere,**	609	**For certes, I am al Venerien**
	I wept continuously, and acted sorry,		For certainly, I am all influenced by Venus
589	**As wyves moten, for it is usage,**	610	**In felinge, and myn herte is Marcien.**
	As wives must do, for it is the custom,		In feeling, and my heart is influenced by Mars.
590	**And with my coverchief covered my visage;**		
	And with my kerchief covered my face,		

611	**Venus me yaf my lust, my likerousnesse,**	632	**But afterward repented me ful sore.**
	Venus me gave my lust, my amorousness,		But afterward I repented very bitterly.
612	**And Mars yaf me my sturdy hardinesse.**	633	**He nolde suffre nothing of my list.**
	And Mars gave me my sturdy boldness.		He would not allow me anything of my desires.
613	**Myn ascendent was Taur, and Mars ther-inne.**	634	**By god, he smoot me ones on the list,**
	My ascendant was Taurus, and Mars was therein.		By God, he hit me once on the ear,
614	**Allas! allas! that ever love was sinne!**	635	**For that I rente out of his book a leef,**
	Alas! Alas! That ever love was sin!		Because I tore a leaf out of his book,
615	**I folwed ay myn inclinacioun**	636	**That of the strook myn ere wex al deef.**
	I followed always my inclination		So that of the stroke my ear became all deaf.
616	**By vertu of my constellacioun;**	637	**Stiborn I was as is a leonesse,**
	By virtue of the state of the heavens at my birth;		I was as stubborn as is a lioness,
617	**That made me I coude noght withdrawe**	638	**And of my tonge a verray Iangleresse,**
	That made me that I could not withdraw		And of my tongue a true chatterbox,
618	**My chambre of Venus from a good felawe.**	639	**And walke I wolde, as I had doon biforn,**
	My chamber of Venus from a good fellow.		And I would walk, as I had done before,
619	**Yet have I Martes mark up-on my face,**	640	**From hous to hous, al-though he had it sworn.**
	Yet have I Mars' mark upon my face,		From house to house, although he had sworn the contrary.
620	**And also in another privee place.**	641	**For which he often tymes wolde preche,**
	And also in another private place.		For which he often times would preach,
621	**For, god so wis be my savacioun,**	642	**And me of olde Romayn gestes teche,**
	For as God may be my salvation,		And teach me of old Roman stories,
622	**I ne loved never by no discrecioun,**	643	**How he, Simplicius Gallus, lefte his wyf,**
	I never loved in moderation,		How he, Simplicius Gallus, left his wife,
623	**But ever folwede myn appetyt,**	644	**And hir forsook for terme of al his lyf,**
	But always followed my appetite,		And forsook her for rest of all his life,
624	**Al were he short or long, or blak or whyt;**	645	**Noght but for open-heeded he hir say**
	Whether he were short, or tall, or black-haired, or blond;		Because of nothing but because he saw her bare-headed
625	**I took no kepe, so that he lyked me,**	646	**Lokinge out at his dore upon a day.**
	I took no notice, provided that he pleased me,		Looking out at his door one day.
626	**How pore he was, ne eek of what degree.**		
	How poor he was, nor also of what rank.		
627	**What sholde I seye, but, at the monthes ende,**	647	**Another Romayn tolde he me by name,**
	What should I say but, at the month's end,		Another Roman he told me by name,
628	**This Ioly clerk Iankin, that was so hende,**	648	**That, for his wyf was at a someres game**
	This jolly clerk, Jankin, that was so courteous,		Who, because his wife was at a midsummer revel
629	**Hath wedded me with greet solempnitee,**	649	**With-oute his witing, he forsook hir eke.**
	Has wedded me with great solemnity,		Without his knowledge, he forsook her also.
630	**And to him yaf I al the lond and fee**	650	**And than wolde he up-on his Bible seke**
	And to him I gave all the land and property		And then he would seek in his Bible
631	**That ever was me yeven ther-bifore;**	651	**That ilke proverbe of Ecclesiaste,**
	That ever was given to me before then;		That same proverb of Ecclesiasticus

652	**Wher he comandeth and forbedeth faste,**
	Where he commands and strictly forbids that,
653	**Man shal nat suffre his wyf go roule aboute;**
	Man should suffer his wife go wander about;
654	**Than wolde he seye right thus, with-outen doute,**
	Then would he say right thus, without doubt,
655	**"Who-so that buildeth his hous al of salwes,**
	"Whoever builds his house all of willow twigs,
656	**And priketh his blinde hors over the falwes,**
	And spurs his blind horse over the open fields,
657	**And suffreth his wyf to go seken halwes,**
	And suffers his wife to go on pilgrimages,
658	**Is worthy to been hanged on the galwes!"**
	Is worthy to be hanged on the gallows!"
659	**But al for noght, I sette noght an hawe**
	But all for nothing, I gave not a hawthorn berry
660	**Of his proverbes nof his olde sawe,**
	For his proverbs nor for his old sayings,
661	**Ne I wolde nat of him corrected be.**
	Nor would I be corrected by him.
662	**I hate him that my vices telleth me,**
	I hate him who tells me my vices,
663	**And so do mo, god woot! of us than I.**
	And so do more of us, God knows, than I.
664	**This made him with me wood al outrely;**
	This made him all utterly furious with me;
665	**I nolde noght forbere him in no cas.**
	I would not put up with him in any way.
666	**Now wol I seye yow sooth, by seint Thomas,**
	Now will I tell you the truth, by Saint Thomas,
667	**Why that I rente out of his book a leef,**
	Why I tore a leaf out of his book,
668	**For which he smoot me so that I was deef.**
	For which he hit me so hard that I was deaf.
669	**He hadde a book that gladly, night and day,**
	He had a book that regularly, night and day,
670	**For his desport he wolde rede alway.**
	For his amusement he would always read.
671	**He cleped it Valerie and Theofraste,**
	He called it Valerie and Theofrastus,
672	**At whiche book he lough alwey ful faste.**
	At which book he always heartily laughed.
673	**And eek ther was som-tyme a clerk at Rome,**
	And also there was once a clerk at Rome,
674	**A cardinal, that highte Seint Ierome,**
	A cardinal, who is called Saint Jerome,
675	**That made a book agayn Iovinian;**
	That made a book against Jovinian;
676	**In whiche book eek ther was Tertulan,**
	In which book also there was Tertullian,
677	**Crisippus, Trotula, and Helowys,**
	Crisippus, Trotula, and Heloise,
678	**That was abbesse nat fer fro Parys;**
	Who was abbess not far from Paris;
679	**And eek the Parables of Salomon,**
	And also the Parables of Salomon,
680	**Ovydes Art, and bokes many on,**
	Ovid's Art, and many other books,
681	**And alle thise wer bounden in o volume.**
	And all these were bound in one volume.
682	**And every night and day was his custume,**
	And every night and day was his custom,
683	**Whan he had leyser and vacacioun**
	When he had leisure and spare time
684	**From other worldly occupacioun,**
	From other worldly occupations,
685	**To reden on this book of wikked wyves.**
	To read in this book of wicked wives.
686	**He knew of hem mo legendes and lyves**
	He knew of them more legends and lives
687	**Than been of gode wyves in the Bible.**
	Than are of good women in the Bible.
688	**For trusteth wel, it is an impossible**
	For trust well, it is an impossibility
689	**That any clerk wol speke good of wyves,**
	That any clerk will speak good of women,
690	**But-if it be of holy seintes lyves,**
	Unless it be of holy saints' lives,
691	**Ne of noon other womman never the mo.**
	Nor of any other woman in any way.
692	**Who peyntede the leoun, tel me who?**
	Who painted the lion, tell me who?
693	**By god, if wommen hadde writen stories,**
	By God, if women had written stories,

694	**As clerkes han with-inne hir oratories,**	713	**Up-on a night Iankin, that was our syre,**
	As clerks have within their studies,		Upon a night Jankin, that was master of our house,
695	**They wolde han writen of men more wikkednesse**	714	**Redde on his book, as he sat by the fyre,**
	They would have written of men more wickedness		Read on his book, as he sat by the fire,
696	**Than all the mark of Adam may redresse.**	715	**Of Eva first, that, for hir wikkednesse,**
	Than all the male sex could set right.		Of Eve first, how for her wickedness
697	**The children of Mercurie and of Venus**	716	**Was al mankinde broght to wrecchednesse,**
	The children of Mercury (clerks) and of Venus (lovers)		All mankind was brought to wretchedness,
698	**Been in hir wirking ful contrarious;**	717	**For which that Iesu Crist him-self was slayn,**
	Are directly contrary in their actions;		For which Jesus Christ himself was slain,
699	**Mercurie loveth wisdom and science,**	718	**That boghte us with his herte-blood agayn.**
	Mercury loves wisdom and knowledge,		Who bought us back with his heart's blood.
700	**And Venus loveth ryot and dispence.**	719	**Lo, here expres of womman may ye finde,**
	And Venus loves riot and extravagant expenditures.		Lo, here clearly of woman you may find
701	**And, for hir diverse disposicioun,**	720	**That womman was the los of al mankinde.**
	And, because of their diverse dispositions,		That woman was the cause of the loss of all mankind.
702	**Ech falleth in otheres exaltacioun;**		
	Each falls in the other's most powerful astronomical sign;	721	**Tho redde he me how Sampson loste his heres,**
703	**And thus, god woot! Mercurie is desolat**		Then he read me how Sampson lost his hair,
	And thus, God knows, Mercury is powerless	722	**Slepinge, his lemman kitte hem with hir sheres;**
704	**In Pisces, wher Venus is exaltat;**		Sleeping, his lover cut it with her shears;
	In Pisces (the Fish), where Venus is exalted;	723	**Thurgh whiche tresoun loste he bothe his yën.**
705	**And Venus falleth ther Mercurie is reysed;**		Through which treason he lost both his eyes.
	And Venus falls where Mercury is raised.		
706	**Therfore no womman of no clerk is preysed.**	724	**Tho redde he me, if that I shal nat lyen,**
	Therefore no woman is praised by any clerk.		Then he read to me, if I shall not lie,
707	**The clerk, whan he is old, and may noght do**	725	**Of Hercules and of his Dianyre,**
	The clerk, when he is old, and can not do		Of Hercules and of his Dianyre,
708	**Of Venus werkes worth his olde sho,**	726	**That caused him to sette himself a-fyre.**
	Any of Venus's works worth his old shoe,		Who caused him to set himself on fire.
709	**Than sit he doun, and writ in his dotage**		
	Then he sits down, and writes in his dotage	727	**No-thing forgat he the penaunce and wo**
710	**That wommen can nat kepe hir mariage!**		He forgot not a bit of the care and the woe
	That women can not keep their marriage!	728	**That Socrates had with hise wyves two;**
			That Socrates had with his two wives;
711	**But now to purpos, why I tolde thee**	729	**How Xantippa caste pisse up-on his heed;**
	But now to the point, why I told thee		How Xantippa caste piss upon his head;
712	**That I was beten for a book, pardee.**	730	**This sely man sat stille, as he were deed;**
	That I was beaten for a book, by God.		This poor man sat still as if he were dead;

731	**He wyped his heed, namore dorste he seyn**
	He wiped his head, no more dared he say,
732	**But "er that thonder stinte, comth a reyn."**
	But "Before thunder stops, there comes a rain!"
733	**Of Phasipha, that was the quene of Crete,**
	Of Phasipha, that was the queen of Crete,
734	**For shrewednesse, him thoughte the tale swete;**
	For sheer malignancy, he thought the tale sweet;
735	**Fy! spek na-more—it is a grisly thing—**
	Fie! Speak no more—it is a grisly thing—
736	**Of hir horrible lust and hir lyking.**
	Of her horrible lust and her pleasure.
737	**Of Clitemistra, for hir lecherye,**
	Of Clitermystra, for her lechery,
738	**That falsly made hir housbond for to dye,**
	That falsely made her husband to die,
739	**He redde it with ful good devocioun.**
	He read it with very good devotion.
740	**He tolde me eek for what occasioun**
	He told me also for what occasion
741	**Amphiorax at Thebes loste his lyf;**
	Amphiorax at Thebes lost his life.
742	**Myn housbond hadde a legende of his wyf,**
	My husband had a legend of his wife,
743	**Eriphilem, that for an ouche of gold**
	Eriphilem, that for a brooch of gold
744	**Hath prively un-to the Grekes told**
	Has secretly unto the Greeks told
745	**Wher that hir housbonde hidde him in a place,**
	Where her husband hid him in a place,
746	**For which he hadde at Thebes sory grace.**
	For which he had at Thebes a sad fate.
747	**Of Lyma tolde he me, and of Lucye,**
	Of Livia told he me, and of Lucie,
748	**They bothe made hir housbondes for to dye;**
	They both made their husbands to die;
749	**That oon for love, that other was for hate;**
	That one for love, that other was for hate;
750	**Lyma hir housbond, on an even late,**
	Livia her husband, on a late evening,
751	**Empoysoned hath, for that she was his fo.**
	Has poisoned, because she was his foe;
752	**Lucya, likerous, loved hir housbond so,**
	Lucia, lecherous, loved her husband so much,
753	**That, for he sholde alwey up-on hir thinke,**
	That, so that he should always think upon her,
754	**She yaf him swich a maner love-drinke,**
	She gave him such a sort of love-drink
755	**That he was deed, er it were by the morwe;**
	That he was dead before it was morning;
756	**And thus algates housbondes han sorwe.**
	And thus always husbands have sorrow.
757	**Than tolde he me, how oon Latumius**
	Then he told me how one Latumius
758	**Compleyned to his felawe Arrius,**
	Complained unto his fellow Arrius,
759	**That in his gardin growed swich a tree,**
	That in his garden grew such a tree,
760	**On which, he seyde, how that his wyves three**
	On which he said how his three wives
761	**Hanged hem-self for herte despitous.**
	Hanged themselves for the malice of their hearts.
762	**"O leve brother," quod this Arrius,**
	"O dear brother," this Arrius said,
763	**"Yif me a plante of thilke blissed tree,**
	"Give me a shoot of that same blessed tree,
764	**And in my gardin planted shal it be!"**
	And in my garden shall it be planted."
765	**Of latter date, of wyves hath he red,**
	Of latter date, of wives has he read,
766	**That somme han slayn hir housbondes in hir bed,**
	That some have slain their husbands in their bed,
767	**And lete hir lechour dighte hir al the night**
	And let her lecher copulate with her all the night
768	**Whyl that the corps lay in the floor up-right.**
	When the corpse lay in the floor flat on its back.
769	**And somme han drive nayles in hir brayn**
	And some have driven nails in their brains

770	**Whyl that they slepte, and thus they han hem slayn.**	788	**And whan I saugh he wolde never fyne**
	While they slept, and thus they had them slain.		And when I saw he would never cease
771	**Somme han hem yeve poysoun in hir drinke.**	789	**To reden on this cursed book al night,**
	Some have given them poison in their drink.		Reading on this cursed book all night,
772	**He spak more harm than herte may bithinke.**	790	**Al sodeynly three leves have I plight**
	He spoke more harm than heart may imagine.		All suddenly have I plucked three leaves
773	**And ther-with-al, he knew of mo proverbes**	791	**Out of his book, right as he radde, and eke,**
	And concerning this he knew of more proverbs		Out of his book, right as he read, and also,
774	**Than in this world ther growen gras or herbes.**	792	**I with my fist so took him on the cheke,**
	Than in this world there grow grass or herbs.		I with my fist so hit him on the cheek,
775	**"Bet is," quod he, "thyn habitacioun**	793	**That in our fyr he fil bakward adoun.**
	"Better is," he said, "thy habitation		That in our fire he fell down backwards.
776	**Be with a leoun or a foul dragoun,**	794	**And he up-stirte as dooth a wood leoun,**
	Be with a lion or a foul dragon,		And he leaped up as does a furious lion,
777	**Than with a womman usinge for to chyde.**	795	**And with his fist he smoot me on the heed,**
	Than with a woman accustomed to scold.		And with his fist he hit me on the head,
778	**Bet is," quod he, "hye in the roof abyde**	796	**That in the floor I lay as I were deed.**
	Better is," he said, "to stay high in the roof,		That on the floor I lay as if I were dead.
779	**Than with an angry wyf doun in the hous;**	797	**And when he saugh how stille that I lay,**
	Than with an angry wife down in the house;		And when he saw how still I lay,
780	**They been so wikked and contrarious;**	798	**He was agast, and wolde han fled his way,**
	They are so wicked and contrary;		He was frightened and would have fled on his way,
781	**They haten that hir housbondes loveth ay."**	799	**Til atte laste out of my swogh I breyde:**
	They always hate what their husbands love."		Until at the last out of my swoon I awoke:
782	**He seyde, "a womman cast hir shame away,**	800	**"O! hastow slayn me, false theef?" I seyde,**
	He said, "A woman casts their shame away,		"O! hast thou slain me, false thief?" I said,
783	**Whan she cast of hir smok;" and forther-mo,**	801	**"And for my land thus hastow mordred me?**
	When she casts off her undergarment;" and furthermore,		"And for my land thus hast thou murdered me?
784	**"A fair womman, but she be chaast also,**	802	**Er I be deed, yet wol I kisse thee."**
	"A fair woman, unless she is also chaste,		Before I am dead, yet will I kiss thee."
785	**Is lyk a gold ring in a sowes nose."**		
	Is like a gold ring in a sow's nose."	803	**And neer he cam, and kneled faire adoun,**
786	**Who wolde wenen, or who wolde suppose**		And near he came, and kneeled gently down,
	Who would believe, or who would suppose	804	**And seyde, "dere suster Alisoun,**
787	**The wo that in myn herte was, and pyne?**		And said, "Dear sister Alisoun,
	The woe that in my heart was, and pain?	805	**As help me god, I shal thee never smyte;**
			So help me God, I shall never (again) smite thee;
		806	**That I have doon, it is thy-self to wyte.**
			What I have done, it is thyself to blame (you drove me to it).
		807	**Foryeve it me, and that I thee biseke"—**
			Forgive it me, and that I beseech thee!"—
		808	**And yet eft-sones I hitte him on the cheke,**
			And yet immediately I hit him on the cheek,

809	**And seyde, "theef, thus muchel am I wreke;**
	And said, "Thief, thus much am I avenged;
810	**Now wol I dye, I may no lenger speke."**
	Now will I die, I may no longer speak."
811	**But atte laste, with muchel care and wo,**
	But at the last, with much care and woe,
812	**We fille acorded, by us selven two.**
	We made an agreement between our two selves.
813	**He yaf me al the brydel in myn hond**
	He gave me all the control in my hand,
814	**To han the governance of hous and lond,**
	To have the governance of house and land,
815	**And of his tonge and of his hond also,**
	And of his tongue, and of his hand also,
816	**And made him brenne his book anon right tho.**
	And made him burn his book immediately right then.
817	**And whan that I hadde geten un-to me,**
	And when I had gotten unto me,
818	**By maistrie, al the soveraynetee,**
	By mastery, all the sovereignty,
819	**And that he seyde, "myn owene trewe wyf,**
	And that he said, "My own true wife,
820	**Do as thee lust the terme of al thy lyf,**
	Do as you please the rest of all thy life,
821	**Keep thyn honour, and keep eek myn estaat"—**
	Guard thy honor, and guard also my reputation"—
822	**After that day we hadden never debaat.**
	After that day we never had an argument.
823	**God help me so, I was to him as kinde**
	As God may help me, I was to him as kind
824	**As any wyf from Denmark un-to Inde,**
	As any wife from Denmark unto India,
825	**And also trewe, and so was he to me.**
	And also true, and so was he to me.
826	**I prey to god that sit in magestee,**
	I pray to God, who sits in majesty,
827	**So blesse his soule, for his mercy dere!**
	So bless his soul for his mercy dear!
828	**Now wol I seye my tale, if ye wol here.'**
	Now will I say my tale, if you will hear.'

Beholde the wordes bitwene the Somonour and the Frere

829	**The Frere lough, whan he hadde herd al this,**
	The Friar laughed, when he had heard all this,
830	**'Now, dame,' quod he, 'so have I Ioye or blis,**
	'Now dame,' he said, 'as I may have joy or bliss,
831	**This is a long preamble of a tale!'**
	This is a long preamble of a tale!'
832	**And whan the Somnour herde the Frere gale,**
	And when the Summoner heard the Friar cry out,
833	**'Lo!' quod the Somnour, 'goddes armes two!**
	'Lo,' said the Summoner, 'By God's two arms!
834	**A frere wol entremette him ever-mo.**
	A friar will always intrude himself (in others' affairs).
835	**Lo, gode men, a flye and eek a frere**
	Lo, good men, a fly and also a friar
836	**Wol falle in every dish and eek matere.**
	Will fall in every dish and also every discussion.
837	**What spekestow of preambulacioun?**
	What speakest thou of perambulation?
838	**What! amble, or trotte, or pees, or go sit doun;**
	What! Amble, or trot, or keep still, or go sit down;
839	**Thou lettest our disport in this manere.'**
	Thou spoil our fun in this manner.'
840	**'Ye, woltow so, sir Somnour?' quod the Frere,**
	'Yes, wilt thou have it thus, sir Summoner?' said the Friar;
841	**'Now, by my feith, I shal, er that I go,**
	'Now, by my faith I shall, before I go,
842	**Telle of a Somnour swich a tale or two,**
	Tell of a summoner such a tale or two
843	**That alle the folk shal laughen in this place.'**
	That all the folk shall laugh in this place.'
844	**'Now elles, Frere, I bishrewe thy face,'**
	'Now otherwise, Friar, I curse thy face,'
845	**Quod this Somnour, 'and I bishrewe me,**
	Said this Summoner, 'and I curse myself,

846 **But if I telle tales two or thre**
Unless I tell tales two or three
847 **Of freres er I come to Sidingborne,**
Of friars before I come to Siitingbourne
848 **That I shal make thyn herte for to morne;**
That I shall make thy heart to mourn;
849 **For wel I wool thy patience is goon.'**
For well I know thy patience is gone.'

850 **Our hoste cryde 'pees! and that anoon!'**
Our Host cried 'Peace! And that right now!'
851 **And seyde, 'lat the womman telle hir tale.**
And said, "Let the woman tell her tale.
852 **Ye fare as folk that dronken been of ale.**
You act like folk that are drunk on ale.

853 **Do, dame, tel forth your tale, and that is best.'**
Do, dame, tell forth your tale, and that is best.'
854 **'Al redy, sir,' quod she, 'right as yow lest,**
'All ready, sir,' she said, 'right as you please,
855 **If I have licence of this worthy Frere.'**
If I have permission of this worthy Friar."
856 **'Yis, dame,' quod he, 'tel forth, and I wol here.'**
'Yes, dame,' he said, 'tell forth, and I will hear.'

Heere endeth the Wyf of Bathe hir Prologe

Canterbury Tales:

The Wife of Bath's Tale

Geoffrey Chaucer

Heere bigynneth the Tale of the Wyf of Bathe

857 **In tholde dayes of the king Arthour,**
In the old days of King Arthur,
858 **Of which that Britons speken greet honour,**
Of whom Britons speak great honor,
859 **All was this land fulfild of fayerye.**
This land was all filled full of supernatural creatures.
860 **The elf-queen, with hir Ioly companye,**
The elf-queen, with her jolly company,
861 **Daunced ful ofte in many a grene mede;**
Danced very often in many a green mead.
862 **This was the olde opinion, as I rede,**
This was the old belief, as I read;
863 **I speke of manye hundred yeres ago;**
I speak of many hundred years ago.
864 **But now can no man see none elves mo.**
But now no man can see any more elves,

865 **For now the grete charitee and prayeres**
For now the great charity and prayers
866 **Of limitours and othere holy freres,**
Of licensed beggars and other holy friars,
867 **That serchen every lond and every streem,**
That overrun every land and every stream,
868 **As thikke as motes in the sonne-beem,**
As thick as specks of dust in the sun-beam,
869 **Blessinge halles, chambres, kichenes, boures,**
Blessing halls, chambers, kitchens, bedrooms,
870 **Citees, burghes, castels, hye toures,**
Cities, towns, castles, high towers,
871 **Thropes, bernes, shipnes, dayeryes,**
Villages, barns, stables, dairies,
872 **This maketh that ther been no fayeryes.**
This makes it that there are no fairies.

873	**For ther as wont to walken was an elf,**	893	**Paraventure, swich was the statut tho;**
	For where an elf was accustomed to walk,		Perhaps such was the statute then;
874	**Ther walketh now the limitour him-self**	894	**But that the quene and othere ladies mo**
	There walks now the licensed begging friar himself		Except that the queen and other ladies as well
875	**In undermeles and in morweninges,**	895	**So longe preyeden the king of grace,**
	In late mornings and in early mornings,		So long prayed the king for grace,
876	**And seyth his matins and his holy thinges**	896	**Til he his lyf him graunted in the place,**
	And says his morning prayers and his holy things		Until he granted him his life right there,
877	**As he goth in his limitacioun.**	897	**And yaf him to the quene al at hir wille,**
	As he goes in his assigned district.		And gave him to the queen, all at her will,
878	**Wommen may go saufly up and doun,**	898	**To chese, whether she wolde him save or spille.**
	Women may go safely up and down.		To choose whether she would him save or put to death.
879	**In every bush, or under every tree;**		
	In every bush or under every tree;	899	**The quene thanketh the king with al hir might,**
880	**Ther is noon other incubus but he,**		The queen thanks the king with all her might,
	There is no other evil spirit but he,	900	**And after this thus spak she to the knight,**
881	**And he ne wol doon hem but dishonour.**		And after this she spoke thus to the knight,
	And he will not do them any harm except dishonor.	901	**Whan that she saugh hir tyme, up-on a day:**
			When she saw her time, upon a day:
882	**And so bifel it, that this king Arthour**	902	**'Thou standest yet,' quod she, 'in swich array,**
	And so it happened that this king Arthur		'Thou standest yet,' she said, 'in such condition,
883	**Hadde in his hous a lusty bacheler,**	903	**That of thy lyf yet hastow no suretee.**
	Had in his house a lusty bachelor,		That of thy life yet thou hast no assurance
884	**That on a day cam rydinge fro river;**	904	**I grante thee lyf, if thou canst tellen me**
	That on one day came riding from hawking,		I grant thee life, if thou canst tell me
885	**And happed that, allone as she was born,**	905	**What thing is it that wommen most desyren?**
	And it happened that, alone as he was born,		What thing it is that women most desire?
886	**He saugh a mayde walkinge him biforn,**	906	**Be war, and keep thy nekke-boon from yren.**
	He saw a maiden walking before him,		Beware, and keep thy neck-bone from iron (axe).
887	**Of whiche mayde anon, maugree hir heed,**	907	**And if thou canst nat tellen it anon,**
	Of which maiden straightway, despite all she could do,		And if thou canst not tell it right now,
888	**By verray force he rafte hir maydenheed;**	908	**Yet wol I yeve thee leve for to gon**
	By utter force, he took away her maidenhead;		Yet I will give thee leave to go
889	**For which oppressioun was swich clamour**	909	**A twelf-month and a day, to seche and lere**
	For which wrong was such clamor		A twelvemonth and a day, to seek to learn
890	**And swich pursute un-to the king Arthour,**	910	**An answere suffisant in this matere.**
	And such demand for justice unto king Arthur,		A satisfactory answer in this matter;
891	**That dampned was this knight for to be deed**	911	**And suretee wol I han, er that thou pace,**
	That this knight was condemned to be dead		And I will have, before thou go, a pledge,
892	**By cours of lawe, and sholde han lost his heed**		
	By course of law, and should have lost his head		

912	Thy body for to yelden in this place.'	930	Whan that we been y-flatered and y-plesed.
	To surrender thy body in this place.'		When we are flattered and pleased.
913	Wo was this knight and sorwefully he syketh;	931	He gooth ful ny the sothe, I wol nat lye;
	Woe was this knight, and sorrowfully he sighs;		He goes very near the truth, I will not lie;
914	But what! he may nat do al as him lyketh.	932	A man shal winne us best with flaterye;
	But what! He can not do all as he pleases.		A man shall win us best with flattery;
915	And at the laste, he chees him for to wende,	933	And with attendance, and with bisinesse,
	And at the last he chose to leave		And with attentions and with solicitude,
916	And come agayn, right at the yeres ende,	934	Been we y-lymed, bothe more and lesse.
	And come again, exactly at the year's end,		We are caught, every one of us.
917	With swich answere as god wolde him purveye;	935	And somme seyn, how that we loven best
	With such answer as God would provide him;		And some say that we love best
918	And taketh his leve, and wendeth forth his weye.	936	For to be free, and do right as us lest,
	And takes his leave, and goes forth on his way.		To be free and do just as we please,
		937	And that no man repreve us of our vyce,
			And that no man reprove us for our vices,
919	He seketh every hous and every place,	938	But seye that we be wyse, and no-thing nyce.
	He seeks every house and every place,		But say that we are wise and not at all silly.
920	Wher-as he hopeth for to finde grace,	939	For trewely, ther is noon of us alle,
	Where he hopes to have the luck		For truly there is not one of us all,
921	To lerne, what thing wommen loven most;	940	If any wight wol clawe us on the galle,
	To learn what thing women love most;		If any one will scratch us on the sore spot,
922	But he ne coude arryven in no cost,	941	That we nil kike, for he seith us sooth;
	But he could not arrive in any region,		That we will not kick back, because he tells us the truth;
923	Wher-as he mighte finde in this matere	942	Assay, and he shal finde it that so dooth.
	Where he might find in this matter		Try it, and whoever so does shall find it true.
924	Two creatures accordinge in-fere.	943	For be we never so vicious with-inne,
	Two creatures agreeing together.		For, be we never so vicious within,
925	Somme seyde, wommen loven best richesse;	944	We wol been holden wyse, and clene of sinne.
	Some said, women love riches best;		We want to be considered wise and clean of sin.
926	Somme seyde, honour, somme seyde, Iolynesse;		
	Some said honor, some said gaiety;	945	And somme seyn, that greet delyt han we
927	Somme, riche array, somme seyden, lust abedde,		And some say that we have great delight
	Some rich clothing, some said lust in bed,	946	For to ben holden stable and eek secree,
928	And ofte tyme to be widwe and wedde.		To be considered steadfast, and also (able to keep a) secret,
	And frequently to be widow and wedded.	947	And in o purpos stedefastly to dwelle,
929	Somme seyde, that our hertes been most esed,		And in one purpose steadfastly to remain,
	Some said that our hearts are most eased	948	And nat biwreye thing that men us telle.
			And not reveal things that men tell us.
		949	But that tale is nat worth a rake-stele;
			But that tale is not worth a rake handle;

950	**Pardee, we wommen conne no-thing hele;**	969	**And sith she dorste telle it to no man,**
	By God, we women can hide nothing;		And since she dared tell it to no man,
951	**Witnesse on Myda; wol ye here the tale?**	970	**Doun to a mareys faste by she ran;**
	Witness on Midas—will you hear the tale?		She ran down to a marsh close by;
952	**Ovyde, amonges othere thinges smale,**	971	**Til she came there, hir herte was a-fyre,**
	Ovid, among other small matters,		Until she came there her heart was afire,
953	**Seyde, Myda hadde, under his longe heres,**	972	**And, as a bitore bombleth in the myre,**
	Said Midas had, under his long hair,		And as a bittern bumbles in the mire,
954	**Growinge up-on his heed two asses eres,**	973	**She leyde hir mouth un-to the water doun:**
	Two ass's ears, growing upon his head,		She laid her mouth down unto the water:
955	**The which vyce he hidde, as he best mighte,**	974	**'Biwreye me nat, thou water, with thy soun,'**
	The which vice he hid as he best could,		'Betray me not, thou water, with thy sound,'
956	**Ful subtilly from every mannes sighte,**	975	**Quod she, 'to thee I telle it, and namo;**
	Very skillfully from every man's sight,		She said; 'to thee I tell it and no others;
957	**That, save his wyf, ther wiste of it na-mo.**	976	**Myn housbond hath longe asses eres two!**
	That, except for his wife, there knew of it no others.		My husband has two long asses ears!
958	**He loved hir most, and trusted hir also;**	977	**Now is myn herte all hool, now is it oute;**
	He loved her most, and trusted her also;		Now is my heart all whole; now is it out;
959	**He preyede hir, that to no creature**	978	**I mighte no lenger kepe it, out of doute,'**
	He prayed her that to no creature		I could no longer keep it, without doubt.'
960	**She sholde tellen of his disfigure.**	979	**Heer may ye se, thogh we a tyme abyde,**
	She should tell of his disfigurement.		Here you may see, though we a time abide,
961	**She swoor him 'nay, for al this world to winne,**	980	**Yet out it moot, we can no conseil hyde;**
	She swore him, 'Nay; for all this world to win,		Yet out it must come; we can hide no secret;
962	**She nolde do that vileinye or sinne,**	981	**The remenant of the tale if ye wol here,**
	She would not do that dishonor or sin,		The remnant of the tale if you will hear,
963	**To make hir housbond han so foul a name;**	982	**Redeth Ovyde, and ther ye may it lere.**
	To make her husband have so foul a reputation;		Read Ovid, and there you may learn it.
964	**She nolde nat telle it for hir owene shame.'**	983	**This knight, of which my tale is specially,**
	She would not tell it for her own shame.'		This knight, of whom my tale is in particular,
965	**But nathelees, hir thoughte that she dyde,**	984	**Whan that he saugh he mighte nat come therby,**
	But nonetheless, she thought that she would die		When he saw he might not come to that,
966	**That she so longe sholde a conseil hyde;**	985	**This is to seye, what wommen loven moost,**
	If she should hide a secret so long;		This is to say, what women love most,
967	**Hir thoughte it swal so sore aboute hir herte,**	986	**With-inne his brest ful sorweful was the goost;**
	She thought it swelled so sore about her heart,		Within his breast very sorrowful was the spirit;
968	**That nedely som word hir moste asterte;**	987	**But hoom he gooth, he mighte nat soiourne.**
	That necessarily some word must escape her;		But home he goes; he could not linger.
		988	**The day was come, that hoomward moste he tourne,**
			The day was come that homeward he must turn,

Things Unattempted Yet in Prose or Rhyme

989	**And in his wey it happed him to ryde,**
	And in his way he happened to ride,
990	**In al this care, under a forest-syde,**
	In all this care, near a forest side,
991	**Wher-as he saugh up-on a daunce go**
	Where he saw upon a dance go
992	**Of ladies foure and twenty, and yet mo;**
	Ladies four and twenty, and yet more;
993	**Toward the whiche daunce he drow ful yerne,**
	Toward the which dance he drew very eagerly,
994	**In hope that som wisdom sholde he lerne.**
	In hope that he should learn some wisdom.
995	**But certeinly, er he came fully there,**
	But certainly, before he came fully there,
996	**Vanisshed was this daunce, he niste where.**
	Vanished was this dance, he knew not where.
997	**No creature saugh he that bar lyf,**
	He saw no creature that bore life,
998	**Save on the grene he saugh sittinge a wyf;**
	Save on the green he saw sitting a woman;
999	**A fouler wight ther may no man devyse.**
	There can no man imagine an uglier creature.
1000	**Agayn the knight this olde wyf gan ryse,**
	At the knight's coming this old wife did rise,
1001	**And seyde, 'sir knight, heer-forth ne lyth no wey.**
	And said, 'Sir knight, there lies no road out of here.
1002	**Tel me, what that ye seken, by your fey?**
	Tell me what you seek, by your faith?
1003	**Paraventure it may the bettre be;**
	Perhaps it may be the better;
1004	**Thise olde folk can muchel thing,' quod she.**
	These old folk know many things,' she said.
1005	**'My leve mooder,' quod this knight certeyn,**
	'My dear mother,' said this knight certainly,
1006	**'I nam but deed, but-if that I can seyn**
	'I am as good as dead unless I can say
1007	**What thing it is that wommen most desyre;**
	What thing it is that women most desire;
1008	**Coude ye me wisse, I wolde wel quyte your hyre.'**
	If you could teach me, I would well repay you.'
1009	**'Plighte me thy trouthe, heer in myn hand,' quod she,**
	'Pledge me thy word here in my hand,' she said,
1010	**'The nexte thing that I requere thee,**
	'The next thing that I require of thee,
1011	**Thou shalt it do, if it lye in thy might;**
	Thou shalt do it, if it lies in thy power;
1012	**And I wol telle it yow er it be night.'**
	And I will tell it to you before it is night.'
1013	**'Have heer my trouthe,' quod the knight, 'I grante.'**
	'Have here my pledged word,' said the knight, 'I agree.'
1014	**'Thanne,' quod she, 'I dar me wel avante,**
	'Then,' she said, 'I dare me well boast
1015	**Thy lyf is sauf, for I wol stonde therby,**
	Thy life is safe, for I will stand thereby,
1016	**Up-on my lyf, the queen wol seye as I.**
	Upon my life, the queen will say as I.
1017	**Lat see which is the proudeste of hem alle,**
	Let's see which is the proudest of them all,
1018	**That wereth on a coverchief or a calle,**
	That wears a kerchief or a hairnet,
1019	**That dar seye nay, of that I shal thee teche;**
	That dares say 'nay' of what I shall teach thee;
1020	**Lat us go forth with-outen lenger speche.'**
	Let us go forth without longer speech.'
1021	**Tho rouned she a pistel in his ere,**
	Then she whispered a message in his ear,
1022	**And bad him to be glad, and have no fere.**
	And commanded him to be glad and have no fear.
1023	**Whan they be comen to the court, this knight**
	When they are come to the court, this knight

1024	**Seyde, 'he had holde his day, as he hadde hight,**
	Said 'he had held his day, as he had promised,
1025	**And redy was his answere,' as he sayde.**
	And his answer was ready,' as he said.
1026	**Ful many a noble wyf, and many a mayde,**
	Very many a noble wife, and many a maid,
1027	**And many a widwe, for that they ben wyse,**
	And many a widow, because they are wise,
1028	**The quene hir-self sittinge as a Iustyse,**
	The queen herself sitting as a justice,
1029	**Assembled been, his answere for to here;**
	Are assembled, to hear his answer;
1030	**And afterward this knight was bode appere.**
	And afterward this knight was commanded to appear.

1031	**To every wight comanded was silence,**
	Silence was commanded to every person,
1032	**And that the knight sholde telle in audience,**
	And that the knight should tell in open court,
1033	**What thing that worldly wommen loven best.**
	What thing (it is) that worldly women love best.
1034	**This knight ne stood nat stille as doth a best,**
	This knight stood not silent as does a beast,
1035	**But to his questioun anon answerde**
	But to his question straightway answered
1036	**With manly voys, that al the court it herde:**
	With manly voice, so that all the court heard it:

1037	**'My lige lady, generally,' quod he,**
	'My liege lady, without exception,' he said,
1038	**'Wommen desyren to have sovereyntee**
	'Women desire to have sovereignty
1039	**As wel over hir housbond as hir love,**
	As well over her husband as her love,
1040	**And for to been in maistrie him above;**
	And to be in mastery above him;
1041	**This is your moste desyr, thogh ye me kille,**
	This is your greatest desire, though you kill me,
1042	**Doth as yow list, I am heer at your wille.'**
	Do as you please; I am here subject to your will.'

1043	**In al the court ne was ther wyf ne mayde,**
	In all the court there was not wife, nor maid,
1044	**Ne widwe, that contraried that he sayde,**
	Nor widow that denied what he said,
1045	**But seyden, 'he was worthy han his lyf.'**
	But said that 'he was worthy to have his life.'
1046	**And with that word up stirte the olde wyf,**
	And with that word up sprang the old woman,
1047	**Which that the knight saugh sittinge in the grene:**
	Whom the knight saw sitting on the green:
1048	**'Mercy,' quod she, 'my sovereyn lady quene!**
	'Mercy,' she said, 'my sovereign lady queen!
1049	**Er that your court departe, do me right.**
	Before your court departs, do me justice.
1050	**I taughte this answere un-to the knight;**
	I taught this answer to the knight;
1051	**For which he plighte me his trouthe there,**
	For which he pledged me his word there,
1052	**The firste thing I wolde of him requere,**
	The first thing that I would ask of him
1053	**He wolde it do, if it lay in his might.**
	He would do, if it lay in his power.
1054	**Bifore the court than preye I thee, sir knight,'**
	Before the court then I pray thee, sir knight,'
1055	**Quod she, 'that thou me take un-to thy wyf;**
	Said she, 'that thou take me as thy wife,
1056	**For wel thou wost that I have kept thy lyf.**
	For well thou know that I have saved thy life.
1057	**If I sey fals, sey nay, up-on thy fey!'**
	If I say false, say nay, upon thy faith!'

1058 **This knight answerde, 'allas! and wey-lawey!**
　　This knight answered, 'Alas and woe is me!
1059 **I woot right wel that swich was my biheste.**
　　I know right well that such was my promise.
1060 **For goddes love, as chees a newe requeste;**
　　For God's love, choose a new request;
1061 **Tak al my good, and lat my body go.'**
　　Take all my goods and let my body go.'

1062 **'Nay than,' quod she, 'I shrewe us bothe two!**
　　'Nay, then,' she said, 'I curse both of us two!
1063 **For thogh that I be foul, and old, and pore,**
　　For though I am ugly, and old, and poor,
1064 **I nolde for al the metal, ne for ore,**
　　I would not for all the metal, nor for ore,
1065 **That under erthe is grave, or lyth above,**
　　That under earth is buried or lies above,
1066 **But-if thy wyf I were, and eek thy love.'**
　　Have anything except that I were thy wife, and also thy love.'

1067 **'My love?' quod he; 'nay, my dampnacioun!**
　　'My love?' he said, 'nay, my damnation!
1068 **Allas! that any of my nacioun**
　　Alas! That any of my family
1069 **Sholde ever so foule disparaged be!'**
　　Should ever be so foully degraded!'
1070 **But al for noght, the ende is this, that he**
　　But all for naught, the end is this, that he
1071 **Constreyned was, he nedes moste hir wedde;**
　　Constrained was; he must by necessity wed her;
1072 **And taketh his olde wyf, and gooth to bedde.**
　　And takes his old wife, and goes to bed.

1073 **Now wolden som men seye, paraventure,**
　　Now would some men say, perhaps,
1074 **That, for my necligence, I do no cure**
　　That because of my negligence I make no effort
1075 **To tellen yow the Ioye and al tharray**
　　To tell you the joy and all the rich display
1076 **That at the feste was that ilke day.**
　　That was at the (wedding) feast that same day.
1077 **To whiche thing shortly answere I shal;**
　　To which thing shortly I shall answer;
1078 **I seye, ther nas no Ioye ne feste at al,**
　　I say there was no joy nor feast at all,
1079 **Ther nas but hevinesse and muche sorwe;**
　　There was nothing but heaviness and much sorrow;
1080 **For prively he wedded hir on a morwe,**
　　For he wedded her in private in the morning,
1081 **And al day after hidde him as an oule;**
　　And all day after hid himself like an owl;
1082 **So wo was him, his wyf looked so foule.**
　　So woeful was he, his wife looked so ugly.

1083 **Greet was the wo the knight hadde in his thoght,**
　　Great was the woe the knight had in his thought,
1084 **Whan he was with his wyf a-bedde y-broght;**
　　When he was brought to bed with his wife;
1085 **He walweth, and he turneth to and fro.**
　　He wallows and he turns to and fro.
1086 **His olde wyf lay smylinge evermo,**
　　His old wife lay smiling evermore,
1087 **And seyde, 'o dere housbond, *benedicite*!**
　　And said, 'O dear husband, bless me!
1088 **Fareth every knight thus with his wyf as ye?**
　　Does every knight behave thus with his wife as you do?
1089 **Is this the lawe of king Arthures hous?**
　　Is this the law of king Arthur's house?
1090 **Is every knight of his so dangerous?**
　　Is every knight of his so aloof?
1091 **I am your owene love and eek your wyf;**
　　I am your own love and your wife;
1092 **I am she, which that saved hath your lyf;**
　　I am she who has saved your life;
1093 **And certes, yet dide I yow never unright;**
　　And, certainly, I did you never wrong yet;

1094	**Why fare ye thus with me this firste night?**	1109	**But for ye speken of swich gentillesse**
	Why behave you thus with me this first night?		But, since you speak of such nobility
1095	**Ye faren lyk a man had lost his wit;**	1110	**As is descended out of old richesse,**
	You act like a man who had lost his wit;		As is descended out of old riches,
1096	**What is my gilt? for goddes love, tel me it,**	1111	**That therfore sholden ye be gentil men,**
	What is my offense? For God's love, tell it,		That therefore you should be noble men,
1097	**And it shal been amended, if I may.'**	1112	**Swich arrogance is nat worth an hen.**
	And it shall be amended, if I can.'		Such arrogance is not worth a hen.
1098	**'Amended?' quod this knight, 'allas! nay, nay!**	1113	**Loke who that is most vertuous alway,**
	'Amended?' said this knight, 'Alas, nay, nay!		Look who is most virtuous always,
1099	**It wol nat been amended never mo!**	1114	**Privee and apert, and most entendeth ay**
	It will not be amended ever more.		In private and public, and most intends ever
1100	**Thou art so loothly, and so old also,**	1115	**To do the gentil dedes that he can,**
	Thou art so loathsome, and so old also,		To do the noble deeds that he can;
1101	**And ther-to comen of so lowe a kinde,**	1116	**And tak him for the grettest gentil man.**
	And moreover descended from such low born lineage,		Take him for the greatest noble man.
1102	**That litel wonder is, thogh I walwe and winde.**	1117	**Crist wol, we clayme of him our gentillesse,**
	That little wonder is though I toss and twist about.		Christ wants us to claim our nobility from him,
1103	**So wolde god myn herte wolde breste!'**	1118	**Nat of our eldres for hir old richesse.**
	So would God my heart would burst!'		Not from our ancestors for their old riches.
		1119	**For thogh they yeve us al hir heritage,**
			For though they give us all their heritage,
		1120	**For which we clayme to been of heigh parage,**
			For which we claim to be of noble lineage,
1104	**'Is this,' quod she, 'the cause of your unreste?'**	1121	**Yet may they nat biquethe, for no-thing,**
	'Is this,' she said, 'the cause of your distress?'		Yet they can not bequeath by any means,
		1122	**To noon of us hir vertuous living,**
			To any of us their virtuous living,
1105	**'Ye, certainly,' quod he, 'no wonder is.'**	1123	**That made hem gentil men y-called be;**
	'Yes, certainly,' he said, 'it is no wonder.'		That made them be called noble men;
1106	**'Now, sire,' quod she, 'I coude amende al this,**	1124	**And bad us folwen hem in swich degree.**
	'Now, sir,' she said, 'I could amend all this,		And commanded us to follow them in such matters.
1107	**If that me liste, er it were dayes three,**	1125	**Wel can the wyse poete of Florence,**
	If I pleased, before three days were past,		Well can the wise poet of Florence,
1108	**So wel ye mighte here yow un-to me.**	1126	**That highte Dant, speken in this sentence;**
	Providing that you might behave well towards me.		Who is called Dante, speak on this matter.
		1127	**Lo in swich maner rym is Dantes tale:**
			Lo, in such sort of rime is Dante's speech:
		1128	**'Ful selde up ryseth by his branches smale**
			'Very seldom grows up from its small branches

1129	**Prowesse of man, for god, of his goodnesse,**	1148	**Sith folk ne doon hir operacioun**
	Nobility of man, for God, of his goodness,		Since folk not do behave as they should
1130	**Wol that of him we clayme our gentillesse;'**	1149	**Alwey, as dooth the fyr, lo! in his kinde.**
	Wants us to claim our nobility from him;'		Always, as does the fire, lo, in its nature.
1131	**For of our eldres may we no-thing clayme**	1150	**For, god it woot, men may wel often finde**
	For from our ancestors we can claim no thing		For, God knows it, men may well often find
1132	**But temporel thing, that man may hurte and mayme.**	1151	**A lordes sone do shame and vileinye;**
	Except temporal things, that may hurt and injure a man.		A lord's son doing shame and dishonor;
		1152	**And he that wol han prys of his gentrye**
1133	**Eek every wight wot this as wel as I,**		And he who will have praise for his noble birth
	Also every person knows this as well as I,	1153	**For he was boren of a gentil hous,**
1134	**If gentillesse were planted naturelly**		Because he was born of a noble house
	If nobility were planted naturally	1154	**And hadde hise eldres noble and vertuous,**
1135	**Un-to a certeyn linage, doun the lyne,**		And had his noble and virtuous ancestors,
	Unto a certain lineage down the line,	1155	**And nil him-selven do no gentil dedis,**
1136	**Privee ne apert, than wolde they never fyne**		And will not himself do any noble deeds,
	Then in private and in public they would never cease	1156	**Ne folwe his gentil auncestre that deed is,**
1137	**To doon of gentillesse the faire offyce;**		Nor follow his noble ancestry that is dead,
	To do the just duties of nobility;	1157	**He nis nat gentil, be he duk or erl;**
1138	**They mighte do no vileinye or vyce.**		He is not noble, be he duke or earl;
	They could do no dishonor or vice.	1158	**For vileyns sinful dedes make a cherl.**
			For churlish sinful deeds make a churl.
1139	**Tak fyr, and ber it in the derkeste hous**	1159	**For gentillesse nis but renomee**
	Take fire and bear it in the darkest house		For nobility is nothing but renown
1140	**Bitwix this and the mount of Caucasus,**	1160	**Of thyne auncestres, for hir heigh bountee,**
	Between this and the mount of Caucasus,		Of thy ancestors, for their great goodness,
1141	**And lat men shette the dores and go thenne;**	1161	**Which is a strange thing to thy persone.**
	And let men shut the doors and go away;		Which is a thing not naturally part of thy person.
1142	**Yet wol the fyr as faire lye and brenne,**	1162	**Thy gentillesse cometh fro god allone;**
	Yet will the fire as brightly blaze and burn,		Thy nobility comes from God alone;
1143	**As twenty thousand men mighte it biholde;**	1163	**Than comth our verray gentillesse of grace,**
	As if twenty thousand men might it behold;		Then our true nobility comes from grace;
1144	**His office naturel ay wol it holde,**	1164	**It was no-thing biquethe us with our place.**
	Its natural function it will always hold,		It was not at all bequeathed to us with our social rank.
1145	**Up peril of my lyf, til that it dye.**		
	On peril of my life (I say), until it dies.	1165	**Thenketh how noble, as seith Valerius,**
			Think how noble, as says Valerius,
1146	**Heer may ye see wel, how that genterye**	1166	**Was thilke Tullius Hostilius,**
	Here may you see well that nobility		Was that same Tullius Hostillius,
1147	**Is nat annexed to possessioun,**	1167	**That out of povert roos to heigh noblesse.**
	Is not joined with possession,		That out of poverty rose to high nobility.

1168	**Redeth Senek, and redeth eek Boëce,**	1187	**He that coveyteth is a povre wight,**
	Read Seneca, and read also Boethius;		He who covets is a poor person,
1169	**Ther shul ye seen expres that it no drede is,**	1188	**For he wolde han that is nat in his might.**
	There shall you see clearly that it is no doubt,		For he would have that which is not in his power.
1170	**That he is gentil that doth gentil dedis;**	1189	**But he that noght hath, ne coveyteth have,**
	That he is noble who does noble deeds;		But he who has nothing, nor covets to have anything,
1171	**And therfore, leve housbond, I thus conclude,**	1190	**Is riche, al-though ye holde him but a knave.**
	And therefore, dear husband, I thus conclude,		Is rich, although you consider him but a knave.
1172	**Al were it that myne auncestres were rude,**	1191	**Verray povert, it singeth proprely;**
	Although it is so that my ancestors were rude,		True poverty, it rightly sings;
1173	**Yet may the hye god, and so hope I,**	1192	**Iuvenal seith of povert merily:**
	Yet may the high God, and so hope I,		Juvenal says of poverty merrily:
1174	**Grante me grace to liven vertuously.**	1193	**"The povre man, whan he goth by the weye,**
	Grant me grace to live virtuously.		'The poor man, when he goes along the roadway,
1175	**Thanne am I gentil, whan that I biginne**	1194	**Bifore the theves he may singe and pleye."**
	Then am I noble, when I begin		Before the thieves he may sing and play."
1176	**To liven vertuously and weyve sinne.**	1195	**Povert is hateful good, and, as I gesse,**
	To live virtuously and abandon sin.		Poverty is a hateful good and, as I guess,
1177	**And ther-as ye of povert me repreve,**	1196	**A ful greet bringer out of bisinesse;**
	And whereas you reprove me for poverty,		A very great remover of cares;
1178	**The hye god, on whom that we bileve,**	1197	**A greet amender eek of sapience**
	The high God, on whom we believe,		A great amender also of wisdom
1179	**In wilful povert chees to live his lyf.**	1198	**To him that taketh it in pacience.**
	In voluntary poverty chose to live his life.		To him that takes it in patience.
1180	**And certes every man, mayden, or wyf,**	1199	**Povert is this, al-though it seme elenge:**
	And certainly every man, maiden, or woman,		Poverty is this, although it may seem miserable:
1181	**May understonde that Iesus, hevene king,**	1200	**Possessioun, that no wight wol chalenge.**
	Can understand that Jesus, heaven's king,		A possession that no one will challenge.
1182	**Ne wolde nat chese a vicious living.**	1201	**Povert ful ofte, whan a man is lowe,**
	Would not choose a vicious form of living.		Poverty very often, when a man is low,
1183	**Glad povert is an honest thing, certeyn;**	1202	**Maketh his god and eek him-self to knowe.**
	Glad poverty is an honest thing, certain;		Makes him know his God and also himself.
1184	**This wol Senek and othere clerkes seyn.**	1203	**Povert a spectacle is, as thinketh me,**
	This will Seneca and other clerks say.		Poverty is an eye glass, as it seems to me,
1185	**Who-so that halt him payd of his poverte,**	1204	**Thurgh which he may his verray frendes see.**
	Whoever considers himself satisfied with his poverty,		Through which one may see his true friends.
1186	**I holde him riche, al hadde he nat a sherte.**	1205	**And therfore, sire, sin that I noght yow greve,**
	I consider him rich, although he had not a shirt.		And therefore, sir, since I do not injure you,

1206	**Of my povert na-more ye me repreve.**
	You (should) no longer reprove me for my poverty.
1207	**Now, sire, of elde ye repreve me;**
	Now, sir, of old age you reprove me;
1208	**And certes, sire, thogh noon auctoritee**
	And certainly, sir, though no authority
1209	**Were in no book, ye gentils of honour**
	Were in any book, you gentlefolk of honor
1210	**Seyn that men sholde an old wight doon favour,**
	Say that men should be courteous to an old person,
1211	**And clepe him fader, for your gentillesse;**
	And call him father, because of your nobility;
1212	**And auctours shal I finden, as I gesse.**
	And authors shall I find, as I guess.
1213	**Now ther ye seye, that I am foul and old,**
	Now where you say that I am ugly and old,
1214	**Than drede you noght to been a cokewold;**
	Than do not fear to be a cuckold;
1215	**For filthe and elde, al-so moot I thee,**
	For filth and old age, as I may prosper,
1216	**Been grete wardeyns up-on chastitee.**
	Are great guardians of chastity.
1217	**But nathelees, sin I knowe your delyt,**
	But nonetheless, since I know your delight,
1218	**I shal fulfille your worldly appetyt.**
	I shall fulfill your worldly appetite.
1219	**Chese now,' quod she, 'oon of thise thinges tweye,**
	'Choose now,' she said, 'one of these two things:
1220	**To han me foul and old til that I deye,**
	To have me ugly and old until I die,
1221	**And be to yow a trewe humble wyf,**
	And be to you a true, humble wife,
1222	**And never yow displese in al my lyf,**
	And never displease you in all my life,
1223	**Or elles ye wol han me yong and fair,**
	Or else you will have me young and fair,
1224	**And take your aventure of the repair**
	And take your chances of the crowd
1225	**That shal be to your hous, by-cause of me,**
	That shall be at your house because of me,
1226	**Or in som other place, may wel be.**
	Or in some other place, as it may well be.
1227	**Now chese your-selven, whether that yow lyketh.'**
	Now choose yourself, whichever you please.'
1228	**This knight avyseth him and sore syketh,**
	This knight deliberates and painfully sighs,
1229	**But atte laste he seyde in this manere,**
	But at the last he said in this manner,
1230	**'My lady and my love, and wyf so dere,**
	'My lady and my love, and wife so dear,
1231	**I put me in your wyse governance;**
	I put me in your wise governance;
1232	**Cheseth your-self, which may be most plesance,**
	Choose yourself which may be most pleasure,
1233	**And most honour to yow and me also.**
	And most honor to you and me also.
1234	**I do no fors the whether of the two;**
	I do not care which of the two;
1235	**For as yow lyketh, it suffiseth me.'**
	For as it pleases you, is enough for me.'
1236	**'Thanne have I gete of yow maistrye,' quod she,**
	'Then have I gotten mastery of you,' she said,
1237	**'Sin I may chese, and governe as me lest?'**
	'Since I may choose and govern as I please?'
1238	**'Ye, certes, wyf,' quod he, 'I holde it best.'**
	'Yes, certainly, wife,' he said, 'I consider it best.'
1239	**'Kis me,' quod she, 'we be no lenger wrothe;**
	'Kiss me,' she said, 'we are no longer angry;
1240	**For, by my trouthe, I wol be to yow bothe,**
	For, by my troth, I will be to you both,
1241	**This is to seyn, ye, bothe fair and good.**
	This is to say, yes, both fair and good.

1242	**I prey to god that I mot sterven wood,**	1253	**His herte bathed in a bath of blisse;**
	I pray to God that I may die insane,		His heart bathed in a bath of bliss;
1243	**But I to yow be al-so good and trewe**	1254	**A thousand tyme a-rewe he gan hir kisse.**
	Unless I to you be as good and true		A thousand time in a row he did her kiss.
1244	**As ever was wyf, sin that the world was newe.**	1255	**And she obeyed him in every thing**
	As ever was wife, since the world was new.		And she obeyed him in every thing
1245	**And, but I be to-morn as fair to sene**	1256	**That mighte doon him plesance or lyking.**
	And unless I am tomorrow morning as fair to be seen		That might do him pleasure or enjoyment.
1246	**As any lady, emperyce, or quene,**	1257	**And thus they lyve unto hir lyves ende**
	As any lady, empress, or queen,		And thus they live unto their lives' end
1247	**That is bitwixe the est and eke the west,**	1258	**In parfit joye; and Jhesu Crist us sende**
	That is between the east and also the west,		In perfect joy; and Jesus Christ us send
1248	**Doth with my lyf and deeth right as yow lest.**	1259	**Housbondes meeke, yonge, and fressh abedde,**
	Do with my life and death right as you please.		Husbands meek, young, and vigorous in bed,
1249	**Cast up the curtin, loke how that it is.'**	1260	**And grace t' overbyde hem that we wedde;**
	Cast up the curtain, look how it is.'		And grace to outlive them whom we wed;
1250	**And whan the knight saugh verraily al this,**	1261	**And eek I praye Jhesu shorte hir lyves**
	And when the knight saw truly all this,		And also I pray Jesus shorten their lives
1251	**That she so fair was, and so yong ther-to,**	1262	**That noght wol be governed by hir wyves;**
	That she so was beautiful, and so young moreover,		That will not be governed by their wives;
1252	**For Ioye he hente hir in his armes two,**	1263	**And olde and angry nygardes of dispence,**
	For joy he clasped her in his two arms,		And old and angry misers in spending,
		1264	**God sende hem soone verray pestilence!**
			God send them soon the very pestilence!

Heere endeth the Wyves Tale of Bathe

Sonnet 18, Sonnet 116, and Sonnet 130

William Shakespeare

Sonnet 18

Shall I compare thee to a summer's day?
Thou art more lovely and more temperate.
Rough winds do shake the darling buds of May,
And summer's lease hath all too short a date.
5 Sometime too hot the eye of heaven shines,
And often is his gold complexion dimmed;
And every fair from fair sometimes declines,
By chance or nature's changing course untrimm'd.
But thy eternal summer shall not fade
10 Nor lose possession of that fair thou ow'st.
Nor shall Death brag thou wander'st in his shade,
When in eternal lines to time thou grow'st.
So long as men can breathe, or eyes can see,
So long lives this, and this gives life to thee

Sonnet 116

Let me not to the marriage of true minds
Admit impediments. Love is not love
Which alters when it alteration finds,
Or bends with the remover to remove.
5 O no! it is an ever-fixéd mark,
That looks on tempests and is never shaken;
It is the star to every wandering bark,
Whose worth's unknown, although his height be taken.
Love's not Time's fool, though rosy lips and cheeks
10 Within his bending sickle's compass come.
Love alters not with his brief hours and weeks,
But bears it out even to the edge of doom.
If this be error and upon me proved,
I never writ, nor no man ever loved.

Sonnet 130

My mistress' eyes are nothing like the sun;
Coral is far more red than her lips' red;
If snow be white, why then her breasts are dun;
If hairs be wires, black wires grow on her head;
5 I have seen roses damasked, red and white,
But no such roses see I in her cheeks;
And in some perfumes is there more delight
Than in the breath that from my mistress reeks.
I love to hear her speak, yet well I know
10 That music hath a far more pleasing sound.
I grant I never saw a goddess go;
My mistress, when she walks, treads on the ground.
And yet, by heaven, I think my love as rare
As any she belied with false compare.

The Canonization

John Donne

For God's sake hold your tongue, and let me love,
   Or chide my palsy, or my gout,
My five grey hairs, or ruined fortune flout,
With wealth your state, your mind with arts improve,
5 Take you a course, get you a place,

William Shakespeare, "Sonnet 116". Copyright in the Public Domain.
William Shakespeare, "Sonnet 18". Copyright in the Public Domain.
William Shakespeare, "Sonnet 130". Copyright in the Public Domain.
John Donne, "The Canonization", from *Songs and Sonnets*. Copyright in the Public Domain.

Observe His Honour, or His Grace,
Or the King's real, or his stamped face
   Contémplate; what you will, approve,
   So you will let me love.

10 Alas, alas, who's injur'd by my love?
   What merchant's ships have my sighs drowned?
Who says my tears have overflowed his ground?
   When did my colds a forward spring remove?
When did the heats which my veins fill
15   Add one more to the plaguy bill?
Soldiers find wars, and lawyers find out still
   Litigious men, which quarrels move,
   Though she and I do love.

Call us what you will, we're made such by love;
20   Call her one, me another fly,
We're tapers too, and at our own cost die,
   And we in us find the eagle and the dove.
   The phoenix riddle hath more wit
   By us: we two being one, are it.
25 So, to one neutral thing both sexes fit,
   We die and rise the same, and prove
   Mysterious by this love.

We can die by it, if not live by love,
   And if unfit for tombs and hearse
30 Our legend be, it will be fit for verse;
   And if no piece of chronicle we prove,
   We'll build in sonnets pretty rooms;
   As well a well-wrought urn becomes
The greatest ashes, as half-acre tombs,
35   And by these hymns, all shall approve
   Us canoniz'd for love:

And thus invoke us: You, whom reverend love
   Made one another's hermitage;
You, to whom love was peace, that now is rage;
40 Who did the whole world's soul contract, and drove
   Into the glasses of your eyes
   (So made such mirrors, and such spies,
That they did all to you epitomize)
   Countries, towns, courts: Beg from above
45   A pattern of your love!

A Valediction: Forbidding Mourning

John Donne

As virtuous men pass mildly, away,
   And whisper to their souls to go,
Whilst some of their sad friends do say,
   The breath goes now, and some say, No;

5 So let us melt, and make no noise,
   No tear-floods, nor sigh-tempests move ;
'Twere profanation of our joys
   To tell the laity our love.

Moving of th' earth brings harms and fears ;
10   Men reckon what it did and meant;
But trepidation of the spheres,
   Though greater far, is innocent.

Dull sublunary lovers' love
   (Whose soul is sense) cannot admit
15 Absence, because it doth remove
   Those things which elemented it.

John Donne, "A Valediction: Forbidding Mourning," from *Songs and Sonnets*. Copyright in the Public Domain.

But we, by a love so much refined,
    That ourselves know not what it is,
Inter-assuréd of the mind,
20   Care less, eyes, lips, and hands to miss.

Our two souls therefore, which are one,
    Though I must go, endure not yet
A breach, but an expansion,
    Like gold to airy thinness beat.

25 If they be two, they are two so
    As stiff twin compasses are two ;

Thy soul, the fixed foot, makes no show
    To move, but doth, if th' other do.

And though it in the centre sit,
30   Yet when the other far doth roam,
It leans and hearkens after it,
    And grows erect, as that comes home.

Such wilt thou be to me, who must
    Like th' other foot, obliquely run ;
35 Thy firmness makes my circle just,
    And makes me end where I begun.

Good Friday, 1613. Riding Westward

John Donne

Let man's soul be a sphere, and then, in this,
Th' intelligence that moves, devotion is
And as the other spheres, by being grown
Subject to foreign motion, lose their own,
5 And being by others hurried every day,
Scarce in a year their natural form obey ;
Pleasure or business, so, our souls admit
For their first mover, and are whirled by it.
Hence is't, that I am carried towards the West,
10 This day, when my soul's form bends to the East.
There I should see a Sun, by rising set,
And by that setting endless day beget:
But that Christ on this cross did rise and fall,
Sin had eternally benighted all.
15 Yet dare I, almost be glad, I do not see
That spectacle, of too much weight for me.

Who sees God's face, that is self-life, must die;
What a death were it then to see God die?
It made his own lieutenant, Nature, shrink;
20 It made his footstool crack, and the sun wink.
Could I behold those hands which span the poles,
And tune all spheres at once, pierced with those holes ?
Could I behold that endless height which is
Zenith to us and to our antipodes,
25 Humbled below us? Or that blood, which is
The seat of all our soul's, if not of His,
Made dirt of dust, or that flesh which was worn
By God for His apparel, ragg'd and torn?
If on these things I durst not look, durst I
30 Up on his miserable mother cast mine eye,

John Donne, "Good Friday, 1613. Riding Westward," Copyright in the Public Domain.

Who was God's partner here, and fnished
    thus
Half of that sacrifice which ransomed us?
Though these things, as I ride, be from
    mine eye,
They're present yet unto my memory,
35 For that looks towards them; and Thou
    look'st towards me,
O Saviour, as Thou hang'st upon the tree.

I turn my back to thee but to receive
Corrections till Thy mercies bid Thee leave.
O think me worth Thine anger, punish me,
40 Burn off my rust and my deformity;
Restore Thine image, so much, by Thy
    grace,
That Thou mays't know me, and I'll turn my
    face.

Lycidas

John Milton

Yet once more, O ye laurels, and once more
Ye Myrtles brown, with Ivy never-sear,
I com to pluck your Berries harsh and crude,
And with forc'd fingers rude,
5   Shatter your leaves before the mellowing year.
Bitter constraint, and sad occasion dear,
Compels me to disturb your season due:
For *Lycidas* is dead, dead ere his prime,
Young Lycidas, and hath not left his peer:
10 Who would not sing for Lycidas? he knew
Himself to sing, and build the lofty rhyme.
He must not flote upon his watry bear
Unwept, and welter to the parching wind,
Without the meed of som melodious tear.

15 Begin then, Sisters of the sacred well,
That from beneath the seat of Jove doth spring,
Begin, and somwhat loudly sweep the string.
Hence with denial vain, and coy excuse,
So may som gentle Muse
20 With lucky words favour my destin'd Urn,
And as he passes turn,
And bid fair peace be to my sable shrowd.
For we were nurst upon the self-same hill,
Fed the same flock, by fountain, shade, and rill.

25 Together both, ere the high Lawns appear'd
Under the opening eye-lids of the morn,
We drove a field, and both together heard
What time the Gray-fly winds her sultry horn,
Batt'ning our flocks with the fresh dews of
    night,
30 Oft till the Star that rose, at Ev'ning, bright
Toward Heav'ns descent had slop'd his westing
    wheel.
Mean while the Rural ditties were not mute,
Temper'd to th' Oaten Flute,
Rough Satyrs danc'd, and Fauns with clov'n
    heel,
35 From the glad sound would not be absent
    long,
And old Damœtas lov'd to hear our song.

But O the heavy change, now thou art gon,
Now thou art gon, and never must return!
Thee Shepherd, thee the Woods, and desert
    Caves,
40 With wilde Thyme and the gadding Vine
    o'regrown,
And all their echoes mourn.

John Milton, "Lycidas," from *Justa Edouardo King Naufrago*. Copyright in the Public Domain.

    The Willows, and the Hazle Copses green,
    Shall now no more be seen,
    Fanning their joyous Leaves to thy soft layes.
45 As killing as the Canker to the Rose,
    Or Taint-worm to the weanling Herds that graze,
    Or Frost to Flowers, that their gay wardrop wear,
    When first the White thorn blows;
    Such, Lycidas, thy loss to Shepherds ear.

50 Where were ye Nymphs when the remorse less deep
    Clos'd o're the head of your lov'd Lycidas?
    For neither were ye playing on the steep,
    Where your old Bards, the famous Druids ly,
    Nor on the shaggy top of Mona high,
55 Nor yet where Deva spreads her wisard stream:
    Ay me, I fondly dream!
    Had ye bin there—for what could that have don?
    What could the Muse her self that Orpheus bore,
    The Muse her self, for her inchanting son
60 Whom Universal nature did lament,
    When by the rout that made the hideous roar,
    His goary visage down the stream was sent,
    Down the swift Hebrus to the Lesbian shore.

    Alas! What boots it with uncessant care
65 To tend the homely slighted Shepherds trade,
    And strictly meditate the thankles Muse,
    Were it not better don as others use,
    To sport with Amaryllis in the shade,
    Or with the tangles of Neæra's hair?
70 Fame is the spur that the clear spirit doth raise
    (That last infirmity of Noble mind)
    To scorn delights, and live laborious dayes;
    But the fair Guerdon when we hope to find,
    And think to burst out into sudden blaze,
75 Comes the blind Fury with th' abhorred shears,
    And slits the thin spun life. But not the praise,
    Phœbus repli'd, and touch'd my trembling ears;
    Fame is no plant that grows on mortal soil,
    Nor in the glistering foil
80 Set off to th' world, nor in broad rumour lies,
    But lives and spreds aloft by those pure eyes,
    And perfet witnes of all judging Jove;
    As he pronounces lastly on each deed,
    Of so much fame in Heav'n expect thy meed.

85 O Fountain *Arethuse*, and thou honour'd flood,
    Smooth-sliding Mincius, crown'd with vocall reeds,
    That strain I heard was of a higher mood:
    But now my Oate proceeds,
    And listens to the Herald of the Sea
90 That came in Neptune's plea,
    He ask'd the Waves, and ask'd the Fellon winds,
    What hard mishap hath doom'd this gentle swain?
    And question'd every gust of rugged wings
    That blows from off each beaked Promontory,
95 They knew not of his story,
    And sage Hippotades their answer brings,
    That not a blast was from his dungeon stray'd,
    The Ayr was calm, and on the level brine,
    Sleek Panope with all her sisters play'd.
100 It was that fatall and perfidious Bark
    Built in th' eclipse, and rigg'd with curses dark,
    That sunk so low that sacred head of thine.

    Next Camus, reverend Sire, went footing slow,
    His Mantle hairy, and his Bonnet sedge,
105 Inwrought with figures dim, and on the edge
    Like to that sanguine flower inscrib'd with woe.
    Ah! Who hath reft (quoth he) my dearest pledge?
    Last came, and last did go,
    The Pilot of the Galilean lake,
110 Two massy Keyes he bore of metals twain,
    (The Golden opes, the Iron shuts amain)
    He shook his Miter'd locks, and stern bespake,
    How well could I have spar'd for thee young swain,
    Anow of such as for their bellies sake,
115 Creep and intrude, and climb into the fold?
    Of other care they little reck'ning make,
    Then how to scramble at the shearers feast,
    And shove away the worthy bidden guest.

Blind mouthes! that scarce themselves know how to hold
120 A Sheep-hook, or have learn'd ought els the least
That to the faithfull Herdmans art belongs!
What recks it them? What need they? They are sped;
And when they list, their lean and flashy songs
Grate on their scrannel Pipes of wretched straw,
125 The hungry Sheep look up, and are not fed,
But swoln with wind, and the rank mist they draw,
Rot inwardly, and foul contagion spread:
Besides what the grim Woolf with privy paw
Daily devours apace, and nothing sed,
130 But that two-handed engine at the door,
Stands ready to smite once, and smite no more.

Return Alpheus, the dread voice is past,
That shrunk thy streams; Return Sicilian Muse,
And call the Vales, and bid them hither cast
135 Their Bels, and Flourets of a thousand hues.
Ye valleys low where the milde whispers use,
Of shades and wanton winds, and gushing brooks,
On whose fresh lap the swart Star sparely looks,
Throw hither all your quaint enameld eyes,
140 That on the green terf suck the honied showres,
And purple all the ground with vernal flowres.
Bring the rathe Primrose that forsaken dies.
The tufted Crow-toe, and pale Jasmine,
The white Pink, and the Pansie freakt with jeat,
145 The glowing Violet.
The Musk-rose, and the well attir'd Woodbine,
With Cowslips wan that hang the pensive hed,
And every flower that sad embroidery wears:
Bid Amaranthus all his beauty shed,
150 And Daffadillies fill their cups with tears,
To strew the Laureat Herse where Lycid lies.
For so to interpose a little ease,
Let our frail thoughts dally with false surmise.

Ay me! Whilst thee the shores and sounding Seas
155 Wash far away, where ere thy bones are hurld,
Whether beyond the stormy Hebrides,
Where thou perhaps under the whelming tide
Visit'st the bottom of the monstrous world;
Or whether thou to our moist vows deny'd,
160 Sleep'st by the fable of Bellerus old,
Where the great vision of the guarded Mount
Looks toward Namancos and Bayona's hold;
Look homeward Angel now, and melt with ruth.
And, O ye Dolphins, waft the haples youth.
165 Weep no more, woful Shepherds weep no more,
For Lycidas your sorrow is not dead,
Sunk though he be beneath the watry floar,
So sinks the day-star in the Ocean bed,
And yet anon repairs his drooping head,
170 And tricks his beams, and with new-spangled Ore,
Flames in the forehead of the morning sky:
So Lycidas sunk low, but mounted high,
Through the dear might of him that walk'd the waves;
Where other groves, and other streams along,
175 With Nectar pure his oozy Lock's he laves,
And hears the unexpressive nuptiall Song,
In the blest Kingdoms meek of joy and love.
There entertain him all the Saints above,
In solemn troops, and sweet Societies
180 That sing, and singing in their glory move,
And wipe the tears for ever from his eyes.
Now Lycidas the Shepherds weep no more;
Hence forth thou art the Genius of the shore,
In thy large recompense, and shalt be good
185 To all that wander in that perilous flood.

Thus sang the uncouth Swain to th' Okes and rills,
While the still morn went out with Sandals gray,
He touch'd the tender stops of various Quills,
With eager thought warbling his Dorick lay:
190 And now the Sun had stretch'd out all the hills,
And now was dropt into the Western bay;
At last he rose, and twitch'd his Mantle blew:
To morrow to fresh Woods, and Pastures new.

Paradise Lost:

Book I

John Milton

The Argument

This first book proposes first, in brief, the whole subject, *man's disobedience, and the loss thereupon of Paradise wherein he was placed. Then touches the prime cause of his fall, the serpent, or rather Satan in the serpent; who revolting from God, and drawing to his side many legions of angels, was by the command of God, driven out of heaven with all his crew into the great deep.* Which action past over, the poem hasts into the midst of things, *presenting Satan with his Angels now fallen into hell,* described here, not in the centre (for heaven and earth may be supposed as yet not made, certainly not yet accursed) *but in a place of utter darkness fitliest called Chaos: Here Satan, with his Angels lying on the burning Lake, thunder-struck and astonished, after a certain space recovers, as from confusion, calls up him who next in order and dignity lay by him; they confer of their miserable fall. Satan awakens all his legions, who lay till then in the same manner confounded; they rise, their numbers, array of Battle, their chief leaders nam'd according to the idols known afterwards in Canaan and the countries adjoyning. To these Satan directs his speech, comforts them with hope yet of regaining Heaven, but tells them lastly of a new world, and new kind of Creature to be created, according to an ancient Prophesey or report in heaven;* (for that Angels were long before this visible creation, was the opinion of many ancient Fathers.) *To find out the truth of this prophesey, and what to determin thereon he refers to a full council. What his associates thence attempt. Pandemonium, the palace of Satan rises, suddenly built out of the deep: The infernal peers there sit in council.*

    Of man's first disobedience, and the fruit
Of that forbidden tree, whose mortal taste
Brought death into the world, and all our woe,
With loss of *Eden*, till one greater Man
5 Restore us, and regain the blissful seat,
Sing Heavenly Muse, that on the secret top
Of *Oreb*, or of *Sinai*, didst inspire
That Shepherd, who first taught the chosen Seed,
In the Beginning how the heavens and Earth
10 Rose out of *Chaos*: Or if *Sion* Hill
Delight thee more, and *Siloa's* Brook that flow'd
Fast by the oracle of God; I thence
Invoke thy aid to my advent'rous song,
That with no middle flight intends to soar
15 Above th' *Aonian* mount, while it pursues
Things unattempted yet in prose or rhyme.
And chiefly thou O spirit, that dost prefer
Before all temples th'upright heart and pure,
Instruct me, for thou know'st; Thou from the first
20 Wast present, and with mighty wings outspread
Dove-like sat'st brooding on the vast abyss
And mad'st it pregnant: What in me is dark

John Milton, "Book 1", from *Paradise Lost*. Copyright in the Public Domain.

      Illumine, what is low raise and support;
      That to the highth of this great argument
25   I may assert eternal Providence,
      And justifie the wayes of God to men.

      Say first, for heaven hides nothing from thy view,
      Nor the deep tract of hell, say first what cause
      Mov'd our grand parents in that happy State,
30   Favour'd of Heaven so highly, to fall off
      From their Creator, and transgress his will
      For one restraint, lords of the world besides?
      Who first seduc'd them to that foul revolt?
      Th' infernal serpent; he it was, whose guile
35   Stirr'd up with envy and revenge, deceiv'd
      The mother of mankind, what time his pride
      Had cast him out from Heaven, with all his host
      Of rebel angels, by whose aid aspiring
      To set himself in glory above his peers,
40   He trusted to have equaled the Most High,
      If he opposed: and with ambitious aim
      Against the throne and monarchy of God
      Rais'd impious war in heaven and Battle proud
      With vain attempt. Him the Almighty power
45   Hurl'd headlong flaming from th' ethereal Skye
      With hideous ruine and combustion down
      To bottomless perdition, there to dwell
      In adamantine chains and penal fire,
      Who durst defie th' Omnipotent to Arms.
50   Nine times the space that measures day and night
      To mortal men, he with his horrid crew
      Lay vanquished, rolling in the fiery gulf
      Confounded though immortal; But his doom
      Reserv'd him to more wrath: for now the thought
55   Both of lost happiness and lasting pain
      Torments him. Round he throws his baleful eyes
      That witness'd huge affliction and dismay
      Mixed with obdurate pride and stedfast hate:
      At once as far as angels ken; he views
60   The dismal situation waste and wilde:
      A Dungeon horrible, on all sides round
      As one great furnace flam'd: yet from those flames
      No light, but rather darkness visible
      Serv'd onely to discover sights of woe,
65   Regions of sorrow, doleful shades, where peace
      And rest can never dwell: hope never comes
      That comes to all: but torture without end
      Still urges, and a fiery deluge, fed
      With ever-burning sulphur unconsum'd,
70   Such place eternal justice had prepar'd
      For those rebellious, here their prison ordain'd
      In utter darkness, and their portion set
      As far remov'd from God and light of Heaven
      As from the Centre thrice to th'utmost pole.
75   O how unlike the place from whence they fell!
      There the companions of his fall, o'erwhelm'd
      With floods and whirlwinds of tempestuous fire,
      He soon discerns; and welt'ring by his side
      One next himself in power, and next in crime,
80   Long after known in *Palestine,* and nam'd
      Beelzebub. To whom th' Arch-Enemy,
      And thence in Heaven called Satan, with bold words
      Breaking the horrid silence thus began.

      If thou beest he—But O how fall'n! how chang'd

85 From him, who in the happy realms of light
Cloth'd with transcendent brightness didst outshine
Myriads though bright; if he, whom mutual league,
United thoughts and counsels, equal hope
And hazard in the glorious enterprize,
90 Joined with me once, now misery hath joined
In equal ruin; into what pit thou seest,
From what highth fallen, so much the stronger prov'd
He with his thunder; and till then who knew
The force of those dire arms? Yet not for those,
95 Nor what the potent Victor in his rage
Can else inflict, do I repent or change,
Though chang'd in outward lustre; that fixt mind,
And high disdain, from sence of injur'd merit,
That with the mightiest rais'd me to contend;
100 And to the fierce contention brought along
Innumerable force of spirits arm'd
That durst dislike his reign, and me preferring
His utmost power with adverse power oppos'd
In dubious Battle on the plains of heaven,
105 And shook his throne. What though the field be lost?
All is not lost; the unconquerable will,
And study of revenge, immortal hate,
And courage never to submit or yield;
(And what is else not to be overcome?)
110 That glory never shall his wrath or might
Extort from me, to bow and sue for grace
With suppliant knee and defy his power,
Who from the terror of this arm so late
Doubted his empire. That were low indeed;
115 That were an ignominy and shame beneath
This downfall; since by fate the strength of gods
And this empyreal substance cannot fail;
Since through experience of this great event
In arms not worse, in foresight much advanced,
120 We may with more successful hope resolve
To wage by force or guile eternal war
Irreconcilable, to our grand foe,
Who now triumphs, and in th' excess of joy
Sole reigning holds the Tyranny of heaven.
125 So spake the apostate angel, though in pain;
Vaunting aloud, but racked with deep despair:
And him thus answer'd soon his bold Compeer.

O Prince, O Chief of many Throned Powers,
That led th' embattelld seraphim to war
130 Under thy conduct, and in dreadful deeds
Fearless, endanger'd heavens perpetual King
And put to proof his high supremacy
Whether upheld by strength, or chance, or fate,
Too well I see and rue the dire event,
135 That with sad overthrow and foul defeat
Hath lost us heaven, and all this mighty host
In horrible destruction laid thus low,
As far as hods and heavenly essences,
Can perish: for the mind and spirit remains
140 Invincible, and vigour soon returns,
Though all our glory extinct, and happy state,
Here swallow'd up in endless misery;
But what if he our conqueror, (whom I now
Of force believe Almighty, since no less
145 Then such could hav o'erpowered such force as ours)
Have left us this our spirit and strength entire
Strongly to suffer and support our pains;
That we may so suffice his vengeful ire,
Or do him mightier service as his thralls
150 By right of war, whate'er his business be,

Here in the heart of hell to work in fire,
Or do his errands in the gloomy deep;
What can it then avail though yet we feel
Strength undiminished, or eternal being,
155 To undergo eternal punishment?
Whereto with speedy words th' Arch-fiend replied:

Fallen Cherub, to be weak is miserable
Doing or suffering: but of this be sure,
To do aught good never will be our task;
160 But ever to do ill our sole delight,
As being the contrary to his high will
Whom we resist. If then his Providence
Out of our evil seek to bring forth good,
Our labour must be to pervert that end,
165 And out of good still to find means of evil:
Which oft times may succeed, so as perhaps
Shall grieve him, if I fail not, and disturb
His inmost counsels from their destin'd aim.
But see! the angry Victor hath recall'd
170 His ministers of vengeance and pursuit
Back to the gates of heaven: The sulphurous hail
Shot after us in storm, o'erblown hath laid
The fiery Surge, that from the precipice
Of heaven receiv'd us falling, and the thunder,
175 Wing'd with red lightning and impetuous rage,
Perhaps hath spent his shafts, and ceases now
To bellow through the vast and boundless deep.
Let us not slip th' occasion, whether scorn,
Or satiate fury yield it from our Foe.
180 Seest thou yon dreary Plain, forlorn and wilde,
The seat of desolation, void of light,

Save what the glimmering of these livid flames
Casts pale and dreadful? Thither let us tend
From off the tossing of these fiery waves;
185 There rest, if any rest can harbour there,
And re-assembling our afflicted Powers,
Consult how we may henceforth most offend
Our enemy; our own loss how repair,
How overcome this dire Calamity,
190 What reinforcement we may gain from Hope,
If not what resolution from despair.

Thus Satan talking to his neerest mate,
With head up-lift above the wave, and eyes
That sparkling blaz'd: his other parts besides
195 Prone on the flood, extended long and large
Lay floating many a rood: in bulk as huge,
As whom the fables name of monstrous size,
Titanian, or *Earth-born*, that warr'd on *Jove*,
Briareus or *Typhon*, whom the den
200 By ancient *Tarsus* held; or that sea-beast
Leviathan, which God of all his works
Created hugest that swim th' ocean stream:
(Him, haply slumb'ring on the *Norway* foam,
The pilot of some small night-founder'd skiff,
205 Deeming some Island, oft, as seamen tell,
With fixed anchor in his scaly rind
Moors by his side under the lee, while night
Invests the Sea, and wished morn delays.)
So stretched out huge in length the arch-fiend lay
210 Chain'd on the burning lake, nor ever thence
Had risen or heav'd his head, but that the will
And high permission of all-ruling Heaven
Left him at large to his own dark designs:
That with reiterated crimes he might
215 Heap on himself damnation, while he sought
Evil to others: and enrag'd might see,
How all his malice serv'd but to bring forth
Infinite goodness, grace and mercy shown
On Man by him seduced, but on himself
220 Treble confusion, wrath, and vengeance

poured.
Forthwith upright he rears from off the Pool
His mighty stature; on each hand the flames
Drivn backward slope their pointing spires, and rolled
In billows, leave i' th'midst a horrid vale.
225 Then with expanded wings he steers his flight
Aloft, incumbent on the dusky air,
That felt unusual weight: till on dry Land
He lights, if it were land that ever burn'd
With solid, as the lake with liquid fire:
230 And such appear'd in hue, as when the force
Of subterranean wind transports a hill
Torn from *Pelorus,* or the shatter'd side
Of thund'ring *Ætna,* whose combustible
And fueled entrails thence conceiving Fire,
235 Sublim'd with mineral fury, aid the winds,
And leave a singed bottom all involv'd
With stench and smoke; Such resting found the sole
Of unblessed feet; him follow'd his next Mate,
Both glorying to have scap't the *Stygian* flood
240 As gods, and by their own recover'd strength;
Not by the suff'rance of supernal power.

Is this the region, this the soil, the clime,
Said then the lost archangel, this the seat,
That we must change for heaven, this mournful gloom
245 For that celestial light? be it so; since he
Who now is sovereign can dispose and bid
What shall be right: farthhest from him is best
Whom reason hath equalld, force hath made supreme
Above his equals. Farewel happy fields
250 Where Joy for ever dwells; hail horrors; hail,
Infernal world: and thou profoundest hell
Receive thy new Possessor! One who brings
A mind not to be chang'd by Place or Time.
The mind is its own place, and in itself
255 Can make a heaven of hell, a hell of heaven.
What matter where, if I be still the same,
And what I should be, all but less then he
Whom thunder hath made greater? Here at least
We shall be free; th' Almighty hath not built
260 Here for his envy; will not drive us hence:
Here we may reign secure; and in my choice
To reign is worth ambition, though in hell:
Better to reign in Hell, then serve in heaven.
But wherefore let we then our faithful friends,
265 Th' associates and copartners of our loss
Lye thus astonished on th' oblivious pool,
And call them not to share with us their part
In this unhappy mansion: or once more
With rallied arms to try what may be yet
270 Regain'd in heaven, or what more lost in Hell?

So *Satan* spake, and him *Beelzebub*
Thus answer'd: Leader of those aarmies bright,
Which but th' Onmipotent none could have foyld,
If once they hear that voice, their liveliest pledge
275 Of hope in fears and dangers, heard so oft
In worst extremes, and on the perilous edge
Of battle when it rag'd, in all assaults
Their surest signal, they will soon resume
New courage, and revive, though now they lie
280 Groveling and prostrate on yon lake of fire,
(As we erewhile,) astounded and amaz'd;
No wonder, fall'n such a pernicious heighth.

He scarce had ceased when the superiour fiend
Was moving toward the shore; his ponder'ous shield
285 Ethereal temper, massy, large, and round,
Behind him cast; the broad circumference
Hung on his shoulders like the moon,

        whose orb
Through optic glass the *Tuscan* artist views
At ev'ning from the top of *Fesole,*
290 Or in *Valdarno,* to descry new lands,
Rivers or mountains in her spotty globe.
His spear, (to equal which the tallest Pine
Hewn on *Norwegian* hills, to be the Mast
Of some great ammiral, were but a wand,)
295 He walkt with to support uneasie steps
Over the burning marle, (not like those steps
On heaven's azure!) and the torrid clime
Smote on him sore besides, vaulted with fire.
Nathless he so endur'd, till on the beach
300 Of that inflamed sea, he stood and call'd
His legions, angel forms, who lay entranced
Thick as autumnal leaves that strew the brooks
In *Vallombrosa,* where th' *Etrurian* shades
High over-arched imbower; or scatter sedge
305 Afloat, when with fierce Winds *Orion* arm'd
Hath vext the Red-Sea coast, whose waves o'erthrew
Busiris and his *Memphian* chivalry,
While with perfidious hatred they pursu'd
The sojourners of *Goshen,* who beheld
310 From the safe shore their floating carkases
And broken Chariot Wheels, so thick bestrown,
Abject and lost lay these, covering the flood,
Under amazement of their hideous change.
He call'd so loud, that all the hollow deep
315 Of hell resounded: Princes, Potentates,
Warriors, the flower of heaven! once yours, now lost,
If such astonishment as this can seize
Eternal spirits; or have ye chosen this place
After the toil of Battle to repose
320 Your wearied virtue, for the ease you find
To slumber here, as in the vales of heaven?
Or in this abject posture have ye sworn
T'dore the Conquerour? who now beholds
Cherube and Seraph rowling in the flood
325 With scatter'd arms and ensigns, till anon
His swift pursuers from heaven gates discern
Th' advantage, and descending tread us down
Thus drooping, or with linked thunderbolts
Transfix us to the bottom of this gulf.
330 Awake, arise, or be for ever fall'n.

They heard, and were abashed, and up they sprung
Upon the wing; as when men wont to watch
On duty, sleeping found by whom they dread,
Rouse and bestir themselves ere well awake.
335 Nor did they not perceive the evil plight
In which they were, or the fierce pains not feel;
Yet to their general's voice they soon obey'd
Innumerable; as when the potent rod
Of *Amrams* son in *Egypts* evil day
340 Wav'd round the coast, up call'd a pitchy cloud
Of *Locusts,* warping on the eastern wind,
That o'er the Realm of impious *Pharaoh* hung
Like night, and darken'd all the Land of *nile*:
So numberless were those bad Angels seen
345 Hov'ring on wing under the cope of hell,
'Twixt upper, nether, and surrounding Fires
Till, as a signal given, th' uplifted Spear
Of their great sultan waving to direct
Thir course, in even balance down they light
350 On the firm brimstone, and fill all the plain:
A multitude, like which the populous north
Pour'd never from her frozen loins, to pass
Rhine or the *Danaw,* when her barbarous Sons
Came like a deluge on the south, and spread
355 Beneath *Gibralter* to the *Lybian* sands.
Forthwith from every squadron, and each band,

The heads and leaders thither haste, where stood
Thir great commander; godlike shapes and forms
Excelling human, princely dignities,
And powers! that erst in heaven sat on thrones; [360]
Though of their Names in heav'nly Records now
Be no memorial blotted out and raz'd
By their rebellion, from the books of life.
Nor had they yet among the sons of *Eve*
Got them new names; till wand'ring o'er the earth, [365]
Through God's high sufferance for the tryal of man,
By falsities and lies the greatest part
Of mankind they corrupted to forsake
God their Creator, and th' invisible
Glory of him that made them, to transform [370]
Oft to the image of a brute, adorn'd
With gay religions full of pomp and gold,
And devils to adore for deities:
Then were they known to men by various names,
And various idols through the heathen world. [375]
Say, Muse, their names then known; who first, who last,
Rous'd from the slumber, on that fiery couch,
At their great Emperor's call as next in worth
Came singly where he stood on the bare strand,
While the promiscuous croud stood yet aloof? [380]
The chief were those who, from the pit of hell
Roaming to seek their prey on earth, durst fix
Their seats long after next thse seat of God,
Thrir Altars by his altar, Gods ador'd
Among the nations round, and durst abide [385]
Jehovah thund'ring out of *Sion*, thron'd
Between the cherubim; yea, often plac'd
Within his sanctuary itself their shrines,
Abominations; and with cursed things
His holy rites, and solemn feasts profan'd, [390]
And with their darkness durst affront his light.
First *Moloch*, horrid king besmear'd with blood
Of human sacrifice, and parents tears,
Though, for the noyse of drums and timbrels loud
Thir children's cries unheard, that passed through fire [395]
To his grim Idol. Him the *Ammonite*
Worshiped in *Rabba* and her watery plain,
In *Argob,* and in *Basan,* to the stream
Of utmost *Arnon*. Nor content with such
Audacious neighbourhood, the wisest heart [400]
Of *Solomon* he led by fraud, to build
His temple right against the temple of God,
On that opprobrious hill; and made his grove
The pleasant valley of *Hinnom, Tophet* thence
And black *Gehenna* called, the type of hell. [405]
Next *Chemos,* th' obscene dread of *Moabs* sons,
From *Aroar* to *Nebo,* and the wild
Of southmost *Abarim*; in *Hesebon*
And *Horonaim, Seon*'s realm, beyond
The flowry dale of *Sibma* clad with vines, [410]
And *Eleale* to th' *Asphaltick* pool.
Peor his other Name, when he entic'd
Israel in *Sittim,* on their march from *Nile*
To do him wanton rites, which cost them woe.
Yet thence his lustful orgies he enlarg'd [415]
Even to that hill of scandal, by the Grove
Of *Moloch* homicide; lust hard by hate;
Till good *Josiah* drove them thence to hell.
With these came they, who from the bordring flood
Of old *Euphrates* to the Brook that parts [420]
Egypt from *Syrian* ground, had general names

Of *Baalim* and *Ashtaroth,* those male,
These Feminine: For spirits when they please
Can either sex assume, or both; so soft
425 And uncompounded is their Essence pure,
Not tied or manacled with joint or limb,
Nor founded on the brittle strength of bones,
Like cumbrous flesh; but in what shape they choose
Dilated or condensed, bright or obscure,
430 Can execute their airy purposes,
And works of love or enmity fulfill.
For those the race of *Israel* oft forsook
Their living strength, and unfrequented left
His righteous Altar, bowing lowly down
435 To bestial Gods; for which their heads as low
Bow'd down in Battle, sunk before the spear
Of despicable foes. With these in troop
Came *Astoreth,* whom the *Phoenicians* call'd
Astarte, queen of heaven, with crescent horns;
440 To whose bright Image nightly by the moon
Sidonian virgins paid their vows and songs,
In *Sion* also not unsung, where stood
Her temple on th' offensive mountain, built
By that uxorious king, whose heart though large,
445 Beguil'd by fair idolatresses, fell
To idols foul. *Thammuz* came next behind,
Whose annual wound in *Lebanon* allur'd
The *Syrian* damsels to lament his fate
In am'rous ditties all a Summer's day,
450 While smooth *Adonis* from his native rock
Ran purple to the sea, suppos'd with blood
Of *Thammuz* yearly wounded: the love-tale
Infected *Sions* daughters with like heat;
Whose wanton passions in the sacred porch
455 *Ezekiel* saw, when, by the vision led
His eye surveyed the dark idolatries
Of alienated *Judah.* Next came one
Who mourn'd in earnest, when the captive ark
Maim'd his brute Image, head and hands lopped off
460 In his own temple, on the grunsel edge,
Where he fell flat, and sham'd his worshipers:
Dagon his name; Sea Monster; upward man
And downward fish: yet had his temple high
Rear'd in *Azotus,* dreaded through the coast
465 Of *Palestine,* in *Gath* and *Ascalon,*
And *Accaron* and *Gaza's* frontier bounds.
Him follow'd *Rimmon,* whose delightful seat
Was fair *Damascus,* on the fertil banks
Of *Abbana* and *Pharphar,* lucid streams;
470 He also against the house of God was bold:
A leper once he lost and gain'd a king,
Ahaz, his sottish conquerour, whom he drew
Gods Altar to disparage and displace
For one of *Syrian* mode, whereon to burn
475 His odious off'rings, and adore the Gods
Whom he had vanquished. After these appear'd
A crew who under names of old renown,
Osiris, Isis, Orus, and their train
With monstrous shapes and sorceries abus'd
480 Fanatic *Egypt,* and her priests, to seek
Thir wand'ring gods disguis'd in brutish forms
Rather then human. Nor did *Israel* 'scape
Th' infection, when their borrow'd gold compos'd
The calf in *Oreb;* and the rebel king
485 Doubl'd that sin in *Bethel,* and in *Dan,*
Lik'ning his Maker to the grazed ox,
Jehovah, who in one night when he pass'd
From *Egypt* marching, equalled with one stroke
Both her first-born and all her bleating gods.
490 *Belial* came last, then whom a spirit more lewd
Fell not from heaven, or more gross to love
Vice for itself: To him no temple stood

Or altar smoked; yet who more oft then he
In temples and at altars, when the *priest*
495 Turns atheist, as did *Eli's* Sons, who fill'd
With lust and violence the house of God.
In courts and palaces he also reigns
And in luxurious cities, where the noise
Of riot ascends above their loftiest towrs,
500 And injury and outrage: and when night
Darkens the streets, then wander forth the sons
Of *Belial,* flown with insolence and wine.
Witness the Streets of *Sodom,* and that night
In *Gibeah,* when the hospitable door
505 Expos'd a Matron to avoid worse rape.

These were the prime in order and in might;
The rest were long to tell, though far renown'd.
Th' *Ionian* Gods, of *Javan's* issue held
Gods, yet confessed later then heaven and earth
510 Thir boasted parents. *Titan,* heavens first born,
With his enormous brood, and birthright seized
By younger *Saturn:* he from mightier *Jove,*
His own and *Rhea's* Son, like measure found;
So Jove usurping reign'd; these first in *Crete*
515 And *Ida* known; thence on the snowy top
Of cold *Olympus* rul'd the middle air
Their highest heaven; or on the *Delphian* cliff,
Or in *Dodona,* and through all the bounds
Of *Doric* land; or who with *Saturn* old
520 Fled over *Adria* to th' *Hesperian* Fields,
And o'er the *Celtic* roam'd the utmost isles.
All these and more came flocking; but with looks
Down cast and damp; yet such wherein appear'd
Obscure some glimps of joy to have found their chief
525 Not in despair, to have found themselves not lost
In loss itself; which on his count'nance cast
Like doubtful hue: but he his wonted pride
Soon recollecting, with high words, that bore
Semblance of worth, not substance, gently rais'd
530 Their fainting courage, and dispell'd their fears.
Then strait commands that at the warlike sound
Of trumpets loud, and clarions be uprear'd
His mighty standard: that proud honour claim'd
Azazel as his right, a cherub tall;
535 Who forthwith from the glittering staff unfurl'd
Th' imperial ensign, which full high advanced
Shon like a Meteor streaming to the wind
With gemms and golden lustre rich emblaz'd,
Seraphic arms and trophies; all the while
540 Sonorous mettal blowing martial sounds:
At which the universal host up sent
A shout that tore hells concave; and beyond
Frighted the reign of *Chaos* and old Night.
All in a moment through the gloom were seen
545 Ten thousand banners rise into the air
With orient colours waving: with them rose
A forest huge of Spears; and thronging helms
Appear'd, and serried shields in thick array,
Of depth immeasurable: anon they move
550 In perfect *Phalanx* to the *Dorian* mood
Of flutes, and soft recorders; such as rais'd
To hight of noblest temper heroes old
Arming to Battle, and instead of rage,
Deliberate valour breath'd, firm and unmov'd
555 With dread of death to flight, or foul retreat;

Nor wanting power to mitigate and swage,
With solemn touches, troubled thoughts, and chase
Anguish and doubt, and fear, and sorrow and pain,
From mortal or immortal minds. Thus they
Breathing united force, with fixed thought
Mov'd on in silence to soft pipes, that charm'd
Thir painful steps o'er the burnt soil: and now
Advanced in view, they stand, a horrid front
Of dreadful length, and dazling arms, in guise
Of warriors old with order'd spear and shield,
Awaiting what command their mighty chief
Had to impose: he through the armed files
Darts his experienced eye, and soon traverse
The whole battalion views, their order due,
Their visages and stature as of gods,
Their number last he sums. And now his heart
Distends with pride, and hard'ning in his strength
Glories: for never since created man,
Met such imbodied force, as nam'd with these
Could merit more then that small infantry
Warr'd on by cranes; though all the giant brood
Of *Phlegra* with th' heroic race were joined,
That fought at *Theb's* and *Ilium,* on each side
Mixt with auxiliar Gods; and what resounds
In fable or *romance* of *Uthers* son,
Begirt with *British* and *Armoric* knights;
And all who since baptiz'd or infidel,
Jousted in *Aspramont* or *Montalban,*
Damasco, or *Morocco,* or *Trebisond;*
Or whom *Biserta* sent from *Afric* shore,
When *Charlemain* with all his peerage fell
By *Fontarabbia.* Thus far these beyond
Compare of mortal prowess, yet observ'd
Their dread commander: he above the rest
In shape and gesture proudly eminent
Stood like a tower; his form had yet not lost
All her original brightness, nor appear'd
Less then arch angel ruin'd, and th' excess
Of glory obscur'd: as when the sun new risen
Looks through the horizontal misty air
shorn of his beams, or from behind the moon
In dim eclipse disastrous twilight sheds
On half the nations, and with fear of change
Perplexes monarchs; darkened so, yet shone
Above them all th' arch angel: but his face
Deep scars of thunder had intrenched, and care
Sat on his faded cheek, but under brows
Of dauntless courage, and considerate pride
Waiting revenge: cruel his eye, but cast
Signs of remorse and passion, to behold
The fellows of his crime, the followers rather
(Far other once beheld in bliss) condemn'd
For ever now to have their lot in pain;
Millions of spirits, for his fault amerced
Of heaven, and from Eternal Splendors flung
For his revolt; yet faithful how they stood,
Their Glory wither'd: as when heavens fire
hath scath'd the forrest oaks, or mountain pines,
With singed top their stately growth, though bare,
Stands on the blasted heath. He now prepar'd
To speak; whereat their doubl'd ranks they bend
From wing to wing, and half enclose him round
With all his peers: attention held them mute:
Thrice he assay'd, and thrice in spite of scorn,

| 620 | Tears, such as angels weep, burst forth; at last
Words interwove with sighs found out their way.

O myriads of immortal spirits; O powers
Matchless, but with th' Almighty, and that strife
Was not inglorious, though th' event was dire,
| 625 | As this place testifies, and this dire change,
Hateful to utter: but what power of mind,
Foreseeing or presaging, from the depth
Of knowledge past or present, could have fear'd,
How such united force of gods, how such
| 630 | As stood like these, could ever know repulse?
For who can yet beleeve, though after loss,
That all these puissant legions, whose exile
Hath emptied heaven, shall fail to reascend
Self-rais'd, and repossess their native seat?
| 635 | For mee be witness all the host of heaven,
If counsels different, or danger shunn'd
By me, have lost our hopes: But he who reigns
Monarch in heaven, till then as one secure
Sat on his throne, upheld by old repute,
| 640 | Consent or custom, and his regal state
Put forth at full, but still his strength conceal'd,
Which tempted our attempt, and wrought our fall.
Henceforth his might we know, and know our own
So as not either to provoke, or dread
| 645 | New war, provoked. Our better part remains
To work in close design, by fraud or guile,
What force effected not: that he no less
At length from us may find, who overcomes
By force, hath overcome but half his foe.
| 650 | Space may produce new worlds; whereof so rife
There went a fame in heaven, that he, ere long,
Intended to create; and therein plant
A generation, whom his choice regard
Should favour equal to the sons of heaven:
Thither, if but to pry, shall be perhaps
| 655 | Our first eruption, thither or elsewhere:
For this infernal pit shall never hold
Celestial spirits in bondage, nor th' abyss
Long under darkness cover. But these thoughts
| 660 | Full counsel must mature: peace is despair'd,
For who can think submission? war then, war
Open or understood, must be resolv'd.

He spake: and to confirm his words outflew
Millions of flaming swords, drawn from the thighs
| 665 | Of mighty cherubim: the sudden blaze
Far round illumin'd hell; highly they rag'd
Against the Highest, and fierce with grasped arms
Clash'd on their sounding Shields the din of war,
Hurling defiance toward the vault of heaven.

| 670 | There stood a hill not far whose grisly top
Belch'd fire and rolling smoke; the rest entire
Shon with a glassy scurff; (undoubted sign
That in his womb was hid metallic ore,
The work of sulphure.) thither wing'd with speed
| 675 | A numerous brigade hasten'd: as when bands
Of pioners with spade and pickaxe arm'd,
Forerun the royal camp, to trench a field,
Or cast a rampart: *Mammon* led them on,
Mammon, the least erected spirit that fell
| 680 | From heav'n: for even in heav'n his looks and thoughts
Were always downward bent, admiring more
The riches of heavens pavement, trod'n gold,
Then aught divine or holy else, enjoy'd

In vision beatific: by him first
685 Men also, and by his suggestion taught,
Ransack'd the centre, and with impious hands
Rifled the bowels of their mother earth
For treasures better hid. Soon had his crew
Opened into the hill a spacious wound
690 And digg'd out ribs of gold. Let none admire
That riches grow in hell; that soil may best
Deserve the precious bane.) And here let those
Who boast in mortal things, and wond'ring tell
Of *Babel,* and the works of *Memphian* kings,
695 Learn how their greatest monuments of fame,
And strength, and art, are easily outdone
By Spirits reprobate, and in an hour,
What in an age they with incessant toil,
And hands innumerable scarce perform.
700 Nigh on the Plain in many cells prepar'd,
That underneath had veins of liquid fire
Sluic'd from the lake, a second multitude
With wondrous art found out the massy ore,
Severing each kind, and scummed the Bullion dross:
705 A third as soon had form'd within the ground
A various mould; and from the boiling cells
By strange conveyance fill'd each hollow nook:
As in an organ, from one blast of wind,
To many a row of pipes the sound-board breathes.
710 Anon out of the earth a fabrick huge
Rose like an exhalation, with the sound
Of dulcet symphonies and voices sweet,
Built like a temple, where *pilasters* round
Were set, and Doric pillars, overlaid
715 With golden architrave; nor did there want
Cornice or frieze, with bossy Sculptures graven:
The Roof was fretted gold. Not *Babylon,*
Nor great *Alcairo* such magnificence
Equall'd in all their glories, to inshrine
720 *Belus,* or *Serapis,* their gods; or seat
Their kings, when *Egypt* with *Assyria* strove
In wealth and luxury. Th' ascending pile
Stood fixt her stately height: and straight the dores
Op'ning their brazen folds discover wide
725 Within her ample spaces o'er the smooth
And level pavement: from the arched roof,
Pendent by suttle magic, many a row
Of starry lamps, and blazing cressets, fed
With *Naphtha* and *Asphaltus* yielded light,
730 As from a sky. The hasty multitude
Admiring enter'd, and the work some praise,
And some the Architect: his hand was known
In heaven by many a Tow'red structure high,
Where scepterd angels held their residence,
735 And sat as princes; whom the supreme King
Exalted to such power, and gave to rule,
Each in his Hierarchy, the orders bright:
Nor was his name unheard, or unador'd,
In ancient *Greece;* and in *Ausonian* land
740 Men call'd him *Mulciber:* and how he fell
From heaven, they fabled, thrown by angry *Jove*
Sheer o'er the chrystal battlements: from morn
To noon he fell, from noon to dewy eve,
A summer's day; and with the setting sun
745 Dropped from the Zenith like a falling star,
On *Lemnos* th' *Ægean* Isle: thus they relate,
Erring; for he with this rebellious rout
Fell long before; nor aught avail'd him now
T'have built in heaven high towrs; nor did he scape
750 By all his engines, but was headlong sent
With his industrious crew to build in hell.

Meanwhile the winged hearalds by command

Of sovereign power, with awful ceremony
And trumpet's sound, throughout the host proclaim
755 A solemn council forthwith to be held
At *Pandemonium*, the high capital
Of Satan and his peers: their summons call'd,
From every band and squared regiment,
By place or choice the worthiest they anon
760 With hunderds, and with thousands, trooping came
Attended: all access was throng'd, the gates
And porches wide, but chief the spacious hall
(Though like a cover'd field, where champions bold
Wont ride in arm'd, and at the Soldan's chair
765 Defied the best of *Paynim* chivalry
To mortal combat, or carreer with lance)
Thick swarm'd, both on the ground, and in the air,
Brushed with the hiss of rustling wings. As bees
In spring time, when the Sun with *Taurus* rides,
770 Pour forth their populous youth about the hive
In clusters; they among fresh dews and flowers
Fly to and fro, or on the smoothed plank,
The suburb of their Straw-built citadel,
New rubbed with balm, expatiate and confer
775 Their state affairs: so thick the airy crowd
Swarm'd and were straiten'd; till the signal given.
Behold a wonder; they but now who seem'd
In bigness to surpass earths giant sons
Now less then smallest dwarfs, in narrow room
780 Throng numberless, like that pygmean race
Beyond the *Indian* mount, or faerie elves,
Whose midnight revels, by a forest side,
Or Fountain some belated peasant sees,
Or dreams he sees, while over-head the Moon
785 Sits Arbitress, and nearer to the Earth
Wheels her pale course; they on their mirth and dance
Intent, with jocund Music charm his ear:
At once with joy and fear his heart rebounds.
Thus incorporeal Spirits to smallest forms
790 Reduc'd their shapes immense: and were at large
Though without number still amidst the hall
Of that infernal court. But far within,
And in their own dimensions like themselves,
The great saraphic lords and cherubim
795 In close recess and secret conclave sat;
A thousand demi-gods on golden seats,
Frequent and full. After short silence then,
And summons read, the great consult began.

End of Book First.

Argument. Milton announces that he intends to follow classical precedents by beginning his epic *in medeas res*, in the middle of things, and only later coming back, by reported action, to beginnings.

Death into the World, and all our woe. This locution echoes fairly closely Virgil's narrative voice in *Aeneid* book 4, announcing that death and woe followed the ersatz nuptials of Aeneas and Dido:

To the same cave come Dido and the Trojan chief. Primal earth and nuptial Juno give the sign; fires flashed in heaven, the witness to their bridal, and on the mountain-top screamed the Nymphs. That day was the first day of death, that the first cause of woe. (Trans. H. Rushton Fairclough in *Virgil* vol. 1 Cambridge, MA: Havard University Press, 1935 407)

Pandemonium. Literally, "all the demons." Milton coins the name for the assembly hall of devils whose erection is recounted at the end of book 1.

one greater Man. The Messiah.

Heavenly Muse. Is the "Heavenly Muse" invoked here the same as the "Urania," traditionally the muse of astronomy. More likely, contemporary readers would have first thought of the "Holy Spirit," as the inspiration of Moses.

Oreb. Moses, "That Shepherd," received the Law on Mt. Horeb (Deuteronomy 4: 10) or its spur, Mt. Sinai (Exodus 19: 20).

adventrous Song. Note the similarities between Milton's opening and the opening lines of Virgil's *Aeneid* and of Homer's *Odyssey*. Milton wants not only to compare his project to the ancient epics, but also himself to those poets and his main character, Adam, to their celebrated heroes. All of these comparisons raise interesting and complicated questions of authority, heroism, and nationalism in art.

chosen seed. The people of Israel. See Exodus 19-20.

In the Beginning. The opening words of both Genesis (Geneva) and the Gospel of John (Geneva).

Sion. To the haunts of the classical muses near the Castalian spring on Mt. Parnassus, Milton prefers to claim Mt. Sion and its brooks Kidron and Siloa, a kind of biblically authorized Parnassus.

out of Chaos. One of Milton's several heterodox positions. Orthodoxy held that God created everything *ex nihilo*, out of nothing (the "void" of Genesis 1:2; See Calvin's *Commentary on Genesis*). Milton borrows the concept of chaos, or unformed matter, from Hesiod and Platonic philosophy. Milton was also a monist, holding that all things were created out of God.

Aonian Mount. Mt. Helicon, in Aonia, sacred to the classical muses.

Line 16. The line ironically (maybe even sarcastically?) recalls the stanza 2 of canto 1 of Ariosto's *Orlando Furioso*.

Dove-like. The Holy Spirit appears as a dove in John 1: 32.

brooding on the vast Abyss. Milton's "brooding" is a better translation of the Hebrew than the familiar "moved upon the face of the waters" of the Authorized version of Genesis 1:2.

pregnant. Milton invites us to imagine the Holy Spirit copulating with the unformed matter of Chaos ("the vast Abyss"). In Milton's monism, distinctions between spirit and matter are not absolute.

Say first. Compare this with Homer's invocation to the muse in the *Iliad* 1.8.

one restraint. That is, the single injunction against eating from the tree of the knowledge of good and evil (Genesis 2: 17).

Lords of the World. According to Genesis 1:28, human beings were created to "have dominion" over the rest of creation.

Hurld headlong flaming. This description recalls Pieter Bruegel's *Fall of the Rebel Angels* (about 1562). See also William Blake's 1808 watercolor illustration of the rebel angels' fall (told by Raphael at 6.864-66).

Adamantine. Unbreakable, rocklike.

Nine times the Space. In Hesiod's *Theogony* 664-735, the Titans take a similar fall.

kenn. Range; which in the case of angels must be presumed to be nearly limitless.

hope never comes. A deliberate echo of Dante's *Inferno* 3.9: "All hope abandon ye who enter here."

thir. Their. Milton's preferred spelling was "thir," and Flannagan reports that "their" was changed to "thir" in later stages of the 1674 edition. The same is true of line 499 and other lines.

from the Center to…the Pole. Milton asks us to refer to the Ptolemaic model of the universe with the earth at the center of nine concentric spheres. On Milton's cosmology, Ptolemaic or Copernican.

Beelzebub. "God of the flies" or "Chief of the devils." See Matthew 10: 25, Mark 3: 22, and Luke 11:15.

call'd Satan. Originally Lucifer, "bringer of light," his name in heaven is changed to Satan, "enemy."

Gods. That is, the strength of empyreal angels, virtually gods.

eternal Warr. To speak of "eternal war" is to be quite doubtful about the prospects for victory.

thralls. Slaves.

rood. A rod, a variable measure of six to eight yards.

Titanian. For Hesiod's story of Zeus's (Jove's) war with the giants, the Titans and Briareos.

Leviathan. See Isaiah 27:1 and Job 41.

incumbent. Literally "pressing upon."

Pelorus. In Sicily, the peninsula of Pelorus is dominated by Mt. Aetna.

Sublim'd with Mineral fury. Vaporized by the volcano's fire.

Stygian. Styx was, in classical mythology, one of the rivers of hell; thus Stygian connotes hellish.

clime. Climate.

The mind is its own place. See Satan's later speech on the relationship between self, mind, and place: 4.75.

serve in heaven. Homer's Odysseus says that when he interviewed Achilles in the underworld, Achilles expressed an attitude opposite to Satan's: "I would rather be a paid servant in a poor man's house and be above ground than king of kings among the dead" (*Odyssey* 11.363-65).

Ethereal temper. Tempered in ethereal (heavenly) fire. Aeneas's shield was said to have been forged in the netherworld by Vulcan and was blazoned with stories of gods and heroes (*Aeneid* 8).

Optic Glass. Telescope. Galileo (1564–1642) was one of the earliest makers of telescopes; he was the first to make one powerful enough to view the surface of the moon.

Tuscan artist. Galileo (1564–1642). Milton visited him and saw his telescope in Valdarno, the valley of the Arno. Galileo's telescope and the observations he made with it supported the Copernican model of the cosmos over the Ptolemaic model, much to the Church's chagrin. Galileo spent most of the last years of his life under house arrest, ordered by the Church.

Fesole. Fiesole, a hill town near Florence.

Valdarno. The Arno valley, where Florence is located.

Ammiral. Admiral or flagship.

Marle. "A kind of soil consisting principally of clay mixed with carbonate of lime, forming a loose unconsolidated mass, valuable as a fertilizer. The marl of lakes is a white, chalky deposit consisting of the mouldering remains of Mollusca, Entomostraca, and partly of fresh-water algae" (*OED2*).

Nathless. Nevertheless.

Vallombrosa. A famously shady valley near Florence.

Etrurian shades. "Etrurian" is another way of saying Etruscan, that is of or from Tuscany, a region of Italy. "Shades" leaves both positive (cool and pleasant) and negative (ghosts) impressions, complicated further by Vallambrosa's suggestion of a valley of shadows or shades (Psalm 23:4 and Dante's *Inferno* 3.112-15).

sedge. Seaweed.

Orion. A "stormy" constellation in *Aeneid* 1. 535 and 4. 73.

Busirus. The Greek name for Pharaoh, in this instance as leader of the Egyptian (Memphian, from Memphis) cavalry (chivalry) who chased the Israelites across the Red Sea and was drowned by the returning seas.

Sojourners of Goshen. The Israelites.

Cherubim and Seraphim. Two orders or ranks of angels. Images of Cherubim stood by the sanctuary in the temple at Jerusalem.

Amrams Son. Moses. See Exodus 10: 12-15.

Cope. "Cope of heaven" was a common expression in Milton's day, indicating "the over-arching canopy or vault of heaven". The cope of hell is even more imaginable as a vaulted ceiling.

thir great Sultan. Satan as Sultan, or "the sovereign or chief ruler of a Muslim country" *OED2*. The poem literally demonizes Islam rulers.

the populous North. In accounts of the fall of Rome, the place from which the invading barbarian hordes were thought to have come.

Rhene or the Danaw. Rhine and Danube rivers. The narrator compares the devils to the hordes of "barbarians" who invaded Rome.

Got them new Names. Many Church Fathers believed the fallen angels came to be known and worshipped as pagan deities.

Devils...for Deities. That is to say that, though nameless at this time and blotted from the book of life in heaven, the fallen angels later came to be named by fallen men as pagan gods.

Moloch. Literally "King."

children's cries unheard. The cries of children being sacrificed to Moloch were drowned out by drums and timbrels.

Ammonite. Non-Hebrew tribe mentioned in Samuel 12: 26-27. The Israelites destroyed the "sons *of Ammon*" near the Moabite border stream of Arnon in Argob and Basan.

Rabba. The capital of the Ammonites, Rabbah; now Amman in Jordan.

Argob, Basan, Arnon. Lands east of the Dead Sea, where Moloch was worshipped, now part of Jordan.

Hill. See Kings 23: 13.

Hinnom. See Jeremiah 19:6. Gehenna, or Gehinnom, is Hebrew for the place or valley of the damned, especially the valley where Moloch was worshipped with human sacrifices.

Chemos. Chemosh a Moabite diety to whom Solomon built a shrine according to: Kings 11:7. See also Numbers 21: 29.

Aroar. Aroer, now Arair in modern Jordan.

Nebo. A southern Moabite town; also the name of the mountain from which Moses first glimpsed the promised land of Canaan (Deuteronomy 32:49).

Abarim. Hill of western Moab, overlooking the Jordan and the Dead Sea.

Hesebon. Heshbon and Horonaim were Amorite cities. Sihon (Milton's Seon) was king of the Amorites.

Sibma. Region east of the Jordan famous for its wine. Elealeh, a nearby city.

Asphaltick Pool. The Dead Sea.

Israel in Sittim. The Isrealites "began to commit whoredom" with the daughters of Moab at Shittim, on the flight from Egypt to Canaan. (Numbers 25: 1-3.)

Hill of scandal. The place just east of the Jerusalem temple, across the Kidron valley, often called the Mount of Olives, where Solomon erected shrines to pagan dieties like Moloch, Baal, Chemosh, and Ashtoreth. King Josiah, according to destroyed these "abominations." 2 Kings 23,

Josiah. See Kings 23: 10.

Brook. According to Fowler, the river Besor.

Baalim and Ashtaroth. Plural forms of Baal and Astarte. Baal-Peor was one of several sites for the worship of Baal, often depicted as a calf or other beasts. Astarte was a middle eastern goddess of fertility and war.

Essence pure. Spirits and angels are incorporeal.

cumbrous. Cumbersome.

Sidonian. Phonician.

Sion. Israel's promised land.

th' offensive Mountain. Presumably the same site as the "Hill of Scandal".

uxorious King. That is, Solomon, who had several hundred wives (uxor being Latin for wife). Milton tends to link adultery with idolatry, as did the biblical authors in the expression, "whoring after false gods."

Thammuz. Tammuz, lover and spouse of Sumerian Inanna (Ishtar in Akkadian and Astarte in the Bible). Often identified with Adonis, his death was celebrated in the spring.

Adonis. The Lebanese river Adonis, red with mud in the summer.

Sions daughters. Israelite women.

the dark Idolatries. See Ezekiel 8: 14.

alienated. That is, alienated from God; apostate.

grunsel. Groundsill or threshold.

Dagon. Philistine sea-God. When the Philistines captured the ark of the Lord and placed it in Dagon's temple, the idol was found dismembered the next morning. See 1 Samuel 5:4.

Azotus. Ashdod, along with Askelon and Ekron, were three of the five principal cities of Philistia; the others were Gath and Gaza.

Rimmon. Hadad, the west Semitic God of weather.

Damascus. Damascus is the capital city of Syria.

A Leper once he lost. When the prophet Elisha told the Syrian Naaman that bathing in the Jordan would cure his leprosy, Naaman scoffed, asking "Are not Abana and Pharpar, rivers of Damascus, better than all the waters of Israel? may I not wash in them, and be clean?"; when he later bathed in the Jordan and was cured, he worshipped the God of Israel. Israel's King Ahaz, however, built an altar to Rimmon (2 Kings 16).

Osiris, Orus, Isis. Osiris was perhaps the most important god of ancient Egypt. Isis was his consort and mother of Horus.

The Calf. Exodus 32: 1-20.

Rebel King. Jereboam. See 1 Kings 12: 28-30.

equal'd with one stroke. See Exodus 12: 12.

Belial. Belial a Vulgate synonym for Satan, but here a separate devil. Also the Hebrew word for "worthless." "Sons of Belial" means good-for-nothings.

Ely's sons. See 1 Samuel 2: 12-25.

flown. Flying free like a sheet, halyard or sail that has come loose in a wind and flies dangerously free without check.

worse rape. See the stories in Genesis 19:4-13 and Judges 19. Milton's notion that rape of men is "worse" than rape of women, even when a "Matron" is raped to death, appears supported by the biblical accounts.

Javan. Japhet's son and therefore Noah's grandson (Genesis 10:2). The Geneva notes to Genesis 10:2 identify Javan as the progenitor of the "Medes and the Grekes," so Milton identifies him with Ion, the progenitor of the Ionian Greeks.

boasted Parents. Heaven and Earth, according to many ancient poets, were the parents of the Titans. Milton casts some doubt here upon these claims with the term "boasted," implying pretence. See Apollodorus' *Library* 1.1.1; also Virgil's *Aeneid* 4.254. According to Hesiod's *Theogony* 126-139, Chaos was the first being, then the earth came to be the foundation of "the deathless ones." The children of Chaos were Erebus (a place of darkness between earth and Hades) and Night, whose union produced Aether (air) and Day. Earth gave birth to Heaven, with whom she later copulated to produce the Titans: Oceanus, Coeus and Crius and Hyperion, Iapetus, Theia, Rhea, Themis, Mnemosyne, gold-crowned Phoebe and lovely Tethys. She also gave birth to Chronus (Saturn), the cyclopes and various other monsters. According to Apollodorus' *Library* 1.1.4-1.1.7, the Titans and Titanides (female Titans) were cast by the gods into Hades and, in revenge for this, Earth spurred them on to rebellion, giving Chronos a special sickle with which he cut off Heaven's testicles and threw them into the sea. Assuming dominion over creation, Cronus (Saturn) coupled with his sister Rhea and she became pregnant with Zeus (Jove) who, according to prophecy, killed his father to become king of the Gods.

Creet. Crete. Rhea, pregnant with Zeus, feared that Chronus would try to destroy the child prophesied to supplant him, so she hid in Crete and bore Zeus in a cave there. She gave the infant Zeus into the care of the Cretans and the nymphs Adrastia and Ida.

Olympus. Mountain in northern Thessaly reputed to be the home of the gods.

Delphian. The oracle of Apollo was at Delphi, the Delphian oracle; that of Zeus was at Dodona.

Doric Land. Greece.

Adria. The Adriatic Sea.

Hesperian Fields. The land of the westering sun, or Italy.

utmost Isles. The British isles.

Azazel. Hebrew word for "scapegoat." See Leviticus 16:8-20. According to some Cabbalistic writers, one of the four standard bearers of Satan's army.

Chaos. In Milton's cosmology, Chaos and Night reigned over the "eternal anarchy," the formless void between hell and heaven.

Phalanx. In Greek antiquity, "a body of heavy-armed infantry drawn up in close order, with shields joined and long spears overlapping; especially famous in the Macedonian army" *OED2*).

Dorian. "Of Doris or Doria, a division of ancient Greece. The Dorian mode in Music was one of the ancient Grecian modes, characterized by simplicity and solemnity; also, the first of the 'authentic' ecclesiastical modes" (*OED2*).

swage. Assuage.

Warr'd on by Cranes. In *Iliad* 3. 1-5, Homer compares the cries of the Trojans to the sound made by cranes in their annual rush to the sea, when they slaughter pygmies in their path.

Phlegra. In Ovid's *Metamorphoses* 10. 233, the giants battle the gods on the plain of Phlegra in Macedonia.

Theb's. The "Heroic Race" are the seven heroes of the Trojan war in Statius' *Thebaid* and Aeschylus' *Seven Against Thebes.*

Uther's Son. King Arthur, son of Uther Pendragon.

Armoric. From Brittany in the north of France.

Aspramont or *Montalban.* Castles in chivalric romances, sites of great international tournaments.

Damasco, Morocco, Trebisond. Sites from chivalric romances of famous tournaments between Christian and pagans or "infidels" (Moslems). These sites and those mentioned above, figure prominently on Arisoto's romance epic: *Orlando Furioso* 17.14 and 18.158.

Biserta. Legendary versions of history tell of Muslims setting out from Bizerte in Tunisia to conquer Carolingian Spain; actually Muslims invaded Spain in 1711, some 30 years before Charlemagne's birth. Modern Fuenterrabia is in northern Spain.

Perplexes Monarchs. Until modern times, eclipses were believed to portend the fall of monarchs and emperors.

amerc't. Deprived.

th' event. The result.

puissant. Powerful and courageous.

custome. Milton frequently scorned the role played by "custom" in politics, religion and law. See *Areopagitica*; and a second place in *Areopagitica*. See also the *Doctrine and Discipline of Divorce* book 1 and book 2; and *The Tenure of Kings and Magistrates*.

fame. Rumor.

Pioners. Pioneers, trench-diggers.

Mammon. His name is Aramaic for "wealth." Milton also alludes to Spenser's Mammon in the *Faerie Queene* 2.7.

downward bent. Compare this to Satan at the bottom of the stairs to heaven in 3.542.

Babel. The famous tower of Babel, erected by Nimrod; see Genesis 11:4 and *PL* 12.38-62.

Memphian. Egyptian. Milton refers to the great pyramids of the Pharaohs.

bossy Sculptures. Embossed and engraved sculptures.

fretted Gold. "Adorned with carving in elaborate patterns; carved or wrought intodecorative patterns." (OED2)

Alcairo. Cairo.

Belus or Serapis. Belus is Latinized Bel, Mesopotamian god of the air, also know to the ancient Hebrews as Baal (Jeremiah 51:44). Sarapis is a Greco-Egyptian god of the sun.

Cressets. Iron basket lamps.

Ausonian land. Italy.

Mulciber. Vulcan or Hephaistos in Greek. The gods' smith. According to legend, Hephaistos was born by Hera, queen of the gods, without any sire. Hera threw him down to Hades, but he was rescued by his own wit with the help of Dionysius. See Pausanius' *Description of Greece* 1.20.3.

they relate. Homer, in *Iliad* 1. 591-5 and Lucretius in *Elegia 7* and *Natram non pati senium* 23, tell the story of Hephaistos's fall.

Pandæmonium. Milton coined the word from familiar Greek lexemes: pan meaning "all"; daimon meaning "demon" or "mortal-to-god go-between"; and ion, meaning "assembly" as in Panathenaion, "assembly of all."

awful. Awe-inspiring.

Bees. Homer describes the Achaean assembly (*Iliad* 2. 87-90) and Virgil the Carthaginians (*Aeneid* 1.430-36) as "busy bees."

Pigmean Race. In his *Natural History* 7. 26, Pliny locates the land of the Pygmies in the mountains beyond the source of the Ganges.

some belated Peasant. Milton echoes the episode of Bottom's dream in Shakespeare's *Midsummer Night's Dream* 4.1.

conclave. The word deliberately alludes to the secret conclave of cardinals who elect the pope, thus insinuating the demonic character of such meetings.

Paradise Lost:

Book II

John Milton

The Argument

The consultation begun, Satan debates whether another battle be to be hazarded for the recovery of heaven: some advise it, others dissuade. A third proposal is preferred, mentioned before by Satan, *to search the truth of that prophesy or tradition in heaven concerning another world, and another kind of creature, equal, or not much inferiour to themselves, about this time to be created: Their doubt who shall be sent on this difficult search:* Satan *their chief, undertakes alone the voyage; is honourd and applauded. The council thus ended, the rest betake them several ways and to several employments, as their inclinations lead them, to entertain the time till* Satan *return. He passes on his journey to hell gates, finds them shut, and who sat there to guard them, by whom at length they are opened, and discover to him the great gulf between hell and heaven: with what difficulty he passes through, directed by* Chaos, *the Power of that place, to the sight of this new world which he sought.*

    High on a throne of royal state, which far
Outshone the wealth of *Ormus* and of *Ind;*
Or where the gorgeous east with richest hand
Showers on her kings *barbaric* pearl and gold,
5   Satan exalted sat, by merit rais'd
To that bad eminence: and from despair
Thus high uplifted beyond hope, aspires
Beyond thus high; insatiate to pursue
Vain war with heaven; and by success untaught,
10   His proud imaginations thus display'd:

Powers and dominions, deities of heaven,
(For since no deep within her gulf can hold
Immortal vigour, though oppressed and fallen,
I give not heaven for lost: from this descent
15   Celestial virtues rising, will appear
More glorious and more dread then from no fall,
And trust themselves to fear no second fate:)
Me, though just right and the fixt laws of heaven
Did first create your leader: next free choice;
20   With what besides, in counsil or in fight,
Hath bin achiev'd of merit: yet this loss
Thus far at least recover'd, hath much more
Established in a safe unenvied throne,
Yielded with full consent. The happier state
25   In heaven, which follows dignity, might draw
Envy from each inferior: but who here
Will envy whom the highest place exposes
Foremost to stand against the thunderer's aim
Your bulwark; and condemns to greatest share

John Milton, "Book 2," from *Paradise Lost*. Copyright in the Public Domain.

30   Of endless pain? Where there is then no good
     For which to strive, no strife can grow up there
     From faction; for none sure will claim in hell
     Precedence; none, whose portion is so small
     Of present pain, that with ambitious mind
35   Will covet more; with this advantage then
     To union, and firm faith, and firm accord,
     More then can be in heaven, we now return
     To claim our just inheritance of old,
     Surer to prosper then prosperity
40   Could have assur'd us; and by what best way,
     Whether of open war or covert guile,
     We now debate: who can advise may speak.

     He ceas'd; and next him *Moloch*, sceptre'd king,
     Stood up, the strongest and the fiercest spirit
45   That fought in heaven, now fiercer by despair:
     His trust was with th' Eternal to be deem'd
     Equal in strength, and rather then be less,
     Cared not to be at all; with that care lost
     Went all his fear: of God, or hell, or worse,
50   He reck'd not; and these words thereafter spake.

     My sentence is for open war: Of wiles,
     More unexpert, I boast not: them let those
     Contrive who need; or when they need, not now.
     For while they sit contriving, shall the rest,
55   Millions that stand in arms, and longing wait
     The signal to ascend, sit ling'ring here

     Heavens fugitives, and for their dwelling-place
     Accept this dark opprobrious den of shame,
     The prison of his tyranny who reigns
60   By our delay? No, let us rather choose
     Arm'd with Hell flames and fury all at once
     O're heavens high towers to force resistless way,
     Turning our tortures into horrid arms
     Against the Torturer; when to meet the noise
65   Of his Almighty engine he shall hear
     Infernal thunder; and for lightning, see
     Black fire and horror shot with equal rage
     Among his angels: and his throne itself
     Mixed with *Tartarean* Sulphur, and strange fire,
70   His own invented torments. But, perhaps,
     The way seems difficult and steep, to scale
     With upright wing against a higher foe.
     Let such bethink them, (if the sleepy drench
     Of that forgetful lake benum not still,)
75   That in our proper motion we ascend
     Up to our native seat: descent and fall
     To us is adverse. Who but felt of late
     When the fierce Foe hung on our broken rear
     Insulating, and pursu'd us through the deep,
80   With what compulsion, and laborious flight
     We sunk thus low? Th' ascent is easy then;
     Th' event is fear'd; should we again provoke
     Our stronger, some worse way his wrath may find
     To our destruction: (if there be in Hell
85   Fear to be worse destroy'd.) What can be worse
     Then to dwell here, driven out from bliss, condemn'd
     In this abhorred deep to utter woe?
     Where pain of unextinguishable fire
     Must exercise us, without hope of end
90   The vassals of his anger, when the scourge
     Inexorably, and the torturing hour,

     Calls us to penance? more destroy'd then thus,
     We should be quite abolished and expire.

What fear we then? what doubt we to incense
95 His utmost ire? which to the height enrag'd,
Will either quite consume us, and reduce
To nothing this essential; happier far.
Then miserable to have eternal being;
Or if our substance be indeed divine,
100 And cannot cease to be, we are at worst
On this side nothing: and by proof we feel
Our power sufficient to disturb his heaven,
And with perpetual inroades to alarme,
Though inaccessible, his fatal throne:
105 Which if not victory, is yet revenge.

He ended frowning, and his look denounc'd
Desperate revenge, and battle dangerous
To less then gods. On th' other side uprose
Belial, in act more graceful and humane:
110 A fairer person lost not heaven; he seem'd
For dignity compos'd, and high exploit:
But all was false and hollow;: though his tongue
Dropt manna, and could make the worse appear
The better reason, to perplex and dash
115 Maturest counsels; for his thoughts were low:
To vice industrious, but to nobler deeds
Timorous and slothful: yet he pleas'd the ear
And with persuasive accent thus began:

I should be much for open war, O peers,
120 As not behind in hate, if what was urg'd
Main reason to persuade immediate war,
Did not dissuade me most: and seem to cast
Ominous conjecture on the whole success;
When he who most excels in fact of arms,
125 In what he counsels, and in what excels,
Mistrustful, grounds his courage on despair,
And utter dissolution, as the scope
Of all his aim, after some dire revenge.
First, what revenge? the towers of heaven are fill'd
130 With armed watch, that render all access
Impregnable; oft on the bordering deep
Encamp their legions; or with obscure wing,
Scout far and wide into the realm of night,
Scorning surprise. Or could we break our way
135 By force, and at our heels all hell should rise
With blackest insurrection, to confound
Heavens purest light; yet our great enemy
All incorruptible would on his throne
Sit unpolluted, and th' ethereal mould
140 Incapable of stain, would soon expel
Her mischief, and purge off the baser fire
Victorious. Thus repuls'd, our final hope
Is flat despair: we must exasperate
Th' Almighty Victor to spend all his rage,
145 And that must end us; that must be our cure
To be no more. Sad cure; for who would loose,
Though full of pain, this intellectual being;
Those thoughts, that wander through eternity.
To perish rather, swallow'd up and lost
150 In the wide womb of uncreated night,
Devoid of sense and motion? And who knows,
Let this be good, whether our angry foe
Can give it, or will ever? how he can,
Is doubtful; that he never will, is sure.
155 Will he, so wise, let loose at once his ire,
Belike through impotence, or unaware,
To give his enemies their wish, and end
Them in his anger, whom his anger saves
To punish endless? Wherefore cease we then?
160 Say they who counsel war; we are decreed,
Reserv'd and destin'd to Eternal woe;
Whatever doing, what can we suffer more;
What can we suffer worse?—Is this then worst,
Thus sitting, thus consulting, thus in arms?
165 What! when we fled amain, pursu'd and struck

With heavens afflicting thunder, and besought
The deep to shelter us? This hell then seem'd
A refuge from those wounds. Or when we lay
Chain'd on the burning lake? That sure was worse.
170 What if the breath that kindled those grim fires,
Awak'd, should blow them into sevenfold rage,
And plunge us in the flames? Or, from above,
Should intermitted vengeance arm again
His red right hand to plague us? What if all
175 Her stores were open'd, and this firmament
Of hell should spout her cataracts of fire?
Impendent horrors; threatning hideous fall
One day upon our heads: while we perhaps
Designing or exhorting glorious warr,
180 Caught in a fiery tempest shall be hurl'd
Each on his rock transfixed, the sport and prey
Of racking whirlwinds: or for ever sunk
Under yon boiling ocean, wrapp't in chains;
There to converse with everlasting groans,
185 Unrespited, unpitied, unrepriev'd,
Ages of hopeless end. This would be worse.
War therefore, open or conceal'd, alike
My voice dissuades: for what can force or guile
With him, or who deceive his mind, whose eye
190 Views all things at one view? He from heav'ns height
All these our motions vain sees and derides:
Not more almighty to resist our might,
Then wise to frustrate all our plots and wiles.
Shall we then live thus vile, the race of Heaven
195 Thus trampled, thus expell'd, to suffer here
Chains and these torments? Better these then worse
By my advice; since fate inevitable
Subdues us, and omnipotent decree,
The victors will. To suffer, as to do,
200 Our strength is equal, nor the law unjust
That so ordains: this was at first resolv'd,
If we were wise, against so great a foe
Contending, and so doubtful what might fall.
I laugh, when those who at the spear are bold
205 And vent'rous, if that fail them, shrink, and fear
What yet they know must follow, to endure
Exile, or ignominy, or bonds, or pain,
The sentence of their conquerour: This is now
Our doom; which if we can sustain and bear,
210 Our supreme foe, in time, may such remit
His anger: and perhaps thus far remov'd,
Not mind us not offending, satisfied
With what is punished; whence these raging fires
Will slacken, if his breath stir not their flames.
215 Our purer essence then will overcome
Their noxious vapour; or inur'd, not feel;
Or chang'd at length, and to the place conform'd
In temper and in nature, will receive
Familiar the fierce heat, and void of pain
220 This horror will grow mild, this darkness, light:
Besides what hope the never-ending flight
Of future dayes may bring, what chance, what change
Worth waiting, since our present lot appears
For happy, though but ill; for ill, not worst;
225 If we procure not to ourselves more woe.

Thus *Belial* with words cloathed in reason's garb
Counsell'd ignoble ease, and peaceful sloth,

Not peace: and after him thus *Mammon* spake.

Either to disenthrone the King of heaven
230 We war, if war be best, or to regain
Our own right lost: Him to unthrone we then
May hope when everlasting Fate shall yeild
To fickle Chance, and *Chaos* judge the strife:
The former vain to hope, argues as vain
235 The latter: for what place can be for us
Within heavens bound, unless heavens Lord supreme
We overpower? Suppose he should relent
And publish grace to all, on promise made
Of new subjection; with what eyes could we
240 Stand in his presence humble, and receive
Strict Laws imposed, to celebrate his throne
With warbled hymns, and to his Godhead sing
Forced Hallelujah's? while he lordly sits
Our envied Sovran, and his Altar breathes
245 Ambrosial odours and ambrosial flowers,
Our servile offerings; this must be our task
In heaven, this our delight; how wearisom
Eternity so spent, in worship paid
To whom we hate. Let us not then pursue
250 By force impossible, by leave obtain'd
Unacceptable, though in heaven, our state
Of splendid vassalage: but rather seek
Our own good from ourselves; and from our own
Live to ourselves, though in this vast recess,
255 Free, and to none accountable: preferring
Hard liberty before the easy yoke
Of servile pomp. Our greatness will appear
Then most conspicuous, when great things of small,
Useful of hurtful, prosperous of adverse
260 We can create; and in what place so e'er
Thrive under evil, and work ease out of pain,
Through labour and endurance. This deep world
Of darkness do we dread? How oft amidst
Thick clouds and dark, doth heavens all-ruling Sire
265 Choose to reside, his glory unobscur'd
And with the majesty of darkness round
Covers his throne; from whence deep thunders roar
Mustering their rage, and heaven resembles Hell?
As he our darkness, cannot we his Light
270 Imitate when we please? This desert soil
Wants not her hidden lustre, gems and gold;
Nor want we skill or art, from whence to raise
Magnificence; and what can heaven show more?
Our torments also may in length of time
275 Become our elements; these piercing fires
As soft as now severe, our temper chang'd
Into their temper; which must needs remove
The sensible of pain. All things invite
To peaceful counsels, and the settled state
280 Of order, how in safety best we may
Compose our present evils, with regard
Of what we are, and were; dismissing quite
All thought of war; ye have what I advise.

He scarce had finished, when such murmur fill'd
285 Th' assembly, as when hollow rocks retain
The sound of blustring winds, which all night long
Had rous'd the sea, now with hoarse cadence lull
Sea-faring men o'erwatched, whose bark by chance,
Or pinnace, anchors in a craggy bay
290 After the tempest: such applause was heard
As *Mammon* ended, and his sentence pleas'd,
Advising peace. For, such another field

They dreaded worse then hell: so much the fear
Of thunder and the sword of *Michael,*
295 Wrought still within them; and no less desire
To found this nether empire, which might rise,
By policy, and long process of time,
In emulation opposite to heaven.
Which when *Beelzebub* perceiv'd, (than whom,
300 *Satan* except, none higher sat,) with grave
Aspect he rose, and in his rising seem'd
A pillar of state: deep on his front engraven,
Deliberation sat and public care;
And princely counsel in his face yet shon,
305 Majestic though in ruin: sage he stood,
With *Atlantean* shoulders fit to bear
The weight of mightiest monarchies; his look
Drew audience and attention still as night,
Or Summers noon-tide air; while thus he spake:

310 Thrones and imperial powers, offspring of heav'n
Ethereal virtues; or these Titles now
Must we renounce, and changing style, be call'd
Princes of hell? For, so the popular vote
Inclines, here to continue, and build up here
315 A growing empire; doubtless; while we dream,
And know not that the King of heaven hath doom'd
This place our dungeon; not our safe retreat
Beyond his Potent arm, to live exempt
From heavens high jurisdiction, in new league
320 Banded against his throne: but to remain
In strictest bondage, though thus far remov'd,
Under th' inevitable curb, reserv'd
His captive multitude: for he, be sure,
In heighth or depth, still first and last will Reign
325 Sole king, and of his kingdom loose no part
By our revolt; but over hell extend
His empire, and with iron sceptre rule
Us here, as with his golden those in heaven.

What sit we then projecting peace and war?
330 War hath determin'd us, and foil'd with loss
Irreparable; terms of peace yet none
Vouchsafed or sought: for what peace will be given
To us enslav'd, but custody severe,
And stripes, and arbitrary punishment
335 Inflicted? and what peace can we return?
But to our power hostility and hate,
Untam'd reluctance, and revenge; though slow,
Yet ever plotting how the Conqueror least
May reap his conquest, and may least rejoice
340 In doing what we most in suffering feel?
Nor will occasion want, nor shall we need
With dangerous expedition, to invade
Heaven, whose high walls fear no assault or siege,
Or ambush from the deep: what if we find
345 Some easier enterprize? There is a place
(If ancient and prophetic fame in heaven
Err not,) another world, the happy seat
Of some new race call'd *Man;* about this time
To be created like to us, though less
350 In power and excellence, but favour'd more
Of him who rules above: so was his will
Pronounc'd among the gods, and by an oath,
That shook heavens whole circumference, confirm'd.
Thither let us bend all our thoughts, to learn
355 What creatures there inhabit, of what mould,

Or substance, how endued, and what their power,
And where their weakness, how attempted best,
By force or suttlety Though heaven be shut,
And heaven's high arbitrator sit secure
360 In his own strength, this place may lie expos'd
The utmost border of his kingdom, left
To their defence who hold it: here perhaps
Some advantageous act may be achiev'd
By sudden onset, either with hell fire
365 To waste his whole creation, or possess
All as our own, and drive as we were driven,
The puny habitants; or if not drive,
Seduce them to our party, that their God
May prove their foe, and with repenting hand
370 Abolish his own works. This would surpass
Common revenge, and interrupt his joy
In our confusion, and our joy upraise
In his disturbance; when his darling sons,
Hurl'd headlong to partake with us, shall curse
375 Their frail original, and faded bliss:
Faded so soon. Advise if this be worth
Attempting, or to sit in darkness here
Hatching vain empires. Thus *Beelzebub*
Pleaded his devilish counsel, first devis'd
380 By *Satan,* and in part propos'd: for whence,
But from the author of all ill, could spring
So deep a malice to confound the race
Of mankind in one root, and earth with hell
To mingle and involve, done all to spite
385 The great Creator? But their spite still serves
His glory to augment. The bold design
Pleas'd highly those infernal states, and joy
Sparkl'd in all their eyes; with full assent
They vote: whereat his speech he thus renews.

390 Well have ye judg'd, well ended long debate,
Synod of gods, and, like to what ye are,
Great things resolv'd; which from the lowest deep
Will once more lift us up, in spite of fate,
Nearer our ancient seat; perhaps in view
395 Of those bright confines, whence with neighbouring arms,
And opportune excursion we may chance
Re-enter heaven: or else in some milde zone
Dwell not unvisited of heavens fair light
Secure, and at the brightning orient beam
400 Purge off this gloom: the soft delicious air,
To heal the scar of these corrosive fires,
Shall breath her balm. But first whom shall we send
In search of this new world? whom shall we find
Sufficient? Who shall tempt with wandering feet
405 The dark, unbottom'd, infinite abyss,
And through the palpable obscure find out
His uncouth way; or spread his airy flight,
Upborne with indefatigable wings,
Over the vast abrupt, ere he arrive
410 The happy isle? What strength, what art can then
Suffice, or what evasion bear him safe
Through the strict senteries, and stations thick
Of angels watching round? Here he had need
All circumspection; and we now no less
415 Choice in our suffrage; for, on whom we send,
The weight of all, and our last hope, relies.

This said, he sat; and expectation held
His look suspence, awaiting who appeared
To second or oppose, or undertake
420 The perilous attempt; but all sat mute,
Pondering the danger with deep thoughts; and each
In other's countenance read his own dismay
Astonished; none, among the choice and prime

Of those heaven-warring champions, could be found
425 So hardy, as to proffer, or accept
Alone the dreadful voyage: till at last
Satan, whom now transcendent glory rais'd
Above his fellows, with Monarchal pride
(Conscious of highest worth) unmov'd thus spake:

430 O progeny of heaven, empyreal thrones;
With reason hath deep silence, and demur,
Seiz'd us, though undismayed: long is the way
And hard, that out of hell leads up to light:
Our prison strong, this huge convex of fire,
435 Outrageous to devour, immures us round
Ninefold: and gates of burning adamant
Barr'd over us prohibit all egress.
These passed, (if any pass,) the void profound
Of unessential night receives him next
440 Wide gaping; and with utter loss of being
Threatens him, plung'd in that abortive gulf.
If thence he 'scape into whatever world,
Or unknown region, what remains him less
Then unknown dangers, and as hard escape?
445 But I should ill become this throne, O Peers!
And this imperial sovereignty, adorn'd
With splendour, arm'd with power, if aught propos'd
And judg'd of public moment, in the shape
Of difficulty, or danger, could deterr
450 Me from attempting. Wherefore do I assume
These Royalties, and not refuse to reign,
Refusing to accept as great a share
Of hazard as of honour due alike
To him who reigns, and so much to him due
455 Of hazard more, as he above the rest
High honour'd sits? Go therefore mighty powers,
Terror of heaven, though fallen; intend at home,
(While here shall be our home,) what best may ease
The present misery, and render hell
460 More tollerable; if there be cure or charm,
To respite or deceive, or slack the pain
Of this ill mansion intermit no watch
Against a wakeful foe, while I abroad,
Through all the coasts of dark destruction, seek
465 Deliverance for us all: this enterprise
None shall partake with me. Thus saying, rose
The monarch, and prevented all reply:
Prudent, least, from his resolution rais'd,
Others among the chief might offer now
470 (Certain to be refused) what erst they fear'd;
And so refus'd, might in opinion stand
His rivals; winning cheap the high repute
Which he through hazard huge must earn. But they
Dreaded not more th' adventure, than his voice
475 Forbidding; and at once with him they rose:
Their rising all at once was as the sound
Of thunder heard remote. Towards him they bend
With awful reverence prone; and as a god
Extoll him equal to the highest in heaven:
480 Nor fail'd they to express how much they prais'd,
That for the general safety he despis'd
His own, (for neither do the spirits damn'd
Loose all their virtue; least bad men should boast
Their specious deeds on earth, which glory excites:
485 Or close ambition varnished o'er with zeal.)
Thus they their doubtful consultations dark
Ended rejoicing in their matchless chief:
As when from mountain-tops the dusky clouds

Ascending, while the north-wind sleeps, O'erspread
490 Heavens cheerful face, the louring element
Scowls o'er the darkened landscape snow, or shower;
If chance the radiant sun with farewell sweet
Extend his evening beam, the fields revive,
The birds their notes renew, and bleating herds
495 Attest their joy, that hill and valley rings.
O shame to men! Devil with Devil damn'd
Firm concord holds, men only disagree
Of Creatures rational, though under hope
Of heavenly grace: and God proclaiming peace,
500 Yet live in hatred, enmity, and strife
Among themselves, and levy cruel wares,
Wasting the earth, each other to destroy:
As if (which might induce us to accord)
Man had not hellish foes now besides,
505 That day and night, for his destruction wait.

The *Stygian* Counsil thus dissolv'd; and forth
In order came the grand infernal peers:
'Midst came their mighty paramount, and seem'd
Alone th' antagonist of heaven, nor less
510 Than hells dread emperour with pomp supreme,
And godlike imitated state, Him round
A globe of fiery seraphim inclos'd,
With bright emblazonry, and horrent arms.
Then of their session ended, they bid cry
515 With trumpets' regal sound the great result:
Toward the four winds four speedy cherubim
Put to their mouths the sounding alchemy
By heralds' voice explain'd: the hollow abyss
Heard far and wide, and all the host of hell
520 With deafning shout return'd them loud acclaim.

Thence more at ease their minds and somewhat rais'd
By false presumptuous hope, the ranged powers
Disband, and wand'ring, each his several way
Pursues, as inclination or sad choice
525 Leads him perplexed, where he may likeliest find
Truce to his restless thoughts, and entertain
The irksome hours, till his great chief return.
Part on the plain, or in the air sublime
Upon the wing; or in swift race contend,
530 As at th' Olympian games; or *Pythian* fields:
Part curb their firey steeds, or shun the goal
With rapid wheels, or fronted brigades form.
As when, to warn proud cities war appears
Wag'd in the troubl'd sky, and armies rush
535 To battle in the clouds, before each van
Prick forth the airy knights, and couch their spears
Till thickest legions close; with feats of arms
From either end of heaven the welkin burns.
Others, with vast *Typhœan* rage, more fell!
540 Rend up both rocks and hills, and ride the air
In whirlwind! hell scarce holds the wild uproar.
As when *Alcides* from *Echalia* crown'd
With conquest, felt th' envenom'd robe, and tore
Through pain up by the roots *Thessalian* Pines,
545 And *Lichas* from the top of *Eta* threw
Into th' *Euboic* Sea. Others, more mild,
Retreated in a silent valley, sing
With notes angelical to many a harp
Their own heroic deeds and hapless fall
550 By doom of battle; and complain that fate
Free virtue should enthrall to force or chance.
Their song was partial; but the harmony

  (What could it less when spirits immortal sing!)
  Suspended hell, and took with ravishment
555 The thronging audience. In discourse more sweet,
  (For Eloquence the soul, song charms the sense,)
  Others apart sat on a hill retir'd,
  In thoughts more elevate, and reason'd high,
  Of providence, foreknowledge, will and fate,
560 Fixt fate, free will, foreknowledge absolute;
  And found no end, in wand'ring mazes lost.
  Of good and evil much they argued then,
  Of happiness, and final misery,
  Passion and apathy, and glory and shame,
565 Vain wisdom all, and false philosophy;
  Yet with a pleasing sorcery could charm
  Pain for a while, or anguish, and excite
  Fallacious hope, or arm th' obdurate breast
  With stubborn patience, as with triple steel.
570 Another part, in squadrons and gross bands,
  On bold adventure to discover wide
  That dismal world, (if any clime perhaps
  Might yield them easier habitation,) bend
  Four ways their flying march, along the banks
575 Of four infernal rivers that disgorge
  Into the burning lake their baleful streams;
  Abhorred *Styx*, the flood of deadly hate;
  Sad *Acheron* of sorrow; black and deep;
  Cocytus, nam'd of lamentation loud
580 Heard on the ruful stream: fierce *Phlegethon*
  Whose waves of torrent fire inflame with rage.
  Far off from these a slow and silent stream,
  Lethe, the River of oblivion rolles
  Her watery Labyrinth? whereof who drinks,
585 Forthwith his former state and being forgets;
  Forgets both joy and grief, pleasure and pain.
  Beyond this flood a frozen continent
  Lies dark and wilde: beat with perpetual storms
  Of whirlwind, and dire hail; which on firm land
590 Thaws not but gathers heap, and ruin seems
  Of ancient pile: all else deep snow and ice:
  A gulf profound; as that *Serbonian* Bog
  Betwixt *Damiata* and mount *Casius* old,

  Where armies whole have sunk: the parching air
595 Burns frore, and cold performs the effect of fire.
  Thither by harpy-footed furies hal'd,
  At certain revolutions, all the damn'd
  Are brought; and feel by turns the bitter change
  Of fierce extremes, extremes by change more fierce;
600 From beds of raging fire to starve in ice
  Their soft ethereal warmth, and there to pine
  Immoveable, infixed, and frozen round,
  Periods of time; thence hurried back to fire.
  They ferry over this *Lethean* sound
605 Both to and fro, their sorrow to augment,
  And wish, and struggle as they pass, to reach
  The tempting stream, with one small drop to lose
  In sweet forgetfulness all pain and woe,
  All in one moment, and so near the brink:
610 But fate withstands, and to oppose th' attempt
  Medusa, with *Gorgonian* terror, guards
  The ford, and of itself the water flies
  All taste of living wight; as once it fled
  The lip of *Tantalus.* Thus roving on,
615 In confus'd march forlorn, th' adventrous bands
  With shudd'ring horror pale, and eyes aghast
  View'd first their lamentable lot and found
  No rest: through many a dark and dreary vale
  They pass'd, and many a region dolorous,
620 O'er many a Frozen, many a firey alpe;

Rocks, caves, lakes, fens, bogs, dens, and shades of death;
A universe of death; which God by curse
Created evil; for evil only good,
Where all life dies, death lives, and nature breed,
625 Perverse, all monstrous, all prodigious things,
Abominable, unutterable, and worse
Then fables yet have feign'd, or fear conceiv'd,
Gorgons and *Hydras,* and *Chimeras* dire.

Mean while the adversary of God and man,
630 *Satan* with thoughts inflam'd of highest design,
Puts on swift wings, and towards the gates of hell
Explores his solitary flight; somtimes
He scours the right-hand coast, somtimes the left,
Now shaves with level wing the deep; then soars
635 Up to the fiery concave touring high.
As when far off at sea a fleet descri'd,
Hangs in the clouds, by *Æquinoctial* winds
Close sailing from *Bengala,* or the isles
Of *Ternate* and *Tidore,* whence merchants bring
640 Their spicy drugs: they on the trading flood
Through the wide *Ethiopian* to the Cape
Ply, stemming nightly toward the Pole: so seem'd
Far off the flying fiend. At last appear
Hell bounds, high-reaching to the horrid roof;
645 And thrice threefold the gates: three folds were brass,
Three iron, three of adamantine rock:
Impenetrable, impal'd with circling fire,
Yet unconsum'd. Before the gates there sat
On either side a formidable shape;
650 The one seem'd woman to the waist, and fair:
But ended foul in many a scaly fold,
Voluminous and vast: a serpent arm'd
With mortal sting; about her middle round
A cry of hell-hounds never ceasing bark'd
655 With wide *Cerberian* mouths full loud, and rung
A hideous peal: yet, when they list, would creep,
If aught disturb'd their noise, into her womb,
And kennel there; yet there still bark'd and howl'd
Within unseen. Far less abhorr'd than these
660 Vex'd *Scylla,* bathing in the Sea that parts
Calabria from the hoarse *Trinacrian* shore,
Nor uglier follow the night-hag, when call'd
In secret, riding through the air she comes,
Lur'd with the smell of infant-blood, to dance
665 With *Lapland* witches, while the laboring moon
Eclipses at their charms. The other shape
(If shape it might be call'd that shape had none
Distinguishable in member, joint, or limb;
Or substance might be call'd that shadow seem'd,
670 For each seem'd either:) black it stood as night,
Fierce as ten furies, terrible as hell,
And shook a dreadful dart: what seem'd his head.
The likeness of a kingly crown had on.
Satan was now at hand, and from his seat
675 The monster, moving onward came as fast
With horrid strides: hell trembled as he strode.
Th' undaunted fiend what this might be admir'd;
Admir'd, not fear'd; God and his Son except,
Created thing nought valued he nor shunn'd
680 And with disdainful look thus first began:

Whence and what art thou, execrable shape,
That dar'st, though grim and terrible, advance
Thy miscreated front athwart my way
To yonder gates? through them I mean to pass,
685 That be assur'd, without leave ask of thee
Retire, or taste thy folly, and learn by proof,
Hell-born, not to contend with spirits of heaven.

To whom the goblin full of wrath reply'd,:
Art thou that traitor-angel, art thou hee,
690 Who first broke peace in heaven and faith, till then
Unbroken; and in proud rebellious arms
Drew after him the third part of heavens sons,
Conjur'd against the Highest; for which both thou
And they, outcast from god, are here condemn'd
695 To waste eternal days in woe and pain?
And reck'n'st thou thyself with spirits of Heaven,
Hell-doom'd, and breath'st defiance here and scorn,
Where I reign king, and to enrage thee more,
Thy king, and lord? Back to thy punishment,
700 False fugitive; and to thy speed add wings;
Lest with a whip of scorpions I pursue
Thy ling'ring, or with one stroke of this dart

Strange horror seize thee, and pangs unfelt before.
So spake the grisly terror, and in shape
705 (So speaking and so threatning,) grew tenfold
More dreadful and deform: on th' other side,
Incenst with indignation, *Satan* stood
Unterrified, and like a comet burn'd,
That fires the length of *Ophiucus* huge
710 In th' artic sky, and from his horrid hair
Shakes pestilence and war. Each at the head
Levell'd his deadly aim; their fatal hands
No second stroke intend: and such a frown
Each cast at th' other, as when two black clouds
715 With heavens artill'ry fraught, come rattling on
Over the *Caspian*; then stand front to front,
Hov'ring a space, till winds the signal blow
To join their dark encounter in mid air:
So frown'd the mighty combatants, that hell
720 Grew darker at their frown: so matched they stood;
For never but once more was either like
To meet so great a foe. And now great deeds
Had been achiev'd, whereof all hell had rung,
Had not the snaky sorceress that sat
725 Fast by hell gate, and kept the fatal key,
Risen, and with hideous outcry rush'd between.

O Father, what intends thy hand, she cry'd,
Against thy only son? What fury, O son,
Possesses thee to bend that mortal dart
730 Against thy Father's head? and knowest for whom;
For him who sits above and laughs the while
At thee ordain'd his drudge, to execute
What e'er his wrath, which he calls Justice, bids;
His wrath which one day will destroy ye both.

735 She spake, and at her words the hellish pest
Forbore: then these to her *Satan* return'd:

So strange thy outcry, and thy words so strange
Thou interposest, that my sudden hand
Prevented, spares to tell thee yet by deeds

740 What it intends; till first I know of thee,
What thing thou art, thus double-form'd, and why
In this infernal vale first met, thou call'st
Me Father, and that fantasm call'st my son:
I know thee not, nor ever saw till now
745 Sight more detestable then him and thee.

T'whom thus the portress of hell-gate reply'd;
Hast thou forgot me then, and do I seem
Now in thine eye so foul? once deem'd so fair
In heaven; when at th'assembly, and in sight
750 Of all the seraphim with thee combin'd
In bold conspiracy against heaven's King,
All on a sudden miserable pain
Surpris'd thee, dim thine eyes, and dizzy swam
In darkness; while thy head flames thick and fast
755 Threw forth; till on the left side op'ning wide,
Likest to thee in shape and count'nance bright,
Then shining heavenly fair, a Goddess arm'd
Out of thy head I sprung: amazement seized
All th' host of heaven; back they recoild, affraid
760 At first, and call'd me *Sin*; and for a sign
Portentous held me: but familiar grown,
I pleas'd, and with attractive graces won
The most averse, thee chiefly, who full oft
(Thyself in me thy perfect image viewing)
765 Becam'st enamour'd, and such joy thou took'st
With me in secret, that my womb conceiv'd
A growing burden. Meanwhile war arose,
And fields were fought in heaven; wherein remain'd
(For what could else?) to our almighty foe
770 Cleer victory; to our part loss, and rout,
Through all the empyrean: down they fell,
Driven headlong from the pitch of heaven, down
Into this deep; and in the general fall
I also: at which time this powerful Key
755 Into my hand was given, with charge to keep
These Gates for ever shut, which none can pass
Without my opening. Pensive here I sat
Alone, but long I sat not, till my womb
Pregnant by thee, and now excessive grown
780 Prodigious motion felt, and rueful throes.
At last this odious offspring whom thou seest,
Thine own begotten, breaking violent way
Tore through my entrails, that with fear and pain
Distorted, all my nether shape thus grew
785 Transform'd, but he my inbred enemy
Forth-issu'd, brandishing his fatal dart
Made to destroy: I fled, and cry'd out *Death*!
Hell trembled at the hideous name, and sigh'd
From all her caves, and back resounded, *Death*!
790 I fled, but he pursu'd (though more, it seems,
Inflam'd with lust then rage) and swifter, far,
Me overtook his mother, all dismayed,
And in embraces forcible, and foule,
Engendering with me, of that rape begot
795 These yelling monsters; that with ceasless cry
Surround me, as thou sawst, hourly conceiv'd,
And hourly born, with sorrow infinite
To me. For when they list, into the womb
That bred them they return; and howle, and gnaw
800 My bowels, their repast; then bursting forth,
Afresh with conscious terrors vex me round,
That rest or intermission none I find.
Before mine eyes in opposition sits
Grim *Death*, my son and foe: who sets them on,
805 And me his parent would full soon devour
For want of other prey, but that he knows

His end with mine involv'd; and knows that I
Should prove a bitter morsel, and his bane,
Whenever that shall be; so Fate pronounc'd.
810 But thou O father, I forewarn thee, shun
His deadly arrow; neither vainly hope
To be invulnerable in those bright arms,
Though temper'd heav'nly; for that mortal dint,
Save he who reigns above, none can resist.

815 She finish'd, and the subtle Fiend his lore
Soon learn'd, now milder, and thus answer'd smooth:
Dear daughter, since thou claim'st me for thy sire,
And my fair son here shows't me, (the dear pledge
Of dalliance had with thee in heaven, and joys
820 Then sweet, now sad to mention, through dire change
Befalln us, unforeseen, unthought of,) know
I come no enemy, but to set free
From out this dark and dismal house of pain,
Both him and thee, and all the heav'nly Host
825 Of spirits that (in our just pretences arm'd,)
Fell with us from on high: from them I go
This uncouth errand sole; and one for all
Myself expose, with lonely steps to tread
Th' unsounded deep, and through the void immense
830 To search with wand'ring quest a place foretold
Should be, and, by concurring signs, ere now
Created vast and round; a place of bliss
In the purlieus of heaven, and therein placed
A race of upstart creatures, to supply
835 Perhaps our vacant room; though more remov'd,
Least heaven surcharg'd with potent multitude
Might hap to move new broiles. Be this or aught
Than this more secret now design'd, I haste
To know; and this once known, shall soon return,
840 And bring ye to the place where thou and death,
Shall dwell at ease, and up and down unseen
Wing silently the buxom air, embalm'd
With odours: there ye shall be fed, and fill'd
Immeasurably, all things shall be your prey.
845 He ceas'd, for both seem'd highly pleas'd, and Death
Grinn'd horrible a ghastly smile, to hear
His famine should be fill'd; and bless'd his maw
Destin'd to that good hour: no less rejoiced
His mother bad, and thus bespake her sire:

850 The key of this infernal pit by due,
And by command of heavens all-powerful King,
I keep: by him forbidden to unlock
These adamantine gates; against all force
Death ready stands to interpose his dart,
855 Fearless to be o'ermatched by living might.
But what I owe to his commands above
Who hates me, and hath hither thrust me down
Into this gloom of *Tartarus* profound,
To sit in hateful office here confin'd,
860 Inhabitant of heaven, and heav'nly-born,
Here in perpetual agony and pain,
With terrors and with clamors compassed round,
Of mine own brood, that on my bowels feed:
Thou art my father, thou my author, thou
865 My being gav'st me; whom should I obey
But thee? whom follow? thou wilt bring me soon
To that new world of light and bliss, among

The gods who live at ease, where I shall reign
At thy right hand voluptuous, as beseems
870 Thy daughter and thy darling, without end.

Thus saying, from her side the fatal key,
Sad instrument of all our woe, she took;
And towards the gate rolling her bestial train,
Forthwith the huge portcullis high up-drew;
875 Which but herself, not all the *Stygian* powers
Could once have mov'd; then in the key-hole turns
Th' intricate wards, and every bolt and bar
Of massy Iron or solid rock with ease
Unfastens: on a sudden open fly
880 With impetuous recoily, and jarring sound
Th' infernal doors, and on their hinges grate
Harsh thunder, that the lowest bottom shook
Of *Erebus*. She opened, but to shut
Excell'd her power; the Gates wide open stood,
885 That with extended wings a banner'd host
Under spread ensigns marching might pass through
With horse and chariots ranked in loose array
So wide they stood; and like a furnace mouth
Cast forth redounding smoke and ruddy flame.
890 Before their eyes in sudden view appear
The secrets of the hoary deep; a dark
Illimitable ocean, without bound,
Without dimension, where length, breadth, and height,
And time and place are lost; where eldest Night
895 And *Chaos*, sncestor's of nature, hold
Eternal *Anarchy,* amidst the noise
Of endless wars, and by confusion stand:
For hot, cold, moist, and dry, four champions fierce
Strive here for mastery, and to battle bring
900 Their embryon Atoms; they around the flag
Of each his faction, in their several clans,
Light-arm'd or heavy, sharp, smooth, swift or slow,
Swarm populous, unnumber'd as the sands
Of *Barca,* or *Cyrene's* torrid soil,
905 Levied to side with warring winds, and poise
Their lighter wings. To whom these most adhere,
Hee rules a moment: *Chaos* umpire sits,
And by decision more imbroiles the fray,
By which he reigns: next him high arbiter
910 *Chance* governs all. Into this wilde abyss,
(The womb of nature and perhaps her Grave,
Of neither sea, nor shore, nor air, nor fire,
But all these in their pregnant causes mixed
Confus'dly, and which thus must ever fight,
915 (Unless th' almighty maker them ordain
His dark materials to create more worlds,)
Into this wild abyss the wary fiend
Stood on the brink of hell, and look'd a-while,
Pond'ring his voyage; (for no narrow frith
920 He had to cross;) nor was his ear less peal'd
With noises loud and ruinous (to compare
Great things with small,) then when *Bellona* storms
With all her batt'ring engines bent to raze
Some capital city; or less than if this frame
925 Of heaven were falling, and these elements
In mutiny had from her axle torn
The steadfast earth. At last his Sail-broad vanes
He spreads for flight, and in the surging smoke
Uplifted spurns the ground: thence many a league,
930 As in a cloudy chair ascending rides
Audacious: but that seat soon failing, meets
A vast vacuity: all unawares,
Flutt'ring his pennons vain, plumb down he drops

Ten thousand fathom deep: and to this hour
935 Down had been falling, had not by ill chance
The strong rebuff of som tumultuous cloud,
Instinct with fire and nitre, hurried him
As many miles aloft: that furie stay'd,
Quenched in a boggy *Syrtis*, neither sea,
940 Nor good dry land, nigh founder'd on he fares,
Treading the crude consistence, half on foot,
Half flying; behooves him now both oar and sail.
As when a gryfon, through the wilderness
With winged course o'er hill or moary dale,
945 Pursues the *Arimaspian,* who by stelth,
Had from his wakeful custody purloind
The guarded gold: So eagerly the fiend
O'er bog or steep, through strait, rough, dense, or rare,
With head, hands, wings, or feet, pursues his way;
950 And swims, or sinks, or wades, or creeps, or flyes.
At length a universal hubbub wil
Of stunning sounds and voices all confus'd,
Borne through the hollow dark assaults his ear
With loudest vehemence: thither he plies,
955 Undaunted to meet there whatever power,
Or spirit, of the nethermost abyss,
Might in that noise reside, of whom to ask
Which way the nearest coast of darkness lies
Bordering on light: when strait behold the throne
960 Of *Chaos,* and his dark pavilion spread
Wide on the wasteful deep: with him enthron'd
Sat aable-vested *Night,* eldest of things,
The consort of his reign: and by them stood
Orcus and *Ades,* and the dreaded name
965 Of *Demogorgon: Rumor* next, and *Chance,*
And *Tumult* and *Confusion* all embroild,
And *Discord* with a thousand various mouths.

T'whom *Satan* turning boldly thus: Ye powers,
And spirits of this nethermost abyss,
970 *Chaos* and *ancient Night,* I come no spy
With purpose to explore or to disturb
The secrets of your realm: but by constraint
Wand'ring this darksome desert, as my way
Lies through your spacious empire up to light,
975 Alone and without guide, half lost, I seek
What readiest path leads where your gloomy bounds
Confine with heaven: or if some other place
From your dominion won, th' ethereal king
Possesses lately, thither to arrive
980 I travel this profound: direct my course;
Directed no mean recompence it brings
To your behoof: if I that region lost,
All usurpation thence expell'd, reduce
To her original darkness and your sway,
985 (Which is my present journey,) and once more
Erect the standard there of *ancient Night*;
Yours be th' advantage all, mine the revenge.

Thus *Satan;* and him thus the anarch old,
With fault'ring speech and visage incompos'd
990 Answer'd: I know thee stranger, who thou art,
That mighty leading angel, who of late
Made head against heavens king, though overthrown.
I saw, and heard: for such a num'rous host
Fled not in silence through the frighted deep,
995 With ruin upon ruin, rout on rout,
Confusion worse confounded: and heaven gates
Pour'd out by millions her victorious bands
Pursuing. I upon my frontieres here

Keep residence; if all I can will serve,
1000 That little which is left so to defend
Encroached on still through our intestine broils
Weak'ning the sceptre of old *Night*: first hell,
Your dungeon stretching far and wide beneath:
Now lately heaven and earth, another World
1005 Hung ore my realm, link'd in a golden chain,
To that side heaven from whence your legions fell:
If that way be your walk, you have not far;
So much the nearer danger; go and speed;
Havock, and spoil, and ruin are my gain.

1010 He ceas'd; and *Satan* staid not to reply,
But glad that now his sea should find a shore,
With fresh alacrity and force renew'd,
Springs upward, like a pyramid of fire
Into the wilde expanse; and through the shock
1015 Of fighting elements, on all sides round
Environ'd wins his way: harder beset,
And more endanger'd, then when *Argo* pass'd
Through *Bosphorus*, betwixt the justling rocks:
Or when *Ulysses* on the Larboard shunn'd
1020 *Charybdis,* and by th' other whirlpool steer'd.
So he with difficulty and labour hard
Moved on, with difficulty and labour he;
But he once passed, soon after, when man fell,
Strange alteration; sin and death, amain,
1025 Following his tract, (such was the will of heaven,)
Pav'd after him a broad and beaten way
Over the dark abyss, whose boiling gulf
Tamely endur'd a bridge of wondrous length,
From Hell continued, reaching th'utmost orb
1030 Of this frail World; by which the spirits perverse
With easy intercourse pass to and fro,
To tempt or punish mortals, except whom
God and good angels guard by special grace.

But now at last the sacred influence
1035 Of light appears, and from the walls of heaven
Shoots far into the bosom of dim night
A glimmering dawn, here nature first begins
Her farthest verge, and *Chaos* to retire,
As from her outmost works a broken foe,
1040 With tumult less, and with less hostile din;
That *Satan* with less toil, and now with ease,
Wafts on the calmer wave by dubious light;
And like a weather-beaten vessel holds
Gladly the Port, though shrouds and tackle torn;
1045 Or in the emptier waste, resembling air,
Weighs his spread wings, at leasure to behold
Far off th' empyreal heaven, extended wide
In circuit, undetermind square or round:
With opal towrs and battlements adorn'd
1050 Of living saphire, (once his native seat;)
And fast by, hanging in a golden chain,
This pendant world, in bigness as a star
Of smallest magnitude, close by the moon.
Thither full fraught with mischievous revenge,
1055 Accursed, and in a cursed hour, he hies.

The End of Book Second.

Throne of Royal State. The opening recalls Spenser's description of the throne of Lucifera, incarnate pride: High above all a cloth of state was spred,
   And a rich throne, as bright as sunny day. (*Faerie Queene* 1.4.8.1-2)

Ormus. An island in the Persian Gulf. Ind is short for India, proverbially home to a splendid court.

by merit rais'd. Both Satan and the Messiah are raised by merit. Satan's merit is ironic, however—he merits punishment, rather than glory.

success. This refers to the outcome, good or bad. Satan so far has remained "untaught" by his "success," which is his banishment to Hell. Note the ironic coupling with "Vain War."

Powers and Dominions. Two orders of angels. See Colossians 1: 16.

Immortal vigor. Satan and the devils, though damned, remain immortal and godlike in their power compared to mortals.

virtues. Though irony is intended here, Satan principally means virtue as "The power or operative influence inherent in a supernatural or divine being" (*OED2*).

a safe unenvied Throne. Who, we might ask would envy Satan's "throne"? Is Satan being ironic unwittingly or at his own expense?

Yielded with full consent. Ironic, as Satan has assumed the throne of Hell without asking or receiving consent.

who here will envy. The angels have fallen because they envied God's power; Satan is here trying to convince his peers not to envy him.

thunderer. A reference to Jove, as in Ovid's *Metamorphoses* 1.228. Here Satan uses this symbol of omnipotence to suggest that God is a tyrant.

Moloch. Described at some length in 1. 392-405.

reck'd not. Cared not.

sentence. Counsel.

unexpert. Inexperienced.

sit lingring. Note the apparent contradiction in Moloch's description of the devils' position. They "stand" in arms, but "sit" awaiting the signal.

Almighty Engin. Moloch refers to the Son's "fierce Chariot".

Tartarean. From Tartarus, the classical underworld.

forgetful Lake. The "oblivious Pool" of 1.266. Also reminiscent of the River Lethe; a drink of this river made the spirits of the dead forget their earthly life. In Dante's *Purgatorio* spirits cleanse themselves of guilt, not the memory of their earthly life.

insulting. Meaning both "assaulting" and "exulting."

Th' ascent is easie. Contrast with the sybil's warning to Aeneas about the descent into hell. Also note the contrast to Dante, who found his ascent difficult (blocked by a leopard, lion and a she-wolf), but his descent into hell unimpeded.

event. Outcome.

exercise. Torment.

Vassals. This could be a reference either to the original Latin meaning of "servant" or "slave," or as Richard Bentley suggests, it could mean "vessels," in allusion to Romans 9: 22.

Penance. Moloch echoes the Roman Catholic tradition of mortification of the flesh, practiced by various monastic orders. Here, Milton condemns this practice as misguided and satanic by association.

essential. Essence.

proof. Experience.

fatal. Maintained by fate.

not Victory is yet Revenge. Even if the devils are not victorious, the attempt to overthrow God is, in itself, an act of revenge.

denounc'd. "To give formal, authoritative, or official information of; to proclaim, announce, declare; to publish, promulgate." (OED2)

Belial. See also Belial's appearances in 1.490; The characterization of Belial is Milton's, but the tradition may have been taken from Reginald Scot's *Discoverie of Witchcraft* (1665).

Manna. The divine substance that God provided as nourishment to the Israelites in Exodus 16 (see Exodus 16:31 for the origin of the name).

fact. Deed or feat.

baser fire. See Deuteronomy 4:24 and Psalms 104:4 for the conception of God as a "consuming fire" and "his angels" as "a flaming fire."

flat. Dull.

doubtful. Is this, as Regina Schwartz suggests, an infernal version of Hamlet's soliloquy? (*Remembering and Repeating* 20).

Belike. Doubtless.

amain. With all of our strength.

Chain'd on the burning Lake. This was how Satan and his follwers found themselves when they first awoke in 1.210.

red right hand. The phrase appears to be a translation of "rubente dextera" from Horace, *Odes* 1.2.2-3.

Each on his rock transfixt. Prometheus was chained to a rock for disobedience to Jove. He was condemned to have his liver eaten each day for having given fire to man. See Aeschylus's *Prometheus Bound.*

sees and derides. This echoes Psalm 2: 4: "He that sitteth in the heavens shall laugh; the Lord shall have them in derision."

temper. Substance.

cloath'd in reasons garb. Milton implies that while Belial's words may sound reasonable and persuasive, his words are actually hollow, like the speaker.

Chaos. In Milton's cosmology, Chaos and Night reigned over the "eternal anarchy," the formless void between hell and heaven. See Regina Schwartz's excellent discussion of Chaos in *Remembering and Repeating: Biblical Creation in Paradise Lost.*

Sovran. Sovereign.

Ambrosial Flowers. In the *Iliad* 4. 3-4, Hebe pours ambrosia for the gods. Thus ambrosia was thought to be the proper food of gods.

Hard liberty. Milton restates this principle in *Samson Agonistes* 268-271. In this context, it echoes the closing words of the invective of the Consul Aemilius Lepidus against the tyrant Cornelius Sulla in 78 B.C.E. as it is found in Sallust's version of that *Oration to the Roman People.* As a republican Milton believed deeply in the virtue of seeking "hard liberty" over subjection to a tyrant, but he equated utter subjection to God with liberty.

Thick clouds and dark. See Chronicles 5: 13, 6:1 and Psalms 18: 11-13.

sensible of pain. The character of pain as interpreted by the senses.

Such applause. This is likely an allusion to Virgil's *Aeneid* 10, where the gods' response to the violent appeals of Juno sounds like the winds that gradually build into a storm.

sword of Michael. Michael's sword is rightfully feared: in the war in Heaven, he wounded even Satan, though Satan quickly healed.

pollicy. Political strategy.

Beelzebub. Compare to Beelzebub's first appearance in Book 1.

Front. Forehead.

Atlantean. The Titan Atlas was forced to support the heavens on his shoulders.

off-spring of heaven. It is hard not to hear a double sense to this phrase: children of heaven and exiles from heaven.

Virtues. "The power or operative influence inherent in a supernatural or divine being." (*OED2*)

stile. Title.

first and last. In Revelation 21: 6, the voice of the Lord says, "I am the Alpha and the Omega, the beginning and the end." There is some irony in a devil quoting this scripture in particular.

Iron Scepter. Psalms 2: 9.

to our power. To the limit of our power.

reluctance. Resistance.

Gods. Angels.

by an Oath. Milton combines biblical representations of God taking an oath by himself "because he could swear by no greater" (Hebrews 6:13; Genesis 22:16) with classical recollections of Zeus shaking Olympus as he makes a vow to Thetis (*Iliad* 1. 530).

endu'd. Endowed.

abolish his own works. See Genesis 6: 7.

confusion. Destruction.

Their frail Original. Adam, the first man. The first edition read "Originals," including Eve as a "frail" one.

By Satan. See book 1. 651.

one root. One man, or Adam.

states. Estates.

They vote. No doubt the first example of "manufactured consent", parading as democracy.

Synod of Gods. A synod is a church council, composed of bishops and other dignitaries. Milton uses Beelzebub's praise to condemn the organization of the Roman Catholic church.

seat. See line 347, where seat refers to home or capital.

tempt. Attempt.

palpable obscure. Exodus 10: 22.

uncouth. Unknown.

abrupt. Used here as a noun: the gap or schism between Heaven and Hell.

suspence. Doubtful.

long is the way. Reinforcement of line 81: the descent into Hell is easy, but the ascent from Hell is difficult.

convex of Fire. Convex refers to the area around Hell; "ninefold" refers to the nine circles of the Styx around the underworld of the *Aeneid* 6. 570, and "gates of burning Adamant" recall Virgil's columns surrounding the gates of Tartarus. This structure of Hell is also employed by Dante in the *Inferno*, where each of the nine circles of Hell hosts different sinners.

unessential. Without essence or being.

abortive. The meaning of this is unclear. It could mean lifeless, or monstrous (destructive). Or the word could also be used as a derivation in the etymological sense, meaning "away from birth," or not created, as in line 439.

moment. Importance.

intend. Attend to or consider.

Mansion. Home. Refer to lines 347 and 394.

Deliverance. In emulation opposite to Christ, Satan claims the role of deliverer and savior.

rais'd. Emboldened.

clos. Close; hidden or secret.

Element. Sky.

lantskip. Landscape.

Stygian. Hellish. From the name of the River Styx, Hell's chief river according to classical legend.

peers. Lords.

th' Antagonist. Close to the literal sense of the name, Satan; adversary.

Globe. Body of heavily armed soldiers.

horrent. Bristling

Alchymie. A metallic composition that imitates gold; thus, by metonymy, a horn made of such a metal. The horns which the fallen angels blow are in imitation of those blown in heaven, not of the same material.

th' Olympian Games or Pythian fields. This alludes to the funeral games at the tomb of Anchises in *Aeneid* 5.776, and the games at the tomb of Patroclus in the *Iliad* 23. 800. The Pythian fields were near Delphi, where the Pythian games, which celebrated the victory of Apollo over the Python, were held. Why would Milton describe contests like these as fit pastimes for devils?

shun the Goal. That is, avoid touching the course marker as they round the turn in a chariot race.

close. Close (engage) in battle.

welkin. The sky.

Typhoean. Monstrous, like Typhon; see also 1.197-199.

Alcides. Hercules.

Lichas from the top of Oeta. Returning victorious from Oechalia, in Laconia, Hercules was brought a gift of the cloak of the centaur Nessus, whom he had years earlier fought and killed. The cloak was poisoned and destroyed him, causing him to throw the innocent Lichas into the sea.

sing.../ Their own Heroic deeds. That is, some practised the arts of epic song and celebrated their own fall in heroic verse.

partial. That is, sung in parts, but paranomasia suggests two other senses: incomplete, and biased.

charms the Sense. In the context of Hell, Satan and the other fallen angels, these songs must be both false and insincere, as Hell is a place of false praise. This is of course in contrast to Heaven.

reason'd high. This recalls the castle of Limbo in Dante's *Inferno* 4.45, where those who lived before Christianity spend eternity.

bold adventure. Some of the devils opt for adventure and exploration.

Styx. Hades's chief river according to Homer's *Odyssey* 10.510. Cocytus, Periphlegeton and Acheron are other rivers of Hades.

Lethe. The River of Oblivion.

gathers heap. That is, gathers mass.

pile. Building.

Serbonian bog. Quicksands around Lake Serbonis at the mouth of the Nile.

Damiata. Damietta, a city at the mouth of the Nile. Casius, a mountain in Egypt, figures in Lucan's *Pharsalia* book 8; identified as the site of Pompey's tomb in Tasso's *Jerusalem Delivered* 15.

frore. Frozen.

th' effect of Fire. Compare to Dante's description of the innermost circles of Hell in *Inferno* 33. 93-117. Instead of fire in Hell, Dante immerses Dis (Lucifer) and the other members of the four rings of the ninth circle in a lake of ice.

harpy-footed Furies. The harpies, who attacked Aeneas and his men, had the faces and breasts of young women, the wings and bodies of birds, and talons for hands (*Aeneid* 3.211-217). See also *Inferno* 13. 12.

starve. Die.

infixt, and frozen round. Here, Milton alludes not to the classical Hell of raging fires, but to Dante's Hell of frozen lakes and beds of ice.

ferry. Alludes to Charon's ferry in Dante's *Inferno* 3. 83.

Medusa. Gorgon who had snakes for hair and whose appearance turned men into stones. See *Odyssey* 11.634.

wight. Body.

Tantalus. Tantalus was condemned in Hell to suffer intense thirst in a pool whose water rose just below the reach of his lips. See *Odyssey* 11. 582-592.

No rest. See Matthew 12: 43.

for evil only good. That is, evil that can be used to construct good.

Gorgons and Hydra's, and Chimera's. The hydra was a nine-headed dragon, the chimera breathed fire, and for the gorgons. See also *Aeneid* 6. 744.

Adversary. Adversary is a lteral translation of the name, Satan.

Explores. Tests or proves.

Ethiopian. The Indian Ocean.

the Trading Flood. The ships imagined here mimic the spice route, from India south and west around the Cape of Good Hope. Ternate and Tidore are two of the Spice Islands near New Guinea.

Cerberian. Like the legendary hell-hound, Cerberus. See Homer's *Iliad* 8.365.

seem'd Woman. Sin owes her serpentine nether parts to conceptions like Spenser's Error: Halfe like a serpent horribly displaide,

But th'other halfe did a woman's shape retaine. (*Faerie Queene* 1.1.14)

But the dogs around Sin's waist, and especially their Cerberean mouths—a literally Ovidian phrase—plainly match Ovid's description of Scylla, the lovely nymph whose body Circe transformed into a mass of yelping hounds from the waist down (*Metamorphoses* 14. 40-74). Finally,-according to Ovid-she became the dangerous reef between Sicily (Trinacria) and the toe of the Italian boot (Calabria).

Night-Hag. Hecate, the goddess of the underworld.

Lapland. Province of northern Finland and legendary home of the witches.

labouring. Undergoing eclipse, a reference to the comtemporary belief that the witches could control the phases of the moon.

The other shape. Death, whom Milton deliberately introduces on line 666, which is the number of the Beast in Revelation 13:18. The inversion of 666, 999, is the line chosen in book 9 for the moment of Adam's fall—9.999.

Furies. The Furies, according to classical legend, were born of the drops of blood that streamed from the testicles of Heaven when his son Cronus cut them in revenge for being thrust into Hades. Their names are Alecto, Tisiphone, and Megaera.

likeness of a Kingly Crown. The description of Death is so full of equivocal expressions that it is difficult to visualize him. As soon as you imagine a feature, you're told it only seem'd or looked that way, but wasn't really. Milton's description of Death may owe something to Pieter Bruegel's depiction of *Mad Meg* (1562), especially in the undefined features and the gigantic maw.

admir'd. Synonymous with wondered.

Spirits of heaven. Satan, though now in Hell, was born in Heaven, unlike Death who was born in Hell. One might wonder why Milton wants to draw attention to this distinction, which leads to such nice observations that Death was conceived, according to this story, in Heaven, and Sin was born in Heaven, not Hell.

the third part of heaven's Sons. See Revelation 12: 3-4.

Conjur'd. Persuaded to rebel.

whip of Scorpions. See 1 Kings 12: 11.

Ophiucus. Ophiuchus; the Serpent-Bearer, a particularly large constellation.

two black Clouds. The two black clouds in Boiardo's *Orlando Innamorato* 1.16 are Orlando and the Tartar king Agricane.

Caspian. A notoriously stormy sea.

never but once more. When each is met by the triumphant Christ, an even greater foe.

only Son. This phrase cannot help but strike us as a parody of Christ's relation to His Father. Indeed, Satan, Sin, and Death unwittingly express an infernal trinity, in "emulation opposite to heaven." As an anti-trinitarian, perhaps Milton also means to mock trintarianism as an infernal falsehood.

spares. Forbears.

left side op'ning wide. The left side is the "sinister" side. Also, Eve is created from one of Adam's left ribs (8. 465).

Out of thy head I sprung. Here, the birth of Sin from Satan echoes the birth of Athena from the head of Zeus.

in me thy perfect image viewing. Sin, the firstborn of Satan, is the perfect image of himself as the Son is said to be the perfect image of the Father. Satan's love for his own image is his love for himself, or narcissism.

Pitch. Height.

own begotten. The phrase echoes (parodically) John 1:14 and John 3:16.

cry'd out Death. Milton's allegory, the only overt allegory in this epic poem, dramatizes the metaphors of James 1:15.

Hell trembl'd at the hideous Name. This is an interesting parody on the end of *Inferno* 3.132, where the "darkened plain" of Hell trembles after Virgil utters the name of God and informs Dante that "no good soul" ever travels on Charon's boat (*Inferno* 3.129-132.) Here, Hell trembles at the mention of Death.

dismaid. This word allows of several punning senses.

Fate pronounc'd. Fate is still regarded as the supreme power.

mortal dint. Death-dealing blow.

dalliance. The word is used to describe Adam's sexual practices with Eve immediately after the fall and also Solomon's less than perfectly licit "dalliance" with his Egyptian wife.

house of pain. As referred to in Job 30: 23.

pretences. Claims.

one for all/ Myself expose. Satan's self-sacrifice parodies the Son's voluntary sacrifice in 3.236.

unfounded. Bottomless.

Purlieues. French word for boundaries.

vacant room. That is, Satan's and the rebel angels' place.

buxom. Unresisting.

Office. Service.

Thou art my Father, thou my Author. Here, Sin addresses Satan in the same manner that Dante addresses Virgil in the beginning of the Inferno: "You are my master and my author" (*Inferno* 1.85), and "you are my guide, my governor, my master" (*Inferno* 2.140).

Gods who live at ease. Compare to Homer's *Iliad* 6. 138 and *Odyssey* 4. 805, where the gods seem to always live at ease. However unattractive a character Sin is, she, unlike Adam, Eve, and even Satan, remains obedient to the person she thinks is her Father and creator.

At thy right hand. Here is the ultimate parody: Satan, Sin, and Death as the Holy Trinity.

Porcullis. Portcullis; outer gate.

Stygian. Styx was, in classical mythology, one of the rivers of hell; thus Stygian connotes hellish.

wards. The notches on a key.

Without dimension. Milton "defines" Chaos by its lack of all forms of dimension, definition, and boundaries. In book 7, creation is the process of setting boundaries and dimensions to the "first matter" of Chaos (book 7.166-67 and 219-233)

hot, cold, moist, and dry. The characteristics of the four humors correspond to the four basic elements.

Barca. Desert between Egypt and Tunis, or according to Orgel, a city in the Lybian desert.

Cyrene. Ancient city near modern Tripoli.

frith. Inlet or estuary.

peal'd. Deafened.

Bellona. Goddess of War.

rase. Raze, destroy.

Vannes. Wings.

pennons. Feathers or wings.

Syrtis. Shifting sands on the North African coast.

Gryfon. Griffins were the guardians of abundant quantities of gold which the Arimaspians constantly tried to steal.

wades, or creeps, or flyes. Satan's difficulty in his ascent out of Hell echoes Dante's difficulty in his ascent up the mountain in Purgatory (*Purgatorio* 4.28-33).

(*Faerie Queene* 1.1.37) (Hughes 261)

Orcus and Ades. Names of the classical god of Hell.

Confine with. Border upon.

Anarch. Anarchy, chaos.

Made head. Fought.

golden Chain. See *Iliad* 8. 15-24 for the legend of the golden chain linking the earth and the heavens.

Argo. Ship of Jason and the Argonauts.

Charybdis. Whirlpool opposite Scylla, the more treacherous whirlpool.

Th'utmost Orbe. The outermost circle of Earth is the orbit of the moon.

this frail World. Earth.

square or round. Too wide to determine if the boundary is straight or curved.

living Sapphire. See Revelations 21: 19.

pendant world. Not only the earth, but the entire created universe.

fraught with. Full freighted

Paradise Lost:

Book III

John Milton

The Argument

God sitting on his throne sees Satan *flying towards this world, then newly created; shows him to the Son who sat at his right hand; foretells the success of* Satan *in perverting mankind: clears his own Justice and wisdom from all imputation, having created man free, and able enough to have withstood his tempter; yet declares his purpose of grace towards him, in regard he fell not of his own malice, as did* Satan, *but by him seduced. The Son of God renders praises to his Father for the manifestation of his gracious purpose towards* Man; *but God again declares, that Grace cannot be extended towards Man without the satisfaction of divine justice; Man hath offended the majesty of God by aspiring to Godhead, and, therefore, with all his progeny devoted to death, must die, unless some one can be found sufficient to answer for his offence, and undergo his punishment. The Son of God freely offers himself a ransom for Man; the Father accepts him,*

John Milton, "Book 3," from *Paradise Lost*. Copyright in the Public Domain.

ordains his incarnation, pronounces his exaltation above all names in heaven and earth; commands all the angels to adore him; they obey, and hymning to their harps in full choir, celebrate the Father and the Son. Meanwhile, Satan alights upon the bare Convex of this worlds outermost Orb; where wand'ring he first finds a place, since called The lymbo of vanity; what persons and things fly up thither; thence comes to the gate of heaven, described ascending by stairs, and the waters above the firmament that flow about it: his passage thence to the orb of the sun: he finds there Uriel, *the regent of that orb; but first changes himself into the shape of a meaner angel; and pretending a zealous desire to behold the new creation and Man whom God had placed here, inquires of him the place of his habitation, and is directed; alights first on Mount* Niphates.

    Hail holy Light, offspring of heaven first-born,
    Or of th' eternal co-eternal beam;
    May I express thee unblam'd? Since God is light,
    And never but in unapproached light
5   Dwelt from eternity; dwelt then in thee,
    Bright effluence of bright essence increate;
    Or hearest thou rather pure ethereal stream,
    Whose fountain who shall tell? Before the sun,
    Before the heavens thou wert, and at the voice
10   Of God, as with a Mantle didst invest
    The rising world of waters dark and deep,
    Won from the void and formless infinite.
    Thee I revisit now with bolder wing,
    Escaped the *Stygian* pool, though long detain'd
15   In that obscure sojourn; while in my flight
    Through utter and through middle darkness borne,
    With other notes then to th' *Orphean* lyre,
    I sung of *chaos,* and *eternal Night;*
    Taught by the heavenly Muse to venture down
20   The dark descent, and up to reascend,
    Though hard, and rare; Thee I revisit safe,
    And feel thy sovereign vital lamp: but thou
    Revisit'st not these eyes, that rolle in vain
    To find thy piercing ray, and find no dawn;
25   So thick a drop serene hath quenched their orbs,
    Or dim suffusion veil'd. Yet not the more
    Cease I to wander where the Muses haunt
    Clear spring, or shady grove, or sunny hill,
    Smit with the love of sacred song: but chief
30   Thee, *Sion,* and the flowery brooks beneath,
    That wash thy hallow'd feet, and warbling flow,
    Nightly I visit: nor sometimes forget
    Those other two equall'd with me in fate,
    (So were I equal'd with them in renown,)
35   Blind *Thamyris* and blind *Mæonides:*
    And *Tiresias* and *Phineus,* prophets old.
    Then feed on thoughts, that voluntary move
    Harmonious numbers; as the wakeful bird
    Sings darkling, and in shadiest covert hid
40   Tunes her nocturnal note. Thus with the year
    Seasons return; but not to me returns
    Day, or the sweet approach of even or morn,
    Or sight of vernal bloom, or summers rose,
    Or flocks, or heards, or human face divine;
45   But cloud instead, and ever-during dark
    Surrounds me; from the cheerful ways of men
    Cut off; and for the book of knowledge fair
    Presented with a universal blank
    Of nature's works, to me expung'd and razd,
50   And wisdom at one entrance quite shut out.
    So much the rather thou celestial light,
    Shine inward, and the mind through all her powers
    Irradiate, there plant eyes; all mist from thence
    Purge and disperse; that I may see and tell
55   Of things invisible to mortal sight.

Now had the Almighty Father from above,
(From the pure empyrean where he sits high thron'd above all height, bent down his eye,
His own works and their works at once to view:
60 About him all the sanctities of heaven
Stood thick as starrs, and from his sight receiv'd
Beatitude past utterance: on his right
The radiant image of his glory sat,
His only Son. On earth he first beheld
65 Our two first parents, (yet the only two
Of mankind,) in the happy garden placed,
Reaping immortal fruits of joy and love;
Uninterrupted joy, unrivall'd love,
In blissful solitude, he then survey'd
70 Hell, and the gulf between, and *Satan* there
Coasting the wall of heaven on this side night,
In the dun air sublime: and ready now
To stoop with wearied wings, and willing feet,
On the bare outside of this world, that seem'd
75 Firm land imbosom'd without firmament;
Uncertain which, in ocean or in air.
Him god beholding from his prospect high,
Wherein past, present, future he beholds,
Thus to his only Son foreseeing spake:

80 Only begotten Son, seest thou what rage
Transports our adversary, whom no bounds
Prescrib'd, no bars of hell, nor all the chains
Heaped on him there, nor yet the main abyss
Wide interrupt, can hold? So bent he seems
85 On desparate revenge, that shall redound
Upon his own rebellious head. And now
Through all restraint broke loos he wings his way
Not far off heaven, in the precincts of light,
Directly towards the new created world,
90 And Man there placed, with purpose to assay
If him by force he can destroy, or worse,
By some false guile pervert: and shall pervert;
For man will hearken to his glozing lies,
And easily transgress the sole command,
95 Sole pledge of his obedience: so will fall,
He and his faithless progeny. Whose fault?
Whose but his own? Ingrate, he had of me
All he could have; I made him just and right;
Sufficient to have stood, though free to fall.
100 Such I created all th' ethereal powers
And spirits, both them who stood, and them who fail'd;
Freely they stood who stood, and fell who fell.
Not free, what proof could they have given sincere
Of true allegiance, constant faith or love,
105 Where only what they needs must do, appear'd;
Not what they would? What praise could they receive?
What pleasure I from such obedience paid,
When will and reason (reason also is choice)
Useless and vain, of freedom both despoil'd,
110 Made passive both, had serv'd necessity,
Not me? They therefore as to right belong'd,
So were created, nor can justly accuse
Their maker, or their making, or their fate,
As if predestination over-rul'd
115 Their will, dispos'd by absolute decree
Or high foreknowledge; they themselves decreed
Their own revolt, not I: if I foreknew,
Foreknowledge had no influence on their fault,
Which had no less prov'd certain unforeknown.
120 So without least impulse or shadow of Fate,
Or aught by me immutably foreseen,

They trespass, authors to themselves in all,
Both what they judge and what they choose; for me
I form'd them free, and free they must remain,
125 Till they enthrall themselves: I else must change
Their nature, and revoke the high decree
Unchangeable, eternal, which ordain'd
Their freedom; they themselves ordain'd their fall.
The first sort by their own suggestion fell,
130 Self-tempted, self-deprav'd: Man falls, deceiv'd,
By th'other first: man therefore, shall find grace,
The other none. In mercy and justice both,
Through heaven and earth, so shall my glory excel,
But mercy first, and last, shall brightest shine.

135 Thus while God spake, ambrosial fragrance fill'd
All heaven, and in the blessed spirits elect
Sense of new joy ineffable diffus'd.
Beyond compare the Son of God was seen
Most glorious: in him all his Father shone
140 Substantially express'd; and in his face
Divine compassion visibly appear'd,
Love without end, and without measure grace;
Which uttering thus he to his father spake:

O Father, gracious was that word which clos'd
145 Thy sovereign sentence, that Man should find grace
For which both heaven and earth shall high extol
Thy praises, with th' innumerable sound
Of hymns and sacred songs, wherewith thy throne
Encompass'd shall resound thee ever blessed.

150 For should Man finally be lost, should man
Thy creature late so lov'd, thy youngest son
Fall circumvented thus by fraud, though joined
With his own folly? that be from thee far,
That far be from thee, Father, who art judge
155 Of all things made, and judgest only right.
Or shall the Adversary thus obtain
His end, and frustrate thine? shall he fulfil
His malice, and thy goodness bring to nought;
Or proud return, though to his heavier doom,
160 Yet with revenge accomplished and to hell
Draw after him the whole race of mankind,
By him corrupted? Or wilt thou thyself
Abolish thy creation, and unmake,
For him, what for thy glory thou hast made?
165 So should thy goodness and thy greatness, both
Be questioned and blasphem'd without defence.

To whom the great Creatour thus replied.
O Son, in whom my soul hath chief delight,
Son of my bosom, Son who art alone
170 My word, my wisdom, and effectual might,
All hast thou spoken as my thoughts are, all
As my eternal purpose hath decreed.
Man shall not quite be lost, but sav'd who will
Yet not of will in him, but grace in me
175 Freely voutsafed; once more I will renew
His lapsed powers, though forfeit and inthrall'd
By sin to foul exorbitant desires;
Upheld by me, yet once more he shall stand
On even ground against his mortal foe:
180 By me upheld, that he may know how frail
His fallen condition is, and to me owe
All his deliverance, and to none but me.
Some I have chosen of peculiar grace
Elect above the rest: so is my will;
185 The rest shall hear me call, and oft be warn'd

Their sinful state, and to appease betimes
Th' incensed Deity while offer'd grace
Invites: for I will clear their senses dark,
What may suffice, and soften stony hearts
190 To pray, repent, and bring obedience due.
To prayer, repentance, and obedience due,
Though but endevor'd with sincere intent,
Mine ear shall not be slow, mine eye not shut;
And I will place within them as a guide
195 My umpire *conscience;* whom if they will hear,
Light after light well us'd they shall attain,
And to the end persisting, safe arrive.
This my long sufferance and my day of grace,
They who neglect and scorn shall never taste;
200 But hard be hardened, blind he blinded more,
That they may stumble on, and deeper fall;
And none but such from mercy I exclude.
But yet all is not done: Man disobeying,
Disloyal breaks his fealty, and sins
205 Against the high supremacy of heaven,
Affecting Godhead, and so losing all,
To expiate his treason hath nought left,
But to destruction, sacred and devote,
He with his whole posterity must die,
210 Die he or justice must; unless for him
Some other able, and as willing, pay
The rigid satisfaction, death for death.
Say heavenly powers, where shall we find such love?
Which of ye will be mortal to redeem
215 Man's mortal crime, and just th' unjust to save?
Dwells in all Heaven charity so dear?

He ask'd, but all the heavenly choir stood mute,
And silence was in heaven: on man's behalf
Patron or intercessor none appear'd,
220 Much less that durst upon his own head draw
The deadly forfeiture, and ransom set.
And now without redemption all mankind
Must have been lost, adjudg'd to death and hell
By doom severe, had not the Son of God,
225 In whom the fulness dwells of love divine,
His dearest mediation thus renew'd:

Father, thy word is past, man shall find grace,
And shall grace not find means, that finds her way,
The speediest of thy winged messengers,
230 To visit all thy creatures, and to all
Comes unprevented, unimplor'd, unsought?
Happy for man, so coming; he her aide
Can never seek, once dead in sins and lost;
Atonement for himself, or offering meet,
235 (Indebted and undone,) hath none to bring.
Behold me then, me for him, life for life
I offer, on me let thine anger fall;
Account me man: I for his sake will leave
Thy bosom, and this glory next to thee
240 Freely put off, and for him lastly die
Well pleas'd, on me let death wreck all his rage;
Under his gloomy power I shall not long
Lie vanquished; thou hast givn me to possess
Life in myself for ever: by thee I live,
245 Though now to Death I yield, and am his due
All that of me can die, yet that debt paid,
Thou wilt not leave me in the loathsome grave
His prey, nor suffer my unspotted soule
For ever with corruption there to dwell;
250 But I shall rise victorious, and subdue
My vanquisher, spoiled of his vanted spoil;
Death his death's wound shall then receive, and stoop
Inglorious, of his mortal sting disarm'd.
I through the ample air in triumph high

255 Shall lead hell captive maugre hell; and show
The powers of darkness bound. Thou at the sight
Pleas'd, out of heaven shalt look down and smile,
While by thee rais'd I ruin all my foes,
Death last, and with his Carcass glut the Grave:
260 Then with the multitude of my redeem'd
Shall enter heaven, long absent, and return,
Father, to see thy face, wherein no cloud
Of anger shall remain; but peace assured,
And reconcilement: wrauth shall be no more
265 Thenceforth, but in thy presence Joy entire.

His words here ended, but his meek aspect
Silent yet spake, and breath'd immortal love
To mortal men, above which only shone
Filial obedience: as a sacrifice
270 Glad to be offer'd, he attends the will
Of his great Father. Admiration seiz'd
All heaven, what this might mean, and whither tend,
Wond'ring; but soon th' Almighty thus replied:

O thou in heaven and Earth the only peace
275 Found out for mankind under wrauth; O thou,
My sole complacence; well thou know'st how dear
To me are all my works, nor man the least,
Though last created; that for him I spare
Thee from my bosom and right hand, to save
280 By loosing thee a while, the whole Race lost.
Thou, therefore, whom thou only canst redeem,
Their nature also to thy nature join;
And be thyself man among men on earth,
Made flesh, when time shall be, of virgin seed,
285 By wondrous birth: be thou in *Adam's* room,
The head of all mankind, though *Adams* son.
As in him perish all men, so in thee
As from a second root, shall be restor'd
As many as are restor'd, without thee, none.
290 His crime makes guilty all his sons; thy merit
Imputed shall absolve them who renounce
Their own both righteous and unrighteous deeds
And live in thee transplanted, and from thee
Receive new life. So man, as is most just,
295 Shall satisfy for Man, be judg'd and die,
And dying rise, and rising with him raise
His Brethren, ransom'd with his own dear life.
So heavenly love shall outdo hellish hate,
Giving to death, and dying to redeeme,
300 So dearly to redeem what Hellish hate
So easily destroy'd, and still destroy's
In those who, when they may, accept not grace.
Nor shalt thou, by descending to assume
Man's nature, lessen or degrade thine own.
305 Because thou hast, though thron'd in high--est bliss
Equal to God, and equally enjoying
Godlike fruition, quitted all to save
A world from utter loss, and hast been found
By merit more then birthright Son of God,
310 Found worthiest to be so by being good,
Far more then great or high; because in thee
Love hath abounded more then Glory abounds;
Therefore thy humiliation shall exalt
With thee thy manhood also to this throne.
315 Here shalt thou sit incarnate, here shalt reign
Both God and Man, Son both of God and Man,

　　　　　Anointed universal King: all power
　　　　　I give thee: reign for ever, and assume
　　　　　Thy merits: under thee, as head supreme
320　　　Thrones, princedoms, powers, dominions I reduce;
　　　　　All knees to thee shall bow, of them that bide
　　　　　In heaven, or earth, or under earth in hell.
　　　　　When thou, attended gloriously from heaven,
　　　　　Shalt in the Sky appear, and from thee send
325　　　The summoning archangels to proclaim
　　　　　Thy dread tribunal: forthwith from all winds
　　　　　The living, and forthwith the cited dead
　　　　　Of all past ages to the general doom
　　　　　Shall hasten, such a peal shall rouse their sleep:
330　　　Then, all thy saints assembled, thou shalt judge
　　　　　Bad men and angels; they arraign'd shall sink
　　　　　Beneath thy sentence; hell, her numbers full,
　　　　　Thenceforth shall be for ever shut. Mean while
　　　　　The world shall burn, and from her ashes spring
335　　　New heaven and earth, wherein the just shall dwell;
　　　　　And, after all their tribulations long,
　　　　　See golden days, fruitful of golden deeds,
　　　　　With joy and love triumphing, and fair truth.
　　　　　Then thou thy regal sceptre shalt lay by,
340　　　For regal scepter then no more shall need;
　　　　　God shall be all in all. But all ye gods,
　　　　　Adore him, who to compass all this dies;
　　　　　Adore the Son, and honour him as me.

　　　　　No sooner had th' Almighty ceased, but all
345　　　The multitude of angels, with a shout
　　　　　Loud as from numbers without number, sweet,
　　　　　As from blessed voices, uttering joy, heaven rung
　　　　　With jubilee, and loud hosanna's fill'd
　　　　　Th' eternal regions. Lowly reverent
350　　　Towards either throne they bow, and to the ground
　　　　　With solemn adoration down they cast
　　　　　Their crowns, inwove with amaranth and gold;
　　　　　Immortal amaranth, a flower which once
　　　　　In Paradise, fast by the tree of life,
355　　　Began to bloom; but soon for man's offence
　　　　　To heaven remov'd, where first it grew, there grows,
　　　　　And flowers aloft, shading the fount of life;
　　　　　And where the river of bliss through midst of heaven
　　　　　Rolls o'er *Elisian* flours her amber stream:
360　　　With these that never fade, the spirits elect
　　　　　Bind their resplendent locks inwreath'd with beams;
　　　　　Now in loose garlands thick thrown off; the bright
　　　　　Pavement, that like a sea of jasper shone,
　　　　　Impurpled with celestial roses smil'd.
365　　　Then crown'd again, their golden harps they took,
　　　　　Harps ever tun'd, that glittering by their side,
　　　　　Like quivers hung, and with præamble sweet
　　　　　Of charming symphony they introduce
　　　　　Their sacred song, and waken raptures high;
370　　　No voice exempt, no voice but well could join
　　　　　Melodious part, such concord is in heaven.

　　　　　Thee, Father, first they sung, omnipotent,
　　　　　Immutable, immortal, infinite,
　　　　　Eternal king; thee author of all being,
375　　　Fountain of light, thyself invisible
　　　　　Amidst the glorious brightness where thou sitt'st
　　　　　Thron'd inaccessible, but when thou shad'st

The full blaze of thy beams, and through a cloud,
Drawn round about thee like a radiant shrine,
380 Dark with excessive bright thy skirts appeer,
Yet dazzle heaven, that brightest seraphim
Approach not, but with both wings veil their eyes.
Thee, next they sang, of all creation first,
Begotten Son, divine similitude,
385 In whose conspicuous count'nance, without cloud
Made visible, th' almighty Father shines,
Whom else no creature can behold: on thee
Impressed the effulgence of his glory abides,
Transfus'd on thee his ample Spirit rests.
390 He heaven of heavens and all the powers therein,
By thee created, and by thee threw down
Th' aspiring dominations: thou that day
Thy Father's dreadful thunder did not spare,
Nor stop thy flaming chariot-wheels, that shook
395 Heavens everlasting frame, while o'er the necks
Thou drov'st of warring angels disarra'd.
Back from pursuit thy powers with loud acclaim
Thee only extol'd, Son of thy Fathers might,
To execute fierce vengeance on his foes
400 Not so on man: him through their malice fallen,
Father of mercy and grace, thou didst not doom
So strictly, but much more to pity incline:
No sooner did thy dear and only Son
Perceive thee purpos'd not to doom frail man
405 So strictly, but much more to pitie enclin'd,
He, to appease thy wrauth, and end the strife
Of mercy and justice in thy face discern'd,
Regardless of the bliss wherein he sat
Second to thee, offer'd himself to die
410 For mans offence. O unexampled love,
Love no where to be found less then divine!
Hail, Son of God, Saviour of men, thy name
Shall be the copious matter of my song
Henceforth, and never shall my harp thy praise
415 Forget, nor from thy Fathers praise disjoin.

Thus they in heaven, above the starry Sphear,
Their happy hours in joy and hymning spent.
Meanwhile upon the firm opacous globe
Of this round world, whose first convex divides
420 The luminous inferior orbs, enclos'd
From *Chaos,* and th' inroad of darkness old,
Satan alighted walks: a globe far off
It seem'd, now seems a boundless continent
Dark, waste, and wild, under the frown of night
425 Starless expos'd, and ever-threat'ning storms
Of *Chaos* blustring round, inclement sky;
Save on that side which from the wall of heaven,
Though distant far some small reflection gaines
Of glimmering air, less vexed, with tempest loud:
430 Here walk'd the fiend at large in spacious field.
As when a vulture, on *Imaus* bred,
Whose snowy ridge the roving *Tartar* bounds,
Dislodging from a region scarce of prey,
To gorge the flesh of lambs, or yeanling kids
435 On hills where flocks are fed, flies toward the springs
Of *Ganges* or *Hydaspes, Indian* streams;
But in his way lights on the barren plains
Of *Sericana,* where *Chineses* drive
With sails and wind their cany wagons light:
440 So on this windy sea of land, the fiend

  Walk'd up and down alone, bent on his prey;
  Alone, for other creature in this place,
  Living or liveless, to be found was none;
  None yet; but store hereafter from the earth
445 Up hither like aerial vapours flew,
  Of all things transitory and vain, when sin
  With vanity had fill'd the works of men:
  Both all things vain, and all who in vain things
  Built their fond hopes of glory or lasting fame,
450 Or happiness in this or th' other life:
  All who have their reward on earth, the fruits
  Of painful superstition and blind zeal,
  Naught seeking but the praise of men, here find
  Fit retribution, empty as their deeds:
455 All th' unaccomplished works of natures hand,
  Abortive, monstrous, or unkindly mixed,
  Dissolv'd on earth, fleet hither, and in vain,
  Till final dissolution, wander here:
  Not in the neighb'ring moon, as some have dream'd;
460 Those argent fields more likely habitants,
  Translated saints or middle spirits hold
  Betwixt th' angelical and human kind.
  Hither of ill-joined sons and daughters born.
  First from the ancient world those giants came,
465 With many a vain exploit, though then renown'd:
  The builders next of *Babel* on the plain
  Of *Sennaar,* and still with vain design
  New *Babels,* had they wherewithall, would build:
  Others came single; he who to be deem'd
470 A God, leap'd fondly into *Ætna's* flames,
  Empedocles, and he who, to enjoy
  Plato's Elysium, leap'd into the sea,
  Cleombrotus, and many more too long,
  Embryos and idiots, eremits and friars
475 White, black and grey, with all their trumpetry.
  Here pilgrims roam, that stray'd so far to seek
  In *Golgotha* him dead, who lives in heaven;
  And they who to be sure of Paradise,
  Dying put on the weeds of *Dominic,*
480 Or in *Franciscan* think to pass disguis'd,
  They pass the planets seven, and pass the fixt,
  And that crystalline sphere whose balance weighs
  The trepidation talked, and that first-mov'd;
  And now Saint *Peter* at heavens wicket seems
485 To wait them with his keys, and now at foot
  Of heavens ascent they lift their feet, when lo
  A violent cross wind from either coast
  Blows them transverse, ten thousand leagues awry
  Into the devious air; then might ye see
490 Cowls, hoods and habits with their wearers, tost
  And flutter'd into rags, then reliques, beads,
  Indulgences, dispenses, pardons, bulls,
  The sport of winds: all these upwhirld aloft,
  Fly o'er the backside of the world far off
495 Into a *Limbo* large and broad, since call'd
  The Paradise of Fools, to few unknown
  Long after: now unpeopled, and untrod;
  All this dark globe the fiend found as he pass'd,
  And long he wander'd, till at last a gleam
500 Of dawning light turn'd thither-ward in haste
  His travell'd steps; far distant he descries,
  Ascending by degrees magnificent
  Up to the wall of heaven a structure high,
  At top whereof, but far more rich, appear'd
505 The work as of a kingly palace gate,
  With frontispice of diamond and gold

Embellished, thick with sparkling orient gemes
The portal shone, inimitable on earth;
By model, or by shading pencil drawn.
510 The stairs were such as whereon *Jacob* saw
Angels ascending and descending, bands
Of guardians bright, when he from *Esau* fled
To *Padan-aram,* in the field of *Luz,*
Dreaming by night under the open sky,
515 And waking cried, *This is the Gate of heaven*
Each stair mysteriously was meant, nor stood
There always, but drawn up to heaven sometimes
Viewless, and underneath a bright sea flow'd
Of jasper, or of liquid pearl, whereon
520 Who after came from Earth, sailing arriv'd,
Wafted by angels, or flew o'er the lake
Rapt in a chariot drawn by fiery steeds.
The stairs were then let down, whether to dare
The fiend by easy ascent, or aggravate
525 His sad exclusion from the doors of bliss:
Direct against which opened from beneath,
Just o'er the blissful seat of Paradise,
A passage down to th' earth, a passage wide,
Wider by far then that of after-times
530 Over Mount *Sion,* and, though that were large,
Over the *promis'd Land* to God so dear,
By which, to visit oft those happy tribes,
On high behests his angels to and fro
Pass'd frequent, and his eye with choice regard,
535 From *Paneas,* the fount of *Jordan's* flood,
To *Beersaba,* where the *Holy Land*
Borders on *Ægypt* and th' *Arabian* shore;
So wide the opening seem'd, where bounds were set
To darkness, such as bound the ocean wave.
540 *Satan* from hence now, on the lower stair,
That scal'd by steps of gold to heaven gate,
Looks down with wonder at the sudden view
Of all this world at once. As when a scout,
Through dark and desert wayes with peril gone
545 All night, at last by break of cheerful dawn
Obtains the brow of some high-climbing hill,
Which to his eye discovers unaware
The goodly prospect of some foreign land
First seen, or some renown'd metropolis
550 With glist'ring spires and pinnacles adorn'd,
Which now the rising sun gilds with his beams.
Such wonder seiz'd, though after heaven seen,
The spirit maligne, but much more envy seiz'd
At sight of all this world beheld so fair.
555 Round he surveys and well might where he stood
So high above the circling canopy
Of night's extended shade, from eastern point
Of *Libra* to the fleecy star, that bears
Andromeda far off *Atlantic* seas
560 Beyond th' *horizon*: then from pole to pole
He views in breadth, and without longer pause
Down right into the world's first region throws
His flight precipitant, and wind's with ease,
Through the pure marble air his oblique way,
565 Amongst innumerable stars, that shone
Stars distant, but nigh hand seem'd other world's:
Or other worlds they seem'd, or happy isles,
Like those *Hesperian* gardens fam'd of old,
Fortunate fields, and groves and flowery vales,

570	Thrice happy isles! But who dwelt happy there
	He stay'd not to inquire. Above them all
	The golden sun, in splendor likest heaven,
	Allur'd his eye; thither his course he bends
	Through the calm firmament, (but up or down)
575	By centre, or eccentric, hard to tell;
	Or longitude,) where the great luminary
	Aloof the vulgar constellations thick,
	That from his lordly eye keep distance due,
	Dispenses light from far; they as they move
580	Their stary dance in numbers that compute
	Days, months, and years, tow'rds his all-cheering lamp
	Turn swift their various motions, or are turn'd
	By his magnetic beam, that gently warms
	The universe, and to each inward part,
585	With gentle penetration, though unseen,
	Shoots invisible virtue even to the deep;
	So wondrously was set his station bright.
	There lands the fiend, a spot like which perhaps
	Astronomer in the sun's lucent orb,
590	Through his glaz'd optic tube yet never saw.
	The place he found beyond expression bright,
	Compar'd with aught on earth, medal or stone:
	Not all parts alike, but all alike inform'd
	With radiant light, as glowing iron with fire;
595	If metal, part seem'd gold, part silver clear;
	If stone, carbuncle most or chrysolite,
	Ruby or topaz, to the twelve that shone
	In *Aaron's* Breast-plate, and a stone besides
	Imagin'd rather oft then elsewhere seen,
600	That stone, or like to that which here below
	Philosophers in vain so long have sought,
	In vain, though by their powerful art they binde
	Volatil *Hermes,* and call up unbound
	In various shapes old *Proteus* from the sea,
605	Draind through a Limbec to his native forme.
	What wonder then if fields and region here
	Breathe forth *elixir* pure, and rivers run
	Potable gold, when with one virtuous touch
	Th' arch-chemic sun so far from us remote,
610	Produces with terrestrial humor mixed
	Here in the dark so many precious things
	Of colour glorious, and effect so rare?
	Here matter new to gaze the Devil met
	Undazzled: far and wide his eye commands,
615	For sight no obstacle found here, nor shade,
	But all sunshine, as when his beams at noon
	Culminate from th' *æquator*, as they now
	Shot upward still direct, whence no way round
	Shadow from body opaque can fall; and th'air,
620	No where so clear, sharpened his visual ray
	To objects distant far, whereby he soon
	Saw within ken a glorious angel stand,
	The same whom *John* saw also in the sun:
	His back was turn'd, but not his brightness hid:
625	Of beaming sunny rays, a golden tiar
	Circled his head, nor less his locks behind
	Illustrious on his shoulders, fledge with wings,
	Lay waving round; on some great charge employ'd
	He seem'd, or fixed in cogitation deep.
630	Glad was the spirit impure as now in hope
	To find who might direct his wand'ring flight
	To Paradise the happy seat of man,
	His journey's end and our beginning woe.
	But first he casts to change his proper shape,
635	Which else might work him danger or delay:
	And now a stripling cherub he appears,
	Not of the prime, yet such as in his face

	Youth smil'd celestial, and to every limb
	Sutable grace diffus'd, so well he feign'd:
640	Under a coronet his flowing hair
	In curls on either cheek played; wings he wore
	Of many a colour'd plume, sprinkled with gold
	His habit fit for speed succinct, and held
	Before his decent steps a silver wand.
645	He drew not nigh unheard; the angel bright,
	Ere he drew nigh, his radiant visage turn'd,
	Admonished by his ear; and strait was known
	Th' archangel *Uriel,* one of the seven
	Who in God's presence, nearest to his throne,
650	Stand ready at command, and are his eyes
	That run through all the heavens, or down to th' earth
	Bear his swift errands over moist and dry,
	O'er sea and land; him *Satan* thus accostes:
	Uriel, for thou of those seven spirits that stand
655	In sight of God's high throne, gloriously bright,
	The first art wont his great authentic will
	Interpreter through highest heaven to bring,
	Where all his sons thy embassy attend;
	And here art likeliest by supreme decree
660	Like honor to obtain, and as his eye
	To visit oft this new creation round;
	Unspeakable desire to see, and know
	All these his wondrous works, but chiefly man,
	His chief delight and favour; him, for whom
665	All these his works so wondrous he ordain'd,
	Hath brought me from the Choirs of cherubim
	Alone thus wand'ring. Brightest seraph, tell
	In which of all these shining orbes hath man
	His fixed seat, or fixed seat hath none,
670	But all these shining orbes his choice to dwell;
	That I may find him, and with secret gaze,
	Or open admiration him behold,
	On whom the great Creator hath bestow'd
	Worlds, and on whom hath all these graces powr'd;
675	That both in him and all things, as is meet,
	The universal Maker we may praise;
	Who justly hath driven out his rebel foes
	To deepest hell; and to repair that loss,
	Created this new happy race of men
680	To serve him better: wise are all his ways.
	So spake the false dissembler unperceiv'd;
	For neither man nor angel can discern
	Hypocrisy, the only evil that walks
	Invisible, except to God alone,
685	By his permissive will, through heaven and earth:
	And oft though wisdom wake, suspicion sleeps
	At wisdom's gate, and to simplicity
	Resigns her charge, while goodness thinks no ill
	Where no ill seems; Which now for once beguil'd
690	*Uriel,* though regent of the sun, and held
	The sharpest sighted spirit of all in heaven;
	Who to the fraudulent impostor foul,
	In his uprightness answer thus return'd.
	Faire Angel, thy desire which tends to know
695	The works of God, thereby to glorify
	The great Work-Master, leads to no excess
	That reaches blame, but rather merits praise
	The more it seems excess, that led thee hither
	From thy empyreal mansion thus alone,
700	To witness with thine eyes what some perhaps,
	Contented with report, hear only in heaven:
	For wonderful indeed are all his works,
	Pleasant to know, and worthiest to be all
	Had in remembrance always with delight:
705	But what created mind can comprehend

Their number, or the wisdom infinite
That brought them forth, but hid their causes deep.
I saw when at his word the formless mass,
This worlds material mould, came to a heap:
710 *Confusion* heard his voice, and wild uproar
Stood rul'd, stood vast infinitude confin'd;
Till at his second bidding darkness fled,
Light shone, and order from disorder sprung.
Swift to their several quarters hasted then
715 The cumbrous elements, earth, flood, air, fire,
And this ethereal quintessence of heaven
Flew upward, spirited with various forms,
That roll'd orbicular, and turn'd to stars
Numberless, as thou seest, and how they move;
720 Each had his place appointed, each his course;
The rest in circuit walls this universe.
Look downward on that Globe, whose hither side
With light from hence, though but reflected, shines;
That place is Earth the seat of man; that light
725 His day, which else as th' other Hemisphere,
Night would invade; but there the neighbouring moon
(So call that opposite fair star) her aid
Timely interposes, and her monthly round,
Still ending, still renewing, through mid heaven,
730 With borrow'd light her countenance triform
Hence fills and empties to enlighten th' earth,
And in her pale dominion checks the night.
That spot to which I point is *Paradise*,
Adams abode, those lofty shades his bower:
735 Thy way thou canst not miss, me mine requires.

Thus said, he turn'd, and *Satan* bowing low,
As to superior Spirits is wont in heaven,
Where honour due and reverence none neglects,
Took leave, and tow'rd the coast of earth beneath,
740 Down from th' ecliptic, sped with hop'd success,
Throws his steep flight in many an airy wheel,
Nor staid, till on *Niphates'* top he lights.

The End of Book Third.

Satan. The name's literal senses are "enemy" or "adversary."

Godhead. In book 9, Satan comes to Eve when she is separated from Adam and tempts her into eating from the forbidden tree of knowledge. Part of his ruse involves promising her eventual Godhead (9.708).

Uriel. Literally the "fire" or "light" of God, Uriel is one of the four archangels of the Hebrew tradition. The others were Michael, Gabriel, and Raphael, and each was assigned one quarter of the world in each of the cardinal directions. The name does not originate in the Bible (Uriel never appears in the Bible), but in the Apocrypha.

Mt. Niphates. A mountain in the Taurus range, in Armenia. Milton refers to it as being near Assyria in 4.126. According to Jordanes' *The Origins and Deeds of the Gods*, Niphates is a mountain range in Asia: "The range has different names among various peoples. The Indian calls it Imaus and in another part Paropamisus. The Parthian calls it first Choatras and afterward Niphates; the Syrian and Armenian call it Taurus; the Scythian names it Caucasus and Rhipaeus, and at its end calls it Taurus. Many other tribes have given names to the range."

holy light. Dante writes a similar invocation to light in *Paradiso* 13. 55 of the *Divine Comedy*.

unblam'd. Milton's narrator expresses some anxiety about getting this address to God as Light just right, anxious not to omit some glory by speaking another, or to misspeak himself at all in addressing one so high, so glorious.

God is light. As in John 1:5.

effluence. Pouring or streaming forth.

increate. Not Created.

Or hear'st thou rather. "Or wouldst thou rather be addressed as…"

Ethereal. Born of or tempered by Heavenly fire, or merely of Heaven.

Before the Heavens. See Genesis 1:3, which states that light was the first created thing.

invest. Envelop.

void and formless. See the description of the "world" before creation in Genesis 1:2.

Stygian. Referring to the river Styx, one of the rivers of Hell, found at the entrance to Hades. Also used in general reference to the underworld of classical mythology. Milton's narrator says that he has left the Hell of books 1 and 2, and now ascends to descrption of heaven, as if he were, as Dante imagines making such a journey himself in *Purgatorio* 1. 1-9.

utter and through middle darkness. A reference to Hell and Chaos. See note for Chaos.

Chaos. Milton borrows the concept of chaos, or unformed matter, from Hesiod and Platonic philosophy (especially the *Timaeus* 53a-b).

the heavenly Muse. Urania, the muse associated with astronomy. Also implies the Holy Spirit. See the earlier invocation to the muse in 1.6.

Orphean. Relating to the legendary orator and poet Orpheus, who travelled to Hades to plead for the release of his young wife, Eurydice.

Sovran. Sovereign.

eyes, that rowle in vain. Milton had been totally blind since 1652. The poet and the narrator are thus almost fully identified.

drop serene. A reference to gutta serena, the medical term for the variety of cataracts which blinded Milton; it in fact refers to any blindness which has no appearance-altering features. These cataracts gave little or no physical clouding or other sign of blindness, but left Milton virtually sightless.

Mt. Sion. A sacred mountain, purported to be the site of Moses's "lore and teaching" from God. Milton apparently prefers its image to that of the usual mountain home of the Muses, Mount Parnassus. See 1.386 and 1.442 and Deuteronomy 4:48.

Thamyris. Homer mentions this blind Thracian in the *Iliad* 2.594.

Maeonides. An archaic form of the name Homer, the blind poet and author of the *Iliad* and the *Odyssey*. The name stems from his apparent homeland of Maeonia.

Tiresias. A sage and prophet who appears in Sophocles' *Oedipus the King* as well as in *Antigone*. A Theban seer, he prophesied the fall of Oedipus, and spoke of his blindness as the facilitator of his state of illumination.

Phineus. A blind Thracian king who enjoyed the gift of prophecy.

numbers. A reference to poetic units and rhythm, namely verses, or when appropriate, used in reference to musical measures.

the wakeful Bird. The nightingale.

darkling. Intended as an adjective, meaning "in the dark".

the Book of knowledg fair. That is, creation as a book of knowledge.

Empyrean. Of or pertaining to the highest Heaven or celestial areas.

stoop. To swoop down, as with a bird of prey.

World. Here the poem refers not to the Earth alone, but rather the sphere of the created universe, beyond which is Chaos or void.

assay. To try.

glozing. Flattering, cajoling, or perverting.

the sole Command. God's command that Adam and Eve leave the tree of knowledge untouched.

Sufficient to have stood, though free to fall. This phrase is the kernel of Milton's sense of free will. The reformation debate about free will and predestination was framed by Erasmus, *On Free Will* (1524), and Luther, *The Bondage of the Will* (1525).

Reason also is choice. See *Areopagitica*.

Predestination. Milton's conception of predestination can be usefully compared to Augustine's in

Anti-Pelagian Writings in the *Nicene and Post-Nicene Fathers*, Series 1, Volume 5.

The first sort. Satan and his angel followers.

Man falls deceiv'd. See Milton's version of Adam's fall in 9. 998.

Spirits elect. The "good" angels are spirits elect. Milton intends this to mean those who have not rebelled with Satan. They are referred to in Timothy 5:21.

Substantially express'd. The Son is the substantial expression of the Father's invisible (5.157) glory. Compare this father-son relation to Adam and Eve's as described in 4.481–491. See also William Blake's 1808 image of the relation of Father to Son.

Adversarie. Literal sense of the name Satan.

Abolish thy Creation. See Genesis 6:6-7 and *PL* 2. 370.

My word, my wisdom, and effectual might. The Son is here defined as the sole agent of God, the outward expression in word, wisdom, and might of an otherwise invisible (see line 375 and 5. 157), ineffable God.

pray, repent, and bring obedience due. See the culmination of this in 10.1081-1096. Compare to Calvin's sense of human beings as totally incapable of right action (*Institutes* 3.22.1-3). Perhaps Milton has the father repeat the point to emphasize this departure from the strict Calvinism typical of his republican associates from the 1640s and 50s.

heavenly Quire stood mute. Compare to the grand consult of devils in book 2.418-20.

man shall find grace. See William Blake's 1808 watercolor illustration of these lines.

unprevented. Here the word retains its Latin root, and should be read as "un-anticipated."

death. The child of the incestuous relationship between Satan and his daughter Sin in 2.746.

maugre. In spite of.

complacence. Pleasure or source of pleasure.

right Hand. Christ sits at the right hand of God. A sign of utmost respect, and simultaneously one of slight inferiority. Milton held the unorthodox view that the Son was not coeternal with the Father, but was begotten by the Father at a particular moment before creation.

Made flesh. Echoes John 1: 14: "The Word was made flesh."

Virgin seed. Referring to the Virgin Mary and the Son's incarnation as a man.

room. In the place of Adam.

Adams Son. Milton's bid to reconcile two of Jesus's common titles: Son of Man and Son of God.

without thee none. Milton, like most of his contemporaries, believed that belief in Jesus Christ was the only salvation from eternal damnation. On this score, at least, he was absolutely intolerant.

imputed. Ascribed by vicarious substitution. This has been read to mean both Christ's taking on man's sin, and man's taking on Christ's virtue to enable salvation.

new life. These lines, 290–94, virtually paraphrase Paul's doctrine in Romans 5: 14-21.

Equal to God. The phrase here modifies "bliss," implying that the Son in heaven enjoys bliss equal to that enjoyed by God, but not necessarily general equality of the Son to God. Though, Milton might have invited a misreading here from more orthodox readers.

merit. Milton presents the Son as Son of God more by virtue of his deeds than by virtue of his begetting. Satan plays a parody of such merit in 2.5.

thy Manhood also. That is, by virtue of dying for men as a mortal, the Son's "manhood," his incarnate self, will be advanced to a heavenly throne every bit as much as his godhood already is. The term "manhood" appears gender specific, as if salvation were principally a manly experience, and only by extension intended for women.

under thee as Head Supreme. All orders of angels and creatures are now to be placed under the Son as "universal king."

from all Winds. From every direction.

cited. Called forth.

Doom. Judgement, with the eschatalogical implications of Judgement Day.

Immortal Amarant. Amaranth, a purple flower which according to legend, could not, as its name implied, ever wither.

Elisian. Elysian refers to Elysium, the classical Greek place reserved for the virtuous departed. The *term* can be extended to any heavenly or divinely joyous place of similar stature to Heaven.

conspicuous. Clearly visible, unlike God who is invisible (5. 157) or barely visible. See also the note above.

effulgence. Splendid radiance.

opacous. Opaque.

first convex. The outer edge of the created universe, bordering on Chaos.

inferior Orbs. The spheres described by our solar system, sun, planets, moons.

Imaus. A mountain in the Himalayan range.

roving Tartar. Genghis Khan.

yeanling. Newborn.

Hydaspes. The Jhelum river in the Punjab. The Ganges is a mjor river of northern India.

Sericana. China, and the Gobi desert, over which people often traveled in sail-powered wagons.

store. A multitude.

Aereal. Of the air, airy.

Not in the neighbouring Moon. Ariosto, in *Orlando Furioso* 34. LXX-LXXIII (1532), imagined such a Limbo of Vanities located on the moon; Milton ridicules this as a "dream."

argent. Silver.

Translated Saints. Enoch (Genesis 5:24) and Elijah (2 Kings 2: 1-11) were both transported to heaven alive.

ill-joynd Sons and Daughters. Genesis 6: 4 tells the story of how a race of giants was born to women who coupled with the "sons of God."

Sennaar. The plain of Shinar from Genesis 10: 10.

Empedocles. Sicilian pre-Socratic philosopher from the fifth century, BCE. In his *Ars Poetica* 464-67, Horace tells the story of how Empedocles threw himself into the volcanic Mt. Aetna to prove himself divine; the volcano spewed out his apparently mortal remains.

Cleombrotus. A youth said to have drowned himself in an ecstatic fervor after reading the Plato's *Phaedo* (Lactantius, *Divine Institutes* 3.18).

White, Black and Grey. The White Friars are the Carmelites, the Black are the Dominicans, and the Grey are the Franciscans. Milton's contempt for these Roman Catholic orders prompts him to place them in this Limbo of Vanities.

Golgotha. The site of the crucifixion. See Matthew 27:33.

weeds. Clothing.

whose ballance weighs. Libra, symbolized by the balance, was located in one of the 55 crystalline spheres of Ptolemaic cosmology. In Ptolemaic cosmology, this balance was said to measure the trepidation, or irregular motion, in the sphere. Traditional cosmologists, committed to a Ptolemaic model, spoke much about "trepidation" as a way of accounting for otherwise unaccounted for celestial motions. For graphic and animated details of Ptolemaic cosmology, see "The Universe of Aristotle and Ptolemy."

that first mov'd. The primum mobile, or prime mover sphere from which the movement of all the other spheres derived. For graphic and animated details of Ptolemaic cosmology, see The Universe of Aristotle and Ptolemy.

Beads. Rosaries, or prayers recited with beads as mempory aids.

Indulgences. Indulgences were special dispensations that could be purchased from Roman Catholic church officials.

Bulls. Certain Papal decrees are called Bulls.

Paradise of Fools. An area devoid of boundaries intended to be the abode of transgressors. *Jacob*. According to Genesis 28, Jacob cheats his older brother Esau by deceiving his father Isaac into blessing him in Esau's stead. Jacob then had a dream of angels ascending a ladder, hence the term "Jacob's Ladder."

Padan-Aram. Home of Jacob's uncle Laban, who provides him sanctuary from the rage of Esau.

mysteriously was meant. That is the steps on the ladder have been interpreted allegorically to signify a graduated set of states of being between earth and heaven.

Who after came from Earth. Enoch (Genesis 5: 21-24) and Elijah (2 Kings 2: 11) are two who were said to have sailed from earth to heaven.

Rapt. Carried away or transported.

Paneas. Also known as the city of Dan, it lies at the source of the Jordan and forms the northern border of Canaan.

Beersaba. Also known as Beersheba, it forms the southern border of Canaan.

Looks down with wonder. Standing at the foot of the stairway to heaven, Satan finds the prospect below him more wonderful.

obtains. Reaches.

the fleecie Starr. The Andromeda nebula; Andromeda and Aries.

other Worlds. That is, from a distance they looked like stars ("shon/ Stars distant"), but closer ("nigh hand") they appeared to be planets ("other worlds").

Hesperian Gardens. As in *A Mask* this refers to the Hesperides, a legendary orchard at the edge of the world where golden fruit grew, as told in Ovid's *Metamorphoses* The isles have been associated with both the Canary Islands and British Isles.

hard to tell. Hard to tell because it depends upon whether one believes a Copernican or a Ptolemaic account of the universe. Milton remains uncommitted on this score. See excellent graphic explanations of the Copernican and Ptolemaic cosmologies.

Longitude. Implying lateral movement. Here, Satan's lateral and vertical movements are both made confusing by the lack of reference to anything else.

the great Luminarie. The sun.

Magnetic beam. By the time Milton is writing book 3 of *Paradise Lost,* Newton had not yet published his theory of universal gravitation, though he had published early versions of his three laws of motion by 1666. Whether Milton knew of Newton's researches and ideas is a matter of some speculation.

Astronomer. Galileo discovered the presence of spots on the sun using his telescope in 1609. Also referred to as the "Tuscan Artist" in 1.288.

Carbuncle. Any red gemstone, with implications of Aaron's Breastplate.

choice. Careful or deliberate.

Chrysolite. Any green gemstone.

the Twelve that shon. Aaron, high priest of Israel and Moses's brother, wore a ceremonial breastplate in which twelve gemstones were set, each one representing a tribe of Israel. See Exodus 28: 17-24.

That stone. Often referred to as "the Philosopher's Stone," long sought after as an alchemical agent capable of turning base metals into gold.

Hermes. Mercury, an element crucial to many alchemical processes. Hermes is also a Greek deity, Mercury being his Roman equivalent, son of Zeus and Maia, and God of Science.

Limbec. Alembic, an apparatus used for distilling. See "Limbeck" in Samuel Norton.

Potable. Suitable for drinking. Drinkable gold is "a preparation of nitro-muriate of gold deoxydized by some volatile oil, formerly esteemed as a cordial medicine; drinkable gold."

Arch-chimic. The first alchemist. In this case the sun and its rays create gemstones in the ground. Timeline of famous alchemists.

Humor. Moisture.

Culminate. Reaching its greatest altitude, its meridian. Here the pre-lapsarian sun rises directly over the equator, creating no shadows and providing Satan with a clear view.

kenn. Range of sight.

The same whom John saw. See Revelation 19:17.

tiar. Tiara; crown.

Cherube. Satan displays his shapeshifting abilities by changing into a Cherub to fool Uriel. Cherubim and seraphim are two orders or ranks of angels. Images of Cherubim stood by the sanctuary in the temple at Jerusalem.

permissive. According to this logic, the difference between what God permits and what he actively wills absolves him from liability for evil and sin.

tends. Intends; wants.

Light. Genesis 1:2 names Light as the first creation.

her countenance triform. "Countenance Triform" is a reference to the three phases of the moon: crescent, full, and waning crescent. They are associated with the goddesses named Luna (Lucina), Diana, and Hecate.

th' Ecliptic. The path of the sun, assuming a Ptolemaic, geocentric cosmos.

Paradise Lost:

Book IV

John Milton

The Argument

Satan *now in prospect of* Eden, *and nigh the place where he must now attempt the bold enterprise which he undertook alone against God and Man, falls into many doubts with himself, and many passions, fear, envy, and despair; but at length confirms himself in evil, journeys on to Paradise, whose outward prospect and situation is described, overleaps the bounds, sits in the shape of a cormorant on the tree of life, as highest in the garden to look about him. The Garden describ'd;* Satans *first sight of* Adam *and* Eve; *his wonder at their excellent form and happy state, but with resolution to work their fall; overhears their discourse, thence gathers that the tree of knowledge was forbidden them to eat of, under penalty of death; and thereon intends to found his temptation, by seducing them to transgress: then leaves them a while, to know further of their state by some other means. Meanwhile* Uriel *descending on a Sun-beam warns* Gabriel, *who had in charge the gate of Paradise, that some evil spirit had escaped the deep, and past at noon by his sphere in the shape of a good angel, down to Paradise, discovered after by his furious gestures in the mount.* Gabriel *promises to find him ere morning. Night coming on,* Adam *and* Eve *discourse of going to their rest: their bower described; their evening worship.* Gabriel, *drawing forth his bands of night-watch to walk the round of Paradise, appoints two strong angels to* Adam's *bower, least the evil spirit should be there doing some harm to* Adam *or* Eve *sleeping; there they find him at the ear of* Eve, *tempting her in a dream, and bring him, though unwilling, to* Gabriel; *by whom questioned, he scornfully answers, prepares resistance, but hindered by a sign from heaven, flies out of Paradise.*

    O for that warning voice, which he who saw
Th' *Apocalypse,* heard cry in heaven aloud,
Then when the Dragon, put to second rout,
Came furious down to be reveng'd on men
5 *Wo to th'nhabitants on Earth,* That now,
While time was, our first parents had bin warn'd
The coming of their secret foe, and scap'd
Haply so scap'd his mortal snare: for now
Satan, now first inflam'd with rage, came down,
10 The tempter ere th' accuser of mankind,
To wreck on innocent frail man his loss
Of that first battle, and his flight to hell.
Yet not rejoicing in his speed, though bold,
Far off and fearless, nor with cause to boast,
15 Begins his dire attempt; which nigh the birth
Now rolling, boils in his tumultuous breast,
And like a devilish engine back recoils
Upon himself: horror and doubt distract
His troubled thoughts, and from the bottom stir
20 The Hell within him; for within him hell

John Milton, "Book 4," from *Paradise Lost*. Copyright in the Public Domain.

He brings, and round about him, nor from hell
One step no more then from himself, can fly
By change of place: now conscience wakes despair
That slumber'd, wakes the bitter memory
25 Of what he was, what is, and what must be
Worse; of worse deeds worse sufferings must ensue.
Sometimes towards *Eden,* which now in his view
Lay pleasant, his griev'd look he fixes sad;
Sometimes tow'rds heaven and the full-blazing sun,
30 Which now sat high in his meridian Tower:
Then much revolving, thus in sighs began.

O thou that with surpassing glory crown'd,
Look'st from thy sole dominion like the god
Of this new world; at whose sight all the stars
35 Hide their diminished heads; to thee I call,
But with no friendly voice, and add thy name
O Sun, to tell thee how I hate thy beams,
That bring to my remembrance from what state
I fell; how glorious once above thy sphere;
40 Till pride and worse ambition threw me down,
Warring in heaven against heavens matchless King.
Ah, wherefore, He deserv'd no such return
From me, whom he created what I was
In that bright eminence, and with his good
45 Upbraided none; nor was his service hard.
What could be less then to afford him praise,
The easiest recompence, and pay him thanks,
How due; yet all his good prov'd ill in me,
And wrought but malice; lifted up so high
50 I dein'd subjection, and thought one step higher
Would set me highest, and in a moment quit
The debt immense of endless gratitude,
So burdensome still paying, still to owe;
Forgetful what from him I still receiv'd,
55 And understood not that a grateful mind
By owing owes not, but still pays, at once
Indebted and dischargd; what burden then?
O had his powerful destiny ordaind
Me some inferior angel, I had stood
60 Then happy; no unbounded hope had rais'd
Ambition. Yet why not? Some other power
As great might have aspir'd, and me though mean,
Drawn to his part; but other powers as great
Fell not, but stand unshaken, from within
65 Or from without, to all temptations arm'd.
Hadst thou the same free will and power to stand?
Thou hadst: whom hast thou then or what to accuse,
But heavens free love dealt equally to all?
Be then his love accursed, since love or hate,
70 To me alike, it deals eternal woe.
Nay curs'd be thou; since against his thy will
Chose freely what it now so justly rues.
Me miserable, Which way shall I fly
Infinite wrath, and infinite despair?
75 Which way I fly is hell; my self am hell;
And in the lowest deep a lower deep
Still threat'ning to devour me, opens wide,
To which the hell I suffer seems a heaven.
O then at last relent: is there no place
80 Left for repentance, none for pardon left?
None left but by submission; and that word
Disdain forbids me, and my dread of shame
Among the spirits beneath, whom I seduc'd
With other promises and other vaunts
85 Than to submit, boasting I could subdue
Th' Omnipotent. Ay me, they little know
How dearly I abide that boast so vain,

Under what torments inwardly I groan:
While they adore me on the throne of hell,
90 With diadem and sceptre high advanc'd
The lower still I fall, only supreme
In misery; such joy ambition finds.
But say I could repent and could obtain
By act of grace my former state; how soon
95 Would height recall high thoughts, how soon unsay
What feign'd submission swore: ease would recant
Vows made in pain, as violent and void.
For never can true reconcilement grow,
Where wounds of deadly hate have peirc'd so deep:
100 Which would but lead me to a worse relapse
And heavier fall: so should I purchase dear
Short intermission bought with double smart.
This knows my punisher; therefore as far
From granting he, as I from begging peace:
105 All hope excluded thus, behold instead
Of us outcast, exil'd, his new delight,
Mankind created, and for him this world.
So farewell, hope, and with hope farewell, fear,
Farewell, remorse: all good to me is lost;
110 Evil be thou my good; by thee at least
Divided empire with heavens king I hold,
By thee, and more then half perhaps will reign;
As man ere long, and this new world shall know.

Thus while he spake, each passion dimm'd his face,
115 Thrice chang'd with pale, ire, envie and despair:
Which marr'd his borrow'd visage, and betrayed
Him counterfet, if any eye beheld:
For heavenly minds from such distempers foul
Are ever clear. Whereof he soon aware,
120 Each perturbation smooth'd with outward calme,
Artificer of fraud; and was the first
That practis'd falsehood under saintly show,
Deep malice to conceal, couched with revenge;
Yet not enough had practis'd to deceive
125 *Uriel* once warn'd; whose eye pursued him down
The way he went, and on th' *Assyrian* mount
Saw him disfigur'd, more then could befall
Spirit of happy sort: his gestures fierce
He mark'd and mad demeanour, then alone,
130 As he suppos'd, all unobserv'd, unseen.
So on he fares: and to the border comes
Of *Eden*, where delicious Paradise,
Now nearer, crowns with her inclosure green,
As with a rural mound, the champaign head
135 Of a steep wilderness; whose hairy sides
With thicket overgrown, grotesque and wild,
Access denied: and over head up grew
Insuperable height of loftiest shade,
Cedar, and pine, and fir, and branching palm
140 A silvan scene, and as the ranks ascend
Shade above shade, a woody theatre
Of stateliest view. Yet higher then their tops
The verdurous wall of Paradise up-sprung:
Which to our general sire gave prospect large
145 Into his neather empire neighb'ring round.
And higher then that wall a circling row
Of goodliest trees, loaden with fairest fruit,
Blossoms and fruits at once of golden hue
Appeared, with gay enamel'd colours mixed:
150 On which the sun more glad impress'd his beams,
Then in fair evening cloud, or humid bow,
When god hath showr'd the earth; so lovely seem'd
That landscape: and of pure now purer air
Meets his approach, and to the heart inspires
155 Vernal delight and joy, able to drive
All sadness but despair: now gentle gales,
Fanning their odoriferous wings, dispense

  Native perfumes, and whisper whence they stole
  Those balmy spoils. As when to them who saile
160 Beyond the *Cape of Hope*, and now are past
  Mozambic, off at sea north-east winds blow
  Sabean odours from the spicy shore
  Of *Araby* the blessed, with such delay
  Well pleas'd they slack their course, and many a league
165 Chear'd with the grateful smell old ocean smiles:
  So entertain'd those odorous sweets the fiend
  Who came their bane: though with them better pleased
  Then *Asmodeus* with the fishy fume
  That drove him, though enamour'd, from the spouse
170 Of *Tobits* son, and with a vengeance sent
  From *Media* post to *Ægypt*, there fast bound.

  Now to th' ascent of that steep savage hill
  Satan had journeyed on, pensive and slow;
  But further way found none, so thick intwin'd,
175 As one continued brake, the undergrowth
  Of shrubs and tangling bushes had perplexed
  All path of Man or Beast that past that way:
  One gate there only was, and that look'd east
  On th' other side; which when th' arch-felon saw
180 Due entrance he disdain'd, and in contempt,
  At one slight bound high overleaped all bound
  Of hill or highest wall, and sheer within
  Lights on his feet. As when a prowling wolf,
  Whom hunger drives to seek new haunt for prey,
185 Watching where shepherds pen their flocks at eve
  In hurdled cotes amid the field secure,
  Leaps o'er the fence with ease into the fold:
  Or as a thief bent to unhoard the cash
  Of some rich burgher, whose substantial doors,
190 Cross-barr'd and bolted fast, fear no assault,
  In at the window climbs, or o'er the tiles;
  So clomb this first grand thief into God's fold;
  So since into his church lewd hirelings climbe;
  Thence up he flew and on the tree of life,
195 (The middle tree and highest there that grew,)
  Sat like a cormorant; yet not true life
  Thereby regain'd, but sat devising death
  To them who lived; nor on the virtue thought
  Of that life-giving plant, but only us'd
200 For prospect, what well us'd had bin the pledge
  Of immortality. So little knows
  Any, but God alone, to value right
  The good before him, but perverts best things
  To worst abuse, or to their meanest use.
205 Beneath him, with new wonder, now he views,
  To all delight of human sense expos'd
  In narrow room, nature's whole wealth, yea more,
  A heaven on earth; for blissful paradise
  Of God the garden was, by him in the east
210 Of *Eden* planted; *Eden* stretchd her line
  From *Auran* eastward to the royal towers
  Of Great *Seleucia*, built by *Grecian* kings,
  Or where the sons of *Eden* long before
  Dwelt in *Telassar*. In this pleasant soil
215 His far more pleasant garden God ordain'd;
  Out of the fertile ground he caused to grow
  All trees of noblest kind, for sight, smell, taste;
  And all amid them stood the tree of life,
  High eminent, blooming ambrosial fruit

220 Of vegetable gold: and next to life,
Our death, the tree of knowledge, grew fast by;
Knowledge of good bought dear by knowing ill.
Southward through *Eden* went a river large,
Nor chang'd his course, but through the shaggy hill
225 Pass'd underneath ingulfed, for God had thrown
That mountain as his garden mould, high rais'd
Upon the rapid current, which through veins
Of porous earth with kindly thirst up drawn,
Rose a fresh fountain, and with many a rill
230 Watered the garden; thence united fell
Down the steep glade, and met the neather flood,
Which from his darksome passage now appears,
And now divided into four main streams,
Runs divers, wand'ring many a famous realm
235 And country, whereof here needs no account:
But rather to tell how, if art could tell,
How from that Sapphire fount the crisped brooks,
Rolling on orient pearl and sands of gold,
With mazy error under pendant shades
240 Ran nectar, visiting each plant, and fed
Flowers worthy of Paradise which not nice art
In beds and curious knots, but nature boon
Powered forth profuse on hill and dale and plain,
Both where the morning sun first warmly smote
245 The open field, and where the unpierced shade
Imbround the noontide bowers: thus was this place,
A happy rural seat of various view:
Groves whose rich trees wept odorous gums and balm,
Others whose fruit burnished with golden rind
250 Hung amiable, *Hesperian* fables true,
If true, here only, and of delicious taste.
Betwixt them lawns, or level downs, and flocks
Grazing the tender herb, were interpos'd,
Or palmie hillock, or the flowery lap
255 Of some irriguous valley spread her store;
Flowers of all hue, and without thorn the rose.
Another side, umbrageous grots and caves
Of cool recess, o'er which the mantling vine
Lays forth her purple grape, and gently creeps
260 Luxuriant: meanwhile murmuring waters fall
Down the slope hills, dispersed, or in a lake,
That to the fringed bank with myrtle crown'd
Her chrystal mirror holds, unite their streams.
The birds their quire apply: airs, vernal aires,
265 Breathing the smell of field and grove, attune
The trembling leaves, while universal *Pan*,
Knit with the *graces* and the *hours* in dance,
Led on th' eternal spring. Not that fair field
Of *Enna*, where *Proserpin* gathering flowers
270 Herself a fairer flower by gloomy *dis*

Was gatherd: which cost *Ceres* all that pain
To seek her through the world; nor that sweet grove
Of *Daphne* by *Orontes*, and th' inspir'd
Castalian spring, might with this Paradise
275 Of *Eden* strive; nor that *Nyseian* isle
Girt with the river *Triton*, where old *Cham*,
Whom gentiles *Ammon* call, and *Lybian Jove*,

Hid *Amalthea,* and her florid son
Young *Bacchus,* from his stepdame *Rhea's* eye;
280 Nor where *Abassin* kings their issue guard,
Mount *Amara,* though this by some suppos'd
True Paradise, under the *Ethiop* line
By *Nilus* head, enclos'd with shining rock,
A whole day's journey high, but wide remote
285 From this *Assyrian* garden, where the fiend
Saw undelighted all delight, all kind
Of living creatures new to sight and strange.
Two of far nobler shape erect and tall,
Godlike erect, with native honour clad
290 In naked majesty seem'd lords of all,
And worthy seem'd; for in their looks divine
The image of their glorious maker shone,
Truth, wisdom, sanctitude severe and pure,
Severe but in true filial freedom plac'd;
295 Whence true authority in men; though both
Not equal, as their sex not equal seem'd;
For contemplation he and valour form'd,
For softness she and sweet attractive grace,
He for God only, she for God in him:
300 His fair large front and eye sublime declar'd
Absolute rule; and hyacinthine locks
Round from his parted forelock manly hung
Clust'ring, but not beneath his shoulders broad:
She as a veil down to the slender waist
305 Her unadorned golden tresses wore
Dishevell'd, but in wanton ringlets wav'd
As the vine curls her tendrils, which impli'd
Subjection, but requir'd with gentle sway,
And by her yielded, by him best receiv'd,
310 Yielded with coy submission, modest pride,
And sweet reluctant amorous delay.
Nor those mysterious parts were then conceal'd,
Then was not guiltie shame, dishonest shame
Of natures works, honor dishonorable:
315 Sin-bred, how have ye troubled all mankind
With shows instead, mere shows of seeming pure,
And banished from man's life his happiest life,
Simplicity and spotless innocence.
So passed they naked on, nor shunn'd the sight
320 Of god or angel, for they thought no ill:
So hand in hand they pass'd, the lovliest pair
That ever since in love's embraces met,
Adam the goodliest man of men since borne
His sons: the fairest of her daughters, *Eve.*
325 Under a tuft of shade, that on a green
Stood whisp'ring soft, by a fresh fountain side,
They sat them down: and after no more toil
Of their sweet gard'ning labour then suffic'd
To recommend coole *Zephyr,* and made ease
330 More easy, wholesome thirst and appetite
More grateful, to their supper fruits they fell,
Nectarine fruits which the compliant boughs
Yielded them, sidelong as they sat recline
On the soft downy bank damask'd with flowers:
335 The savory pulp they chew, and in the rind
Still as they thirsted scoop the brimming stream;
Nor gentle purpose, nor endearing smiles
Wanted, nor youthful dalliance as beseems
Fair couple, linked in happy nuptial league,
340 Alone as they. About them frisking play'd
All beasts of th' earth, since wild, and of all chase
In wood or wilderness, forest or den;
Sporting the lion ramp'd, and in his paw

Dandled the kid; bears, tigers, ounces, pards,
345 Gambol'd before them; the unwieldy elephant,
To make them mirth, us'd all his might, and wreath'd
His lithe proboscis; close the serpent sly
Insinuating, wove with Gordian twine
His breaded train, and of his fatal guile
350 Gave proof unheeded; others on the grass
Couched, and now fill'd with pasture, gazing sat,
Or bedward ruminating; for the sun
Declin'd was hasting now with prone carreer
To th' ocean isles, and in th' ascending scale
355 Of heaven the stars that usher evening rose:
When *Satan,* still in gaze, as first he stood,
Scarce thus at length fail'd speech recover'd sad:

O hell, What doe mine eyes with grief behold?
Into our room of bliss thus high advanced
360 Creatures of other mould; earth-born perhaps,
Not spirits, yet to heavenly spirits bright
Little inferior; whom my thoughts pursue
With wonder, and could love, so lively shines
In them divine resemblance, and such grace
365 The hand that form'd them on their shape hath pour'd.
Ah gentle pair, ye little think how nigh
Your change approaches, when all these delights
Will vanish, and deliver ye to woe;
More woe, the more your taste is now of joy:
370 Happy, but for so happy ill secur'd
Long to continue, and this high seat your heaven,
Ill-fenced for heaven to keep out such a foe
As now is enter'd; yet no purpos'd foe
To you whom I could pity thus forlorn,
375 Though I unpitied: league with you I seek,
And mutual amity so straight, so close,
That I with you must dwell, or you with me
Henceforth; my dwelling haply may not please
Like this fair Paradise, your sense, yet such
380 Accept your Maker's work; He gave it me,
Which I as freely give; hell shall unfold,
To entertain you two, her widest gates,
And send forth all her kings; there will be room,
Not like these narrow limits, to receive
385 Your numerous offspring; if no better place,
Thank him who puts me loath to this revenge
On you who wrong me not for him who wrong'd.
And should I at your harmless innocence
Melt, as I doe, yet public reason just,
390 Honour and empire with revenge enlarg'd,
By conq'ring this new world, compels me now
To do what else (though damn'd) I should abhore.

So spake the fiend, and with necessity,
(The dtyrants plea,) excus'd his devilish deeds.
395 Then from his lofty stand on that high tree,
Down he alights among the sportful herd
Of those four-footed kinds; himself now one,
Now other, as their shape serv'd best his end
Nearer to view his prey, and unespied
400 To mark what of their state he more might learn
By word or action marked: about them round
A lion now he stalks with fiery glare;
Then as a tiger, who by chance hath spied
In some purlieu two gentle fawns at play,
405 Strait couches close, then rising changes oft

His couchant watch, as one who chose his ground,
Whence rushing he might surest seize them both
Griped in each paw: when *Adam,* first of men,
To first of women *Eve* thus moving speech,
410 Turn'd him, all ear, to hear new utterance flow:

Sole partner and sole part of all these joys,
Dearer thyself then all: needs must the power
That made us, and for us this ample world
Be infinitly good, and of his good
415 As liberal, and free as infinite;
That rais'd us from the dust, and placed us here
In all this happiness, who at his hand
Have nothing merited, nor can perform
Aught whereof he hath need: he who requires
420 From us no other service then to keep
This one, this easy charge, of all the trees
In Paradise that bear delicious fruit
So various, not to taste that only tree
Of knowledge, planted by the tree of life,
425 So near grows death to life, whate'er death is;
Some dreadful thing no doubt; for well thou know'st
God hath pronounced it death to taste that tree,
The only sign of our obedience left,
Among so many signes of power and rule,
430 Conferred upon us; and dominion given
Over all other creatures that possess
Earth, air, and sea. Then let us not think hard
One easy prohibition, who enjoy
Free leave so large to all things else, and choice
435 Unlimited of manifold delights:
But let us ever praise him, and extol
His bounty, following our delightful task,
To prune these growing plants, and tend these flowers,
Which were it toilsome, yet with thee were sweet.

440 To whom thus *Eve* replied: O thou for whom,
And from whom, I was formd flesh; of thy flesh;
And without whom am to no end; my guide
And head, what thou hast said is just and right.
For we to him indeed all praises owe,
445 And daily thanks; I chiefly who enjoy
So far the happier lot, enjoying thee
Pre-eminent by so much odds: while thou
Like consort to thyself canst no where find.
That day I oft remember, when from sleep
450 I first awaked, and found myself repos'd
Under a shade of flowers, much wond'ring where
And what I was, whence thither brought, and how.
Not distant far from thence a murmuring sound
Of waters issued from a cave, and spread
455 Into a liquid plain, then stood unmov'd
Pure as th'expanse of heaven: I thither went,
With unexperienced thought, and laid me down
On the green bank, to look into the clear
Smooth lake, that to me seem'd another sky.
460 As I bent down to look, just opposite,
A shape within the watry gleam appear'd
Bending to look on me: I started back;
It started back: but pleas'd I soon returnd,
Pleas'd it return'd as soon with answering looks
465 Of sympathy and love: there I had fixt
Mine eyes till now, and pin'd with vain desire,

Had not a voice thus warn'd me, what thou seest,
What there thou seest, fair creature, is thyself;
With thee it came and goes: but follow me,
And I will bring thee where no shadow stays
Thy coming, and thy soft embraces; he
Whose image thou art: him thou shalt enjoy,
Inseparably thine, to him shalt bear
Multitudes like thy self, and thence be call'd
Mother of human race. What could I do,
But follow straight, invisibly thus led
Till I espied thee, fair indeed and tall,
Under a plata'n, yet, methought less fair,
Less winning soft, less amiably mild,
Then that smooth watr'y image: back I turn'd,
Thou following cryd'st aloud, Return, fair *Eve*,
Whom fliest thou? Whom thou fliest, of him thou art,
His flesh, his bone; to give thee being I lent
Out of my side to thee, nearest my heart,
Substantial life, to have thee by my side
Henceforth an individual solace dear:
Part of my soul I seek thee; and thee claim
My other half. With that thy gentle hand
Seiz'd mine; I yielded; and from that time see
How beauty is excell'd by manly grace,
And wisdom, which alone is truly fair.

So spake our general mother, and with eyes
Of conjugal attraction unreprov'd,
And meek surrender, half imbracing lean'd
On our first father: half her swelling breast
Naked met his under the flowing gold
Of her loose tresses hid: he in delight
Both of her Beauty and submissive charms,
Smil'd with superior love, as *Jupiter*
On *Juno* smiles, when he impregns the clouds
That shed *may* flowers; and press'd her matron lip
With kisses pure: aside the devil turn'd
For envy, yet with jealous leer malign
Eyed them askance; and to himself thus plain'd:

Sight hateful, sight tormenting. Thus these two
Imparadised in one another's arms,
(The happier *Eden*,) shall enjoy their fill
Of bliss on bliss: while I to hell am thrust,
Where neither joy nor love, but fierce desire,
Amongst our other torments not the least,
Still unfulfill'd with pain of longing pines.
Yet let me not forget what I have gain'd
From their own mouths; all is not theirs it seems:
One fatal tree there stands of knowledge call'd,
Forbidden them to taste. Knowledge forbidden?
Suspicious, reasonless. Why should their lord
Envy them that? Can it be sin to know?
Can it be death? And do they only stand
By ignorance? Is that their happy state,
The proof of their obedience and their faith?
O fair foundation laid whereon to build
Their ruin! Hence I will excite their minds
With more desire to know, and to reject
Envious commands, invented with design
To keep them low whom knowledge might exalt
Equal with gods: aspiring to be such,
They taste and die: what likelier can ensue?
But first with narrow search I must walk round
This garden, and no corner leave unspied;
A chance but chance may lead where I may meet

  Some wand'ring spirit of heaven, by fountain side
  Or in thick shade retir'd, from him to Draw
  What further would be learned. Live while ye may,
  Yet happy pair; enjoy, till I return,
535 Short pleasures, for long woes are to succeed.

  So saying, his proud step he scornful turn'd,
  But with sly circumspection, and began
  Through wood, through waste, o'er hill, o'er dale, his roam,
  Meanwhile in utmost longitude, where heaven
540 With earth and ocean meets, the setting sun
  Slowly descended; and with right aspect
  Against the eastern gate of Paradise
  Levell'd his evening rays: it was a rock
  Of alablaster, pil'd up to the clouds,
545 Conspicuous far; winding with one ascent
  Accessible from earth, one entrance high:
  The rest was craggy cliff, that overhung
  Still as it rose, impossible to climb.
  Betwixt these rocky pillars *Gabriel* sat,
550 Chief of th' angelic guards, awaiting night:
  About him exercis'd heroic games
  Th' unarmed youth of heaven, but nigh at hand
  Celestial armory, shields, helms, and speares
  Hung high with diamond flaming, and with gold.
555 Thither came *Uriel*, gliding through the even
  On a sun-beam, swift as a shooting star
  In *autumn* thwarts the night, when vapors fir'd
  Impress the air, and shows the mariner
  From what point of his compass to beware
560 Impetuous winds: he thus began in haste:

  Gabriel, to thee thy course by lot hath given
  Charge and strict watch that to this happy place
  No evil thing approach or enter in.
  This day at height of noon came to my spheare
565 A spirit, zealous, as he seem'd, to know
  More of th' almighty's works, and chiefly man,
  Gods latest image: I describ'd his way,
  Bent all on speed, and markt his airy gait;
  But in the mount that lies from *Eden* north,
570 Where he first lighted, soon discern'd his looks
  Alien from heaven, with passions foul obscur'd:
  Mine eye pursued him still, but under shade
  Lost sight of him. One of the banished crew,
  I fear, hath ventur'd from the deep, to raise
575 New troubles; him thy care must be to find.

  To whom the winged warrior thus return'd:
  Uriel, no wonder if thy perfet sight,
  Amid the suns bright circle where thou sitst,
  See far and wide: in at this gate none pass
580 The vigilance here plac'd, but such as come
  Well known from heaven; and since meridian hour
  No creature thence: if spirit of other sort,
  So minded, have o'erleap'd these earthy bounds
  On purpose, hard thou know'st it to exclude
585 Spiritual substance with corporeal bar.
  But if within the circuit of these walks,
  In whatsoever shape he lurk, of whom
  Thou tellst, by morrow dawning I shall know.

  So promis'd he: and *Uriel* to his charge
590 Return'd on that bright beam, whose point now raised
  Bore him slope downward to the sun now fallen
  Beneath th' *Azores*; whither the prime orb,
  Incredible how swift, had thither roll'd

Diurnal, or this less volubil Earth
595 By shorter flight to th' East, had left him there
Arraying with reflected purple and gold
The clouds that on his western throne attend.

Now came still evening on, and twilight gray
Had in her sober livery all things clad:
600 Silence accompanied; for beast, and bird,
They to their grassy couch, these to their nests
Were slunk, all but the wakeful nightingale;
She all night long her amorous descant sung;
Silence was pleas'd: now glow'd the firmament
605 With living sapphires: *Hesperus* that led
The starry Host, rode brightest, till the moon
Rising in clouded majesty, at length,
Apparent queen, unveil'd her peerless light,
And o'er the dark her silver mantle threw.

610 When *Adam* thus to *Eve*: fair consort, th' hour
Of night, and all things now retir'd to rest,
Mind us of like repose; since god hath set
Labour and rest, as day and night, to men
Successive, and the timely dew of sleep,
615 Now falling with soft slumbrous weight inclines
Our eyelids; other creatures all day long
Rove idle unemploy'd, and less need rest:
Man hath his daily work of body, or mind,
Appointed, which declares his dignity,
620 And the regard of heaven on all his ways;
While other animals unactive range,
And of their doings God takes no account.
To-morrow ere fresh Morning streak the east
With first approach of light, we must be risen,
625 And at our pleasant labour, to reform
Yon flowery arbours, yonder allies green,
Our walk at noon, with branches overgrown:
That mock our scant manuring, and require
More hands then ours to lop their wanton growth:
630 Those blossoms also, and those dropping gums,
That lie bestrown unsightly and unsmooth,
Ask riddance, if we mean to tread with ease:
Meanwhile, as nature wills, night bids us rest.

To whom thus *Eve*, with perfect beauty adornd.
635 My author and disposer, what thou bid'st
Unargu'd I obey; so god ordains:
God is thy law, thou mine; to know no more
Is woman's happiest knowledge and her praise.
With thee conversing I forget all time;
640 All seasons and their change, all please alike:
Sweet is the breath of morn, her rising sweet,
With charm of earliest birds; pleasant the sun,
When first on this delightful land he spreads
His orient beams, on herb, tree, fruit, and flower,
645 Glist'ring with dew; fragrant the fertile earth
After soft showers; and sweet the coming on
Of grateful evening mild, then silent night,
With this her solemn bird, and this fair moon,
And these the gems of heaven, her starrye train:
650 But neither breath of morn when she ascends
With charm of earliest birds: nor rising sun
On this delightful land, nor herb, fruit, flower,

Glistring with dew: nor fragrance after showers:
Nor grateful evening mild, nor silent night
655 With this her solemn Bird, nor walk by moon,
Or glittering starlight, without thee is sweet.
But wherfore all night long shine these? For whom
This glorious sight, when sleep hath shut all eyes?

To whom our general Ancestor repli'd.
660 Daughter of god and man, accomplished *Eve*,
Those have their course to finish, round the earth
By morrow evening, and from land to land
In order, though to nations yet unborn,
Minist'ring light prepar'd, they set and rise;
665 Least total darkness should by night regain
Her old possession, and extinguish life
In nature and all things, which these soft fires
Not only enlighten, but with kindly heat
Of various influence foment and warm,
670 Temper or nourish, or in part shed down
Their stellar virtue on all kinds that grow
On earth, made hereby apter to receive
Perfection from the suns more potent Ray.
These then, though unbeheld in deep of night,
675 Shine not in vain; nor think, though men were none,
That heaven would want spectators, god want praise,
Millions of spiritual creatures walk the earth
Unseen, both when we wake and when we sleep:
All these with ceaseless praise his works behold
680 Both day and night. How often, from the steep
Of echoing hill or thicket have we heard
Celestial voices, to the midnight air,
Sole, or responsive each to others note,
Singing their great creator? Oft in bands
685 While they keep watch, or nightly rounding walk,
With heavenly touch of instrumental sounds,
In full harmonic number joind, their songs
Divide the night, and lift our thoughts to heaven.

Thus talking, hand in hand alone they pass'd
690 On to their blissful bower: it was a place
Chosen by the sovereign planter, when he fram'd
All things to mans delightful use: the roof
Of thickest covert was inwoven shade,
Laurel and myrtle, and what higher grew,
695 Of firm and fragrant leaf: on either side
Acanthus, and each odorous bushy shrub
Fenc'd up the verdant wall: each beauteous flower,
Iris all hues, roses, and jessamine,
Rear'd high their flourish'd heads between, and wrought
700 Mosaic: underfoot the violet,
Crocus, and hyacinth with rich inlay
Broider'd the ground; more colour'd then with stone
Of costliest emblem: other creature here;
Beast, bird, insect, or worm durst enter none;
705 Such was their awe of man. In shady bower
More sacred, and sequester'd, though but feign'd,
Pan or *Silvanus* never slept; nor nymph,
Nor *Faunus*, haunted. Here, in close recess
With flowers, garlands, and sweet smelling herbs,
710 Espoused *Eve* deck'd first her nuptial bed:
And heavenly choirs the hymenean sung,
What day the genial angel to our sire
Brought her in naked beauty more adorn'd,

More lovely then *Pandora*: whom the gods
715 Endow'd with all their gifts, and o, too like
In sad event, when to th' unwiser son
Of *Japhet* brought by *Hermes*, she ensnar'd
Mankind with her fair looks, to be aveng'd
On him who had stole *Jove's* authentic fire.

720 Thus, at their shady lodge arriv'd, both stood,
Both turn'd, and under open sky ador'd
The god that made both sky, air, earth and heaven
Which they beheld; the moon's resplendent globe,
And starry pole, thou also mad'st the night,
725 Maker omnipotent, and thou the day,
Which we in our appointed work employ'd
Have finish'd happy in our mutual help,
And mutual love, the crown of all our bliss
Ordain'd by thee, and this delicious place,
730 For us too large: where thy abundance wants
Partakers, and uncropp'd falls to the ground.
But thou hast promis'd from us two a race
To fill the earth, who shall with us extoll
Thy goodness infinite, both when we wake,
735 And when we seek, as now, thy gift of sleep.

This said unanimous, and other Rites
Observing none, but adoration pure
Which God likes best, into their inmost bower
Handed they went; and eas'd the putting off
740 These troublesome disguises which we wear,
Straight side by side were laid, nor turnd I weene,
Adam from his fair spouse; nor *Eve* the rites
Mysterious of connubial love refus'd:
Whatever hypocrites austerely talk
745 Of purity and place and innocence:
Defaming as impure what god declares
Pure; and commands to some, leaves free to all.
Our maker bids increase; who bids abstain,
But our destroyer, foe to God and man?
750 Hail wedded love, mysterious law, true source
Of human offspring, sole propriety,
In Paradise; of all things common else.
By thee adulterous lust was driven from men
Among the bestial herds to range, by thee,
755 Founded in reason, loyal, just, and pure,
Relations dear, and all the charities
Of father, son, and brother first were known.
Far be it, that I should write thee sin or blame,
Or think thee unbefitting holiest place
760 Perpetual fountain of domestic sweets,
Whose bed is undefil'd and chaste pronounc'd,
Present, or past; as saints and patriarchs us'd.
Here love his golden shafts employes, here lights
His constant lamp, and waves his purple wings,
765 Reigns here and revels: not in the bought smile
Of harlots, loveless, joyless, unindeard,
Casual fruition; nor in court amours,
Mix'd dance, or wanton mask, or midnight ball,
Or serenade, which the starv'd lover sings
770 To his proud fair, best quitted with disdain.
These lulld by nightingales embracing slept;
And on their naked limbs the flowery roof
Shower'd roses, which the morn repair'd. Sleep on
Bless'd pair; and o yet happiest if ye seek
775 No happier state, and know to know no more.

Now had night measur'd with her shadowy cone
Half way up hill this vast sublunar vault:
And from their ivory port the cherubim

    Forth issuing at th' accustomd hour, stood arm'd
780 To their night watches in warlike parade,
    When *Gabriel* to his next in power thus spake:

    Uzziel, half these draw off, and coast the south
    With strictest watch: these other wheel the north;
    Our circuit meets full west. As flame they part,
785 Half wheeling to the shield, half to the spear.
    From these, two strong and subtle spirits he call'd
    That neer him stood, and gave them thus in charge.

    Ithuriel and *Zephon*, with wingd speed
    Search through this garden, leave un searcht no nook,
790 But chiefly where those two fair creatures lodge,
    Now laid perhaps asleep secure of harme.
    This eevning from the sun's decline arriv'd
    Who tells of some infernal spirit seen
    Hitherward bent (who could have thought?) Escap'd
795 The barrs of hell, on errand bad no doubt:
    Such where ye find, sieze fast, and hither bring.

    So saying, on he led his radiant files,
    Daz'ling the moon; these to the bower direct
    In search of whom they sought: him there they found
800 Squat like a toad, close at the eare of *Eve*;
    Assaying by his devilish art to reach
    The organs of her fancie, and with them forge
    Illusions as he list, phantasms and dreams,
    Or if, inspiring venom, he might taint
805 Th' animal spirits that from pure blood arise
    Like gentle breaths from rivers pure, thence raise
    At least distemperd, discontented thoughts,
    Vaine hopes, vaine aimes, inordinate desires
    Blown up with high conceits ingendring pride.
810 Him thus intent *ithuriel* with his spear.
    Touch'd lightly; for no falshood can endure
    Touch of celestial temper, but returns
    Of force to its own likeness: up he starts
    Discoverd and surpriz'd. As when a spark
815 Lights on a heap of nitrous powder, laid
    Fit for the tun some magazin to store
    Against a rumord warr, the smuttie graine
    With sudden blaze diffus'd, inflames the air:
    So started up in his own shape the fiend.
820 Back stept those two fair angels half amazed,
    So sudden to behold the griesly king;
    Yet thus, unmovd with fear, accost him soon:

    Which of those rebell spirits adjudg'd to hell,
    Com'st thou, escap'd thy prison? and transform'd,
825 Why sat'st thou like an enemy in wait
    Here watching at the head of these that sleep?

    Know ye not then said *Satan*, fill'd with scorn;
    Know ye not me? Ye knew me once no mate
    For you, there sitting where ye durst not soar:
830 Not to know me argues yourselves unknown,
    The lowest of your throng: or if ye know,
    Why ask ye, and superfluous begin
    Your message, like to end as much in vain?
    To whom thus *Zephon*, answering scorn with scorn:
835 Think not, revolted spirit, thy shape the same,

Or undiminish'd brightness, to be known
As when thou stoodst in heaven upright and pure;
That glory then, when thou no more wast good,
Departed from thee; and thou resemble'st now
840 Thy sin and place of doom obscure and foul.
But come, for thou, be sure, shalt give account
To him who sent us, whose charge is to keep
This place inviolable, and these from harm.

So spake the cherub, and his grave rebuke,
845 Severe in youthful beauty, added grace
Invincible: abash'd the devil stood,
And felt how awful goodness is, and saw
Virtue in her shape how lovly, saw, and pin'd
His loss; but chiefly to find here observ'd
850 His lustre visibly impair'd: yet seem'd
Undaunted. If I must contend, said he,
Best with the best, the sender not the sent,
Or all at once; more glory will be won,
Or less be lost. Thy fear, said *Zephon* bold,
855 Will save us trial what the least can doe
Single against thee wicked, and thence weak.

The fiend replie'd not, overcome with rage;
But like a proud steed reind, went haughty on,
Champing his iron curb: to strive or fly
860 He held it vain; awe from above had quell'd
His heart, not else dismay'd. Now drew they nigh
The western point, where those half-rounding guards
Just met, and closing stood in squadron join'd
Awaiting next command. To whom their chief,
865 *Gabriel* from the front thus call'd aloud.

O friends, I hear the tread of nimble feet
Hasting this way, and now by glimpse discern
Ithuriel and *Zephon* through the shade,
And with them comes a third of regal port,
870 But faded splendor wan; who by his gait
And fierce demeanour, seems the prince of hell,
Not likely to part hence without contest;
Stand firm, for in his look defiance lowers.

He scarce had ended, when those two approach'd,
875 And brief related whom they brought, where found,
How busied, in what form and posture couch'd.

To whom with stern regard thus *Gabriel* spake:
Why hast thou, *Satan*, broke the bounds prescrib'd
To thy transgressions, and disturb'd the charge
880 Of others, who approve not to transgress
By thy example, but have power and right
To question thy bold entrance on this place;
Employ'd it seems to violate sleep, and those
Whose dwelling god hath planted here in bliss?

885 To whom thus *Satan* with contemptuous brow:
Gabriel, thou hadst in heaven th' esteem of wise,
And such I held thee; but this question ask'd
Puts me in doubt. Lives there who loves his pain?
Who would not, finding way, break loose from hell,
890 Though thither doom'd? Thou wouldst thyself, no doubt,
And boldly venture to whatever place

Farthest from pain, where thou might'st hope to change
Torment with ease, and; soonest recompence
Dole with delight, which in this place i sought;
895 To thee no reason, who know'st only good,
But evil hast not tried, and wilt object
His will who bound us? Let him surer bar
His iron gates, if he intends our stay
In that dark durance: thus much what was ask'd.
900 The rest is true, they found me where they say;
But that implies not violence or harm.

Thus he in scorn. The warlike angel mov'd,
Disdainfully half-smiling thus replied:
O loss of one in heaven to judge of wise,
905 Since *Satan* fell, whom folly overthrew,
And now returns him from his prison scap'd,
Gravely in doubt whether to hold them wise
Or not, who ask what boldness brought him hither
Unlicens'd from his bounds in hell prescrib'd;
910 So wise he judges it to fly from pain
However, and to scape his punishment.
So judge thou still, presumptuous, till the wrath,
Which thou incurr'st by flying, meet thy flight
Sevenfold, and scourge that wisdom back to hell,
915 Which taught thee yet no better, that no pain
Can equal anger infinite provok'd.
But wherefore thou alone? Wherefore with thee
Came not all hell broke loose? Is pain to them
Less pain, less to be fled, or thou then they
920 Less hardy to endure? Courageous chief,
The first in flight from pain, hadst thou alleg'd
To thy deserted host this cause of flight,
Thou surely hadst not come sole fugitive.

To which the Fiend thus answer'd frowning stern:
925 Not that I less endure, or shrink from pain,
Insulting angel, well thou know'st I stood
Thy fiercest, when in battle to thy aid
The blasting vollied thunder made all speed,
And seconded thy else not dreaded spear:
930 But still thy words at random, as before,
Argue thy inexperience what behoves
From hard assays and ill successes past
A faithful leader, not to hazard all
Through wayes of danger by himself untri'ed,
935 I, therefore, I alone first undertook
To wing the desolate abyss, and spy
This new created world, whereof in hell
Fame is not silent, here in hope to find
Better abode, and my afflicted Powers
940 To settle here on Earth, or in mid air;
Though for possession put to try once more
What thou and thy gay legions dare against;
Whose easier business were to serve their lord
High up in heaven, with songs to hymn his throne,
945 And practis'd distances to cringe, not fight.

To whom the warrior angel, soon replied.
To say and strait unsay, pretending first
Wise to flie pain, professing next the spy,
Argues no leader, but a liar trac'd,
950 *Satan*, and couldst thou faithful add? O name,
O sacred name of faithfulness profan'd!
Faithful to whom? To thy rebellious crew?
Army of fiends, fit body to fit head;
Was this your discipline and faith engag'd,
955 Your military obedience, to dissolve
Allegeance to th' acknowledg'd power supreme?

And thou sly hypocrite, who now wouldst seem
Patron of liberty, who more then thou
Once fawn'd, and cring'd, and servielly ador'd
960 Heavens awful monarch? Wherefore but in hope
To dispossess him, and thy self to reign?
But mark what I arreed thee now-Avaunt.
Fly thither whence thou fledst: if from this hour
Within these hallowd limits thou appear,
965 Back to th' infernal pit I drag thee chain'd,
And seal thee so, as henceforth not to scorn
The facile gates of hell too slightly barr'd.

So threatn'd he, but Satan to no threats
Gave heed, but waxing more in rage replied.

970 Then when I am thy captive talk of chains,
Proud limitarie cherub, but ere then
Far heavier load thy self expect to feel
From my prevailing arm, though heaven's King
Ride on thy wings, and thou with thy compeers,
975 Us'd to the yolke, draw'st His triumphant wheels
In progress through the rode of heaven star-pav'd.

While thus he spake, th' angelic squadron bright
Turnd fiery red, sharp'ning in mooned hornes
Their phalanx, and began to hem him round
980 With ported spears, as thick as when a field
Of *Ceres* ripe for harvest waving bends
Her bearded Grove of ears, which way the wind
Swayes them; the careful plowman doubting stands
Lest on the threshing-floor his hopeful sheaves
985 Prove chaff. On th'other side *Satan* alarm'd
Collecting all his might dilated stood,
Like *Teneriff* or *Atlas* unremov'd:
His stature reacht the sky, and on his crest
Sat horror plum'd; nor wanted in his graspe
990 What seem'd both spear and shield: Now dreadful deeds
Might have ensu'd, nor only Paradise
In this commotion, but the starry cope
Of heaven perhaps, or all the elements,
At least had gone to rack, disturb'd, and torne
995 With violence of this conflict, had not soon
Th' eternal to prevent such horrid fray,
Hung forth in heaven his golden scales, yet seen
Betwixt *Astrea* and the *Scorpion* sign,
Wherein all things created first he weigh'd,
1000 The pendulous round earth with balanc'd air
In counterpoise, now ponders all events,
Battles and realms: in these he put two weights,
The sequel each of parting and of fight;
The latter quick up flew, and kick't the beam;
1005 Which *Gabriel* spying, thus bespake the fiend:

Satan, I know thy strength, and thou know'st mine,
Neither our own but given; what folly then
To boast what arms can do, since thine no more
Then heaven permits, nor mine, though doubld now
1010 To trample thee as mire: for proof look up,
And read thy lot in yon celestial sign,
Where thou art weigh'd, and shown how light, how weak,
If thou resist. The fiend look'd up and knew
His mounted scale aloft: nor more; but fled
1015 Murm'ring, and with him fled the shades of night.

The End of Book Fourth.

Cormorant. Voracious sea-bird symbolic of insatiable greed.

furious gestures. Satan's uncontrollable anger gives away his disguise to Uriel.

warning voice. Milton refers to John's parable of the defeat of Satan in Revelation 12: 3-12.

while time was. While there was time.

scap'd. Escaped.

Haply. Perhaps.

wreck. Avenge.

rowling. Satan's plan turns over or rolls in his mind.

devillish Engine. In this case, a cannon.

Hell within him. These lines echo Mephistopheles' famous speeches in Marlowe's *Doctor Faustus*:

Hell hath no limits, nor is circumscrib'd,
In one selfe place: but where we are is hell,
And where hell is there must we ever be.

Eden. Paradise; Eden is Hebrew for "pleasure."

Meridian Tow'r. Noon.

revolving. Meditating.

thou that with surpassing Glory crownd. Satan addresses the Sun; see line 37.

like the God. Satan, though he certainly knows better, entertains what later will be called a pagan conception of God: the sun as a god.

whom he created what I was. This is an example of Satan contradicting himself. Compare to 5.860 where he claims that angels are "self-begot." Satan seems, in these few lines of soliloquy, to be unusually candid, admitting his mistake to himself if to no one else.

sdeind. Disdained, scorned.

quit. Satisfy; repay.

still. In lines 53 and 54 "still" should be interpreted as "always." Note also the immediate contradiction to lines 46–47; how does this sudden shift of thought come about?

mean. Inferior.

dealt equally. This soliloquy, lines 32–68, repays close attention and analysis, especially an attempt to trace first the logic, then the psychology of each twist and turn, as suggested in line 115 below. For example, in line 67 Satan verges on concluding he has no one to blame but himself, but he finishes his sentence in line 68 by accusing, of all things, "heavens free Love."

Chose freely. Satan, for at least a brief moment, agrees with God's description of the rebellion in 3.102: "Freely they stood who stood, and fell who fell."

at last relent. Lines 79-80 appear to echo Claudius's attempts at repentance in *Hamlet* 3.3.40 and following. The phrase "place for repentance" also echoes the language of Hebrews 12: 17 concerning Esau's sale of his birthright, a story found in Genesis 25: 24-34. Satan, however, cannot repent, because repentance, according to Milton's God, is not possible without divine prompting; see *PL* 3.174-191.

vaunts. Boasts.

Mankind created. The notion is that human beings were created by God to take the place in the creation left void by the fallen angels. This idea surfaces also in 3.678-79 and below in line 359.

Artificer of fraud. Satan is the source of all lies. Refer to 3.681-690.

couch't. Hidden, suppressed.

Assyrian mount. Mount Niphates. See 3.742.

champain head. Open country.

grottesque. From Italian "grotto," thus meaning grotto-esque, not necessarily implying ugliness as we often understand the word today. Nevertheless, words like "wilderness," "wild," and "overgrown" may challenge received notions of what Paradise looked like.

Theatre. Milton's use of the words "Scene" and "Theatre" suggest Eden as a stage upon which the tragic drama of the Fall will take place.

vendurous. Composed of rich green vegetation.

general Sire. Adam.

nether Empire. That is, all the lower parts of the world outside of the garden of Eden. The idea of Adam as an emperor is derived from God's injunction in Genesis 1: 28 to "subdue" and "have dominion" over all creation.

enamell'd. Bright and shiny.

humid Bow. Rainbow.

That Landscape. Milton's descriptions of Eden may owe something to Hieronymus Bosch's depiction of a Garden of Earthly Delights.

of. From.

Cape of Hope. The Cape of Good Hope. This whole passage describing Eden's delights also suggests the effects those delights might have both on Satan (he is past Hope) and on mortals. It also evokes once again the exoticism of lands associated with the spice trade as in 2.640.

Sabean. Referring to Biblical Sheba, which is modern-day Yemen.

grateful. Pleasant.

Asmodeus. Milton invokes the story of Tobias from the apocryphal Book of Tobit. Tobias, traveling in Persia, married Sara whose seven former husbands were killed on their wedding night by her demon lover, Asmodeus. Raphael advised Tobias to burn the heart and liver of a fish to drive the demon away.

brake. Shrubbery.

one slight bound. The ease with which Satan enters Paradise, despite the appointed angelic guard, has often been the topic of critical comment. How are we supposed to understand this feature of Eden—walled, but not adequately walled? The following similes (wolf and burglar) complicate the question.

sheer. Wholly or completely.

first grand Thief. The extended similes raise lots of questions. Are we invited to think of God as a less than adequate shepherd and mankind as sheep? Or of God as overlooking windows or roof access and human being as his lifeless gold?

lewd Hirelings. Milton compares Satan's leap into Eden to the entrance of "lewd hirelings" (self-serving clergymen) into the Church. A similar image of self-serving clergy as wolves appears in *Lycidas* 113-131.

Cormorant. Voracious sea-bird symbolic of insatiable greed.

For prospect. Satan so radically misperceives and so misuses the Tree of Life that it serves him merely as a convenient perch while he plans to bring Death into the world.

Line. Boundary. Paradise was thought to lie between the Tigris and Euphrates rivers in what today is Iraq.

Auran. Harran, a village in the eastern part of ancient Israel where Abraham is believed to have lived, now in southeastern Turkey.

Seleucia. City founded by one of Alexander the Great's generals and located on the Tigris river in modern-day Iraq.

Telassar. Believed to be a City in Eden (Kings 19: 12; Isaiah 37: 12).

bought dear by knowing ill. On the intimate connection between knowing good and knowing evil, see *Areopagitica*.

a River large. Genesis 2: 10 mentions such a river in Eden, dividing into four streams. The fountain is Milton's imagination.

shaggie. Heavily forested.

crisped. Rippling.

error. Wandering.

nice Art. "Art" here has a negative connotation, implying artifice or deceit. "Nice" here connotes extravagant or flaunting. Milton implies that intricately planned man-made gardens are inferior to the profuse and less apparently organized abundance of nature in Eden.

Beds and curious Knots. Tudor formal gardens were often very intricate affairs, carefully planned and tended. The late 17th and 18th century began to prefer more natural looking landscapes and views.

boon. Graciously bestowed favour.

Imbround. Browned, darkened.

Hesperian Fables. Referring to the stories of Hesperian gardens, a legendary orchard at the edge of the world where golden fruit grew, as told in Ovid's *Metamorphoses*. The isles have been associated with both the Canary Islands and British Isles.

irriguous. Naturally irrigated.

umbrageous. Shady.

mantling. Covering, providing shade.

quire. Choir.

Universal Pan. A personification of Nature. In the Nativity Ode, Milton imagines Christ as the antitype to the shepherd's Pan (88–90).

the Graces and the Hours. The Graces, in Greek religion, were a group of goddesses of fertility. The name refers to the "pleasing" or "charming" appearance of a fertile field or garden. The number of Graces varied in different legends, but usually there were three: Aglaia (Brightness), Euphrosyne (Joyfulness), and Thalia (Bloom). They are said to be daughters of Zeus and Hera (or Eurynome, daughter of Oceanus) or of Helios and Aegle, a daughter of Zeus. According to Hesiod, the Horae were the children of Zeus, the king of the gods, and Themis, a Titaness, and their names (Eunomia, Dike, Eirene—that is, Good Order, Justice, Peace) indicate the extension of their functions from nature to the events of human life. At Athens they were apparently two in number: Thallo and Carpo, the goddesses of the flowers of spring and of the fruits of summer. Their yearly festival was the Horaea. In later mythology the Horae became the four seasons, daughters of the sun god, Helios, and the moon goddess, Selene, each represented with the conventional attributes. See Botticelli's *Primavera*.

Proserpin. Milton refers to the stories of Proserpina in Ovid's *Metamorphosis* and the Homeric *Hymn to Demeter*. Proserpina, daughter of Zeus and Ceres, is carried away by Dis (Pluto) while gathering flowers in Enna, Sicily. Ceres, the goddess of corn, prevented any crops from growing while she searched for her daughter. Finally, Dis agreed to return Proserpina to her mother for six months each year. Thus, the crops only grow for half a year. These might be called negative similes, since each comparison is evoked by "Not" or "nor."

Daphne. The gardens of Daphne on the river Orontes in Syria were known for their magnificent cypress and laurel trees, which were watered by a springs, dedicated to Apollo and named after the Castalian Spring on Mt. Parnassus. According to Ovid (*Metamorphoses* 1.450-68), upon Phoebus Apollo's attempt to rape her, Daphne tried to run away and then turned into a laurel tree. See Bernini's *Apollo e Dafne*

Nyseian Isle. An island where Ammon, the son of Saturn and king of Lybia, had his son Bacchus brought up to protect him from his stepmother Rhea. Ammon was identified with Jove and Noah's son Ham.

Abbasin. Abyssinian.

issue. Children

Amara. In Milton's time, Amara, a hill in modern day Ethiopia, was by some thought to be Paradise located on the equator (the "Ethiop Line").

erect. Milton repeats the word, "erect," as if standing erect were as much, or more, a matter of nobility and godlikeness as it is simply a matter of walking on two, rather than four legs.

image of their glorious Maker shon. In Milton's view, does God's image in man signify or constitute human superiority over the rest of creation? In *Tetrachordon*, Milton defines more precisely what he takes to be the "Image of God" (*Tetrachordon* Gen. 1.27). This opening description of Adam and Eve runs together the two accounts from Genesis: Genesis 1: 26-31 which describes the creation of mankind as both male and female at once; and Genesis 2, which describes the creation of Adam first, then Eve from Adam.

filial freedom. Apparently both Adam and Eve enjoy the same "filial freedom," that is, the freedom characteristic of children and heirs of the Father. Filius is Latin for son and filia for daughter, so the English word, "filial" may be read as including both genders and so referring to both Adam and Eve, as "men" in line 295 appears to include Eve as well as Adam, as in the word, "mankind." But note how the tenor of the passage shifts at precisely this point.

Not equal. This line and those that follow have occasioned a great deal of commentary in recent years. See especially Turner, *One Flesh*; McColley, *Milton's Eve*; and most helpful: Nyquist, "The Genesis of Gendered Subjectivity in the Divorce Tracts and in *Paradise Lost*." Milton appears to follow Pauline teaching on marriage (1 Timothy 2:11) fairly closely, at least *his* understanding of Pauline teaching. Milton was very likely aware of popular pamphlets that argued the equality (even sometimes superiority) of women.

seem'd. The use of "seemed" in this passage is worth close attention. Sometimes it implies a theory of the perfect coincidence of appearance and reality in prelapsarian Paradise; other times it may be taken to refer to the way things looked to Satan, who is the implied observer throughout this passage.

contemplation he. Many readers have noted that these two lines appear to describe Adam as a looker and a doer (contemplation and valour) and Eve as one looked at and acted upon (attractive and soft). Indeed Adam shows a strong interest in abstruse subjects when he talks with the archangel Raphael (book 8.15-40) and Eve prefers to participate in conversations that are not entirely abstract, but include touching and feeling as well (8.52-57).

shee for God in him. Adam was created in God's image, while Eve was subsequently created from Adam.

Front. Forehead, as if a large forehead indicated intelligence.

sublime. Oriented heavenward.

Hyacinthin Locks. The poem compares Adam to Hyacinthus, the boy beloved of Apollo in Orpheus's song from Ovid's *Metamorphoses* 10.163-219. Milton likens Adam to Apollo's "beloved" as an example of ideal male beauty. Milton often alludes to Orpheus (*Lycidas* 58–63, *A Mask* 84–88, "At a Solemn Music") as a classical example of the power of poetic song. Homer describes Odysseus's head and hair in a similar fashion at just those moments when Athena pays special attentions to him (*Odyssey* 6. 231: "she also made the hair grow thick on the top of his head, and flow down in curls like hyacinth blossoms"). The word "Clustring" also alludes to a similar description of the "fair clustering tresses" Venus bestows upon Aeneas in the *Aeneid* 1.590-91. See a yellow hyacinth in bloom. On hair length for men and women, see also 1 Corinthians 11:15.

veil. It seems odd that Eve needs a veil considering lines 312 and 313.

Disheveld. As with the vegetation in Paradise which apparently requires the attention of a gardener, so we are surprised to find Eve's hair described as dishevelled, or wanton.

coy. Shy or reserved.

modest pride. The physical portrayal of Adam and Eve is complex, like these oxymoronic expressions. Milton's description of Adam focuses on his head, suggesting Adam's most important characteristic is his intellect; Eve's "unadorned golden tresses" pull the focus away from her head to her entire body, implying her primary characteristic is her beauty and grace, though we shall later be instructed, as was Eve, just how far "manly grace and wisdom" exceed female beauty and how wisdom alone can be called "truly fair".

mysterious parts. That is, their genitals. Milton chooses the word "mysterious" to remind readers that "connubial rites" (line 743) are truly (though allegorically or typologically) about the relations between Christ and his church (Ephesians 5:31-32), "mysteriously meant," like the stairs that lead to heaven (3.516).

dishonest. Impure or unchaste.

meer shows. In his divorce tracts Milton complained incessantly about women whose false shows of modesty and shamefastness led the men who married them into the worst hell imaginable—marriage to an unfit partner. See *The Doctrine and Discipline of Divorce*.

Gardning labour. We might be surprised at first that Milton thinks there was labor in Paradise, but Milton, like many of us, loved to work and thought it a source of pleasure. Milton also specifies that prelapsarian work, in proper amounts, also enhanced other pleasures, like that of feeling a cool wind, taking rest, satisfying a thirst, or an appetite for food.

Zephyr. West wind.

recline. Reclining.

damaskt. Ornamented with variegated pattern or design.

gentle purpose. Conversation. Milton insisted in his *Doctrine and Discipline of Divorce* that "fit conversation" is the chief purpose for which marriage was instituted and woman created.

Wanted. Lacking.

youthful dalliance. See other instances of the word "dalliance". Is "dalliance" an alternative to "gentle purpose"?

Dandl'd the Kid. Isaiah 11:6-10 describes a future Paradise where all beasts will lie down and play together, even with children.

Ounces, Pards. Lynxes and leopards.

Proboscis. Trunk.

Gordian twine. As hard to untie as the Gordian knot, which Alexander the Great cut.

breaded. Braided.

ruminating. Chewing the cud.

Ocean Isles. The Azores in the mid North Atlantic.

our room. Satan refers to the "vacant room" of the fallen angels. The idea is that mankind and his world was created to "repair" the loss of the fallen angels.

Little inferior. Satan echoes the sense of Psalm 8: "Thou hast made him a little lower than the angels, and hast crowned him with glory and honour." See also *Hamlet* "What a piece of work is a man!"

gentle pair. See William Blake's 1808 watercolor illustration of these lines.

Long to continue. Adam and Eve enjoy happiness, but, says Satan, this happiness is not well enough protected to continue for long.

Ill fenc't. Again, Paradise is not well protected enough to prevent Satan from entering.

League. A compact for protection of common interests.

send forth all her Kings. The lines echo Isaiah 14: 9, but the tone with which Satan echoes the prophet is worth pondering.

wrong me. Satan refuses to accept responsibility for his act of revenge, instead blaming God by essentially using the childish argument "he made me do it."

public reason. Reason of state, a perversion of the Ciceronian principle (*Laws* 3.3.8) that the good of the people is the supreme law.

Tyrants plea. For Milton's theory of the origins of tyranny and the emptiness of this excuse, see 12.95.

himself now one,/ Now other. That is, Satan tries on the shapes of various animals as he approaches the bower without being detected.

Purlieu. A piece of land bordering a forest.

couchant. Lying down.

Turn'd him all ear. That is, Satan is now "all ears" for Adam's speech?

dust. Adam was made by God from the dust of the earth and Eve made from his rib according to Genesis 2. See also Genesis 3: 19: "for dust thou art, and unto dust shalt thou return."

dreadful thing. Adam has not yet witnessed death; though he understands it is a "dreadful thing," his knowledge of it is limited.

Dominion. This recalls Genesis 1: 26, in which God intends Adam to have dominion over "every creeping thing that creepeth upon the earth."

without whom am to no end. Milton was not alone in believing that the only purpose for which woman was created is to remedy a man's loneliness. See *The Doctrine and Discipline of Divorce*. The phrase "flesh of thy flesh" directly echoes Adam's words in Genesis 2: 23.

my Guide. Milton's Eve echoes the Pauline teaching about men and women, husbands and wives. See 1 Corinthians 11: 3; see also verses 8 and 9.

odds. The amount by which one thing exceeds or excels another.

Like consort to thyself canst nowhere find. Adam, we learn in book 8, specifically asked God to supply him with an equal partner, one like himself (8.381-397). Yet here Eve implies that Adam is so much her superior as to have no equal on earth and so no like consort. Is Eve mistaken?

what. Eve refers to herself as "what" and Adam as "who"; overall, there are slight but revealing differences between the first questions that come to Eve's mind and those that come to Adam's mind.

expanse of heaven. Eve is incorporating knowledge retrospectively; What is here expressed as a simile, she took for an identity when new waked to consciouness (line 459).

A Shape. Milton echoes here in Eve's actions the myth of Narcissus in Ovid's *Metamorphoses*.

What there thou seest fair Creature is thy self. This may be read as implying that Eve's self (apart from Adam as she presently is) is no deeper a thing than her appearance.

staies. Awaits.

Whose image thou art. That is, Adam. Eve, like Adam, carries the image of God, but for Eve this *image is derivative*; she is more immediately in Adam's image than in God's. See this point made explicit in *Tetrachordon*.

invisibly thus led. Eve does not recognize the voice as God, but it is one of the chief features of God's beauty to be invisible (5. 157). Milton may be suggesting a natural tendency in Eve to follow and obey.

espi'd thee. Eve, we remember is talking to Adam.

Platan. Plane tree.

watry image. "Watry" may pun here on the sense of watered down or less clear since Eve's image in the lake is merely a reflection of her image, which is in turn a reflection of Adam's inward "manly grace and wisdom," which is, in turn, the image of God in Adam.

individual. Inseparable.

truly fair. A distinction is formed here between "faire" as properly applied to Eve (481) and "truly fair" which applies only to "wisdom," a quality essentially invisible though capable of demonstration. Eve is fair, beautiful on the outside, but Adam's inward "wisdom" is "truly fair," that is, more like the image of God, partly, paradoxically, because it is an invisible, inner quality.

unreprov'd. Innocent.

Beauty and submissive Charms. Beauty alone, however attractive, does not delight Adam as much as beauty combined with submission.

Jupiter. King of gods and sky.

Juno. Jupiter's queen, and, allegorically, the air.

impregns. Impregnates.

Ey'd them askance. Milton reminds the reader that Satan has been watching Adam and Eve for nearly all of book 4, emphasizing Satan's voyeurism.

plaind. Complained, whined.

fierce desire. Desire here is implicitly distinguished from love.

can it be sin to know. Satan already prepares his temptation arguments. The sin, of course, is not knowledge or even desire for knowledge, but disobedience.

Envious commands. Satan ascribes his own feelings of envy to God, claiming that God denies Adam and Eve knowledge of good and evil because He envies them.

narrow. Precise, careful.

utmost Longitude. Farthest point in the west.

right aspect. Facing a given direction.

Alablaster. Alabaster (white stone).

Gabriel. Gabriel is one of the four archangels of the Hebrew tradition. The others were Michael, Uriel, and Raphael; each was assigned one quarter of the world in each of the cardinal directions. Gabriel also serves as a heavenly messenger; see Luke 1:19 and Daniel 8.

Heroic Games. Contrast the angels' games with the corrupt and warlike athletics of the demons in Hell in 2.528-538.

thwarts. Flies across.

vapors fir'd. Heat lightning.

Gods latest Image. The angels, and especially the Son, are the earlier versions of God's image.

describ'd. Noticed.

with passions foul obscur'd. See Milton's description of Satan's "furious gestures" in the Argument at the beginning of book 4.

Meridian hour. Noon.

Spiritual substance. Presumably this is why Satan cannot be kept out of Paradise since he is made of "Spiritual substance." But what besides the spirits of Hell is Gabriel's squad supposed to guard against?

slope downward. Since the sun is now below the horizon, Uriel slides down on a beam as he returns to his station in the sun.

Azores. See note for "Ocean Isles."

prime Orb. The sun. Milton does not commit himself to either a Ptolemaic or Copernican cosmology.

Diurnal. In a day.

less volubil. Less capable of easy rotation; the narrator's description here favors a Ptolemaic cosmology without totally excluding a Copernican explanation of sunsets. See note above.

Hesperus. The evening star.

Apparent. Manifest.

eye-lids. Possibly borrowed from Spenser's *The Faerie Queene* 1.1.36: "the sad humour loading their eye liddes."

daily work. God commands Adam and Eve to "dress" and "keep" Eden in Genesis 2: 15. The dignity of work, along with walking erect, speaking language and enjoying God's special attention are features that distinguish humans from beasts in Milton's world-view.

Allies. Alleys.

manuring. Tillage, cultivation; though Milton may also mean us to imagine that Adam and Eve fertilized their garden with manure.

More hands then ours. Milton reckons that for Paradise to be truly perfect, there must be work available for Adam's children, since work is one of life's great pleasures, and a distinctly human dignity.

Ask riddance. Must be removed.

conversing. See Milton's definition of the purpose of marriage and woman's creation in the *Doctrine and Discipline of Divorce—*" an apt and cheerful conversation."

seasons. Times of the day; seasonal changes began only after the Fall of man.

charm. Song.

Daughter of God and Man. Adam is probably to be understood literally here; God and Adam are Eve's parents.

foment. Nurture with heat.

spiritual Creatures. Adam suggests the presence of guardian angels on Earth at all times, who praise the beauty of God's creation while man is asleep and unable to do so.

harmonic number joind. The angelic singers seem like the Muses in Hesiod's *Theogony*, who sing the greatness of their father Zeus, the earth and heaven, in ceaseless concert as they mount the cloudy slope of Olympus in the darkness.

hand in hand alone. That is to say no other creatures follow them into their bower.

Gessamin. Jasmine.

flourisht. Blooming.

stone of costliest Emblem. Stone with inlaid work.

feign'd. Invented or imagined.

Faunus. Pan, Silvanus, and Faunus are all satyrs, beings with the form of a goat from the waist down, from Greek and Roman mythology.

Hymanaen. Marriage song.

genial Angel. Implies that there is a guardian angel protecting the bower of Adam and Eve.

Pandora. Pandora, according to pagan legend the first woman, was created by Jove's request to avenge Prometheus (foresight), who stole fire from heaven. She was endowed with gifts by the gods, given a box filled with evils, and sent to marry Epimetheus (hindsight), a brother of Prometheus. Although warned against it, Epimetheus opened the box and all life's evils flew out. Pandora and Eve are "like in sad event" in that they are both associated with tragic events.

Japhet. Noah's son Japhet, identified here with the legendary Titan Iapetus, father of Prometheus and Epimetheus.

Pole. Sky.

Thou. Adam and Eve addres God in their spontaneous (and spontaneously poetic) evening prayers of thanksgiving and praise.

wants. Lacks.

weene. Suppose.

handed. Joined hand in hand.

connubial Love. Milton probably shocked his earliest readers by suggesting that Adam and Eve had sexual relations before the fall, but we should also note how carefully he has kept anything like sexual desire out of this description: Adam, we are told, did not "turn" from his wife, and Eve did not "refuse" the "Rites mysterious" (referring to Ephesians 5: 31-32) The activity sounds like obedience to God's command (line 747) rather than sexual desire.

bids increase. "Be fruitful, and multiply, and replenish the earth" (Genesis 1:28).

mysterious Law. The poem alludes to Paul's interpretation of "one flesh" (Genesis 2:24) in Ephesians 5: 31-32. For other instances of the word, "mysterious,"

propriety. Property.

bed is undefil'd. The narrator quotes from Hebrews 13:4. The Greek underlying "undefiled" is amiantos, a word also used in Hebrews 7:26, James 1:27, and 1 Peter 1:4.

Love. Milton's description of "Love" is similar to Ovid's representation of Cupid.

shafts. Arrows.

fruition. Copulation.

starv'd. Of love; a sneering jab at the courtly love convention of (male) lovesickness in the face of a lady's proud refusal.

know to know no more. One of many warnings to abstain from desiring to know too much.

Cone. The earth's shadow forms a cone if the sun is below the horizon. Here, it is at 45 degrees, so it is nine o'clock, post meridian.

Port. Gate.

Uzziel. A cabbalistic angel; his name means "strength of a god." The only Uzziel in the Bible is a mortal being.

wheel. Circle.

Ithuriel and Zephon. Meaning "discovery of god" and "searcher," respectively. An angel named Ithuriel is not mentioned in the Bible and though the name Zephon appears in the Bible, he is not an angel.

close at the eare. The source of the dream Eve complains of having in 5. 32-93. See William Blake's 1808 watercolor illustration of these lines.

animal spirits. Robert Burton described the theory of spirits, "The natural are begotten in the liver, and thence dispersed through the veins…The vital spirits are made in the heart…The animal spirits formed the vital, brought up to the brain, and diffused by the nerves, to the subordinate members, give sense and motion to them all" (*Anatomy of Melancholy*).

conceits. Thoughts.

nitrous Powder. Gunpowder.

Fit for the Tun. Ready to be stored in a barrel.

Against. In anticipation of.

started up. Milton's simile emphasizes Satan's underlying carelessness and lack of reason. Satan explodes upward like a pile of gunpowder in storage merely for a "rumord Warr"; the conflagration is destructive yet unnecessary and aimless.

argues. Indicates. Satan attests that failure of angels to recognize him indicates their obscure position in Heaven as he is known by all "important" angels. He fails to understand that sin has so deformed his physical being that he is essentially unrecognizable.

obscure. Dark, but also unknown.

Cherube. Zephon is apparently a cherub by rank. Cherubim and seraphim are two orders or ranks of angels. Images of Cherubim stood by the sanctuary in the temple at Jerusalem.

port. Manner.

gate. Gait.

charge. Refers to Adam and Eve, whom Gabriel is in charge of protecting.

thou hadst in heaven th' esteem of wise. Gabriel is famous in Heaven for his wisdom. Satan is being childishly sarcastic, telling Gabriel that if he is so smart, he should know why Satan left Hell and came to Paradise.

Farthest from pain. Satan admits his own cowardice, saying he ran from Hell to escape its torments and avoid his punishment. This directly contradicts Satan's speech to the other fallen angels in 2.445-60 in which he claims he will only undertake the journey because the honor of leadership carries the responsibility of accepting hazardous challenges when they arise.

durance. Forced confinement.

mov'd. Irate.

O loss of one in heaven to judge of wise. Gabriel answers Satan's sarcasm with some of his own: Satan and his wise judgment are, he sarcastically remarks, a great loss to Heaven.

However. By any means.

Which thou incurr'st by flying. In his soliloquy early in book 4, Satan acknowledges that he expects to be punished even further for his escape from Hell; see lines 75–78.

surely. Gabriel's heavy sarcasm continues here; he sees through Satan's lie and takes the opportunity to insult him, mockingly calling Satan "courageous Chief" when his cowardice is quite evident.

afflicted Powers. Satan's beaten forces. See 1.186.

gay Legions. Satan attempts to mock Gabriel and the other angels by implying that the splendor of the Heavenly armies is merely for show.

cringe. Allowing space to bow.

trac't. Detected.

Patron of liberty. Satan may depict some of the disappointment Milton felt in another apparent patron of liberty, Oliver Cromwell. See the Britannica article from which the following assessment is quoted: "In the spring of 1657 heCromwell was tempted by an offer of the crown by a majority in Parliament on the ground that it fitted in better with existing institutions and the English common law. In the end he refused to become king because he knew that it would offend his old republican officers. Nevertheless, in the last year and a half of his life he ruled according to a form of government known as "the Petition and Advice." This in effect made him a constitutional monarch with a House of Lords whose members he was allowed to nominate as well as an elected House of Commons."

arreede. Advise.
avant. Depart.
facil. Easily yielding.
limitarie. Boundary-guarding.
progress. Procession.
mooned. Shaped like a crescent.
ported Spears. Held at guard or ready position.
Ceres. Goddess of grain.
careful. Apprehensive.
Least. Lest.
Teneriff or Atlas. Teneriff, a mountain in the Canary Islands, once thought to be the highest in the world. Atlas, a mountain in Morocco, once believed to support the sky.
wanted. Lacked.
Cope. Dome.
gon to rack. Been ruined.
Scales. Milton remembered the golden scales in which Zeus weighed and compared the destinies of the Greeks and Trojans (*Iliad* 8. 69-72,) and of Hector against Achilles (*Iliad* 22. 209), or the weighing of Aeneas' fate against that of Turnus (*Aeneid* 12. 725-727), but he gives the conception cosmic scope by identifying the scales with the constellation of Libra which stands between the Virgin and the Scorpion in the Zodiac.
ponders. Weighs.
sequel. Outcome.
Neither our own but giv'n. That is, all power, like all grace, flows from God alone according to Milton's theology.

Paradise Lost:

Book V

John Milton

The Argument

*M*orning approached, Eve *relates to* Adam *her troublesome dream; he likes it not, yet comforts her. They come forth to their day labours: Their Morning hymn at the door of their bower. God, to render man inexcusable sends* Raphael *to admonish him of his obedience; of his free estate; of his enemy near at hand, who he is, and why his enemy; and whatever else may avail* Adam *to know.* Raphael *comes down to Paradise: his appearance described, his coming discerned by* Adam *afar off sitting at the door of his bower; he goes out to meet him, brings him to his lodge, entertains him with the choicest fruits of Paradise got together by* Eve; *their discourse at table.* Raphael *performs his message, minds* Adam *of his state and of his enemy; relates, at Adam's request, who that enemy is, and how he came to be so, beginning from his first revolt in heaven, and the occasion thereof; how he drew his legions after him to*

John Milton, "Book 5," from *Paradise Lost*. Copyright in the Public Domain.

the parts of the north, and there incited them to rebel with him, persuading all but only Abdiel *a seraph, who in argument dissuades and opposes him, then forsakes him.*

  Now morn her rosie steps in th' eastern clime
  Advancing, sow'd the earth with orient pearl,
  When *Adam* wak'd, so custom'd, for his sleep
  Was airy light, from pure digestion bred,
5   And temperate vapours bland, which th' only sound
  Of leaves and fuming rills, *Aurora's* fan,
  Lightly dispers'd, and the shrill matin song
  Of birds on every bough: so much the more
  His wonder was to find unwaken'd *Eve*
10   With tresses discompos'd, and glowing cheek,
  As through unquiet rest: he, on his side
  Leaning half rais'd, with looks of cordial love,
  Hung over her enamour'd; and beheld
  Beauty, which whether waking or asleep,
15   Shot forth peculiar graces; then with voice
  Mild, as when *Zephyrus* on *Flora* breathes,
  Her hand soft touching, whisper'd thus: Awake
  My fairest, my espous'd, my latest found,
  Heavens last best gift, my ever new delight,
20   Awake, the morning shines and the fresh field
  Calls us; we lose the prime, to mark how spring
  Our tended plants, how blows the citron grove,
  What drops the myrrh, and what the balmy reed,
  How nature paints her colours, how the bee
25   Sits on the bloom extracting liquid sweet.

  Such whispering wak'd her, but with startl'd eye
  On *Adam*, whom embracing, thus she spake:

  O sole, in whom my thoughts find all repose,
  My glory, my perfection, glad I see
30   Thy face, and morn return'd; for I this night
  (Such night till this, I never pass'd,) have dream'd,
  If dream'd, not, as I oft am wont, of thee,
  Works of day past, or morrow's next design,
  But of offense and trouble, which my mind
35   Knew never till this irksome night: methought
  Close at mine ear one call'd me forth to walk
  With gentle voice; I thought it thine: it said,
  Why sleepst thou, *Eve*? Now is the pleasant time,
  The cool, the silent, save where silence yields
40   To the night-warbling bird, that now awake
  Tunes sweetest his love-labor'd song; now reigns
  Full orb'd the moon, and with more pleasing light
  Shadowy sets off the face of things; in vain,
  If none regard; heaven wakes with all his eyes,
45   Whom to behold but thee, nature's desire?
  In whose sight all things joy, with ravishment
  Attracted by thy beauty still to gaze.
  I rose as at thy call, but found thee not:
  To find thee I directed then my walk;

50   And on, methought, alone I pass'd through ways
  That broughte me on a sudden to the tree
  Of interdicted knowledge: fair it seem'd,
  Much fairer to my fancy then by day;
  And as I wond'ring lookt, beside it stood
55   One shap'd and wing'd like one of those from heaven

By us oft seen: his dewy locks distill'd
Ambrosia; on that tree he also gaz'd;
And O fair plant, said he, with fruit surcharg'd,
Deigns none to ease thy load and taste thy sweet?
60 Nor god, nor man? is knowledge so despis'd?
Or envy, or what reserve forbids to taste?
Forbid who will, none shall from me withhold
Longer thy offer'd good, why else set here?
This said he paus'd not, but with vent'rous arm
65 He pluck'd, he tasted; me damp horror chill'd
At such bold words vouch'd with a deed so bold:
But he thus overjoy'd; O fruit divine,
Sweet of thyself, but much more sweet thus cropt,
Forbidde'n here, it seems, as only fit
70 For god's, yet able to make gods of men:
And why not gods of men, since good, the more
Communicated, more abundant grows,
The author not impair'd, but honour'd more?
Here, happy creature, fair angelic *Eve*,
75 Partake thou also; happy though thou art,
Happier thou may'st be, worthier canst not be:
Taste this, and be henceforth among the gods,
Thy self a goddess, not to earth confin'd,
But sometimes in the air, as wee, sometimes
80 Ascend to heaven, by merit thine, and see

What life the gods live there, and such live thou.
So saying, he drew nigh, and to me held,
Even to my mouth of that same fruit held part
Which he had pluck'd; the pleasant savory smell
85 So quicken'd appetite, that I, methought,
Could not but taste. Forthwith up to the clouds
With him I flew, and underneath beheld
The earth outstretch'd immense, a prospect wide
And various: wond'ring at my flight and change
90 To this high exaltation; suddenly
My guide was gone, and I, methought, sunk down,
And fell asleep; but O how glad I wak'd
To find this but a dream. Thus *Eve* her night
Related, and thus *Adam* answer'd sad:

95 Best image of myself and dearer half,
The trouble of thy thoughts this night in sleep
Affects me equally; nor can I like
This uncouth dream, of evil sprung I fear;
Yet evil whence? In thee can harbour none,
100 Created pure. But know, that in the soul
Are many lesser faculties that serve
Reason as chief; among these fancy next
Her office holds; of all external things,
Which the five watchful senses represent,
105 She forms imaginations, airy shapes,
Which reason joining or disjoining, frames
All what we affirm or what deny, and call
Our knowledge or opinion; then retires
Into her private Cell when nature rests.
110 Oft in her absence mimic fancy wakes
To imitate her; but misjoining shapes,
Wild work produces oft, and most in dreams,
Ill matching words and deeds long past or late.
Some such resemblances methinks I find
115 Of our last evening's talk, in this thy dream,
But with addition strange: yet be not sad:
Evil into the mind of God or man
May come and go, so unapprov'd, and leave
No spot or blame behind: which gives me hope,

120 That what in sleep thou didst abhor to dream,
Waking thou never wilt consent to do.
Be not disheartend then, nor cloud those looks,
That wont to be more cheerful and serene,
Then when fair morning first smiles on the world;
125 And let us to our fresh imployments rise
Among the groves, the fountains, and the flowers
That open now their choicest bosom'd onely smells,
Reserv'd from night, and kept for thee in store.

So cheer'd he his fair spouse, and she was cheer'd,
130 But silently a gentle tear let fall
From either eye, and wip'd them with her hair;
Two other precious drops that ready stood,
Each in their crystal sluice, he ere they fell
Kiss'd as the gracious signs of sweet remorse
135 And pious awe, that fear'd to have offended.

So all was clear'd, and to the field they haste.
But first, from under shady arborous roof,
Soon as they forth were come to open sight
Of day-spring, and the sun, who scarce uprisen,
140 With wheels yet hov'ring o're the ocean brim,
Shot parallel to the earth his dewy ray,
Discov'ring in wide landscape all the east
Of paradise and *Edens* happy plains,
Lowly they bow'd adoring, and began
145 Their orisons, each morning duly paid
In various style; for neither various style
Nor holy rapture wanted they to praise

Their Maker, in fit strains pronounc'd or sung
Unmeditated, such prompt eloquence
150 Flow'd from their lips, in prose or numerous verse;
More tuneable then needed lute or harp
To add more sweetness; and they thus began;

These are thy glorious works, parent of good,
Almighty, thine this universal frame,
155 Thus wondrous fair; thyself how wondrous then;
Unspeakable, who sitts't above these heavens
To us invisible, or dimly seen
In these thy lowest works: yet these declare
Thy goodness beyond thought, and power divine;
160 Speak, ye who best can tell, ye sons of light,
Angels; for ye behold him, and with songs
And choral symphonies, day without night,
Circle his throne rejoicing, ye in heaven:
On earth join all ye creatures to extoll
165 Him first, him last, him midst, and without end.
Fairest of stars, last in the train of night,
If better thou belong not to the dawn,
Sure pledge of day, that crown'st the smiling morn
With thy bright circlet, praise him in thy sphere,
170 While day arises, that sweet hour of prime.
Thou sun, of this great World both eye and soul,
Acknowledge him thy greater, sound his praise
In thy eternal course, both when thou climb'st,
And when high noon hast gaind, and when thou fall'st.
175 Moon that now meet'st the orient sun, now flist
With the fixt stars, fixt in their orb that flies;

And ye five other wand'ring fires, that move
In mystic dance not without song, resound
His praise, who out of darkness call'd up light,
180 Air, and ye elements, the eldest birth
Of nature's womb, that in quaternion run
Perpetual circle, multiform; and mix,
And nourish all things; let your ceaseless change
Vary to our great Maker still new praise.
185 Ye mists and exhalations that now rise
From hill or steaming lake, dusky or grey,
Till the sun paint your fleecy skirts with gold,
In honour to the world's great Author rise;
Whether to deck with clouds th' uncolour'd sky,
190 Or wet the thirsty earth with falling showers,
Rising or falling still advance his praise.
His praise ye winds, that from four quarters blow,
Breathe soft or loud; and wave your tops ye pines,
With every plant; in sign of worship wave.
195 Fountains, and ye, that warble, as ye flow,
Melodious murmurs, warbling tune his praise.
Join voices all ye living souls; ye birds,
That singing up to heaven-gate ascend,
Bear on your wings and in your notes his praise.
200 Ye that in waters glide, and ye that walk
The earth, and stately tread, or lowly creep;
Witness if I be silent, morn or even,
To hill, or valley, fountain or fresh shade,
Made vocal by my song, and taught his praise.
205 Hail universal Lord, be bounteous still
To give us only good; and if the night
Have gather'd aught of evil, or conceal'd,
Disperse it, as now light dispels the dark.

So pray'd they, innocent; and to their thoughts
210 Firm peace recover'd soon, and wonted calm.
On to their morning's rural work they haste,
Among sweet dews and flowers; where any row
Of fruit-trees overwoody reach'd too far
Their pamper'd boughs, and needed hands to check
215 Fruitless embraces: or they led the vine
To wed her elm; she spous'd about him twines
Her marriageable arms, and with her brings
Her dower th' adopted clusters, to adorn
His barren leaves. Them thus employed beheld
220 With pity heaven's high King, and to him call'd
Raphael, the sociable spirit, that deign'd
To travel with *Tobias*, and secur'd
His marriage with the seventimes-wedded maid.

Raphael, said he, thou hear'st what stir on earth
225 *Satan* from hell scap't through the darksome gulf
Hath rais'd in paradise, and how disturb'd
This night the human pair; how he designs
In them at once to ruin all mankind.
Go, therefore, half this day as friend with friend
230 Converse with *Adam*, in what bower or shade
Thou find'st him, from the heat of noon retir'd,
To respite his day-labour with repast,
Or with repose; and such discourse bring on,
As may advise him of his happy state,
235 Happiness in his power left free to will,
Left to his own free will; his will, though free,
Yet mutable; whence warn him to beware

He swerve not, too secure: tell him withal
His danger, and from whom; what enemy
240 Late fallen himself from heaven, is plotting now
The fall of others from like state of bliss;
By violence? No, for that shall be withstood;
But by deceit and lies: this let him know,
Lest wilfully transgressing he pretend
245 Surprisal, unadmonish'd, unforewarnd.

So spake th' eternal father, and fulfilld
All justice: nor delayed the wing'd saint
After his charge receiv'd; but from among
Thousand celestial ardors, where he stood
250 Veil'd with his gorgeous wings, up springing light
Flew through the midst of heaven; th'angelic choirs
On each hand parting, to his speed gave way
Through all th' empyreal road; till at the gate
Of heaven arriv'd, the gate self-opend wide,
255 On golden hinges turning, as by work
Divine the sovereign Architect had fram'd.
From hence, no cloud, or, to obstruct his sight,
Star interpos'd, however small, he sees,
Not unconform to other shining globs,
260 Earth and the garden of God, with cedars crown'd
Above all hills. As when by night the Glass
Of *Galileo*, less assur'd, observes
Imagin'd lands and regions in the moon:
Or pilot from amidst the *Cyclades*,
265 *Delos* or *Samos* first appearing kens
A cloudy spot. Down thither prone in flight
He speeds, and through the vast ethereal sky
Sailes between worlds and worlds; with steady wing
Now on the polar winds, then with quick fan
270 Winnows the buxom air; till within soar
Of tow'ring eagles, to all the fowles he seems
A *phœnix*, gaz'd by all, as that sole Bird
When to inshrine his reliques in the sun's
Bright temple, to *Ægyptian Thebe's* he flies.
275 At once on th' eastern cliff of Paradise
He lights, and to his proper shape returns,
A seraph wing'd; six wings he wore to shade
His lineaments divine; the pair that clad
Each shoulder broad, came mantling o'er his breast
280 With regal ornament; the middle pair
Girt like a starry zone his waist, and round
Skirted his loins and thighs with downy gold
And colours dipped in heaven; the third his feet
Shaddow'd from either heel with feather'd mail,
285 Sky-tinctur'd grain. Like *Maia's* son he stood,
And shook his plumes, that heavenly fragrance fill'd
The circuit wide. Straight knew him all the bands
Of angels under watch; and to his state,
And to his message high, in honour rise;
290 For on some message high they guess'd him bound.
Their glittering tents he pass'd, and now is come
Into the blissful field, through groves of myrrh,
And flowering odours, cassia, nard, and balm;
A wilderness of sweets; for Nature here
295 Wanton'd as in her prime, and play'd at will
Her virgin fancies, pouring forth more sweet,
Wild above rule or art; enormous bliss.
Him through the spicy forest onward come,
Adam discern'd, as in the door he sat

300   Of his cool bower, while now the mounted sun
Shot down direct his fervid rays, to warm
Earths' inmost womb, more warmth then *Adam* needs:
And *Eve* within, due at her hour, prepar'd
For dinner savory fruits, of taste to please
305   True appetite, and not disrelish thirst
Of nect'rous draughts between, from milky stream,
Berry or grape: to whom thus *Adam* call'd:

Haste hither *Eve*, and, worth thy sight behold,
Eastward among those trees, what glorious shape,
310   Comes this way moving; seems another morn
Risen on mid-noon: some great behest from heaven
To us perhaps he brings, and will vouchsafe
This day to be our guest. But go with speed,
And what thy stores contain, bring forth, and pour
315   Abundance, fit to honour and receive
Our heavenly stranger: well we may afford
Our givers their own gifts, and large bestow
From large bestow'd, where nature multiplies
Her fertile growth, and by disburd'ning grows
320   More fruitful, which instructs us not to spare.

To whom thus *Eve*: *Adam*, earth's hallow'd mould,
Of god inspir'd, small store will serve, where store
All seasons, ripe for use hangs on the stalk;
Save what by frugal storing firmness gains
325   To nourish, and superfluous moist consumes:
But I will haste, and from each bough and brak,
Each plant and juiciest gourd will pluck such choice
To entertain our angel guest, as he
Beholding shall confess, that here on earth
330   God hath dispens'd his bounties as in heaven.

So saying, with dispatchful looks in haste
She turns, on hospitable thoughts intent
What choice to chuse for delicacie best,
What order, so contriv'd as not to mix
335   Tastes, not well join'd, inelegant, but bring
Taste after taste, upheld with kindliest change:
Bestirs her then, and from each tender stalk
Whatever earth all bearing mother, yields
In *India* East or West, or middle shore
340   In *Pontus* or the *Punic* coast, or where
Alcinous reign'd, fruit of all kinds, in coat,
Rough, or smooth rind, or bearded husk, or shell
She gathers, tribute large, and on the board
Heaps with unsparing hand; for drink the grape
345   She crushes, inoffensive must, and meathes
From many a berry, and from sweet kernels pres'd
She tempers dulcet creams; nor these to hold
Wants her fit vessels pure; then strews the ground
With rose and odours from the shrub unfum'd.
350   Meawhile our primitive great sire, to met
His god-like guest, walks forth, without more train
Accompanied then with his own complete
Perfections: in himself was all his state,
More solemn then the tedious pomp that waits
355   On princes, when their rich retinue long
Of horses led, and grooms besmear'd with gold,
Dazzles the crowd, and sets them all agape.
Nearer his presence *Adam*, though not awed,

Yet with submiss approach, and reverence meek,
360 As to a superior nature, bowing low

Thus said: Native of heaven, for other place
None can then heaven such glorious shape contain;

Since, by descending from the thrones above,
Those happy places thou hast deign'd awhile
365 To want, and honour these, vouchsafe with us
Two only, who yet by sovereign gift possess
This spacious ground, in yonder shady bower
To rest, and what the garden choicest bears
To sit and taste, till this meridian heat
370 Be over, and the sun more cool decline.

Whom thus th' angelic virtue answer'd mild.
Adam, I therefore came; nor art thou such
Created, or such place hast here to dwell,
As may not oft invite, though spirits of heaven
375 To visit thee; lead on then where thy bower
O'ershades; for these midhours, till evening rise,
I have at will. So to the silvan lodge
They came, that like *Pomona's* arbour smil'd
With flowerets deck'd and fragrant smells; but *Eve*
380 Undeck'd, save with herself, more lovely fair
Then wood-nymph, or the fairest goddess feign'd
Of three that in mount *Ida* naked strove,
Stood to entertain her guest from heaven: no veil
She needed, virtue proof; no thought infirm
385 Alter'd her cheek. On whom the angel *Hail*
Bestow'd, the holy salutation us'd
Long after to bless'd *Mary*, second *Eve*.

Hail mother of mankind, whose fruitful womb
Shall fill the world more numerous with thy sons,
390 Than with these various fruits the trees of God
Have heap'd this table. Rais'd of grassy turf
Their table was, and mossy seats had round;
And on her ample square from side to side
All *Autumn* pil'd, though *spring* and *Autumn* here
395 Danc'd hand in hand. A while discourse they hold,
No fear lest dinner cool; when thus began
Our author. Heavenly stranger, pleas'd to taste
These bounties, which our nourisher, from whom
All perfet good, unmeasur'd out, descends,
400 To us for food and for delight, hath caus'd
Th' earth to yeild; unsavory food perhaps
To spiritual natures; only this I know,
That one celestial Father gives to all.

To whom the angel: therefore what he gives
405 (Whose praise be ever sung;) to man in part
Spiritual, may of purest spirits be found
No ingrateful food: and food alike those pure
Intelligential substances require,
As doth your rational; and both contain
410 Within them every lower faculty
Of sense, whereby they hear, see, smell, touch, taste.
Tasting concoct, digest, assimilate,
And corporeal to incorporeal turn.
For know, whatever was created, needs
415 To be sustain'd and fed; of elements,
The grosser feeds the purer, earth the sea,
Earth and the sea feed air, the air those fires
Ethereal, and as lowest first the moon;

Whence in her visage round, those spots unpurg'd
420 Vapours not yet into her substance turn'd.
Nor doth the moon no nourishment exhale
From her moist continent to higher orbs.
The sun, that light imparts to all, receives
From all his alimental recompense
425 In humid exhalations, and at even
Sups with the ocean; though in heaven the trees
Of life ambrosial frutage bear, and vines
Yield nectar; though from off the boughs each morn
We brush mellifluous dewes, and find the ground
430 Cover'd with pearly grain: yet God hath here
Varied his bounty so with new delights,
As may compare with heaven; and to taste
Think not I shall be nice. So down they sat,
And to their viands fell; nor seemingly
435 The angel, nor in mist, the common gloss
Of theologians, but with keen dispatch
Of real hunger, and concoctive heat
To transubstantiate; what redounds, transpires
Through spirits with ease; nor wonder, if by fire
440 Of sooty coal, th; empiric alchimist
Can turn, or holds it possible to turn,
Metals of drossiest ore to perfet gold,
As from the mine. Meanwhile at table *Eve*
Minister'd naked, and their flowing cups
445 With pleasant liquors crown'd: O innocence
Deserving Paradise; If ever, then,
Then had the sons of God excuse to have been
Enamour'd at that sight; but in those hearts
Love unlibidinous reign'd, nor jealousy
Was understood, the injur'd lovers hell.

450 Thus when with meats and drinks they had suffic'd
Not burd'nd nature, sudden mind arose
In *Adam*, not to let th' occasion pass,
Given him by this great conference, to know
455 Of things above his world, and of their being
Who dwell in heaven, whose excellence he saw
Transcend his own so far, whose radiant forms
Divine effulgence, whose high power so far
Exceeded human, and his wary speech
460 Thus to th' empyreal minister he fram'd;

Inhabitant with god, now know I well
Thy favour, in this honour done to man,
Under whose lowly roof thou hast vouchsaf'd
To enter, and these earthly fruits to taste,
465 Food not of angels, yet accepted so,
As that more willingly thou couldst not seem
At heaven's high feasts to have fed: yet what compare?

To whom the winged hierarch repli'd;
O *Adam*, one almighty is, from whom
470 All things proceed, and up to him return,
If not deprav'd from good, created all
Such to perfection, one first matter all,
Endued with various forms various degrees,
Of substance, and in things that live, of life;
475 But more refin'd, more spiritous, and pure,
As nearer to him plac'd or nearer tending,
Each in their several active spheres assign'd
Till body up to spirit work, in bounds
Proportion'd to each kind. So from the root
480 Springs lighter the green stalk, from thence the leaves
More airy, last the bright consummate flower
Spirits odorous breathes: flowers and their fruit,
Mans nourishment, by gradual scale sublim'd
To vital spirits aspire, to animal,
485 To intellectual, give both life and sense,
Fancy and understanding; whence the soul

    Reason receives, and reason is her being,
Discursive, or intuitive; discourse
Is oftest yours, the latter most is ours,
490 Differing but in degree, of kind the same.
Wonder not, then, what God for you saw good
If I refuse not, but convert, as you,
To proper substance: time may come, when men
With angels may participate, and find
495 No inconvenient diet, nor too light fare;
And from these corporal nutriments perhaps
Your bodies may at last turn all to spirit,
Improv'd by tract of time, and wing'd ascend
Ethereal, as wee, or may at choice
500 Here or in heavenly paradises dwell;
If ye be found obedient, and retain
Unalterably firm his love entire,
Whose progeny you are. Meanwhile enjoy
Your fill what happiness this happy state
505 Can comprehend, incapable of more.

To whom the patriarch of mankind replied:
O favourable spirit, propitious guest,
Well hast thou taught the way that might direct
Our knowledge, and the scale of nature set
510 From centre to circumference, whereon,
In contemplation of created things,
By steps we may ascend to god. But say,
What meant that caution join'd, *If ye be found*
Obedient? Can we want obedience then
515 To him, or possibly his love desert,
Who form'd us from the dust, and plac'd us here,
Full to the utmost measure of what bliss
Human desires can seek or apprehend?

To whom the angel: Son of heaven and earth,
520 Attend: that thou art happy, owe to God;
That thou continue'st such, owe to thyself,
That is, to thy obedience; therein stand.
This was that caution given thee; be advis'd.
God made thee perfect, not immutable;
525 And good he made thee, but to persevere
He left it in thy power, ordain'd thy will
By nature free, not over rul'd by fate
Inextricable, or strict necessity:
Our voluntary service he requires,
530 Not our necessitated; such with him
Finds no acceptance, nor can find: for how
Can hearts not fre, be tried whether they serve
Willing or no, who will but what they must
By destiny, and can no other choose?
535 Myself, and all th' angelic host that stand
In sight of god enthron'd, our happy state
Hold, as you yours, while our obedience holds;
On other surety none; freely we serve,
Because we freely love, as in our will
540 To love or not; in this we stand or fall:
And some are fallen, to disobedience fallen,
And so from heaven to deepest hell; O fall
From what high state of bliss into what woe.

To whom our great progenitor: Thy words
545 Attentive, and with more delighted ear
Divine instructor, I have heard, then when
Cherubic songs by night from neighbouring hills
Aerial music send: nor knew I not
To be both will and deed created free;
550 Yet that we never shall forget to love
Our Maker, and obey him whose command
Single is yet so just, my constant thoughts
Assur'd me and still assure: though what thou tell'st
Hath pas's'd in heaven, some doubt within me move,
555 But more desire to hear, if thou consent,
The full relation, which must needs be strange,
Worthy of sacred silence to be heard;
And we have yet large day, for scarce the sun
Hath finish'd half his journey, and scarce begins

	His other half in the great zone of heaven.		Stream in the air, and for distinction serve
560		590	
	Thus *Adam* made request; and *Raphael*,		Of hierarchies, of orders, and degrees;
	After short pause assenting, thus began:		Or in their glittering tissues bear emblaz'd
			Holy memorials, acts of zeal and love
	High matter thou enjoin'st me, O prime of men,		Recorded eminent. Thus when in orbs
	Sad task and hard; for how shall I relate	595	Of circuit inexpressible they stood,
565	To human sense th'invisible exploits		Orb within orb, the Father infinite,
	Of waring spirits? How, without remorse		By whom in bliss imbosom'd sat the Son,
	The ruin of so many, glorious once,		Amidst, as from a flaming mount, whose top
	And perfect while they stood? How, last, unfold		Brightness had made invisible, thus spake:
	The secrets of another world, perhaps	600	Hear all ye angels, progeny of light,
570	Not lawful to reveal? Yet for thy good		Thrones, dominations, princedoms, virtues, powers,
	This is dispenc'd: and what surmounts the reach		Hear my decree, which unrevok't shall stand.
	Of human sense, I shall delineate so,		This day I have begot whom I declare
	By likening spiritual to corporal forms,		My only son, and on this holy hill
	As may express them best; though what if earth	605	Him have anointed, whom ye now behold
575	Be but the shadow of heaven, and things therein,		At my right hand; your Head I him appoint;
	Each to other like, more then on earth is thought?		And by myself have sworn to him shall bow
			All knees in heaven, and shall confess him Lord.
	As yet this world was not, and *Chaos* wild		Under his great vicegerent reign abide
	Reign'd where these heavens now roll, where earth now rests	610	United as one individual soul,
	Upon her centre pois'd, when on a day,		For ever happy. Him who disobeys,
580	(For time, though in eternity, appli'd		Me disobeyes, breaks union, and that day
	To motion, measures all things durable		Cast out from God and blessed vision, falls
	By present, past, and future,) on such day		Into utter darkness, deep ingulf'd, his place
	As heavens great year brings forth, th' empyreal host	615	Ordain'd, without redemption, without end.
	Of angels by imperial summons call'd,		
585	Innumerable, before th' almighty's throne		So spake th' omnipotent, and with his words
	Forthwith from all the ends of heaven appear'd		All seem'd well pleas'd; all seem'd, but were not all.
	Under their hierarchs in orders bright:		That day, as other solemn dayes, they spent
	Ten thousand thousand ensigns high advanc'd,		In song and dance about the sacred hill;
	Standards and gonfalons 'twixt van and reare	620	Mystical dance, which yonder starry sphere
			Of planets and of fixt in all her wheeles
			Resembles nearest, mazes intricate,
			Eccentric, intervolv'd, yet regular

Then most, when most, irregular they seem
And in their motions harmony divine
So smooths her charming tones, that God's own ear
Listens delighted. Evening now approach'd
(For we have also our evening and our morn,
We ours for change delectable, not need;)
Forthwith from dance to sweet repast they turn
Desirous; all in circles as they stood,
Tables are set, and on a sudden pil'd
With angel's food, and rubied nectar flows
In pearl, in diamond, and massy gold,
Fruit of delicious vines, the growth of heaven.
On flowers repos'd, and with fresh flowerets crown'd,
They eat, they drink, and in communion sweet
Quaff immortality and joy, secure
Of surfit where full measure only bounds
Excess, before th' all bounteous king, who shower'd
With copious hand, rejoicing in their joy.
Now, when ambrosial night with clouds exhal'd
From that high mount of god, whence light and shade
Spring both, the face of brightest heaven had chang'd
To grateful twilight, (for night comes not there
In darker veil) and roseate dews dispos'd
All but the unsleeping eyes of God to rest,
Wide over all the plain, and wider far
Then all this globous earth in plain outspred,
(Such are the courts of God,) th' angelic throng,
Disper'st in bands, and files their camp extend
By living streams among the trees of life,
Pavilions numberless, and sudden rear'd,
Celestial tabernacles, where they slept
Fann'd with cool winds, save those who in their course
Melodious hymns about the sovran throne
Alternate all night long: but not so wak'd
Satan, (so call him now, his former name
Is heard no more in heaven;) he of the first,
If not the first archangel, great in power,
In favour and pre-eminence, yet fraught
With envy against the Son of God, that day
Honour'd by his great father, and proclaim'd
Messiah King anointed, could not bear,
Through pride that sight, & thought him self impair'd.
Deep malice thence conceiving, and disdain,
Soon as midnight brought on the dusky hour
Friendliest to sleep and silence, he resolv'd
With all his Legions to dislodge, and leave
Unworshipp'd, unobey'd the throne supreme
Contemptuous, and his next subordinate
Awak'ning, thus to him in secret spake:

Sleep'st thou, companion dear; what sleep can close
Thy eye-lids? And remember'st what decree
Of yesterday, so late hath pass'd the lips
Of heavens Almighty. Thou to me thy thoughts
Wast wont, I mine to thee was wont to impart;
Both waking we were one; how then can now
Thy sleep dissent? New laws thou seest impos'd;
New laws from him who reigns, new minds may raise
In us who serve, new counsels, to debate
What doubtful may ensue: more in this place
To utter is not safe. Assemble thou
Of all those myriads which we lead the chief;
Tell them that, by command, ere yet dim night

Her shadowy cloud withdraws, I am to haste,
And all who under me their banners wave,
Homeward with flying march where we possess
The quarters of the North: there to prepare
690 Fit entertainment to receive our King,
The great *Messiah*, and his new commands,
Who speedily through all the hierarchies
Intends to pass triumphant, and give laws.

So spake the false archangel, and infus'd
695 Bad influence into th' unwary breast
Of his associate: he together calls,
Or several one by one, the regent powers,
Under him regent; tells, as he was taught,
That the Most High commanding, now ere night,
700 Now ere dim night had disincumberd heaven,
The great hierarchal standard was to move;
Tells the suggested cause, and casts between
Ambiguous words and jealousies, to sound
Or taint integrity. But all obey'd
705 The wonted signal, and superior voice
Of their great potentate; for great indeed
His name, and high was his degree in heaven;
His count'nance, as the morning star that guides
The starry flock, allur'd them, and with lies
710 Drew after him the third part of heavens host.
Meanwhile th' eternal eye, whose sight discerns
Abstrusest thoughts, from forth his holy mount,
And from within the golden lamps that burn
Nightly before him, saw, without their light,
715 Rebellion rising; saw in whom, how spread
Among the sons of morn, what multitudes
Were banded to oppose his high decree;
And, smiling, to his only son thus said:

Son, thou in whom my glory I behold
720 In full resplendence, Heir of all my might,
Nearly it now concerns us to be sure
Of our omnipotence, and with what arms
We mean to hold what anciently we claim
Of deity or empire; such a foe
725 Is rising, who intends to erect his throne
Equal to ours, throughout the spacious north;
Nor so content, hath in his thought to try,
In battle, what our power is, or our right.
Let us advise, and to this hazard draw
730 With speed what force is left, and all employ
In our defense, lest unawares we lose
This our high place, our sanctuary, our hill.

To whom the Son with calm aspect and cleer
Light'ning divine, ineffable, serene,
735 Made answer: mighty Father, thou thy foes
Justly hast in derision, and, secure,
Laugh'st at their vain designes and tumults vain,
Matter to me of glory, whom their hate
Illustrates, when they see all regal power
740 Giv'n me to quell their pride, and in event
Know whether I be dext'rous to subdue
Thy rebels, or be found the worst in heaven.

So spake the Son: but *Satan* with his powers
Far was advanc'd on winged speed, an host
745 Innumerable as the stars of night,
Or stars of morning, dew-drops, which the sun
Impearls on every leaf, and every flower.
Regions they pass'd, the mighty regencies
Of seraphim, and potentates, and thrones,
750 In their triple degrees; regions to which
All thy dominion, *Adam*, is no more
Then what this garden is to all the earth,
And all the sea, from one entire globose
Stretch'd into longitude; which, having pass'd,
755 At length into the limits of the north

They came, and *Satan* to his royal seat
High on a hill, far blazing, as a mount
Rais'd on a mount, with pyramids and towers
From diamond quarries hewn, and rocks of gold;
760 The palace of great *Lucifer*, (so call
That structure in the Dialect of men
Interpreted) which not long after he,
Affecting all equality with God,
In imitation of that mount whereon
765 *Messiah* was declar'd in sight of heaven,
The mountain of the Congregation call'd;
For thither he assembled all his train,
Pretending so commanded, to consult
About the great reception of their King
770 Thither to come, and with calumnious art
Of counterfeted truth thus held their ears:

Thrones, dominations, princedoms, virtues, powers;
If these magnific titles yet remain
Not merely titular, since by decree
775 Another now hath to himself engross'd
All power, and us eclips'd under the name
Of King Anointed; for whom all this haste
Of midnight march, and hurried meeting here;
This only to consult how we may best,
780 With what may be devis'd of honours new,
Receive him, coming to receive from us
Knee-tribute, yet unpaid; prostration vile,
Too much to one, but double how endur'd,
To one, and to his image now proclaim'd?
785 But what if better counsels might erect
Our minds and teach us to cast off this yoke?
Will ye submit your necks; and choose to bend
The supple knee? Ye will not, if I trust
To know ye right, or if ye know yourselves
790 Natives and sons of heaven possessd before
By none, and if not equal all, yet free,
Equally free; for orders and degrees
Jar not with liberty, but well consist.
Who can in reason then, or right assume
795 Monarchy over such as live by right
His equals, if in power and splendor less,
In freedom equal? Or can introduce
Law and edict on us, who without law
Ere not? Much less for this to be our Lord,
800 And look for adoration, to th' abuse
Of those imperial titles, which assert
Our being ordain'd to govern, not to serve.

Thus far his bold discourse without control
Had audience; when among the seraphim
805 *Abdiel*, then whom none with more zeal ador'd
The Deity, and divine commands obey'd,
Stood up, and in a flame of zeal severe,
The current of his fury thus oppos'd:

O argument blasphemous, false and proud;
810 Words which no ear ever to hear in heaven
Expected, least of all from thee, ingrate
In place thyself so high above thy peers.
Canst thou with impious obloquy condemn
The just decree of God, pronounc'd and sworn,
815 That to his only Son by right endu'd
With regal sceptre, every soul in heaven
Shall bend the knee, and in that honour due
Confess him rightful king? Unjust thou saist
Flatly unjust, to binde with laws the free,
820 And equal over equals to let reigne,
One over all with unsucceeded power.
Shalt thou give law to god, shalt thou dispute
With him the points of libertie, who made
Thee what thou art, and formd the pow'rs of heaven
825 Such as he pleasd, and circumscrib'd their being?
Yet by experience taught we know how good,
And of our good, and of our dignitie
How provident he is, how far from thought
To make us less, bent rather to exalt

830 Our happy state under one head more neer
United. But to grant it thee unjust,
That equal over equals monarch reigne:
Thy self though great and glorious dost thou count,
Or all angelic nature joind in one,
835 Equal to him begotten son, by whom
As by his word the mighty father made
All things, ev'n thee, and all the spirits of heaven
By him created in their bright degrees,
Crownd them with glory, and to their glory nam'd
840 Thrones, dominations, princedoms, virtues, powers,
Essential powers, nor by his reign obscur'd,
But more illustrious made, since he the head
One of our number thus reduc't becomes,
His laws our laws, all honour to him done
845 Returns our own. Cease then this impious rage,
And tempt not these; but hast'n to appease
Th' incensed father, and th' incensed son,
While pardon may be found in time besought.

So spake the fervent angel, but his zeale
850 None seconded, as out of season judg'd,
Or singular and rash, whereat rejoic'd
Th' apostat, and more haughty thus repli'd:
That we were form'd then saist thou? And the work
Of secondary hands, by task transfer'd
855 From Father to his Son? Strange point and new;
Doctrine which we would know whence learn'd: who saw
When this creation was? Remember'st thou
Thy making, while the Maker gave thee being?
We know no time when we were not as now;
860 Know none before us, self-begot, self-rais'd
By our own quick'ning power, when fatal course
Had circl'd his full orb, the birth mature
Of this our native heaven, ethereal sons.
Our puissance is our own; our own right hand
865 Shall teach us highest deeds, by proof to try
Who is our equal: then thou shalt behold
Whether by supplication we intend
Address, and to begirt th' Almighty throne
Beseeching or besieging. This report,
870 These tidings carrie to th' anointed King;
And fly, ere evil intercept thy flight.

He said, and, as the sound of waters deep,
Hoarce murmur echo'd to his words applause
Through the infinite host; nor less for that
875 The flaming seraph, fearless, though alone
Encompass'd round with foes, thus answer'd bold:

O alienate from God, O spirit accurs'd,
Forsak'n of all good; I see thy fall
Determind, and thy hapless crew involv'd
880 In this perfidious fraud, contagion spread
Both of thy crime and punishment: henceforth
No more be troubl'd how to quit the yoke
Of gods *Messiah*; those indulgent laws
Will not now be vouchsaf'd: other decrees
885 Against thee are gone forth without recall;
That golden scepter which thou didst reject
Is now an iron rod to bruise and break
Thy disobedience. Well thou didst advise:
Yet not for thy advise; or threats I fly
890 These wicked tents devoted, least the wrath
Impendent, raging into sudden flame,
Distinguish not: for soon expect to feel
His thunder on thy head, devouring fire.
Then who created thee lamenting learn,
895 When who can uncreate thee thou shalt know.

So spake the seraph *Abdiel,* faithful found
Among the faithless, faithful only he
Among innumerable false, unmov'd,
Unshak'n, unseduc'd, unterrified

900 His loyalty he kept, his love, his zeal;
Nor number, nor example with him wrought
To swerve from truth, or change his constant mind
Though single. From amidst them forth he pass'd,
Long way through hostile scorn, which he sustain'd

905 Superior, nor of violence fear'd aught;
And with retorted scorn his back he turn'd
On those proud towers to swift destruction doom'd.

End of Book Fifth.

Raphael. The archangel Rapahel serves as a messenger between Heaven and Earth. In Hebrew, Raphael means "God has healed." He appears in the Apocryphal *Book of Tobit* where Raphael assumes the form of a man and helps Tobias ward off the demon Asmodeus. The other chief archangels are Michael, Gabriel, and Uriel; each was assigned one quarter of the world in each of the cardinal directions.

rosie steps. Milton echoes Homer's "rosy-fingered dawn" (*Odyssey* 2.1). *Orient Pearle.* This may invoke either the pearl-like quality of eastern (oriental) morning light, or the dew that appears with the dawn.

Aurora. Aurora personifies the dawn and her "fan" stirring the leaves, along with morning birdsong, wakes Adam.

Matin Song. Morning song, with some suggestion of the liturgical sense of morning prayer.

peculiar. In other words, graces belonging exclusively to Eve's beauty. The image of Eve's beauty "shooting" forth graces is repeated in book 8.62-63, when we are asked to imagine that her graces "shot Darts of desire." The significance of Eve's beauty and its relations to Adam's inward beauty are the topic of Eve's discourse in book 4.489-491.

Zephyrus. The westwind personified; and Eve personified as Flora, his wife, as in Ovid's *Fasti*.

prime. The very beginning of the day; sunrise.

blows. Blooms.

balmie reed. A balm-producing reed, probably balsam. The balsam tree also makes myrrh, another aromatic resin.

My Glorie, my Perfection. Eve addresses Adam as one who completes (perfects) her, implying she is not complete in herself, though she sometimes seems so to Adam (8.548). Perhaps this is because Adam felt himself incomplete before Eve's creation (8.355-366), but Eve must be taught to think herself incomplete (4.489-491).

dream'd. See William Blake's watercolor illustration of Eve sleeping with Satan close by.

in vain. The tempting voice contradicts Adam's bedtime response to Eve the night before (4.668-680). Adam had said that the stars shine not in vain even though he and Eve may sleep. Others enjoy the sights. Why, then, does Eve think the voice is Adam's? The tempter's first tactic is to encourage Eve to be unsatisfied with Adam's wisdom.

Whom to behold but thee. The tempting voice suggests, contrary to the voice she heard on her first waking day (4.467-472), that her beauty is admired and desired by all creation.

Ambrosia. In classical legend, ambrosia is not only the food of the gods, but also the healing oil with which they anoint themselves and specially chosen mortals.

reserve. Restriction.

Ascend to heaven. The tempter here promises precisely what Raphael later says will inevitably be theirs one day, if they remain obedient:

My Guide was gon. Presumably the tempter is broken off in mid-temptation at that moment when Ithuriel and Zephon touch Satan, "squat like a Toad" and return him to his proper (fallen) shape (4.810-814).

Image of myself. Adam refers to Eve as his best image (4.471-72), much as the Son is spoken of as the Father's image in 3.139-142. But the symmetry does not hold when we consider that the Son is not only the best image of the Father, but also the executor of all his power.

Eve may be Adam's "best image," but she is never appointed Adam's exclusive executive.

uncouth. Unfamiliar, as yet unknown.

Fancy. In 8.461, Milton refers to fancy as "internal sight." It can be taken as another word for "imagination" or the power to see things that are not in the physical world.

deeds long past. It is well worth comparing Adam's theory of dreams to Freud's in "On Dreams" part 1: "During the epoch which may be described as pre-scientific, men had no difficulty in finding an explanation of dreams. When they remembered a dream after waking up, they regarded it as either a favourable or a hostile manifestation of higher powers, daemonic and divine. When modes of thought belonging to natural science began to flourish, all this ingenious mythology was transformed into psychology, and to-day only a small minority of educated people doubt that dreams are a product of the dreamer's own mind." Adam's theory is clearly the pre-scientific one Freud describes, but still it is hard for us not to think Eve's unconscious somehow had a part in producing the dream, especially when Adam recognizes "resemblances" from their bedtime discourse.

our last Eevnings talk. Adam refers to their talk in 4.657-688.

so unapprov'd. Adam invokes much the same principle to defend himself against Raphael's implicit accusation, in book 8. 608-11, that Adam has succumbed in passion to Eve's beauty. Even more to the point, Adam's explanation of how evil thoughts and temptations can come into one's mind and leave no trace of sin resembles quite closely Augustine's meditations on sexy dreams and noctornal emissions in his *Confessions*

bosom'd. Hidden.

with her haire. Wiping tears with hair is bound to evoke the image of Mary Magdalene in Luke 7:38.

sweet remorse. But, we might well ask, remorse for what? fear for what offense? Adam has pronounced Eve offenseless, spotless and blameless (119), or has he only hoped that she is? Augustine describes his feeling of remorse following his wet dreams in much the same way: "And it is by this difference between sleeping and waking that we discover that it was not we who did it, while we still feel sorry that in some way it was done in us" (*Confessions*)

arborous roof. The "arborous roof" Milton refers to is first mentioned as "their blissful bower" in 4.690.

Landscape. Landscape.

Orisons. Morning prayers.

various style. Adam and Eve do not pray according to set forms, of course. They pray spontaneously and ardently, though their prayers may at times resemble what later became set forms (especially those drawn from scripture.)

numerous Verse. Milton equates harmonic or rythmical verse with verse having a numerical structure, suggesting that mathematical considerations played a part in constructing the epic as a whole. He refers to "Harmonious numbers" in 3.38.

invisible. This concept of creation as the visible expression of God's invisible goodness and power is a Christian commonplace.

Sons of Light. The Sons of Light also figure in "Nativity Ode" 119.

Fairest of Stars. The morning star called Lucifer (light-bringer) by day and Hesperus by night. It is the brightest star in Homer's *Iliad* 22. 315.

when thou fallst. Adam, it appears, certainly assumes a Ptolemaic, geocentric, cosmology.

five other wand'ring Fires. Here the term "fires" refers to planets. The five planets that they refer to are Venus, Mercury, Mars, Jupiter and Saturn.

Perpetual Circle. Plato's *Timaeus* (49c) proposes the notion that the four elements could reversibly transform into one another. This idea comes up again in this book when Raphael describes the organization of the universe (415-426). Einstein's theory that all matter originally derived from energy, is partly (and oddly) consistent with Raphael's account below.

my Song. The first couple's morning prayers echo, in form, David's psalms of praise, especially Psalm 148. This is also the form of the "Benedicite omnia opera domini domino", a popular part of matins and included in the 1559 *Book of Common Prayer* for Morning Prayers.

wed her Elm. The classical image of the vine wedded to the elm is found in Horace's *Odes* 2.15.4-5 and Virgil's *Georgics* 2.367. Here it also is meant to resemble the relationship between Eve (vine) and Adam (elm) as in 4.307.

secure. With excessive confidence that all is safe.

Celestial Ardors. Other angels.

self-opend. Compare this description of the gate to Heaven with Milton's description of the gates of Hell, "on their hinges grate/ Harsh thunder" 2.881-2.

Glass/ Of Galileo. Galileo was the first to study the moon carefully through a telescope.

Cyclades. The Cyclades are a group of islands in the Aegean with the island of Delos at its center. The island of Samos lies northeast of the Cyclades.

Fann. Wing.

Towring. The "tower" of an eagle is the circular flight it takes upward. At this point in his descent, Raphael has reached the highest altitude of any bird's flight.

sole Bird. There existed one phoenix only. It immolated itself approximately every 500 years at the city of the sun, Heliopolis. Like most people of his day, Milton identified Heliopolis with the Egyptian city, Thebes.

Seraph. In addition to cherubim and thrones, seraphim constituted the loftiest triad of the nine orders of angels. Seraphim are described in Isaiah 6:2.

Zone. Belt. The most famous starry belt is Orion's.

Maia's son. In classical mythology the heavenly messenger was Hermes or Mercury. Maia, daughter of Atlas, bore Hermes to Zeus. Milton echoes here the visit Hermes makes to Odysseus in *Odyssey* 10.275 to warn him about, and give him herbal protection against, Circe's charms. Virgil's *Aeneid* 4.318-340 tells of Mercury's mission to Aeneas in Carthage to encourage him to abandon Dido and Carthage and resume his destiny as an empire founder.

state. Rank.

Cassia. A plant with a fragrance like cinnamon.

Nard. Spikenard, a plant from which fragrant ointment was made.

Wantond. Flourished innocently, but the word still sounds ominous.

more warmth then Adam needs. In other words, it got uncomfortably hot at noon in Eden. This, of course, is no imperfection, for Adam was meant to retire to his "coole bower" each noontide for repast and rest.

Our heavenly stranger. Milton's story of entertaining a heavenly guest is modeled partly on the story of Abraham and Sarah entertaining "the Lord" in Genesis 18.

kindliest. Most in harmony with nature.

India East or West. India or the West Indies.

middle shoare. The lands surrounding the Mediterranean Sea. Pontus, the shore of the Black Sea, is to the north, and Punic, the African coast, is to the south.

Alcinous. He is the king of Phaiakia in Homer's *Odyssey* 7.115-34. Odysseus visits his paradisal garden of perpetual harvest.

inoffensive moust. Unfermented (and therefore alcohol-free) grape juice.

unfum'd. Not burned. That is, there is no incense here.

Pomona's. Pamona, the Roman goddess of fruit.

Undeckt. Naked. Milton emphasizes Eve's nakedness here quite a bit. Adam, of course, was naked too, but Milton feels no need to comment frequently on this.

three that in Mount Ida naked strove. When the Trojan prince Paris was selected to judge the beauty contest, held on Mount Ida, in which Juno, Minerva, and Venus competed, he selected Venus. Her prize was a golden apple; his reward was the most beautiful mortal woman, Helen, whom he abducted from her husband, Menelaus, and thus began the Trojan war

Haile. The angel of the annunciation greets Mary with the word "hail" in Luke 1: 28.

with thy Sons. The blessings of female fertility are assumed to be sons, not daughters, and Raphael blesses Eve's fruitful womb without saying anything about Adam's loins.

Spring and Autumn. In Eden, crops which we think of as seasonal were harvested continuously.

lest Dinner coole. Though she prepared food, nowhere does Milton indicate that Eve cooked food, therefore it need not cool.

Authour. Progenitor, Adam.

perfet good unmeasur'd out, descends. These lines echo James 1: 17.

ingrateful. Displeasing.

Intelligential substances. Angels, according to Milton's metaphysics, are purely intelligential beings; humans are rational beings with some mixture of animal substance;

concoct, digest, assimilate. These are the three stages of digestion. The first stage is literally the digestion of food in the stomach, the second is the transfer to the blood, and the third is the incorporation into the body.

sups. Milton refers to the classical notion that the sun feeds on the ocean. His cosmology specifies that the Moon feeds on Earth's exhalations, and the Sun on the exhalations of all the other planets, in a grand cosmic pecking order.

nice. Fasitidious.

transubstantiate. Milton refers to the turning of one substance into another, most often to a finer one, but the technical term evokes the Roman Catholic doctrine of transubstantiation which holds that bread, at the moment of sacerdotal consecration, literally becomes the body of Christ. Milton appears to propose a different, and to his way of thinking less superstitious, notion of transubstantiation.

transpires. Having argued that angels may eat earthly food with real hunger and real digestion, Milton feels bound to account for the waste products of digestion—"what redounds." Apparently these are gotten rid of with ease.

Empiric. Experimental.

Ministerd naked. See William Blake's 1808 watercolor illustration of these lines.

crown'd. Filled to the brim.

the Sons of God. The story of "The Sons of God" from Genesis 6 has occasioned a wide variety of interpretations. Some commentators, following the Book of Enoch (Chapter 7), took the "Sons of God" to be angels who had lusted after women, coupled with them and produced a race of giants. Milton alludes to this reading even as he denies it credence. See John Rumrich's interesting comments on this passage in *Milton Unbound*. Rumrich ignores the more obvious point that in Aristotelian (and Thomistic) ethics, the bodily pleasures of appetite—sex, food and drink—almost always are linked as a set of pleasures presenting special ethical problems because they are pleasures taken in "necessary" activities.

suffic'd/ Not burd'nd Nature. That is, they had eaten just enough to restore their energy and not so much as to make them sleepy or thick-headed. This is precisely the temperance in food and drink recommended by Aristotle in the *Nicomachean Ethics*

one first matter all. This phrase is taken as the most explicit pronouncement of Milton's monism. The entire universe including man, beast, earth, and angels all originated from the "one first matter" of God himself. Milton describes a continuum with God, the most spiritous, at one end of the spectrum, and earth, the least spiritous, at the other.

If ye be found obedient. Adam and Eve, says Raphael, will naturally ascend to heaven as ever more spiritous beings as time goes on, provided only they remain obedient.

Whose progenie. This phrase is found in Paul's sermon to the Athenians in Acts

perfet, not immutable. Adam is perfect in that he is complete and capable of obedience, but can choose to disobey.

thy will. Milton presents a discussion of predestination versus free will, a subject he touched on in *The Christian Doctrine*: "in assigning the gift of free will, God suffered both men and angels to stand or fall at their own uncontrolled choice."

Cherubic. Cherubim are the highest order of angels, praising God continually.

to reveal?. Classical epics often included large sections of reported action. Here Raphael tells Adam of Satan's original rebellion; in subsequent books he will tell the stories of war in heaven (book 6) and creation (book 7). For classical examples of this mode consider Aeneas' relation to Dido the story of the fall of Troy in books 2 and 3 of the *Aeneid*. Also significant is the reported action in the middle books of Homer's *Odyssey* 9-12.

Each to other like. Raphael here describes the method by which he will relate to Adam matters that "surmount" the reach of human sense. He will speak in similitudes where necessary, a kind of obligatory allegory. But what if, he adds, things on earth are truly but shadows or allegories of things in heaven? This notion is a Christian version of Plato's idea in the *Republic* though unlike Plato it stresses likenesses over differences, and Milton's monism repudiates the notion of an ontological divide between heavenly and earthly things.

great Year. The great year is time it takes the "fixed stars" to complete one revolution of the heavens. Plato's estimate has sometimes been reckoned to be 36,000 solar years.

Gonfalons. Banners that hang from a crosspiece, gonfalons often are used in liturgical and military processions.

circuit inexpressible. A circumference so large that is indescribable.

a flaming Mount. Milton's heavenly mount resembles Mt. Sinai, upon which Moses received the Law (Exodus 19: 16-20: 20).

This day I have begot. Milton's words echo Psalm 2: 6-7. For Luther's interesting commentary on this passage ("But here, when the eternal Father, who is a Spirit, speaks this word about His own Son, it cannot be understood"). Another important Bible passage having to do with the Son's elevation and begottenness is Hebrews 1.

Vice-gerent. Ruler's representative.

shall confess him Lord. These lines echo Philippians 2: 9-11.

who disobeyes. These lines suggest that the Son's begetting, anointing, and installation as Lord of Heaven is the equivalent in heaven of the forbidden fruit on earth. Praising the Son is the heavenly pledge of obedience.

Eccentric. Moving in an orbit that circles a point other than the main center earth; this eccentric center itself moves around earth, its planet describing a complicated spiral pattern. Eccentrics were modifications of Ptolemiac cosmology introduced to account for apparent anomalies in celestial motion.

heard no more in heaven. The names of the apostate angels are no longer heard in Heaven after their fall. In book 1, Milton lists their "new names"—the names of pagan gods (1.361 and following).

anointed. The literal meaning of "Messiah."

impaird. Lowered in rank.

his next subordinate. Beezlebub. See 1.79.

Quarters of the North. The idea that Satan resides in the North is derived from Isaiah 14: 12, 13.

So spake. Readers may do well to try to imagine Raphael imitating the voice of Satan, the rebel angel, as he recites Satan's blasphemous words.

Morning Star. Lucifer.

the third part. See book 2. 692.

Abstrusest. Most hidden.

smiling. The tone of the speech that follows requires special attention from readers. The Son hears a tone of justified "derision" (736) in the Father's speech, suggesting that the words of concern about losing their "high place" (731-32) by a surprise attack should probably be read sarcastically.

Illustrates. Glorifies; adds luster to.

their triple Degrees. Milton alludes to Dionysus the Areopagite's conception of the heirarchy of angels from *The Celestial Hierarchy*.

Stretcht into Longitude. That is, flattened into a map, as in a Mercator projection.

Affecting. Pretending.

double. Tribute now to both the Father and the Son.

liberty. Satan says that although they constitute a heirarchy, they they are all equally free. However, he complains that the anointing of a king (the Son) impairs their liberty.

who without law/ Erre not. Satan questions why there is a need to impose laws on those who do right even in the absence of law; this is similar to some popular antinomian arguments of the 1640's and 50's.

Abdiel. The name Abdiel appears in Chronicles 5: 15. He does not appear in the Bible as an angel, let alone a seraph, one of the two highest ranks of angels. The name most likely comes from the Hebrew word meaning, "Servant of God."

ingrate. Precisely the word the Father uses to describe a disobedient Adam (3.97).

unsucceeded. Eternal.

equal over equals. Adam similarly objects to Nimrod's arrogant usurpation of authority in 12.63 when Michael shows and then explains to him the tyrannies of the future.

by whom/ As by his Word. Abdiel cites the Son as the agent of God, his executive word, in creation of all things, including him.

strange point and new. This is precisely the doctrine taught by Raphael in book 7.

Ethereal Sons. Satan suggests that God did not create the angels, but rather the natural course of things which is marked by one revolution of the great year. "Fatal" is intended to mean inevitable.

Golden Scepter. God's benevolent rule. In *Of Reformation* 2, Milton writes: "let him advise how he can reject the pastorly rod and sheephook of Christ, and those cords of love, and not fear to fall under the iron sceptre of his anger, that will dash him to pieces like a potsherd."

I fly. Abdiel flees the scene not because he has been frightened by Satan's threats but because he does not want to be caught in God's wrath as it descends on the guilty. Abdiel's words echo those of Moses in Numbers 16:26, when he urges the Israelites to run from the rebels Korah, Dathan, and Abiram, "Depart from the tents of these wicked men, and touch nothing of theirs, lest you be involved in their sins."

To His Coy Mistress

Andrew Marvell

Had we but world enough, and time,
This coyness, lady, were no crime
We would sit down, and think which way
To walk, and pass our long love's day.
5 Thou by the Indian Ganges' side
Shouldst rubies find; I by the tide
Of Humber would complain. I would
Love you ten years before the flood,
And you should, if you please, refuse
10 Till the conversion of the Jews.
My vegetable love should grow
Vaster than empires and more slow;
An hundred years should go to praise
Thine eyes, and on thy forehead gaze;
15 Two hundred to adore each breast,
But thirty thousand to the rest;
An age at least to every part,
And the last age should show your heart.
For, lady, you deserve this state,
20 Nor would I love at lower rate.
    But at my back I always hear
Time's wingéd chariot hurrying near;
And yonder all before us lie
Deserts of vast eternity.
25 Thy beauty shall no more be found;
Nor, in thy marble vault, shall sound

Andrew Marvell, "To His Coy Mistress," Copyright in the Public Domain.

My echoing song: then worms shall try
That long-preserved virginity,
And your quaint honour turn to dust,
30   And into ashes all my lust:
The grave's a fine and private place,
But none, I think, do there embrace.
    Now therefore, while the youthful hue
Sits on thy skin like morning dew,
35   And while thy willing soul transpires
At every pore with instant fires,

Now let us sport us while we may,
And now, like amorous birds of prey,
Rather at once our time devour
40   Than languish in his slow-chapped power.
Let us roll all our strength and all
Our sweetness up into one ball,
And tear our pleasures with rough strife
Thorough the iron gates of life:
45   Thus, though we cannot make our sun
Stand still, yet we will make him run.

A Modest Proposal

for Preventing the Children of Poor People in Ireland, From Being a Burden to Their Parents or Country, and for Making Them Beneficial to the Public

Jonathan Swift

It is a melancholy object to those who walk through this great town or travel in the country, when they see the streets, the roads, and cabin doors, crowded with beggars of the female sex, followed by three, four, or six children, all in rags and importuning every passenger for an alms. These mothers, instead of being able to work for their honest livelihood, are forced to employ all their time in strolling to beg sustenance for their helpless infants: who as they grow up either turn thieves for want of work, or leave their dear native country to fight for the Pretender in Spain, or sell themselves to the Barbadoes.

I think it is agreed by all parties that this prodigious number of children in the arms, or on the backs, or at the heels of their mothers, and frequently of their fathers, is in the present deplorable state of the kingdom a very great additional grievance; and, therefore, whoever could find out a fair, cheap, and easy method of making these children sound, useful members of the commonwealth, would deserve so well of the public as to have his statue set up for a preserver of the nation. But my intention is very far from being confined to provide only for the children of professed beggars; it is of a much greater extent, and shall take in the whole number of infants at a certain age who are born of parents in effect as little able to support them as those who demand our charity in the streets.

As to my own part, having turned my thoughts for many years upon this important subject, and maturely weighed the several schemes of other projectors, I have always found them grossly mistaken in the computation. It is true, a child just dropped

---

Jonathan Swift, "A Modest Proposal For Preventing The Children of Poor People in Ireland From Being A burden to Their Parents or Country, and For Making Them Beneficial to The Public," Copyright in the Public Domain.

from its dam may be supported by her milk for a solar year, with little other nourishment; at most not above the value of two shillings which the mother may certainly get, or the value in scraps, by her lawful occupation of begging; and it is exactly at one year old that I propose to provide for them in such a manner as instead of being a charge upon their parents or the parish, or wanting food and raiment for the rest of their lives, they shall on the contrary contribute to the feeding, and partly to the clothing, of many thousands.

There is likewise another great advantage in my scheme, that it will prevent those voluntary abortions, and that horrid practice of women murdering their bastard children, alas, too frequent among us, sacrificing the poor innocent babes, I doubt more to avoid the expense than the shame, which would move tears and pity in the most savage and inhuman breast.

The number of souls in this kingdom being usually reckoned one million and a half, of these I calculate there may be about two hundred thousand couple whose wives are breeders; from which number I subtract thirty thousand couple, who are able to maintain their own children, (although I apprehend there cannot be so many, under the present distresses of the kingdom;) but this being granted, there will remain an hundred and seventy thousand breeders. I again subtract fifty thousand for those women who miscarry, or whose children die by accident or disease within the year. There only remains one hundred and twenty thousand children of poor parents annually born. The question therefore is, how this number shall be reared and provided for, which, as I have already said, under the present situation of affairs, is utterly impossible by all the methods hitherto proposed. For we can neither employ them in handicraft or agriculture; we neither build houses (I mean in the country) nor cultivate land: they can very seldom pick up a livelihood by stealing, till they arrive at six years old, except where they are of towardly parts: although I confess they learn the rudiments much earlier: during which time, they can however be properly looked upon only as probationers, as I have been informed by a principal gentleman in the county of Cavan, who protested to me that he never knew above one or two instances under the age of six, even in a part of the kingdom so renowned for the quickest proficiency in that art.

I am assured by our merchants, that a boy or a girl before twelve years old is no salable commodity; and even when they come to this age they will not yield above three pounds, or three pounds and half-a-crown at most on the exchange; which cannot turn to account either to the parents or kingdom, the charge of nutriment and rags having been at least four times that value.

I shall now therefore humbly propose my own thoughts, which I hope will not be liable to the least objection.

I have been assured by a very knowing American of my acquaintance in London, that a young healthy child well nursed is at a year old a most delicious, nourishing, and wholesome food, whether stewed, roasted, baked, or boiled; and I make no doubt that it will equally serve in a fricasse or a ragout.

I do therefore humbly offer it to public consideration that of the hundred and twenty thousand children already computed, twenty thousand may be reserved for breed, whereof only one-fourth part to be males; which is more than we allow to sheep, black cattle or swine; and my reason is, that these children are seldom the fruits of marriage, a circumstance not much regarded by our savages, therefore one male will be sufficient to serve four females. That the remaining hundred thousand may, at a year old, be offered in the sale to the persons of quality and fortune through the kingdom; always advising the mother to let them suck plentifully in the last month, so as to render them plump and fat for a good table. A child will make two dishes at an entertainment for friends; and when the family dines alone, the fore or hind quarter will make a reasonable dish, and seasoned with a little pepper or salt will be very good boiled on the fourth day, especially in winter.

I have reckoned upon a medium that a child just born will weigh twelve pounds, and in a solar year, if tolerably nursed, increaseth to twenty-eight pounds.

I grant this food will be somewhat dear, and therefore very proper for landlords, who, as they have already devoured most of the parents, seem to have the best title to the children.

Infants' flesh will be in season throughout the year, but more plentiful in March, and a little before and after: for we are told by a grave author, an eminent French physician, that fish being a prolific diet, there are more children born in Roman Catholic countries about nine months after Lent than at any other season; therefore, reckoning a year after Lent, the markets will be more glutted than usual, because the number of popish infants is at least three to one in this kingdom; and therefore it will have one other collateral advantage, by lessening the number of papists among us.

I have already computed the charge of nursing a beggar's child (in which list I reckon all cottagers, labourers, and four-fifths of the farmers) to be about two shillings per annum, rags included; and I believe no gentleman would repine to give ten shillings for the carcass of a good fat child, which, as I have said, will make four dishes of excellent nutritive meat, when he hath only some particular friend or his own family, to dine with him. Thus the squire will learn to be a good landlord, and grow popular among his tenants; the mother will have eight shillings net profit, and be fit for work till she produces another child.

Those who are more thrifty (as I must confess the times require) may flay the carcass; the skin of which artificially dressed, will make admirable gloves for ladies, and summer boots for fine gentlemen.

As to our city of Dublin, shambles may be appointed for this purpose in the most convenient parts of it, and butchers we may be assured will not be wanting; although I rather recommend buying the children alive, and dressing them hot from the knife, as we do roasting pigs.

A very worthy person, a true lover of his country, and whose virtues I highly esteem, was lately pleased in discoursing on this matter to offer a refinement upon my scheme. He said that many gentlemen of this kingdom, having of late destroyed their deer, he conceived that the want of venison might be well supplied by the bodies of young lads and maidens, not exceeding fourteen years of age nor under twelve; so great a number of both sexes in every country being now ready to starve for want of work and service; and these to be disposed of by their parents, if alive, or otherwise by their nearest relations. But with due deference to so excellent a friend, and so deserving a patriot, I cannot be altogether in his sentiments; for as to the males, my American acquaintance assured me, from frequent experience, that their flesh was generally tough and lean, like that of our schoolboys by continual exercise, and their taste disagreeable; and to fatten them would not answer the charge. Then as to the females, it would, I think, with humble submission be a loss to the public, because they soon would become breeders themselves; and besides, it is not improbable that some scrupulous people might be apt to censure such a practice (although indeed very unjustly), as a little bordering upon cruelty; which, I confess, hath always been with me the strongest objection against any project, however so well intended.

But in order to justify my friend, he confessed that this expedient was put into his head by the famous Psalmanazar, a native of the island Formosa, who came from thence to London above twenty years ago, and in conversation told my friend, that in his country when any young person happened to be put to death, the executioner sold the carcass to persons of quality as a prime dainty; and that in his time the body of a plump girl of fifteen, who was crucified for an attempt to poison the emperor, was sold to his Imperial Majesty's prime minister of state, and other great mandarins of the court, in joints from the gibbet, at four hundred crowns. Neither indeed can I deny, that if the same use were made of several plump young girls in this town, who without one single groat to their fortunes, cannot stir abroad without a chair, and appear at playhouse and assemblies in foreign fineries which they never will pay for, the kingdom would not be the worse.

Some persons of a desponding spirit are in great concern about that vast number of poor people, who are aged, diseased, or maimed, and I have been desired to employ my thoughts what course may be taken to ease the nation of so grievous an encumbrance. But I am not in the least pain upon that matter, because it is very well known that they are every day dying and rotting by cold and famine, and filth and vermin, as fast as can be reasonably expected. And as to the young laborers, they are now in as hopeful a condition; they cannot get work, and consequently pine away for want of nourishment, to a degree that if at any time they are accidentally hired to common labor, they have not strength to perform it; and thus the country and themselves are happily delivered from the evils to come.

I have too long digressed, and therefore shall return to my subject. I think the advantages by the proposal which I have made are obvious and many, as well as of the highest importance.

For first, as I have already observed, it would greatly lessen the number of papists, with whom we are yearly overrun, being the principal breeders of the nation as well as our most dangerous enemies; and who stay at home on purpose with a design to deliver the kingdom to the Pretender, hoping to take their advantage by the absence of so many good protestants, who have chosen rather to leave their country than stay at home and pay tithes against their conscience to an Episcopal curate.

Secondly, the poorer tenants will have something valuable of their own, which by law may be made liable to distress and help to pay their landlord's rent, their corn and cattle being already seized, and money a thing unknown.

Thirdly, whereas the maintenance of an hundred thousand children, from two years old and upward, cannot be computed at less than ten shillings a piece per annum, the nation's stock will be thereby increased fifty thousand pounds per annum, beside the profit of a new dish introduced to the tables of all gentlemen of fortune in the kingdom who have any refinement in taste. And the money will circulate among ourselves, the goods being entirely of our own growth and manufacture.

Fourthly, the constant breeders, beside the gain of eight shillings sterling per annum by the sale of their children, will be rid of the charge of maintaining them after the first year.

Fifthly, this food would likewise bring great custom to taverns; where the vintners will certainly be so prudent as to procure the best receipts for dressing it to perfection, and consequently have their houses frequented by all the fine gentlemen, who justly value themselves upon their knowledge in good eating: and a skilful cook, who understands how to oblige his guests, will contrive to make it as expensive as they please.

Sixthly, this would be a great inducement to marriage, which all wise nations have either encouraged by rewards or enforced by laws and penalties. It would increase the care and tenderness of mothers toward their children, when they were sure of a settlement for life to the poor babes, provided in some sort by the public, to their annual profit instead of expense. We should see an honest emulation among the married women, which of them could bring the fattest child to the market. Men would become as fond of their wives during the time of their pregnancy, as they are now of their mares in foal, their cows in calf, their sows when they are ready to farrow; nor offer to beat or kick them (as is too frequent a practice) for fear of a miscarriage.

Many other advantages might be enumerated. For instance, the addition of some thousand carcasses in our exportation of barreled beef, the propagation of swine's flesh, and improvement in the art of making good bacon, so much wanted among us by the great destruction of pigs, too frequent at our tables; which are no way comparable in taste or magnificence to a well- grown, fat, yearling child, which roasted whole will make a considerable figure at a lord mayor's feast or any other public entertainment. But this and many others I omit, being studious of brevity.

Supposing that one thousand families in this city would be constant customers for infants' flesh, besides others who might have it at merry meetings, particularly at weddings and christenings, I compute that Dublin would take off annually about twenty thousand carcasses; and the rest of the kingdom (where probably they will be sold somewhat cheaper) the remaining eighty thousand.

I can think of no one objection, that will possibly be raised against this proposal, unless it should be urged, that the number of people will be thereby much lessened in the kingdom. This I freely own, and 'twas indeed one principal design in offering it to the world. I desire the reader will observe, that I calculate my remedy for this one individual kingdom of Ireland, and for no other that ever was, is, or I think, ever can be, upon Earth. Therefore let no man talk to me of other expedients: of taxing our absentees at five shillings a pound: of using neither cloaths, nor houshold furniture, except what is of our own growth and manufacture: of utterly rejecting the materials and instruments that promote foreign luxury: of curing the expensiveness of pride, vanity, idleness, and gaming in our women: of introducing a vein of parsimony, prudence and temperance: of learning to love our country, wherein we differ even from Laplanders, and the inhabitants of Topinamboo: of quitting our animosities and factions, nor acting any longer like the Jews, who were murdering one another at the very moment their city was taken: of being a little cautious not to sell our country and consciences for nothing: of teaching landlords to have at least one degree of mercy towards their tenants: lastly, of putting a spirit of honesty, industry, and skill into our shop keepers: who, if a resolution could now be taken to buy only our native goods, would immediately unite to cheat and exact upon us in the price, the measure, and the goodness, nor could ever yet be brought to make one fair proposal of just dealing, though often and earnestly invited to it.

Therefore I repeat, let no man talk to me of these and the like expedients, 'till he hath at least some glympse of hope, that there will ever be some hearty and sincere attempt to put them into practice.

But, as to myself, having been wearied out for many years with offering vain, idle, visionary thoughts, and at length utterly despairing of success, I fortunately fell upon this proposal: which, as it is wholly new, so it hath something solid and real, of no expence and little trouble, full in our own power, and whereby we can incur no danger in disobliging England. For this kind of commodity will not bear exportation, and flesh being of too tender a consistence, to admit a long continuance in salt, although perhaps I could name a country, which would be glad to eat up our whole nation without it.

After all, I am not so violently bent upon my own opinion as to reject any offer proposed by wise men, which shall be found equally innocent, cheap, easy, and effectual. But before something of that kind shall be advanced in contradiction to my scheme, and offering a better, I desire the author, or authors will be pleased maturely to consider two points. First, as things now stand, how they will be able to find food and raiment for an hundred thousand useless mouths and backs. And secondly, there being a round million of creatures in human figure throughout this kingdom, whose whole subsistence put into a common stock would leave them in debt two millions of pounds sterling, adding those who are beggars by profession to the bulk of farmers, cottagers, and laborers, with their wives and children who are beggars in effect; I desire those politicians who dislike my overture, and may perhaps be so bold as to attempt an answer, that they will first ask the parents of these mortals, whether they would not at this day think it a great happiness to have been sold for food, at a year old in the manner I prescribe, and thereby have avoided such a perpetual scene of misfortunes as they have since gone through by the oppression of landlords, the impossibility of paying rent without money or trade, the want of common sustenance, with neither house nor clothes to cover them from the inclemencies of the weather, and the most inevitable prospect of entailing the like or greater miseries upon their breed for ever.

I profess, in the sincerity of my heart, that I have not the least personal interest in endeavoring to promote this necessary work, having no other motive than the public good of my country, by advancing our trade, providing for infants, relieving the poor, and giving some pleasure to the rich. I have no children by which I can propose to get a single penny; the youngest being nine years old, and my wife past child-bearing.

The Rape of the Lock
An heroi-comical poem

Alexander Pope

Nolueram, Belinda, tuos violare capillos;
sed juvat hoc precibus me tribuisse tuis.
                                       -Martial

To Mrs. Arabella Fermor

Madam,

It will be in vain to deny that I have some regard for this piece, since I dedicate it to you. Yet you may bear me witness, it was intended only to divert a few young ladies, who have good sense and good humour enough to laugh not only at their sex's little unguarded follies, but at their own. But as it was communicated with the air of a secret, it soon found its way into the world. An imperfect copy having been offered to a Bookseller, you had the good-nature for my sake to consent to the publication of one more correct: This I was forced to, before I had executed half my design, for the Machinery was entirely wanting to complete it.

The machinery, Madam, is a term invented by the Critics, to signify that part which the deities, angels, or dæmons are made to act in a poem: For the ancient Poets are in one respect like many modern ladies: let an action be never so trivial in itself, they always make it appear of the utmost importance. These machines I determined to raise on a very new and odd foundation, the Rosicrucian doctrine of Spirits.

I know how disagreeable it is to make use of hard words before a lady; but 'tis so much the concern of a Poet to have his works understood, and particularly by your Sex, that you must give me leave to explain two or three difficult terms.

The Rosicrucians are a people I must bring you acquainted with. The best account I know of them is in a French book call'd *Le Comte de Gabalis*,

Alexander Pope, "The Rape of the Lock." Copyright in the Public Domain.

which both in its title and size is so like a novel, that many of the fair sex have read it for one by mistake. According to these gentlemen, the four Elements are inhabited by spirits, which they call Sylphs, Gnomes, Nymphs, and Salamanders. The Gnomes or Dæmons of earth delight in mischief; but the Sylphs whose habitation is in the air, are the best-conditioned creatures imaginable. For they say, any mortals may enjoy the most intimate familiarities with these gentle Spirits, upon a condition very easy to all true Adepts, an inviolate preservation of Chastity.

As to the following cantos, all the passages of them are as fabulous, as the vision at the beginning, or the transformation at the end; (except the loss of your hair, which I always mention with reverence). The Human persons are as fictitious as the airy ones; and the character of Belinda, as it is now managed, resembles you in nothing but in beauty.

If this poem had as many graces as there are in your person, or in your mind, yet I could never hope it should pass thro' the world half so uncensured as you have done. But let its fortune be what it will, mine is happy enough, to have given me this occasion of assuring you that I am, with the truest esteem, Madam,

Your most obedient, Humble Servant,

A. Pope

Canto I

What dire offence from am'rous causes springs,
What mighty contests rise from trivial things,
I sing—This verse to Caryl, Muse! is due:
This, ev'n Belinda may vouchsafe to view:
5   Slight is the subject, but not so the praise,
If she inspire, and he approve my lays.
    Say what strange motive, Goddess! could compel
A well-bred lord t' assault a gentle belle?
Oh say what stranger cause, yet unexplored,
10 Could make a gentle belle reject a lord?
In tasks so bold, can little men engage,
And in soft bosoms dwells such mighty rage?
    Sol thro' white curtains shot a timorous ray,
And oped those eyes that must eclipse the day,
15 Now lap dogs give themselves the rousing shake,
And sleepless lovers, just at twelve, awake:
Thrice rung the bell, the slipper knock'd the ground,
And the press'd watch return'd a silver sound.
Belinda still her downy pillow pressed,
20 Her guardian Sylph prolong'd the balmy rest:
'Twas he had summoned to her silent bed
The morning dream that hover'd o'er her head.
A youth more glitt'ring than a birthnight beau,
(That ev'n in slumber caus'd her cheek to glow)
25 Seem'd to her ear his winning lips to lay,
And thus in whispers said, or seem'd to say:
    Fairest of mortals, thou distinguish'd care
Of thousand bright Inhabitants of air!
If e'er one vision touch'd thy infant thought,
Of all the nurse and all the priest have taught,
30 Of airy elves by moonlight shadows seen,
The silver token, and the circled green,
Or virgins visited by angel-pow'rs,
With golden crowns and wreaths of heav'nly flow'rs;
Hear and believe! thy own importance know,
35 Nor bound thy narrow views to things below.
Some secret truths, from learned pride conceal'd,
To maids alone and children are reveal'd:
What tho' no credit doubting wits may give?
The fair and innocent shall still believe.
40 Know, then, unnumber'd spirits round thee fly,
The light Militia of the lower sky:
These, tho' unseen, are ever on the wing,
Hang o'er the box, and hover round the Ring.
Think what an equipage thou hast in air,
45 And view with scorn two pages and a chair.
As now your own, our beings were of old,
And once enclos'd in woman's beauteous mold;
Thence, by a soft transition, we repair
From earthly vehicles to these of air.
50 Think not, when Woman's transient breath is fled
That all her vanities at once are dead:
Succeeding vanities she still regards,
And tho' she plays no more, o'erlooks the cards.
Her joy in gilded chariots, when alive,
55 And love of ombre, after death survive.
For when the Fair in all their pride expire,
To their first elements their souls retire:
The Sprites of fiery termagants in flame

  Mount up, and take a Salamander's name.
60 Soft yielding minds to water glide away,
 And sip, with Nymphs, their elemental tea.
 The graver Prude sinks downward to a Gnome,
 In search of mischief still on earth to roam.
 The light coquettes in Sylphs aloft repair,
65 And sport and flutter in the fields of air.
  "Know further yet; whoever fair and chaste
 Rejects mankind, is by some Sylph embrac'd:
 For Spirits, freed from mortal laws, with ease
 Assume what sexes and what shapes they please.
70 What guards the purity of melting maids,
 In courtly balls, and midnight masquerades,
 Safe from the treach'rous friend, the daring spark,
 The glance by day, the whisper in the dark,
 When kind occasion prompts their warm desires,
75 When music softens, and when dancing fires?
 'Tis but their Sylph, the wise Celestials know,
 Tho' Honour is the word with men below.
  "Some nymphs there are, too conscious of their face,
 For life predestin'd to the Gnomes' embrace.
80 These swell their prospects and exalt their pride,
 When offers are disdain'd, and love deny'd:
 Then gay ideas crowd the vacant brain,
 While peers, and dukes, and all their sweeping train,
 And garters, stars, and coronets appear,
85 And in soft sounds, 'your Grace' salutes their ear.
 'Tis these that early taint the female soul,
 Instruct the eyes of young Coquettes to roll,
 Teach infant cheeks a bidden blush to know,
 And little hearts to flutter at a beau.
90 "Oft, when the world imagine women stray,
 The Sylphs thro' mystic mazes guide their way,
 Thro' all the giddy circle they pursue,
 And old impertinence expel by new.
 What tender maid but must a victim fall
95 To one man's treat, but for another's ball?
 When Florio speaks what virgin could withstand,
 If gentle Damon did not squeeze her hand?
 With varying vanities, from ev'ry part,
 They shift the moving toyshop of their heart;
100 Where wigs with wigs, with sword-knots sword-knots strive,
 Beaux banish beaux, and coaches coaches drive.
 This erring mortals Levity may call;
 Oh blind to truth! the Sylphs contrive it all.
105 Of these am I, who thy protection claim,
 A watchful sprite, and Ariel is my name.
 Late, as I rang'd the crystal wilds of air,
 In the clear mirror of thy ruling star
 I saw, alas! some dread event impend,
110 Ere to the main this morning sun descend,
 But Heaven reveals not what, or how, or where:
 Warn'd by the Sylph, oh pious maid, beware!
 This to disclose is all thy guardian can:
 Beware of all, but most beware of Man!"
115 He said; when Shock, who thought she slept too long,
 Leaped up, and wak'd his mistress with his tongue.
 'Twas then, Belinda, if report say true,
 Thy eyes first open'd on a billet-doux;
 Wounds, charms, and ardors were no sooner read,
120 But all the vision vanish'd from thy head.
 And now, unveil'd, the toilet stands displayed,
 Each silver vase in mystic order laid.
 First, robed in white, the nymph intent adores,
 With head uncover'd, the cosmetic powers.
125 A heavenly image in the glass appears;
 To that she bends, to that her eyes she rears.
 Th' inferior priestess, at her altar's side,
 Trembling begins the sacred rites of Pride.
 Unnumbered treasures ope at once, and here
130 The various off'rings of the world appear;
 From each she nicely culls with curious toil,
 And decks the Goddess with the glitt'ring spoil.
 This casket India's glowing gems unlocks,
 And all Arabia breathes from yonder box.
135 The tortoise here and elephant unite,
 Transformed to combs, the speckled, and the white.
 Here files of pins extend their shining rows,
 Puffs, powders, patches, bibles, billet-doux.
 Now awful Beauty puts on all its arms;
140 The fair each moment rises in her charms,
 Repairs her smiles, awakens ev'ry grace,
 And calls forth all the wonders of her face;
 Sees by degrees a purer blush arise,
 And keener lightnings quicken in her eyes.
145 The busy Sylphs surround their darling care,
 These set the head, and those divide the hair,
 Some fold the sleeve, whilst others plait the gown;
 And Betty's prais'd for labours not her own.

Canto II

    Not with more glories, in th' etherial plain,
The Sun first rises o'er the purpled main,
Than, issuing forth, the rival of his beams
Launch'd on the bosom of the silver Thames.
5 Fair nymphs, and well-dressed youths around her shone,
But ev'ry eye was fix'd on her alone.
On her white breast a sparkling cross she wore,
Which Jews might kiss, and infidels adore.
Her lively looks a sprightly mind disclose,
10 Quick as her eyes, and as unfix'd as those:
Favours to none, to all she smiles extends;
Oft she rejects, but never once offends.
Bright as the sun, her eyes the gazers strike,
And, like the sun, they shine on all alike.
15 Yet graceful ease, and sweetness void of pride,
Might hide her faults, if Belles had faults to hide:
If to her share some female errors fall,
Look on her face, and you'll forget 'em all.
    This Nymph, to the destruction of mankind,
20 Nourish'd two locks, which graceful hung behind
In equal curls, and well conspir'd to deck
With shining ringlets the smooth ivory neck.
Love in these labyrinths his slaves detains,
And mighty hearts are held in slender chains.
25 With hairy springes we the birds betray,
Slight lines of hair surprise the finny prey,
Fair tresses man's imperial race ensnare,
And beauty draws us with a single hair.
    Th' advent'rous Baron the bright locks admir'd;
30 He saw, he wish'd, and to the prize aspir'd.
Resolv'd to win, he meditates the way,
By force to ravish, or by fraud betray;
For when success a lover's toil attends,
Few ask, if fraud or force attain'd his ends.
35   For this, ere Phœbus rose, he had implor'd
Propitious Heaven, and every power adored,
But chiefly Love—to Love an Altar built,
Of twelve vast French romances, neatly gilt.
There lay three garters, half a pair of gloves;
40 And all the trophies of his former loves:
With tender billet-doux he lights the pyre,
And breathes three am'rous sighs to raise the fire.
Then prostrate falls, and begs with ardent eyes
Soon to obtain, and long possess the prize:
45 The pow'rs gave ear, and granted half his pray'r,
The rest, the winds dispers'd in empty air.
    But now secure the painted vessel glides,
The sunbeams trembling on the floating tides,
While melting music steals upon the sky,
50 And soften'd sounds along the waters die;
Smooth flow the waves, the zephyrs gently play,
Belinda smil'd, and all the world was gay.
All but the Sylph—with careful thoughts oppressed,
Th' impending woe sat heavy on his breast.
He summons straight his denizens of air;
55 The lucid squadrons round the sails repair:
Soft o'er the shrouds aërial whispers breathe,
That seem'd but zephyrs to the train beneath.
Some to the sun their insect-wings unfold,
60 Waft on the breeze, or sink in clouds of gold;
Transparent forms too fine for mortal sight,
Their fluid bodies half dissolv'd in light,
Loose to the wind their airy garments flew,
Thin glitt'ring textures of the filmy dew,
65 Dipt in the richest tincture of the skies,
Where light disports in ever-mingling dyes,
While ev'ry beam new transient colours flings,
Colours that change whene'er they wave their wings.
Amid the circle, on the gilded mast,
70 Superior by the head, was Ariel plac'd;
His purple pinions opening to the sun,
He rais'd his azure wand, and thus begun:
    Ye Sylphs and Sylphids, to your chief give ear!
Fays, Fairies, Genii, Elves, and Dæmons, hear!
75 Ye know the spheres and various tasks assign'd
By laws eternal to th' aërial kind.
Some in the fields of purest æther play,
And bask and whiten in the blaze of day.
Some guide the course of wand'ring orbs on high,
80 Or roll the planets thro' the boundless sky.
Some less refin'd, beneath the moon's pale light
Pursue the stars that shoot athwart the night,
Or suck the mists in grosser air below,
Or dip their pinions in the painted bow,
85 Or brew fierce tempests on the wintry main,
Or o'er the glebe distil the kindly rain.
Others on earth o'er human race preside,
Watch all their ways, and all their actions guide:
Of these the chief the care of nations own,
90 And guard with arms divine the British Throne.
    Our humbler province is to tend the Fair,

    Not a less pleasing, tho' less glorious care:
    To save the powder from too rude a gale,
    Nor let th' imprison'd essences exhale;
95 To draw fresh colours from the vernal flow'rs
    To steal from rainbows e'er they drop in show'rs
    A brighter wash; to curl their waving hairs,
    Assist their blushes, and inspire their airs;
    Nay oft, in dreams, invention we bestow,
100 To change a Flounce, or add a Furbelow.
      "This day, black omens threat the brightest fair,
    That e'er deserv'd a watchful spirit's care;
    Some dire disaster, or by force, or slight;
    But what, or where, the fates have wrapt in night.
105 Whether the nymph shall break Diana's law,
    Or some frail China jar receive a flaw,
    Or stain her honour or her new brocade,
    Forget her pray'rs, or miss a masquerade,
    Or lose her heart, or necklace, at a ball;
110 Or whether Heav'n has doom'd that Shock must fall.
    Haste, then, ye spirits! to your charge repair:
    The flutt'ring fan be Zephyretta's care;
    The drops to thee, Brillante, we consign;
    And, Momentilla, let the watch be thine;
115 Do thou, Crispissa, tend her fav'rite Lock;
    Ariel himself shall be the guard of Shock.
      "To fifty chosen Sylphs, of special note,
    We trust th' important charge, the petticoat:
    Oft have we known that sevenfold fence to fail,
120 Tho' stiff with hoops, and arm'd with ribs of whale:
    Form a strong line about the silver bound,
    And guard the wide circumference around.
      Whatever spirit, careless of his charge,
    His post neglects, or leaves the fair at large,
125 Shall feel sharp vengeance soon o'ertake his sins,
    Be stopp'd in vials, or transfix'd with pins;
    Or plung'd in lakes of bitter washes lie,
    Or wedg'd whole ages in a bodkin's eye;
    Gums and pomatums shall his flight restrain,
130 While clogg'd he beats his silken wings in vain;
    Or alum styptics with contracting power
    Shrink his thin essence like a rivel'd flow'r:
    Or, as Ixion fix'd, the wretch shall feel
    The giddy motion of the whirling mill,
135 In fumes of burning chocolate shall glow,
    And tremble at the sea that froths below!"
      He spoke; the spirits from the sails descend;
    Some, orb in orb, around the nymph extend;
    Some thread the mazy ringlets of her hair;
140 Some hang upon the pendants of her ear:
    With beating hearts the dire event they wait,
    Anxious, and trembling for the birth of Fate.

Canto III

    Close by those meads, for ever crown'd with flow'rs,
    Where Thames with pride surveys his rising tow'rs,
    There stands a structure of majestic frame,
    Which from the neighb'ring Hampton takes its name.
5   Here Britain's statesmen oft the fall foredoom
    Of foreign tyrants and of nymphs at home;
    Here thou, great Anna! whom three realms obey.
    Dost sometimes counsel take—and sometimes tea.
      Hither the heroes and the nymphs resort,
10 To taste awhile the pleasures of a court;
    In various talk th' instructive hours they past,
    Who gave the ball, or paid the visit last;
    One speaks the glory of the British Queen,
    And one describes a charming Indian screen;
15 A third interprets motions, looks, and eyes;
    At ev'ry word a reputation dies.
    Snuff, or the fan, supply each pause of chat,
    With singing, laughing, ogling, and *all that*.
      Meanwhile, declining from the noon of day,
20 The sun obliquely shoots his burning ray;
    The hungry Judges soon the sentence sign,
    And wretches hang that jury-men may dine;
    The merchant from th' Exchange returns in peace,
    And the long labours of the Toilet cease.
25 Belinda now, whom thirst of fame invites,
    Burns to encounter two advent'rous Knights,
    At Ombre singly to decide their doom;
    And swells her breast with conquests yet to come.
    Straight the three bands prepare in arms to join,
30 Each band the number of the sacred nine.
    Soon as she spreads her hand, th' aërial guard
    Descend, and sit on each important card:
    First Ariel perch'd upon a Matadore,
    Then each, according to the rank they bore;
35 For Sylphs, yet mindful of their ancient race,
    Are, as when women, wondrous fond of place.
      Behold, four Kings in majesty rever'd,
    With hoary whiskers and a forky beard;
40 And four fair Queens whose hands sustain a flow'r,
    Th' expressive emblem of their softer pow'r;
    Four Knaves in garbs succinct, a trusty band,
    Caps on their heads, and halberts in their hand;

And particolour'd troops, a shining train,
Draw forth to combat on the velvet plain.
45 The skilful Nymph reviews her force with care:
Let Spades be trumps! she said, and trumps they were.
Now move to war her sable Matadores,
In show like leaders of the swarthy Moors.
Spadillio first, unconquerable Lord!
50 Led off two captive trumps, and swept the board.
As many more Manillio forc'd to yield,
And march'd a victor from the verdant field.
Him Basto follow'd, but his fate more hard
Gain'd but one trump and one Plebeian card.
55 With his broad sabre next, a chief in years,
The hoary Majesty of Spades appears,
Puts forth one manly leg, to sight reveal'd,
The rest, his many-colour'd robe conceal'd.
The rebel Knave, who dares his prince engage,
60 Proves the just victim of his royal rage.
Ev'n mighty Pam, that Kings and Queens o'erthrew
And mow'd down armies in the fights of Lu,
Sad chance of war! now destitute of aid,
Falls undistinguish'd by the victor spade!
65 Thus far both armies to Belinda yield;
Now to the Baron fate inclines the field.
His warlike Amazon her host invades,
Th' imperial consort of the crown of Spades.
The Club's black Tyrant first her victim dy'd,
70 Spite of his haughty mien, and barb'rous pride:
What boots the regal circle on his head,
His giant limbs, in state unwieldy spread;
That long behind he trails his pompous robe,
And, of all monarchs, only grasps the globe?
75 The Baron now his Diamonds pours apace;
Th' embroider'd King who shows but half his face,
And his refulgent Queen, with pow'rs combin'd
Of broken troops an easy conquest find.
Clubs, Diamonds, Hearts, in wild disorder seen,
80 With throngs promiscuous strow the level green.
Thus when dispers'd a routed army runs,
Of Asia's troops, and Afric's sable sons,
With like confusion different nations fly,
Of various habit, and of various dye,
85 The pierc'd battalions dis-united fall,
In heaps on heaps; one fate o'erwhelms them all.
The Knave of Diamonds tries his wily arts,
And wins (oh shameful chance!) the Queen of Hearts.
At this, the blood the virgin's cheek forsook,
90 A livid paleness spreads o'er all her look;
She sees, and trembles at th' approaching ill,
Just in the jaws of ruin, and Codille.
And now (as oft in some distemper'd State)
On one nice Trick depends the gen'ral fate.
95 An Ace of Hearts steps forth: The King unseen
Lurk'd in her hand, and mourn'd his captive Queen:
He springs to Vengeance with an eager pace,
And falls like thunder on the prostrate Ace.
The nymph exulting fills with shouts the sky;
100 The walls, the woods, and long canals reply.
Oh thoughtless mortals! ever blind to fate,
Too soon dejected, and too soon elate.
Sudden, these honours shall be snatch'd away,
And curs'd for ever this victorious day.
105 For lo! the board with cups and spoons is crown'd,
The berries crackle, and the mill turns round;
On shining Altars of Japan they raise
The silver lamp; the fiery spirits blaze:
110 From silver spouts the grateful liquors glide,
While China's earth receives the smoking tide:
At once they gratify their scent and taste,
And frequent cups prolong the rich repast.
Straight hover round the Fair her airy band;
115 Some, as she sipp'd, the fuming liquor fann'd,
Some o'er her lap their careful plumes display'd,
Trembling, and conscious of the rich brocade.
Coffee, (which makes the politician wise,
And see thro' all things with his half-shut eyes)
120 Sent up in vapours to the Baron's brain
New Stratagems, the radiant Lock to gain.
Ah cease, rash youth! desist ere't is too late,
Fear the just Gods, and think of Scylla's Fate!
Chang'd to a bird, and sent to flit in air,
She dearly pays for Nisus' injur'd hair!
125 But when to mischief mortals bend their will,
How soon they find fit instruments of ill!
Just then, Clarissa drew with tempting grace
A two-edg'd weapon from her shining case:
130 So Ladies in Romance assist their Knight,
Present the spear, and arm him for the fight.
He takes the gift with rev'rence, and extends
The little engine on his fingers' ends;
This just behind Belinda's neck he spread,
135 As o'er the fragrant steams she bends her head.
Swift to the Lock a thousand Sprites repair,
A thousand wings, by turns, blow back the hair;

And thrice they twitch'd the diamond in her ear;
Thrice she look'd back, and thrice the foe drew near.
140 Just in that instant, anxious Ariel sought
The close recesses of the Virgin's thought;
As on the nosegay in her breast reclin'd,
He watch'd th' ideas rising in her mind,
Sudden he view'd, in spite of all her art,
145 An earthly Lover lurking at her heart.
Amaz'd, confus'd, he found his pow'r expir'd,
Resign'd to fate, and with a sigh retir'd.
The Peer now spreads the glitt'ring Forfex wide,
T' inclose the Lock; now joins it, to divide.
150 Ev'n then, before the fatal engine clos'd,
A wretched Sylph too fondly interpos'd;
Fate urg'd the shears, and cut the Sylph in twain,
(But airy substance soon unites again)
The meeting points the sacred hair dissever
From the fair head, for ever, and for ever!
155 Then flash'd the living lightning from her eyes,
And screams of horror rend th' affrighted skies.
Not louder shrieks to pitying heav'n are cast,
When husbands, or when lapdogs breathe their last;
160 Or when rich China vessels fall'n from high,
In glitt'ring dust and painted fragments lie!
"Let wreaths of triumph now my temples twine"
The victor cry'd, the glorious Prize is mine!
While fish in streams, or birds delight in air,
165 Or in a coach and six the British Fair,
As long as Atalantis shall be read,
Or the small pillow grace a Lady's bed,
While visits shall be paid on solemn days,
When num'rous wax-lights in bright order blaze,
170 While nymphs take treats, or assignations give,
So long my honour, name, and praise shall live!
What Time would spare, from Steel receives its date,
And monuments, like men, submit to fate!
Steel could the labour of the Gods destroy,
175 And strike to dust th' imperial tow'rs of Troy;
Steel could the works of mortal pride confound,
And hew triumphal arches to the ground.
What wonder then, fair nymph! thy hairs should feel,
The conqu'ring force of unresisted Steel?

Canto IV

But anxious cares the pensive nymph oppress'd,
And secret passions labour'd in her breast.
Not youthful kings in battle seiz'd alive,
Not scornful virgins who their charms survive,
5 Not ardent lovers robb'd of all their bliss,
Not ancient ladies when refus'd a kiss,
Not tyrants fierce that unrepenting die,
Not Cynthia when her manteau's pinn'd awry,
E'er felt such rage, resentment, and despair,
10 As thou, sad Virgin! for thy ravish'd Hair.
For, that sad moment, when the Sylphs withdrew
And Ariel weeping from Belinda flew,
Umbriel, a dusky, melancholy sprite,
15 As ever sully'd the fair face of light,
Down to the central earth, his proper scene,
Repair'd to search the gloomy Cave of Spleen.
Swift on his sooty pinions flits the Gnome,
20 And in a vapour reach'd the dismal dome.
No cheerful breeze this sullen region knows,
The dreaded East is all the wind that blows.
Here in a grotto, shelter'd close from air,
And screen'd in shades from day's detested glare,
25 She sighs for ever on her pensive bed,
Pain at her side, and Megrim at her head.
Two handmaids wait the throne: alike in place,
But differing far in figure and in face.
30 Here stood Ill-nature like an ancient maid,
Her wrinkled form in black and white array'd;
With store of pray'rs, for mornings, nights, and noons,
Her hand is fill'd; her bosom with lampoons.
There Affectation, with a sickly mien,
35 Shows in her cheek the roses of eighteen,
Practis'd to lisp, and hang the head aside.
Faints into airs, and languishes with pride,
On the rich quilt sinks with becoming woe,
Wrapt in a gown, for sickness, and for show.
40 The fair ones feel such maladies as these,
When each new night-dress gives a new disease.
A constant vapour o'er the palace flies;
Strange phantoms rising as the mists arise;
45 Dreadful, as hermit's dreams in haunted shades,
Or bright, as visions of expiring maids.
Now glaring fiends, and snakes on rolling spires,

Pale spectres, gaping tombs, and purple fires:
Now lakes of liquid gold, Elysian scenes,
50 And crystal domes, and angels in machines.
   Unnumber'd throngs on every side are seen,
Of bodies chang'd to various forms by Spleen.
Here living teapots stand, one arm held out,
55 One bent; the handle this, and that the spout:
A Pipkin there, like Homer's Tripod walks;
Here sighs a Jar, and there a Goose-pie talks;
Men prove with child, as pow'rful fancy works,
And maids turn'd bottles, call aloud for corks.
60 Safe past the Gnome thro' this fantastic band,
A branch of healing Spleenwort in his hand.
Then thus address'd the Power: "Hail, wayward Queen!
Who rule the sex to fifty from fifteen:
65 Parent of vapours and of female wit,
Who give th' hysteric, or poetic fit,
On various tempers act by various ways,
Make some take physic, others scribble plays;
Who cause the proud their visits to delay,
70 And send the godly in a pet to pray.
A nymph there is, that all thy pow'r disdains,
And thousands more in equal mirth maintains.
But oh! if e'er thy Gnome could spoil a grace,
Or raise a pimple on a beauteous face,
75 Like citron-waters matrons cheeks inflame,
Or change complexions at a losing game;
If e'er with airy horns I planted heads,
Or rumpled petticoats, or tumbled beds,
Or caus'd suspicion when no soul was rude,
80 Or discompos'd the head-dress of a Prude,
Or e'er to costive lap-dog gave disease,
Which not the tears of brightest eyes could ease:
Hear me, and touch Belinda with chagrin,
That single act gives half the world the spleen."
85   The Goddess with a discontented air
Seems to reject him, tho' she grants his pray'r.
A wond'rous bag with both her hands she binds,
Like that where once Ulysses held the winds;
90 There she collects the force of female lungs,
Sighs, sobs, and passions, and the war of tongues.
A vial next she fills with fainting fears,
Soft sorrows, melting griefs, and flowing tears.
The Gnome rejoicing bears her gifts away,
95 Spreads his black wings, and slowly mounts to day.
   Sunk in Thalestris' arms the nymph he found,
Her eyes dejected and her hair unbound.
Full o'er their heads the swelling bag he rent,
100 And all the Furies issu'd at the vent.
Belinda burns with more than mortal ire,
And fierce Thalestris fans the rising fire.
"O wretched maid!" she spread her hands, and cry'd,
(While Hampton's echoes, "Wretched maid!" reply'd),
105 "Was it for this you took such constant care
The bodkin, comb, and essence to prepare?
For this your locks in paper durance bound,
For this with torturing irons wreath'd around?
For this with fillets strain'd your tender head,
110 And bravely bore the double loads of lead?
Gods! shall the ravisher display your hair,
While the Fops envy, and the Ladies stare!
Honour forbid! at whose unrivall'd shrine
Ease, pleasure, virtue, all our sex resign.
115 Methinks already I your tears survey,
Already hear the horrid things they say,
Already see you a degraded toast,
And all your honour in a whisper lost!
How shall I, then, your helpless fame defend?
120 'T will then be infamy to seem your friend!
And shall this prize, th' inestimable prize,
Expos'd thro' crystal to the gazing eyes,
And heighten'd by the diamond's circling rays,
On that rapacious hand for ever blaze?
125 Sooner shall grass in Hyde-park Circus grow,
And wits take lodgings in the sound of Bow;
Sooner let earth, air, sea, to Chaos fall,
Men, monkeys, lap-dogs, parrots, perish all!"
130   She said; then raging to Sir Plume repairs,
And bids her Beau demand the precious hairs;
(Sir Plume of amber snuff-box justly vain,
And the nice conduct of a clouded cane)
With earnest eyes, and round unthinking face,
135 He first the snuffbox open'd, then the case,
And thus broke out—"My Lord, why, what the devil?
Z—ds! damn the lock! 'fore Gad, you must be civil!
Plague on't! 't is past a jest—nay prithee, pox!
Give her the hair"—he spoke, and rapp'd his box.
140   "It grieves me much" reply'd the Peer again,
"Who speaks so well should ever speak in vain.
But by this Lock, this sacred Lock I swear,
(Which never more shall join its parted hair;
145 Which never more its honours shall renew,

Clipp'd from the lovely head where late it grew)
That while my nostrils draw the vital air,
This hand, which won it, shall for ever wear."
He spoke, and speaking, in proud triumph spread
150 The long-contended honours of her head.
But Umbriel, hateful Gnome! forbears not so;
He breaks the vial whence the sorrows flow.
Then see! the nymph in beauteous grief appears,
155 Her eyes half-languishing, halfdrown'd in tears;
On her heav'd bosom hung her drooping head,
Which, with a sigh, she rais'd; and thus she said.
    "Forever curs'd be this detested day,
Which snatch'd my best, my fav'rite curl away!
160 Happy! ah ten times happy had I been,
If Hampton Court these eyes had never seen!
Yet am not I the first mistaken maid,
By love of courts to num'rous ills betray'd.
Oh had I rather unadmired remain'd
165 In some lone isle, or distant Northern land;
Where the gilt Chariot never marks the way,
Where none learn ombre, none e'er taste bohea!
There kept my charms conceal'd from mortal eye,
Like roses, that in deserts bloom and die.
170 What mov'd my mind with youthful Lords to roam?
Oh had I stay'd, and said my pray'rs at home!
'Twas this, the morning omens seem'd to tell,
Thrice from my trembling hand the patch-box fell;
The tott'ring China shook without a wind.
175 Nay, Poll sat mute, and Shock was most unkind!
A Sylph too warn'd me of the threats of fate,
In mystic visions, now believ'd too late!
See the poor remnants of these slighted hairs!
My hands shall rend what ev'n thy rapine spares:
180 These in two sable ringlets taught to break,
Once gave new beauties to the snowy neck;
The sister-lock now sits uncouth, alone,
And in its fellow's fate foresees its own;
Uncurl'd it hangs, the fatal shears demands,
185 And tempts once more thy sacrilegious hands.
Oh hadst thou, cruel! been content to seize
Hairs less in sight, or any hairs but these!"

Canto V

She said: the pitying audience melt in tears.
But Fate and Jove had stopp'd the Baron's ears.
190 In vain Thalestris with reproach assails,
For who can move when fair Belinda fails?
Not half so fix'd the Trojan could remain,
While Anna begg'd and Dido rag'd in vain.
Then grave Clarissa graceful wav'd her fan;
195 Silence ensu'd, and thus the nymph began.
    "Say why are Beauties prais'd and honour'd most,
The wise man's passion, and the vain man's toast?
Why deck'd with all that land and sea afford,
Why Angels call'd, and Angel-like ador'd?
200 Why round our coaches crowd the white-glov'd beaux,
Why bows the side-box from its inmost rows;
How vain are all these glories, all our pains,
Unless good sense preserve what beauty gains:
That men may say, when we the front-box grace:
205 'Behold the first in virtue as in face!'
Oh! if to dance all night, and dress all day,
Charm'd the small-pox, or chas'd old-age away;
Who would not scorn what housewife's cares produce,
Or who would learn one earthly thing of use?
210 To patch, nay ogle, might become a Saint,
Nor could it sure be such a sin to paint.
But since, alas! frail beauty must decay,
Curl'd or uncurl'd, since locks will turn to grey;
Since painted, or not painted, all shall fade,
215 And she who scorns a man, must die a maid;
What then remains but well our pow'r to use,
And keep good-humour still whate'er we lose?
And trust me, dear! good humour can prevail,
When airs, and flights, and screams, and scolding fail.
220 Beauties in vain their pretty eyes may roll;
Charms strike the sight, but merit wins the soul."
So spoke the Dame, but no applause ensu'd;
Belinda frown'd, Thalestris call'd her Prude.
"To arms, to arms!" the fierce Virago cries,
225 And swift as lightning to the combat flies.
All side in parties, and begin th' attack;
Fans clap, silks rustle, and tough whalebones crack;
Heroes' and Heroines' shouts confus'dly rise,
And bass, and treble voices strike the skies.
230 No common weapons in their hands are found,
Like Gods they fight, nor dread a mortal wound.
    So when bold Homer makes the Gods engage,
And heav'nly breasts with human passions rage;
'Gainst Pallas, Mars; Latona, Hermes arms;
235 And all Olympus rings with loud alarms:
Jove's thunder roars, heav'n trembles all around,

Blue Neptune storms, the bellowing deeps resound:
Earth shakes her nodding tow'rs, the ground gives way.
And the pale ghosts start at the flash of day!
240   Triumphant Umbriel on a sconce's height
Clapp'd his glad wings, and sate to view the fight:
Propp'd on the bodkin spears, the Sprites survey
The growing combat, or assist the fray.
    While thro' the press enrag'd Thalestris flies,
245 And scatters death around from both her eyes,
A beau and Witling perish'd in the throng,
One died in metaphor, and one in song.
"O cruel nymph! a living death I bear,"
Cry'd Dapperwit, and sunk beside his chair.
250 A mournful glance Sir Fopling upwards cast,
"Those eyes are made so killing"—was his last.
Thus on Mæander's flow'ry margin lies
Th' expiring Swan, and as he sings he dies.
    When bold Sir Plume had drawn Clarissa down,
255 Chloe stepp'd in, and kill'd him with a frown;
She smil'd to see the doughty hero slain,
But, at her smile, the Beau reviv'd again.
Now Jove suspends his golden scales in air,
Weighs the Men's wits against the Lady's hair;
260 The doubtful beam long nods from side to side;
At length the wits mount up, the hairs subside.
    See, fierce Belinda on the Baron flies,
With more than usual lightning in her eyes:
Nor fear'd the Chief th' unequal fight to try,
265 Who sought no more than on his foe to die.
But this bold Lord with manly strength endu'd,
She with one finger and a thumb subdu'd:
Just where the breath of life his nostrils drew,
A charge of Snuff the wily virgin threw;
270 The Gnomes direct, to ev'ry atom just,
The pungent grains of titillating dust.
Sudden, with starting tears each eye o'erflows,
And the high dome re-echoes to his nose.
"Now meet thy fate," incens'd Belinda cry'd,
275 And drew a deadly bodkin from her side.
(The same, his ancient personage to deck,
Her great great grandsire wore about his neck,
In three seal-rings; which after, melted down,
Form'd a vast buckle for his widow's gown:
280 Her infant grandame's whistle next it grew,
The bells she jingled, and the whistle blew;
Then in a bodkin grac'd her mother's hairs,
Which long she wore, and now Belinda wears.)

    "Boast not my fall" he cry'd "insulting foe!
285 Thou by some other shalt be laid as low,
Nor think, to die dejects my lofty mind:
All that I dread is leaving you behind!
Rather than so, ah let me still survive,
And burn in Cupid's flames—but burn alive."
290   "Restore the Lock!" she cries; and all around
"Restore the Lock!" the vaulted roofs rebound.
Not fierce Othello in so loud a strain
Roar'd for the handkerchief that caus'd his pain.
But see how oft ambitious aims are cross'd,
295 And chiefs contend 'till all the prize is lost!
The lock, obtain'd with guilt, and kept with pain,
In ev'ry place is sought, but sought in vain:
With such a prize no mortal must be blessed,
So Heaven decrees! with Heaven who can contest?
300   Some thought it mounted to the lunar sphere,
Since all things lost on earth are treasur'd there.
There Hero's wits are kept in pond'rous vases,
And beau's in snuffboxes and tweezercases.
There broken vows and deathbed alms are found,
305 And lovers' hearts with ends of riband bound,
The courtier's promises, and sick man's pray'rs,
The smiles of harlots, and the tears of heirs,
Cages for gnats, and chains to yoke a flea,
Dry'd butterflies, and tomes of casuistry.
310   But trust the Muse—she saw it upward rise,
Tho' mark'd by none but quick, poetic eyes:
(So Rome's great founder to the heav'ns withdrew,
To Proculus alone confess'd in view);
A sudden star, it shot thro' liquid air,
315 And drew behind a radiant trail of hair.
Not Berenice's locks first rose so bright,
The heavens bespangling with dishevelled light.
The Sylphs behold it kindling as it flies,
And pleas'd pursue its progress thro' the skies.
320 This the beau monde shall from the Mall survey,
And hail with music its propitious ray.
This the blest lover shall for Venus take,
And send up vows from Rosamonda's Lake.
This Partridge soon shall view in cloudless skies,
325 When next he looks thro' Galileo's eyes;
And hence th' egregious wizard shall foredoom
The fate of Louis, and the fall of Rome.

Then cease, bright Nymph! to mourn thy ravish'd hair,
Which adds new glory to the shining sphere!
330 Not all the tresses that fair head can boast,
Shall draw such envy as the Lock you lost.
For, after all the murders of your eye,
When, after millions slain, yourself shall die:
When those fair suns shall set, as set they must,
335 And all those tresses shall be laid in dust,
This Lock, the Muse shall consecrate to fame,
And midst the stars inscribe Belinda's name.

An Essay on Criticism

Alexander Pope

Part I

'Tis hard to say, if greater want of skill
Appear in writing or in judging ill,
But of the two less dang'rous is th' offense
To tire our patience, than mislead our sense
5 Some few in that but numbers err in this,
Ten censure wrong for one who writes amiss;
A fool might once himself alone expose,
Now one in verse makes many more in prose.

'Tis with our judgments as our watches, none
10 Go just alike, yet each believes his own.
In poets as true genius is but rare
True taste as seldom is the critic's share
Both must alike from Heaven derive their light,
These born to judge, as well as those to write.
15 Let such teach others who themselves excel,
And censure freely who have written well.
Authors are partial to their wit, 'tis true,
But are not Critics to their judgment too?

Yet if we look more closely, we shall find
20 Most have the seeds of judgment in their mind
Nature affords at least a glimmering light
The lines, tho' touch'd but faintly, are drawn right,
But as the slightest sketch, if justly traced
Is by ill-colouring but the more disgraced
25 So by false learning is good sense defaced
Some are bewilder'd in the maze of schools
And some made coxcombs nature meant but fools
In search of wit these lose their common sense
And then turn Critics in their own defence
30 Each burns alike, who can, or cannot write
Or with a rival's, or an eunuch's spite
All fools have still an itching to deride,
And fain would be upon the laughing side.
If Mævius scribble in Apollo's spite,
35 There are who judge still worse than he can write.

Some have at first for wits, then poets past,
Turn'd Critics next, and prov'd plain fools at last.
Some neither can for wits nor critics pass,
As heavy mules are neither horse nor ass.
40 Those half-learn'd witlings, numerous in our isle,
As half-form'd insects on the banks of Nile
Unfinish'd things, one knows not what to call
Their generation's so equivocal
To tell them, would a hundred tongues require,
45 Or one vain wit's, that might a hundred tire.

But you who seek to give and merit fame,
And justly bear a Critic's noble name,

Alexander Pope, "An Essay on Criticism." Copyright in the Public Domain.

Be sure yourself and your own reach to know,
How far your genius, taste, and learning go;
50 Launch not beyond your depth, but be discreet,
And mark that point where sense and dulness meet.

Nature to all things fix'd the limits fit
And wisely curb'd proud man's pretending wit.
As on the land while here the ocean gains,
55 In other parts it leaves wide sandy plains
Thus in the soul while memory prevails,
The solid power of understanding fails
Where beams of warm imagination play,
The memory's soft figures melt away
60 One science only will one genius fit
So vast is art, so narrow human wit
Not only bounded to peculiar arts,
But oft in those confin'd to single parts.
Like kings we lose the conquests gain'd before,
65 By vain ambition still to make them more
Each might his sev'ral province well command,
Would all but stoop to what they understand.

First follow nature, and your judgment frame
By her just standard, which is still the same
70 Unerring nature, still divinely bright,
One clear, unchang'd, and universal light,
Life, force, and beauty, must to all impart,
At once the source, and end, and test of art.
Art from that fund each just supply provides,
75 Works without show, and without pomp presides:
In some fair body thus th' informing soul
With spirits feeds, with vigour fills the whole,
Each motion guides and ev'ry nerve sustains
Itself unseen, but in th' effects, remains.
80 Some, to whom Heaven in wit has been profuse,
Want as much more, to turn it to its use;
For wit and judgment often are at strife,
Tho' meant each other's aid, like man and wife.
'Tis more to guide, than spur the muse's steed
85 Restrain his fury, than provoke his speed
The winged courser, like a gen'rous horse,
Shows most true mettle when you check his course.

Those rules of old discovered, not devis'd,
Are nature still, but nature methodized;
90 Nature, like liberty, is but restrained
By the same laws which first herself ordain'd.

Hear how learn'd Greece her useful rules indites,
When to repress, and when indulge our flights:
High on Parnassus' top her sons she show'd,
95 And pointed out those arduous paths they trod;
Held from afar, aloft, th' immortal prize,
And urg'd the rest by equal steps to rise.
Just precepts thus from great examples giv'n,
She drew from them what they deriv'd from Heaven.
The generous critic fann'd the poet's fire,
100 And taught the world with reason to admire.
Then criticism the muse's handmaid prov'd,
To dress her charms, and make her more belov'd:
But following wits from that intention stray'd,
Who could not win the mistress, wooed the maid
105 Against the poets their own arms they turn'd,
Sure to hate most the men from whom they learn'd.
So modern 'pothecaries, taught the art
By doctor's bills to play the doctor's part
Bold in the practice of mistaken rules
110 Prescribe, apply, and call their masters fools.
Some on the leaves of ancient authors prey,
Nor time nor moths e'er spoiled so much as they.
Some dryly plain, without invention's aid,
Write dull receipts how poems may be made
115 These leave the sense their learning to display,
And those explain the meaning quite away.

You then whose judgment the right course would steer,
Know well each ancient's proper character
His fable, subject, scope in ev'ry page;
120 Religion, country, genius of his age
Without all these at once before your eyes,
Cavil you may, but never criticize.
Be Homers works your study and delight,
Read them by day, and meditate by night
125 Thence form your judgment, thence your maxims bring,
And trace the muses upward to their spring.
Still with itself compar'd, his text peruse,
And let your comment be the Mantuan Muse.

When first young Maro in his boundless mind,
130 A work t' outlast immortal Rome design'd,

Perhaps he seem'd above the critic's law,
And but from Nature's fountains scorn'd to draw
But when t' examine ev'ry part he came
Nature and Homer were he found, the same.
135 Convinc'd, amazed, he checks the bold design
And rules as strict his labour'd work confine
As if the Stagirite o'erlook'd each line.
Learn hence for ancient rules a just esteem;
To copy nature is to copy them.
140 Some beauties yet no Precepts can declare,
For there's a happiness as well as care.
Music resembles poetry, in each
Are nameless graces which no methods teach,
And which a master-hand alone can reach
If, where the rules not far enough extend,
145 (Since rules were made but to promote their end),
Some lucky licence answer to the full
Th' intent propos'd, that licence is a rule.
Thus Pegasus, a nearer way to take
May boldly deviate from the common track
150 From vulgar bounds with brave disorder part,
And snatch a grace beyond the reach of art,
Which without passing thro' the judgment, gains
The heart, and all its end at once attains.
In prospects thus, some objects please our eyes,
155 Which out of nature's common order rise,
The shapeless rock, or hanging precipice.
Great wits sometimes may gloriously offend,
And rise to faults true Critics dare not mend.
But tho' the Ancients thus their rules invade,
160 (As Kings dispense with laws themselves have made),
Moderns, beware! or if you must offend
Against the precept, ne'er transgress its end;
Let it be seldom, and compell'd by need,
And have, at least, their precedent to plead.
165 The critic else proceeds without remorse,
Seizes your fame, and puts his laws in force.

I know there are, to whose presumptuous thoughts
Those freer beauties, even in them, seem faults.
Some figures monstrous and misshap'd appear,
170 Consider'd singly, or beheld too near,
Which, but proportion'd to their light, or place,
Due distance reconciles to form and grace.
A prudent chief not always must display
His powers in equal ranks, and fair array.
175 But with th' occasion and the place comply,

Conceal his force, nay seem sometimes to fly.
Those oft are stratagems which error seem,
Nor is it Homer nods, but we that dream.
180 Still green with bays each ancient altar stands,
Above the reach of sacrilegious hands
Secure from flames, from envy's fiercer rage,
Destructive war, and all-involving age.
See, from each clime the learn'd their incense bring;
Hear, in all tongues consenting Pæans ring!
185 In praise so just let ev'ry voice be join'd,
And fill the general chorus of mankind.
Hail! bards triumphant! born in happier days;
Immortal heirs of universal praise!
Whose honours with increase of ages grow,
190 As streams roll down, enlarging as they flow;
Nations unborn your mighty names shall sound,
And worlds applaud that must not yet be found!
Oh may some spark of your celestial fire,
The last, the meanest of your sons inspire,
195 (That on weak wings, from far, pursues your flights;
Glows while he reads, but trembles as he writes),
To teach vain wits a science little known,
To admire superior sense, and doubt their own!

Part II

200 Of all the causes which conspire to blind
Man's erring judgment, and misguide the mind,
What the weak head with strongest bias rules,
Is Pride, the never-failing voice of fools.
Whatever nature has in worth denied,
She gives in large recruits of needful pride;
205 For as in bodies, thus in souls, we find
What wants in blood and spirits, swell'd with wind:
Pride, where wit fails, steps in to our defense,
And fills up all the mighty void of sense.
If once right reason drives that cloud away,
210 Truth breaks upon us with resistless day.
Trust not yourself: but your defects to know,
Make use of ev'ry friend—and ev'ry foe.

A little learning is a dang'rous thing;
Drink deep, or taste not the Pierian spring.
215 There shallow draughts intoxicate the brain,
And drinking largely sobers us again.
Fir'd at first sight with what the Muse imparts,

In fearless youth we tempt the heights of arts,
While from the bounded level of our mind
220 Short views we take, nor see the lengths behind;
But more advanc'd, behold with strange surprise
New distant scenes of endless science rise!
So pleas'd at first the tow'ring Alps we try,
Mount o'er the vales, and seem to tread the sky,
225 Th' eternal snows appear already past,
And the first clouds and mountains seem the last;
But, those attain'd, we tremble to survey
The growing labours of the lengthen'd way,
Th' increasing prospect tires our wand'ring eyes,
230 Hills peep o'er hills, and Alps on Alps arise!

A perfect Judge will read each work of Wit
With the same spirit that its author writ
Survey the whole, nor seek slight faults to find
Where Nature moves, and rapture warms the mind;
235 Nor lose, for that malignant dull delight,
The gen'rous pleasure to be charm'd with wit.
But in such lays as neither ebb, nor flow,
Correctly cold, and regularly low,
That shunning faults, one quiet tenour keep,
240 We cannot blame indeed—but we may sleep.
In wit, as nature, what affects our hearts
Is not th' exactness of peculiar parts;
'Tis not a lip, or eye, we beauty call,
But the joint force and full result of all.
245 Thus when we view some well-proportion'd dome,
(The world's just wonder, and ev'n thine, O Rome!)
No single parts unequally surprize,
All comes united to th' admiring eyes;
No monstrous height, or breadth, or length appear;
250 The whole at once is bold, and regular.

Whoever thinks a faultless piece to see,
Thinks what ne'er was, nor is, nor e'er shall be.
In every work regard the writer's end,
Since none can compass more than they intend;
255 And if the means be just, the conduct true,
Applause, in spight of trivial faults, is due:
As men of breeding, sometimes men of wit,
To avoid great errors, must the less commit,
Neglect the rules each verbal critic lays,
260 For not to know some trifles, is a praise.
Most critics, fond of some subservient art,
Still make the whole depend upon a part:
They talk of principles, but notions prize,
And all to one lov'd folly sacrifice.

265 Once on a time, La Mancha's knight, they say,
A certain bard encount'ring on the way,
Discours'd in terms as just, with looks as sage,
As e'er could Dennis of the Grecian stage;
Concluding all were desp'rate sots and fools,
270 Who durst depart from Aristotle's rules.
Our author, happy in a judge so nice,
Produc'd his play, and begg'd the knight's advice;
Made him observe the subject, and the plot,
The manners, passions, unities; what not?
275 All which, exact to rule, were brought about,
Were but a combat in the lists left out.
"What! leave the Combat out?" exclaims the knight:
"Yes, or we must renounce the Stagirite."
"Not so, by Heav'n" he answers in a rage,
280 "Knights, squires, and steeds, must enter on the stage."
"So vast a throng the stage can ne'er contain."
"Then build a new, or act it in a plain."

Thus critics, of less judgment than caprice,
Curious not knowing, not exact but nice,
285 Form short Ideas; and offend in arts
(As most in manners) by a love to parts.

Some to *conceit* alone their taste confine,
And glitt'ring thoughts struck out at ev'ry line;
Pleas'd with a work where nothing's just or fit,
290 One glaring chaos and wild heap of wit.
Poets like painters, thus, unskill'd to trace
The naked nature and the living grace,
With gold and jewels cover ev'ry part,
And hide with ornaments their want of art.
295 True wit is Nature to advantage dress'd,
What oft was thought, but ne'er so well expressed;
Something, whose truth convinc'd at sight we find,
That gives us back the image of our mind.
As shades more sweetly recommend the light,
300 So modest plainness sets off sprightly wit.
For works may have more wit than does 'em good,
As bodies perish thro' excess of blood.

Others for language all their care express,
And value books, as women men, for dress:
305 Their praise is still—the style is excellent:

The sense, they humbly take upon content.
Words are like leaves; and where they most abound,
Much fruit of sense beneath is rarely found.
False Eloquence, like the prismatic glass,
310 Its gaudy colours spreads on ev'ry place;
The face of Nature we no more survey,
All glares alike, without distinction gay.
But true expression, like th' unchanging sun,
Clears and improves whate'er it shines upon,
315 It gilds all objects, but it alters none.
Expression is the dress of thought, and still
Appears more decent, as more suitable:
A vile conceit in pompous words express'd
Is like a clown in regal purple dress'd:
320 For different styles with different subjects sort,
As several garbs with country, town, and court.
Some by old words to fame have made pretense,
Ancients in phrase, mere moderns in their sense
Such labour'd nothings, in so strange a style,
325 Amaze th' unlearn'd, and make the learned smile
Unlucky, as Fungoso in the play,
These sparks with awkward vanity display
What the fine gentleman wore yesterday;
And but so mimic ancient wits at best,
330 As apes our grandsire in their doublets dressed.
In words, as fashions, the same rule will hold;
Alike fantastic, if too new, or old.
Be not the first by whom the new are tried,
Nor yet the last to lay the old aside

335 But most by Numbers judge a poet's song
And smooth or rough, with them is right or wrong;
In the bright Muse though thousand charms conspire,
Her voice is all these tuneful fools admire,
Who haunt Parnassus but to please their ear,
340 Not mend their minds; as some to church repair,
Not for the doctrine, but the music there
These equal syllables alone require,
Though oft the ear the open vowes, tire;
While expletives their feeble aid do join;
345 And ten low words oft creep in one dull line,
While they ring round the same unvary'd chimes,
With sure returns of still expected rhymes,
Where e'er you find "the cooling western breeze,"
In the next line it "whispers through the trees"
350 If crystal streams "with pleasing murmurs creep"
The reader's threaten'd (not in vain) with "sleep"

Then, at the last and only couplet fraught
With some unmeaning thing they call a thought,
A needless Alexandrine ends the song
355 That, like a wounded snake, drags its slow length along.
Leave such to tune their own dull rhymes, and know
What's roundly smooth or languishingly slow;
And praise the easy vigour of a line,
Where Denham's strength, and Waller's sweetness join.
360 True ease in writing comes from art, not chance,
As those move easiest who have learn'd to dance.
'Tis not enough no harshness gives offence,
The sound must seem an Echo to the sense:
Soft is the strain when Zephyr gently blows,
365 And the smooth stream in smoother numbers flows,
But when loud surges lash the sounding shore,
The hoarse, rough verse should like the torrent roar,
When Ajax strives some rock's vast weight to throw,
The line too labours, and the words move slow;
370 Not so, when swift Camilla scours the plain,
Flies o'er th' unbending corn, and skims along the main.
Hear how Timotheus' varied lays surprise,
And bid alternate passions fall and rise!
While, at each change, the son of Libyan Jove
375 Now burns with glory, and then melts with love,
Now his fierce eyes with sparkling fury glow,
Now sighs steal out, and tears begin to flow:
Persians and Greeks like turns of nature found,
And the world's victor stood subdu'd by Sound!
380 The pow'r of music all our hearts allow,
And what Timotheus was, is Dryden now.

Avoid extremes; and shun the fault of such,
Who still are pleas'd too little or too much.
At ev'ry trifle scorn to take offence,
385 That always shows great pride, or little sense;
Those heads, as stomachs, are not sure the best,
Which nauseate all, and nothing can digest.
Yet let not each gay turn thy rapture move;
For fools admire, but men of sense approve:
390 As things seem large which we thro' mists descry,
Dullness is ever apt to magnify.

Some foreign writers, some our own despise;

The ancients only, or the moderns prize.
Thus wit, like faith, by each man is applied
395 To one small sect, and all are damn'd beside.
Meanly they seek the blessing to confine,
And force that sun but on a part to shine,
Which not alone the southern wit sublimes,
But ripens spirits in cold northern climes.
400 Which from the first has shone on ages past,
Enlights the present, and shall warm the last,
Tho' each may feel increases and decays,
And see now clearer and now darker days.
Regard not then if wit be old or new,
405 But blame the false, and value still the true.

Some ne'er advance a judgment of their own,
But catch the spreading notion of the town,
They reason and conclude by precedent,
And own stale nonsense which they ne'er invent.
410 Some judge of author's names, not works, and then
Nor praise nor blame the writings, but the men.
Of all this servile herd the worst is he
That in proud dullness joins with quality,
A constant critic at the great man's board,
415 To fetch and carry nonsense for my lord.
What woful stuff this madrigal would be,
In some starv'd hackney sonnetteer, or me!
But let a lord once own the happy lines,
How the wit brightens! how the style refines!
420 Before his sacred name flies ev'ry fault,
And each exalted stanza teems with thought!

The vulgar thus through imitation err;
As oft the learn'd by being singular.
So much they scorn the crowd that if the throng
425 By chance go right, they purposely go wrong:
So schismatics the plain believers quit,
And are but damn'd for having too much wit.

Some praise at morning what they blame at night,
But always think the last opinion right.
430 A muse by these is like a mistress used,
This hour she's idolized, the next abused;
While their weak heads like towns unfortified,
'Twixt sense and nonsense daily change their side.
Ask them the cause, they're wiser still, they say;
435 And still to-morrow's wiser than to-day.
We think our fathers fools, so wise we grow,
Our wiser sons, no doubt, will think us so.
Once school-divines this zealous isle o'erspread;
Who knew most Sentences, was deepest read,
440 Faith, Gospel, all, seem'd made to be disputed,
And none had sense enough to be confuted:
Scotists and Thomists, now, in peace remain,
Amidst their kindred cobwebs in Duck Lane.
If Faith itself has different dresses worn,
445 What wonder modes in wit should take their turn?
Oft,' leaving what is natural and fit,
The current folly proves the ready wit;
And authors think their reputation safe,
Which lives as long as fools are pleas'd to laugh.

450 Some valuing those of their own side or mind,
Still make themselves the measure of mankind:
Fondly we think we honor merit then,
When we but praise ourselves in other men.
455 Parties in wit attend on those of state,
And public faction doubles private hate.
Pride, malice, folly, against Dryden rose,
In various shapes of parsons, critics, Beaux;
But sense surviv'd, when merry jests were past;
For rising merit will buoy up at last.
460 Might he return, and bless once more our eyes,
New Blackmores and new Milbourns must arise:
Nay should great Homer lift his awful head,
Zoilus again would start up from the dead
Envy will merit, as its shade, pursue;
465 But like a shadow, proves the substance true;
For envied wit, like Sol eclipsed, makes known
Th' opposing body's grossness, not its own,
When first that sun too pow'rful beams displays,
It draws up vapours which obscure its rays,
470 But even those clouds at last adorn its way,
Reflect new glories, and augment the day.

Be thou the first true merit to befriend
His praise is lost, who stays, till all commend.
Short is the date, alas, of modern rhymes,
475 And 'tis but just to let them live betimes.
No longer now that golden age appears,
When Patriarch-wits surviv'd a thousand years:
Now length of Fame (our second life) is lost
And bare threescore is all ev'n that can boast,
480 Our sons their fathers' failing language see,
And such as Chaucer is, shall Dryden be,
So when the faithful pencil has designed

    Some bright Idea of the master's mind
    Where a new world leaps out at his command
485 And ready nature waits upon his hand
    When the ripe colours soften and unite
    And sweetly melt into just shade and light
    When mellowing years their full perfection give
    And each bold figure just begins to live
490 The treach'rous colours the fair art betray
    And all the bright creation fades away!

    Unhappy wit, like most mistaken things
    Atones not for that envy which it brings
    In youth alone its empty praise we boast,
495 But soon the short lived vanity is lost:
    Like some fair flower the early spring supplies.
    That gaily blooms, but ev'n in blooming dies.
    What is this Wit, which must our cares employ?
    The owner's wife, that other men enjoy
500 Then most our trouble still when most admir'd,
    And still the more we give, the more requir'd
    Whose fame with pains we guard, but lose with ease,
    Sure some to vex, but never all to please,
    'Tis what the vicious fear, the virtuous shun,
505 By fools 'tis hated, and by knaves undone!

    If wit so much from ignorance undergo,
    Ah let not learning too commence its foe!
    Of old, those met rewards who could excel,
    And such were praised who but endeavour'd well:
510 Tho' triumphs were to gen'rals only due,
    Crowns were reserv'd to grace the soldiers too.
    Now, they who reach Parnassus' lofty crown,
    Employ their pains to spurn some others down;
    And while self-love each jealous writer rules,
515 Contending wits become the sport of fools:
    But still the worst with most regret commend,
    For each ill author is as bad a friend
    To what base ends, and by what abject ways,
    Are mortals urg'd thro' sacred lust of praise!
520 Ah ne'er so dire a thirst of glory boast,
    Nor in the critic let the man be lost.
    Good-nature and good-sense must ever join;
    To err is human, to forgive, divine.

525 But if in noble minds some dregs remain
    Not yet purg'd off, of spleen and sour disdain;
    Discharge that rage on more provoking crimes,
    Nor fear a dearth in these flagitious times.
    No pardon vile obscenity should find,
    Tho' wit and art conspire to move your mind;
530 But dullness with obscenity must prove
    As shameful sure as impotence in love.
    In the fat age of pleasure, wealth, and ease
    Sprung the rank weed, and thriv'd with large increase:
    When love was all an easy monarch's care;
535 Seldom at council, never in a war
    Jilts rul'd the state, and statesmen farces writ;
    Nay wits had pensions, and young Lords had wit:
    The Fair sate panting at a Courtier's play,
    And not a mask went unimprov'd away:
540 The modest fan was lifted up no more,
    And virgins smil'd at what they blush'd before.
    The following licence of a foreign reign
    Did all the dregs of bold Socinus drain,
    Then unbelieving priests reform'd the nation,
545 And taught more pleasant methods of salvation;
    Where Heaven's free subjects might their rights dispute,
    Lest God himself should seem too absolute:
    Pulpits their sacred satire learn'd to spare,
    And vice admir'd to find a flatt'rer there!
550 Encourag'd thus, wit's Titans brav'd the skies,
    And the press groan'd with licens'd blasphemies.
    These monsters, critics! with your darts engage,
    Here point your thunder, and exhaust your rage!
    Yet shun their fault, who, scandalously nice,
555 Will needs mistake an author into vice;
    All seems infected that th' infected spy,
    As all looks yellow to the jaundic'd eye.

Part III

    Learn then what morals critics ought to show,
    For 'tis but half a judge's task, to know.
560 'Tis not enough, taste, judgment, learning, join;
    In all you speak, let truth and candour shine:
    That not alone what to your sense is due
    All may allow; but seek your friendship too.

    Be silent always when you doubt your sense;
565 And speak, tho' sure, with seeming diffidence:
    Some positive, persisting fops we know,
    Who, if once wrong, will needs be always so;

But you, with pleasure own your errors past,
And make each day a critic on the last.

570 'Tis not enough, your counsel still be true;
Blunt truths more mischief than nice falsehoods do;
Men must be taught as if you taught them not,
And things unknown propos'd as things forgot.
Without good breeding, truth is disapprov'd;
575 That only makes superior sense belov'd.

Be niggards of advice on no pretence;
For the worst avarice is that of sense.
With mean complacence ne'er betray your trust,
Nor be so civil as to prove unjust.
580 Fear not the anger of the wise to raise;
Those best can bear reproof, who merit praise.

'Twere well might critics still this freedom take,
But Appius reddens at each word you speak,
And stares, tremendous, with a threat'ning eye,
585 Like some fierce tyrant in old tapestry.
Fear most to tax an honourable fool,
Whose right it is, uncensur'd, to be dull;
Such, without wit, are poets when they please,
As without learning they can take degrees.
590 Leave dang'rous truths to unsuccessful satires,
And flattery to fulsome dedicators,
Whom, when they praise, the world believes no more,
Than when they promise to give scribbling o'er.
'Tis best sometimes your censure to restrain,
595 And charitably let the dull be vain:
Your silence there is better than your spite,
For who can rail so long as they can write?
Still humming on, their drowsy course they keep,
And lash'd so long, like tops, are lash'd asleep.
600 False steps but help them to renew the race,
As, after stumbling, jades will mend their pace.
What crowds of these, impenitently bold,
In sounds and jingling syllables grown old,
Still run on poets, in a raging vein,
605 Even to the dregs and squeezings of the brain,
Strain out the last dull droppings of their sense,
And rhyme with all the rage of Impotence.

Such shameless bards we have; and yet't is true,
There are as mad abandon'd critics too.
610 The bookful blockhead, ignorantly read,
With loads of learned lumber in his head,
With his own tongue still edifies his ears,
And always list'ning to himself appears.
All books he reads, and all he reads assails.
615 From Dryden's Fables down to Durfey's Tales.
With him, most authors steal their works, or buy;
Garth did not write his own Dispensary.
Name a new Play, and he's the Poet's friend,
Nay show'd his faults but when would Poets mend?
620 No place so sacred from such fops is barr'd,
Nor is Paul's Church more safe than Paul's Churchyard:
Nay, fly to Altars; there they'll talk you dead:
For Fools rush in where angels fear to tread
Distrustful sense with modest caution speaks,
625 It still looks home, and short excursions makes;
But rattling nonsense in full volleys breaks,
And never shock'd, and never turn'd aside,
Bursts out, resistless, with a thund'ring tide.

630 But where's the man, who counsel can bestow,
Still pleas'd to teach, and yet not proud to know?
Unbiased, or by favor, or by spite;
Not dully prepossess'd, nor blindly right;
Tho' learn'd, well-bred; and tho' well-bred, sincere,
Modestly bold, and humanly severe:
635 Who to a friend his faults can freely show,
And gladly praise the merit of a foe?
Blest with a taste exact, yet unconfin'd;
A knowledge both of books and human kind:
Gen'rous converse; a soul exempt from pride;
640 And love to praise, with reason on his side?

Such once were Critics; such the happy few,
Athens and Rome in better ages knew.
The mighty Stagirite first left the shore,
Spread all his sails, and durst the deeps explore:
645 He steer'd securely, and discover'd far,
Led by the light of the Mæonian Star.
Poets, a race long unconfin'd, and free,
Still fond and proud of savage liberty,
Receiv'd his laws; and stood convinc'd 'twas fit,
650 Who conquer'd Nature, should preside o'er Wit.

Horace still charms with graceful negligence,
And without method talks us into sense,
Will, like a friend, familiarly convey
The truest notions in the easiest way.

655 He, who supreme in judgment, as in wit,
Might boldly censure, as he boldly writ,
Yet judg'd with coolness, tho' he sung with fire;
His Precepts teach but what his works inspire.
Our critics take a contrary extreme
660 They judge with fury, but they write with phlegm:
Nor suffers Horace more in wrong translations
By wits, than critics in as wrong quotations.

See dionysius Homer's thoughts refine,
And call new beauties forth from every line!

665 Fancy and art in gay Petronius please,
The scholar's learning, with the courtier's ease.

In grave Quintilian's copious work, we find
The justest rules, and clearest method join'd:
Thus useful arms in magazines we place,
670 All rang'd in order, and dispos'd with grace,
But less to please the eye, than arm the hand,
Still fit for use, and ready at command.

Thee, bold Longinus! all the Nine inspire,
And bless their critic with a poet's fire.
675 An ardent judge, who zealous in his trust,
With warmth gives sentence, yet is always just;
Whose own example strengthens all his laws;
And is himself that great sublime he draws.

680 Thus long succeeding critics justly reign'd,
Licence repress'd, and useful laws ordain'd.
Learning and Rome alike in empire grew;
And Arts still follow'd where her eagles flew;
From the same foes, at last, both felt their doom,
And the same age saw Learning fall, and Rome.
685 With tyranny, then superstition join'd,
As that the body, this enslav'd the mind;
Much was believ'd, but little understood,
And to be dull was constru'd to be good;
A second deluge Learning thus o'er-run,
690 And the monks finish'd what the Goths begun.

At length Erasmus, that great injur'd name,
(The glory of the priesthood, and the shame!)
Stemm'd the wild torrent of a barbrous age,
And drove those holy Vandals off the stage.

695 But see! each muse, in Leo's golden days,
Starts from her trance, and trims her wither'd bays,
Rome's ancient genius, o'er its ruins spread,
Shakes off the dust, and rears his rev'rend head.
Then Sculpture and her sister arts revive;
700 Stones leap'd to form, and rocks began to live;
With sweeter notes each rising temple rung;
A Raphael painted, and a Vida sung.
Immortal Vida! on whose honour'd brow
The poet's bays and critic's ivy grow:
705 Cremona now shal ever boast thy name,
As next in place to Mantua, next in fame!

But soon by impious arms from Latium chas'd,
Their ancient bounds the banish'd muses pass'd;
Thence arts o'er all the northern world advance,
710 But critic-learning flourish'd most in France:
The rules a nation, born to serve, obeys;
And Boileau still in right of Horace sways.
But we, brave Britons, foreign laws despis'd,
And kept unconquer'd, and unciviliz'd;
715 Fierce for the liberties of wit, and bold,
We still defy'd the Romans, as of old.
Yet some there were, among the sounder few
Of those who less presum'd, and better knew,
Who durst assert the juster ancient cause,
720 And here restor'd wit's fundamental laws.
Such was the Muse, whose rules and practice tell,
"Nature's chief masterpiece is writing well.
Such was Roscommon, not more learn'd than good,
With manners gen'rous as his noble blood;
725 To him the wit of Greece and Rome was known,
And every author's merit, but his own.
Such late was Walsh the muse's judge and friend,
Who justly knew to blame or to commend
To failings mild, but zealous for desert;
730 The clearest head, and the sincerest heart.
This humble praise, lamented shade! receive,
This praise at least a grateful muse may give:
The muse, whose early voice you taught to sing,
Prescribed her heights, and pruned her tender wing,
735 (Her guide now lost) no more attempts to rise,
But in low numbers short excursions tries:
Content, if hence th' unlearn'd their wants may view,
The learned reflect on what before they knew
Careless of censure, nor too fond of fame,
740 Still pleas'd to praise, yet not afraid to blame,
Averse alike to flatter, or offend,
Not free from faults, nor yet too vain to mend.

Elegy Written in a Country Churchyard

Thomas Gray

The Curfew tolls the knell of parting day,
    The lowing herd wind slowly o'er the lea,
The plowman homeward plods his weary way,
    And leaves the world to darkness and to me.

5   Now fades the glimmering landscape on the sight,
    And all the air a solemn stillness holds,
Save where the beetle wheels his droning flight,
    And drowsy tinklings lull the distant folds;

Save that from yonder ivy-mantled tower
10   The moping owl does to the moon complain
Of such, as wandering near her secret bower,
    Molest her ancient solitary reign.

Beneath those rugged elms, that yew-tree's shade,
    Where heaves the turf in many a mouldering heap,
15   Each in his narrow cell for ever laid,
    The rude forefathers of the hamlet sleep.

The breezy call of incense-breathing morn,
    The swallow twittering from the straw-built shed,
The cock's shrill clarion, or the echoing horn,
20   No more shall rouse them from their lowly bed.

For them no more the blazing hearth shall burn,
    Or busy housewife ply her evening care;
No children run to lisp their sire's return,
    Or climb his knees the envied kiss to share.

25   Oft did the harvest to their sickle yield,
    Their furrow oft the stubborn glebe has broke;
How jocund did they drive their team afield!
    How bowed the woods beneath their sturdy stroke!

Let not Ambition mock their useful toil,
30   Their homely joys, and destiny obscure;
Nor Grandeur hear with a disdainful smile
    The short and simple annals of the poor.

The boast of heraldry, the pomp of power,
    And all that beauty, all that wealth e'er gave,
35   Awaits alike the inevitable hour:
    The paths of glory lead but to the grave.

Nor you, ye proud, impute to these the fault,
    If memory o'er their tomb no trophies raise,
Where through the long-drawn aisle and
    Little Lamb God bless thee fretted vault
40   The pealing anthem swells the note of praise.

Can storied urn or animated bust
    Back to its mansion call the fleeting breath?
Can Honour's voice provoke the silent dust,
    Or Flattery soothe the dull cold ear of Death?

45   Perhaps in this neglected spot is laid
    Some heart once pregnant with celestial fire;
Hands that the rod of empire might have swayed,
    Or waked to ecstasy the living lyre.
But Knowledge to their eyes her ample page
50   Rich with the spoils of time did ne'er unroll;
Chill Penury repressed their noble rage,
    And froze the genial current of the soul.

Full many a gem of purest ray serene
    The dark unfathomed caves of ocean bear:
55   Full many a flower is born to blush unseen,
    And waste its sweetness on the desert air.

Thomas Gray, "Elegy Written in a Country Churchyard." Copyright in the Public Domain.

Some village Hampden, that with dauntless breast
　　The little tyrant of his fields withstood;
Some mute inglorious Milton here may rest,
60　　Some Cromwell guiltless of his country's blood.

The applause of listening senates to command,
　　The threats of pain and ruin to despise,
To scatter plenty o'er a smiling land,
　　And read their history in a nation's eyes,

65　Their lot forbade: nor circumscribed alone
　　Their glowing virtues, but their crimes confined;
Forbade to wade through slaughter to a throne,
　　And shut the gates of mercy on mankind,

The struggling pangs of conscious truth to hide,
70　　To quench the blushes of ingenuous shame,
Or heap the shrine of Luxury and Pride
　　With incense kindled at the Muse's flame.

Far from the madding crowd's ignoble strife,
　　Their sober wishes never learned to stray;
75　Along the cool sequestered vale of life
　　They kept the noiseless tenor of their way.

Yet even these bones from insult to protect
　　Some frail memorial still erected nigh,
With uncouth rhymes and shapeless sculpture decked,
80　　Implores the passing tribute of a sigh.

Their name, their years, spelt by the unlettered Muse,
　　The place of fame and elegy supply:
And many a holy text around she strews,
　　That teach the rustic moralist to die.

85　For who, to dumb Forgetfulness a prey,
　　This pleasing anxious being e'er resigned,
Left the warm precincts of the cheerful day,
　　Nor cast one longing ling'ring look behind?
On some fond breast the parting soul relies,
90　　Some pious drops the closing eye requires;
Even from the tomb the voice of Nature cries,
　　Even in our Ashes live their wonted Fires.

For thee, who, mindful of the unhonored dead,
　　Dost in these lines their artless tale relate;
95　If chance, by lonely contemplation led,
　　Some kindred spirit shall inquire thy fate,

Haply some hoary-headed swain may say,
　　"Oft have we seen him at the peep of dawn
Brushing with hasty steps the dews away
100　　To meet the sun upon the upland lawn.

"There at the foot of yonder nodding beech
　　That wreathes its old fantastic roots so high,
His listless length at noontide would he stretch,
　　And pore upon the brook that babbles by.

105　"Hard by yon wood, now smiling as in scorn,
　　Muttering his wayward fancies he would rove,
Now drooping, woeful wan, like one forlorn,
　　Or crazed with care, or crossed in hopeless love.

"One morn I missed him on the customed hill,
110　　Along the heath and near his favorite tree;
Another came; nor yet beside the rill,
　　Nor up the lawn, nor at the wood was he;
" he next with dirges due in sad array
　　Slow through the church way path we saw him borne.
115　Approach and read (for thou canst read) the lay
　　Graved on the stone beneath yon aged thorn:"

The Epitaph.

Here rests his head upon the lap of Earth
　　A youth to Fortune and to Fame unknown.
Fair Science frowned not on his humble birth,
120　　And Melancholy marked him for her own.
Large was his bounty, and his soul sincere,
　　Heaven did a recompense as largely send:
He gave to Misery all he had, a tear,
　　He gained from Heaven ('twas all he wished) a friend.
125　No farther seek his merits to disclose,
　　Or draw his frailties from their dread abode
(There they alike in trembling hope repose),
　　The bosom of his Father and his God.

The Lamb

William Blake

    Little Lamb, who made thee?
    Dost thou know who made thee?
Gave thee life & bid thee feed,
By the stream & o'er the mead;
5 Gave thee clothing of delight,
Softest clothing wooly bright;
Gave thee such a tender voice,
Making all the vales rejoice!
    Little Lamb who made thee?
10   Dost thou know who made thee?

    Little Lamb I'll tell thee,
    Little Lamb I'll tell thee!
He is calléd by thy name,
For he calls himself a Lamb:
15 He is meek & he is mild,
He became a little child:
I a child & thou a lamb,
We are called by his name.
    Little Lamb God bless thee!
    Little Lamb God bless thee!

1789

William Blake, "The Lamb", from *Songs of Innocence*. Copyright in the Public Domain.

The Tyger

William Blake

Tyger! Tyger! burning bright
In the forests of the night,
What immortal hand or eye
Could frame thy fearful symmetry?

5 In what distant deeps or skies

Burnt the fire of thine eyes?
On what wings dare he aspire?
What the hand dare seize the fire?

And what shoulder, & what art,
10 Could twist the sinews of thy heart?

William Blake, "The Tyger," from *Songs of Experience*. Copyright in the Public Domain.

And when thy heart began to beat,
What dread hand? & what dread feet?

What the hammer? what the chain?
In what furnace was thy brain?
15 What the anvil? what dread grasp
Dare its deadly terrors clasp?

When the stars threw down their spears
And water'd heaven with their tears,
20 Did he smile his work to see?
Did he who made the Lamb make thee?

Tyger! Tyger! burning bright
In the forests of the night,
What immortal hand or eye
Dare frame thy fearful symmetry?
—1790–92
1794

London

William Blake

I wander thro' each charter'd street,
Near where the charter'd Thames does flow,
And mark in every face I meet
Marks of weakness, marks of woe.

5 In every cry of every man,
In every Infant's cry of fear,
In every voice, in every ban,[1]
The mind-forg'd manacles I hear.

How the Chimney-sweeper's cry
10 Every blackning Church appalls;
And the hapless Soldier's sigh
Runs in blood down Palace walls.

But most thro' midnight streets I hear
How the youthful Harlot's curse
15 Blasts the new-born Infant's tear,[2]
And blights with plagues the Marriage hearse.[3]
1794

---

[1] The various meanings of "ban" are relevant (political and legal prohibition, curse, public condemnation) as well as "banns" (marriage proclamation).

[2] Most critics read this line as implying prenatal blindness, resulting from a parent's venereal disease (the "plagues" of line 16) by earlier infection from the harlot.

[3] In the older sense of "hearse": converts the marriage bed into a bier. Or possibly, since the current sense of the word had also come into use in Blake's day, "converts the marriage coach into a funeral hearse."

William Blake, "London," from *Songs of Experience*. Copyright in the Public Domain.

Lines Composed a Few Miles Above Tintern Abbey

William Wordsworth

On Revisiting the Banks of the Wye During a Tour, July 13, 1798.

    Five years have past; five summers, with the length
    Of five long winters! and again I hear
    These waters, rolling from their mountain-springs
    With a soft inland murmur.—Once again
5   Do I behold these steep and lofty cliffs,
    That on a wild secluded scene impress
    Thoughts of more deep seclusion; and connect
    The landscape with the quiet of the sky.
    The day is come when I again repose
10   Here, under this dark sycamore, and view
    These plots of cottage-ground, these orchard-tufts,
    Which at this season, with their unripe fruits,
    Are clad in one green hue, and lose themselves
    'Mid groves and copses. Once again I see
15   These hedge-rows, hardly hedge-rows, little lines
    Of sportive wood run wild: these pastoral farms,
    Green to the very door; and wreaths of smoke
    Sent up, in silence, from among the trees!
    With some uncertain notice, as might seem
20   Of vagrant dwellers in the houseless woods,
    Or of some Hermit's cave, where by his fire
    The Hermit sits alone.

              These beauteous forms,
    Through a long absence, have not been to me
    As is a landscape to a blind man's eye;
25   But oft, in lonely rooms, and 'mid the din
    Of towns and cities, I have owed to them
    In hours of weariness, sensations sweet,
    Felt in the blood, and felt along the heart;
    And passing even into my purer mind,
30   With tranquil restoration—feelings too
    Of unremembered pleasure: such, perhaps,
    As have no slight or trivial influence
    On that best portion of a good man's life,
    His little, nameless, unremembered, acts
35   Of kindness and of love. Nor less, I trust,
    To them I may have owed another gift,
    Of aspect more sublime; that blessed mood,
    In which the burthen of the mystery,
    In which the heavy and the weary weight
40   Of all this unintelligible world,
    Is lightened:—that serene and blessed mood,
    In which the affections gently lead us on,—
    Until, the breath of this corporeal frame
    And even the motion of our human blood
45   Almost suspended, we are laid asleep
    In body, and become a living soul;
    While with an eye made quiet by the power
    Of harmony, and the deep power of joy,
    We see into the life of things.

William Wordsworth, "Tintern Abbey," from *Lyrical Ballads, With a Few Other Poems.* Copyright in the Public Domain.

            If this
50 Be but a vain belief, yet, oh! how oft—
   In darkness and amid the many shapes
   Of joyless daylight; when the fretful stir
   Unprofitable, and the fever of the world,
   Have hung upon the beatings of my heart—
55 How oft, in spirit, have I turned to thee,
   O sylvan Wye! thou wanderer thro' the woods,
   How often has my spirit turned to thee!
   And now, with gleams of half-extinguished thought,
   With many recognitions dim and faint,
60 And somewhat of a sad perplexity,
   The picture of the mind revives again;
   While here I stand, not only with the sense
   Of present pleasure, but with pleasing thoughts
   That in this moment there is life and food
65 For future years. And so I dare to hope,
   Though changed, no doubt, from what I was when first
   I came among these hills; when like a roe
   I bounded o'er the mountains, by the sides
   Of the deep rivers, and the lonely streams,
70 Wherever nature led—more like a man
   Flying from something that he dreads, than one
   Who sought the thing he loved. For nature then
   (The coarser pleasures of my boyish days,
   And their glad animal movements all gone by)
75 To me was all in all.—I cannot paint
   What then I was. The sounding cataract
   Haunted me like a passion; the tall rock,
   The mountain, and the deep and gloomy wood,
   Their colours and their forms, were then to me
80 An appetite; a feeling and a love,
   That had no need of a remoter charm,
   By thought supplied, nor any interest
   Unborrowed from the eye.—That time is past,
   And all its aching joys are now no more,
85 And all its dizzy raptures.[1] Not for this
   Faint[2] I, nor mourn nor murmur; other gifts
   Have followed; for such loss, I would believe,
   Abundant recompense. For I have learned
   To look on nature, not as in the hour
90 Of thoughtless youth; but hearing oftentimes
   The still, sad music of humanity,
   Nor harsh nor grating, though of ample power
   To chasten and subdue. And I have felt
   A presence that disturbs me with the joy
95 Of elevated thoughts; a sense sublime
   Of something far more deeply interfused,
   Whose dwelling is the light of setting suns,
   And the round ocean and the living air,
   And the blue sky, and in the mind of man:
100 A motion and a spirit, that impels
   All thinking things, all objects of all thought,
   And rolls through all things. Therefore am I still
   A lover of the meadows and the woods,
   And mountains; and of all that we behold
105 From this green earth; of all the mighty world
   Of eye, and ear,—both what they half create,[3]
   And what perceive; well pleased to recognize

---

[1] Lines 66ff. contain Wordsworth's famed description of the three stages of his growing up, defined in terms of his evolving relations to the natural scene: the young boy's purely physical responsiveness (lines 73–74); the postadolescent's aching, dizzy, and equivocal passions—a love that is more like dread (lines 67–72, 75–85: this was his state of mind on the occasion of his first visit); his present state (lines 85ff.), in which for the first time he adds thought to sense.

[2] Lose heart.

[3] This view that the "creative sensibility" contributes to its own perceptions is often reiterated in *The Prelude*.

In nature and the language of the sense,
The anchor of my purest thoughts, the nurse,
110 The guide, the guardian of my heart, and soul
Of all my moral being.

                Nor perchance,
If I were not thus taught, should I the more
Suffer my genial spirits[4] to decay:
For thou art with me here upon the banks
115 Of this fair river; thou my dearest Friend,[5]
My dear, dear Friend; and in thy voice I catch
The language of my former heart, and read
My former pleasures in the shooting lights
Of thy wild eyes. Oh! yet a little while
120 May I behold in thee what I was once,
My dear, dear Sister! and this prayer I make,
Knowing that Nature never did betray
The heart that loved her; 'tis her privilege,
Through all the years of this our life, to lead
125 From joy to joy: for she can so inform
The mind that is within us, so impress
With quietness and beauty, and so feed
With lofty thoughts, that neither evil tongues,
Rash judgments, nor the sneers of selfish men,
130 Nor greetings where no kindness is, nor all
The dreary intercourse of daily life,
Shall e'er prevail against us, or disturb
Our cheerful faith, that all which we behold
Is full of blessings. Therefore let the moon
135 Shine on thee in thy solitary walk;
And let the misty mountain winds be free
To blow against thee: and, in after years,
When these wild ecstasies shall be matured
Into a sober pleasure; when thy mind
140 Shall be a mansion for all lovely forms,
Thy memory be as a dwelling place
For all sweet sounds and harmonies; oh! then,
If solitude, or fear, or pain, or grief
Should be thy portion, with what healing thoughts
145 Of tender joy wilt thou remember me,
And these my exhortations! Nor, perchance—
If I should be where I no more can hear
Thy voice, nor catch from thy wild eyes these gleams
Of past existence[6]—wilt thou then forget
150 That on the banks of this delightful stream
We stood together; and that I, so long
A worshipper of Nature, hither came
Unwearied in that service; rather say
With warmer love—oh! with far deeper zeal
155 Of holier love. Nor wilt thou then forget,
That after many wanderings, many years
Of absence, these steep woods and lofty cliffs,
And this green pastoral landscape, were to me
More dear, both for themselves and for thy sake!

                            July 1798
                                1798

---

[4] Creative powers. ("Genial" is here the adjectival form of the noun "genius.")

[5] His sister, Dorothy.

[6] I.e., reminders of his own "past existence" five years earlier (see lines 116–19).

The World is Too Much With Us

William Wordsworth

The world is too much with us; late and soon,
Getting and spending, we lay waste our powers;
Little we see in Nature that is ours;
We have given our hearts away, a sordid boon![1]
5 This Sea that bares her bosom to the moon;
The winds that will be howling at all hours,
And are up-gathered now like sleeping flowers;
10 For this, for everything, we are out of tune;
It moves us not.—Great God! I'd rather be
A Pagan suckled in a creed outworn;
So might I, standing on this pleasant lea,
Have glimpses that would make me less forlorn;
Have sight of Proteus rising from the sea;
Or hear old Triton blow his wreathed horn.

1802–04
1807

---

[1] Gift; it is the act of giving the heart away that is sordid.

William Wordsworth, "The World is Too Much With Us," from *Poems in Two Volumes*. Copyright in the Public Domain.

London, 1802

William Wordsworth

Milton! thou shouldst be living at this hour:[1]
England hath need of thee: she is a fen
Of stagnant waters: altar, sword, and pen,
Fireside, the heroic wealth of hall and bower,
5 Have forfeited their ancient English dower
Of inward happiness. We are selfish men;
Oh! raise us up, return to us again;

---

[1] One of a series "written immediately after my return from France to London, when I could not but be struck, as here described, with the vanity and parade of our own country...as contrasted with the quiet, and I may say the desolation, that the revolution had produced in France" [Wordsworth's note].

William Wordsworth, "London, 1802," from *Poems in Two Volumes*. Copyright in the Public Domain.

And give us manners, virtue, freedom, power.
Thy soul was like a Star, and dwelt apart;
10 Thou hadst a voice whose sound was like the sea:
Pure as the naked heavens, majestic, free,
So didst thou travel on life's common way,
In cheerful godliness; and yet thy heart
The lowliest duties on herself did lay.

        Sept.1802
        1807

Composed upon Westminster Bridge, September 3, 1802

William Wordsworth

Earth has not any thing to show more fair:[1]
Dull would he be of soul who could pass by
A sight so touching in its majesty;
This City now doth, like a garment, wear
5 The beauty of the morning; silent, bare,
Ships, towers, domes, theatres, and temples lie
Open unto the fields, and to the sky;
All bright and glittering in the smokeless air.
Never did sun more beautifully steep
10 In his first splendour, valley, rock, or hill;
Ne'er saw I, never felt, a calm so deep!
The river glideth at his own sweet will:
Dear God! the very houses seem asleep;
And all that mighty heart is lying still!

        1802
        1807

---

[1] The date of this experience was not Sept. 3, but July 31, 1802; its occasion was a trip to France (see Dorothy Wordsworth's *Grasmere Journals,* July 1802, p. 297). The conflict of feelings attending Wordsworth's brief return to France, where he had once been a revolutionist and the lover of Annette Vallon, evoked a number of personal and political sonnets, among them the two that follow.

William Wordsworth, "Composed Upon Westminster Bridge," from *Poems in Two Volumes*. Copyright in the Public Domain.

Ode on a Grecian Urn

John Keats

Thou still unravished bride of quietness,[1]
    Thou foster-child of silence and slow time,
Sylvan[2] historian, who canst thus express
    A flowery tale more sweetly than our rhyme:
5 What leaf-fringed legend haunts about thy shape
    Of deities or mortals, or of both,
        In Tempe or the dales of Arcady?[3]
    What men or gods are these? What maidens loth?
What mad pursuit? What struggle to escape?
10   What pipes and timbrels? What wild ecstasy?

Heard melodies are sweet, but those unheard
    Are sweeter; therefore, ye soft pipes, play on;
Not to the sensual ear,[4] but, more endeared,
    Pipe to the spirit ditties of no tone:
15 Fair youth, beneath the trees, thou canst not leave
    Thy song, nor ever can those trees be bare;
        Bold lover, never, never canst thou kiss,
Though winning near the goal—yet, do not grieve;
    She cannot fade, though thou hast not thy bliss,
20   For ever wilt thou love, and she be fair!

Ah, happy, happy boughs! that cannot shed
    Your leaves, nor ever bid the spring adieu;
And, happy melodist, unweariéd,
    For ever piping songs for ever new;
25 More happy love! more happy, happy love!
    For ever warm and still to be enjoy'd,
    For ever panting, and for ever young;
All breathing human passion far above,
    That leaves a heart high-sorrowful and cloyed,

---

[1] This urn, with its sculptured reliefs of Dionysian ecstasies, panting young lovers in flight and pursuit, a pastoral piper under spring foliage, and the quiet procession of priest and townspeople, resembles parts of various vases, sculptures, and paintings, but it existed in all its particulars only in Keats's imagination. In the urn—which captures moments of intense experience in attitudes of grace and immobilizes them in marble—Keats found the perfect correlative for his concern with the longing for permanence in a world of change. The interpretation of the details with which he develops this concept, however, is hotly disputed, all the way from the opening phrase—is "still" an adverb ("as yet") or an adjective ("motionless")?—to the two concluding lines, which have already accumulated as much critical dis¬cussion as the "two-handed engine" in Milton's Lycidas or the cruxes in Shakespeare's plays. These disputes testify to the enigmatic richness of meaning in the five stanzas, as well as to the fact that the ode has become a central point of reference in the criticism of the English lyric.

[2] Rustic, representing a woodland scene.

[3] The valleys of Arcadia, a state in ancient Greece often used as a symbol of the pastoral ideal. "Tempe": a beautiful valley in Greece that has come to represent supreme rural beauty.

[4] The ear of sense (as opposed to that of the "spirit," or imagination).

John Keats, "Ode on a Grecian Urn." Copyright in the Public Domain.

30 A burning forehead, and a parching tongue.

Who are these coming to the sacrifice?
　　To what green altar, O mysterious priest,
Lead'st thou that heifer lowing at the skies,
　　And all her silken flanks with garlands dressed?
35 What little town by river or sea shore,
　　Or mountain-built with peaceful citadel,
　　　Is emptied of this folk, this pious morn?
And, little town, thy streets forevermore
　　Will silent be; and not a soul to tell
40 　　　Why thou art desolate, can e'er return.

O Attic[5] shape! Fair attitude! with brede
　　Of marble men and maidens overwrought,[6]
With forest branches and the trodden weed;
　　Thou, silent form, dost tease us out of thought
45 As doth eternity: Cold Pastoral!
　　When old age shall this generation waste,
　　　Thou shalt remain, in midst of other woe
Than ours, a friend to man, to whom thou say'st,
"Beauty is truth, truth beauty,"[7]—that is all
50 　　　Ye know on earth, and all ye need to know.
　　　　　　　　　　　　　　　　1819
　　　　　　　　　　　　　　　　1820

---

[5] Greek. Attica was the region of Greece in which Athens was located.

[6] Ornamented all over ("overwrought") with an interwoven pattern ("brede").

[7] The quotation marks around this phrase are found in the volume of poems Keats published in 1820, but there are no quotation marks in the version printed in *Annals of the Fine Arts* that same year or in the transcripts of the poem made by Keats's friends. This discrepancy has multiplied the diversity of critical interpretations of the last two lines. Critics disagree whether the whole of these lines is said by the urn, or "Beauty is truth, truth beauty" by the urn and the rest by the lyric speaker; whether the "ye" in the last line is addressed to the lyric speaker, to the readers, to the urn, or to the figures on the urn; whether "all ye know" is that beauty is truth, or this plus the statement in lines 46–48; and whether "beauty is truth" is a profound metaphysical proposition, an overstatement representing the limited point of view of the urn, or simply nonsensical.

Dover Beach

Matthew Arnold

The sea is calm tonight.
The tide is full, the moon lies fair
Upon the straits; on the French coast the light
Gleams and is gone; the cliffs of England stand,
5 Glimmering and vast, out in the tranquil bay.
Come to the window, sweet is the night air!
Only, from the long line of spray
Where the sea meets the moon-blanched land,
Listen! you hear the grating roar[1]
10 Of pebbles which the waves draw back, and fling,
At their return, up the high strand,
Begin, and cease, and then again begin,
With tremulous cadence slow, and bring
The eternal note of sadness in.

15 Sophocles long ago
Heard it on the Aegean, and it brought
Into his mind the turbid ebb and flow
Of human misery;[2] we
Find also in the sound a thought,
20 Hearing it by this distant northern sea.

The Sea of Faith
Was once, too, at the full, and round earth's shore
Lay like the folds of a bright girdle furled.[3]
But now I only hear
25 Its melancholy, long, withdrawing roar,

Retreating, to the breath
Of the night-wind, down the vast edges drear
And naked shingles[4] of the world.
Ah, love, let us be true
30 To one another! for the world, which seems
To lie before us like a land of dreams,
So various, so beautiful, so new,
Hath really neither joy, nor love, nor light,
Nor certitude, nor peace, nor help for pain;
35 And we are here as on a darkling plain

---

[1] Cf. Wordsworth, *It Is a Beauteous Evening,* lines 6–8: "Listen! the mighty Being is awake,/And doth with his eternal motion make / A sound like thunder—everlastingly."

[2] Some of Sophocles' plays include episodes featuring "human misery" which may have influenced Arnold's lines. Editors cite as possible sources: *Antigone* (lines 583 ff.); *Oedipus at Colonus* (lines 120 ff); and especially *The Women of Trachis* (lines 112 ff.).

[3] This difficult line means, in general, that at high tide the sea envelops the land closely. Its forces are "gathered" up (to use Wordsworth's term for it) like the "folds" of bright clothing ("girdle") that have been compressed ("furled"). At ebb tide, as the sea retreats, it is unfurled and spread out. It still surrounds the shoreline but not as an "enclasping flow" (as in To Marguerite—Continued).

[4] Beaches covered with pebbles.

Matthew Arnold, "Dover Beach," from *New Poems*. Copyright in the Public Domain.

Swept with confused alarms of struggle and flight,
Where ignorant armies[5] clash by night.

ca. 1851
1867

---

[5] Perhaps alluding to battles in Arnold's own time such as occurred during the revolutions of 1848 in Europe, or at the Siege of Rome by the French in 1849 (the date of composition of the poem is unknown, although generally assumed to be 1851.) But the passage also refers back to another battle, one that occurred more than two thousand years earlier when an Athenian army was attempting an invasion of Sicily at nighttime. As this "night battle" was described by Thucydides in his *History of the Peloponnesian War* (vii, Ch.44), the invaders became confused by darkness and slaughtered many of their own men. Hence "ignorant armies."

Poems

Emily Dickinson

258

There's a certain Slant of light,
Winter Afternoons—
That oppresses, like the Heft[1]
Of Cathedral Tunes—

5 Heavenly Hurt, it gives us—
We can find no scar,
But internal difference,
Where the Meanings, are—

None may teach it—Any—
10 'Tis the Seal Despair—
An imperial affliction
Sent us of the Air—

When it comes, the Landscape listens—
Shadows—hold their breath—
15 When it goes, 'tis like the Distance
On the look of Death—

1861
1890

---

[1] Weight.

273

He put the Belt around my life—
I heard the Buckle snap—
And turned away, imperial,
My Lifetime folding up—
5 Deliberate, as a Duke would do
A Kingdom's Title Deed—
Henceforth, a Dedicated sort—
A Member of the Cloud.

Yet not too far to come at call—
10 And do the little Toils
That make the Circuit of the Rest—
And deal occasional smiles
To lives that stoop to notice mine—
And kindly ask it in—
15 Whose invitation, know you not
For Whom I must decline?

1861
1891

287

A Clock stopped—
Not the Mantel's—

Emily Dickinson, Poems: 258, 273, 287, 301, 303, 311, 401, 414, 435, 441, 448, 449, 465, 505, 709, 712, 732, 745, 754, 764, 976, 986. Copyright in the Public Domain.

Geneva's[2] farthest skill
Can't put the puppet bowing—
5   That just now dangled still—

An awe came on the Trinket!
The Figures hunched, with pain—
Then quivered out of Decimals—
Into Degreeless Noon—

10   It will not stir for Doctors—
This Pendulum of snow—
This Shopman importunes it—
While cool—concernless No—

Nods from the Gilded pointers—
15   Nods from the Seconds slim—
Decades of Arrogance between
The Dial life—
And Him—

                                  1861
                                  1896

301

I reason, Earth is short—
And Anguish—absolute—
And many hurt,
But, what of that?

5   I reason, we could die—
The best Vitality
Cannot excel Decay,
But, what of that?

I reason, that in Heaven—
10   Somehow, it will be even—
Some new Equation, given—
But, what of that?

                               1862
                               1890

303

The Soul selects her own Society—
Then—shuts the Door—
To her divine Majority—
Present no more—

5   Unmoved—she notes the
Chariots—pausing—
At her low Gate—
Unmoved—an Emperor be kneeling
Upon her Mat—

10   I've known her—from an ample nation—
Choose One—
Then—close the Valves of her attention
Like Stone—

                                1862
                                1890

311

It sifts from Leaden Sieves—
It powders all the Wood.
It fills with Alabaster Wool
The Wrinkles of the Road—

5   It makes an Even Face
Of Mountain, and of Plain—
Unbroken Forehead from the East
Unto the East again—
It reaches to the Fence—
10   It wraps it Rail by Rail
Till it is lost in Fleeces—
It deals Celestial Vail[3]

To Stump, and Stack—and Stem—
A Summer's empty Room—
15   Acres of Joints, where Harvests were,
Recordless, but for them—

It Ruffles Wrists of Posts
As Ankles of a Queen—

---

[2] Geneva, Switzerland—renowned for its clockmakers.

[3] Veil.

　　　　Then stills its Artisans—like Ghosts—
20　　　Denying they have been—
　　　　　　　　　　　　　　1862
　　　　　　　　　　　　　　1891

341

After great pain, a formal feeling comes—
The Nerves sit ceremonious, like Tombs—
The stiff Heart questions was it He, that bore,
And Yesterday, or Centuries before?
5　The Feet, mechanical, go round—
Of Ground, or Air, or Ought—
A Wooden way
Regardless grown,
A Quartz contentment, like a stone—

10　This is the Hour of Lead—
Remembered, if outlived,
As Freezing persons, recollect the Snow—
First—Chill—then Stupor—then the letting go—
　　　　　　　　　　　　　　1862
　　　　　　　　　　　　　　1929

401

What Soft—Cherubic Creatures—
These Gentlewomen are—
One would as soon assault a Plush[4]—
Or violate a Star—

5　Such Dimity[5] Convictions—
A Horror so refined
Of freckled Human Nature—
Of Deity—ashamed[6]—

It's such a common—Glory—
10　A Fisherman's—Degree—
Redemption—Brittle Lady—
Be so—ashamed of Thee—
　　　　　　　　　　　　　　1862
　　　　　　　　　　　　　　1896

407

One need not be a Chamber-to be Haunted—
One need not be a House—
The Brain has Corridors—surpassing
Material Place—

5　Far safer, of a midnight meeting
External Ghost
Than its interior confronting—
That cooler Host—

Far safer, through an Abbey gallop,
10　The Stones a'chase
Than Unarmed, one's a'self encounter—
In lonesome Place—

Ourself behind ourself, concealed—
Should startle most—
15　Assassin hid in our Apartment
Be Horror's least.

The Body—borrows a Revolver—
He bolts the Door—
O'erlooking a superior spectre—
20　Or More—
　　　　　　　　　　　　　　1863
　　　　　　　　　　　　　　1891

414

'Twas like a Maelstrom,[7] with a notch,
That nearer, every Day,
Kept narrowing its boiling Wheel
Until the Agony

---

[4] Cloth with a long, soft pile.

[5] Cotton fabric, delicate and sheer.

[6] "For whosoever shall be ashamed of me and of my words, of him shall the Son of man be ashamed, when he shall come in his own glory...." Luke 9:26.

[7] A violent whirlpool.

5 Toyed coolly with the final inch
  Of your delirious Hem—
  And you dropt, lost,
  When something broke—
  And let you from a Dream—

10 As if a Goblin with a Gauge—
  Kept measuring the Hours—Until you felt your Second
  Weigh, helpless, in his Paws—

  And not a Sinew—stirred—could help,
  And sense was setting numb—
15 When God—remembered—and the Fiend
  Let go, then, Overcome—

  As if your Sentence stood—pronounced—
  And you were frozen led
  From Dungeon's luxury of Doubt
20 To Gibbets,[8] and the Dead—

  And when the Film had stitched your eyes
  A Creature gasped "Reprieve"!
  Which Anguish was the utterest—then—
  To perish, or to live?

         1862
         1945

435

  Much Madness is divinest Sense—
  To a discerning Eye—
  Much Sense—the starkest Madness—
  'Tis the Majority
5 In this, as All, prevail—
  Assent—and you are sane—
  Demur—you're straightway dangerous—
  And handled with a Chain—

         1862
         1890

---

[8] Wooden frameworks on which criminals are hanged and left on display as a warning.

441

  This is my letter to the World
  That never wrote to Me—
  The simple News that Nature told-
  With tender Majesty

5 Her Message is committed
  To Hands I cannot see—
  For love of Her-Sweet—countrymen—
  Judge tenderly—of Me

         1862
         1890

448

  This was a Poet—It is That
  Distills amazing sense
  From ordinary Meanings—
  And Attar so immense

5 From the familiar species
  That perished by the Door—
  We wonder it was not Ourselves
  Arrested it—before—

  Of Pictures, the Discloser—
10 The Poet—it is He—
  Entitles Us—by Contrast—
  To ceaseless Poverty—

  Of Portion—so unconscious—
  The Robbing—could not harm—
  Himself—to Him—a Fortune—
  Exterior—to Time—

         1862
         1929

449

  I died for Beauty—but was scarce
  Adjusted in the Tomb
  When One who died for Truth, was lain

In an adjoining Room—

5   He questioned softly "Why I failed"?
"For Beauty," I replied—
"And I—for Truth—Themself are One—
We Bretheren, are," He said—

And so, as Kinsmen, met a Night—
10   We talked between the Rooms—
Until the Moss had reached our lips—
And covered up—our names—
                             1862
                             1890

465

I heard a Fly buzz—when I died-
The Stillness in the Room
Was like the Stillness in the Air—
Between the Heaves of Storm—

5   The Eyes around—had wrung them dry—
And Breaths were gathering firm
For that last Onset—
When the King Be witnessed—in the Room—

I willed my Keepsakes—Signed away
10   What portion of me be
Assignable—and then it was
There interposed a Fly—

With Blue—uncertain stumbling Buzz—
Between the light—and me—
15   And then the Windows failed—and then
I could not see to see—
                             1862
                             1896

505

I would not paint—a picture—
I'd rather be the One
Its bright impossibility
To dwell—delicious—on—
5   And wonder how the fingers feel
Whose rare—celestial—stir—
Evokes so sweet a Torment—
Such sumptuous—Despair—

10   I would not talk, like Cornets—
I'd rather be the One
Raised softly to the Ceilings—
And out, and easy on—
Through Villages of Ether—
15   Myself endued Balloon
By but a lip of Metal—
The pier to my Pontoon—

Nor would I be a Poet—
It's finer—own the Ear—
20   Enamored—impotent—content—
The License to revere,
A privilege so awful
What would the Dower be,
Had I the Art to stun myself
25   With Bolts of Melody!
                             1862
                             1945

709

Publication—is the Auction
Of the Mind of Man—
Poverty—be justifying
For so foul a thing

5   Possibly—but We—would rather
From Our Garret go
White—Unto the White Creator—
Than invest—Our Snow—

Thought belong to Him who gave it—
10   Then—to Him Who bear
It's Corporeal illustration—Sell
The Royal Air—

In the Parcel—Be the Merchant
Of the Heavenly Grace—
15 But reduce no Human Spirit
To Disgrace of Price—

1863
1929

712

Because I could not stop for Death—
He kindly stopped for me—
The Carriage held but just Ourselves—
And Immortality.

5 We slowly drove—He knew no haste
And I had put away
My labor and my leisure too,
For His Civility—

We passed the School, where Children strove
10 At Recess—in the Ring—
We passed the Fields of Gazing Grain—
We passed the Setting Sun—

Or rather—He passed Us—
The Dews drew quivering and chill—
15 For only Gossamer, my Gown—
My Tippet—only Tulle

We paused before a House that seemed
A Swelling of the Ground—
The Roof was scarcely visible—
20 The Cornice—in the Ground—

Since then—'tis Centuries—and yet
Feels shorter than the Day
I first surmised the Horses' Heads
Were toward Eternity—

1863
1890

732

She rose to His Requirement—dropt
The Playthings of Her Life
To take the honorable Work
Of Woman, and of Wife—

5 If ought She missed in Her new Day,
Of Amplitude, or Awe—
Or first Prospective—Or the Gold
In using, wear away,
It lay unmentioned—as the Sea
10 Develope Pearl, and Weed,
But only to Himself—be known
The Fathoms they abide—

1863
1890

745

Renunciation—is a piercing Virtue—
The letting go
A Presence—for an Expectation—
Not now—
5 The putting out of Eyes—
Just Sunrise—
Lest Day—
Day's Great Progenitor—
Outvie
10 Renunciation—is the Choosing
Against itself—
Itself to justify
Unto itself—
When larger function—
15 Make that appear—
Smaller—that Covered Vision—Here—

1863
1929

754

My life had stood—a Loaded Gun—
In Corners—till a Day
The Owner passed—identified—

     And carried Me away—

5   And now We roam in Sovereign Woods—
     And now We hunt the Doe—
     And every time I speak for Him—
     The Mountains straight reply—

     And do I smile, such cordial light
10   Upon the Valley glow—
     It is as a Vesuvian face
     Had let its pleasure through—

     And when at Night—Our good Day done—
     I guard My Master's Head—
15   'Tis better than the Eider-Duck's
     Deep Pillow—to have shared—

     To foe of His—I'm deadly foe—
     None stir the second time—
     On whom I lay a Yellow Eye—
20   Or an emphatic Thumb—

     Though I than He—may longer live
     He longer must—than I—
     For I have but the power to kill,
     Without—the power to die—
                                    1863
                                    1929

764

Presentiment—is that long Shadow—on the Lawn—
Indicative that Suns go down—

The Notice to the startled Grass

That Darkness—is about to pass—
                                    1862
                                    1890

976

Death is a Dialogue between
The Spirit and the Dust.
"Dissolve" says Death—The Spirit "Sir
I have another Trust"—

5   Death doubts it—Argues from the Ground—
    The Spirit turns away
    Just laying off for evidence
    An Overcoat of Clay.
                                    1864
                                    1890

986

    A narrow Fellow in the Grass
    Occasionally rides—
    You may have met Him—did you not
    His notice sudden is—

5   The Grass divides as with a Comb—
    A spotted shaft is seen—
    And then it closes at your feet
    And opens further on—

    He likes a Boggy Acre
10 A Floor too cool for corn—
    Yet when a Boy, and Barefoot—
    I more than once at Noon
    Have passed, I thought, a Whip lash

God's Grandeur

Gerard Manley Hopkins

The world is charged with the grandeur of God.
    It will flame out, like shining from shook foil;
    It gathers to a greatness, like the ooze of oil
Crushed. Why do men then now not reck his rod?
5   Generations have trod, have trod, have trod;
    And all is seared with trade; Bleared, smeared with toil;
    And wears man's smudge and shares man's smell: the soil
Is bare now, nor can foot feel, being shod.
And for all this, nature is never spent;
10 There lives the dearest freshness deep down things;
And though the last lights off the black West went
    Oh, morning, at the brown brink eastward, springs—
Because the Holy Ghost over the bent
    World broods with warm breast and with ah! bright wings.

Gerard Manley Hopkins, "God's Grandeur," from *Poems of Gerard Manley Hopkins*. Copyright in the Public Domain.

The Windhover

Gerard Manley Hopkins

To Christ our Lord[1]

I caught this morning morning's minion,[2] king-dom of daylight's dauphin,[3] dapple-dawn-drawn Falcon, in his riding
Of the rolling level underneath him steady air, and striding

---

[1] Kestrel, a small falcon noted for hovering in the air.
[2] Darling.
[3] A prince who is heir to the French throne.

Gerard Manley Hopkins, "The Windhover," from *Poems of Gerard Manley Hopkins*. Copyright in the Public Domain.

High there, how he rung upon the rein of a wimpling[4] wing
In his ecstasy! then off, off forth on swing,
  As a skate's heel sweeps smooth on a bow-bend: the hurl and gliding
  Rebuffed the big wind. My heart in hiding
Stirred for a bird,—the achieve of, the mastery of the thing!

Brute beauty and valour and act, oh, air, pride, plume, here
Buckle![5] and the fire that breaks from thee then, a billion
Times told lovelier, more dangerous, O my chevalier![6]

  No wonder of it: shéer plód makes plough down sillion[7]
Shine, and blue-bleak embers, ah my dear,
  Fall, gall[8] themselves, and gash gold-vermilion.

                                        1877
                                        1918

---

[4] Rippling. "Rung upon the rein": circled at the end of a rein.

[5] The verb can be read as imperative or indicative. All three meanings are relevant: to prepare for action, to fasten together, to collapse.
[6] Knight.
[7] The ridge between two furrows of a plowed field.
[8] Break the surface of.

The Second Coming

William Butler Yeats

Turning and turning in the widening gyre[1]
The falcon cannot hear the falconer;
Things fall apart; the center cannot hold;
Mere anarchy is loosed upon the world,
The blood-dimmed tide is loosed, and everywhere
The ceremony of innocence is drowned;
The best lack all conviction, while the worst
Are full of passionate intensity.[2]

Surely some revelation is at hand;
Surely the Second Coming is at hand.

---

[1] This poem expresses Yeats's sense of the dissolution of the civilization of his time, the end of one cycle of history and the approach of another. He called each cycle of history a "gyre" (line 1)—literally a circular or spiral turn (Yeats pronounced it with a hard *g*). The birth of Christ brought to an end the cycle that had lasted from what Yeats called the "Babylonian mathematical starlight" (2000 B.C.) to the dissolution of Greco-Roman culture. "What if the irrational return?" Yeats asked in his prose work *A Vision*. "What if the circle begin again?" He speculates that "we may be about to accept the most implacable authority the world has known."

[2] Lines 4–8 refer to the Russian Revolution of 1917. "The ceremony of innocence" suggests Yeats's view of ritual as the basis of civilized living. Cf. the last stanza of *A Prayer for My Daughter* (p. 1883).

William Butler Yeats, "The Second Coming," from *The Dial*. Copyright in the Public Domain.

The Second Coming! Hardly are those words out
When a vast image out of *Spiritus Mundi*[3]
Troubles my sight: somewhere in sands of the desert
A shape with lion body and the head of a man,
A gaze blank and pitiless as the sun,
Is moving its slow thighs, while all about it
Reel shadows of the indignant desert birds.
The darkness drops again; but now I know
That twenty centuries of stony sleep
Were vexed to nightmare by a rocking cradle,[4]
And what rough beast, its hour come round at last,
Slouches towards Bethlehem to be born?

January 1919
1920–1921

---

[3] The spirit or soul of the universe, with which all individual souls are connected through the "Great Memory," which Yeats held to be a universal subconscious in which the human race preserves its past memories. It is thus a source of symbolic images for the poet.

[4] I.e., the cradle of the infant Christ.

Sailing to Byzantium

William Butler Yeats

That is no country for old men. The young[1]
In one another's arms, birds in the trees
—Those dying generations—at their song,
The salmon-falls, the mackerel-crowded seas,
Fish, flesh, or fowl, commend all summer long
Whatever is begotten, born, and dies.
Caught in that sensual music all neglect
Monuments of unageing intellect.

An aged man is but a paltry thing,
A tattered coat upon a stick, unless
Soul clap its hands and sing, and louder sing
For every tatter in its mortal dress,
Nor is there singing school but studying
Monuments of its own magnificence;

---

[1] Yeats wrote in A Vision: "I think that if I could be given a month of antiquity and leave to spend it where I chose, I would spend it in Byzantium [modern Istanbul] a little before Justinian opened St. Sophia and closed the Academy of Plato [i.e., ca. a.d. 535]....I think that in early Byzantium, maybe never before or since in recorded history, religious, aesthetic, and practical life were one, that architects and artificers...spoke to the multitude in gold and silver. The painter, the mosaic worker, the worker in gold and silver, the illuminator of sacred books were almost impersonal, almost perhaps without the consciousness of individual design, absorbed in their subject matter and that the vision of a whole people."

William Butler Yeats, "Sailing to Byzantium," from *The Tower*. Copyright © 1928 by The Estate of William Butler Yeats.

15   And therefore I have sailed the seas and come
To the holy city of Byzantium.

O sages standing in God's holy fire
As in the gold mosaic of a wall,[2]
Come from the holy fire, perne in a gyre,[3]
20   And be the singing-masters of my soul.
Consume my heart away; sick with desire
And fastened to a dying animal
It knows not what it is; and gather me
Into the artifice of eternity.

Once out of nature I shall never take
My bodily form from any natural thing,
But such a form as Grecian goldsmiths make
Of hammered gold and gold enamelling
To keep a drowsy Emperor awake;[4]
Or set upon a golden bough to sing
To lords and ladies of Byzantium
Of what is past, or passing, or to come.

                              September 1926
                                       1927

---

[2] Yeats had in mind the mosaic frieze of the holy martyrs in the church of San Apollinare Nuovo at Ravenna, which he had visited in 1907.

[3] I.e., whirl round in a spiral motion. "Perne" (or "pirn") is literally a bobbin, reel, or spool, on which something is wound. It became a favorite word of Yeats's, used as a verb meaning "to spin round"; he associated the spinning with the spinning of fate.

[4] "I have read somewhere," Yeats wrote, "that in the Emperor's palace at Byzantium was a tree made of gold and silver, and artificial birds that sang." Cf. also Hans Christian Andersen's Emperor's Nightingale, which may have been in Yeats's mind at the time.

"Out, Out—"

Robert Frost

The buzz saw snarled and rattled in the yard
And made dust and dropped stove-length sticks of wood,
Sweet-scented stuff when the breeze drew across it.
And from there those that lifted eyes could count
5   Five mountain ranges one behind the other
Under the sunset far into Vermont.
And the saw snarled and rattled, snarled and rattled,

Robert Frost, "Out, Out—". Copyright in the Public Domain.

    As it ran light, or had to bear a load.
    And nothing happened: day was all but done.
10 Call it a day, I wish they might have said
    To please the boy by giving him the half hour
    That a boy counts so much when saved from work.
    His sister stood beside them in her apron
    To tell them "Supper." At the word, the saw,
15 As if to prove saws knew what supper meant,
    Leaped out at the boy's hand, or seemed to leap—
    He must have given the hand. However it was,
    Neither refused the meeting. But the hand!
    The boy's first outcry was a rueful laugh,
20 As he swung toward them holding up the hand
    Half in appeal, but half as if to keep
    The life from spilling. Then the boy saw all—
    Since he was old enough to know, big boy
    Doing a man's work, though a child at heart—
25 He saw all spoiled. "Don't let him cut my hand off—
    The doctor, when he comes. Don't let him, sister!"
    So. But the hand was gone already.
    The doctor put him in the dark of ether.
    He lay and puffed his lips out with his breath.
30 And then—the watcher at his pulse took fright.
    No one believed. They listened at his heart.
    Little—less—nothing!—and that ended it.
    No more to build on there. And they, since they
    Were not the one dead, turned to their affairs.

Stopping By Woods on a Snowy Evening

Robert Frost

    Whose woods these are I think I know.
    His house is in the village though;
    He will not see me stopping here
    To watch his woods fill up with snow.

5 My little horse must think it queer
    To stop without a farmhouse near
    Between the woods and frozen lake
    The darkest evening of the year.

    He gives his harness bells a shake
10 To ask if there is some mistake.
    The only other sound's the sweep
    Of easy wind and downy flake.

    The woods are lovely, dark and deep.
    But I have promises to keep,
15 And miles to go before I sleep,
    And miles to go before I sleep.

Robert Frost, "Stopping by Woods on a Snowy Evening," from *New Hampshire*. Copyright © 1923 by Henry Holt & Company.

Home Burial

Robert Frost

He saw her from the bottom of the stairs
Before she saw him. She was starting down,
Looking back over her shoulder at some fear.
She took a doubtful step and then undid it
5 To raise herself and look again. He spoke
Advancing toward her: "What is it you see
From up there always?—for I want to know."
She turned and sank upon her skirts at that,
And her face changed from terrified to dull.
10 He said to gain time: "What is it you see?"
Mounting until she cowered under him.
"I will find out now—you must tell me, dear."
She, in her place, refused him any help,
With the least stiffening of her neck and silence.
15 She let him look, sure that he wouldn't see,
Blind creature; and awhile he didn't see.
But at last he murmured, "Oh," and again, "Oh."

"What is it—what?" she said.
    "Just that I see."
"You don't," she challenged. "Tell me what it is."

20 "The wonder is I didn't see at once.
I never noticed it from here before.
I must be wonted[1] to it—that's the reason.
The little graveyard where my people are!
So small the window frames the whole of it.

---

[1] Accustomed.

25 Not so much larger than a bedroom, is it?
There are three stones of slate and one of marble,
Broad-shouldered little slabs there in the sunlight
On the sidehill. We haven't to mind those.
But I understand: it is not the stones,
30 But the child's mound—"

    "Don't, don't, don't, don't," she cried.

She withdrew, shrinking from beneath his arm
That rested on the banister, and slid downstairs;
35 And turned on him with such a daunting look,
He said twice over before he knew himself:
"Can't a man speak of his own child he's lost?"

"Not you!—Oh, where's my hat? Oh, I don't need it!
I must get out of here. I must get air.—
40 I don't know rightly whether any man can."

"Amy! Don't go to someone else this time.
Listen to me. I won't come down the stairs."

He sat and fixed his chin between his fists.
"There's something I should like to ask you, dear."

Robert Frost, "Home Burial." Copyright in the Public Domain.

45 "You don't know how to ask it."

"Help me, then."

Her fingers moved the latch for all reply.

"My words are nearly always an offense.
I don't know how to speak of anything
50 So as to please you. But I might be taught,
I should suppose. I can't say I see how.
A man must partly give up being a man
With womenfolk. We could have some arrangement
By which I'd bind myself to keep hands off
55 Anything special you're a-mind to name.
Though I don't like such things 'twixt those that love.
Two that don't love can't live together without them.
But two that do can't live together with them."
She moved the latch a little. "Don't—don't go.
60 Don't carry it to someone else this time.
Tell me about it if it's something human.
Let me into your grief. I'm not so much
Unlike other folks as your standing there
Apart would make me out. Give me my chance.
65 I do think, though, you overdo it a little.
What was it brought you up to think it the thing
To take your mother-loss of a first child
So inconsolably—in the face of love.
You'd think his memory might be satisfied-"

70 "There you go sneering now!"

"I'm not, I'm not!
You make me angry. I'll come down to you.
God, what a woman! And it's come to this,
A man can't speak of his own child that's dead."

75 "You can't because you don't know how to speak.
If you had any feelings, you that dug
With your own hand—how could you?—his little grave;
I saw you from that very window there,
Making the gravel leap and leap in air,
80 Leap up, like that, like that, and land so lightly
And roll back down the mound beside the hole.
I thought, Who is that man? I didn't know you.
And I crept down the stairs and up the stairs
To look again, and still your spade kept lifting.
85 Then you came in. I heard your rumbling voice
Out in the kitchen, and I don't know why,
But I went near to see with my own eyes.
You could sit there with the stains on your shoes
Of the fresh earth from your own baby's grave
90 And talk about your everyday concerns.
You had stood the spade up against the wall
Outside there in the entry, for I saw it."

"I shall laugh the worst laugh I ever laughed.
I'm cursed. God, if I don't believe I'm cursed."

95 "I can repeat the very words you were saying:
'Three foggy mornings and one rainy day
Will rot the best birch fence a man can build.'
Think of it, talk like that at such a time!
What had how long it takes a birch to rot
100 To do with what was in the darkened parlor?
You *couldn't* care! The nearest friends can go
With anyone to death, comes so far short
They might as well not try to go at all.

	No, from the time when one is sick to death,
105	One is alone, and he dies more alone.
	Friends make pretense of following to the grave,
	But before one is in it, their minds are turned
	And making the best of their way back to life
	And living people, and things they understand.
110	But the world's evil. I won't have grief so
	If I can change it. Oh, I won't, I won't!"

	"There, you have said it all and you feel better.
	You won't go now. You're crying. Close the door.
	The heart's gone out of it: why keep it up?
115	Amy! There's someone coming down the road!"

	"*You*—oh, you think the talk is all. I must go—
	Somewhere out of this house, How can I make you—"

	"If—you—do!" She was opening the door wider.
	"Where do you mean to go? First tell me that.
120	I'll follow and bring you back by force. I *will!*—"

1914

The Road Not Taken

Robert Frost

	Two roads diverged in a yellow wood,
	And sorry I could not travel both
	And be one traveler, long I stood
	And looked down one as far as I could
5	To where it bent in the undergrowth;

	Then took the other, as just as fair,
	And having perhaps the better claim,
	Because it was grassy and wanted wear;
	Though as for that the passing there
10	Had worn them really about the same,

	And both that morning equally lay
	In leaves no step had trodden black.
	Oh, I kept the first for another day!
	Yet knowing how way leads on to way,
15	I doubted if I should ever come back.

	I shall be telling this with a sigh
	Somewhere ages and ages hence:
	Two roads diverged in a wood, and I—
	I took the one less traveled by,
20	And that has made all the difference.

Robert Frost, "The Road Not Taken," from *Mountain Interval*. Copyright in the Public Domain.

The Love Song Of J. Alfred Prufrock

T.S. Eliot

S'io credesse che mia risposta fosse
A persona che mai tornasse al mondo,
Questa fiamma staria senza piu scosse.
Ma perciocche giammai di questo fondo
Non torno vivo alcun, s'i'òdo il vero,
Senza tema d'infamia ti rispondo.[1]

Let us go then, you and I,
When the evening is spread out against the sky
Like a patient etherised upon a table;
Let us go through certain half-deserted streets,
5   The muttering retreats
Of restless nights in one-night cheap hotels
And sawdust restaurants with oyster-shells:
Streets that follow like a tedious argument
Of insidious intent
10   To lead you to an overwhelming question…[2]
Oh, do not ask, "What is it?"
Let us go and make our visit.

In the room the women come and go
Talking of Michelangelo.

15   The yellow fog that rubs its back upon the window-panes,
The yellow smoke that rubs its muzzle on the window-panes,
Licked its tongue into the corners of the evening,
Lingered upon the pools that stand in drains,
Let fall upon its back the soot that falls from chimneys,
20   Slipped by the terrace, made a sudden leap,
And seeing that it was a soft October night,
Curled once about the house, and fell asleep.

And indeed there will be time
For the yellow smoke that slides along the street
25   Rubbing its back upon the window-panes;
There will be time, there will be time
To prepare a face to meet the faces that you meet;
There will be time to murder and create,
And time for all the works and days[3] of hands
30   That lift and drop a question on your plate;
Time for you and time for me,
And time yet for a hundred indecisions,
And for a hundred visions and revisions,
Before the taking of a toast and tea.

35   In the room the women come and go

---

[1] "If I thought my reply were to one who could ever return to the world, this flame would shake no more; but since, if what I hear is true, none ever did return alive from this depth, I answer you without fear of infamy." The flame (or spirit) of Guido de Montefeltro, suffering in Hades for his sins, confesses to the poet Dante (Inferno, Canto XXVII, lines 61–66).

[2] Here, and throughout, the ellipsis points are Eliot's and do not indicate omissions by the editor.

[3] A reference to *Works and Days,* a poem, by the ancient Greek poet Hesiod, on the rural life and labors of a peasant.

T. S. Eliot, "The Love Song of J. Alfred Prufrock," from *Poetry: A Magazine of Verse.* Copyright in the Public Domain.

Talking of Michelangelo.

And indeed there will be time
To wonder, "Do I dare?" and, "Do I dare?"
Time to turn back and descend the stair,
40   With a bald spot in the middle of my hair—
(They will say: "How his hair is growing thin!")
My morning coat, my collar mounting firmly to the chin,
My necktie rich and modest, but asserted by a simple pin—
(They will say: "But how his arms and legs are thin!")
45   Do I dare
Disturb the universe?
In a minute there is time
For decisions and revisions which a minute will reverse.

For I have known them all already, known them all—
50   Have known the evenings, mornings, afternoons,
I have measured out my life with coffee spoons;
I know the voices dying with a dying fall
Beneath the music from a farther room.
So how should I presume?

55   And I have known the eyes already, known them all—
The eyes that fix you in a formulated phrase,
And when I am formulated, sprawling on a pin,

When I am pinned and wriggling on the wall,
Then how should I begin
60   To spit out all the butt-ends of my days and ways?
And how should I presume?

And I have known the arms already, known them all—
Arms that are braceleted and white and bare
(But in the lamplight, downed with light brown hair!)
65   Is it perfume from a dress
That makes me so digress?
Arms that lie along a table, or wrap about a shawl.
And should I then presume?
And how should I begin?

* * *

70   Shall I say, I have gone at dusk through narrow streets
And watched the smoke that rises from the pipes
Of lonely men in shirt-sleeves, leaning out of windows?…

I should have been a pair of ragged claws
Scuttling across the floors of silent seas.

* * *

75   And the afternoon, the evening, sleeps so peacefully!
Smoothed by long fingers,
Asleep…tired…or it malingers,
Stretched on the floor, here beside you and me.
Should I, after tea and cakes and ices,
80   Have the strength to force the moment to its crisis?

But though I have wept and fasted, wept and prayed,
Though I have seen my head (grown slightly bald) brought in upon a platter,[4]
I am no prophet—and here's no great matter;
I have seen the moment of my greatness flicker,

---

[4] The prophet John the Baptist was beheaded and his head brought on a platter to Salome, the daughter of Herodias. Matthew 14:1-11.

85   And I have seen the eternal Footman hold my coat, and snicker,
     And in short, I was afraid.

     And would it have been worth it, after all,
     After the cups, the marmalade, the tea,
     Among the porcelain, among some talk of you and me,
90   Would it have been worth while,
     To have bitten off the matter with a smile,
     To have squeezed the universe into a ball⁵
     To roll it towards some overwhelming question,
     To say: "I am Lazarus, come from the dead,⁶
95   Come back to tell you all, I shall tell you all"—
     If one, settling a pillow by her head,
     Should say: "That is not what I meant at all.
     That is not it, at all."

     And would it have been worth it, after all,
     Would it have been worth while,
100 After the sunsets and the dooryards and the sprinkled streets,
     After the novels, after the teacups, after the skirts that trail along the floor—
     And this, and so much more?—
     It is impossible to say just what I mean!
105 But as if a magic lantern threw the nerves in patterns on a screen:
     Would it have been worth while
     If one, settling a pillow or throwing off a shawl,
     And turning toward the window, should say:
     "That is not it at all,
110 That is not what I meant, at all."

※ ※ ※

     No! I am not Prince Hamlet, nor was meant to be;
     Am an attendant lord, one that will do
     To swell a progress,⁷ start a scene or two,
     Advise the prince: no doubt, an easy tool,
     Deferential, glad to be of use,
115 Politic, cautious, and meticulous;
     Full of high sentence,⁸ but a bit obtuse;
     At times, indeed, almost ridiculous—
     Almost, at times, the Fool.

     I grow old…I grow old…
120 I shall wear the bottoms of my trousers rolled.⁹
     Shall I part my hair behind? Do I dare to eat a peach?
     I shall wear white flannel trousers, and walk upon the beach.
     I have heard the mermaids¹⁰ singing, each to each.

     I do not think that they will sing to me.

125 I have seen them riding seaward on the waves
     Combing the white hair of the waves blown back
     When the wind blows the water white and black.

     We have lingered in the chambers of the sea
130 By sea-girls wreathed with seaweed red and brown
     Till human voices wake us, and we drown

                                              1910–1911
                                              1915–1917

---

⁵ An allusion to the poem "To His Coy Mistress," by the English poet Andrew Maxwell (1621–1678): "Let us roll all our strength and all / Our sweetness up into one ball…"

⁶ Jesus raised Lazarus from the dead. John 11:1-44.

⁷ To be part of a royal procession.

⁸ Judgment, pronouncement.

⁹ To form fashionable cuffs.

¹⁰ Mythical alluring creatures, half woman and half fish.

The Waste Land

T.S. Eliot

"Nam Sibyllam quidem cumis ego ipse oculis meis vidi in ampulla pendere, et cum illi pueri dicerent: Σίβλλα τί θέλεις; responded illa: ἀποθανείν θέλω."[1]

For Ezra Pound
il miglior fabbro.[2]

I. The Burial Of The Dead[3]

April is the cruellest month, breeding
Lilacs out of the dead land, mixing
Memory and desire, stirring
Dull roots with spring rain.
5 Winter kept us warm, covering
Earth in forgetful snow, feeding
A little life with dried tubers.
Summer surprised us, coming over the Starnbergersee[4]
With a shower of rain; we stopped in the colonnade,
10 And went on in sunlight, into the Hofgarten,[5]
And drank coffee, and talked for an hour.
Bin gar keine Russin, stamm' aus Litauen, echt deutsch.[6]
And when we were children, staying at the archduke's,
My cousin's, he took me out on a sled,
15 And I was frightened. He said, Marie,
Marie, hold on tight. And down we went.
In the mountains, there you feel free.
I read, much of the night, and go south in the winter.

What are the roots that clutch, what branches grow
20 Out of this stony rubbish? Son of man,
You cannot say, or guess, for you know only
A heap of broken images, where the sun beats,
And the dead tree gives no shelter, the cricket no relief,
And the dry stone no sound of water. Only
25 There is shadow under this red rock,
(Come in under the shadow of this red rock),
And I will show you something different from either
Your shadow at morning striding behind you

---

[1] "For I myself saw with my own eyes the Sibyl of Cumae [in Italy] hanging in a bottle; and when the boys cried to her, 'Sibyl, what do you want?' she used to reply, 'I want to die.'" (Petronius, *Satyricon*, Chapter XLVIII). The Sibyl, a prophetess, had been given long life by Apollo, but she had failed to ask for eternal youth and health.

[2] "The better craftsman," a quotation from Dante's *Purgatorio* (Canto XXVI, line 117). Pound had assisted Eliot in writing "The Waste Land."

[3] The title of the services for the dead in *The Book of Common Prayer* of the Church of England.

[4] Lake near Munich, Germany.

[5] Public park in Munich.

[6] German: I'm not Russian; I come from Lithuania, pure German.

T. S. Eliot, "The Waste Land," from *The Criterion*. Copyright in the Public Domain.

Or your shadow at evening rising to meet you;
30 I will show you fear in a handful of dust.

> *Frisch weht der Wind*
> *Der Heimat zu.*
> *Mein Irisch Kind,*
> *Wo weilest du?*[7]

35 "You gave me hyacinths[8] first a year ago;
"They called me the hyacinth girl."
—Yet when we came back, late, from the Hyacinth garden,
Your arms full, and your hair wet, I could not
Speak, and my eyes failed, I was neither
40 Living nor dead, and I knew nothing,
Looking into the heart of light, the silence.
Oed' und leer das Meer.[9]

Madame Sosostris, famous clairvoyante,
Had a bad cold, nevertheless
45 Is known to be the wisest woman in Europe,
With a wicked pack of cards.[10] Here, said she,
Is your card, the drowned Phoenician Sailor,
(Those are pearls that were his eyes.[11] Look!)
Here is Belladonna, the Lady of the Rocks,
50 The lady of situations.
Here is the man with three staves, and here the Wheel,
And here is the one-eyed merchant, and this card,
Which is blank, is something he carries on his back,
Which I am forbidden to see. I do not find
55 The Hanged Man. Fear death by water.
I see crowds of people, walking round in a ring.
Thank you. If you see dear Mrs. Equitone,
Tell her I bring the horoscope myself:
One must be so careful these days.

60 Unreal City,
Under the brown fog of a winter dawn,
A crowd flowed over London Bridge, so many,
I had not thought death had undone so many.[12]
Sighs, short and infrequent, were exhaled,
65 And each man fixed his eyes before his feet.
Flowed up the hill and down King William Street,
To where Saint Mary Woolnoth[13] kept the hours
With a dead sound on the final stroke of nine.
There I saw one I knew, and stopped him, crying: "Stetson!
70 "You who were with me in the ships at Mylae![14]
"That corpse you planted last year in your garden,
"Has it begun to sprout? Will it bloom this year?
"Or has the sudden frost disturbed its bed?
"O keep the Dog far hence, that's friend to men,
75 "Or with his nails he'll dig it up again![15]
"*You! hypocrite lecteur!—mon semblable,—mon frere!*"[16]

---

[7] "Fresh blows the wind / To the homeland / My Irish child; / Where are you waiting?" See Eliot's note, I, line 31 (page 1178).

[8] A flower named for Hyacinthus, ancient Greek fertility god. The Hyacinthia, a resurrection festival in his honor, was celebrated in July to commemorate the seasonal rebirth and growth of vegetation.

[9] "Desolate and empty the sea."

[10] Tarot cards, used in fortune-telling. See Eliot's note, I, line 46.

[11] From Shakespeare's *The Tempest* (Act I, Scene ii, line 398).

[12] A quotation from Dante's *Inferno*. See Eliot's note, I, line 63.

[13] London church.

[14] Site of a Roman naval victory over the Carthaginians (260 B.C.).

[15] An adaptation from John Webster's *The White Devil* (1612): "But keep the wolf far thence, that's foe to men, / For with his nails he'll dig them up again." (Act V, Scene iv, lines 97–98).

[16] French: "hypocrite reader!—my likeness,—my brother!"

II. A Game Of Chess

      The Chair she sat in, like a burnished throne,
      Glowed on the marble,[17] where the glass
      Held up by standards wrought with fruited vines
80   From which a golden Cupidon[18] peeped out
      (Another hid his eyes behind his wing)
      Doubled the flames of seven branched candelabra
      Reflecting light upon the table as
      The glitter of her jewels rose to meet it,
85   From satin cases poured in rich profusion.
      In vials of ivory and coloured glass
      Unstoppered, lurked her strange synthetic perfumes,
      Unguent, powdered, or liquid—troubled, confused
      And drowned the sense in odours; stirred by the air
90   That freshened from the window, these ascended
      In fattening the prolonged candle-flames,
      Flung their smoke into the laquearia,[19]
      Stirring the pattern on the coffered ceiling.
      Huge sea-wood fed with copper
95   Burned green and orange, framed by the coloured stone,
      In which sad light a carved dolphin swam.
      Above the antique mantel was displayed
      As though a window gave upon the sylvan scene[20]
      The change of Philomel,[21] by the barbarous king
100 So rudely forced; yet there the nightingale
      Filled all the desert with inviolable voice
      And still she cried, and still the world pursues,
      "Jug Jug"[22] to dirty ears.
      And other withered stumps of time
105 Were told upon the walls; staring forms
      Leaned out, leaning, hushing the room enclosed.
      Footsteps shuffled on the stair.
      Under the firelight, under the brush, her hair
      Spread out in fiery points
110 Glowed into words, then would be savagely still.

      "My nerves are bad to-night. Yes, bad. Stay with me.
      "Speak to me. Why do you never speak? Speak.
      "What are you thinking of? What thinking? What?
115 "I never know what you are thinking. Think."
      I think we are in rats' alley
      Where the dead men lost their bones.

      "What is that noise?"
                            The wind under the door.
      "What is that noise now? What is the wind doing?"
120   Nothing again nothing.
                                 "Do
      "You know nothing? Do you see nothing?
      Do you remember "Nothing?"

                                I remember
125 Those are pearls that were his eyes.

---

[17] An adaptation of the description of Cleopatra's barge in Shakespeare's *Antony and Cleopatra*: "The barge she sat in, like a burnish'd throne, / Burn'd on the water." (Act II, Scene ii, lines 196–197).

[18] A statue of Cupid, Roman god of love.

[19] Fretted ceiling. See Eliot's note, II, line 92.

[20] A reference to *Paradise Lost* (Book IV, line 140) where Milton describes the Garden of Eden.

[21] In classical legend Philomel was raped by Tereus, King of Thrace. The gods then turned her into a nightingale. The story is told in Ovid's *Metamorphoses*.

[22] Words traditionally used in English poetry to represent the song of the nightingale.

"Are you alive, or not? Is there nothing in your head?"
                    But
O O O O that Shakespeherian Rag—
It's so elegant
130 So intelligent[23]

"What shall I do now? What shall I do?
"I shall rush out as I am, and walk the street
"With my hair down, so. What shall we do to-morrow?
"What shall we ever do?"
135   The hot water at ten.
And if it rains, a closed car at four.
And we shall play a game of chess,
Pressing lidless eyes and waiting for a knock upon the door.

When Lil's husband got demobbed,[24] I said—
140 I didn't mince my words, I said to her myself,
HURRY UP PLEASE ITS TIME[25]
Now Albert's coming back, make yourself a bit smart.
He'll want to know what you done with that money he gave you
To get yourself some teeth. He did, I was there.
145 You have them all out, Lil, and get a nice set,
He said, I swear, I can't bear to look at you.
And no more can't I, I said, and think of poor Albert,
He's been in the army four years, he wants a good time,
And if you don't give it him, there's others will, I said.
150 Oh is there, she said. Something o' that, I said.
Then I'll know who to thank, she said, and give me a straight look.
HURRY UP PLEASE ITS TIME
If you don't like it you can get on with it, I said,
Others can pick and choose if you can't.
155 But if Albert makes off, it won't be for lack of telling.
You ought to be ashamed, I said, to look so antique.
(And her only thirty-one.)
I can't help it, she said, pulling a long face,
It's them pills I took, to bring it off, she said
160 (She's had five already, and nearly died of young George.)
The chemist[26] said it would be all right, but I've never been the same.
You are a proper fool, I said.
Well, if Albert won't leave you alone, there it is, I said,
What you get married for if you don't want children?
165 HURRY UP PLEASE ITS TIME
Well, that Sunday Albert was home, they had a hot gammon,[27]
And they asked me in to dinner, to get the beauty of it hot—
HURRY UP PLEASE ITS TIME
HURRY UP PLEASE ITS TIME
170 Goonight Bill. Goonight Lou. Goonight May. Goonight. Ta ta. Goonight. Goonight.
Good night, ladies, good night, sweet ladies,
good night, good night.[28]

III. The Fire Sermon

The river's tent is broken: the last fingers of leaf

---

[23] Lines adapted from the lyrics of *That Shakesperian Rag*, a popular song of 1912.

[24] Demobilized from the army.

[25] English pubkeeper's call to announce closing time.

[26] English "pharmacist."

[27] Smoked ham.

[28] From the speech by Ophelia, after she has gone mad. Shakespeare, *Hamlet* (Act IV, Scene v, lines 72–74).

Clutch and sink into the wet bank. The wind
175 Crosses the brown land, unheard. The nymphs are departed.
Sweet Thames, run softly, till I end my song.[29]
The river bears no empty bottles, sandwich papers,
Silk handkerchiefs, cardboard boxes, cigarette ends
Or other testimony of summer nights. The nymphs are departed.
180 And their friends, the loitering heirs of city directors;[30]
Departed, have left no addresses.
By the waters of Leman I sat down and wept[31]...
Sweet Thames, run softly till I end my song,
Sweet Thames, run softly, for I speak not loud or long.
185 But at my back in a cold blast I hear[32]
The rattle of the bones, and chuckle spread from ear to ear.

A rat crept softly through the vegetation
Dragging its slimy belly on the bank
While I was fishing in the dull canal
190 On a winter evening round behind the gashouse
Musing upon the king my brother's wreck
And on the king my father's death before him.[33]
White bodies naked on the low damp ground
And bones cast in a little low dry garret,
195 Rattled by the rat's foot only, year to year.
But at my back from time to time I hear
The sound of horns and motors, which shall bring
Sweeney to Mrs. Porter[34] in the spring.
O the moon shone bright on Mrs. Porter
200 And on her daughter
They wash their feet in soda water
Et, O ces voix d'enfants, chantant dans la coupole![35]

Twit twit twit
Jug jug jug jug jug jug
205 So rudely forc'd.
Tereu[36]

Unreal City
Under the brown fog of a winter noon
Mr. Eugenides,[37] the Smyrna[38] merchant
210 Unshaven, with a pocket full of currants
C.i.f. London: documents at sight,[39]
Asked me in demotic[40] French
To luncheon at the Cannon Street Hotel
Followed by a weekend at the Metropole.

---

[29] A quotation from Edmund Spenser's "Prothalamion" (1596), which describes an elegant procession of nymphs down the river Thames.

[30] Directors of business firms in the City, the financial district of London.

[31] From the lamentations of the Jews exiled from Palestine: "By the rivers of Babylon, there we sat down, yea, we wept, when we remembered Zion." Psalm 137. Eliot substitutes "Leman," the French name for Lake Geneva, Switzerland.

[32] Adapted from "To His Coy Mistress," by Andrew Marvell (1621-1678): "But at my back I always hear / Time's winged chariot hurrying near" (lines 21-22).

[33] Adapted from the words of Ferdinand, son of the King of Naples, in Shakespeare's *The Tempest* (Act I, Scene ii, lines 389–391): "Sitting on a bank, / Weeping against the King my father's wreck, / This music crept by me upon the waters."

[34] Here, as elsewhere in Eliot's poetry, Sweeney represents crude humankind. Mrs. Porter and her daughter were whores described in a bawdy song popular with British troops in World War I. See Eliot's note, III, line 199.

[35] French: "And, O those voices of children [choirboys] singing in the dome." From "Parsifal," a sonnet by Paul Verlaine (1844–1896).

[36] A conventional representation, with "jug, jug," of the nightingale's song and an allusion to King Tereus, the despoiler of Philomela.

[37] Greek for *wellborn*.

[38] Seaport in Turkey.

[39] Business terms used in the buying and selling of commodities. See Eliot's note, III, line 210.

[40] Vulgar.

215　　At the violet hour, when eyes and back
　　　　Turn upward from the desk, when the human engine waits
　　　　Like a taxi throbbing waiting
　　　　I Tiresias, though blind, throbbing between two lives,[41]
　　　　Old man with wrinkled female breasts, can see
220　　At the violet hour, the evening hour that strives
　　　　Homeward, and brings the sailor home from sea,[42]
　　　　The typist home at teatime, clears her breakfast, lights
　　　　Her stove, and lays out food in tins.
　　　　Out of the window perilously spread
225　　Her drying combinations[43] touched by the sun's last rays,
　　　　On the divan are piled (at night her bed)
　　　　Stockings, slippers, camisoles, and stays.[44]
　　　　I Tiresias, old man with wrinkled dugs[45]
　　　　Perceived the scene, and foretold the rest—
230　　I too awaited the expected guest.
　　　　He, the young man carbuncular,[46] arrives,
　　　　A small house agent's clerk, with one bold stare,
　　　　One of the low on whom assurance sits
　　　　As a silk hat on a Bradford millionaire.[47]
235　　The time is now propitious, as he guesses,
　　　　The meal is ended, she is bored and tired,
　　　　Endeavours to engage her in caresses
　　　　Which still are unreproved, if undesired.
　　　　Flushed and decided, he assaults at once;
240　　Exploring hands encounter no defence;
　　　　His vanity requires no response,
　　　　And makes a welcome of indifference.
　　　　(And I Tiresias have foresuffered all
　　　　Enacted on this same divan or bed;
245　　I who have sat by Thebes below the wall
　　　　And walked among the lowest of the dead.)[48]
　　　　Bestows one final patronising kiss,
　　　　And gropes his way, finding the stairs unlit…

　　　　She turns and looks a moment in the glass,
250　　Hardly aware of her departed lover;
　　　　Her brain allows one half-formed thought to pass:
　　　　"Well now that's done: and I'm glad it's over."
　　　　When lovely woman stoops to folly and
　　　　Paces about her room again, alone,
255　　She smoothes her hair with automatic hand,
　　　　And puts a record on the gramophone.[49]

　　　　"This music crept by me upon the waters"[50]
　　　　And along the Strand,[51] up Queen Victoria Street.
　　　　O City, City, I can sometimes hear
260　　Beside a public bar in Lower Thames Street,
　　　　The pleasant whining of a mandoline
　　　　And a clatter and a chatter from within
　　　　Where fishmen lounge at noon: where the walls

---

[41] Tiresias, a blind prophet in Greek myth, had been transformed into a woman for seven years. See Eliot's note, III, line 218.

[42] Eliot refers (see his note) to "Sappho's lines," probably a reference to her poem to Hesperus, the Evening Star that brings "home all things the bright morning dispersed." Eliot may also have had in mind the lines from "Requiem" by Robert Louis Stevenson (1850–1894): "Home is the sailor, home from the sea."

[43] One-piece underwear.

[44] Camisoles: short, sleeveless underwear. Stays: corset with bone stiffeners.

[45] Breasts.

[46] Afflicted with carbuncles, boils.

[47] One of the newly rich from the English industrial city of Bradford.

[48] Tiresias made his prophecies in Thebes, where he lived, and in Hades, the underworld, after his death.

[49] An ironic adaptation from Oliver Goldsmith's *The Vicar of Wakefield* (Chapter 24): "When lovely woman stoops to folly, / And finds too late that men betray; / What charm can soothe her melancholy? / What art can wash her guilt away?"

[50] From *The Tempest*. See footnote 34 above.

[51] A London street.

	Of Magnus Martyr[52] hold
265	Inexplicable splendour of Ionian white and gold.
	The river sweats
	Oil and tar
	The barges drift
	With the turning tide
270	Red sails
	Wide
	To leeward, swing on the heavy spar.
	The barges wash
	Drifting logs
275	Down Greenwich Reach[53]
	Past the Isle of Dogs.[54]
	Weialala leia
	Wallala leialala[55]
	Elizabeth and Leicester[56]
280	Beating oars
	The stern was formed
	A gilded shell
	Red and gold
	The brisk swell
285	Rippled both shores
	Southwest wind
	Carried down stream
	The peal of bells
	White towers
290	Weialala leia
	Wallala leialala
	"Trams[57] and dusty trees.
	Highbury bore me. Richmond and Kew
	Undid me.[58] By Richmond I raised my knees
295	Supine on the floor of a narrow canoe."
	"My feet are at Moorgate,[59] and my heart
	Under my feet. After the event
	He wept. He promised 'a new start.'
	I made no comment. What should I resent?"
300	"On Margate Sands.[60]
	I can connect
	Nothing with nothing.
	The broken fingernails of dirty hands.
	My people humble people who expect
305	Nothing."
	la la
	To Carthage then I came[61]
	Burning burning burning burning[62]
310	O Lord Thou pluckest me out[63]
	O Lord Thou pluckest
	burning

IV. Death By Water

	Phlebas the Phoenician, a fortnight dead,
	Forgot the cry of gulls, and the deep sea swell
315	And the profit and loss.
	A current under sea

---

[52] A London church built by Sir Christopher Wren (1632–1723). See Eliot's note, III, line 264.

[53] The Thames River at Greenwich.

[54] A peninsula in the Thames.

[55] The refrain in the song of the Rhine-maidens from the opera *Die Cotter dammerung,* by Richard Wagner (1813–1883)

[56] Queen Elizabeth I of England and Robert Dudley, the Earl of Leicester. Their boat-ride on the Thames (see Eliot's note, III, line 279) is contrasted to the three sordid love affairs that follow (lines 292–308).

[57] Streetcars.

[58] Highbury: London suburb; Richmond and Kew: park and resort areas near London. Eliot echoes the lines from Dante, "Siena bore me; Maremma undid me," used also by Ezra Pound in one of his "Hugh Selwyn Mauberley" poems.

[59] Slum area of London.

[60] A seaside resort on the Thames.

[61] From St. Augustine's *Confessions* (Book III, Chapter i). See Eliot's note, III, line 307.

62 From the Fire Sermon of Buddha, which calls for a life free of fiery passion. See Eliot's note, III, line 308.

[63] In his *Confessions,* St. Augustine thanks the Lord for plucking him from his broiling, unholy loves. See Eliot's note, III, line 309.

Picked his bones in whispers. As he rose and fell
He passed the stages of his age and youth
Entering the whirlpool.
         Gentile or jew
320 O you who turn the wheel[64] and look to windward,
Consider Phlebas, who was once handsome and tall as you.

V. What The Thunder Said[65]

After the torchlight red on sweaty faces
After the frosty silence in the gardens
After the agony in stony places
325 The shouting and the crying
Prison and palace and reverberation
Of thunder of spring over distant mountains
He who was living is now dead[66]
We who were living are now dying
330 With a little patience

Here is no water but only rock
Rock and no water and the sandy road
The road winding above among the mountains
Which are mountains of rock without water
335 If there were water we should stop and drink
Amongst the rock one cannot stop or think
Sweat is dry and feet are in the sand
If there were only water amongst the rock
Dead mountain mouth of carious[67] teeth that cannot spit
340 Here one can neither stand nor lie nor sit
There is not even silence in the mountains
But dry sterile thunder without rain
There is not even solitude in the mountains
But red sullen faces sneer and snarl
345 From doors of mudcracked houses
      If there were water

And no rock
If there were rock
And also water
350 And water
A spring
A pool among the rock
If there were the sound of water only
Not the cicada
355 And dry grass singing
But sound of water over a rock
Where the hermit-thrush sings in the pine trees
Drip drop drip drop drop drop drop
But there is no water
360 Who is the third, who walks always beside you?[68]
When I count, there are only you and I together
But when I look ahead up the white road
There is always another one walking beside you
Gliding wrapt in a brown mantle, hooded
365 I do not know whether a man or a woman
—But who is that on the other side of you?
What is that sound high in the air[69]
Murmur of maternal lamentation
Who are those hooded hordes swarming
370 Over endless plains, stumbling in cracked earth
Ringed by the flat horizon only
What is the city over the mountains
Cracks and reforms and bursts in the violet air
Falling towers
375 Jerusalem Athens Alexandria
Vienna London
Unreal

---

[64] The wheel of fortune or (more likely) a ship's steersman's wheel.

[65] In the Indian *Upanishads*, the Lord speaks through the thunder.

[66] Lines 322–328 refer to Christ's ordeal after The Last Supper and His martyrdom.

[67] Decayed.

[68] After His crucifixion, Christ appeared before two travelers to Emmaus. Luke 24:13-31. See also Eliot's note, V, line 360.

[69] Lines 367–377 allude to the upheavals resulting from the Russian Revolution that threatened the centers of civilization: Jerusalem, Athens, Alexandria, etc. See Eliot's note, V, lines 366–77.

A woman drew her long black hair out tight
And fiddled whisper music on those strings
380 And bats with baby faces in the violet light
Whistled, and beat their wings
And crawled head downward down a blackened wall
And upside down in air were towers
Tolling reminiscent bells, that kept the hours
385 And voices singing out of empty cisterns and exhausted wells.

In this decayed hole among the mountains
In the faint moonlight, the grass is singing
Over the tumbled graves, about the chapel
There is the empty chapel,[70] only the wind's home.
390 It has no windows, and the door swings,
Dry bones can harm no one.
Only a cock stood on the rooftree
Co co rico co co rico[71]
In a flash of lightning. Then a damp gust
395 Bringing rain

Ganga[72] was sunken, and the limp leaves
Waited for rain, while the black clouds
Gathered far distant, over Himavant.[73]
The jungle crouched, humped in silence.
400 Then spoke the thunder
Da

Datta:[74] what have we given?
My friend, blood shaking my heart
The awful daring of a moment's surrender
405 Which an age of prudence can never retract
By this, and this only, we have existed
Which is not to be found in our obituaries
Or in memories draped by the beneficent spider
Or under seals broken by the lean solicitor
410 In our empty room
Da

Dayadhvam:[75] I have heard the key
Turn in the door once and turn once only
We think of the key, each in his prison
415 Thinking of the key, each confirms a prison
Only at nightfall, aethereal rumours
Revive for a moment a broken Coriolanus[76]
Da

Damyata:[77] The boat responded
420 Gaily, to the hand expert with sail and oar
The sea was calm, your heart would have responded
Gaily, when invited, beating obedient
To controlling hands

            I sat upon the shore
425 Fishing,[78] with the arid plain behind me
Shall I at least set my lands in order?[79]
London Bridge is falling down falling down falling down
Poi s'ascose nel foco che gli affina[80]
Quando fiam uti chelidon[81]—O swallow swallow
430 *Le Prince d'Aquitaine à la tour abolie*[82]

---

[70] The Chapel Perilous wherein the knight was prepared for his quest for the Holy Grail.

[71] The sound of the cock's crow (French version), indicating the coming of dawn and renewal.

[72] The Ganges River.

[73] The Himalaya Mountains.

[74] Sanskrit: "Give." From the words of the thunder in the *Upanishads*.

[75] Sanskrit: "Sympathize."

[76] Roman general and title character of Shakespeare's *Coriolanus*. He was ruined by his pride and the ingratitude of the masses.

[77] Sanskrit: "Control yourselves."

[78] The Fisher King, to whom Eliot alludes, is, like Christ, a symbol of resurrection. See Eliot's note, V, line 425.

[79] "Thus saith the Lord, Set thine house inorder: for thou shalt die, and not live." Isaiah 38:1.

[80] Italian: Then he hid himself in the flame that purifies them," i.e., the flame that destroys lust. Dante, *Purgatorio* (Canto XXVI, *line* 148).

[81] "When shall I be like the swallow?" From the anonymous Latin poem (fourth century?) "Pervigilium Veneris" ("The Vigil of Venus"), celebrating love and the return of spring. See Eliot's note, V, line 429.

[82] French: "The Prince of Aquitaine at the ruined tower." From the sonnet "El Desdichado" by Gerard de Nerval (1808–1855).

These fragments I have shored against my ruins
Why then Ile fit you.[83] Hieronymo's mad againe.[84]

Datta. Dayadhvam. Damyata.

Shantih shantih shantih[85]

1914-1922
1922

---

[83] From *The Spanish Tragedy* by Thomas Kyd (1557?-1595?). The words are spoken by Hieron-ymo, who seeks revenge for the murder of his son.

[84] The subtitle of *The Spanish Tragedy*.

[85] Sanskrit: "The Peace which passeth understanding." See Eliot's note, V, line 434.

Dulce et Decorum Est

Wilfred Owen

1 Bent double, like old beggars under sacks,
Knock-kneed, coughing like hags, we cursed through sludge,
Till on the haunting flares we turned our backs,
And towards our distant rest began to trudge
5 Men marched asleep. Many had lost their boots
But limped on, blood-shod. All went lame, all blind;
Drunk with fatigue; deaf even to the hoots
Of gas-shells dropping softly behind.

Gas! GAS! Quick, boys—An ecstasy of fumbling
10 Fitting the clumsy helmets just in time,
But someone still was yelling out and stumbling
And floundering like a man in fire or lime.—
Dim through the misty panes and thick green light
As under a green sea, I saw him drowning.
15 In all my dreams before my helpless sight
He plunges at me, guttering, choking, drowning.

If in some smothering dreams, you too could pace
Behind the wagon that we flung him in,
And watch the white eyes writhing in his face
20 His hanging face, like a devils sick of sin,
If you could hear, at every jolt, the blood
Gome gargling from the froth-corrupted lungs
Bitter as the cud
Of vile, incurable sores on innocent tongues,—
25 My friend, you would not tell with such high zest
To children ardent for some desperate glory,
The old lie: *Dulce et decorum est Pro patria mori.*

Wilfred Owen, "Dulce et Decorum Est," Copyright in the Public Domain.

Musée des Beaux Arts

W. H. Auden

About suffering they were never wrong,
The Old Masters: how well they understood
Its human position; how it takes place
While someone else is eating or opening a window or just walking dully along;

How, when the aged are reverently, passionately waiting
For the miraculous birth, there always must be
Children who did not specially want it to happen, skating
On a pond at the edge of the wood:
They never forgot
That even the dreadful martyrdom must run its course
Anyhow in a corner, some untidy spot
Where the dogs go on with their doggy life and the torturer's horse
Scratches its innocent behind on a tree.

In Brueghel's Icarus,[1] for instance: how everything turns away
Quite leisurely from the disaster; the plow man may
Have heard the splash, the forsaken cry,
But for him it was not an important failure; the sun shone
As it had to on the white legs disappearing into the green
Water; and the expensive delicate ship that must have seen
Something amazing, a boy falling out of the sky,
Had somewhere to get to and sailed calmly on.

---

[1] This poem describes and comments on Pieter Brueghel's painting Landscape with the Fall of Icarus. According to myth, Daedalus and his son Icarus made wings, whose feathers they attached with wax, to escape Crete. Icarus flew so near the sun that the wax melted and he fell into the sea.

W. H. Auden, "Musée des Beaux-Arts," from *Collected Poems*. Copyright © 2007 by The Estate of W. H. Auden. .

Skunk Hour

Robert Lowell

(For Elizabeth Bishop)

Nautilus Island's hermit
heiress still lives through winters in her
   Spartan cottage;
her sheep still graze above the sea.
Her son's a bishop. Her farmer
is first selectman in our village;
she's in her dotage.

Thirsting for
the hierarchic privacy
of Queen Victoria's century,
she buys up all
the eyesores facing her shore,
and lets them fall.

The season's ill—
we've lost our summer millionaire,
who seemed to leap from an L. L. Bean°
catalogue. His nine-knot yawl
was auctioned off to lobstermen.
A red fox stain covers Blue Hill.

And now our fairy
decorator brightens his shop for fall;
his fishnet's filled with orange cork,
orange, his cobbler's bench and awl;
there is no money in his work,
he'd rather marry.

One dark night,
my Tudor Ford climbed the hill's skull;
I watched for love-cars. Lights turned
   down,
they lay together, hull to hull,
where the graveyard shelves on the town....
My mind's not right.

A car radio bleats,
"Love, O careless Love...." I hear
my ill-spirit sob in each blood cell,
as if my hand were at its throat....
I myself am hell;
nobody's here—

only skunks, that search
in the moonlight for a bite to eat.
They march on their soles up Main Street:
white stripes, moonstruck eyes' red fire
under the chalk-dry and spar spire
of the Trinitarian Church,

I stand on top
of our back steps and breathe the rich air—
a mother skunk with her column of kittens
   swills the garbage pail.
She jabs her wedge-head in a cup
of sour cream, drops her ostrich tail,
and will not scare.

Robert Lowell, "Skunk Hour,",= from *Partisan Review*. Copyright © 1958 by Partisan Review, Inc.

Diving into the Wreck

Adrienne Rich

First having read the book of myths,
and loaded the camera,
and checked the edge of the knife-blade,
I put on
the body-armor of black rubber
the absurd flippers
the grave and awkward mask.
I am having to do this
not like Cousteau with his
assiduous team
aboard the sun-flooded schooner
but here alone.

There is a ladder.
The ladder is always there
hanging innocently
close to the side of the schooner.
We know what it is for,
we who have used it.
Otherwise
it is a piece of maritime floss
some sundry equipment.

I go down.
Rung after rung and still
the oxygen immerses me
the blue light
the clear atoms
of our human air.
I go down.
My flippers cripple me,
I crawl like an insect down the ladder
and there is no one
to tell me when the ocean
will begin.

First the air is blue and then
it is bluer and then green and then
black I am blacking out and yet
my mask is powerful
it pumps my blood with power
the sea is another story
the sea is not a question of power
I have to learn alone
to turn my body without force
in the deep element.

And now: it is easy to forget
what I came for
among so many who have always
lived here
swaying their crenellated fans
between the reefs
and besides
you breathe differently down here.

I came to explore the wreck.
The words are purposes.
The words are maps.
I came to see the damage that was done
and the treasures that prevail.
I stroke the beam of my lamp
slowly along the flank
of something more permanent
than fish or weed

the thing I came for:
the wreck and not the story of the wreck
the thing itself and not the myth
the drowned face always staring

Adrienne Rich, "Diving Into the Wreck," from *Diving into the Wreck: Poems 1971–1972*. Copyright © 1973 by W. W. Norton & Company, Inc. Permission to reprint granted by the publisher.

65	toward the sun		whose drowned face sleeps with open eyes
	the evidence of damage		whose breasts still bear the stress
	worn by salt and sway into this threadbare beauty	80	whose silver, copper, vermeil cargo lies
	the ribs of the disaster		obscurely inside barrels
	curving their assertion		half-wedged and left to rot
70	among the tentative haunters.		we are the half-destroyed instruments
			that once held to a course
	This is the place.	85	the water-eaten log
	And I am here, the mermaid whose dark hair		the fouled compass
	streams black, the merman in his armored body		We are, I am, you are
	We circle silently		by cowardice or courage
75	about the wreck		the one who find our way
	we dive into the hold.	90	back to this scene
	I am she: I am he		carrying a knife, a camera
			a book of myths
			in which
			our names do not appear.

Daddy

Sylvia Plath

	You do not do, you do not do		And a head in the freakish Atlantic
	Any more, black shoe		Where it pours bean green over blue
	In which I have lived like a foot		In the waters off beautiful Nauset.
	For thirty years, poor and white,		I used to pray to recover you.
5	Barely daring to breathe or Achoo.	15	Ach, du.
	Daddy, I have had to kill you.		In the German tongue, in the Polish town
	You died before I had time—		Scraped flat by the roller
	Marble-heavy, a bag full of God,		Of wars, wars, wars.
	Ghastly statue with one gray toe		But the name of the town is common.
10	Big as a Frisco seal	20	My Polack friend

Sylvia Plath, "Daddy," from *The Collected Poems*. Published by Harper & Row, 1981. Copyright by The Estate of Sylvia Plath. Permission to reprint granted by the rights holder.

Says there are a dozen or two.
So I never could tell where you
Put your foot, your root,
I never could talk to you.
25 The tongue stuck in my jaw.

It stuck in a barb wire snare.
Ich, ich, ich, ich,
I could hardly speak.
I thought every German was you.
30 And the language obscene

An engine, an engine
Chuffing me off like a Jew.
A Jew to Dachau, Auschwitz, Belsen.
I began to talk like a Jew.
35 I think I may well be a Jew.

The snows of the Tyrol, the clear beer of
    Vienna
Are not very pure or true.
With my gypsy ancestress and my weird
    luck
And my Taroc pack and my Taroc pack
40 I may be a bit of a Jew.

I have always been scared of *you*,
With your Luftwaffe, your gobbledygoo.
And your neat mustache
And your Aryan eye, bright blue.
45 Panzer-man, panzer-man, O You—

Not God but a swastika
So black no sky could squeak through.
Every woman adores a Fascist,
The boot in the face, the brute
50 Brute heart of a brute like you.

You stand at the blackboard, daddy,
In the picture I have of you,
A cleft in your chin instead of your foot
But no less a devil for that, no not
55 Any less the black man who

Bit my pretty red heart in two.
I was ten when they buried you.
At twenty I tried to die
And get back, back, back to you.
60 I thought even the bones would do.

But they pulled me out of the sack,
And they stuck me together with glue,
And then I knew what to do.
I made a model of you,
65 A man in black with a Meinkampf look

And a love of the rack and the screw.
And I said I do, I do.
So daddy, I'm finally through.
The black telephone's off at the root,
70 The voices just can't worm through.

If I've killed one man, I've killed two—
The vampire who said he was you
And drank my blood for a year,
Seven years, if you want to know.
75 Daddy, you can lie back now.

There's a stake in your fat black heart
And the villagers never liked you.
They are dancing and stamping on you.
They always *knew* it was you.
80 Daddy, daddy, you bastard, I'm through.

Lady Lazarus

Sylvia Plath

I have done it again.
One year in every ten
I manage it—

A sort of walking miracle, my skin
Bright as a Nazi lampshade,
My right foot

A paperweight,
My face a featureless, fine
Jew linen.

Peel off the napkin
O my enemy.
Do I terrify?—

The nose, the eye pits, the full set of teeth?
The sour breath
Will vanish in a day.

Soon, soon the flesh
The grave cave ate will be
At home on me

And I a smiling woman.
I am only thirty.
And like the cat I have nine times to die.

This is Number Three.
What a trash
To annihilate each decade.

What a million filaments.
The peanut-crunching crowd
Shoves in to see

Them unwrap me hand and foot—
The big strip tease.
Gentlemen, ladies,

These are my hands,
My knees.
I may be skin and bone,

Nevertheless, I am the same, identical woman.
The first time it happened I was ten.
It was an accident.

The second time I meant
To last it out and not come back at all.
I rocked shut

As a seashell.
They had to call and call
And pick the worms off me like sticky pearls.

Dying
Is an art, like everything else.
I do it exceptionally well.

I do it so it feels like hell.
I do it so it feels real.
I guess you could say I've a call.

It's easy enough to do it in a cell.
It's easy enough to do it and stay put.

Sylvia Plath, "Lady Lazarus," from *The Collected Poems*. Published by Harper & Row, 1981. Copyright by The Estate of Sylvia Plath. Permission to reprint granted by the rights holder.

It's the theatrical

Comeback in broad day
To the same place, the same face, the same brute
Amused shout:

'A miracle!'
That knocks me out.
There is a charge

For the eyeing of my scars, there is a charge
For the hearing of my heart—
It really goes.

And there is a charge, a very large charge
For a word or a touch
Or a bit of blood

Or a piece of my hair or my clothes.
So, so, Herr Doktor.
So, Herr Enemy.

I am your opus,
I am your valuable,
The pure gold baby

That melts to a shriek.
I turn and burn.
Do not think I underestimate your great concern.

Ash, ash—
You poke and stir.
Flesh, bone, there is nothing there—

A cake of soap,
A wedding ring,
A gold filling.

Herr God, Herr Lucifer
Beware
Beware.

Out of the ash
I rise with my red hair
And I eat men like air.

Section II
FICTION

Young Goodman Brown

Nathaniel Hawthorne

Young Goodman Brown came forth at sunset into the street at Salem village; but put his head back, after crossing the threshold, to exchange a parting kiss with his young wife. And Faith, as the wife was aptly named, thrust her own pretty head into the street, letting the wind play with the pink ribbons of her cap while she called to Goodman Brown.

"Dearest heart," whispered she, softly and rather sadly, when her lips were close to his ear, "prithee put off your journey until sunrise and sleep in your own bed to-night. A lone woman is troubled with such dreams and such thoughts that she's afeared of herself sometimes. Pray tarry with me this night, dear husband, of all nights in the year."

"My love and my Faith," replied young Goodman Brown, "of all nights in the year, this one night must I tarry away from thee. My journey, as thou callest it, forth and back again, must needs be done 'twixt now and sunrise. What, my sweet, pretty wife, dost thou doubt me already, and we but three months married?"

"Then God bless you!" said Faith, with the pink ribbons; "and may you find all well when you come back."

"Amen!" cried Goodman Brown. "Say thy prayers, dear Faith, and go to bed at dusk, and no harm will come to thee."

So they parted; and the young man pursued his way until, being about to turn the corner by the meeting-house, he looked back and saw the head of Faith still peeping after him with a melancholy air, in spite of her pink ribbons.

"Poor little Faith!" thought he, for his heart smote him. "What a wretch am I to leave her on such an errand! She talks of dreams, too. Methought as she spoke there was trouble in her face, as if a dream had warned her what work is to be done to-night. But no, no; 't would kill her to think it. Well, she's a blessed angel on earth, and after this one night I'll cling to her skirts and follow her to heaven."

With this excellent resolve for the future, Goodman Brown felt himself justified in making more haste on his present evil purpose. He had taken a dreary road, darkened by all the gloomiest trees of the forest, which barely stood aside to let the narrow path creep through, and closed immediately behind. It was all as lonely as could be; and there is this peculiarity in such a solitude, that the traveller knows not who may be concealed by the innumerable trunks and the thick boughs overhead; so that with lonely footsteps he may yet be passing through an unseen multitude.

"There may be a devilish Indian behind every tree," said Goodman Brown to himself; and he glanced fearfully behind him as he added, "What if the devil himself should be at my very elbow!"

His head being turned back, he passed a crook of the road, and, looking forward again, beheld the figure of a man, in grave and decent attire, seated at the foot of an old tree. He arose at Goodman Brown's approach and walked onward side by side with him.

"You are late, Goodman Brown," said he. "The clock of the Old South was striking as I came through Boston, and that is full fifteen minutes agone."

"Faith kept me back a while," replied the young man, with a tremor in his voice, caused by the

Nathaniel Hawthorne, "Young Goodman Brown." Copyright in the Public Domain.

sudden appearance of his companion, though not wholly unexpected.

It was now deep dusk in the forest, and deepest in that part of it where these two were journeying. As nearly as could be discerned, the second traveller was about fifty years old, apparently in the same rank of life as Goodman Brown, and bearing a considerable resemblance to him, though perhaps more in expression than features. Still they might have been taken for father and son. And yet, though the elder person was as simply clad as the younger, and as simple in manner too, he had an indescribable air of one who knew the world, and who would not have felt abashed at the governor's dinner table or in King William's court, were it possible that his affairs should call him thither. But the only thing about him that could be fixed upon as remarkable was his staff, which bore the likeness of a great black snake, so curiously wrought that it might almost be seen to twist and wriggle itself like a living serpent. This, of course, must have been an ocular deception, assisted by the uncertain light.

"Come, Goodman Brown," cried his fellow-traveller, "this is a dull pace for the beginning of a journey. Take my staff, if you are so soon weary."

"Friend," said the other, exchanging his slow pace for a full stop, "having kept covenant by meeting thee here, it is my purpose now to return whence I came. I have scruples touching the matter thou wot'st of."

"Sayest thou so?" replied he of the serpent, smiling apart. "Let us walk on, nevertheless, reasoning as we go; and if I convince thee not thou shalt turn back. We are but a little way in the forest yet."

"Too far! too far!" exclaimed the goodman, unconsciously resuming his walk. "My father never went into the woods on such an errand, nor his father before him. We have been a race of honest men and good Christians since the days of the martyrs; and shall I be the first of the name of Brown that ever took this path and kept"—

"Such company, thou wouldst say," observed the elder person, interpreting his pause. "Well said, Goodman Brown! I have been as well acquainted with your family as with ever a one among the Puritans; and that's no trifle to say. I helped your grandfather, the constable, when he lashed the Quaker woman so smartly through the streets of Salem; and it was I that brought your father a pitch-pine knot, kindled at my own hearth, to set fire to an Indian village, in King Philip's war.[1] They were my good friends, both; and many a pleasant walk have we had along this path, and returned merrily after midnight. I would fain be friends with you for their sake."

"If it be as thou sayest," replied Goodman Brown, "I marvel they never spoke of these matters; or, verily, I marvel not, seeing that the least rumor of the sort would have driven them from New England. We are a people of prayer, and good works to boot, and abide no such wickedness."

"Wickedness or not," said the traveller with the twisted staff, "I have a very general acquaintance here in New England. The deacons of many a church have drunk the communion wine with me; the selectmen of divers towns make me their chairman; and a majority of the Great and General Court are firm supporters of my interest. The governor and I, too—But these are state secrets."

"Can this be so?" cried Goodman Brown, with a stare of amazement at his undisturbed companion. "Howbeit, I have nothing to do with the governor and council; they have their own ways, and are no rule for a simple husbandman like me. But, were I to go on with thee, how should I meet the eye of that good old man, our minister, at Salem village? Oh, his voice would make me tremble both Sabbath day and lecture day."

Thus far the elder traveller had listened with due gravity; but now burst into a fit of irrepressible mirth, shaking himself so violently that his snake-like staff actually seemed to wriggle in sympathy.

"Ha! ha! ha!" shouted he again and again; then composing himself, "Well, go on, Goodman Brown, go on; but, prithee, don't kill me with laughing."

"Well, then, to end the matter at once," said Goodman Brown, considerably nettled, "there is my wife, Faith. It would break her dear little heart; and I'd rather break my own."

---

[1] King Philip, a Wampanoag chief, spearheaded the most destructive Indian war ever waged against the New England colonists (1675–76).

"Nay, if that be the case," answered the other, "e'en go thy ways, Goodman Brown. I would not for twenty old women like the one hobbling before us that Faith should come to any harm."

As he spoke he pointed his staff at a female figure on the path, in whom Goodman Brown recognized a very pious and exemplary dame, who had taught him his catechism in youth, and was still his moral and spiritual adviser, jointly with the minister and Deacon Gookin.

"A marvel, truly that Goody Cloyse should be so far in the wilderness at nightfall," said he. "But with your leave, friend, I shall take a cut through the woods until we have left this Christian woman behind. Being a stranger to you, she might ask whom I was consorting with and whither I was going."

"Be it so," said his fellow-traveller. "Betake you to the woods, and let me keep the path."

Accordingly the young man turned aside, but took care to watch his companion, who advanced softly along the road until he had come within a staff's length of the old dame. She, meanwhile, was making the best of her way, with singular speed for so aged a woman, and mumbling some indistinct words—a prayer, doubtless—as she went. The traveller put forth his staff and touched her withered neck with what seemed the serpent's tail.

"The devil!" screamed the pious old lady.

"Then Goody Cloyse knows her old friend?" observed the traveller, confronting her and leaning on his writhing stick.

"Ah, forsooth, and is it your worship indeed?" cried the good dame. "Yea, truly is it, and in the very image of my old gossip, Goodman Brown, the grandfather of the silly fellow that now is. But—would your worship believe it?—my broomstick hath strangely disappeared, stolen, as I suspect, by that unhanged witch, Goody Cory, and that, too, when I was all anointed with the juice of smallage, and cinquefoil, and wolf's bane"—

"Mingled with fine wheat and the fat of a new-born babe," said the shape of old Goodman Brown.

"Ah, your worship knows the recipe," cried the old lady, cackling aloud. "So, as I was saying, being all ready for the meeting, and no horse to ride on, I made up my mind to foot it; for they tell me there is a nice young man to be taken into communion to-night. But now your good worship will lend me your arm, and we shall be there in a twinkling."

"That can hardly be," answered her friend. "I may not spare you my arm, Goody Cloyse; but here is my staff, if you will."

So saying, he threw it down at her feet, where, perhaps, it assumed life, being one of the rods which its owner had formerly lent to the Egyptian magi. Of this fact, however, Goodman Brown could not take cognizance. He had cast up his eyes in astonishment, and, looking down again, beheld neither Goody Cloyse nor the serpentine staff, but his fellow-traveller alone, who waited for him as calmly as if nothing had happened.

"That old woman taught me my catechism," said the young man; and there was a world of meaning in this simple comment.

They continued to walk onward, while the elder traveller exhorted his companion to make good speed and persevere in the path, discoursing so aptly that his arguments seemed rather to spring up in the bosom of his auditor than to be suggested by himself. As they went, he plucked a branch, of maple to serve for a walking stick, and began to strip it of the twigs and little boughs, which were wet with evening dew. The moment his fingers touched them they became strangely withered and dried up as with a week's sunshine. Thus the pair proceeded, at a good free pace, until suddenly, in a gloomy hollow of the road, Goodman Brown sat himself down on the stump of a tree and refused to go any farther.

"Friend," he said, stubbornly, "my mind is made up. Not another step will I budge on this errand. What if a wretched old woman do choose to go to the devil when I thought she was going to heaven: is that any reason, why I should quit my dear Faith and go after her?"

"You will think better of this by and by," said his acquaintance, composedly. "Sit here and rest yourself a while; and when you feel like moving again, there is my staff to help you along."

Without more words, he threw his companion the maple stick, and was as speedily out of sight as if he had vanished into the deepening gloom. The young man sat a few moments by the roadside, applauding himself greatly, and thinking with how clear a conscience he should meet the minister in his morning walk, nor shrink from the eye of good old Deacon Gookin. And what calm sleep would be his that very night, which was to have been spent so wickedly, but so purely and sweetly now, in the arms of Faith! Amidst these pleasant and praiseworthy meditations, Goodman Brown heard the tramp of horses along the road, and deemed it advisable to conceal himself within the verge of the forest, conscious of the guilty purpose that had brought him thither, though now so happily turned from it.

On came the hoof tramps and the voices of the riders, two grave old voices, conversing soberly as they drew near. These mingled sounds appeared to pass along the road, within a few yards of the young man's hiding-place; but, owing doubtless to the depth of the gloom at that particular spot, neither the travellers nor their steeds were visible. Though their figures brushed the small boughs by the wayside, it could not be seen that they intercepted, even for a moment, the faint gleam from the strip of bright sky athwart which they must have passed. Goodman Brown alternately crouched and stood on tiptoe, pulling aside the branches and thrusting forth his head as far as he durst without discerning so much as a shadow. It vexed him the more, because he could have sworn, were such a thing possible, that he recognized the voices of the minister and Deacon Gookin, jogging along quietly, as they were wont to do, when bound to some ordination or ecclesiastical council. While yet within hearing, one of the riders stopped to pluck a switch.

"Of the two, reverend sir," said the voice like the deacon's, "I had rather miss an ordination dinner than to-night's meeting. They tell me that some of our community are to be here from Falmouth and beyond, and others from Connecticut and Rhode Island, besides several of the Indian powwows, who, after their fashion, know almost as much deviltry as the best of us. Moreover, there is a goodly young woman to be taken into communion."

"Mighty well, Deacon Gookin!" replied the solemn old tones of the minister. "Spur up, or we shall be late. Nothing can be done, you know, until I get on the ground."

The hoofs clattered again; and the voices, talking so strangely in the empty air, passed on through the forest, where no church had ever been gathered or solitary Christian prayed. Whither, then, could these holy men be journeying so deep into the heathen wilderness? Young Goodman Brown caught hold of a tree for support, being ready to sink down on the ground, faint and overburdened with the heavy sickness of his heart. He looked up to the sky, doubting whether there really was a heaven above him. Yet there was the blue arch, and the stars brightening in it.

"With heaven above and Faith below, I will yet stand firm against the devil!" cried Goodman Brown.

While he still gazed upward into the deep arch of the firmament and had lifted his hands to pray, a cloud, though no wind was stirring, hurried across the zenith and hid the brightening stars. The blue sky was still visible, except directly overhead, where this black mass of cloud was sweeping swiftly northward. Aloft in the air, as if from the depths of the cloud, came a confused and doubtful sound of voices. Once the listener fancied that he could distinguish the accents of towns-people of his own, men and women, both pious and ungodly, many of whom he had met at the communion table, and had seen others rioting at the tavern. The next moment, so indistinct were the sounds, he doubted whether he had heard aught but the murmur of the old forest, whispering without a wind. Then came a stronger swell of those familiar tones, heard daily in the sunshine at Salem village, but never until now from a cloud of night. There was one voice, of a young woman, uttering lamentations, yet with an uncertain sorrow, and entreating for some favor, which, perhaps, it would grieve her to obtain; and all the unseen multitude, both saints and sinners, seemed to encourage her onward.

"Faith!" shouted Goodman Brown, in a voice of agony and desperation; and the echoes of the forest mocked him, crying, "Faith! Faith!" as if bewildered wretches were seeking her all through the wilderness.

The cry of grief, rage, and terror was yet piercing the night, when the unhappy husband held his breath for a response. There was a scream, drowned immediately in a louder murmur of voices, fading into far-off laughter, as the dark cloud swept away, leaving the clear and silent sky above Goodman Brown. But something fluttered lightly down through the air and caught on the branch of a tree. The young man seized it, and beheld a pink ribbon.

"My Faith is gone!" cried he after one stupefied moment. "There is no good on earth; and sin is but a name. Come, devil; for to thee is this world given."

And, maddened with despair, so that he laughed loud and long, did Goodman Brown grasp his staff and set forth again, at such a rate that he seemed to fly along the forest path rather than to walk or run. The road grew wilder and drearier and more faintly traced, and vanished at length, leaving him in the heart of the dark wilderness, still rushing onward with the instinct that guides mortal man to evil. The whole forest was peopled with frightful sounds—the creaking of the trees, the howling of wild beasts, and the yell of Indians; while sometimes the wind tolled like a distant church bell, and sometimes gave a broad roar around the traveller, as if all Nature were laughing him to scorn. But he was himself the chief horror of the scene, and shrank not from its other horrors.

"Ha! ha! ha!" roared Goodman Brown when the wind laughed at him. "Let us hear which will laugh loudest. Think not to frighten me with your deviltry. Come witch, come wizard, come Indian powwow, come devil himself, and here comes Goodman Brown. You may as well fear him as he fear you."

In truth, all through the haunted forest there could be nothing more frightful than the figure of Goodman Brown. On he flew among the black pines, brandishing his staff with frenzied gestures, now giving vent to an inspiration of horrid blasphemy, and now shouting forth such laughter as set all the echoes of the forest laughing like demons around him. The fiend in his own shape is less hideous than when he rages in the breast of man. Thus sped the demoniac on his course, until, quivering among the trees, he saw a red light before him, as when the felled trunks and branches of a clearing have been set on fire, and throw up their lurid blaze against the sky, at the hour of midnight. He paused, in a lull of the tempest that had driven him onward, and heard the swell of what seemed a hymn, rolling solemnly from a distance with the weight of many voices. He knew the tune; it was a familiar one in the choir of the village meeting-house. The verse died heavily away, and was lengthened by a chorus, not of human voices, but of all the sounds of the benighted wilderness pealing in awful harmony together. Goodman Brown cried out, and his cry was lost to his own ear by its unison with the cry of the desert.

In the interval of silence he stole forward until the light glared full upon his eyes. At one extremity of an open space, hemmed in by the dark wall of the forest, arose a rock, bearing some rude, natural resemblance either to an altar or a pulpit, and surrounded by four blazing pines, their tops aflame, their stems untouched, like candles at an evening meeting. The mass of foliage that had overgrown the summit of the rock was all on fire, blazing high into the night and fitfully illuminating the whole field. Each pendent twig and leafy festoon was in a blaze. As the red light arose and fell, a numerous congregation alternately shone forth, then disappeared in shadow, and again grew, as it were, out of the darkness, peopling the heart of the solitary woods at once.

"A grave and dark-clad company," quoth Goodman Brown.

In truth they were such. Among them, quivering to and fro between gloom and splendor, appeared faces that would be seen next day at the council board of the province, and others which, Sabbath after Sabbath, looked devoutly heavenward, and benignantly over the crowded pews, from the holiest pulpits in the land. Some affirm that the lady of the governor was there. At least there were high dames well known to her, and wives of honored husbands, and widows, a great multitude, and ancient maidens, all of excellent repute, and fair young girls, who trembled lest their mothers should espy them. Either the sudden gleams of light flashing over the obscure field bedazzled Goodman Brown, or he recognized a score of the church members of Salem village famous for their especial sanctity. Good old Deacon Gookin had arrived, and waited at the skirts of that venerable saint, his revered pastor. But, irreverently consorting with these grave, reputable, and pious people, these elders of the church, these chaste dames and dewy virgins, there were men of dissolute lives and women of spotted fame, wretches given over to all mean and filthy vice, and suspected even of horrid crimes. It was strange to see that the good shrank not from the wicked, nor were the sinners abashed by the saints. Scattered also among their pale-faced enemies were the Indian priests, or powwows, who had often scared their native forest with more hideous incantations than any known to English witchcraft.

"But where is Faith?" thought Goodman Brown; and, as hope came into his heart, he trembled.

Another verse of the hymn arose, a slow and mournful strain, such as the pious love, but joined to words which expressed all that our nature can conceive of sin, and darkly hinted at far more. Unfathomable to mere mortals is the lore of fiends. Verse after verse was sung; and still the chorus of the desert swelled between like the deepest tone of a mighty organ; and with the final peal of that dreadful anthem there came a sound, as if the roaring wind, the rushing streams, the howling beasts, and every other voice of the unconcerted wilderness were mingling and according with the voice of guilty man in homage to the prince of all. The four blazing pines threw up a loftier flame, and obscurely discovered shapes and visages of horror on the smoke wreaths above the impious assembly. At the same moment the fire on the rock shot redly forth and formed a flowing arch above its base, where now appeared a figure. With reverence be it spoken, the figure bore no slight similitude, both in garb and manner, to some grave divine of the New England churches.

"Bring forth the converts!" cried a voice that echoed through the field and rolled into the forest.

At the word, Goodman Brown stepped forth from the shadow of the trees and approached the congregation, with whom he felt a loathful brotherhood by the sympathy of all that was wicked in his heart. He could have well-nigh sworn that the shape of his own dead father beckoned him to advance, looking downward from a smoke wreath, while a woman, with dim features of despair, threw out her hand to warn him back. Was it his mother? But he had no power to retreat one step, nor to resist, even in thought, when the minister and good old Deacon Gookin seized his arms and led him to the blazing rock. Thither came also the slender form of a veiled female, led between Goody Cloyse, that pious teacher of the catechism, and Martha Carrier, who had received the devil's promise to be queen of hell. A rampant hag was she. And there stood the proselytes beneath the canopy of fire.

"Welcome, my children," said the dark figure, "to the communion of your race. Ye have found thus young your nature and your destiny. My children, look behind you!"

They turned; and flashing forth, as it were, in a sheet of flame, the fiend worshippers were seen; the smile of welcome gleamed darkly on every visage.

"There," resumed the sable form, "are all whom ye have reverenced from youth. Ye deemed them holier than yourselves and shrank from your own sin, contrasting it with their lives of righteousness and prayerful aspirations heavenward. Yet here are they all in my worshipping assembly. This night it shall be granted you to know their secret deeds: how hoary-bearded elders of the church have whispered wanton words to the young maids of their households; how many a woman, eager for widows' weeds, has given her husband a drink at bedtime and let him sleep his last sleep in her bosom; how beardless youths have made haste to inherit their fathers' wealth; and how fair damsels—blush not, sweet ones—have dug little graves in the garden, and bidden me, the sole guest, to an infant's funeral. By the sympathy of your human hearts for sin ye shall scent out all the places—whether in church, bedchamber, street, field, or forest—where crime has been committed, and shall exult to behold the whole earth one stain of guilt, one mighty blood spot. Far more than this. It shall be yours to penetrate, in every bosom, the deep mystery of sin, the fountain of all wicked arts, and which inexhaustibly supplies more evil impulses than human power—than my power at its utmost—can make manifest in deeds. And now, my children, look upon each other."

They did so; and, by the blaze of the hell-kindled torches, the wretched man beheld his Faith, and the wife her husband, trembling before that unhallowed altar.

"Lo, there ye stand, my children," said the figure, in a deep and solemn tone, almost sad with its despairing awfulness, as if his once angelic nature could yet mourn for our miserable race. "Depending upon one another's hearts, ye had still hoped that virtue were not all a dream. Now are ye undeceived. Evil is the nature of mankind. Evil must be your only happiness. Welcome again, my children, to the communion of your race."

"Welcome," repeated the fiend worshippers, in one cry of despair and triumph.

And there they stood, the only pair, as it seemed, who were yet hesitating on the verge of wickedness in this dark world. A basin was hallowed, naturally, in the rock. Did it contain water, reddened by the lurid light? or was it blood? or, perchance, a liquid flame? Herein did the shape of evil dip his hand and prepare to lay the mark of baptism upon their foreheads, that they might be partakers of the mystery of sin, more conscious of the secret guilt of others, both in deed and thought, than they could now be of their own. The husband cast one look at his pale wife, and Faith at him. What polluted wretches would the next glance show them to each other, shuddering alike at what they disclosed and what they saw!

"Faith! Faith!" cried the husband, "look up to heaven, and resist the wicked one."

Whether Faith obeyed he knew not. Hardly had he spoken when he found himself amid calm night and solitude, listening to a roar of the wind which died heavily away through the forest. He staggered against the rock, and felt it chill and damp; while a hanging twig, that had been all on fire, besprinkled his cheek with the coldest dew.

The next morning young Goodman Brown came slowly into the street of Salem village, staring around him like a bewildered man. The good old minister was taking a walk along the graveyard to get an appetite for breakfast and meditate his sermon, and bestowed a blessing, as he passed, on Goodman Brown. He shrank from the venerable saint as if to avoid an anathema. Old Deacon Gookin was at domestic worship, and the holy words of his prayer were heard through the open window. "What God doth the wizard pray to?" quoth Goodman Brown. Goody Cloyse, that excellent old Christian, stood in the early sunshine at her own lattice, catechizing a little girl who had brought her a pint of morning's milk. Goodman Brown snatched away the child as from the grasp of the fiend himself. Turning the corner by the meeting-house, he spied the head of Faith, with the pink ribbons, gazing anxiously forth, and bursting into such joy at sight of him that she skipped along the street and almost kissed her husband before the whole village. But Goodman Brown looked sternly and sadly into her face, and passed on without a greeting.

Had Goodman Brown fallen asleep in the forest and only dreamed a wild dream of a witch-meeting?

Be it so if you will; but, alas! it was a dream of evil omen for young Goodman Brown. A stern, a sad, a darkly meditative, a distrustful, if not a desperate man did he become from the night of that fearful dream. On the Sabbath day, when the congregation were singing a holy psalm, he could not listen because an anthem of sin rushed loudly upon his ear and drowned all the blessed strain. When the minister spoke from the pulpit with power and fervid eloquence, and, with his hand on the open Bible, of the sacred truths of our religion, and of saint-like lives and triumphant deaths, and of future bliss or misery unutterable, then did Goodman Brown turn pale, dreading lest the roof should thunder down upon the gray blasphemer and his hearers. Often awaking suddenly at midnight, he shrank from the bosom of Faith; and at morning or eventide, when the family knelt down at prayer, he scowled and muttered to himself, and gazed sternly at his wife, and turned away. And when he had lived long, and was borne to his grave a hoary corpse, followed by Faith, an aged woman, and children and grandchildren, a goodly procession, besides neighbors not a few, they carved no hopeful verse upon his tombstone, for his dying hour was gloom.

1835

The Cask of Amontillado

Edgar Allan Poe

The thousand injuries of Fortunato I had borne as I best could; but when he ventured upon insult, I vowed revenge. You, who so well know the nature of my soul, will not suppose, however, that I gave utterance to a threat. At length I would be avenged; this was a point definitely settled—but the very definitiveness with which it was resolved precluded the idea of risk. I must not only punish, but punish with impunity. A wrong is unredressed when retribution overtakes its redresser. It is equally unredressed when the avenger fails to make himself felt as such to him who has done the wrong.

It must be understood, that neither by word nor deed had I given Fortunato cause to doubt my good-will. I continued, as was my wont, to smile in his face, and he did not perceive that my smile now was at the thought of his immolation.

He had a weak point—this Fortunato—although in other regards he was a man to be respected and even feared. He prided himself on his connoisseurship in wine. Few Italians have the true virtuoso spirit. For the most part their enthusiasm is adopted to suit the time and opportunity—to practise imposture upon the British and Austrian millionnaires. In painting and gemmary Fortunato, like his countrymen, was a quack—but in the matter of old wines he was sincere. In this respect I did not differ from him materially: I was skilful in the Italian vintages myself, and bought largely whenever I could.

It was about dusk, one evening during the supreme madness of the carnival season, that I encountered my friend. He accosted me with excessive warmth, for he had been drinking much. The man wore motley. He had on a tight-fitting parti-striped dress, and his head was surmounted by the conical cap and bells. I was so pleased to see him, that I thought I should never have done wringing his hand.

I said to him: "My dear Fortunato, you are luckily met. How remarkably well you are looking to-day! But I have received a pipe[1] of what passes for Amontillado, and I have my doubts"

"How?" said he. "Amontillado? A pipe? Impossible! And in the middle of the carnival!"

"I have my doubts," I replied; "and I was silly enough to pay the full Amontillado price without consulting you in the matter. You were not to be found, and I was fearful of losing a bargain."

"Amontillado!"

"I have my doubts."

"Amontillado!"

"And I must satisfy them."

"Amontillado!"

"As you are engaged, I am on my way to Luchesi. If any one has a critical turn, it is he. He will tell me—"

"Luchesi cannot tell Amontillado from Sherry."

"And yet some fools will have it that his taste is a match for your own."

"Come, let us go."

"Whither?"

"To your vaults."

"My friend, no; I will not impose upon your good nature. I perceive you have an engagement. Luchesi—"

"I have no engagement;—come."

---

[1] A large cask or keg.

Edgar Allan Poe, "The Cask of Amontillado," from *Godey's Lady's Book*. Copyright in the Public Domain.

"My friend, no. It is not the engagement, but the severe cold with which I perceive you are afflicted. The vaults are insufferably damp. They are encrusted with nitre."

"Let us go, nevertheless. The cold is merely nothing. Amontillado! You have been imposed upon. And as for Luchesi, he cannot distinguish Sherry from Amontillado."

Thus speaking, Fortunato possessed himself of my arm. Putting on a mask of black silk, and drawing a roquelaire[2] closely about my person, I suffered him to hurry me to my palazzo.

There were no attendants at home; they had absconded to make merry in honor of the time. I had told them that I should not return until the morning, and had given them explicit orders not to stir from the house. These orders were sufficient, I well knew, to insure their immediate disappearance, one and all, as soon as my back was turned.

I took from their sconces two flambeaux, and giving one to Fortunato, bowed him through several suites of rooms to the archway that led into the vaults. I passed down a long and winding staircase, requesting him to be cautious as he followed. We came at length to the foot of the descent, and stood together on the damp ground of the catacombs of the Montresors.

The gait of my friend was unsteady, and the bells upon his cap jingled as he strode.

"The pipe?" said he.

"It is farther on," said I; "but observe the white web-work which gleams from these cavern walls."

He turned toward me, and looked into my eyes with two filmy orbs that distilled the rheum of intoxication.

"Nitre?" he asked, at length.

"Nitre," I replied. "How long have you had that cough?"

"Ugh! ugh! ugh!—ugh! ugh! ugh!—ugh! ugh! ugh!—ugh! ugh! ugh!—ugh! ugh! ugh!"

My poor friend found it impossible to reply for many minutes.

"It is nothing," he said, at last.

"Come," I said, with decision, "we will go back; your health is precious. You are rich, respected, admired, beloved; you are happy, as once I was. You are a man to be missed. For me it is no matter. We will go back; you will be ill, and I cannot be responsible. Besides, there is Luchesi—"

"Enough," he said; "the cough is a mere nothing; it will not kill me. I shall not die of a cough."

"True—true," I replied; "and, indeed, I had no intention of alarming you unnecessarily; but you should use all proper caution. A draught of this Medoc will defend us from the damps."

Here I knocked off the neck of a bottle which I drew from a long row of its fellows that lay upon the mould.

"Drink," I said, presenting him the wine.

He raised it to his lips with a leer. He paused and nodded to me familiarly, while his bells jingled.

"I drink," he said, "to the buried that repose around us."

"And I to your long life."

He again took my arm, and we proceeded.

"These vaults," he said, "are extensive."

"The Montresors," I replied, "were a great and numerous family."

"I forget your arms."

"A huge human foot d'or,[3] in a field azure; the foot crushes a serpent rampant whose fangs are imbedded in the heel."

"And the motto?"

"Nemo me impune lacessit."[4]

"Good!" he said.

The wine sparkled in his eyes and the bells jingled. My own fancy grew warm, with the Medoc. We had passed through walls of piled bones, with casks and puncheons intermingling into the inmost recesses of the catacombs. I paused again, and this time I made bold to seize Fortunato by an arm above the elbow.

"The nitre!" I said; "see, it increases. It hangs like moss upon the vaults. We are below the river's bed. The drops of moisture trickle among the bones.

---

[2] A short cloak.

[3] Of gold

[4] "No one wounds me with impunity"; the motto of the royal arms of Scotland.

Come, we will go back ere it is too late. Your cough—"

"It is nothing," he said; "let us go on. But first, another draught of the Medoc."

I broke and reached him a flagon of De Grâve. He emptied it at a breath. His eyes flashed with a fierce light. He laughed and threw the bottle upward with a gesticulation I did not understand.

I looked at him in surprise. He repeated the movement—a grotesque one.

"You do not comprehend?" he said.

"Not I," I replied.

"Then you are not of the brotherhood."

"How?"

"You are not of the masons."

"Yes, yes," I said; "yes, yes."

"You? Impossible! A mason?"

"A mason," I replied.

"A sign," he said.

"It is this," I answered, producing a trowel from beneath the folds of my roquelaire.

"You jest," he exclaimed, recoiling a few paces. "But let us proceed to the Amontillado."

"Be it so," I said, replacing the tool beneath the cloak, and again offering him my arm. He leaned upon it heavily. We continued our route in search of the Amontillado. We passed through a range of low arches, descended, passed on, and descending again, arrived at a deep crypt, in which the foulness of the air caused our flambeaux rather to glow than flame.

At the most remote end of the crypt there appeared another less spacious. Its walls had been lined with human remains, piled to the vault overhead, in the fashion of the great catacombs of Paris. Three sides of this interior crypt were still ornamented in this manner. From the fourth the bones had been thrown down, and lay promiscuously upon the earth, forming at one point a mound of some size. Within the wall thus exposed by the displacing of the bones, we perceived a still interior recess, in depth about four feet, in width three, in height six or seven. It seemed to have been constructed for no especial use within itself, but formed merely the interval between two of the colossal supports of the roof of the catacombs, and was backed by one of their circumscribing walls of solid granite.

It was in vain that Fortunato, uplifting his dull torch, endeavored to pry into the depth of the recess. Its termination the feeble light did not enable us to see.

"Proceed," I said; "herein is the Amontillado. As for Luchesi—"

"He is an ignoramus," interrupted my friend, as he stepped unsteadily forward, while I followed immediately at his heels. In an instant he had reached the extremity of the niche, and finding his progress arrested by the rock, stood stupidly bewildered. A moment more and I had fettered him to the granite. In its surface were two iron staples, distant from each other about two feet, horizontally From one of these depended a short chain, from the other a padlock. Throwing the links about his waist, it was but the work of a few seconds to secure it. He was too much astounded to resist. Withdrawing the key I stepped back from the recess.

"Pass your hand," I said, "over the wall; you cannot help feeling the nitre. Indeed it is very damp. Once more let me implore you to return. No? Then I must positively leave you. But I must first render you all the little attentions in my power."

"The Amontillado!" ejaculated my friend, not yet recovered from his astonishment.

"True," I replied; "the Amontillado."

As I said these words I busied myself among the pile of bones of which I have before spoken. Throwing them aside, I soon uncovered a quantity of building stone and mortar. With these materials and with the aid of my trowel, I began vigorously to wall up the entrance of the niche.

I had scarcely laid the first tier of the masonry when I discovered that the intoxication of Fortunato had in a great measure worn off. The earliest indication I had of this was a low moaning cry from the depth of the recess. It was *not* the cry of a drunken man. There was then a long and obstinate silence. I laid the second tier, and the third, and the fourth; and then I heard the furious vibrations of the chain. The noise lasted for several minutes, during which, that I might hearken to it with the more satisfaction, I ceased my labors and sat down upon the bones.

When at last the clanking subsided, I resumed the trowel, and finished without interruption the fifth, the sixth, and the seventh tier. The wall was now nearly upon a level with my breast. I again paused, and holding the flambeaux over the masonwork, threw a few feeble rays upon the figure within.

A succession of loud and shrill screams, bursting suddenly from the throat of the chained form, seemed to thrust me violently back. For a brief moment I hesitated—I trembled. Unsheathing my rapier, I began to grope with it about the recess; but the thought of an instant reassured me. I placed my hand upon the solid fabric of the catacombs, and felt satisfied. I reapproached the wall. I replied to the yells of him who clamored. I reechoed—I aided—I surpassed them in volume and in strength. I did this, and the clamorer grew still.

It was now midnight, and my task was drawing to a close. I had completed the eighth, the ninth, and the tenth tier. I had finished a portion of the last and the eleventh; there remained but a single stone to be fitted and plastered in. I struggled with its weight; I placed it partially in its destined position. But now there came from out the niche a low laugh that erected the hairs upon my head. It was succeeded by a sad voice, which I had difficulty in recognizing as that of the noble Fortunato. The voice said—

"Ha! ha! ha!—he! he!—a very good joke indeed—an excellent jest. We will have many a rich laugh about it at the palazzo—he! he! he!—over our wine—he! he! he!"

"The Amontillado!" I said.

"He! he! he!—he! he! he!—yes, the Amontillado. But is it not getting late? Will not they be awaiting us at the palazzo, the Lady Fortunato and the rest? Let us be gone."

"Yes," I said, "let us be gone."

For the love of God, Montresor!

"Yes," I said, "for the love of God!"

But to these words I hearkened in vain for a reply. I grew impatient. I called aloud:

"Fortunato!"

No answer. I called again:

"Fortunato!"

No answer still, I thrust a torch through the remaining aperture and let it fall within. There came forth in return only a jingling of the bells. My heart grew sick—on account of the dampness of the catacombs. I hastened to make an end of my labor. I forced the last stone into its position; I plastered it up. Against the new masonry I re-erected the old rampart of bones. For the half of a century no mortal has disturbed them. *In pace requiescat!*[5]

1846

---

[5] In peace may he rest (Latin)

The Black Cat

Edgar Allan Poe

For the most wild, yet most homely narrative which I am about to pen, I neither expect nor solicit belief. Mad indeed would I be to expect it, in a case where my very senses reject their own evidence. Yet, mad am I not—and very surely do I not dream. But to-morrow I die, and to-day I would unburden my soul. My immediate purpose is to place before the world, plainly, succinctly, and without comment, a series of mere household events. In their consequences, these events have terrified—have tortured—have destroyed me. Yet I will not attempt to expound them. To me, they have presented little but Horror—to many they will seem less terrible than *barroques*. Hereafter, perhaps, some intellect may be found which will reduce my phantasm to the common-place—some intellect more calm, more logical, and far less excitable than my own, which will perceive, in the circumstances I detail with awe, nothing more than an ordinary succession of very natural causes and effects.

From my infancy I was noted for the docility and humanity of my disposition. My tenderness of heart was even so conspicuous as to make me the jest of my companions. I was especially fond of animals, and was indulged by my parents with a great variety of pets. With these I spent most of my time, and never was so happy as when feeding and caressing them. This peculiarity of character grew with my growth, and, in my manhood, I derived from it one of my principal sources of pleasure. To those who have cherished an affection for a faithful and sagacious dog, I need hardly be at the trouble of explaining the nature or the intensity of the gratification thus derivable. There is something in the unselfish and self-sacrificing love of a brute, which goes directly to the heart of him who has had frequent occasion to test the paltry friendship and gossamer fidelity of mere *Man*.

I married early, and was happy to find in my wife a disposition not uncongenial with my own. Observing my partiality for domestic pets, she lost no opportunity of procuring those of the most agreeable kind. We had birds, goldfish, a fine dog, rabbits, a small monkey, and a *cat*.

This latter was a remarkably large and beautiful animal, entirely black, and sagacious to an astonishing degree. In speaking of his intelligence, my wife, who at heart was not a little tinctured with superstition, made frequent allusion to the ancient popular notion, which regarded all black cats as witches in disguise. Not that she was ever *serious* upon this point—and I mention the matter at all for no better reason than that it happens, just now, to be remembered.

Pluto—this was the cat's name—was my favorite pet and playmate. I alone fed him, and he attended me wherever I went about the house. It was even with difficulty that I could prevent him from following me through the streets.

Our friendship lasted, in this manner, for several years, during which my general temperament and character—through the instrumentality of the Fiend Intemperance—had (I blush to confess it) experienced a radical alteration for the worse. I grew, day by day, more moody, more irritable, more regardless of the feelings of others. I suffered myself to use intemperate language to my wife. At length, I even offered her personal violence. My pets, of course, were made to feel the change in my

Edgar Allan Poe, The Black Cat", from *The Saturday Evening Post*. Published by Saturday Evening Post Society, 1843. Copyright in the Public Domain.

disposition. I not only neglected, but ill-used them. For Pluto, however, I still retained sufficient regard to restrain me from maltreating him, as I made no scruple of maltreating the rabbits, the monkey, or even the dog, when by accident, or through affection, they came in my way. But my disease grew upon me—for what disease is like Alcohol!—and at length even Pluto, who was now becoming old, and consequently somewhat peevish—even Pluto began to experience the effects of my ill temper.

One night, returning home, much intoxicated, from one of my haunts about town, I fancied that the cat avoided my presence. I seized him; when, in his fright at my violence, he inflicted a slight wound upon my hand with his teeth. The fury of a demon instantly possessed me. I knew myself no longer. My original soul seemed, at once, to take its flight from my body; and a more than fiendish malevolence, gin-nurtured, thrilled every fibre of my frame. I took from my waistcoat-pocket a pen-knife, opened it, grasped the poor beast by the throat, and deliberately cut one of its eyes from the socket! I blush, I burn, I shudder, while I pen the damnable atrocity.

When reason returned with the morning—when I had slept off the fumes of the night's debauch—I experienced a sentiment half of horror, half of remorse, for the crime of which I had been guilty; but it was, at best, a feeble and equivocal feeling, and the soul remained untouched. I again plunged into excess, and soon drowned in wine all memory of the deed.

In the meantime the cat slowly recovered. The socket of the lost eye presented, it is true, a frightful appearance, but he no longer appeared to suffer any pain. He went about the house as usual, but, as might be expected, fled in extreme terror at my approach. I had so much of my old heart left, as to be at first grieved by this evident dislike on the part of a creature which had once so loved me. But this feeling soon gave place to irritation. And then came, as if to my final and irrevocable overthrow, the spirit of PERVERSENESS. Of this spirit philosophy takes no account. Yet I am not more sure that my soul lives, than I am that perverseness is one of the primitive impulses of the human heart—one of the indivisible primary faculties, or sentiments, which give direction to the character of Man. Who has not, a hundred times, found himself committing a vile or a silly action, for no other reason than because he knows he should *not*? Have we not a perpetual inclination, in the teeth of our best judgment, to violate that which is Law, merely because we understand it to be such? This spirit of perverseness, I say, came to my final overthrow. It was this unfathomable longing of the soul to vex itself—to offer violence to its own nature—to do wrong for the wrong's sake only—that urged me to continue and finally to consummate the injury I had inflicted upon the unoffending brute. One morning, in cold blood, I slipped a noose about its neck and hung it to the limb of a tree;—hung it with the tears streaming from my eyes, and with the bitterest remorse at my heart;—hung it *because* I knew that it had loved me, and because I felt it had given me no reason of offence;—hung it *because* I knew that in so doing I was committing a sin—a deadly sin that would so jeopardize my immortal soul as to place it—if such a thing were possible—even beyond the reach of the infinite mercy of the Most Merciful and Most Terrible God.

On the night of the day on which this cruel deed was done, I was aroused from sleep by the cry of fire. The curtains of my bed were in flames. The whole house was blazing. It was with great difficulty that my wife, a servant, and myself, made our escape from the conflagration. The destruction was complete. My entire worldly wealth was swallowed up, and I resigned myself thenceforward to despair.

I am above the weakness of seeking to establish a sequence of cause and effect, between the disaster and the atrocity. But I am detailing a chain of facts—and wish not to leave even a possible link imperfect. On the day succeeding the fire, I visited the ruins. The walls, with one exception, had fallen in. This exception was found in a compartment wall, not very thick, which stood about the middle of the house, and against which had rested the head of my bed. The plastering had here, in great measure, resisted the action of the fire—a fact which I attributed to its having been recently spread. About this wall a dense crowd were collected, and many persons seemed to be examining a particular portion of it with very minute and eager attention. The words "strange!" "singular!" and other similar expressions, excited my curiosity. I approached and saw, as if graven in *bas-relief* upon the white surface, the figure of a gigantic *cat*. The impression was given with an accuracy truly marvellous. There was a rope about the animal's neck.

When I first beheld this apparition—for I could scarcely regard it as less—my wonder and my terror were extreme. But at length reflection came to my aid. The cat, I remembered, had been hung in a garden adjacent to the house. Upon the alarm of fire, this garden had been immediately filled by the crowd—by some one of whom the animal must have been cut from the tree and thrown, through an open window, into my chamber. This had probably been done with the view of arousing me from sleep. The falling of other walls had compressed the victim of my cruelty into the substance of the freshly-spread plaster; the lime of which, with the flames, and the ammonia from the carcass, had then accomplished the portraiture as I saw it.

Although I thus readily accounted to my reason, if not altogether to my conscience, for the startling fact just detailed, it did not the less fail to make a deep impression upon my fancy. For months I could not rid myself of the phantasm of the cat; and, during this period, there came back into my spirit a half-sentiment that seemed, but was not, remorse. I went so far as to regret the loss of the animal, and to look about me, among the vile haunts which I now habitually frequented, for another pet of the same species, and of somewhat similar appearance, with which to supply its place.

One night as I sat, half stupified, in a den of more than infamy, my attention was suddenly drawn to some black object, reposing upon the head of one of the immense hogsheads of gin, or of rum, which constituted the chief furniture of the apartment. I had been looking steadily at the top of this hogshead for some minutes, and what now caused me surprise was the fact that I had not sooner perceived the object thereupon. I approached it, and touched it with my hand. It was a black cat—a very large one—fully as large as Pluto, and closely resembling him in every respect but one. Pluto had not a white hair upon any portion of his body; but this cat had a large, although indefinite splotch of white, covering nearly the whole region of the breast.

Upon my touching him, he immediately arose, purred loudly, rubbed against my hand, and appeared delighted with my notice. This, then, was the very creature of which I was in search. I at once offered to purchase it of the landlord; but this person made no claim to it—knew nothing of it—had never seen it before.

I continued my caresses, and, when I prepared to go home, the animal evinced a disposition to accompany me. I permitted it to do so; occasionally stooping and patting it as I proceeded. When it reached the house it domesticated itself at once, and became immediately a great favorite with my wife.

For my own part, I soon found a dislike to it arising within me. This was just the reverse of what I had anticipated; but—I know not how or why it was—its evident fondness for myself rather disgusted and annoyed me. By slow degrees, these feelings of disgust and annoyance rose into the bitterness of hatred. I avoided the creature; a certain sense of shame, and the remembrance of my former deed of cruelty, preventing me from physically abusing it. I did not, for some weeks, strike, or otherwise violently ill use it; but gradually—very gradually—I came to look upon it with unutterable loathing, and to flee silently from its odious presence, as from the breath of a pestilence.

What added, no doubt, to my hatred of the beast, was the discovery, on the morning after I brought it home, that, like Pluto, it also had been deprived of one of its eyes. This circumstance, however, only endeared it to my wife, who, as I have already said, possessed, in a high degree, that humanity of feeling which had once been my distinguishing trait, and the source of many of my simplest and purest pleasures.

With my aversion to this cat, however, its partiality for myself seemed to increase. It followed my footsteps with a pertinacity which it would be difficult to make the reader comprehend. Whenever I sat, it would crouch beneath my chair, or spring upon my knees, covering me with its loathsome caresses. If I arose to walk it would get between my feet and thus nearly throw me down, or, fastening its long and sharp claws in my dress, clamber, in this manner, to my breast. At such times, although I longed to destroy it with a blow, I was yet withheld from so doing, partly by a memory of my former crime, but chiefly—let me confess it at once—by absolute *dread* of the beast.

This dread was not exactly a dread of physical evil—and yet I should be at a loss how otherwise to define it. I am almost ashamed to own—yes, even in this felon's cell, I am almost ashamed to own—that the terror and horror with which the animal inspired me, had been heightened by one of the merest chimeras it would be possible to conceive. My wife had called my attention, more than once, to the character of the mark of white hair, of which I have spoken, and which constituted the sole visible difference between the strange beast and the one I had destroyed. The reader will remember that this mark, although large, had been originally very indefinite; but, by slow degrees—degrees nearly imperceptible, and which for a long time my reason struggled to reject as fanciful—it had, at length, assumed a rigorous distinctness of outline. It was now the representation of an object that I shudder to name—and for this, above all, I loathed, and dreaded, and would have rid myself of the monster *had I dared*—it was now, I say, the image of a hideous—of a ghastly thing—of the GALLOWS!—oh, mournful and terrible engine of Horror and of Crime—of Agony and of Death!

And now was I indeed wretched beyond the wretchedness of mere Humanity. And *a brute beast*—whose fellow I had contemptuously destroyed—*a brute beast* to work out for me—for me a man, fashioned in the image of the High God—so much of insufferable woe! Alas! neither by day nor by night knew I the blessing of Rest any more! During the former the creature left me no moment alone; and, in the latter, I started, hourly, from dreams of unutterable fear, to find the hot breath of *the thing* upon my face, and its vast weight—an incarnate nightmare that I had no power to shake off—incumbent eternally upon my *heart*!

Beneath the pressure of torments such as these, the feeble remnant of the good within me succumbed. Evil thoughts became my sole intimates—the darkest and most evil of thoughts. The moodiness of my usual temper increased to hatred of all things and of all mankind; while from the sudden, frequent, and ungovernable outbursts of a fury to which I now blindly abandoned myself, my uncomplaining wife, alas, was the most usual and the most patient of sufferers.

One day she accompanied me, upon some household errand, into the cellar of the old building which our poverty compelled us to inhabit. The cat followed me down the steep stairs, and, nearly throwing me headlong, exasperated me to madness. Uplifting an axe, and forgetting, in my wrath, the childish dread which had hitherto stayed my hand, I aimed a blow at the animal which, of course, would have proved instantly fatal had it descended as I wished. But this blow was arrested by the hand of my wife. Goaded, by the interference, into a rage more than demoniacal, I withdrew my arm from her grasp and buried the axe in her brain. She fell dead upon the spot, without a groan.

This hideous murder accomplished, I set myself forthwith, and with entire deliberation, to the task of concealing the body. I knew that I could not remove it from the house, either by day or by night, without the risk of being observed by the neighbors. Many projects entered my mind. At one period I thought of cutting the corpse into minute fragments, and destroying them by fire. At another, I resolved to dig a grave for it in the floor of the cellar. Again, I deliberated about casting it in the well in the yard—about packing it in a box, as if merchandize, with the usual arrangements, and so getting a porter to take it from the house. Finally I hit upon what I considered a far better expedient than either of these. I determined to wall it up in the cellar, as the monks of the Middle Ages are recorded to have walled up their victims.

For a purpose such as this the cellar was well adapted. Its walls were loosely constructed, and had lately been plastered throughout with a rough plaster, which the dampness of the atmosphere had prevented from hardening. Moreover, in one of the walls was a projection, caused by a false chimney, or fireplace, that had been filled up, and made to resemble the rest of the cellar. I made no doubt that I could readily displace the bricks at this point, insert the corpse, and wall the whole up as before, so that no eye could detect any thing suspicious.

And in this calculation I was not deceived. By means of a crow bar I easily dislodged the bricks, and, having carefully deposited the body against the inner wall, I propped it in that position, while, with little trouble, I relaid the whole structure as it originally stood. Having procured mortar, sand, and hair, with every possible precaution, I prepared a plaster which could not be distinguished from the old, and with this I very carefully went over the new brick-work. When I had finished, I felt satisfied that all was right. The wall did not present the slightest appearance of having been disturbed. The rubbish on the floor was picked up with the minutest care. I looked around triumphantly, and said to myself—"Here at least, then, my labor has not been in vain."

My next step was to look for the beast which had been the cause of so much wretchedness; for I had, at length, firmly resolved to put it to death. Had I been able to meet with it, at the moment, there could have been no doubt of its fate; but it appeared that the crafty animal had been alarmed at the violence of my previous anger, and forebore to present itself in my present mood. It is impossible to describe, or to imagine, the deep, the blissful sense of relief which the absence of the detested creature occasioned in my bosom. It did not make its appearance during the night; and thus for one night at least, since its introduction into the house, I soundly and tranquilly slept; aye, *slept* even with the burden of murder upon my soul!

The second and the third day passed, and still my tormentor came not. Once again I breathed as a freeman. The monster, in terror, had fled the premises for ever! I should behold it no more! My happiness was supreme! The guilt of my dark deed disturbed me but little. Some few inquiries had been made, but these had been readily answered. Even a search had been instituted—but of course nothing was to be discovered. I looked upon my future felicity as secured.

Upon the fourth day of the assassination, a party of the police came, very unexpectedly, into the house, and proceeded again to make rigorous investigation of the premises. Secure, however, in the inscrutability of my place of concealment, I felt no embarrassment whatever. The officers bade me accompany them in their search. They left no nook or corner unexplored. At length, for the third or fourth time, they descended into the cellar. I quivered not in a muscle. My heart beat calmly as that of one who slumbers in innocence. I walked the cellar from end to end. I folded my arms upon my bosom, and roamed easily to and fro. The police were thoroughly satisfied and prepared to depart. The glee at my heart was too strong to be restrained. I burned to say if but one word, by way of triumph, and to render doubly sure their assurance of my guiltlessness.

"Gentlemen," I said at last, as the party ascended the steps, "I delight to have allayed your suspicions. I wish you all health, and a little more courtesy. By the bye, gentlemen, this—this is a very well-constructed house," (In the rabid desire to say something easily, I scarcely knew what I uttered at all),—"I may say an *excellently* well-constructed house. These walls—are you going, gentlemen?—these walls are solidly put together"; and here, through the mere frenzy of bravado, I rapped heavily, with a cane which I held in my hand, upon that very portion of the brick-work behind which stood the corpse of the wife of my bosom.

But may God shield and deliver me from the fangs of the Arch-Fiend! No sooner had the reverberation of my blows sunk into silence, than I was answered by a voice from within the tomb!—by a cry, at first muffled and broken, like the sobbing of a child, and then quickly swelling into one long, loud, and continuous scream, utterly anomalous and inhuman—a howl—a wailing shriek, half of horror and half of triumph, such as might have arisen only out of hell, conjointly from the throats of the dammed in their agony and of the demons that exult in the damnation.

Of my own thoughts it is folly to speak. Swooning, I staggered to the opposite wall. For one instant the party upon the stairs remained motionless, through extremity of terror and of awe. In the next, a dozen stout arms were toiling at the wall. It fell bodily. The corpse, already greatly decayed and clotted with gore, stood erect before the eyes of the spectators. Upon its head, with red extended mouth and solitary eye of fire, sat the hideous beast whose craft had seduced me into murder, and whose informing voice had consigned me to the hangman. I had walled the monster up within the tomb.

Bartleby, the Scrivener:

A Story of Wall Street

Herman Melville

I am a rather elderly man. The nature of my avocations, for the last thirty years, has brought me into more than ordinary contact with what would seem an interesting and somewhat singular set of men, of whom, as yet, nothing, that I know of, has ever been written—I mean, the law-copyists or scriveners. I have known very many of them, professionally and privately, and, if I pleased, could relate divers histories, at which good-natured gentlemen might smile, and sentimental souls might weep. But I waive the biographies of all other scriveners, for a few passages in the life of Bartleby, who was a scrivener, the strangest I ever saw, or heard of. While, of other law-copyists I might write the complete life, of Bartleby nothing of that sort can be done. I believe that no materials exist, for a full and satisfactory biography of this man. It is an irreparable loss to literature. Bartleby was one of those beings of whom nothing is ascertainable, except from the original sources, and, in his case, those are very small. What my own astonished eyes saw of Bartleby, *that* is all I know of him, except, indeed, one vague report, which will appear in the sequel.

Ere introducing the scrivener, as he first appeared to me, it is fit I make some mention of myself, my *employés,* my business, my chambers, and general surroundings, because some such description is indispensable to an adequate understanding of the chief character about to be presented. Imprimis:[1] I am a man who, from his youth upwards, has been filled with a profound conviction that the easiest way of life is the best. Hence, though I belong to a profession proverbially energetic and nervous, even to turbulence, at times, yet nothing of that sort have I ever suffered to invade my peace. I am one of those unambitious lawyers who never address a jury, or in any way draw down public applause; but, in the cool tranquillity of a snug retreat, do a snug business among rich men's bonds, and mortgages, and title-deeds. All who know me, consider me an eminently *safe* man. The late John Jacob Astor, a personage

---

[1] In the first place (Latin)

Herman Melville, "Bartleby the Scrivener: A Story of Wall Street", from Putnam's Magazine. Copyright in the Public Domain.

little given to poetic enthusiasm, had no hesitation in pronouncing my first grand point to be prudence; my next, method. I do not speak it in vanity, but simply record the fact, that I was not unemployed in my profession by the late John Jacob Astor; a name which, I admit, I love to repeat; for it hath a rounded and orbicular sound to it, and rings like unto bullion. I will freely add, that I was not insensible to the late John Jacob Astor's good opinion.

Some time prior to the period at which this little history begins, my avocations had been largely increased. The good old office, now extinct in the State of New York, of a Master in Chancery, had been conferred upon me. It was not a very arduous office, but very pleasantly remunerative. I seldom lose my temper; much more seldom indulge in dangerous indignation at wrongs and outrages; but I must be permitted to be rash here and declare, that I consider the sudden and violent abrogation of the office of Master in Chancery, by the new Constitution, as a premature act; inasmuch as I had counted upon a life-lease of the profits, whereas I only received those of a few short years. But this is by the way.

My chambers were up stairs, at No.—Wall Street. At one end, they looked upon the white wall of the interior of a spacious skylight shaft, penetrating the building from top to bottom.

This view might have been considered rather tame than otherwise, deficient in what landscape painters call "life." But, if so, the view from the other end of my chambers offered, at least, a contrast, if nothing more. In that direction, my windows commanded an unobstructed view of a lofty brick wall, black by age and everlasting shade; which wall required no spy-glass to bring out its lurking beauties, but, for the benefit of all near-sighted spectators, was pushed up to within ten feet of my window-panes. Owing to the great height of the surrounding buildings, and my chambers being on the second floor, the interval between this wall and mine not a little resembled a huge square cistern.

At the period just preceding the advent of Bartleby, I had two persons as copyists in my employment, and a promising lad as an office-boy. First, Turkey; second, Nippers; third, Ginger Nut. These may seem names, the like of which are not usually found in the Directory. In truth, they were nicknames, mutually conferred upon each other by my three clerks, and were deemed expressive of their respective persons or characters. Turkey was a short, pursy Englishman of about my own age—that is, somewhere not far from sixty. In the morning, one might say, his face was of a fine florid hue, but after twelve o'clock, meridian—his dinner hour—it blazed like a grate full of Christmas coals; and continued blazing—but, as it were, with a gradual wane—till six o'clock, P.M., or thereabouts; after which, I saw no more of the proprietor of the face, which, gaining its meridian with the sun, seemed to set with it, to rise, culminate, and decline the following day, with the like regularity and undiminished glory. There are many singular coincidences I have known in the course of my life, not the least among which was the fact, that, exactly when Turkey displayed his fullest beams from his red and radiant countenance, just then, too, at that critical moment, began the daily period when I considered his business capacities as seriously disturbed for the remainder of the twenty-four hours. Not that he was absolutely idle, or averse to business then; far from it. The difficulty was, he was apt to be altogether too energetic. There was a strange, inflamed, flurried, flighty recklessness of activity about him. He would be incautious in dipping his pen into his inkstand. All his blots upon my documents were dropped there after twelve o'clock, meridian. Indeed, not only would he be reckless, and sadly given to making blots in the afternoon, but, some days, he went further, and was rather noisy. At such times, too, his face flamed with augmented blazonry, as if cannel coal had been heaped on anthracite. He made an unpleasant racket with his chair; spilled his sand-box; in mending his pens, impatiently split them all to pieces, and threw them on the floor in a sudden passion; stood up, and leaned over his table, boxing his papers about in a most indecorous manner, very sad to behold in an elderly man like him. Nevertheless, as he was in many ways a most valuable person to me, and all the time before twelve o'clock, meridian, was the quickest, steadiest creature, too, accomplishing a great deal of work in a style not easily to be matched—for these reasons, I was willing to overlook his eccentricities, though, indeed, occasionally, I remonstrated with him. I did this very gently, however, because, though the civilest, nay, the blandest and most reverential of men in the morning, yet, in the afternoon, he was disposed, upon provocation, to be slightly rash with his tongue—in fact, insolent. Now, valuing his morning services as I did, and resolved not to lose them—yet, at the same time, made uncomfortable by his inflamed ways after twelve o'clock—and being a man of peace, unwilling by my admonitions to call forth unseemly retorts from him, I took upon me, one Saturday noon (he was always worse on Saturdays) to hint to him, very kindly, that, perhaps, now that he was growing old, it might be well to abridge his labors; in short, he need not come to my chambers after twelve o'clock, but, dinner over, had best go home to his lodgings, and rest himself till tea-time. But no; he insisted upon his afternoon devotions. His countenance became intolerably fervid, as he oratorically assured me—gesticulating with a long ruler at the other end of the room—that if his services in the morning were useful, how indispensable, then, in the afternoon?

"With submission, sir," said Turkey, on this occasion, "I consider myself your right-hand man. In the morning I but marshal and deploy my columns; but in the afternoon I put myself at their head, and gallantly charge the foe, thus"—and he made a violent thrust with the ruler.

"But the blots, Turkey," intimated I.

"True; but, with submission, sir, behold these hairs! I am getting old. Surely, sir, a blot or two of a warm afternoon is not to be severely urged against gray hairs. Old age—even if it blot the page—is honorable. With submission, sir, we *both* are getting old."

This appeal to my fellow-feeling was hardly to be resisted. At all events, I saw that go he would not. So, I made up my mind to let him stay, resolving, nevertheless, to see to it that, during the afternoon, he had to do with my less important papers.

Nippers, the second on my list, was a whiskered, sallow, and, upon the whole, rather piratical-looking young man, of about five-and-twenty. I always deemed him the victim of two evil powers—ambition and indigestion. The ambition was evinced by a certain impatience of the duties of a mere copyist, an unwarrantable usurpation of strictly professional affairs such as the original drawing up of legal documents. The indigestion seemed betokened in an occasional nervous testiness and grinning irritability, causing the teeth to audibly grind together over mistakes committed in copying; unnecessary maledictions, hissed, rather than spoken, in the heat of business; and especially by a continual discontent with the height of the table where he worked. Though of a very ingenious mechanical turn, Nippers could never get this table to suit him. He put chips under it, blocks of various sorts, bits of pasteboard, and at last went so far as to attempt an exquisite adjustment, by final pieces of folded blotting paper. But no invention would answer. If, for the sake of easing his back, he brought the table-lid at a sharp angle well up towards his chin, and wrote there like a man using the steep roof of a Dutch house for his desk, then he declared that it stopped the circulation in his arms. If now he lowered the table to his waistbands, and stooped over it in writing, then there was a sore aching in his back. In short, the truth of the matter was, Nippers knew not what he wanted. Or, if he wanted anything, it was to be rid of a scrivener's table altogether. Among the manifestations of his diseased ambition was a fondness he had for receiving visits from certain ambiguous-looking fellows in seedy coats, whom he called his clients. Indeed, I was aware that not only was he, at times, considerable of a ward-politician, but he occasionally did a little business at the justices' courts, and was not unknown on the steps of the Tombs.[2] I have good reason to believe, however, that one individual who called upon him at my chambers, and who, with a grand air, he insisted was his client, was no other than a dun, and the alleged title-deed, a bill. But, with all his failings, and the annoyances he caused me, Nippers, like his compatriot Turkey, was a very useful man to me; wrote a neat, swift hand; and, when he chose, was not deficient in a gentlemanly sort of deportment. Added to this, he always dressed in a gentlemanly sort of way; and so, incidentally, reflected credit upon my chambers. Whereas, with

---

[2] A prison in New York City.

respect to Turkey, I had much ado to keep him from being a reproach to me. His clothes were apt to look oily, and smell of eating-houses. He wore his pantaloons very loose and baggy in summer. His coats were execrable, his hat not to be handled. But while the hat was a thing of indifference to me, inasmuch as his natural civility and deference, as a dependent Englishman, always led him to doff it the moment he entered the room, yet his coat was another matter. Concerning his coats, I reasoned with him; but with no effect. The truth was, I suppose, that a man with so small an income could not afford to sport such a lustrous face and a lustrous coat at one and the same time. As Nippers once observed, Turkey's money went chiefly for red ink. One winter day, I presented Turkey with a highly respectable-looking coat of my own—a padded gray coat, of a most comfortable warmth, and which buttoned straight up from the knee to the neck. I thought Turkey would appreciate the favor, and abate his rashness and obstreperousness of afternoons. But no; I verily believe that buttoning himself up in so downy and blanket-like a coat had a pernicious effect upon him upon the same principle that too much oats are bad for horses. In fact, precisely as a rash, restive horse is said to feel his oats, so Turkey felt his coat. It made him insolent. He was a man whom prosperity harmed.

Though, concerning the self-indulgent habits of Turkey, I had my own private surmises, yet, touching Nippers, I was well persuaded that, whatever might be his faults in other respects, he was, at least, a temperate young man. But, indeed, nature herself seemed to have been his vintner, and, at his birth, Charged him so thoroughly with an irritable, brandy-like disposition, that all subsequent potations were needless. When I consider how, amid the stillness of my chambers, Nippers would sometimes impatiently rise from his seat, and stooping over his table, spread his arms wide apart, seize the whole desk, and move it, and jerk it, with a grim, grinding motion on the floor, as if the table were a perverse voluntary agent, intent on thwarting and vexing him, I plainly perceive that, for Nippers, brandy-and-water were altogether superfluous.

It was fortunate for me that, owing to its peculiar cause—indigestion—the irritability and consequent nervousness of Nippers were mainly observable in the morning, while in the afternoon he was comparatively mild. So that, Turkey's paroxysms only coming on about twelve o'clock, I never had to do with their eccentricities at one time. Their fits relieved each other, like guards. When Nippers' was on, Turkey's was off; and *vice versa*. This was a good natural arrangement, under the circumstances.

Ginger Nut, the third on my list, was a lad, some twelve years old. His father was a carman, ambitious of seeing his son on the bench instead of a cart, before he died. So he sent him to my office, as student at law, errand-boy, cleaner, and sweeper, at the rate of one dollar a week. He had a little desk to himself, but he did not use it much. Upon inspection, the drawer exhibited a great array of the shells of various sorts of nuts. Indeed, to this quick-witted youth, the whole noble science of the law was contained in a nutshell. Not the least among the employments of Ginger Nut, as well as one which he discharged with the most alacrity, was his duty as cake and apple purveyor for Turkey and Nippers. Copying lawpapers being proverbially a dry, husky sort of business, my two scriveners were fain to moisten their mouths very often with Spitzenbergs, to be had at the numerous stalls nigh the Custom House and Post Office. Also, they sent Ginger Nut very frequently for that peculiar cake—small, flat, round, and very spicy—after which he had been named by them. Of a cold morning, when business was but dull, Turkey would gobble up scores of these cakes, as if they were mere wafers—indeed, they sell them at the rate of six or eight for a penny—the scrape of his pen blending with the crunching of the crisp particles in his mouth. Of all the fiery afternoon blunders and flurried rashness of Turkey, was his once moistening a ginger-cake between his lips, and clapping it on to a mortgage, for a seal. I came within an ace of dismissing him then. But he mollified me by making an oriental bow, and saying—

"With submission, sir, it was generous of me to find you in stationery on my own account."

Now my original business—that of a conveyancer and title hunter, and drawer-up of recondite documents of all sorts—was considerably increased by receiving the Master's office. There was now great work for scriveners. Not only must I push the clerks already with me, but I must have additional help.

In answer to my advertisement, a motionless young man one morning stood upon my office threshold, the door being open, for it was summer. I can see that figure now—pallidly neat, pitiably respectable, incurably forlorn! It was Bartleby.

After a few words touching his qualifications, I engaged him, glad to have among my corps of copyists a man of so singularly sedate an aspect, which I thought might operate beneficially upon the flighty temper of Turkey, and the fiery one of Nippers.

I should have stated before that ground-glass folding-doors divided my premises into two parts, one of which was occupied by my scriveners, the other by myself. According to my humor, I threw open these doors, or closed them. I resolved to assign Bartleby a corner by the folding-doors, but on my side of them, so as to have this quiet man within easy call, in case any trifling thing was to be done. I placed his desk close up to a small side-window in that part of the room, a window which originally had afforded a lateral view of certain grimy brickyards and bricks, but which, owing to subsequent erections, commanded at present no view at all, though it gave some light. Within three feet of the panes was a wall, and the light came down from far above, between two lofty buildings, as from a very small opening in a dome. Still further to a satisfactory arrangement, I procured a high green folding screen, which might entirely isolate Bartleby from my sight, though not remove him from my voice. And thus, in a manner, privacy and society were conjoined.

At first, Bartleby did an extraordinary quantity of writing. As if long famishing for something to copy, he seemed to gorge himself on my documents. There was no pause for digestion. He ran a day and night line, copying by sunlight and by candle-light. I should have been quite delighted with his application, had he been cheerfully industrious. But he wrote on silently, palely, mechanically.

It is, of course, an indispensable part of a scrivener's business to verify the accuracy of his copy, word by word. Where there are two or more scriveners in an office, they assist each other in this examination, one reading from the copy, the other holding the original. It is a very dull, wearisome, and lethargic affair. I can readily imagine that, to some sanguine temperaments, it would be altogether intolerable. For example, I cannot credit that the mettlesome poet, Byron, would have contentedly sat down with Bartleby to examine a law document of, say five hundred pages, closely written in a crimpy hand.

Now and then, in the haste of business, it had been my habit to assist in comparing some brief document myself, calling Turkey or Nippers for this purpose. One object I had, in placing Bartleby so handy to me behind the screen, was, to avail myself of his services on such trivial occasions. It was on the third day, I think, of his being with me, and before any necessity had arisen for having his own writing examined, that, being much hurried to complete a small affair I had in hand, I abruptly called to Bartleby. In my haste and natural expectancy of instant compliance, I sat with my head bent over the original on my desk, and my right hand sideways, and somewhat nervously extended with the copy, so that, immediately upon emerging from his retreat, Bartleby might snatch it and proceed to business without the least delay.

In this very attitude did I sit when I called to him, rapidly stating what it was I wanted him to do—namely, to examine a small paper with me. Imagine my surprise, nay, my consternation, when, without moving from his privacy, Bartleby, in a singularly mild, firm voice, replied, "I would prefer not to."

I sat awhile in perfect silence, rallying my stunned faculties. Immediately it occurred to me that my ears had deceived me, or Bartleby had entirely misunderstood my meaning. I repeated my request in the clearest tone I could assume; but in quite as clear a one came the previous reply, "I would prefer not to."

"Prefer not to," echoed I, rising in high excitement, and crossing the room with a stride. "What do you mean? Are you moonstruck? I want you to help me compare this sheet here—take it," and I thrust it towards him.

"I would prefer not to," said he.

I looked at him steadfastly. His face was leanly composed; his gray eye dimly calm. Not a wrinkle of agitation rippled him. Had there been the least uneasiness, anger, impatience, or impertinence in his manner; in other words, had there been anything ordinarily human about him, doubtless I should have violently dismissed him from the premises. But as it was, I should have as soon thought of turning my pale plaster-of-paris bust of Cicero out of doors. I stood gazing at him awhile, as he went on with his own writing, and then reseated myself at my desk. This is very strange, thought I. What had one best do? But my business hurried me. I concluded to forget the matter for the present, reserving it for my future leisure. So, calling Nippers from the other room, the paper was speedily examined.

A few days after this, Bartleby concluded four lengthy documents, being quadruplicates of a week's testimony taken before me in my High Court of Chancery. It became necessary to examine them. It was an important suit, and great accuracy was imperative. Having all things arranged, I called Turkey, Nippers, and Ginger Nut, from the next room, meaning to place the four copies in the hands of my four clerks, while I should read from the original. Accordingly, Turkey, Nippers, and Ginger Nut had taken their seats in a row, each with his document in his hand, when I called to Bartleby to join this interesting group.

"Bartleby! quick, I am waiting."

I heard a slow scrape of his chair legs on the uncarpeted floor, and soon he appeared standing at the entrance of his hermitage.

"What is wanted?" said he, mildly.

"The copies, the copies," said I, hurriedly. "We are going to examine them. There"—and I held towards him the fourth quadruplicate.

"I would prefer not to," he said, and gently disappeared behind the screen.

For a few moments I was turned into a pillar of salt, standing at the head of my seated column of clerks. Recovering myself, I advanced towards the screen, and demanded the reason for such extraordinary conduct.

"*Why* do you refuse?"

"I would prefer not to."

With any other man I should have flown outright into a dreadful passion, scorned all further words, and thrust him ignominiously from my presence. But there was something about Bartleby that not only strangely disarmed me, but, in a wonderful manner, touched and disconcerted me. I began to reason with him.

"These are your own copies we are about to examine. It is labor saving to you, because one examination will answer for your four papers. It is common usage. Every copyist is bound to help examine his copy. Is it not so? Will you not speak? Answer!"

"I prefer not to," he replied in a flute-like tone. It seemed to me that, while I had been addressing him, he carefully revolved every statement that I made; fully comprehended the meaning; could not gainsay the irresistible conclusion; but, at the same time, some paramount consideration prevailed with him to reply as he did.

"You are decided, then, not to comply with my request—a request made according to common usage and common sense?"

He briefly gave me to understand, that on that point my judgment was sound. Yes: his decision was irreversible.

It is not seldom the case that, when a man is browbeaten in some unprecedented and violently unreasonable way, he begins to stagger in his own plainest faith. He begins, as it were, vaguely to surmise that, wonderful as it may be, all the justice and all the reason is on the other side. Accordingly, if any disinterested persons are present, he turns to them for some reinforcement for his own faltering mind.

"Turkey," said I, "what do you think of this? Am I not right?"

"With submission, sir," said Turkey, in his blandest tone, "I think that you are."

"Nippers," said I, "what do *you* think of it?"

"I think I should kick him out of the office."

(The reader of nice perceptions will have perceived that, it being morning, Turkey's answer is couched in polite and tranquil terms, but Nippers replies in ill-tempered ones. Or, to repeat a previous sentence, Nippers' ugly mood was on duty, and Turkey's off.)

"Ginger Nut," said I, willing to enlist the smallest suffrage in my behalf, "what do *you* think of it?"

"I think, sir, he's a little *luny*," replied Ginger Nut, with a grin.

"You hear what they say," said I, turning towards the screen, "come forth and do your duty."

But he vouchsafed no reply. I pondered a moment in sore perplexity. But once more business hurried me. I determined again to postpone the consideration of this dilemma to my future leisure. With a little trouble we made out to examine the papers without Bartleby, though at every page or two Turkey deferentially dropped his opinion, that this proceeding was quite out of the common; while Nippers, twitching in his chair with a dyspeptic nervousness, ground out, between his set teeth, occasional hissing maledictions against the stubborn oaf behind the screen. And for his (Nippers') part, this was the first and the last time he would do another man's business without pay.

Meanwhile Bartleby sat in his hermitage, oblivious to everything but his own peculiar business there.

Some days passed, the scrivener being employed upon another lengthy work. His late remarkable conduct led me to regard his ways narrowly. I observed that he never went to dinner; indeed, that he never went anywhere. As yet I had never, of my personal knowledge, known him to be outside of my office. He was a perpetual sentry in the corner. At about eleven o'clock though, in the morning, I noticed that Ginger Nut would advance towards the opening in Bartleby's screen, as if silently beckoned thither by a gesture invisible to me where I sat. The boy would then leave the office, jingling a few pence, and reappear with a handful of ginger-nuts, which he delivered in the hermitage, receiving two of the cakes for his trouble.

He lives, then, on ginger-nuts, thought I; never eats a dinner, properly speaking; he must be a vegetarian, then, but no; he never eats even vegetables, he eats nothing but ginger-nuts. My mind then ran on in reveries concerning the probable effects upon the human constitution of living entirely on ginger-nuts. Ginger-nuts are so called, because they contain ginger as one of their peculiar constituents, and the final flavoring one. Now, what was ginger? A hot, spicy thing. Was Bartleby hot and spicy? Not at all. Ginger, then, had no effect upon Bartleby. Probably he preferred it should have none.

Nothing so aggravates an earnest person as a passive resistance. If the individual so resisted be of a not inhumane temper, and the resisting one perfectly harmless in his passivity, then, in the better moods of the former, he will endeavor charitably to construe to his imagination what proves impossible to be solved by his judgment. Even so, for the most part, I regarded Bartleby and his ways. Poor fellow! thought I, he means no mischief; it is plain he intends no insolence; his aspect sufficiently evinces that his eccentricities are involuntary. He is useful to me. I can get along with him. If I turn him away, the chances are he will fall in with some less indulgent employer, and then he will be rudely treated, and perhaps driven forth miserably to starve. Yes. Here I can cheaply purchase a delicious self-approval. To befriend Bartleby; to humor him in his strange wilfulness, will cost me little or nothing, while I lay up in my soul what will eventually prove a sweet morsel for my conscience. But this mood was not invariable with me. The passiveness of Bartleby sometimes irritated me. I felt strangely goaded on to encounter him in new opposition—to elicit some angry spark from him answerable to my own. But, indeed, I might as well have essayed to strike fire with my knuckles against a bit of Windsor soap. But one afternoon the evil impulse in me mastered me, and the following little scene ensued:

"Bartleby," said I, "when those papers are all copied, I will compare them with you."

"I would prefer not to."

"How? Surely you do not mean to persist in that mulish vagary?"

No answer.

I threw open the folding-doors nearby, and turning upon Turkey and Nippers, exclaimed:

"Bartleby a second time says, he won't examine his papers. What do you think of it, Turkey?"

It was afternoon, be it remembered. Turkey sat glowing like a brass boiler; his bald head steaming; his hands reeling among his blotted papers.

"Think of it?" roared Turkey. "I think I'll just step behind his screen, and black his eyes for him!"

So saying, Turkey rose to his feet and threw his arms into a pugilistic position. He was hurrying away to make good his promise, when I detained him, alarmed at the effect of incautiously rousing Turkey's combativeness after dinner.

"Sit down, Turkey," said I, "and hear what Nippers has to say. What do you think of it, Nippers? Would I not be justified in immediately dismissing Bartleby?"

"Excuse me, that is for you to decide, sir. I think his conduct quite unusual, and, indeed, unjust, as regards Turkey and myself. But it may only be a passing whim."

"Ah," exclaimed I, "you have strangely changed your mind, then—you speak very gently of him now."

"All beer," cried Turkey; "gentleness is effects of beer—Nippers and I dined together to-day. You see how gentle *I* am, sir. Shall I go and black his eyes?"

"You refer to Bartleby, I suppose. No, not to-day, Turkey," I replied; "pray, put up your fists."

I closed the doors, and again advanced towards Bartleby. I felt additional incentives tempting me to my fate. I burned to be rebelled against again. I remembered that Bartleby never left the office.

"Bartleby," said I, "Ginger Nut is away; just step around to the Post Office, won't you?" (it was but a three minutes' walk) "and see if there is anything for me."

"I would prefer not to."

"You will not?"

"I *prefer* not."

I staggered to my desk, and sat there in a deep study. My blind inveteracy returned. Was there any other thing in which I could procure myself to be ignominiously repulsed by this lean, penniless wight? my hired clerk? What added thing is there, perfectly reasonable, that he will be sure to refuse to do?

"Bartleby!"

No answer.

"Bartleby," in a louder tone.

No answer.

"Bartleby," I roared.

Like a very ghost, agreeably to the laws of magical invocation, at the third summons, he appeared at the entrance of his hermitage.

"Go to the next room, and tell Nippers to come to me."

"I would prefer not to," he respectfully and slowly said, and mildly disappeared.

"Very good, Bartleby," said I, in a quiet sort of serenely-severe self-possessed tone, intimating the unalterable purpose of some terrible retribution very close at hand. At the moment I half intended something of the kind. But upon the whole, as it was drawing towards my dinner-hour, I thought it best to put on my hat and walk home for the day, suffering much from perplexity and distress of mind.

Shall I acknowledge it? The conclusion of this whole business was, that it soon became a fixed fact of my chambers, that a pale young scrivener, by the name of Bartleby, had a desk there; that he copied for me at the usual rate of four cents a folio (one hundred words); but he was permanently exempt from examining the work done by him, that duty being transferred to Turkey and Nippers, out of compliment, doubtless, to their superior acuteness; moreover, said Bartleby was never, on any account, to be dispatched on the most trivial errand of any sort; and that even if entreated to take upon him such a matter, it was generally understood that he would "prefer not to"—in other words, that he would refuse point blank.

As days passed on, I became considerably reconciled to Bartleby. His steadiness, his freedom from all dissipation, his incessant industry (except when he chose to throw himself into a standing revery behind his screen), his great stillness, his unalterableness of demeanor under all circumstances, made him a valuable acquisition. One prime thing was this—*he was always there*—first in the morning, continually through the day, and the last at night. I had a singular confidence in his honesty. I felt my most precious papers perfectly safe in his hands. Sometimes, to be sure, I could not, for the very soul of me, avoid falling into sudden spasmodic passions with him. For it was exceeding difficult to bear in mind all the time those strange peculiarities, privileges, and unheard-of exemptions, forming the tacit stipulations on Bartleby's part under which he remained in my office. Now and then, in the eagerness of dispatching pressing business, I would inadvertently summon Bartleby, in a short, rapid tone, to put his finger, say, on the incipient tie of a bit of red tape with which I was about compressing some papers. Of course, from behind the screen the usual answer, "I prefer not to," was sure to come; and then, how could a human creature, with the common infirmities of our nature, refrain from bitterly exclaiming upon such perverseness—such unreasonableness? However, every added repulse of this sort which I received only tended to lessen the probability of my repeating the inadvertence.

Here it must be said, that, according to the custom of most legal gentlemen occupying chambers in densely populated law buildings, there were several keys to my door. One was kept by a woman residing in the attic, which person weekly scrubbed and daily swept and dusted my apartments. Another was kept by Turkey for convenience sake. The third I sometimes carried in my own pocket. The fourth I knew not who had.

Now, one Sunday morning I happened to go to Trinity Church, to hear a celebrated preacher, and finding myself rather early on the ground I thought I would walk round to my chambers for a while. Luckily I had my key with me; but upon applying it to the lock, I found it resisted by something inserted from the inside. Quite surprised, I called out; when to my consternation a key was turned from within; and thrusting his lean visage at me, and holding the door ajar, the apparition of Bartleby appeared, in his shirt-sleeves, and otherwise in a strangely tattered *dishabille*, saying quietly that he was sorry, but he was deeply engaged just then, and preferred not admitting me at present. In a brief word or two, he moreover added, that perhaps I had better walk round the block two or three times, and by that time he would probably have concluded his affairs.

Now, the utterly unsurmised appearance of Bartleby, tenanting my law-chambers of a Sunday morning, with his cadaverously gentlemanly *nonchalance*, yet withal firm and self-possessed, had such a strange effect upon me, that incontinently I slunk away from my own door, and did as desired. But not without sundry twinges of impotent rebellion against the mild effrontery of this unaccountable scrivener. Indeed, it was his wonderful mildness chiefly, which not only disarmed me, but unmanned me, as it were. For I consider that one, for the time, is sort of unmanned when he tranquilly permits his hired clerk to dictate to him, an order him away from his own premises. Further-more , I was full of uneasiness as to what Bartleby could possibly be doing in my office in his shirt-sleeves, and in an otherwise dismantled condition on a Sunday morning. Was anything amiss going on? Nay, that was out of the question. It was not be thought of for a moment that Bartleby was an immoral person. But what could he be doing there?—copying? Nay again, whatever might be his eccentricities, Bartleby was an eminently decorous person. He would be the last man to sit down to his desk in any state approaching to nudity. Besides, it was Sunday; and there was something about Bartleby that forbade the supposition that he would by any secular occupation violate the proprieties of the day.

Nevertheless, my mind was not pacified; and full of a restless curiosity, at last I returned to the door. Without hindrance I inserted my key, opened it, and entered. Bartleby was not to be seen. I looked round anxiously, peeped behind his screen; but it was very plain that he was gone. Upon more closely examining the place, I surmised that for an indefinite period Bartleby must have ate, dressed, and slept in my office, and that too without plate, mirror, or bed,. The cushioned seat of a rickety old sofa in one corner bore the faint impress of a lean, reclining form. Rolled away under his desk, I found a blanket; under the empty grate, a blacking box and brush; on a chair, a tin basin, with soap and ragged towel; in a newspaper a few crumbs of ginger-nuts and a morsel of cheese. Yes, thought I, it is evident enough that Bartleby has been making his home here, keeping bachelor's hall all by himself. Immediately then the thought came sweeping across me, what miserable friendlessness and loneliness are here revealed! His poverty is great; but his solitude, how horrible! Think of it. Of a Sunday, Wall Street is deserted as Petra,[3] and every night of every day it is an emptiness. This building, too, which of week-days hums

---

[3] A city in what is now Jordan, once the center of an Arab kingdom. It was deserted for more than ten centuries, until its rediscovery by explorers in 1812.

with industry and life, at nightfall echoes with sheer vacancy, and all through Sunday is forlorn. And here Bartleby makes his home; sole spectator of a solitude which he has seen all populous—a sort of innocent and transformed Marius[4] brooding among the ruins of Carthage!

For the first time in my life a feeling of overpowering stinging melancholy seized me. Before, I had never experienced aught but a not unpleasing sadness. The bond of a common humanity now drew me irresistibly to gloom. A fraternal melancholy! For both I and Bartleby were sons of Adam. I remembered the bright silks and sparkling faces I had seen that day, in gala trim, swan-like sailing down the Mississippi of Broadway; and I contrasted them with the pallid copyist, and thought to myself, Ah, happiness courts the light, so we deem the world is gay; but misery hides aloof, so we deem that misery there is none. These sad fancyings—chimeras, doubtless, of a sick and silly brain—led on to other and more special thoughts, concerning the eccentricities of Bartleby. Presentiments of strange discoveries hovered round me. The scrivener's pale form appeared to me laid out, among uncaring strangers, in its shivering winding-sheet.

Suddenly I was attracted by Bartleby's closed desk, the key in open sight left in the lock.

I mean no mischief, seek the gratification of no heartless curiosity, thought I; besides, the desk is mine, and its contents, too, so I will make bold to look within. Everything was methodically arranged, the papers smoothly placed. The pigeon-holes were deep, and removing the files of documents, I groped into their recesses. Presently I felt something there, and dragged it out. It was an old bandanna handkerchief, heavy and knotted. I opened it, and saw it was a saving's bank.

I now recalled all the quiet mysteries which I had noted in the man. I remembered that he never spoke but to answer; that, though at intervals he had considerable time to himself, yet I had never seen him reading—no, not even a newspaper; that for long periods he would stand looking out, at his pale window behind the screen, upon the dead brick wall; I was quite sure he never visited any refectory or eating-house; while his pale face clearly indicated that he never drank beer like Turkey; or tea and coffee even, like other men; that he never went anywhere in particular that I could learn; never went out for a walk, unless, indeed, that was the case at present; that he had declined telling who he was, or whence he came, or whether he had any relatives in the world; that though so thin and pale, he never complained of ill-health. And more than all, I remembered a certain unconscious air of pallid—how shall I call it?—of pallid haughtiness, say, or rather an austere reserve about him, which has positively awed me into my tame compliance with his eccentricities, when I had feared to ask him to do the slightest incidental thing for me, even though I might know, from his long-continued motionlessness, that behind his screen he must be standing in one of those dead-wall reveries of his.

Revolving all these things, and coupling them with the recently discovered fact, that he made my office his constant abiding place and home, and not forgetful of his morbid moodiness; revolving all these things, a prudential feeling began to steal over me. My first emotions had been those of pure melancholy and sincerest pity; but just in proportion as the forlornness of Bartleby grew and grew to my imagination, did that same melancholy merge into fear, that pity into repulsion. So true it is, and so terrible, too, that up to a certain point the thought or sight of misery enlists our best affections; but, in certain special cases, beyond that point it does not. They err who would assert that invariably this is owing to the inherent selfishness of the human heart. It rather proceeds from a certain hopelessness of remedying excessive and organic ill. To a sensitive being, pity is not seldom pain. And when at last it is perceived that such pity cannot lead to effectual succor, common sense bids the soul be rid of it. What I saw that morning persuaded me that the scrivener was the victim of innate and incurable disorder. I might give alms to his body; but his body did not

---

[4] Gaius Marius (1577–86 B.C.), a Roman general, several times elected consul. Marius's greatest military successes came in the Jugurthine War, in Africa. Later, when his opponents gained power and he was banished, he fled to Africa. Carthage was a city in North Africa.

pain him; it was his soul that suffered, and his soul I could not reach.

I did not accomplish the purpose of going to Trinity Church that morning. Somehow, the things I had seen disqualified me for the time from church-going. I walked homeward, thinking what I would do with Bartleby. Finally, I resolved upon this—I would put certain calm questions to him the next morning, touching his history, etc., and if he declined to answer them openly and unreservedly (and I supposed he would prefer not), then to give him a twenty dollar bill over and above whatever I might owe him, and tell him his services were no longer required; but that if in any other way I could assist him, I would be happy to do so, especially if he desired to return to his native place, wherever that might be, I would willingly help to defray the expenses. Moreover, if, after reaching home, he found himself at any time in want of aid, a letter from him would be sure of a reply.

The next morning came.

"Bartleby," said I, gently calling to him behind his screen.

No reply.

"Bartleby," said I, in a still gentler tone, "come here; I am not going to ask you to do anything you would prefer not to do—I simply wish to speak to you."

Upon this he noiselessly slid into view.

"Will you tell me, Bartleby, where you were born?"

"I would prefer not to."

"Will you tell me *anything* about yourself?"

"I would prefer not to."

"But what reasonable objection can you have to speak to me? I feel friendly towards you."

He did not look at me while I spoke, but kept his glance fixed upon my bust of Cicero, which, as I then sat, was directly behind me, some six inches above my head.

"What is your answer, Bartleby?" said I, after waiting a considerable time for a reply, during which his countenance remained immovable, only there was the faintest conceivable tremor of the white attenuated mouth.

"At present I prefer to give no answer," he said, and retired into his hermitage.

It was rather weak in me I confess, but his manner, on this occasion, nettled me. Not only did there seem to lurk in it a certain calm disdain, but his perverseness seemed ungrateful, considering the undeniable good usage and indulgence he had received from me.

Again I sat ruminating what I should do. Mortified as I was at his behavior, and resolved as I had been to dismiss him when I entered my office, nevertheless I strangely felt something superstitious knocking at my heart, and forbidding me to carry out my purpose, and denouncing me for a villain if I dared to breathe one bitter word against this forlornest of mankind. At last, familiarly drawing my chair behind his screen, I sat down and said: "Bartleby, never mind, then, about revealing your history; but let me entreat you, as a friend, to comply as far as may be with the usages of this office. Say now, you will help to examine papers tomorrow or next day: in short, say now, that in a day or two you will begin to be a little reasonable:—say so, Bartleby."

"At present I would prefer not to be a little reasonable," was his mildly cadaverous reply.

Just then the folding-doors opened, and Nippers approached. He seemed suffering from an unusually bad night's rest, induced by severer indigestion than common. He overheard those final words of Bartleby.

"*Prefer not*, eh?" gritted Nippers—"I'd *prefer* him, if I were you, sir," addressing me—"I'd *prefer* him; I'd give him preferences, the stubborn mule! What is it, sir, pray, that he *prefers* not to do now?"

Bartleby moved not a limb.

"Mr. Nippers," said I, "I'd prefer that you would withdraw for the present."

Somehow, of late, I had got into the way of involuntarily using this word "prefer" upon all sorts of not exactly suitable occasions. And I trembled to think that my contact with the scrivener had already and seriously affected me in a mental way. And what further and deeper aberration might it not yet produce? This apprehension had not been without efficacy in determining me to summary measures.

As Nippers, looking very sour and sulky, was departing, Turkey blandly and deferentially approached.

"With submission, sir," said he, "yesterday I was thinking about Bartleby here, and I think that if he would but prefer to take a quart of good ale every day, it would do much towards mending him, and enabling him to assist in examining his papers."

"So you have got the word, too," said I, slightly excited.

"With submission, what word, sir?" asked Turkey, respectfully crowding himself into the contracted space behind the screen, and by so doing, making me jostle the scrivener. "What word, sir?"

"I would prefer to be left alone here," said Bartleby, as if offended at being mobbed in his privacy.

"*That's* the word, Turkey," said I—"that's it."

"Oh, *prefer*? oh yes—queer word. I never use it myself. But, sir, as I was saying, if he would but prefer—"

"Turkey," interrupted I, "you will please withdraw."

"Oh certainly, sir, if you prefer that I should."

As he opened the folding-door to retire, Nippers at his desk caught a glimpse of me, and asked whether I would prefer to have a certain paper copied on blue paper or white. He did not in the least roguishly accent the word "prefer." It was plain that it involuntarily rolled from his tongue. I thought to myself, surely I must get rid of a demented man, who already has in some degree turned the tongues, if not the heads of myself and clerks. But I thought it prudent not to break the dismission at once.

The next day I noticed that Bartleby did nothing but stand at his window in his dead-wall revery. Upon asking him why he did not write, he said that he had decided upon doing no more writing.

"Why, how now? what next?" exclaimed I, "do no more writing?"

"No more."

"And what is the reason?"

"Do you not see the reason for yourself?" he indifferently replied.

I looked steadfastly at him, and perceived that his eyes looked dull and glazed. Instantly it occurred to me, that his unexampled diligence in copying by his dim window for the first few weeks of his stay with me might have temporarily impaired his vision.

I was touched. I said something in condolence with him. I hinted that of course he did wisely in abstaining from writing for a while; and urged him to embrace that opportunity of taking wholesome exercise in the open air. This, however, he did not do. A few days after this, my other clerks being absent, and being in a great hurry to dispatch certain letters by the mail, I thought that, having nothing else earthly to do, Bartleby would surely be less inflexible than usual, and carry these letters to the Post Office. But he blankly declined. So, much to my inconvenience, I went myself.

Still added days went by. Whether Bartleby's eyes improved or not, I could not say. To all appearance, I thought they did. But when I asked him if they did he vouchsafed no answer. At all events, he would do no copying. At last, in replying to my urgings, he informed me that he had permanently given up copying.

"What!" exclaimed I; "suppose your eyes should get entirely well—better than ever before—would you not copy then?"

"I have given up copying," he answered, and slid aside.

He remained as ever, a fixture in my chamber. Nay—if that were possible—he became still more of a fixture than before. What was to be done? He would do nothing in the office; why should he stay there? In plain fact, he had now become a millstone to me, not only useless as a necklace, but afflictive to bear. Yet I was sorry for him. I speak less than truth when I say that, on his own account, he occasioned me uneasiness. If he would but have named a single relative or friend, I would instantly have written, and urged their taking the poor fellow away to some convenient retreat. But he seemed alone, absolutely alone in the universe. A bit of wreck in the mid-Atlantic. At length, necessities connected with my business tyrannized over all other considerations. Decently as I could, I told Bartleby that in six days' time he must unconditionally leave the office. I warned him to take measures, in the interval, for procuring some other abode. I offered to assist him in this endeavor, if he himself would but take the first step towards a removal. "And when you finally quit me, Bartleby," added I, "I shall see that you go not away entirely unprovided. Six days from this hour, remember."

At the expiration of that period, I peeped behind the screen, and lo! Bartleby was there.

I buttoned up my coat, balanced myself; advanced slowly towards him, touched his shoulder, and said, "The time has come; you must quit this place; I am sorry for you; here is money; but you must go."

"I would prefer not," he replied, with his back still towards me.

"You *must*."

He remained silent.

Now I had an unbounded confidence in this man's common honesty. He had frequently restored to me sixpences and shillings carelessly dropped upon the floor, for I am apt to be very reckless in such shirt-button affairs. The proceeding, then, which followed will not be deemed extraordinary.

"Bartleby," said I, "I owe you twelve dollars on account; here are thirty-two; the odd twenty are yours—Will you take it?" and I handed the bills towards him.

But he made no motion.

"I will leave them here, then," putting them under a weight on the table. Then taking my hat and cane and going to the door, I tranquilly turned and added—"After you have removed your things from these offices, Bartleby, you will of course lock the door—since every one is now gone for the day but you—and if you please, slip your key underneath the mat, so that I may have it in the morning. I shall not see you again; so good-bye to you. If, hereafter, in your new place of abode, I can be of any service to you, do not fail to advise me by letter. Good-bye, Bartleby, and fare you well."

But he answered not a word; like the last column of some ruined temple, he remained standing mute and solitary in the middle of the otherwise deserted, room.

As I walked home in a pensive mood, my vanity got the better of my pity. I could not but highly plume myself on my masterly management in getting rid of Bartleby. Masterly I call it, and such it must appear to any dispassionate thinker. The beauty of my procedure seemed to consist in its perfect quietness.

There was no vulgar bullying, no bravado of any sort, no choleric hectoring, and striding to and fro across the apartment, jerking out vehement commands for Bartleby to bundle himself off with his beggarly traps. Nothing of the kind. Without loudly bidding Bartleby depart—as an inferior genius might have done—I *assumed* the ground that depart he must; and upon that assumption built all I had to say. The more I thought over my procedure, the more I was charmed with it. Nevertheless, next morning, upon awakening, I had my doubts—I had somehow slept off the fumes of vanity. One of the coolest and wisest hours a man has, is just after he awakes in the morning. My procedure seemed as sagacious as ever—but only in theory. How it would prove in practice—there was the rub. It was truly a beautiful thought to have assumed Bartleby's departure; but, after all, that assumption was simply my own, and none of Bartleby's. The great point was, not whether I had assumed that he would quit me, but whether he would prefer to do so. He was more a man of preferences than assumptions.

After breakfast, I walked down town, arguing the probabilities *pro* and *con*. One moment I thought it would prove a miserable failure, and Bartleby would be found all alive at my office as usual; the next moment it seemed certain that I should find his chair empty. And so I kept veering about. At the corner of Broadway and Canal Street, I saw quite an excited group of people standing in earnest conversation.

"I'll take odds he doesn't," said a voice as I passed.

"Doesn't go?—done!" said I, "put up your money."

I was instinctively putting my hand in my pocket to produce my own, when I remembered that this was an election day. The words I had overheard bore no reference to Bartleby, but to the success or non-success of some candidate for the mayoralty. In my intent frame of mind, I had, as it were, imagined that all Broadway shared in my excitement, and were debating the same question with me. I passed on, very thankful that the uproar of the street screened my momentary absent-mindedness.

As I had intended, I was earlier than usual at my office door. I stood listening for a moment. All was still. He must be gone. I tried the knob. The door was locked. Yes, my procedure had worked to a charm; he indeed must be vanished. Yet a certain melancholy mixed with this: I was almost sorry for my brilliant success. I was fumbling under the door mat for the key, which Bartleby was to have left there for me, when accidentally my knee knocked against a panel, producing a summoning sound, and in response a voice came to me from within—"Not yet; I am occupied."

It was Bartleby.

I was thunderstruck. For an instant I stood like the man who, pipe in mouth, was killed one cloudless afternoon long ago in Virginia, by summer lightning; at his own warm open window he was killed, and remained leaning out there upon the dreamy afternoon, till someone touched him, when he fell.

"Not gone!" I murmured at last. But again obeying that wondrous ascendancy which the inscrutable scrivener had over me, and from which ascendancy, for all my chafing, I could not completely escape, I slowly went down stairs and out into the street, and while walking round the block, considered what I should next do in this unheard-of perplexity. Turn the man out by an actual thrusting I could not; to drive him away by calling him hard names would not do; calling in the police was an unpleasant idea; and yet, permit him to enjoy his cadaverous triumph over me—this, too, I could not think of. What was to be done? or, if nothing could be done, was there anything further that I could *assume* in the matter? Yes, as before I had prospectively assumed that Bartleby would depart, so now I might retrospectively assume that departed he was. In the legitimate carrying out of this assumption, might enter my office in a great hurry, and pretending not to see Bartleby at all, walk straight against him as if he were air. Such a proceeding would in a singular degree have the appearance of a home-thrust. It was hardly possible that Bartleby could withstand such an application of the doctrine of assumption. But upon second thoughts the success of the plan seemed rather dubious. I resolved to argue the matter over with him again.

"Bartleby," said I, entering the office, with a quietly severe expression, "I am seriously displeased. I am pained, Bartleby. I had thought better of you. I had imagined you of such a gentlemanly organization, that in any delicate dilemma a slight hint would suffice—in short, an assumption. But it appears I am deceived. Why," I added, unaffectedly starting, "you have not even touched that money yet," pointing to it, just where I had left it the evening previous.

He answered nothing.

"Will you, or will you not, quit me?" I now demanded in a sudden passion, advancing close to him.

"I would prefer *not* to quit you," he replied, gently emphasizing the *not*.

"What earthly right have you to stay here? Do you pay any rent? Do you pay my taxes? Or is this property yours?"

He answered nothing.

"Are you ready to go on and write now? Are your eyes recovered? Could you copy a small paper for me this morning? or help examine a few lines? or step round to the Post Office? In a word, will you do anything at all, to give a coloring to your refusal to depart the premises?"

He silently retired into his hermitage.

I was now in such a state of nervous resentment that I thought it but prudent to check myself at present from further demonstrations. Bartleby and I were alone. I remembered the tragedy of the unfortunate Adams and the still more unfortunate Colt in the solitary office of the latter; and how poor Colt, being dreadfully incensed by Adams, and imprudently permitting himself to get wildly excited, was at unawares hurried into his fatal act—an act which certainly no man could possibly deplore more than the actor himself.[5] Often it had occurred to me in my ponderings upon the subject that had that altercation taken place in the public street, or at a private residence, it would not have terminated as it did. It was the circumstance of being alone in a solitary office, up stairs, of a building entirely unhallowed by humanizing domestic associations—an uncarpeted office, doubtless, of a dusty, haggard

---

[5] John C. Colt murdered Samuel Adams in January 1842. Later that year, after his conviction, Colt committed suicide a half-hour before he was to be hanged. The case received wide and sensationalistic press coverage at the time.

sort of appearance—this it must have been, which greatly helped to enhance the irritable desperation of the hapless Colt.

But when this old Adam of resentment rose in me and tempted me concerning Bartleby, I grappled him and threw him. How? Why, simply by recalling the divine injunction: "A new commandment give I unto you, that ye love one another." Yes, this it was that saved me. Aside from higher considerations, charity often operates as a vastly wise and prudent principle—a great safeguard to its possessor. Men have committed murder for jealousy's sake, and anger's sake, and hatred's sake, and selfishness' sake, and spiritual pride's sake; but no man, that ever I heard of, ever committed a diabolical murder for sweet charity's sake. Mere self-interest, then, if no better motive can be enlisted, should, especially with high-tempered men, prompt all beings to charity and philanthropy. At any rate, upon the occasion in question, I strove to drown my exasperated feelings towards the scrivener by benevolently construing his conduct. Poor fellow, poor fellow! thought I, he don't mean anything; and besides, he has seen hard times, and ought to be indulged.

I endeavored, also, immediately to occupy myself, and at the same time to comfort my despondency I tried to fancy, that in the course of the morning, at such time as might prove agreeable to him, Bartleby, of his own free accord, would emerge from his hermitage and take up some decided line of march in the direction of the door. But no. Half-past twelve o'clock came; Turkey began to glow in the face, overturn his inkstand, and become generally obstreperous; Nippers abated down into quietude and courtesy; Ginger Nut munched his noon apple; and Bartleby remained standing at his window in one of his profoundest dead-wall reveries. Will it be credited? Ought I to acknowledge it? That afternoon I left the office without saying one further word to him.

Some days now passed, during which, at leisure intervals I looked a little into "Edwards[6] on the Will," and "Priestley[7] on Necessity." Under the circumstances, those books induced a salutary feeling. Gradually I slid into the persuasion that these troubles of mine, touching the scrivener, had been all predestined from eternity, and Bartleby was billeted upon me for some mysterious purpose of an all-wise Providence, which it was not for a mere mortal like me to fathom. Yes, Bartleby, stay there behind your screen, thought I; I shall persecute you no more; you are harmless and noiseless as any of these old chairs; in short, I never feel so private as when I know you are here. At last I see it, I feel it; I penetrate to the predestined purpose of my life. I am content. Others may have loftier parts to enact; but my mission in this world, Bartleby, is to furnish you with office-room for such period as you may see fit to remain.

I believe that this wise and blessed frame of mind would have continued with me, had it not been for the unsolicited and uncharitable remarks obtruded upon me by my professional friends who visited the rooms. But thus it often is, that the constant friction of illiberal minds wears out at last the best resolves of the more generous. Though to be sure, when I reflected upon it, it was not strange that people entering my office should be struck by the peculiar aspect of the unaccountable Bartleby, and so be tempted to throw out some sinister observations concerning him. Sometimes an attorney, having business, with me, and calling at my office, and, finding no one but the scrivener there, would undertake to obtain some sort of precise information from him touching my whereabouts; but without heeding his idle talk, Bartleby would remain standing immovable in the middle of the room. So after contemplating him in

---

[6] Jonathan Edwards, *Freedom of the Will* (1754). Edwards was an important American theologian, a rigidly orthodox Calvinist who believed in the doctrine of predestination and a leader of the Great Awakening, the religious revival that swept the North American colonies in the 1740s.

[7] Joseph Priestley (1733–1803), English scientist and clergyman. Priestley began as a Unitarian but developed his own radical ideas on "natural determinism." As a scientist, he did early experiments with electricity and was one of the first to discover the existence of oxygen. As a political philosopher, he championed the French Revolution—a cause so unpopular in England that he had to flee that country and spend the last decade of his life in the United States.

that position for a time, the attorney would depart, no wiser than he came.

Also, when a reference was going on, and the room full of lawyers and witnesses, and business driving fast, some deeply-occupied legal gentleman present, seeing Bartleby wholly unemployed, would request him to run round to his (the legal gentleman's) office and fetch some papers for him. Thereupon, Bartleby would tranquilly decline, and yet remain idle as before. Then the lawyer would give a great stare, and turn to me. And what could I say? At last I was made aware that all through the circle of my professional acquaintance, a whisper of wonder was running round, having reference to the strange creature I kept at my office. This worried me very much. And as the idea came upon me of his possibly turning out a long-lived man, and keeping occupying my chambers, and denying my authority; and perplexing my visitors; and scandalizing my professional reputation; and casting a general gloom over the premises; keeping soul and body together to the last upon his savings (for doubtless he spent but half a dime a day), and in the end perhaps outlive me, and claim possession of my office by right of his perpetual occupancy: as all these dark anticipations crowded upon me more and more, and my friends continually intruded their relentless remarks upon the apparition in my room; a great change was wrought in me. I resolved to gather all my faculties together, and forever rid me of this intolerable incubus.

Ere revolving any complicated project, however, adapted to this end, I first simply suggested to Bartleby the propriety of his permanent departure. In a calm and serious tone, I commended the idea to his careful and mature consideration. But, having taken three days to meditate upon it, he apprised me, that his original determination remained the same; in short, that he still preferred to abide with me.

What shall I do? I now said to myself, buttoning up my coat to the last button. What shall I do? what ought I to do? what does conscience say I *should* do with this man, or, rather, ghost. Rid myself of him, I must; go, he shall. But how? You will not thrust him, the poor, pale, passive mortal you will not thrust such a helpless creature out of your door? you will not dishonor yourself by such cruelty? No, I will not, I cannot do that. Rather would I let him live and die here, and then mason up his remains in the wall. What, then, will you do? For all your coaxing, he will not budge. Bribes he leaves under your own paper-weight on your table; in short, it is quite plain that he prefers to cling to you.

Then something severe, something unusual must be done. What! surely you will not have him collared by a constable, and commit his innocent pallor to the common jail? And upon what ground could you procure such a thing to be done?—a vagrant, is he? What! he a vagrant, a wanderer, who refuses to budge? It is because he will not be a vagrant, then, that you seek to count him *as* a vagrant. That is too absurd. No visible means of support: there I have him. Wrong again: for indubitably he *does* support himself, and that is the only unanswerable proof that any man can show of his possessing the means so to do. No more, then. Since he will not quit me, I must quit him. I will change my offices; I will move elsewhere, and give him fair notice, that if I find him on my new premises I will then proceed against him as a common trespasser.

Acting accordingly, next day I thus addressed him: "I find these chambers too far from the City Hall; the air is unwholesome. In a word, I propose to remove my offices next week, and shall no longer require your services. I tell you this now, in order that you may seek another place."

He made no reply, and nothing more was said.

On the appointed day I engaged carts and men, proceeded to my chambers, and, having but little furniture, everything was removed in a few hours. Throughout, the scrivener remained standing behind the screen, which I directed to be removed the last thing. It was withdrawn; and, being folded up like a huge folio, left him the motionless occupant of a naked room. I stood in the entry watching him a moment, while something from within me upbraided me.

I re-entered, with my hand in my pocket—and—and my heart in my mouth.

"Good-bye, Bartleby; I am going—good-bye, and God some way bless you; and take that," slipping something in his hand. But it dropped upon the floor, and then—strange to say—I tore myself from him whom I had so longed to be rid of.

Established in my new quarters, for a day or two I kept the door locked, started at every footfall in the passages. When I returned to my rooms, after any little absence, I would pause at the threshold for an instant, and attentively listen, ere applying my key. But these fears were needless. Bartleby never came nigh me.

I thought all was going well, when a perturbed-looking stranger visited me, inquiring whether I was the person who had recently occupied rooms at No.—Wall Street.

Full of forebodings, I replied that I was.

"Then, sir," said the stranger, who proved a lawyer, "you are responsible for the man you left there. He refuses to do any copying; he refuses to do anything; he says he prefers not to; and he refuses to quit the premises."

"I am very sorry, sir," said I, with assumed tranquillity, but an inward tremor, "but, really, the man you allude to is nothing to me—he is no relation or apprentice of mine, that you should hold me responsible for him."

"In mercy's name, who is he?"

"I certainly cannot inform you. I know nothing about him. Formerly I employed him as a copyist; but he has done nothing for me now for some time past."

"I shall settle him, then—good morning, sir."

Several days passed, and I heard nothing more; and, though I often felt a charitable prompting to call at the place and see poor Bartleby, yet a certain squeamishness, of I know not what, withheld me.

All is over with him, by this time, thought I, at last, when, through another week, no further intelligence reached me. But, coming to my room the day after, I found several persons waiting at my door in a high state of nervous excitement.

"That's the man here—he comes," cried the foremost one, whom I recognized as the lawyer who had previously called upon me alone.

"You must take him away, sir, at once," cried a portly person among them, advancing upon me, and whom I knew to be the landlord of No.—Wall Street. "These gentlemen, my tenants, cannot stand it any longer; Mr. B—" pointing to the lawyer, "has turned him out of his room, and he now persists in haunting the building generally, sitting upon the banisters of the stairs by day, and sleeping in the entry by night. Everybody is concerned; clients are leaving the offices; some fears are entertained of a mob; something you must do, and that without delay."

Aghast at this torrent, I fell back before it, and would fain have locked myself in my new quarters. In vain I persisted that Bartleby was nothing to me— no more than to any one else. In vain—I was the last person known to have anything to do with him, and they held me to the terrible account. Fearful, then, of being exposed in the papers (as one person present obscurely threatened), I considered the matter, and, at length, said, that if the lawyer would give me a confidential interview with the scrivener, in his (the lawyer's) own room, I would, that afternoon, strive my best to rid them of the nuisance they complained of.

Going up stairs to my old haunt, there was Bartleby silently sitting upon the banister at the landing.

"What are you doing here, Bartleby?" said I.

"Sitting upon the banister," he mildly replied.

I motioned him into the lawyer's room, who then left us.

"Bartleby," said I, "are you aware that you are the cause of great tribulation to me, by persisting in occupying the entry after being dismissed from the office?"

No answer.

"Now one of two things must take place. Either you must do something, or something must be done to you. Now what sort of business would you like to engage in? Would you like to re-engage in copying for some one?"

"No; I would prefer not to make any change."

"Would you like a clerkship in a dry-goods store?"

"There is too much confinement about that. No, I would not like a clerkship; but I am not particular."

"Too much confinement," I cried, "why, you keep yourself confined all the time!"

"I would prefer not to take a clerkship," he rejoined, as if to settle that little item at once.

"How would a bar-tender's business suit you? There is no trying of the eye-sight in that."

"I would not like it at all; though, as I said before, I am not particular."

His unwonted wordiness inspired me. I returned to the charge.

"Well, then, would you like to travel through the country collecting bills for the merchants? That would improve your health."

"No, I would prefer to be doing something else."

"How, then, would going as a companion to Europe, to entertain some young gentleman with your conversation—how would that suit you?"

"Not at all. It does not strike me that there is anything definite about that. I like to be stationary. But I am not particular."

"Stationary you shall be, then," I cried, now losing all patience, and, for the first time in all my exasperating connections with him, fairly flying into a passion. "If you do not go away from these premises before night, I shall feel bound—indeed, I *am* bound—to—to—to quit the premises myself!" I rather absurdly concluded, knowing not with what possible threat to try to frighten his immobility into compliance. Despairing of all further efforts, I was precipitately leaving him, when a final thought occurred to me—one which had not been wholly unindulged before.

"Bartleby," said I, in the kindest tone I could assume under such exciting circumstances, "will you go home with me now not to my office, but my dwelling—and remain there till we can conclude upon some convenient arrangement for you at our leisure? Come, let us start now, right away."

"No: at present I would prefer not to make any change at all."

I answered nothing; but, effectually dodging every one by the suddenness and rapidity of my flight, rushed from the building, ran up Wall Street towards Broadway, and, jumping into the first omnibus, was soon removed from pursuit. As soon as tranquillity returned, I distinctly perceived that I had now done all that I possibly could, both in respect to the demands of the landlord and his tenants, and with regard to my own desire and sense of duty, to benefit Bartleby, and shield him from rude persecution. I now strove to be entirely care-free and quiescent; and my conscience justified me in the attempt; though, indeed, it was not so successful as I could have wished. So fearful was I of being again hunted out by the incensed landlord and his exasperated tenants, that, surrendering my business to Nippers, for a few days, I drove about the upper part of the town and through the suburbs, in my rock-away; crossed over to Jersey City and Hoboken, and paid fugitive visits to Manhattanville and Astoria. In fact, I almost lived in my rockaway for the time.

When again I entered my office, lo, a note from the landlord lay upon the desk. I opened it with trembling hands. It informed me that the writer had sent to the police, and had Bartleby removed to the Tombs as a vagrant. Moreover, since I knew more about him than any one else, he wished me to appear at that place, and make a suitable statement of the facts. These tidings had a conflicting effect upon me. At first I was indignant; but, at last, almost approved. The landlord's energetic, summary disposition, had led him to adopt a procedure which I do not think I would have decided upon myself; and yet, as a last resort, under such peculiar circumstances, it seemed the only plan.

As I afterwards learned, the poor scrivener, when told that he must be conducted to the Tombs, offered not the slightest obstacle, but, in his pale, unmoving way, silently acquiesced.

Some of the compassionate and curious bystanders joined the party; and headed by one of the constables arm-in-arm with Bartleby, the silent procession filed its way through all the noise, and heat, and joy of the roaring thoroughfares at noon.

The same day I received the note, I went to the Tombs, or, to speak more properly, the Halls of Justice. Seeking the right officer, I stated the purpose of my call, and was informed that the individual I described was, indeed, within. I then assured the functionary that Bartleby was a perfectly honest man, and greatly to be compassionated, however unaccountably eccentric. I narrated all I knew, and closed by suggesting the idea of letting him remain in as indulgent confinement as possible, till something less harsh might be done—though, indeed,

I hardly knew what. At all events, if nothing else could be decided upon, the alms-house must receive him. I then begged to have an interview.

Being under no disgraceful charge, and quite serene and harmless in all his ways, they had permitted him freely to wander about the prison, and, especially, in the inclosed grass-platted yards thereof. And so I found him there, standing all alone in the quietest of the yards, his face towards a high wall, while all around, from the narrow slits of the jail windows, I thought I saw peering out upon him the eyes of murderers and thieves.

"Bartleby!"

"I know you," he said, without looking round—"and I want nothing to say to you."

"It was not I that brought you here, Bartleby," said I, keenly pained at his implied suspicion. "And to you, this should not be so vile a place. Nothing reproachful attaches to you by being here. And see, it is not so sad a place as one might think. Look, there is the sky, and here is the grass."

"I know where I am," he replied, but would say nothing more, and so I left him.

As I entered the corridor again, a broad meat-like man, in an apron, accosted me, and, jerking his thumb over my shoulder, said "Is that your friend?"

"Yes."

"Does he want to starve? If he does, let him live on the prison fare, that's all."

"Who are you?" asked I, not knowing what to make of such an unofficially speaking person in such a place.

"I am the grub-man. Such gentlemen as have friends here, hire me to provide them with something good to eat."

"Is this so?" said I, turning to the turnkey.

He said it was.

"Well, then," said I, slipping some silver into the grub-man's hands (for so they called him), "I want you to give particular attention to my friend there; let him have the best dinner you can get. And you must be as polite to him as possible."

"Introduce me, will you?" said the grub-man, looking at me with an expression which seemed to say he was all impatience for an opportunity to give a specimen of his breeding.

Thinking it would prove of benefit to the scrivener, I acquiesced; and, asking the grub-man his name, went up with him to Bartleby.

"Bartleby, this is a friend; you will find him very useful to you."

"Your sarvant, sir, your sarvant," said the grubman, making a low salutation behind his apron. "Hope you find it pleasant here, sir; nice grounds—cool apartments—hope you'll stay with us some time—try to make it agreeable. What will you have for dinner to-day?"

"I prefer not to dine to-day," said Bartleby, turning away. "It would disagree with me; I am unused to dinners." So saying, he slowly moved to the other side of the inclosure, and took up a position fronting the dead-wall.

"How's this?" said the grub-man, addressing me with a stare of astonishment. "He's odd, ain't he?"

"I think he is a little deranged," said I, sadly.

"Deranged? deranged is it? Well, now, upon my word, I thought that friend of yourn was a gentleman forger; they are always pale and genteel-like, them forgers. I can't help pity 'em—can't help it, sir. Did you know Monroe Edwards?" he added, touchingly, and paused. Then, laying his hand piteously on my shoulder, sighed, "he died of consumption at Sing-Sing. So you weren't acquainted with Monroe?"

"No, I was never socially acquainted with any forgers. But I cannot stop longer. Look to my friend yonder. You will not lose by it. I will see you again."

Some few days after this, I again obtained admission to the Tombs, and went through the corridors in quest of Bartleby; but without finding him.

"I saw him coming from his cell not long ago," said a turnkey, "may be he's gone to loiter in the yards."

So I went in that direction.

"Are you looking for the silent man?" said another turnkey, passing me. "Yonder he lies—sleeping in the yard there. 'Tis not twenty minutes since I saw him lie down."

The yard was entirely quiet. It was not accessible to the common prisoners. The surrounding walls, of amazing thickness, kept off all sounds behind them. The Egyptian character of the masonry weighed upon me with its gloom. But a soft imprisoned turf grew under foot. The heart of the eternal pyramids, it seemed, wherein, by some strange magic, through the clefts, grass-seed, dropped by birds, had sprung.

Strangely huddled at the base of the wall, his knees drawn up, and lying on his side, his head touching the cold stones, I saw the wasted Bartleby. But nothing stirred. I paused; then went close up to him; stooped over, and saw that his dim eyes were open; otherwise he seemed profoundly sleeping. Something prompted me to touch him. I felt his hand, when a tingling shiver ran up my arm and down my spine to my feet.

The round face of the grub-man peered upon me now. "His dinner is ready. Won't he dine to-day, either? Or does he live without dining?"

"Lives without dining," said I, and closed the eyes.

"Eh!—He's asleep, ain't he?"

"With kings and counselors,"[8] murmured I.

There would seem little need for proceeding further in this history. Imagination will readily supply the meagre recital of poor Bartleby's interment. But, ere parting with the reader, let me say, that if this little narrative has sufficiently interested him, to awaken curiosity as to who Bartleby was, and what manner of life he led prior to the present narrator's making his acquaintance, I can only reply, that in such curiosity I fully share, but am wholly unable to gratify it. Yet here I hardly know whether I should divulge one little item of rumor, which came to my ear a few months after the scrivener's decease. Upon what basis it rested, I could never ascertain; and hence, how true it is I cannot now tell. But, inasmuch as this vague report has not been without a certain suggestive interest to me, however sad, it may prove the same with some others; and so I will briefly mention it. The report was this: that Bartleby had been a subordinate clerk in the Dead Letter Office at Washington, from which he had been suddenly removed by a change in the administration. When I think over this rumor, hardly can I express the emotions which seize me. Dead letters! does it not sound like dead men? Conceive a man by nature and misfortune prone to a pallid hopelessness, can any business seem more fitted to heighten it than that of continually handling these dead letters, and assorting them for the flames? For by the cart-load they are annually burned. Sometimes from out the folded paper the pale clerk takes a ring—the finger it was meant for, perhaps, moulders in the grave; a bank-note sent in swiftest charity—he whom it would relieve, nor eats nor hungers any more; pardon for those who died despairing; hope for those who died unhoping; good tidings for those who died stifled by unrelieved calamities. On errands of life, these letters speed to death.

Ah, Bartleby! Ah, humanity!

1853

---

[8] A reference to Job 3:14. Job, who has lost his family and all his property and been stricken by a terrible disease, wishes he had never been born: "then had I been at rest with kings and counselors of the earth, which built desolate places for themselves."

A Simple Heart

Gustave Flaubert

1

For half a century the women of Pont-l'Évêque envied Mme Aubain her maidservant Félicité.

In return for a hundred francs a year she did all the cooking and the housework, the sewing, the washing, and the ironing. She could bridle a horse, fatten poultry, and churn butter, and she remained faithful to her mistress, who was by no means an easy person to get on with.

Mme Aubain had married a young fellow who was good-looking but badly-off, and who died at the beginning of 1809, leaving her with two small children and a pile of debts. She then sold all her property except for the farms of Toucques and Geffosses, which together brought in five thousand francs a year at the most, and left her house at Saint-Melaine for one behind the covered market which was cheaper to run and had belonged to her family.

This house had a slate roof and stood between the alley-way and a lane leading down to the river. Inside there were differences in level which were the cause of many a stumble. A narrow entrance-hall separated the kitchen from the parlor, where Mme Aubain sat all day long in a wicker easy-chair by the window. Eight mahogany chairs were lined up against the white-painted wainscoting, and under the barometer stood an old piano loaded with a pyramid of boxes and cartons. On either side of the chimney-piece, which was carved out of yellow marble in the Louis Quinze style, there was a tapestry-covered arm-chair, and in the middle was a clock designed to look like a temple of Vesta. The whole room smelt a little musty, as the floor was on a lower level than the garden.

On the first floor was "Madame's" bedroom—very spacious, with a patterned wallpaper of pale flowers and a portrait of "Monsieur" dressed in what had once been the height of fashion. It opened into a smaller room in which there were two cots, without mattresses. Then came the drawing-room, which was always shut up and full of furniture covered with dust-sheets. Next there was a passage leading to the study, where books and papers filled the shelves of a book-case in three sections built round a big writing-table of dark wood. The two end panels were hidden under pen-and-ink drawings, landscapes in gouache, and etchings by Audran,[2] souvenirs of better days and bygone luxury. On the second floor a dormer window gave light to Félicité's room, which looked out over the fields.

Every day Félicité got up at dawn, so as not to miss Mass, and worked until evening without stopping. Then, once dinner was over, the plates and dishes put away, and the door bolted, she piled ashes on the log fire and went to sleep in front of the hearth, with her rosary in her hands. Nobody could be more stubborn when it came to haggling over prices, and as for cleanliness, the shine on her saucepans was the despair of all the other servants. Being of a thrifty nature, she ate slowly, picking up from the table the crumbs from her loaf of bread—a twelve pound loaf which was baked specially for her and lasted twenty days.

All the year round she wore a kerchief of printed calico fastened behind with a pin, a bonnet which covered her hair, grey stockings, a red skirt, and

Gustave Flaubert, "A Simple Heart," from *Three Tales*, pp. 21–56. Copyright in the Public Domain.

over her jacket a bibbed apron such as hospital nurses wear.

Her face was thin and her voice was sharp. At twenty-five she was often taken for forty; once she reached fifty, she stopped looking any age in particular. Always silent and upright and deliberate in her movements, she looked like a wooden doll driven by clock-work.

2

Like everyone else, she had had her love-story. Her father, a mason, had been killed when he fell off some scaffolding. Then her mother died, and when her sisters went their separate ways a farmer took her in, sending her, small as she was, to look after the cows out in the fields. She went about in rags, shivering with cold, used to lie flat on the ground to drink water out of the ponds, would be beaten for no reason at all, and was finally turned out of the house for stealing thirty sous, a theft of which she was innocent. She found work at another farm, looking after the poultry, and as she was liked by her employers the other servants were jealous of her.

One August evening—she was eighteen at the time—they took her off to the fête at Colleville. From the start she was dazed and bewildered by the noise of the fiddles, the lamps in the trees, the medley of gaily coloured dresses, the gold crosses and lace, and the throng of people jigging up and down. She was standing shyly on one side when a smart young fellow, who had been leaning on the shaft of a cart, smoking his pipe, came up and asked her to dance. He treated her to cider, coffee, girdle-cake, and a silk neckerchief, and imagining that she knew what he was after, offered to see her home. At the edge of a field of oats, he pushed her roughly to the ground. Thoroughly frightened, she started screaming for help. He took to his heels.

Another night, on the road to Beaumont, she tried to get past a big, slow-moving waggon loaded with hay, and as she was squeezing by she recognized Théodore.

He greeted her quite calmly, saying that she must forgive him for the way he had behaved to her, as "it was the drink that did it."

She did not know what to say in reply and felt like running off.

Straight away he began talking about the crops and the notabilities of the commune, saying that his father had left Colleville for the farm at Les Écots, so that they were now neighbours.

"Ah !" she said.

He added that his family wanted to see him settled but that he was in no hurry and was waiting to find a wife to suit his fancy. She lowered her head. Then he asked her if she was thinking of getting married. She answered with a smile that it was mean of him to make fun of her.

"But I'm not making fun of you!" he said. "I swear I'm not!"

He put his left arm round her waist, and she walked on supported by his embrace. Soon they slowed down. There was a gentle breeze blowing, the stars were shining, the huge load of hay was swaying about in front of them, and the four horses were raising clouds of dust as they shambled along. Then, without being told, they turned off to the right. He kissed her once more and she disappeared into the darkness.

The following week Théodore got her to grant him several rendezvous.

They would meet at the bottom of a farm-yard, behind a wall, under a solitary tree. She was not ignorant of life as young ladies are, for the animals had taught her a great deal; but her reason and an instinctive sense of honour prevented her from giving way. The resistance she put up inflamed Théodore's passion to such an extent that in order to satisfy it (or perhaps out of sheer naïveté) he proposed to her. At first she refused to believe him, but he swore that he was serious.

Soon afterwards he had a disturbing piece of news to tell her: the year before, his parents had paid a man to do his military service for him, but now he might be called up again any day, and the idea of going into the army frightened him. In Félicité's eyes this cowardice of his appeared to be a proof of his affection, and she loved him all the more for it. Every night she would steal out to meet him, and every night Théodore would plague her with his worries and entreaties.

In the end he said that he was going to the Prefecture himself to make inquiries, and that he would come and tell her how matters stood the following Sunday, between eleven and midnight.

At the appointed hour she hurried to meet her sweetheart, but found one of his friends waiting for her instead.

He told her that she would not see Théodore again. To make sure of avoiding conscription, he had married a very rich old woman, Mme Lehoussais; of Toucques.

Her reaction was an outburst of frenzied grief. She threw herself on the ground, screaming and calling on God, and lay moaning all alone in the open until sunrise. Then she went back to the farm and announced her intention of leaving. At the end of the month, when she had received her wages, she wrapped her small belongings up in a kerchief and made her way to Pont-l'Évêque.

In front of the inn there, she sought information from a woman in a widow's bonnet, who, as it happened, was looking for a cook. The girl did not know much about cooking, but she seemed so willing and expected so little that finally Mme Aubain ended up by saying: "Very well, I will take you on."

A quarter of an hour later Félicité was installed in her house.

At first she lived there in a kind of fearful awe caused by "the style of the house" and by the memory of "Monsieur" brooding over everything. Paul and Virginie, the boy aged seven and the girl barely four, seemed to her to be made of some precious substance. She used to carry them about pick-a-back, and when Mme Aubain told her not to keep on kissing them she was cut to the quick. All the same, she was happy now, for her pleasant surroundings had dispelled her grief.

On Thursdays, a few regular visitors came in to play Boston, and Félicité got the cards and the foot-warmers ready beforehand. They always arrived punctually at eight, and left before the clock struck eleven.

Every Monday morning the second-hand dealer who lived down the alley put all his junk out on the pavement. Then the hum of voices began to fill the town, mingled with the neighing of horses, the bleating of lambs, the grunting of pigs, and the rattle of carts in the streets.

About midday, when the market was in full swing, a tall old peasant with a hooked nose and his cap on the back of his head would appear at the door. This was Robelin, the farmer from Geffosses. A little later, and Liébard, the farmer from Toucques, would arrive—a short, fat, red-faced fellow in a grey jacket and leather gaiters fitted with spurs.

Both men had hens or cheeses they wanted to sell to "Madame." But Félicité was up to all their tricks and invariably outwitted them, so that they went away full of respect for her.

From time to time Mme Aubain had a visit from an uncle of hers, the Marquis de Grémanville, who had been ruined by loose living and was now living at Falaise on his last remaining scrap of property. He always turned up at lunch-time, accompanied by a hideous poodle which dirtied all the furniture with its paws. However hard he tried to behave like a gentleman, even going so far as to raise his hat every time he mentioned "my late father," the force of habit was usually too much for him, for he would start pouring himself one glass after another and telling bawdy stories. Félicité used to push him gently out of the house, saying politely: "You've had quite enough, Monsieur de Grémanville. See you another time!" and shutting the door on him.

She used to open it with pleasure to M. Bourais, who was a retired solicitor. His white tie and his bald head, his frilled shirt and his ample brown frock-coat, the way he had of rounding his arm to take a pinch of snuff, and indeed everything about him made an overwhelming impression on her such as we feel when we meet some outstanding personality.

As he looked after "Madame's" property, he used to shut himself up with her for hours in "Monsieur's" study. He lived in dread of compromising his reputation, had a tremendous respect for the Bench, and laid claim to some knowledge of Latin.

To give the children a little painless instruction, he made them a present of a geography book with illustrations. These represented scenes in different parts of the world, such as cannibals wearing feather head-dresses, a monkey carrying off a young lady,

Bedouins in the desert, a whale being harpooned, and so on.

Paul explained these pictures to Félicité, and that indeed was all the education she ever had. As for the children, they were taught by Guyot, a poor devil employed at the Town Hall, who was famous for his beautiful handwriting, and who had a habit of sharpening his penknife on his boots.

When the weather was fine the whole household used to set off early for a day at the Geffosses farm.

The farm-yard there was on a slope, with the house in the middle; and the sea, in the distance, looked like a streak of grey. Félicité would take some slices of cold meat out of her basket, and they would have their lunch in a room adjoining the dairy. It was all that remained of a country house which had fallen into ruin, and the wallpaper hung in shreds, fluttering in the draught. Mme Aubain used to sit with bowed head, absorbed in her memories, so that the children were afraid to talk. "Why don't you run along and play?" she would say, and away they went.

Paul climbed up into the barn, caught birds, played ducks and drakes on the pond, or banged with a stick on the great casks, which sounded just like drums.

Virginie fed the rabbits, or scampered off to pick cornflowers, showing her little embroidered knickers as she ran.

One autumn evening they came home through the fields. The moon, which was in its first quarter, lit up part of the sky, and there was some mist floating like a scarf over the winding Toucques. The cattle, lying out in the middle of the pasture, looked peacefully at the four people walking by. In the third field a few got up and made a half circle in front of them.

"Don't be frightened!" said Félicité, and crooning softly, she stroked the back of the nearest animal. It turned about and the others did the same. But while they were crossing the next field they suddenly heard a dreadful bellowing. It came from a bull which had been hidden by the mist, and which now came Towards the two women.

Mme Aubain started to run.

"No! No!" said Félicité. "Not so fast!"

All the same they quickened their pace, hearing behind them a sound of heavy breathing which came nearer and nearer. The bull's hooves thudded like hammers on the turf, and they realized that it had broken into a gallop. Turning round, Félicité tore up some clods of earth and flung them at its eyes. It lowered its muzzle and thrust its horns forward, trembling with rage and bellowing horribly.

By now Mme Aubain had got to the end of the field with her two children and was frantically looking for a way over the high bank. Félicité was still backing away from the bull, hurling clods of turf which blinded it, and shouting: "Hurry! Hurry!"

Mme Aubain got down into the ditch, pushed first Virginie and then Paul up the other side, fell once or twice trying to climb the bank, and finally managed it with a valiant effort.

The bull had driven Félicité back against a gate, and its slaver was spurting into her face. In another second it would have gored her, but she just had time to slip between two of the bars, and the great beast halted in amazement.

This adventure was talked about at Pont-l'Évêque for a good many years, but Félicité never prided herself in the least on what she had done, as it never occurred to her that she had done anything heroic.

Virginie claimed all her attention, for the fright had affected the little girl's nerves, and M. Poupart, the doctor, recommended sea-bathing at Trouville.

In those days the resort had few visitors. Mme Aubain made inquiries, consulted Bourais, and got everything ready as though for a long journey.

Her luggage went off in Liébard's cart the day before she left. The next morning he brought along two horses, one of which had a woman's saddle with a velvet back, while the other carried a cloak rolled up to make a kind of seat on its crupper. Mme Aubain sat on this, with Liébard in front. Félicité looked after Virginie on the other horse, and Paul mounted M. Lechaptois's donkey, which he had lent them on condition they took great care of it.

The road was so bad that it took two hours to travel the five miles to Toucques. The horses sank into the mud up to their pasterns and had to jerk their hind-quarters to get out; often they stumbled in the ruts, or else they had to jump. In some places, Liébard's mare came to a sudden stop, and while he waited patiently for her to move off again, he talked about the people whose properties bordered the road, adding moral reflexions to each story. For instance, in the middle of Toucques, as they were passing underneath some windows set in a mass of nasturtiums, he shrugged his shoulders and said:

"There's a Madame Lehoussais lives here. Now instead of taking a young man, she…"

Félicité did not hear the rest, for the horses had broken into a trot and the donkey was galloping along. All three turned down a bridle-path, a gate swung open, a couple of boys appeared, and everyone dismounted in front of a manure-heap right outside the farm-house door.

Old Mother Liébard welcomed her mistress with every appearance of pleasure. She served up a sirloin of beef for lunch, with tripe and black pudding, a fricassee of chicken, sparkling cider, a fruit tart and brandy-plums, garnishing the whole meal with compliments to Madame, who seemed to be enjoying better health, to Mademoiselle, who had turned into a "proper little beauty," and to Monsieur Paul, who had "filled out a lot." Nor did she forget their deceased grandparents, whom the Liébards had known personally, having been in the family's service for several generations.

Like its occupants, the farm had an air of antiquity. The ceiling-beams were worm-eaten, the walls black with smoke, and the window-panes grey with dust. There was an oak dresser laden with all sorts of odds and ends—jugs, plates, pewter bowls, wolf-traps, sheep-shears, and an enormous syringe which amused the children. In the three yards outside there was not a single tree without either mushrooms at its base or mistletoe in its branches. Several had been blown down and had taken root again at the middle; all of them were bent under the weight of their apples. The thatched roofs, which looked like brown velvet and varied in thickness, weathered the fiercest winds, but the cart-shed was tumbling down. Mme Aubain said that she would have it seen to, and ordered the animals to be reharnessed.

It took them another half-hour to reach Trouville. The little caravan dismounted to make their way along the Scores, a cliff jutting right out over the boats moored below; and three minutes later they got to the end of the quay and entered the courtyard of the Golden Lamb, the inn kept by Mère David.

After the first few days Virginie felt stronger, as a result of the change of air and the sea-bathing. Not having a costume, she went into the water in her chemise and her maid dressed her afterwards in a customs officer's hut which was used by the bathers.

In the afternoons they took the donkey and went off beyond the Roches-Noires, in the direction of Hennequeville. To begin with, the path went uphill between gentle slopes like the lawns in a park, and then came out on a plateau where pasture land and ploughed fields alternated. On either side there were holly-bushes standing out from the tangle of brambles, and here and there a big dead tree spread its zigzag branches against the blue sky.

They almost always rested in the same field, with Deauville on their left, Le Havre on their right, and the open sea in front. The water glittered in the sunshine, smooth as a mirror, and so still that the murmur it made was scarcely audible; unseen sparrows could be heard twittering, and the sky covered the whole scene with its huge canopy. Mme Aubain sat doing her needlework, Virginie plaited rushes beside her, Félicité gathered lavender, and Paul, feeling profoundly bored, longed to get up and go.

Sometimes they crossed the Toucques in a boat and hunted for shells. When the tide went out, sea-urchins, ormers, and jelly-fish were left behind; and the children scampered around, snatching at the foam-flakes carried on the wind. The sleepy waves, breaking on the sand, spread themselves out along the shore. The beach stretched as far as the eye could see, bounded on the land side by the dunes which separated it from the Marais, a broad meadow in the shape of an arena. When they came back that way, Trouville, on the distant hillside, grew bigger at every step, and with its medley of oddly assorted houses seemed to blossom out in gay disorder.

On exceptionally hot days they stayed in their room? The sun shone In dazzling bars of light between the slats of the blind. There was not a sound to be heard in the village, and not a soul to be seen down in the street. Everything seemed more peaceful in the prevailing silence. In the distance caulkers were hammering away at the boats, and the smell of tar was wafted along by a sluggish breeze.

The principal amusement consisted in watching the fishing-boats come in. As soon as they had passed the buoys, they started tacking. With their canvas partly lowered and their foresails blown out like balloons they glided through the splashing waves as far as the middle of the harbour, where they suddenly dropped anchor. Then each boat came alongside the quay, and the crew threw ashore their catch of quivering fish. A line of carts stood waiting, and women in cotton bonnets rushed forward to take the baskets and kiss their men.

One day one of these women spoke to Félicité, who came back to the inn soon after in a state of great excitement. She explained that she had found one of her sisters—and Nastasie Barette, now Leroux, made her appearance, with a baby at her breast, another child holding her right hand, and on her left a little sailor-boy, his arms akimbo and his cap over one ear.

Mme Aubain sent her off after a quarter of an hour. From then on they were forever hanging round the kitchen or loitering about when the family went for a walk, though the husband kept out of sight.

Félicité became quite attached to them. She bought them a blanket, several shirts, and a stove; and it was clear that they were bent on getting all they could out of her.

This weakness of hers annoyed Mme Aubain, who in any event disliked the familiar way in which the nephew spoke to Paul. And so, as Virginie had started coughing and the good weather was over, she decided to go back to Pont-l'Évêque.

M. Bourais advised her on the choice of a school; Caen was considered the best, so it was there that Paul was sent. He said good-bye bravely, feeling really rather pleased to be going to a place where he would have friends of his own.

Mme Aubain resigned herself to the loss of her son, knowing that it was unavoidable. Virginie soon got used to it. Félicité missed the din he used to make, but she was given something new to do which served as a distraction; from Christmas onwards she had to take the little girl to catechism every day.

3

After genuflecting at the door, she walked up the centre aisle under the nave, opened the door of Mme Aubain's pew, sat down, and started looking about her.

The choir stalls were all occupied, with the boys on the right and the girls on the left, while the curé stood by the lectern. In one of the stained-glass windows in the apse the Holy Ghost looked down on the Virgin; another window showed her kneeling before the Infant Jesus; and behind the tabernacle there was a wood-carving of St. Michael slaying the dragon.

The priest began with a brief outline of sacred history. Listening to him, Félicité saw in imagination the Garden of Eden, the Flood, the Tower of Babel, cities burning, peoples dying, and idols being overthrown; and this dazzling vision left her with a great respect for the Almighty and profound fear of His wrath.

Then she wept as she listened to the story of the Passion. Why had they crucified Him, when He loved children, fed the multitudes, healed the blind, and had chosen out of humility to be born among the poor, on the litter of a stable? The sowing of the seed, the reaping of the harvest, the pressing of the grapes—all those familiar things of which the Gospels. The speak had their place in her life. God had sanctified them in passing, so that she loved the lambs more tenderly for love of the Lamb of God, and the doves for the sake of the Holy Ghost,

She found it difficult, however, to imagine what the Holy Ghost looked like, for it was not just a bird but a fire as well, and sometimes a breath. She wondered whether that was its light she had seen flitting about the edge of the marshes at night, whether that was its breath she had felt driving the clouds across the sky, whether that was its voice she had heard in the sweet music of the bells. And she sat in silent adoration, delighting in the coolness of the walls and the quiet of the church.

Of dogma she neither understood nor even tried to understand anything. The curé discoursed, the children repeated their lesson, and she finally dropped off to sleep, waking up suddenly at the sound of their sabots clattering across the flagstones as they left the church.

It was in this manner, simply by hearing it expounded, that she learnt her catechism, for her religious education had been neglected in her youth. From then on she copied all Virginie's observances, fasting when she did and going to confession with her. On the feast of Corpus Christi the two of them made an altar of repose together.

The preparations for Virginie's first communion caused her great anxiety. She worried over her shoes, her rosary, her missal, and her gloves. And how she trembled as she helped Mme Aubain to dress the child!

All through the Mass her heart was in her mouth. One side of the choir was hidden from her by M. Bourais, but directly opposite her she could see the flock of maidens, looking like a field of snow with their white crowns perched on top of their veils; and she recognized her little darling from a distance by her dainty neck and her rapt attitude. The bell tinkled. Every head bowed low, and there was a silence. Then, to the thunderous accompaniment of the organ, choir and congregation joined in singing the *Agnus Dei*. Next the boys' procession began, and after that the girls got up from their seats. Slowly, their hands joined in prayer, they went towards the brightly lit altar, knelt on the first step, received the Host one by one, and went back to their places in the same order. When it was Virginie's turn, Félicité leant forward to see her, and in one of those imaginative flights born of real affection, it seemed to her that she herself was in the child's place. Virginie's face, became her own, Virginie's dress clothed her, Virginie's heart was beating in her breast; and as she closed her eyes and opened her mouth, she almost fainted away.

Early next morning she went to the sacristy and asked M. le Curé to give her communion She received the sacrament with all due reverence, but did not feel the same rapture as she had the day before.

Mme Aubain wanted her daughter to possess every accomplishment, and since Guyot could not teach her English or music, she decided to send her as a boarder to the Ursuline Convent at Honfleur.

Virginie raised no objection, but Félicité went about sighing at Madame's lack of feeling. Then she thought that perhaps her mistress was right: such matters, after all, lay outside her province.

Finally the day arrived when an old waggonette stopped at their door, and a nun got down from it who had come to fetch Mademoiselle. Félicité hoisted the luggage up on top, gave the driver some parting instructions, and put six pots of jam, a dozen pears, and a bunch of violets in the boot.

At the last moment Virginie burst into a fit of sobbing. She threw her arms round her mother, who kissed her on the forehead, saying: "Come now, be brave, be brave." The step was pulled up and the carriage drove away.

Then Mme Aubain broke down, and that evening all her friends, M. and Mme Lormeau, Mme Lechaptois, the Roche feuille sisters, M. de Houppeville, and Bourais, came in to console her.

To begin with she missed her daughter badly. But she hid a letter from her three times a week, wrote back on the other days, walked round her garden, did a little reading, and thus contrived to fill the empty hours.

As for Félicité, she went into Virginie's room every morning from sheer force of habit and looked round it. It upset her not having to brush the child's hair any more, tie her bootlaces, or tuck her up in bed; and she missed seeing her sweet face all the time and holding her hand when they went out together. For want of something to do, she tried making lace, but her fingers were too clumsy and broke the threads. She could not settle to anything, lost her sleep, and, to use her own words, was "eaten up inside."

To "occupy her mind," she asked if her nephew Victor might come and see her, and permission was granted.

He used to arrive after Mass on Sunday, his cheeks flushed, his chest bare, and smelling of the countryside through which he had come. She laid a place for him straight away, opposite hers, and they had lunch together. Eating as little as possible herself, in order to save the expense, she stuffed him so full of food that he fell asleep after the meal. When the first bell for vespers rang, she woke him up, brushed his trousers, tied his tie, and set off for church, leaning on his arm with all a mother's pride.

His parents always told him to get something out of her—a packet of brown sugar perhaps, some soap, or a little brandy, sometimes even money. He brought her his clothes to be mended, and she did the work gladly, thankful for anything that would force him to come again.

In August his father took him on a coasting trip. The children's holidays were just beginning, and it cheered her up to have them home again. But Paul was turning capricious and Virginie was getting too old to be addressed familiarly—a state of affairs which put a barrier of constraint between them.

Victor went to Morlaix, Dunkirk, and Brighton in turn, and brought her a present after each trip. The first time it was a box covered with shells, the second a coffee cup, the third a big gingerbread man. He was growing quite handsome, with his trim figure, his little moustache, his frank open eyes, and the little leather cap that he wore on the back of his head like a pilot. He kept her amused by telling her stories full of nautical jargon.

One Monday—it? was the fourteenth of July 1819, a date she never forgot—Victor told her that he had signed on for an ocean voyage, and that on the Wednesday night he would be taking the Honfleur packet to join his schooner, which was due to sail shortly from Le Havre. He might be away, he said, for two years.

The prospect of such a long absence made Félicité extremely unhappy, and she felt she must bid him godspeed once more. So on the Wednesday evening, when Madame's dinner was over, she put on her clogs and swiftly covered the ten miles between Pont-l'Évêque and Honfleur.

When she arrived at the Calvary she turned right instead of left, got lost in the shipyards, and had to retrace her steps. Some people she spoke to advised her to hurry. She went right round the harbour, which was full of boats, constantly tripping over moorings. Then the ground fell away, rays of light criss-crossed in front of her, and for a moment she thought she was going mad, for she could see horses up in the sky.

On the quayside more horses were neighing, frightened by the sea. A derrick was hoisting them into the air and dropping them into one of the boats, which was already crowded with passengers elbowing their way between barrels of cider, baskets of cheese, and sacks of grain. Hens were cackling and the captain swearing, while a cabin-boy stood leaning on the cats-head, completely indifferent to it all. Félicité, who had not recognized him, shouted: "Victor!" and he raised his head. She rushed forward, but at that very moment the gangway was pulled ashore.

The packet moved out of the harbour with women singing as they hauled it along, its ribs creaking and heavy waves lashing its bows. The sail swung round, hiding everyone on board from view, and against the silvery, moonlit sea the boat appeared as a dark shape that grew ever fainter, until at last it vanished in the distance.

As Félicité was passing the Calvary, she felt a longing to commend to God's mercy all that she held most dear; and she stood there praying for a long time, her face bathed in tears, her eyes fixed upon the clouds. The town was asleep, except for the customs officers walking up and down. Water was pouring ceaselessly through the holes in the sluice-gate, making as much noise as a torrent. The clocks struck two.

The convent parlour would not be open before daybreak, and Madame would be annoyed if she were late; so, although she would have liked to give a kiss to the other child, she set off for home. The maids at the inn were just waking up as she got to Pont-l'Évêque.

So the poor lad was going to be tossed by the waves for months on end! His previous voyages had caused her no alarm. People came back from England and Brittany; but America, the Colonies, the Islands, were all so far away, somewhere at the other end of the world.

From then on Félicité thought of nothing but her nephew. On sunny days she hoped he was not too thirsty, and when there was a storm she was afraid he would be struck by lightning. Listening to the wind howling in the chimney or blowing slates off the roof, she saw him being buffeted by the very same storm, perched on the top of a broken mast, with his whole body bent backwards under a sheet of foam; or again—and these were reminiscences of the illustrated geography book—he was being eaten by savages, captured by monkeys in a forest, or dying on a desert shore. But she never spoke of her worries.

Mme Aubain had worries of her own about her daughter. The good nuns said that she was an affectionate child, but very delicate. The slightest emotion upset her, and she had to give up playing the piano.

Her mother insisted on regular letters from the convent. One morning when the postman had not called, she lost patience and walked up and down the room, between her chair and the window. It was really extraordinary! Four days without any news!

Thinking her own example would comfort her, Félicité said:

"I've been six months, Madame, without news."

"News of whom?"

The servant answered gently:

"Why—of my nephew."

"Oh, your nephew!" And Mme Aubain started pacing up and down again, with a shrug of her shoulders that seemed to say: "I wasn't thinking of him—and indeed, why should I? Who cares about a young, good-for-nothing cabin-boy? Whereas my daughter—why, just think!"

Although she had been brought up the hard way, Félicité was indignant with Madame, but she soon forgot. It struck her as perfectly natural to lose one's head where the little girl was concerned. For her, the two children were of equal importance; they were linked together in her heart by a single bond, and their destinies should be the same.

The chemist told her that Victor's ship had arrived at Havana: he had seen this piece of information in a newspaper.

Because of its association with cigars, she imagined Havana as a place where nobody did anything but smoke, and pictured Victor walking about among crowds of Negroes in a cloud of tobacco-smoke. Was it possible, she wondered, "in case of need" to come back by land? And how far was it from Pont-l'Évêque? To find out she asked M. Bourais.

He reached for his atlas, and launched forth into an explanation of latitudes and longitudes, smiling like the pedant he was at Félicité's bewilderment. Finally he pointed with his pencil at a minute black dot inside a ragged oval patch, saying:

"There it is."

She bent over the map, but the network of coloured lines meant nothing to her and only tired her eyes;. So when Bourais asked her to tell him what was puzzling her, she begged him to show her the house where Victor was living. He threw up his hands, sneezed, and roared with laughter, delighted to come across such simplicity. And Félicité—whose intelligence was so limited that she probably expected to see an actual portrait of her nephew—could not make out why he was laughing.

It was a fortnight later that Liébard came into the kitchen at market-time, as he usually did, and handed her a letter from her brother-in-law. As neither of them could read, she turned to her mistress for help.

Mme Aubain, who was counting the stitches in her knitting, put it down and unsealed the letter. She gave a start, and, looking hard at Félicité, said quietly: "They have some bad news for you…Your nephew."

He was dead. That was all the letter had to say.

Félicité dropped on to a chair, leaning her head against the wall and closing her eyelids, which suddenly turned pink. Then, with her head bowed, her hands dangling, and her eyes she kept repeating: "Poor little lad! Poor little lad!"

Liébard looked at her and sighed. Mme Aubain was trembling slightly. She suggested that she should go and see her sister at Trouville, but Félicité shook her head to indicate that there was no need for that.

There was a silence. Old Liébard thought it advisable to go.

Then Félicité said: "It doesn't matter a bit, not to them it doesn't."

Her head fell forward again, and from time to time she unconsciously picked up the knitting needles lying on the work-table.

Some women went past carrying a tray full of dripping linen.

Catching sight of them through the window, she remembered her own washing; she had passed the lye through it the day before and today it needed rinsing. So she left the room.

Her board and tub were on the bank of the Toucques. She threw a pile of chemises down by the water's edge, rolled up her sleeves, and picked up her battledore. The lusty blows she gave with it could be heard in all the neighbouring gardens.

The fields were empty, the river rippling in the wind; at the bottom long weeds were waving to and fro, like the hair of corpses floating in the water. She held back her grief, and was very brave until the evening; but in her room she gave way to it completely, lying on her mattress with her face buried in the pillow and her fists pressed against her temples.

Long afterwards she learnt the circumstances of Victor's death from the captain of his ship. He had gone down with yellow fever, and they had bled him too much at the hospital. Four doctors had held him at once. He had died straight away, and the chief doctor had said: "Good! There goes another!"

His parents had always treated him cruelly. She preferred not to see them again, and they made no advances, either because they had forgotten about her or out of the callousness of the poor.

Meanwhile Virginie was growing weaker. Difficulty in breathing, fits of coughing, protracted bouts of fever, and mottled patches on the cheekbones all indicated some deep seated complaint. M. Poupart had advised a stay in Provence. Mme Aubain decided to follow this suggestion, and, if it had not been for the weather at Pont-l'Évêque, she would have brought her daughter home at once.

She arranged with a jobmaster to drive her out to the convent every Tuesday. There was a terrace in the garden, overlooking the Seine, and there Virginie, leaning on her mother's arm, walked up and down over the fallen vine leaves. Sometimes, while she was looking at the sails in the distance, or at the long stretch of horizon from the Château de Tancarville to the lighthouses of Le Havre, the sun would break through the clouds and make her blink. Afterwards they would rest in the arbor. Her mother had secured a little cask of excellent Malaga, and, laughing at the idea of getting tipsy, Virginie used to drink a thimbleful, but no more.

Her strength revived. Autumn slipped by, and Félicité assured Mme Aubain that there was nothing to fear. But one evening, coming back from some errand in the neighbourhood, she found M. Poupart's gig standing at the door. He was in the hall, and Mme Aubain was tying on her bonnet.

"Give me my foot-warmer, purse, gloves. Quickly now!"

Virginie had pneumonia and was perhaps past recovery.

"Not yet!" said The doctor; and the two of them got into the carriage with snow-flakes swirling around them. Night was falling and it was very cold.

Félicité rushed into the church to light a candle, and then ran after the gig. She caught up with it an hour later, jumped lightly up behind, and hung on to the fringe. But then a thought stuck her: the Courtyard had not been locked up, and burglars might get in. So she jumped down again.

At dawn the next day she went to the doctor's. He had come home and gone out again on his rounds. Then she waited at the inn, thinking that somebody who was a stranger to the district might call there with a letter. Finally, when it was twilight, she got into the coach for Lisieux.

The convent was at the bottom of a steep lane. When she was half way down the hill, she heard a strange sound which she recognized as a death-bell tolling.

"It's for somebody else," she thought, as she banged the door-knocker hard.

After a few minutes she heard the sound of shuffling feet, the door opened a little way, and a nun appeared.

The good sister said with an air of compunction that "she had just passed away." At that moment the bell of Saint-Léonard was tolled more vigorously than ever.

Félicité went up to the second floor. From the doorway of the room she could see Virginie lying on her back, her hands clasped together, her mouth open, her head tilted back under a black crucifix that leant over her, her face whiter than the curtains that hung motionless on either side. Mme Aubain was clinging to the foot of the bed and sobbing desperately. The Mother Superior stood on the right. Three candlesticks on the chest of drawers added touches of red to the scene, and fog was whitening the windows. Some nuns led Mme Aubain away.

For two nights Félicité never left the dead girl. She said the same prayers over and over again, sprinkled holy water on the sheets, then sat down again to watch. At the end of her first vigil, she noticed that the child's face had gone yellow, the lips were turning blue, the nose looked sharper, and the eyes were sunken. She kissed them several times, and would not have been particularly surprised if Virginie had opened them again: to minds like hers the supernatural is a simple matter. She laid her out, wrapped her in a shroud, put her in her coffin, placed a wreath on her, and spread out her hair. It was fair and amazingly long for her age. Félicité cut off a big lock, half of which she slipped into her bosom, resolving never to part with it.

The body was brought back to Pont-l'Évêque at the request of Mme Aubain, who followed the hearse in a closed carriage.

After the Requiem Mass, it took another three-quarters of an hour to reach the cemetery. Paul walked in front, sobbing. Then came M. Bourais, and after him the principal inhabitants of the town, the women all wearing long black veils, and Félicité. She was thinking about her nephew; and since she had been unable to pay him these last honours, she felt an added grief, just as if they were burying him with Virginie.

Mme Aubain's despair passed all bounds. First of all she rebelled against God, considering it unfair of Him to have taken her daughter from her—for she had never done any harm, and her conscience was quite clear. But was it? She ought to have taken Virginie to the south; other doctors would have saved her life. She blamed herself, wished she could have joined her daughter, and cried out in anguish in her dreams. One dream in particular obsessed her. Her husband, dressed like a sailor, came back from a long voyage, and told her amid tears that he had been ordered to take Virginie away—whereupon they put their heads together to discover somewhere to hide her.

One day she came in from the garden utterly distraught. A few minutes earlier—and she pointed to the spot—father and daughter had appeared to her, doing nothing, but simply looking at her.

For several months she stayed in her room in a kind of stupor. Félicité scolded her gently telling her that she must take care of herself for her son's sake, and also in remembrance of "her."

"Her?" repeated Mme Aubain, as if she were waking from a sleep. "Oh, yes, of course! You don't forget her, do you!" This was an allusion to the cemetery, where she herself was strictly forbidden to go.

Félicité went there every day. She would set out on the stroke of four, going past the houses, up the hill, and through the gate, until she came to Virginie's grave. There was a little column of pink marble with a tablet at its base, and a tiny garden enclosed by chains. The beds were hidden under a carpet of flowers. She watered their leaves and changed the sand, going down on her knees to fork the ground thoroughly. The result was that when Mme Aubain was able to come here, she experienced a feeling of relief, a kind of consolation.

Then the years slipped by, each one like the last, with nothing to vary the rhythm of the great festivals: Easter, the Assumption, All Saints' Day. Domestic events marked dates that later served as points of reference. Thus in 1825 a couple of glaziers white-washed the hall; in 1827 a piece of the roof fell into the courtyard and nearly killed a man; and in the summer of 1828 it was Madame's turn to provide the bread for consecration. About this time Bourais went away in a mysterious fashion; and one by one the old acquaintances disappeared: Guyot, Liébard, Mme Lechaptois, Robelin, and" Uncle Grémanville, who had been paralysed for a long time.

One night the driver of the mail-coach brought Pont-l'Évêque news of the July Revolution. A few days later a new sub prefect was appointed. This was the Baron de Larsonnière, who had been a consul in America, and who brought with him, besides his wife, his sister-in-law and three young ladies who were almost grown-up. They were to be seen on their lawn, dressed in loose-fitting smocks; and they had a Negro servant and a parrot. They paid a call on Mme Aubain, who made a point of returning it. As soon as Félicité saw them coming, she would run and tell her mistress. But only onething could really awaken her interest, and that was her son's letters.

He seemed to be incapable of following any career and spent all his time in taverns. She paid his debts, but he contracted new ones, and the sighs Mme Aubain heaved as she knitted by the window reached Félicité at her spinning-wheel in the kitchen.

The two women used to walk up and down together beside the espalier, forever talking of Virginie and debating whether such and such a thing would have appealed to her, or what she would have said on such and such an occasion.

All her little belongings were in a cupboard in the children's bedroom. Mme Aubain went through them as seldom as possible. One summer day she resigned herself to doing so, and the moths were sent fluttering out of the cupboard.

Virginie's frocks hung in a row underneath a shelf containing three dolls, a few hoops, a set of toy furniture, and the wash-basin she had used. Besides the frocks, they took out her petticoats, her stockings and her handkerchiefs, and spread them out on the two beds before folding them up again. The sunlight streamed in on these pathetic objects, bringing out the stains and showing up the creases made by the child's movements. The air was warm, the sky was blue, a blackbird was singing, and everything seemed to be utterly at peace.

They found a little chestnut-coloured hat, made of plush with a long nap; but the moths had ruined it. Félicité asked if she might have it. The two women looked at each other and their eyes filled with tears. Then the mistress opened her arms, the maid threw herself into them, and they clasped each other in a warm embrace, satisfying their grief in a kiss which made them equal.

It was the first time that such a thing had happened, for Mme Aubain was not of a demonstrative nature. Félicité was as grateful as if she had received a great favour, and henceforth loved her mistress with dog-like devotion and religious veneration.

Her heart grew softer as time went by.

When she heard the drums of a regiment coming down the street she stood at the door with a jug of cider and offered the soldiers a drink. She looked after the people who went down with cholera. She watched over the Polish refugees, and one of them actually expressed a desire to marry her. But they fell out, for when she came back from the Angelus one morning, she found that he had got into her kitchen and was calmly eating an oil-and-vinegar salad.

After the Poles it was Père Colmiche, an old man who was said to have committed fearful atrocities in '93. He lived by the river in a ruined pig-sty. The boys of the town used to peer at him through the cracks in the walls, and threw pebbles at him which landed on the litter where he lay, constantly shaken by fits of coughing. His hair was extremely long, his eyelids inflamed, and on one arm there was a swelling bigger than his head. Félicité brought him some linen, tried to clean out his filthy hovel, and even wondered if she could install him in the wash-house without annoying Madame. When the tumour had burst, she changed his dressings every day, brought him some cake now and then, and put him out in the sun on a truss of hay. The poor old fellow would thank her in a faint whisper, slavering and trembling all the while, fearful of losing her and stretching his hands out as soon as he saw her moving away.

He died, and she had a Mass said for the repose of his soul.

That same day a great piece of good fortune came her way. Just as she was serving dinner, Mme de Larsonnière's Negro appeared carrying the parrot in its cage, complete with perch, chain, and padlock. The Baroness had written a note informing Mme Aubain that her husband had been promoted to a Prefecture and they were leaving that evening; she begged her to accept the parrot as a keepsake and a token of her regard.

This bird had engrossed Félicité's thoughts for a long time, for it came from America, and that word reminded her of Victor. So she had asked asked the Negro all about it, and once she had even gone so far as to say: "How pleased Madame would be if it were hers!"

The Negro had repeated this remark to his mistress, who, unable to take the parrot with her, was glad to get rid of it in this way.

4

His name was Loulou. His body was green, the tips of his wings were pink, his poll blue, and his breast golden.

Unfortunately he had a tiresome mania for biting his perch, and also used to pull his feathers out, scatter his droppings everywhere, and upset his bath water. He annoyed Mme Aubain and so she gave him to Félicité for good.

Félicité started training him, and soon he could say: "Nice boy! Your servant, sir! Hail, Mary!" He was put near the door, and several people who spoke to him said how strange it was that he did not answer to the name of Jacquot, as all parrots were called Jacquot. They likened him to a turkey or a block of wood, and every sneer cut Félicité to the quick. How odd, she thought, that Loulou should be so stubborn, refusing to talk whenever anyone looked at him!

For all that, he liked having people around him, because on Sundays, while the Rochefeuille sisters, M. Houppeville and some new friends—the apothecary Onfroy, M. Varin, and Captain Mathieu—were having their game of cards, he would beat on the window-panes with his wings and make such a din that it was impossible to hear oneself speak.

Bourais's face obviously struck him as terribly funny, for as soon as he saw it he was seized with uncontrollable laughter. His shrieks rang round the courtyard, the echo repeated them, and the neighbours came to their windows and started laughing too. To avoid being seen by the bird, M. Bourais used to creep along by the wall, hiding his face behind his hat, until he got to the river, and then come into the house from the garden. The looks he gave the parrot were far from tender.

Loulou had once been cuffed by the butcher's boy for poking his head into his basket; and since then he was always trying to give him a nip through his shirt. Fabu threatened to wring his neck, although he was not a cruel fellow, in spite of his tattooed arms and bushy whiskers. On the contrary, he rather liked the parrot, so much so indeed that in a spirit of jovial camaraderie he tried to teach him a few swearwords. Félicité, alarmed at this development, put the bird in the kitchen. His little chain was removed and he was allowed to wander all over the house.

Coming downstairs, he used to rest the curved part of his beak on each step and then raise first his right foot, then his left; and Félicité was afraid that this sort of gymnastic performance would make him giddy. He fell ill and could neither talk nor eat for there was a swelling under his tongue such as hens sometimes have. She cured him by pulling this pellicule out with her finger-nails. One day M. Paul was silly enough to blow the smoke of his cigar at him; another time Mme Lormeau started teasing him with the end of her parasol, and he caught hold of the ferrule with his beak. Finally he got lost.

Félicité had put him down on the grass in the fresh air, and left him there for a minute. When she came back, the parrot had gone. First of all she looked for him in the bushes by the river and on the rooftops, paying no attention to her mistress's shouts of: "Be careful, now! must be mad!" Next she went over all the gardens in Pont-l'Évêque, stopping passers by and asking them: "You don't happen to have seen my parrot by any chance?" Those who did not know him already were given a description of the bird. Suddenly she thought she could make out something green flying about behind the mills at the foot of the hill. But up on the hill there was nothing to be seen. A pedlar told her that he had come upon the parrot a short time before in Mère Simon's shop at Saint-Melaine. She ran all the way there, but no one knew what she was talking about. Finally she came back home, worn out, her shoes falling to pieces, and death in her heart. She was sitting beside Madame on the garden-seat and telling her what she had been doing, when she felt something light drop on her shoulder. It was Loulou! What he had been up to, no one could discover: perhaps he had just gone for a little walk round the town.

Félicité was slow to recover from this fright, and indeed never really got over it.

As the result of a chill she had an attack of quinsy, and soon after that her ears were affected. Three years later she was deaf, and she spoke at the top of her voice, even in church. Although her sins could have been proclaimed over the length and breadth of the diocese without dishonour to her or offence to others, M. le Curé thought it advisable to hear her confession in the sacristy.

Imaginary buzzings in the head added to her troubles. Often her mistress would say: "Heavens, how stupid you are!" and she would reply: "Yes, Madame," at the same time looking all around her for something.

The little circle of her ideas grew narrower and narrower, and the pealing of bells and the lowing of cattle went out of her life. Every living thing moved about in a ghostly silence, Only one sound reached her ears now, and that was the voice of the parrot.

As if to amuse her, he would reproduce the click-clack of the turn-spit, the shrill call of a man selling fish, and the noise of the saw at the joiner's across the way; and when the bell rang he would imitate Mme Aubain's "Félicité! The door, the door!"

They held conversations with each other, he repeating *ad nauseam* the three phrases in his repertory, she replying with words which were just as disconnected but which came from the heart. In her isolation, Loulou was almost a son or a lover to her. He used to climb up her fingers, peck at her lips, and hang on to her shawl; and as she bent over him, wagging her head from side to side as nurses do, the great wings of her bonnet and the wings of the bird quivered in unison.

When clouds banked up in the sky and there was a rumbling of thunder, he would utter piercing cries, no doubt remembering the sudden downpours in his native forests. The sound of the rain falling roused him to frenzy. He would flap excitedly around, shoot up to the ceiling, knocking everything over, and fly out of the window to splash about in the garden. But he would soon come back to perch on one of the fire dogs, hopping about to dry his feathers and showing tail and beak in turn.

One morning in the terrible winter of 1837, when she had put him in front of the fire because of the cold she found him dead in the middle of his cage, hanging head down with his claws caught in the bars. He had probably died of a stroke, but she thought he had been poisoned with parsley, and despite the absence of any proof, her suspicions fell on Fabu.

She wept so much that her mistress said to her: "Why don't you have him stuffed ?"

Félicité asked the chemist's advice, remembering that he had always been kind to the parrot. He wrote to Le Havre, and a man called Fellacher agreed to do the job. As parcels sometimes went astray on the mail-coach, she decided to take the parrot as far as Honfleur herself.

On either side of the road stretched an endless succession of apple trees, all stripped of their leaves, and there was ice in the ditches. Dogs were barking around the farms; and Félicité, with her hands tucked under her mantlet, her little black sabots and her basket, walked briskly along the middle of the road.

She crossed the forest, passed Le Haut-Chêne, and got as far as Saint-Gatien.

Behind her, in a cloud of dust, and gathering speed as the horses galloped downhill, a mail-coach swept along like a whirlwind. When he saw this woman making no attempt to get out of the way, the driver poked his head out above the hood, and he and the postilion shouted at her. His four horses could not be held in and galloped faster, the two leaders touching her as they went by. With a jerk of the reins the driver threw them to one side, and then, in a fury, he raised his long whip and gave her such a lash, from head to waist, that she fell flat on her back.

The first thing she did on regaining consciousness was to open her basket. Fortunately nothing had happened to Loulou. She felt her right cheek burning, and when she touched it her hand turned red; it was bleeding.

She sat down on a heap of stones and dabbed her face with her handkerchief. Then she ate a crust of bread which she had taken the precaution of putting in her basket, and tried to forget her wound by looking at the bird.

As she reached the top of the hill at Ecquemauville, she saw the lights of Honfleur twinkling in the darkness like a host of stars, and the shadowy expanse of the sea beyond. Then a sudden feeling of faintness made her stop; and the misery of her childhood, the disappointment of her first love, the departure of her nephew, and the death of Virginie all came back to her at once like the waves of a rising tide, and, welling up in her throat, choked her.

When she got to the boat she insisted speaking to the captain, and without telling him what was in her parcel, asked him to take good care of it.

Fellacher kept the parrot a long time. Every week he promised it for the next; after six months he announced that a box had been sent off, and nothing more was heard of it. It looked as though Loulou would never come back, and Félicité told herself: "They've stolen him for sure!"

At last he arrived looking quite magnificent, perched on a branch screwed into a mahogany base, one foot in the air, his head cocked to one side, and biting a nut which the taxidermist, out of a love of the grandiose, had gilded.

Félicité shut him up in her room.

This place, to which few people were ever admitted, contained such a quantity of religious bric-à-brac and miscellaneous oddments that it looked like a cross between a chapel and a bazaar.

A big wardrobe prevented the door from opening properly. Opposite the window that overlooked the garden was a little round one looking on to the courtyard. There was a table beside the bed, with a water-jug, a couple of combs, and a block of blue soap in a chipped plate. On the walls there were rosaries, medals, several pictures of the Virgin, and a holy-water stoup made out of a coconut. On the chest of drawers, which was draped with a cloth just like an altar, was the shell box Victor had given her, and also a watering-can and a ball, some copybooks, the illustrated geography book, and a pair of ankle-boots. And on the nail looking-glass, fastened by its ribbons, hung the little plush hat.

Félicité carried this form of veneration to such lengths that she even kept one of Monsieur's frock-coats. All the old rubbish Mme Aubain had no more use for, she carried off to her room. That was how there came to be artificial flowers along the edge of the chest of drawers, and a portrait of the Comte d'Artois in the window-recess.

With the aid of a wall-bracket, Loulou was installed on a chimney-breast that jutted out into the room. Every morning when she awoke, she saw him in the light of the dawn, and then she remembered the old days, and the smallest details of insignificant actions, not in sorrow but in absolute tranquillity.

Having no intercourse with anyone, she lived in the torpid state of a sleep-walker. The Corpus Christi processions roused her from this condition, for she would go round the neighbours collecting candlesticks and mats to decorate the altar of repose which they used to set up in the street.

In church she was forever gazing at the Holy Ghost, and one day she noticed that it had something of the parrot about it. This resemblance struck her as even more obvious in a colour print depicting the baptism of Our Lord. With its red wings and its emerald-green body, it was the very image of Loulou.

She bought the print and hung it in the place of the Comte d'Artois, so that she could include them both in a single glance. They were linked together in her mind, the parrot being sanctified by this connection with the Holy Ghost, which itself acquired new life and meaning in her eyes. God the Father could not have chosen a dove as a means of expressing Himself since doves cannot talk, but rather one of Loulou's ancestors. And although Félicité used to say her prayers with her eyes on the picture, from time she would turn slightly towards the bird.

She wanted to join the Children of Mary, but Mme Aubain dissuaded her from doing so.

An important event now loomed up—paul's wedding.

After starting as a lawyer's clerk, he had been in business, in the Customs, and in Inland Revenue, and had even begun trying to get into the Department of Woods and Forests, when, at the age of thirty-six, by some heaven-sent inspiration, he suddenly discovered his real vocation—in the Wills and Probate Department. There he proved so capable that one of the auditors had offered him his daughter in marriage and promised to use his influence on his behalf.

Paul, grown serious-minded, brought her to see his mother. She criticized the way things were done at Pont-l'Évêque, put on airs, and hurt Félicité's feelings. Mme Aubain was relieved to see her go.

The following week came news of M. Bourais's death in an inn in Lower Brittany. Rumours that he had committed suicide were confirmed, and doubts arose as to his honesty. Mme Aubain went over her accounts and was soon conversant with the full catalogue of his misdeeds—embezzlement of interest, secret sales of timber, forged receipts, etc. Besides all this, he was the father of an illegitimate child, and had had "relations with a person at Dozule"

These infamies upset Mme Aubain greatly. In March 1853 she was afflicted with a pain in the chest; her tongue seemed to be covered with a film; leeches failed to make her breathing any easier; and on the ninth evening of her illness she died. She had just reached the age of seventy-two.

She was thought to be younger because of her brown hair, worn in bandeaux round her pale, pock-marked face. There were few friends to mourn her, for she had a haughty manner which put people off. Yet Félicité wept for her as servants rarely weep for their masters. That Madame should die before her upset her ideas, seemed to be contrary to the order of things, monstrous and unthinkable.

Ten days later—the time it took to travel hot-foot from Besançon—the heirs arrived. The daughter-in-law ransacked every drawer, picked out some pieces of furniture and sold the rest; and then back they went to the Wills and Probate Department.

Madame's arm-chair, her pedestal table, her foot-warmer, and the eight chairs had all gone. Yellow squares in the centre of the wall-panels showed where the pictures had hung. They had carried off the two cots with their mattresses, and no trace remained in the cupboard of all Virginie's things. Félicité climbed the stairs to her room, numbed with sadness.

The next day there was a notice on the door, and the apothecary shouted in her ear that the house was up for sale.

She swayed on her feet, and was obliged to sit down.

What distressed her most of all was the idea of leaving her room, which was so suitable for poor Loulou. Fixing an anguished look on him as she appealed to the Holy Ghost, she contracted the idolatrous habit of kneeling in front of the parrot to say her prayers. Sometimes the sun, as it came through the little window, caught his glass eye, so that it shot out a great luminous ray which sent her into ecstasies.

She had a pension of three hundred and eighty francs a year which her mistress had left her. The garden kept her in vegetables. As for clothes, she had enough to last her till the end of her days, and she saved on lighting by going to bed as soon as darkness fell.

She went out as little as possible, to avoid the second-hand dealer's shop, where some of the old furniture was on display. Ever since her fit of giddiness, she had been dragging one leg; and as her strength was failing, Mère Simon, whose grocery business had come to grief, came in every morning to chop wood and pump water for her.

Her eyes grew weaker. The shutters were not opened any more. Years went by, and nobody rented the house and nobody bought it.

For fear of being evicted, Félicité never asked for any repairs to be done. The laths in the roof rotted, and all through one winter her bolster was wet. After Easter she began spitting blood.

When this happened Mère Simon called in a doctor. Félicité wanted to know what was the matter with her, but she was so deaf that only one word reached her: "Pneumonia." It was a word she knew, and she answered gently: "Ah! like Madame," thinking it natural that she should follow in her mistress's footsteps.

The time to set up the altars of repose was drawing near.

The first altar was always at the foot of the hill, the second in front of the post office, the third about half-way up the street. There was some argument as to the siting of this one, and finally the women of the parish picked on Mme Aubain's courtyard.

The fever and the tightness of the chest grew worse. Félicité fretted over not doing anything for the altar. If only she could have put something on it! Then she thought of the parrot. The neighbours protested that it would not be seemly, but the curé gave his permission, and this made her so happy that she begged him to accept Loulou, the only thing of value she possessed, when she died.

From Tuesday to Saturday, the eve of Corpus Christi, she coughed more and more frequently. In the evening her face looked pinched and drawn, her lips stuck to her gums, and she started vomiting. At dawn the next day, feeling very low, she sent for a priest.

Three good women stood by her while she was given extreme unction. Then she said that she had to speak to Fabu.

He arrived in his Sunday best, very ill at ease in this funereal atmosphere.

"Forgive me," she said, making an effort to stretch out her arm. "I thought it was you who had killed him."

What could she mean by such nonsense? To think that she had suspected a man like him of murder. He got very indignant and was obviously going to make a scene.

"Can't you see", they said, "that she isn't in her right mind anymore?"

From time to time Félicité would start talking to shadows. The women went away. Mère Simon had her lunch.

A little later she picked Loulou up and held him out to Félicité, saying:

"Come now, say good-bye to him."

Although the parrot was not a corpse, the worms were eating him up. One of his wings was broken, and the stuffing was coming out of his stomach. But she was blind by now, and she kissed him on the forehead and pressed him against her cheek. Mère Simon took him away from her to put him on the altar.

5

The scents of summer came up from the meadows; there was a buzzing of flies; the sun was glittering in the river and warming the slates of the roof. Mère Simon had come back into the room and was gently nodding off to sleep.

The noise of church bells woke her up; the congregation was coming out from vespers. Félicité's delirium abated. Thinking of the procession, she could see it as clearly as if she had been following it.

All the school-children, the choristers, and the firemen were walking along the pavements, while advancing up the middle of the street came the church officer armed with his halberd, the beadle carrying a great cross, the schoolmaster keeping an eye on the boys, and the nun fussing over her little girls—three of the prettiest, looking like curly-headed angels, were throwing rose-petals into the air. Then came the deacon, with both arms outstretched, conducting the band, and a couple of censor-bearers who turned round at every step to face the Holy Sacrament, which the curé, wearing his splendid chasuble, was carrying under a canopy of poppy-red velvet held aloft by four churchwardens. A crowd of people surged along behind, between the white cloths covering the walls of the houses, and eventually they got to the bottom of the hill.

A cold sweat moistened Félicité's temples. Mère Simon sponged it up with a cloth, telling herself that one day she would have to go the same way.

The hum of the crowd increased in volume, was very loud for a moment, then faded away.

A fusillade shook the window-panes. It was the postilions saluting the monstrance. Félicité rolled her eyes and said as loud as she could: 'Is he all right?'—worrying about the parrot.

She entered into her death-agony. Her breath, coming ever faster, with a rattling sound, made her sides heave. Bubbles of froth appeared at the corners of her mouth, and her whole body trembled.

Soon the booming of the ophicleides, the clear voices of the children, and the deep voices of the men could be heard near at hand. Now and then everything was quiet, and the tramping of feet, deadened by a carpet of flowers, sounded like a flock moving across pasture-land.

The clergy appeared in the courtyard. Mère Simon climbed on to a chair to reach the little round window, from which she had a full view of the altar below.

It was hung with green garlands and adorned with a flounce in English needle point lace. In the middle was a little frame containing some relics, there were two orange-trees at the corners, and all the way along stood silver candlesticks and china vases holding sunflowers, lilies, peonies, foxgloves, and bunches of hydrangea. This pyramid of bright colours stretched from the first floor right down to the carpet which was spread out over the pavement. Some rare objects caught the eye: a silver-gilt sugar-basin wreathed in violets, some pendants of Alençon gems gleaming on a bed of moss, and two Chinese screens with landscape decorations. Loulou, hidden under roses, showed nothing but his blue poll, which looked like a plaque of lapis lazuli.

The churchwardens, the choristers, and the children lined up along the three sides of the courtyard. The priest went slowly up the steps and placed his great shining gold sun on the lace altar-cloth. Everyone knelt down. There was a deep silence. And the censers, swinging at full tilt, slid up and down their chains.

A blue cloud of incense was wafted up into Félicité's room. She opened her nostrils wide and breathed it in with a mystical, sensuous fervour. Then she closed her eyes. Her lips smiled. Her heart-beats grew slower and slower, each a little fainter and gentler, like a fountain running dry, an echo fading away. And as she breathed her last, she thought she could see, in the opening heavens, a gigantic parrot hovering above her head.

The Necklace

Guy de Maupassant

She was one of those pretty and charming girls born, as though fate had blundered over her, into a family of artisans. She had no marriage portion, no expectations, no means of getting known, understood, loved, and wedded by a man of wealth and distinction; and she let herself be married off to a little clerk in the Ministry of Education. Her tastes were simple because she had never been able to afford any other, but she was as unhappy as though she had married beneath her; for women have no caste or class, their beauty, grace, and charm serving them for birth or family, their natural delicacy, their instinctive elegance, their nimbleness of wit, are their only mark of rank, and put the slum girl on a level with the highest lady in the land.

She suffered endlessly, feeling herself born for every delicacy and luxury. She suffered from the poorness of her house, from its mean walls, worn chairs, and ugly curtains. All these things, of which other women of her class would not even have been aware, tormented and insulted her. The sight of the little Breton girl who came to do the work in her little house aroused heart-broken regrets and hopeless dreams in her mind. She imagined silent antechambers, heavy with Oriental tapestries, lit by torches in lofty bronze sockets, with two tall footmen in knee-breeches sleeping in large arm-chairs,

Guy de Maupassant, "The Necklace," from http://www.eastoftheweb.com/short-stories/UBooks/Neck.shtml#top. Copyright © by East of the Web. Permission to reprint granted by the publisher.

overcome by the heavy warmth of the stove. She imagined vast saloons hung with antique silks, exquisite pieces of furniture supporting priceless ornaments, and small, charming, perfumed rooms, created just for little parties of intimate friends, men who were famous and sought after, whose homage roused every other woman's envious longings.

When she sat down for dinner at the round table covered with a three-days-old cloth, opposite her husband, who took the cover off the soup-tureen, exclaiming delightedly: "Aha! Scotch broth! What could be better?" she imagined delicate meals, gleaming silver, tapestries peopling the walls with folk of a past age and strange birds in faery forests; she imagined delicate food served in marvellous dishes, murmured gallantries, listened to with an inscrutable smile as one trifled with the rosy flesh of trout or wings of asparagus chicken.

She had no clothes, no jewels, nothing. And these were the only things she loved; she felt that she was made for them. She had longed so eagerly to charm, to be desired, to be wildly attractive and sought after.

She had a rich friend, an old school friend whom she refused to visit, because she suffered so keenly when she returned home. She would weep whole days, with grief, regret, despair, and misery.

* * *

One evening her husband came home with an exultant air, holding a large envelope in his hand.

"Here's something for you," he said.

Swiftly she tore the paper and drew out a printed card on which were these words:

"The Minister of Education and Madame Ramponneau request the pleasure of the company of Monsieur and Madame Loisel at the Ministry on the evening of Monday, January the 18th."

Instead of being delighted, as her husband hoped, she flung the invitation petulantly across the table, murmuring:

"What do you want me to do with this?"

"Why, darling, I thought you'd be pleased. You never go out, and this is a great occasion. I had tremendous trouble to get it. Every one wants one; it's very select, and very few go to the clerks. You'll see all the really big people there."

She looked at him out of furious eyes, and said impatiently: "And what do you suppose I am to wear at such an affair?"

He had not thought about it; he stammered:

"Why, the dress you go to the theatre in. It looks very nice, to me…"

He stopped, stupefied and utterly at a loss when he saw that his wife was beginning to cry. Two large tears ran slowly down from the corners of her eyes towards the corners of her mouth.

"What's the matter with you? What's the matter with you?" he faltered.

But with a violent effort she overcame her grief and replied in a calm voice, wiping her wet cheeks:

"Nothing. Only I haven't a dress and so I can't go to this party. Give your invitation to some friend of yours whose wife will be turned out better than I shall."

He was heart-broken.

"Look here, Mathilde," he persisted. "What would be the cost of a suitable dress, which you could use on other occasions as well, something very simple?"

She thought for several seconds, reckoning up prices and also wondering for how large a sum she could ask without bringing upon herself an immediate refusal and an exclamation of horror from the careful-minded clerk.

At last she replied with some hesitation:

"I don't know exactly, but I think I could do it on four hundred francs."

He grew slightly pale, for this was exactly the amount he had been saving for a gun, intending to get a little shooting next summer on the plain of Nanterre with some friends who went lark-shooting there on Sundays.

Nevertheless he said: "Very well. I'll give you four hundred francs. But try and get a really nice dress with the money."

The day of the party drew near, and Madame Loisel seemed sad, uneasy and anxious. Her dress was ready, however. One evening her husband said to her:

"What's the matter with you? You've been very odd for the last three days."

"I'm utterly miserable at not having any jewels, not a single stone, to wear," she replied. "I shall look absolutely no one. I would almost rather not go to the party."

"Wear flowers," he said. "They're very smart at this time of the year. For ten francs you could get two or three gorgeous roses."

She was not convinced.

"No…there's nothing so humiliating as looking poor in the middle of a lot of rich women."

"How stupid you are!" exclaimed her husband. "Go and see Madame Forestier and ask her to lend you some jewels. You know her quite well enough for that."

She uttered a cry of delight.

"That's true. I never thought of it."

Next day she went to see her friend and told her her trouble.

Madame Forestier went to her dressing-table, took up a large box, brought it to Madame Loisel, opened it, and said:

"Choose, my dear."

First she saw some bracelets, then a pearl necklace, then a Venetian cross in gold and gems, of exquisite workmanship. She tried the effect of the jewels before the mirror, hesitating, unable to make up her mind to leave them, to give them up. She kept on asking:

"Haven't you anything else?"

"Yes. Look for yourself. I don't know what you would like best."

Suddenly she discovered, in a black satin case, a superb diamond necklace; her heart began to beat covetously. Her hands trembled as she lifted it. She fastened it round her neck, upon her high dress, and remained in ecstasy at sight of herself.

Then, with hesitation, she asked in anguish:

"Could you lend me this, just this alone?"

"Yes, of course."

She flung herself on her friend's breast, embraced her frenziedly, and went away with her treasure. The day of the party arrived. Madame Loisel was a success. She was the prettiest woman present, elegant, graceful, smiling, and quite above herself with happiness. All the men stared at her, inquired her name, and asked to be introduced to her. All the Under-Secretaries of State were eager to waltz with her. The Minister noticed her.

She danced madly, ecstatically, drunk with pleasure, with no thought for anything, in the triumph of her beauty, in the pride of her success, in a cloud of happiness made up of this universal homage and admiration, of the desires she had aroused, of the completeness of a victory so dear to her feminine heart.

She left about four o'clock in the morning. Since midnight her husband had been dozing in a deserted little room, in company with three other men whose wives were having a good time. He threw over her shoulders the garments he had brought for them to go home in, modest everyday clothes, whose poverty clashed with the beauty of the ball-dress. She was conscious of this and was anxious to hurry away, so that she should not be noticed by the other women putting on their costly furs.

Loisel restrained her.

"Wait a little. You'll catch cold in the open. I'm going to fetch a cab."

But she did not listen to him and rapidly descended the staircase. When they were out in the street they could not find a cab; they began to look for one, shouting at the drivers whom they saw passing in the distance.

They walked down towards the Seine, desperate and shivering. At last they found on the quay one of those old nightprowling carriages which are only to be seen in Paris after dark, as though they were ashamed of their shabbiness in the daylight.

It brought them to their door in the Rue des Martyrs, and sadly they walked up to their own apartment. It was the end, for her. As for him, he was thinking that he must be at the office at ten.

She took off the garments in which she had wrapped her shoulders, so as to see herself in all her glory before the mirror. But suddenly she uttered a cry. The necklace was no longer round her neck!

"What's the matter with you?" asked her husband, already half undressed.

She turned towards him in the utmost distress.

"I…I…I've no longer got Madame Forestier's necklace…"

He started with astonishment.

"What!…Impossible!"

They searched in the folds of her dress, in the folds of the coat, in the pockets, everywhere. They could not find it.

"Are you sure that you still had it on when you came away from the ball?" he asked.

"Yes, I touched it in the hall at the Ministry."

"But if you had lost it in the street, we should have heard it fall."

"Yes. Probably we should. Did you take the number of the cab?"

"No. You didn't notice it, did you?"

"No."

They stared at one another, dumbfounded. At last Loisel put on his clothes again.

"I'll go over all the ground we walked," he said, "and see if I can't find it."

And he went out. She remained in her evening clothes, lacking strength to get into bed, huddled on a chair, without volition or power of thought.

Her husband returned about seven. He had found nothing.

He went to the police station, to the newspapers, to offer a reward, to the cab companies, everywhere that a ray of hope impelled him.

She waited all day long, in the same state of bewilderment at this fearful catastrophe.

Loisel came home at night, his face lined and pale; he had discovered nothing.

"You must write to your friend," he said, "and tell her that you've broken the clasp of her necklace and are getting it mended. That will give us time to look about us."

She wrote at his dictation.

By the end of a week they had lost all hope.

Loisel, who had aged five years, declared:

"We must see about replacing the diamonds."

Next day they took the box which had held the necklace and went to the jewellers whose name was inside. He consulted his books.

"It was not I who sold this necklace, Madame; I must have merely supplied the clasp."

Then they went from jeweller to jeweller, searching for another necklace like the first, consulting their memories, both ill with remorse and anguish of mind.

In a shop at the Palais-Royal they found a string of diamonds which seemed to them exactly like the one they were looking for. It was worth forty thousand francs. They were allowed to have it for thirty-six thousand.

They begged the jeweller not to sell it for three days. And they arranged matters on the understanding that it would be taken back for thirty-four thousand francs, if the first one were found before the end of February.

Loisel possessed eighteen thousand francs left to him by his father. He intended to borrow the rest.

He did borrow it, getting a thousand from one man, five hundred from another, five louis here, three louis there. He gave notes of hand, entered into ruinous agreements, did business with usurers and the whole tribe of money-lenders. He mortgaged the whole remaining years of his existence, risked his signature without even knowing if he could honour it, and, appalled at the agonising face of the future, at the black misery about to fall upon him, at the prospect of every possible physical privation and moral torture, he went to get the new necklace and put down upon the jeweller's counter thirty-six thousand francs.

When Madame Loisel took back the necklace to Madame Forestier, the latter said to her in a chilly voice: "You ought to have brought it back sooner; I might have needed it."

She did not, as her friend had feared, open the case. If she had noticed the substitution, what would she have thought? What would she have said? Would she not have taken her for a thief?

* * *

Madame Loisel came to know the ghastly life of abject poverty. From the very first she played her part heroically. This fearful debt must be paid off. She would pay it. The servant was dismissed. They changed their flat; they took a garret under the roof.

She came to know the heavy work of the house, the hateful duties of the kitchen. She washed the plates, wearing out her pink nails on the coarse pottery and the bottoms of pans. She washed the dirty linen, the shirts and dish-cloths, and hung them out to dry on a string; every morning she took the dustbin down into the street and carried up the water, stopping on each landing to get her breath. And, clad like a poor woman, she went to the fruiterer, to the grocer, to the butcher, a basket on her arm, haggling, insulted, fighting for every wretched halfpenny of her money.

Every month notes had to be paid off, others renewed, time gained.

Her husband worked in the evenings at putting straight a merchant's accounts, and often at night he did copying at twopence-halfpenny a page.

And this life lasted ten years.

At the end of ten years everything was paid off, everything, the usurer's charges and the accumulation of superimposed interest.

Madame Loisel looked old now. She had become like all the other strong, hard, coarse women of poor households. Her hair was badly done, her skirts were awry, her hands were red. She spoke in a shrill voice, and the water slopped all over the floor when she scrubbed it. But sometimes, when her husband was at the office, she sat down by the window and thought of that evening long ago, of the ball at which she had been so beautiful and so much admired.

What would have happened if she had never lost those jewels. Who knows? Who knows? How strange life is, how fickle! How little is needed to ruin or to save!

One Sunday, as she had gone for a walk along the Champs-Elysees to freshen herself after the labours of the week, she caught sight suddenly of a woman who was taking a child out for a walk. It was Madame Forestier, still young, still beautiful, still attractive.

Madame Loisel was conscious of some emotion. Should she speak to her? Yes, certainly. And now that she had paid, she would tell her all. Why not?

She went up to her.

"Good morning, Jeanne."

The other did not recognise her, and was surprised at being thus familiarly addressed by a poor woman.

"But…Madame…" she stammered. "I don't know…you must be making a mistake."

"No…I am Mathilde Loisel."

Her friend uttered a cry.

"Oh!…my poor Mathilde, how you have changed!…"

"Yes, I've had some hard times since I saw you last; and many sorrows…and all on your account."

"On my account!…How was that?"

"You remember the diamond necklace you lent me for the ball at the Ministry?"

"Yes. Well?"

"Well, I lost it."

"How could you? Why, you brought it back."

"I brought you another one just like it. And for the last ten years we have been paying for it. You realise it wasn't easy for us; we had no money… Well, it's paid for at last, and I'm glad indeed."

Madame Forestier had halted.

"You say you bought a diamond necklace to replace mine?"

"Yes. You hadn't noticed it? They were very much alike."

And she smiled in proud and innocent happiness.

Madame Forestier, deeply moved, took her two hands.

"Oh, my poor Mathilde! But mine was imitation. It was worth at the very most five hundred francs!…"

The Yellow Wallpaper

Charlotte Perkins Gilman

It is very seldom that mere ordinary people like John and myself secure ancestral halls for the summer.

A colonial mansion, a hereditary estate, I would say a haunted house and reach the height of romantic felicity—but that would be asking too much of fate!

Still I will proudly declare that there is something queer about it.

Else, why should it be let so cheaply? And why have stood so long untenanted?

John laughs at me, of course, but one expects that in marriage.

John is practical in the extreme. He has no patience with faith, an intense horror of superstition, and he scoffs openly at any talk of things not to be felt and seen and put down in figures.

John is a physician, and *perhaps*—(I would not say it to a living soul of course, but this is dead paper and a great relief to my mind)—*perhaps* that is one reason I do not get well faster.

You see, he does not believe I am sick!

And what can one do?

If a physician of high standing, and one's own husband, assures friends and relatives that there is really nothing the matter with one but temporary nervous depression—a slight hysterical tendency—what is one to do?

My brother is also a physician, and also of high standing, and he says the same thing.

So I take phosphates or phosphites—whichever it is, and tonics, and journeys, and air, and exercise, and am absolutely forbidden to "work" until I am well again.

Personally, I disagree with their ideas.

Personally, I believe that congenial work, with excitement and change, would do me good.

But what is one to do?

I did write for a while in spite of them; but it *does* exhaust me a good deal—having to be so sly about it, or else meet with heavy opposition.

I sometimes fancy that in my condition if I had less opposition and more society and stimulus—but John says the very worst thing I can do is to think about my condition, and I confess it always makes me feel bad.

So I will let it alone and talk about the house.

The most beautiful place! It is quite alone, standing well back from the road, quite three miles from the village. It makes me think of English places that you read about, for there are hedges and walls and gates that lock, and lots of separate little houses for the gardeners and people.

There is a *delicious* garden! I never saw such a garden—large and shady, full of box-bordered paths, and lined with long grape-covered arbors with seats under them.

There were greenhouses, too, but they are all broken now.

There was some legal trouble, I believe, something about the heirs and co-heirs; anyhow, the place has been empty for years.

That spoils my ghostliness, I am afraid, but I don't care—there is something strange about the house—I can feel it.

I even said so to John one moonlight evening, but he said what I felt was a *draught,* and shut the window.

Charlotte Perkins Gilman, "The Yellow Wallpaper," from *The New England Magazine*. Copyright in the Public Domain.

I get unreasonably angry with John sometimes. I'm sure I never used to be so sensitive. I think it is due to this nervous condition.

But John says if I feel so, I shall neglect proper self-control; so I take pains to control myself—before him, at least, and that makes me very tired.

I don't like our room a bit. I wanted one downstairs that opened on the piazza and had roses all over the window, and such pretty old-fashioned chintz hangings! but John would not hear of it.

He said there was only one window and not room for two beds, and no near room for him if he took another.

He is very careful and loving, and hardly lets me stir without special direction.

I have a schedule prescription for each hour in the day; he takes all care from me, and so I feel basely ungrateful not to value it more.

He said we came here solely on my account, that I was to have perfect rest and all the air I could get. "Your exercise depends on your strength, my dear," said he, "and your food somewhat on your appetite; but air you can absorb all the time." So we took the nursery at the top of the house.

It is a big, airy room, the whole floor nearly, with windows that look all ways, and air and sunshine galore. It was nursery first and then playroom and gymnasium, I should judge; for the windows are barred for little children, and there are rings and things in the walls.

The paint and paper look as if a boys' school had used it. It is stripped off—the paper—in great patches all around the head of my bed, about as far as I can reach, and in a great place on the other side of the room low down. I never saw a worse paper in my life.

One of those sprawling flamboyant patterns committing every artistic sin.

It is dull enough to confuse the eye in following, pronounced enough to constantly irritate and provoke study and when you follow the lame uncertain curves for a little distance they suddenly commit suicide—plunge off at outrageous angles, destroy themselves in unheard of contradictions.

The color is repellant, almost revolting; a smouldering unclean yellow strangely faded by the slow-turning sunlight.

It is a dull yet lurid orange in some places, a sickly sulphur tint in others.

No wonder the children hated it! I should hate it myself if I had to live in this room long.

There comes John, and I must put this away,—he hates to have me write a word.

* * *

We have been here two weeks, and I haven't felt like writing before since that first day.

I am sitting by the window now, up in this atrocious nursery, and there is nothing to hinder my writing as much as I please, save lack of strength.

John is away all day, and even some nights when his cases are serious.

I am glad my case is not serious!

But these nervous troubles are dreadfully depressing.

John does not know how much I really suffer. He knows there is no *reason* to suffer, and that satisfies him.

Of course it is only nervousness. It does weigh on me so not to do my duty in any way!

I meant to be such a help to John, such a real rest and comfort, and here I am a comparative burden already!

Nobody would believe what an effort it is to do what little I am able,—to dress and entertain, and order things.

It is fortunate Mary is so good with the baby. Such a dear baby!

And yet I *cannot* be with him, it makes me so nervous.

I suppose John never was nervous in his life. He laughs at me so about this wall-paper!

At first he meant to repaper the room, but afterward he said that I was letting it get the better of me, and that nothing was worse for a nervous patient than to give way to such fancies.

He said that after the wall-paper was changed it would be the heavy bedstead, and then the barred windows, and then that gate at the head of the stairs, and so on.

"You know the place is doing you good," he said, "and really, dear, I don't care to renovate the house just for a three months' rental."

"Then do let us go downstairs," I said, "there are such pretty rooms there.

Then he took me in his arms and called me a blessed little goose, and said he would go down cellar, if I wished, and have it whitewashed into the bargain.

But he is right enough about the beds and windows and things.

It is an airy and comfortable room as anyone need wish, and, of course, I would not be so silly as to make him uncomfortable just for a whim.

I'm really getting quite fond of the big room, all but that horrid paper.

Out of one window I can see the garden, those mysterious deep-shaded arbors, the riotous old-fashioned flowers, and bushes and gnarly trees.

Out of another I get a lovely view of the bay and a little private wharf belonging to the estate. There is a beautiful shaded lane that runs down there from the house. I always fancy I see people walking in these numerous paths and arbors, but John has cautioned me not to give way to fancy in the least. He says that with my imaginative power and habit of story-making, a nervous weakness like mine is sure to lead to all manner of excited fancies, and that I ought to use my will and good sense to check the tendency. So I try.

I think sometimes that if I were only well enough to write a little it would relieve the press of ideas and rest me.

But I find I get pretty tired when I try.

It is so discouraging not to have any advice and companionship about my work. When I get really well, John says we will ask Cousin Henry and Julia down for a long visit; but he says he would as soon put fireworks in my pillow-case as to let me have those stimulating people about now.

I wish I could get well faster.

But I must not think about that. This paper looks to me as if it *knew* What a vicious influence it had!

There is a recurrent spot where the pattern lolls like a broken neck and two bulbous eyes stare at you upside down.

I get positively angry with the impertinence of it and the everlastingness. Up and down and sideways they crawl, and those absurd unblinking eyes are everywhere There is one place where two breadths didn't match, and the eyes go all up and down the line, one a little higher than the other.

I remember what a kindly wink the knobs of our big, old bureau used to have, and there was one chair that always seemed like a strong friend.

I used to feel that if any of the other things looked too fierce I could always hop into that chair and be safe

The furniture in this room is no worse than inharmonious, however, for we had to bring it all from downstairs. I suppose when this was used as a playroom they had to take the nursery things out, and no wonder! I never saw such ravages as the children have made here.

The wall-paper, as I said before, is torn off in spots, and it sticketh closer than a brother—they must have had perseverance as well as hatred.

Then the floor is scratched and gouged and splintered, the plaster itself is dug out here and there, and this great heavy bed which is all we found in the room, looks as if it had been through the wars.

But I don't mind it a bit—only the paper.

There comes John's sister. Such a dear girl as she is, and so careful of me! I must not let her find me writing.

She is a perfect and enthusiastic housekeeper, and hopes for no better profession. I verily believe she thinks it is the writing which made me sick!

But I can write when she is out, and see her a long way off from these windows.

There is one that commands the road, a lovely shaded winding road, and one that just looks off over the country. A lovely country, too, full of great elms and velvet meadows.

This wallpaper has a kind of sub-pattern in a different shade, a particularly irritating one, for you can only see it in certain lights, and not clearly then.

But in the places where it isn't faded and where the sun is just so—I can see a strange, provoking, formless sort of figure, that seems to skulk about behind that silly and conspicuous front design.

There's sister on the stairs!

* * *

Well, the Fourth of July is over! The people are all gone and I am tired out. John thought it might do me good to see a little company, so we just had mother and Nellie and the children down for a week.

Of course I didn't do a thing. Jennie sees to everything now.

But it tired me all the same.

John says if I don't pick up faster he shall send me to Weir Mitchell[1] in the fall.

But I don't want to go there at all. I had a friend who was in his hands once, and she says he is just like John and my brother, only more so!

Besides, it is such an undertaking to go so far.

I don't feel as if it was worthwhile to turn my hand over for anything, and I'm getting dreadfully fretful and querulous.

I cry at nothing, and cry most of the time.

Of course I don't when John is here, or anybody else, but when I am alone.

And I am alone a good deal just now. John is kept in town very often by serious cases, and Jennie is good and lets me alone when I want her to.

So I walk a little in the garden or down that lovely lane, sit on the porch under the roses, and lie down up here a good deal.

I'm getting really fond of the room in spite of the wallpaper. Perhaps *because* of the wallpaper.

It dwells in my mind so.

I lie here on this great immovable bed—it is nailed down, I believe—and follow that pattern about by the hour. It is as good as gymnastics, I assure you. I start, we'll say, at the bottom, down in the corner over there where has not been touched, and I determine for the thousandth time that I *will* follow that pointless pattern to some sort of a conclusion.

I know a little of the principle of design, and I know this thing was not arranged on any laws of radiation, or alternation, or repetition, or symmetry, or anything else that I ever heard of.

It is repeated, of course, by the breadths, but not otherwise.

Looked at in one way each breadth stands alone, the bloated curves and flourishes—a kind of "debased Romanesque" with *delirium tremens*—go waddling up and down in isolated columns of fatuity.

But, on the other hand, they connect diagonally, and the sprawling outlines run off in great slanting waves of optic horror, like a lot of wallowing seaweeds in full chase.

The whole thing goes horizontally, too, at least it seems so, and I exhaust myself in trying to distinguish the order of its going in that direction.

They have used a horizontal breadth for a frieze, and that adds wonderfully to the confusion.

There is one end of the room where it is almost intact, and there, when the crosslights fade and the low sun shines directly upon it, I can almost fancy radiation after all,—the interminable grotesques seem to form around a common centre and rush off in headlong plunges of equal distraction.

It makes me tired to follow it. I will take a nap I guess.

* * *

I don't know why I should write this.
I don't want to.
I don't feel able.

And I know John would think it absurd. But I *must* say what I feel and think in some way—it is such a relief!

But the effort is getting to be greater than the relief.

Half the time now I am awfully lazy, and lie down ever so much.

John says I mustn't lose my strength, and has me take cod liver oil and lots of tonics and things, to say nothing of ale and wine and rare meat.

---

[1] Dr. S. Weir Mitchell (1829–1914) was an eminent Philadelphia neurologist who advocated "rest cures" for cervous disorders. He was the author of *Diseases of the, Nervous System Especially of Women* (1881).

Dear John! He loves me very dearly, and hates to have me sick. I tried to have a real earnest reasonable talk with him the other day, and tell him how I wish he would let me go and make a visit to Cousin Henry and Julia.

But he said I wasn't able to go, nor able to stand it after I got there; and I did not make out a very good case for myself, for I was crying before I had finished.

It is getting to be a great effort for me to think straight. Just this nervous weakness I suppose.

And dear John gathered me up in his arms, and just carried me upstairs and laid me on the bed, and sat by me and read to me till it tired my head.

He said I was his darling and his comfort and all he had, and that I must take care of myself for his sake, and keep well.

He says no one but myself can help me out of it, that I must use my will and self-control and not let any silly fancies run away with me.

There's one comfort, the baby is well and happy, and does not have to occupy this nursery with the horrid wallpaper.

If we had not used it, that blessed child would have! What a fortunate escape! Why, I wouldn't have a child of mine, an impressionable little thing, live in such a room for worlds.

I never thought of it before, but it is lucky that John kept me here after all, I can stand it so much easier than a baby, you see.

Of course I never mention it to them any more—I am too wise—but I keep watch of it all the same.

There are things in that wallpaper that nobody knows but me, or ever will.

Behind that outside pattern the dim shapes get clearer every day.

It is always the same shape, only very numerous.

And it is like a woman stooping down and creeping about behind that pattern. I don't like it a bit. I wonder—I begin to think—I wish John would take me away from here!

* * *

It is so hard to talk with John about my case, because he is so wise, and because he loves me so.

But I tried it last night.

It was moonlight. The moon shines in all around just as the sun does.

I hate to see it sometimes, it creeps so slowly, and always comes in by one window or another.

John was asleep and I hated to waken him, so I kept still and watched the moonlight on that undulating wallpaper till I felt creepy.

The faint figure behind seemed to shake the pattern, just as if she wanted to get out.

I got up softly and went to feel and see if the paper *did* move, and when I came back John was awake.

"What is it, little girl?" he said. "Don't go walking about like that—you'll get cold."

I thought it was a good time to talk, so I told him that I really was not gaining here, and that I wished he would take me away.

"Why, darling!" said he, "our lease will be up in three weeks, and I can't see how to leave before.

"The repairs are not done at home, and I cannot possibly leave town just now. Of course if you were in any danger, I could and would, but you really are better, dear, whether you can see it or not. I am a doctor, dear, and I know. You are gaining flesh and color, your appetite is better, I feel really much easier about you."

"I don't weigh a bit more," said I, "nor as much; and my appetite may be better in the evening when you are here but it is worse in the morning when you are away!"

"Bless her little heart!" said he with a big hug, "she shall be as sick as she pleases! But now let's improve the shining hours by going to sleep, and talk about it in the morning!"

"And you won't go away?" I asked gloomily.

"Why, how can I, dear? It is only three weeks more and then we will take a nice little trip of a few days while Jennie is getting the house ready. Really dear you are better!"

"Better in body perhaps—" I began, and stopped short, for he sat up straight and looked at me with such a stern, reproachful look that I could not say another word.

"My darling," said he, "I beg you, for my sake and for our child's sake, as well as for your own, that you will never for one instant let that idea enter your mind! There is nothing so dangerous, so fascinating, to a temperament like yours. It is a false and foolish fancy. Can you trust me as a physician when I tell you so?"

So of course I said no more on that score, and we went to sleep before long. He thought I was asleep first, but I wasn't, and lay there for hours trying to decide whether that front pattern and the back pattern really did move together or separately.

* * *

On a pattern like this, by daylight, there is a lack of sequence, a defiance of law, that is a constant irritant to a normal mind.

The color is hideous enough, and unreliable enough, and infuriating enough, but the pattern is torturing.

You think you have mastered it, but just as you get well underway in following, it turns a back-somersault and there you are. It slaps you in the face, knocks you down, and tramples upon you. It is like a bad dream.

The outside pattern is a florid arabesque, reminding one of a fungus. If you can imagine a toadstool in joints, an interminable string of toadstools, budding and sprouting in endless convolutions—why, that is something like it.

That is, sometimes!

There is one marked peculiarity about this paper, a thing nobody seems to notice but myself, and that is that it changes as the light changes.

When the sun shoots in through the east window— I always watch for that first long, straight ray—it changes so quickly that I never can quite believe it.

That is why I watch it always.

By moonlight—the moon shines in all night when there is a moon—I wouldn't know it was the same paper.

At night in any kind of light, in twilight, candle-light, lamplight, and worst of all by moonlight, it becomes bars! The outside pattern I mean, and the woman behind it is as plain as can be.

I didn't realize for a long time what the thing was that showed behind, that dim sub-pattern, but now I am quite sure it is a woman.

By daylight she is subdued, quiet. I fancy it is the pattern that keeps her so still. It is so puzzling. It keeps me quiet by the hour.

I lie down ever so much now. John says it is good for me, and to sleep all I can.

Indeed he started the habit by making me lie down for an hour after each meal.

It is a very bad habit I am convinced, for you see I don't sleep.

And that cultivates deceit, for I don't tell them I'm awake—O, no!

The fact is I am getting a little afraid of John.

He seems very queer sometimes, and even Jennie has an inexplicable look.

It strikes me occasionally, just as a scientific hypothesis,—that perhaps it is the paper!

I have watched John when he did not know I was looking, and come into the room suddenly on the most innocent excuses, and I've caught him several times *looking at the paper!* And Jennie too. I caught Jennie with her hand on it once.

She didn't know I was in the room, and when I asked her in a quiet, a very quiet voice, with the most restrained manner possible, what she was doing with the paper—she turned around as if she had been caught stealing, and looked quite angry—asked me why I should frighten her so!

Then she said that the paper stained everything it touched, that she had found yellow smooches on all my clothes and John's, and she wished we would be more careful!

Did not that sound innocent? But I know she was studying that pattern, and I am determined that nobody shall find it out but myself!

* * *

Life is very much more exciting now than it used to be. You see I have something more to expect, to look forward to, to watch. I really do eat better, and am more quiet than I was.

John is so pleased to see me improve! He laughed a little the other day, and said I seemed to be flourishing in spite of my wall-paper.

I turned it off with a laugh. I had no intention of telling him it was *because* of the wall-paper—he would make fun of me. He might even want to take me away.

I don't want to leave now until I have found it out. There is a week more, and I think that will be enough.

I'm feeling ever so much better! I don't sleep much at night, for it is so interesting to watch developments; but I sleep a good deal in the daytime.

In the daytime it is tiresome and perplexing.

There are always new shoots on the fungus, and new shades of yellow all over it. I cannot keep count of them, though I have tried conscientiously.

It is the strangest yellow, that wall-paper! It makes me think of all the yellow things I ever saw—not beautiful ones like buttercups, but old foul, bad yellow things.

But there is something else about that paper—the smell! I noticed it the moment we came into the room, but with so much air and sun it was not bad. Now we have had a week of fog and rain, and whether the windows are open or not, the smell is here.

It creeps all over the house.

I find it hovering in the dining-room, skulking in the parlor, hiding in the hall, lying in wait for me on the stairs.

It gets into my hair.

Even when I go to ride, if I turn my head suddenly and surprise it—there is that smell!

Such a peculiar odor, too! I have spent hours in trying to analyze it, to find what it smelled like.

It is not bad—at first, and very gentle, but quite the subtlest, most enduring odor I ever met.

In this damp weather it is awful, I wake up in the night and find it hanging over me.

It used to disturb me at first. I thought seriously of burning the house—to reach the smell.

But now I am used to it. The only thing I can think of that it is like is the *color* of the paper! A yellow smell.

There is a very funny mark on this wall, low down, near the mopboard. A streak that runs round the room. It goes behind every piece of furniture, except the bed, a long, straight, even *smooch*, as if it had been rubbed over and over.

I wonder how it was done and who did it, and what they did it for. Round and round and round—round and round and round—it makes me dizzy!

* * *

I really have discovered something at last.

Through watching so much at night, when it changes so, I have finally found out.

The front pattern *does* move—and no wonder! The woman behind shakes it!

Sometimes I think there are a great many women behind, and sometimes only one, and she crawls around fast, and her crawling shakes it all over.

Then in the very bright spots she keeps still, and in the very shady spots she just takes hold of the bars and shakes them hard.

And she is all the time trying to climb through. But nobody could climb through that pattern—it strangles so; I think that is why it has so many heads.

They get through, and then the pattern strangles them off and turns them upside down, and makes their eyes white!

If those heads were covered or taken off it would not be half so bad.

* * *

I think that woman gets out in the daytime!

And I'll tell you why—privately—I've seen her!

I can see her out of every one of my windows!

It is the same woman, I know, for she is always creeping, and most women do not creep by daylight.

I see her in that long shaded lane, creeping up and down. I see her in those dark grape arbors, creeping all around the garden.

I see her on that long road under the trees, creeping along, and when a carriage comes she hides under the blackberry vines.

I don't blame her a bit. It must be very humiliating to be caught creeping by daylight!

I always lock the door when I creep by daylight. I can't do it at night, for I know John would suspect something at once.

And John is so queer now, that I don't want to irritate him. I wish he would take another room! Besides, I don't want anybody to get that woman out at night but myself.

I often wonder if I could see her out of all the windows at once.

But, turn as fast as I can, I can only see out of one at one time.

And though I always see her, she *may* be able to creep faster than I can turn!

I have watched her sometimes away off in the open country, creeping as fast as a cloud shadow in a high wind.

* * *

If only that top pattern could be gotten off from the under one! I mean to try it, little by little.

I have found out another funny thing, but I shan't tell it this time! It does not do to trust people too much.

There are only two more days to get this paper off, and I believe John is beginning to notice. I don't like the look in his eyes.

And I heard him ask Jennie a lot of professional questions, about me. She had a very good report to give.

She said I slept a good deal in the daytime.

John knows I don't sleep very well at night, for all I'm so quiet!

He asked me all sorts of questions too, and pretended to be very loving and kind.

As if I couldn't see through him!

Still, I don't wonder he acts so, sleeping under this paper for three months.

It only interests me, but I feel sure John and Jennie are secretly affected by it.

* * *

Hurrah! This is the last day, but it is enough. John is to stay in town over night, and won't be out until this evening.

Jennie wanted to sleep with me—the sly thing! But I told her I should undoubtedly rest better for a night all alone.

That was clever, for really I wasn't alone a bit! As soon as it was moonlight and that poor thing began to crawl and shake the pattern, I got up and ran to help her.

I pulled and she shook, I shook and she pulled, and before morning we had peeled off yards of that paper.

A strip about as high as my head and half around the room.

And then when the sun came and that awful pattern began to laugh at me, I declared I would finish it to-day!

We go away to-morrow, and they are moving all my furniture down again to leave things as they were before.

Jennie looked at the wall in amazement, but I told her merrily that I did it out of pure spite at the vicious thing.

She laughed and said she wouldn't mind doing it herself, but I must not get tired.

How she betrayed herself that time!

But I am here, and no person touches this paper but me,—not *alive!*

She tried to get me out of the room—it was too patent! But I said it was so quiet and empty and clean now that I believed I would lie down again and sleep all I could, and not to wake me even for dinner—I would call when I woke.

So now she is gone, and the servants are gone, and the things are gone, and there is nothing left but that great bedstead nailed down, with the canvas mattress we found on it.

We shall sleep downstairs to-night, and take the boat home to-morrow.

I quite enjoy the room, now it is bare again.

How those children did tear about here!

This bedstead is fairly gnawed!

But I must get to work.

I have locked the door and thrown the key down into the front path.

I don't want to go out, and I don't want to have anybody come in, till John comes.

I want to astonish him.

I've got a rope up here that even Jennie did not find. If that woman does get out, and tries to get away, I can tie her!

But I forgot I could not reach far without anything to stand on!

This bed will not move!

I tried to lift and push it until I was lame, and then I got so angry I bit off a little piece at one corner—but it hurt my teeth.

Then I peeled off all the paper I could reach standing on the floor. It sticks horribly and the pattern just enjoys it! All those strangled heads and bulbous eyes and waddling fungus growths just shriek with derision!

I am getting angry enough to do something desperate. To jump out of the window would be admirable exercise, but the bars are too strong even to try.

Besides I wouldn't do it. Of course not. I know well enough that a step like that is improper and might be misconstrued.

I don't like to *look* out of the windows even—there are so many of those creeping women, and they creep so fast.

I wonder if they all come out of that wall-paper as I did?

But I am securely fastened now by my well-hidden rope—you don't get *me* out in the road there!

I suppose I shall have to get back behind the pattern when it comes night, and that is hard!

It is so pleasant to be out in this great room and creep around as I please!

I don't want to go outside. I won't, even if Jennie asks me to.

For outside you have to creep on the ground, and everything is green instead of yellow.

But here I can creep smoothly on the floor, and my shoulder just fits in that long smooch around the wall, so I cannot lose my way.

Why, there's John at the door!

It is no use, young man, you can't open it!

How he does call and pound!

Now he's crying for an axe.

It would be a shame to break down that beautiful door!

"John dear!" said I in the gentlest voice, "the key is down by the front steps, under a plantain leaf!"

That silenced him for a few moments.

Then he said—very quietly indeed, "Open the door, my darling!"

"I can't," said I. "The key is down by the front door under a plantain leaf!"

And then I said it again, several times, very gently and slowly, and said it so often that he had to go and see, and he got it of course, and came in. He stopped short by the door.

"What is the matter?" he cried. "For God's sake, what are you doing!"

I kept on creeping just the same, but I looked at him over my shoulder.

"I've got out at last," said I, "in spite of you and Jane. And I've pulled off most of the paper, so you can't put me back!"

Now why should that man have fainted? But he did, and right across my path by the wall, so that I had to creep over him every time

1892

The Open Boat

A Tale Intended to be After the Fact, Being the Experience of Four Men From the Sunk Steamer *Commodore*.

Stephen Crane

I

None of them knew the color of the sky. Their eyes glanced level, and were fastened upon the waves that swept toward them. These waves were of the hue of slate, save for the tops, which were of foaming white, and all of the men knew the colors of the sea. The horizon narrowed and widened, and dipped and rose, and at all times its edge was jagged with waves that seemed thrust up in points like rocks.

Many a man ought to have a bath-tub larger than the boat which here rode upon the sea. These waves were most wrongfully and barbarously abrupt and tall, and each froth-top was a problem in small boat navigation.

The cook squatted in the bottom and looked with both eyes at the six inches of gunwale which separated him from the ocean. His sleeves were rolled over his fat forearms, and the two flaps of his unbuttoned vest dangled as he bent to bail out the boat. Often he said: "Gawd! That was a narrow clip." As he remarked it he invariably gazed eastward over the broken sea.

The oiler, steering with one of the two oars in the boat, sometimes raised himself suddenly to keep clear of water that swirled in over the stern. It was a thin little oar and it seemed often ready to snap.

The correspondent, pulling at the other oar, watched the waves and wondered why he was there.

The injured captain, lying in the bow, was at this time buried in that profound dejection and indifference which comes, temporarily at least, to even the bravest and most enduring when, willy nilly, the firm fails, the army loses, the ship goes down. The mind of the master of a vessel is rooted deep in the timbers of her, though he command for a day or a decade, and this captain had on him the stern impression of a scene in the grays of dawn of seven turned faces, and later a stump of a top-mast with a white ball on it that slashed to and fro at the waves, went low and lower, and down. Thereafter there was something strange in his voice. Although steady, it was deep with mourning, and of a quality beyond oration or tears.

"Keep 'er a little more south, Billie," said he.

"'A little more south,' sir," said the oiler in the stern.

A seat in this boat was not unlike a seat upon a bucking broncho, and, by the same token, a broncho is not much smaller. The craft pranced and reared, and plunged like an animal. As each wave came, and she rose for it, she seemed like a horse making at a fence outrageously high. The manner of her scramble over these walls of water is a mystic thing, and, moreover, at the top of them were ordinarily these problems in white water, the foam racing down from the summit of each wave, requiring a new leap, and a leap from the air. Then, after scornfully bumping a crest, she would slide, and race, and splash down a long incline and arrive bobbing and nodding in front of the next menace.

A singular disadvantage of the sea lies in the fact that after successfully surmounting one wave you discover that there is another behind it just

---

Stephen Crane, "The Open Boat," from *Scribner's Magazine*. Published by Charles Scribner's Sons, 1897. Copyright in the Public Domain.

as important and just as nervously anxious to do something effective in the way of swamping boats. In a ten-foot dingey one can get an idea of the resources of the sea in the line of waves that is not probable to the average experience, which is never at sea in a dingey. As each slaty wall of water approached, it shut all else from the view of the men in the boat, and it was not difficult to imagine that this particular wave was the final outburst of the ocean, the last effort of the grim water. There was a terrible grace in the move of the waves, and they came in silence, save for the snarling of the crests.

In the wan light, the faces of the men must have been gray. Their eyes must have glinted in strange ways as they gazed steadily astern. Viewed from a balcony, the whole thing would doubtlessly have been weirdly picturesque. But the men in the boat had no time to see it, and if they had had leisure there were other things to occupy their minds. The sun swung steadily up the sky, and they knew it was broad day because the color of the sea changed from slate to emerald-green, streaked with amber lights, and the foam was like tumbling snow. The process of the breaking day was unknown to them. They were aware only of this effect upon the color of the waves that rolled toward them.

In disjointed sentences the cook and the correspondent argued as to the difference between a life-saving station and a house of refuge. The cook had said: "There's a house of refuge just north of the Mosquito Inlet Light, and as soon as they see us, they'll come off in their boat and pick us up."

"As soon as who see us?" said the correspondent.

"The crew," said the cook.

"Houses of refuge don't have crews," said the correspondent. "As I understand them, they are only places where clothes and grub are stored for the benefit of shipwrecked people. They don't carry crews."

"Oh, yes, they do," said the cook.

"No, they don't," said the correspondent.

"Well, we're not there yet, anyhow," said the oiler, in the stern.

"Well," said the cook, "perhaps it's not a house of refuge that I'm thinking of as being near Mosquito Inlet Light. Perhaps it's a life-saving station."

"We're not there yet," said the oiler, in the stern.

II

As the boat bounced from the top of each wave, the wind tore through the hair of the hatless men, and as the craft plopped her stern down again the spray slashed past them. The crest of each of these waves was a hill, from the top of which the men surveyed, for a moment, a broad tumultuous expanse; shining and wind-riven. It was probably splendid. It was probably glorious, this play of the free sea, wild with lights of emerald and white and amber.

"Bully good thing it's an on-shore wind," said the cook. "If not, where would we be? Wouldn't have a show."

"That's right," said the correspondent.

The busy oiler nodded his assent.

Then the captain, in the bow, chuckled in a way that expressed humor, contempt, tragedy, all in one. "Do you think we've got much of a show, now, boys?" said he.

Whereupon the three were silent, save for a trifle of hemming and hawing. To express any particular optimism at this time they felt to be childish and stupid, but they all doubtless possessed this sense of the situation in their mind. A young man thinks doggedly at such times. On the other hand, the ethics of their condition was decidedly against any open suggestion of hopelessness. So they were silent.

"Oh, well," said the captain, soothing his children, "we'll get ashore all right."

But there was that in his tone which made them think, so the oiler quoth: "Yes! If this wind holds!"

The cook was bailing: "Yes! If we don't catch hell in the surf."

Canton flannel gulls flew near and far. Sometimes they sat down on the sea, near patches of brown seaweed that rolled over the waves with a movement like carpets on line in a gale. The birds sat comfortably in groups, and they were envied by some in the dingey, for the wrath of the sea was no more to them than it was to a covey of prairie chickens a thousand miles inland. Often they came very close and stared at the men with black bead-like eyes. At these times they were uncanny and sinister in their unblinking scrutiny, and the men hooted angrily at them, telling them to be gone. One came, and evidently decided to alight on the top of the captain's head. The bird flew parallel to the boat and did not circle, but made short sidelong jumps in the air in chicken-fashion. His black eyes were wistfully fixed upon the captain's head. "Ugly brute," said the oiler to the bird. "You look as if you were made with a jack-knife." The cook and the correspondent swore darkly at the creature. The captain naturally wished to knock it away with the end of the heavy painter, but he did not dare do it, because anything resembling an emphatic gesture would have capsized this freighted boat, and so with his open hand, the captain gently and carefully waved the gull away. After it had been discouraged from the pursuit the captain breathed easier on account of his hair, and others breathed easier because the bird struck their minds at this time as being somehow grewsome and ominous.

In the meantime the oiler and the correspondent rowed. And also they rowed.

They sat together in the same seat, and each rowed an oar. Then the oiler took both oars; then the correspondent took both oars; then the oiler; then the correspondent. They rowed and they rowed. The very ticklish part of the business was when the time came for the reclining one in the stern to take his turn at the oars. By the very last star of truth, it is easier to steal eggs from under a hen than it was to change seats in the dingey. First the man in the stern slid his hand along the thwart and moved with care, as if he were of Sèvres. Then the man in the rowing seat slid his hand along the other thwart. It was all done with the most extraordinary care. As the two sidled past each other, the whole party kept watchful eyes on the coming wave, and the captain cried: "Look out now! Steady there!"

The brown mats of sea-weed that appeared from time to time were like islands, bits of earth. They were travelling, apparently, neither one way nor the other. They were, to all intents stationary. They informed the men in the boat that it was making progress slowly toward the land.

The captain, rearing cautiously in the bow, after the dingey soared on a great swell, said that he had seen the lighthouse at Mosquito Inlet. Presently the cook remarked that he had seen it. The correspondent was at the oars, then, and for some reason he too wished to look at the lighthouse, but his back was toward the far shore and the waves were important, and for some time he could not seize an opportunity to turn his head. But at last there came a wave more gentle than the others, and when at the crest of it he swiftly scoured the western horizon.

"See it?" said the captain.

"No," said the correspondent, slowly, "I didn't see anything."

"Look again," said the captain. He pointed. "It's exactly in that direction."

At the top of another wave, the correspondent did as he was bid, and this time his eyes chanced on a small still thing on the edge of the swaying horizon. It was precisely like the point of a pin. It took an anxious eye to find a lighthouse so tiny.

"Think we'll make it, Captain?"

"If this wind holds and the boat don't swamp, we can't do much else," said the captain.

The little boat, lifted by each towering sea, and splashed viciously by the crests, made progress that in the absence of sea-weed was not apparent to those in her. She seemed just a wee thing wallowing, miraculously, top-up, at the mercy of five oceans. Occasionally, a great spread of water, like white flames, swarmed into her.

"Bail her, cook," said the captain, serenely.

"All right, Captain," said the cheerful cook.

III

It would be difficult to describe the subtle brotherhood of men that was here established on the seas. No one said that it was so. No one mentioned it. But it dwelt in the boat, and each man felt it warm him. They were a captain, an oiler, a cook, and a correspondent, and they were friends, friends in a more curiously iron-bound degree than may be common. The hurt captain, lying against the water-jar in the bow, spoke always in a low voice and calmly, but he could never command a more ready and swiftly obedient crew than the motley three of the dingey. It was more than a mere recognition of what was best for the common safety. There was surely in it a quality that was personal and heartfelt. And after this devotion to the commander of the boat there was this comradeship that the correspondent, for instance, who had been taught to be cynical of men, knew even at the time was the best experience of his life. But no one said that it was so. No one mentioned it.

"I wish we had a sail," remarked the captain. "We might try my overcoat on the end of an oar and give you two boys a chance to rest." So the cook and the correspondent held the mast and spread wide the overcoat. The oiler steered, and the little boat made good way with her new rig. Sometimes the oiler had to scull sharply to keep a sea from breaking into the boat, but otherwise sailing was a success.

Meanwhile the light-house had been growing slowly larger. It had now almost assumed color, and appeared like a little gray shadow on the sky. The man at the oars could not be prevented from turning his head rather often to try for a glimpse of this little gray shadow.

At last, from the top of each wave the men in the tossing boat could see land. Even as the light-house was an upright shadow on the sky, this land seemed but a long black shadow on the sea. It certainly was thinner than paper. "We must be about opposite New Smyrna," said the cook, who had coasted this shore often in schooners. "Captain, by the way, I believe they abandoned that life-saving station there about a year ago."

"Did they?" said the captain.

The wind slowly died away. The cook and the correspondent were not now obliged to slave in order to hold high the oar. But the waves continued their old impetuous swooping at the dingey, and the little craft, no longer under way, struggled woundily over them. The oiler or the correspondent took the oars again.

Shipwrecks are *apropos* of nothing. If men could only train for them and have them occur when the men had reached pink condition, there would be less drowning at sea. Of the four in the dingey none had slept any time worth mentioning for two days and two nights previous to embarking in the dingey, and in the excitement of clambering about the deck of a foundering ship they had also forgotten to eat heartily.

For these reasons, and for others, neither the oiler nor the correspondent was fond of rowing at this time. The correspondent wondered ingenuously how in the name of all that was sane could there be people who thought it amusing to row a boat. It was not an amusement; it was a diabolical punishment, and even a genius of mental aberrations could never conclude that it was anything but a horror to the muscles and a crime against the back. He mentioned to the boat in general how the amusement of rowing struck him, and the weary-faced oiler smiled in full sympathy. Previously to the foundering, by the way, the oiler had worked double-watch in the engine-room of the ship.

"Take her easy, now, boys," said the captain. "Don't spend yourselves. If we have to run a surf you'll need all your strength, because we'll sure have to swim for it. Take your time."

Slowly the land arose from the sea. From a black line it became a line of black and a line of white, trees, and sand. Finally, the captain said that he could make out a house on the shore. "That's the house of refuge, sure," said the cook. "They'll see us before long, and come out after us."

The distant light-house reared high. "The keeper ought to be able to make us out now, if he's looking through a glass," said the captain. "He'll notify the life-saving people."

"None of those other boats could have got ashore to give word of the wreck," said the oiler, in a low voice. "Else the life-boat would be out hunting us."

Slowly and beautifully the land loomed out of the sea. The wind came again. It had veered from the northeast to the southeast. Finally, a new sound struck the ears of the men in the boat. It was the low thunder of the surf on the shore. "We'll never be able to make the light-house now," said the captain. "Swing her head a little more north, Billie," said the captain.

"'A little more north,' sir," said the oiler.

Whereupon the little boat turned her nose once more down the wind, and all but the oarsman watched the shore grow. Under the influence of this expansion doubt and direful apprehension was leaving the minds of the men. The management of the boat was still most absorbing, but it could not prevent a quiet cheerfulness. In an hour, perhaps, they would be ashore.

Their back-bones had become thoroughly used to balancing in the boat and they now rode this wild colt of a dingey like circus men. The correspondent thought that he had been drenched to the skin, but happening to feel in the top pocket of his coat, he found therein eight cigars. Four of them were soaked with sea-water; four were perfectly scatheless. After a search, somebody produced three dry matches, and thereupon the four waifs rode in their little boat, and with an assurance of an impending rescue shining in their eyes, puffed at the big cigars and judged well and ill of all men. Everybody took a drink of water.

IV

"Cook," remarked the captain, "there don't seem to be any signs of life about your house of refuge."

"No," replied the cook. "Funny they don't see us!"

A broad stretch of lowly coast lay before the eyes of the men. It was of low dunes topped with dark vegetation. The roar of the surf was plain, and sometimes they could see the white lip of a wave as it spun up the beach. A tiny house was blocked out black upon the sky. Southward, the slim light-house lifted its little gray length.

Tide, wind, and waves were swinging the dingey northward. "Funny they don't see us," said the men.

The surf's roar was here dulled, but its tone was, nevertheless, thunderous and mighty. As the boat swam over the great rollers, the men sat listening to this roar. "We'll swamp sure," said everybody.

It is fair to say here that there was not a life-saving station within twenty miles in either direction, but the men did not know this fact and in consequence they made dark and opprobrious remarks concerning the eyesight of the nation's life-savers. Four scowling men sat in the dingey and surpassed records in the invention of epithets.

"Funny they don't see us."

The light-heartedness of a former time had completely faded. To their sharpened minds it was easy to conjure pictures of all kinds of incompetency and blindness and indeed, cowardice. There was the shore of the populous land, and it was bitter and bitter to them that from it came no sign.

"Well," said the captain, ultimately, "I suppose we'll have to make a try for ourselves. If we stay out here too long, we'll none of us have strength left to swim after the boat swamps."

And so the oiler, who was at the oars, turned the boat straight for the shore. There was a sudden tightening of muscles. There was some thinking.

"If we don't all get ashore—" said the captain. "If we don't all get ashore, I suppose you fellows know where to send news of my finish?"

They then briefly exchanged some addresses and admonitions. As for the reflections of the men, there was a great deal of rage in them. Perchance they might be formulated thus: "If I am going to be drowned—if I am going to be drowned—if I am going to be drowned, why, in the name of the seven mad gods who rule the sea, was I allowed to come thus far and contemplate sand and trees? Was I brought here merely to have my nose dragged away as I was about to nibble the sacred cheese of life? It is preposterous. If this old ninny-woman, Fate, cannot do better than this, she should be deprived of the management of men's fortunes. She is an old hen who knows not her intention. If she has decided to drown me, why did she not do it in the beginning and save me all this trouble. The whole affair is absurd…But, no, she cannot mean to drown me. She dare not drown me. She cannot drown me. Not after all this work." Afterward the man might have had an impulse to shake his fist at the clouds: "Just you drown me, now, and then hear what I call you!"

The billows that came at this time were more formidable. They seemed always just about to break and roll over the little boat in a turmoil of foam. There was a preparatory and long growl in the speech of them. No mind unused to the sea would have concluded that the dingey could ascend these sheer heights in time. The shore was still afar. The oiler was a wily surfman. "Boys," he said, swiftly, "she won't live three minutes more and we're too far out to swim. Shall I take her to sea again, Captain?"

"Yes! Go ahead!" said the captain.

This oiler, by a series of quick miracles, and fast and steady oarsmanship, turned the boat in the middle of the surf and took her safely to sea again.

There was a considerable silence as the boat bumped over the furrowed sea to deeper water. Then somebody in gloom spoke. "Well, anyhow, they must have seen us from the shore by now."

The gulls went in slanting flight up the wind toward the gray desolate east. A squall, marked by dingy clouds, and clouds brick-red, like smoke from a burning building, appeared from the southeast.

"What do you think of those life-saving people? Ain't they peaches?"

"Funny they haven't seen us."

"Maybe they think we're out here for sport! Maybe they think we're fishin.' Maybe they think we're damned fools."

It was a long afternoon. A changed tide tried to force them southward, but wind and wave said northward. Far ahead, where coast-line, sea, and sky formed their mighty angle, there were little dots which seemed to indicate a city on the shore.

"St. Augustine?"

The captain shook his head. "Too near Mosquito Inlet."

And the oiler rowed, and then the correspondent rowed. Then the oiler rowed. It was a weary business. The human back can become the seat of more aches and pains than are registered in books for the composite anatomy of a regiment. It is a limited area, but it can become the theatre of innumerable muscular conflicts, tangles, wrenches, knots, and other comforts.

"Did you ever like to row, Billie?" asked the correspondent.

"No," said the oiler. "Hang it."

When one exchanged the rowing-seat for a place in the bottom of the boat, he suffered a bodily depression that caused him to be careless of everything save an obligation to wiggle one finger. There was cold sea-water swashing to and fro in the boat, and he lay in it. His head, pillowed on a thwart, was within an inch of the swirl of a wave crest, and sometimes a particularly obstreperous sea came in-board and drenched him once more. But these matters did not annoy him. It is almost certain that if the boat had capsized he would have tumbled comfortably out upon the ocean as if he felt sure it was a great soft mattress.

"Look! There's a man on the shore!"

"Where?"

"There! See 'im? See 'im?"

"Yes, sure! He's walking along."

"Now he's stopped. Look! He's facing us!"

"He's waving at us!"

"So he is! By thunder!"

"Ah, now, we're all right! Now we're all right! There'll be a boat out here for us in half an hour."

"He's going on. He's running. He's going up to that house there."

The remote beach seemed lower than the sea, and it required a searching glance to discern the little black figure. The captain saw a floating stick and they rowed to it. A bath-towel was by some weird chance in the boat, and, tying this on the stick, the captain waved it. The oarsman did not dare turn his head, so he was obliged to ask questions.

"What's he doing now?"

"He's standing still again. He's looking, I think… There he goes again. Toward the house…Now he's stopped again."

"Is he waving at us?"

"No, not now! He was, though."

"Look! There comes another man!"

"He's running."

"Look at him go, would you."

"Why, he's on a bicycle. Now he's met the other man. They're both waving at us. Look!"

"There comes something up the beach."

"What the devil is that thing?"

"Why, it looks like a boat."

"Why, certainly it's a boat."

"No, it's on wheels."

"Yes, so it is. Well, that must be the life-boat. They drag them along shore on a wagon."

"That's the life-boat, sure."

"No, by, it's—it's an omnibus."

"I tell you it's a life-boat."

"It is not! It's an omnibus. I can see it plain. See? One of these big hotel omnibuses."

"By thunder, you're right. It's an omnibus, sure as fate. What do you suppose they are doing with an omnibus? Maybe they are going around collecting the life-crew, hey?"

"That's it, likely. Look! There's a fellow waving a little black flag. He's standing on the steps of the omnibus. There come those other two fellows. Now they're all talking together. Look at the fellow with the flag. Maybe he ain't waving it."

"That ain't a flag, is it? That's his coat. Why, certainly, that's his coat."

"So it is. It's his coat. He's taken it off and is waving it around his head. But would you look at him swing it."

"Oh, say, there isn't any life-saving station there. That's just a winter resort hotel omnibus that has brought over some of the boarders to see us drown."

"What's that idiot with the coat mean? What's he signaling, anyhow?"

"It looks as if he were trying to tell us to go north. There must be a life-saving station up there."

"No! He thinks we're fishing. Just giving us a merry hand. See? Ah, there, Willie."

"Well, I wish I could make something out of those signals. What do you suppose he means?"

"He don't mean anything. He's just playing."

"Well, if he'd just signal us to try the surf again, or to go to sea and wait, or go north, or go south, or go to hell—there would be some reason in it. But look at him. He just stands there and keeps his coat revolving like a wheel. The ass!"

"There come more people."

"Now there's quite a mob. Look! Isn't that a boat?"

"Where? Oh, I see where you mean. No, that's no boat."

"That fellow is still waving his coat."

"He must think we like to see him do that. Why don't he quit it. It don't mean anything."

"I don't know. I think he is trying to make us go north. It must be that there's a life-saving station there somewhere."

"Say, he ain't tired yet. Look at 'im wave."

"Wonder how long he can keep that up. He's been revolving his coat ever since he caught sight of us. He's an idiot. Why aren't they getting men to bring a boat out. A fishing boat—one of those big yawls—could come out here all right. Why don't he do something?"

"Oh, it's all right, now."

"They'll have a boat out here for us in less than no time, now that they've seen us."

A faint yellow tone came into the sky over the low land. The shadows on the sea slowly deepened. The wind bore coldness with it, and the men began to shiver.

"Holy smoke!" said one, allowing his voice to express his impious mood, "if we keep on monkeying out here! If we've got to flounder out here all night!"

"Oh, we'll never have to stay here all night! Don't you worry. They've seen us now, and it won't be long before they'll come chasing out after us."

The shore grew dusky. The man waving a coat blended gradually into this gloom, and it swallowed in the same manner the omnibus and the group of people. The spray, when it dashed uproariously over the side, made the voyagers shrink and swear like men who were being branded.

"I'd like to catch the chump who waved the coat. I feel like soaking him one, just for luck."

"Why? What did he do?"

"Oh, nothing, but then he seemed so damned cheerful."

In the meantime the oiler rowed, and then the correspondent rowed, and then the oiler rowed. Gray-faced and bowed forward, they mechanically, turn by turn, plied the leaden oars. The form of the light-house had vanished from the southern horizon, but finally a pale star appeared, just lifting from the sea. The streaked saffron in the west passed before the all-merging darkness, and the sea to the east was black. The land had vanished, and was expressed only by the low and drear thunder of the surf.

"If I am going to be drowned—if I am going to be drowned—if I am going to be drowned, why, in the name of the seven mad gods, who rule the sea, was I allowed to come thus far and contemplate sand and trees? Was I brought here merely to have my nose dragged away as I was about to nibble the sacred cheese of life?"

The patient captain, drooped over the water-jar, was sometimes obliged to speak to the oarsman.

"Keep her head up! Keep her head up!"

"'Keep her head up,' sir." The voices were weary and low.

This was surely a quiet evening. All save the oarsman lay heavily and listlessly in the boat's bottom. As for him, his eyes were just capable of noting the tall black waves that swept forward in a most sinister silence, save for an occasional subdued growl of a crest.

The cook's head was on a thwart, and he looked without interest at the water under his nose. He was deep in other scenes. Finally he spoke. "Billie," he murmured, dreamfully, "what kind of pie do you like best?"

V

"Pie," said the oiler and the correspondent, agitatedly. "Don't talk about those things, blast you!"

"Well," said the cook, "I was just thinking about ham sandwiches, and—"

A night on the sea in an open boat is a long night. As darkness settled finally, the shine of the light, lifting from the sea in the south, changed to full gold. On the northern horizon a new light appeared, a small bluish gleam on the edge of the waters. These two lights were the furniture of the world. Otherwise there was nothing but waves.

Two men huddled in the stern, and distances were so magnificent in the dingey that the rower was enabled to keep his feet partly warmed by thrusting them under his companions. Their legs indeed extended far under the rowing-seat until they touched the feet of the captain forward. Sometimes, despite the efforts of the tired oarsman, a wave came piling into the boat, an icy wave of the night, and the chilling water soaked them anew. They would twist their bodies for a moment and groan, and sleep the dead sleep once more, while the water in the boat gurgled about them as the craft rocked.

The plan of the oiler and the correspondent was for one to row until he lost the ability, and then arouse the other from his sea-water couch in the bottom of the boat.

The oiler plied the oars until his head drooped forward, and the overpowering sleep blinded him. And he rowed yet afterward. Then he touched a man in the bottom of the boat, and called his name. "Will you spell me for a little while?" he said, meekly.

"Sure, Billie," said the correspondent, awakening and dragging himself to a sitting position. They exchanged places carefully, and the oiler, cuddling down to the sea-water at the cook's side, seemed to go to sleep instantly.

The particular violence of the sea had ceased. The waves came without snarling. The obligation of the man at the oars was to keep the boat headed so that the tilt of the rollers would not capsize her, and to preserve her from filling when the crests rushed past. The black waves were silent and hard to be seen in the darkness. Often one was almost upon the boat before the oarsman was aware.

In a low voice the correspondent addressed the captain. He was not sure that the captain was awake, although this iron man seemed to be always awake. "Captain, shall I keep her making for that light north, sir?"

The same steady voice answered him. "Yes. Keep it about two points off the port bow."

The cook had tied a life-belt around himself in order to get even the warmth which this clumsy cork contrivance could donate, and he seemed almost stove-like when a rower, whose teeth invariably chattered wildly as soon as he ceased his labor, dropped down to sleep.

The correspondent, as he rowed, looked down at the two men sleeping under foot. The cook's arm was around the oiler's shoulders, and, with their fragmentary clothing and haggard faces, they were the babes of the sea, a grotesque rendering of the old babes in the wood.

Later he must have grown stupid at his work, for suddenly there was a growling of water, and a crest came with a roar and a swash into the boat, and it was a wonder that it did not set the cook afloat in his life-belt. The cook continued to sleep, but the oiler sat up, blinking his eyes and shaking with the new cold.

"Oh, I'm awful sorry, Billie," said the correspondent, contritely.

"That's all right, old boy," said the oiler, and lay down again and was asleep.

Presently it seemed that even the captain dozed, and the correspondent thought that he was the one man afloat on all the oceans. The wind had a voice as it came over the waves, and it was sadder than the end.

There was a long, loud swishing astern of the boat, and a gleaming trail of phosphorescence, like blue flame, was furrowed on the black waters. It might have been made by a monstrous knife.

Then there came a stillness, while the correspondent breathed with the open mouth and looked at the sea.

Suddenly there was another swish and another long flash of bluish light, and this time it was alongside the boat, and might almost have been reached with an oar. The correspondent saw an enormous fin speed like a shadow through the water, hurling the crystalline spray and leaving the long glowing trail.

The correspondent looked over his shoulder at the captain. His face was hidden, and he seemed to be asleep. He looked at the babes of the sea. They certainly were asleep. So, being bereft of sympathy, he leaned a little way to one side and swore softly into the sea.

But the thing did not then leave the vicinity of the boat. Ahead or astern, on one side or the other, at intervals long or short, fled the long sparkling streak, and there was to be heard the whirloo of the dark fin. The speed and power of the thing was greatly to be admired. It cut the water like a gigantic and keen projectile.

The presence of this biding thing did not affect the man with the same horror that it would if he had been a picnicker. He simply looked at the sea dully and swore in an undertone.

Nevertheless, it is true that he did not wish to be alone with the thing. He wished one of his companions to awaken by chance and keep him company with it. But the captain hung motionless over the water-jar and the oiler and the cook in the bottom of the boat were plunged in slumber.

VI

"If I am going to be drowned—if I am going to be drowned—if I am going to be drowned, why, in the name of the seven mad gods, who rule the sea, was I allowed to come thus far and contemplate sand and trees?"

During this dismal night, it may be remarked that a man would conclude that it was really the intention of the seven mad gods to drown him, despite the abominable injustice of it. For it was certainly an abominable injustice to drown a man who had worked so hard, so hard. The man felt it would be a crime most unnatural. Other people had drowned at sea since galleys swarmed with painted sails, but still—

When it occurs to a man that nature does not regard him as important, and that she feels she would not maim the universe by disposing of him, he at first wishes to throw bricks at the temple, and he hates deeply the fact that there are no bricks and no temples. Any visible expression of nature would surely be pelleted with his jeers.

Then, if there be no tangible thing to hoot he feels, perhaps, the desire to confront a personification and indulge in pleas, bowed to one knee, and with hands supplicant, saying: "Yes, but I love myself."

A high cold star on a winter's night is the word he feels that she says to him. Thereafter he knows the pathos of his situation.

The men in the dingey had not discussed these matters, but each had, no doubt, reflected upon them in silence and according to his mind. There was seldom any expression upon their faces save the general one of complete weariness. Speech was devoted to the business of the boat.

To chime the notes of his emotion, a verse mysteriously entered the correspondent's head. He had even forgotten that he had forgotten this verse, but it suddenly was in his mind.

> *A soldier of the Legion lay dying in Algiers,*
> *There was lack of woman's nursing, there was dearth of woman's tears;*
> *But a comrade stood beside him, and he took that comrade's hand,*
> *And he said: "I never more shall see my own, my native land."*

In his childhood, the correspondent had been made acquainted with the fact that a soldier of the Legion lay dying in Algiers, but he had never regarded the fact as important. Myriads of his schoolfellows had informed him of the soldier's plight, but the dinning had naturally ended by making him perfectly indifferent. He had never considered it his affair that a soldier of the Legion lay dying in Algiers, nor had it appeared to him as a matter for sorrow. It was less to him than breaking of a pencil's point.

Now, however, it quaintly came to him as a human, living thing. It was no longer merely a picture of a few throes in the breast of a poet, meanwhile drinking tea and warming his feet at the grate; it was an actuality—stern, mournful, and fine.

The correspondent plainly saw the soldier. He lay on the sand with his feet out straight and still. While his pale left hand was upon his chest in an attempt to thwart the going of his life, the blood came between his fingers. In the far Algerian distance, a city of low square forms was set against a sky that was faint with the last sunset hues. The correspondent, plying the oars and dreaming of the slow and slower movements of the lips of the soldier, was moved by a profound and perfectly impersonal comprehension. He was sorry for the soldier of the Legion who lay dying in Algiers.

The thing which had followed the boat and waited had evidently grown bored at the delay. There was no longer to be heard the slash of the cutwater, and there was no longer the flame of the long trail. The light in the north still glimmered, but it was apparently no nearer to the boat. Sometimes the boom of the surf rang in the correspondent's ears, and he turned the craft seaward then and rowed harder. Southward, someone had evidently built a watch-fire on the beach. It was too low and too far to be seen, but it made a shimmering, roseate reflection upon the bluff back of it, and this could be discerned from the boat. The wind came stronger, and sometimes a wave suddenly raged out like a mountain-cat and there was to be seen the sheen and sparkle of a broken crest.

The captain, in the bow, moved on his water-jar and sat erect. "Pretty long night," he observed to the correspondent. He looked at the shore. "Those life-saving people take their time."

"Did you see that shark playing around?"

"Yes, I saw him. He was a big fellow, all right."

"Wish I had known you were awake."

Later the correspondent spoke into the bottom of the boat.

"Billie!" There was a slow and gradual disentanglement. "Billie, will you spell me?"

"Sure," said the oiler.

As soon as the correspondent touched the cold comfortable sea-water in the bottom of the boat, and had huddled close to the cook's life-belt he was deep in sleep, despite the fact that his teeth played all the popular airs. This sleep was so good to him that it was but a moment before he heard a voice call his name in a tone that demonstrated the last stages of exhaustion. "Will you spell me?"

"Sure, Billie."

The light in the north had mysteriously vanished, but the correspondent took his course from the wide-awake captain.

Later in the night they took the boat farther out to sea, and the captain directed the cook to take one oar at the stern and keep the boat facing the seas. He was to call out if he should hear the thunder of the surf. This plan enabled the oiler and the correspondent to get respite together. "We'll give those boys a chance to get into shape again," said the captain. They curled down and, after a few preliminary chatterings and trembles, slept once more the dead sleep. Neither knew they had bequeathed to the cook the company of another shark, or perhaps the same shark.

As the boat caroused on the waves, spray occasionally bumped over the side and gave them a fresh soaking, but this had no power to break their repose. The ominous slash of the wind and the water affected them as it would have affected mummies.

"Boys," said the cook, with the notes of every reluctance in his voice, "she's drifted in pretty close. I guess one of you had better take her to sea again." The correspondent, aroused, heard the crash of the toppled crests.

As he was rowing, the captain gave him some whiskey and water, and this steadied the chills out of him. "If I ever get ashore and anybody shows me even a photograph of an oar—"

At last there was a short conversation.

"Billie…Billie, will you spell me?"

"Sure," said the oiler.

VII

When the correspondent again opened his eyes, the sea and the sky were each of the gray hue of the dawning. Later, carmine and gold was painted upon the waters. The morning appeared finally, in its splendor with a sky of pure blue, and the sunlight flamed on the tips of the waves.

On the distant dunes were set many little black cottages, and a tall white wind-mill reared above them. No man, nor dog, nor bicycle appeared on the beach. The cottages might have formed a deserted village.

The voyagers scanned the shore. A conference was held in the boat. "Well," said the captain, "if no help is coming, we might better try a run through the surf right away. If we stay out here much longer we will be too weak to do anything for ourselves at all." The others silently acquiesced in this reasoning. The boat was headed for the beach. The correspondent wondered if none ever ascended the tall wind-tower, and if then they never looked seaward. This tower was a giant, standing with its back to the plight of the ants. It represented in a degree, to the correspondent, the serenity of nature amid the struggles of the individual—nature in the wind, and nature in the vision of men. She did not seem cruel to him, nor beneficent, nor treacherous, nor wise. But she was indifferent, flatly indifferent. It is, perhaps, plausible that a man in this situation, impressed with the unconcern of the universe, should see the innumerable flaws of his life and have them taste wickedly in his mind and wish for another chance. A distinction between right and wrong seems absurdly clear to him, then, in this new ignorance of the grave-edge, and he understands that if he were given another opportunity he would mend his conduct and his words, and be better and brighter during an introduction, or at a tea.

"Now, boys," said the captain, "she is going to swamp sure. All we can do is to work her in as far as possible, and then when she swamps, pile out and scramble for the beach. Keep cool now and don't jump until she swamps sure."

The oiler took the oars. Over his shoulders he scanned the surf. "Captain," he said, "I think I'd better bring her about, and keep her head-on to the seas and back her in."

"All right, Billie," said the captain. "Back her in." The oiler swung the boat then and, seated in the stern, the cook and the correspondent were obliged to look over their shoulders to contemplate the lonely and indifferent shore.

The monstrous inshore rollers heaved the boat high until the men were again enabled to see the white sheets of water scudding up the slanted beach. "We won't get in very close," said the captain. Each time a man could wrest his attention from the rollers, he turned his glance toward the shore, and in the expression of the eyes during this contemplation there was a singular quality. The correspondent, observing the others, knew that they were not afraid, but the full meaning of their glances was shrouded.

As for himself, he was too tired to grapple fundamentally with the fact. He tried to coerce his mind into thinking of it, but the mind was dominated at this time by the muscles, and the muscles said they did not care. It merely occurred to him that if he should drown it would be a shame.

There were no hurried words, no pallor, no plain agitation. The men simply looked at the shore. "Now, remember to get well clear of the boat when you jump," said the captain.

Seaward the crest of a roller suddenly fell with a thunderous crash, and the long white comber came roaring down upon the boat.

"Steady now," said the captain. The men were silent. They turned their eyes from the shore to the comber and waited. The boat slid up the incline, leaped at the furious top, bounced over it, and swung down the long back of the waves. Some water had been shipped and the cook bailed it out.

But the next crest crashed also. The tumbling boiling flood of white water caught the boat and whirled it almost perpendicular. Water swarmed in from all sides. The correspondent had his hands on the gunwale at this time, and when the water entered at that place he swiftly withdrew his fingers, as if he objected to wetting them.

The little boat, drunken with this weight of water, reeled and snuggled deeper into the sea.

"Bail her out, cook! Bail her out," said the captain.

"All right, Captain," said the cook.

"Now, boys, the next one will do for us, sure," said the oiler. "Mind to jump clear of the boat."

The third wave moved forward, huge, furious, implacable. It fairly swallowed the dingey, and almost simultaneously the men tumbled into the sea. A piece of life-belt had lain in the bottom of the boat, and as the correspondent went overboard he held this to his chest with his left hand.

The January water was icy, and he reflected immediately that it was colder than he had expected to find it off the coast of Florida. This appeared to his dazed mind as a fact important enough to be noted at the time. The coldness of the water was sad; it was tragic. This fact was somehow mixed and confused with his opinion of his own situation that it seemed almost a proper reason for tears. The water was cold.

When he came to the surface he was conscious of little but the noisy water. Afterward he saw his companions in the sea. The oiler was ahead in the race. He was swimming strongly and rapidly. Off to the correspondent's left, the cook's great white and corked back bulged out of the water, and in the rear the captain was hanging with his one good hand to the keel of the overturned dingey.

There is a certain immovable quality to a shore, and the correspondent wondered at it amid the confusion of the sea.

It seemed also very attractive, but the correspondent knew that it was a long journey, and he paddled leisurely. The piece of life-preserver lay under him, and sometimes he whirled down the incline of a wave as if he were on a hand-sled.

But finally he arrived at a place in the sea where travel was beset with difficulty. He did not pause swimming to inquire what manner of current had caught him, but there his progress ceased. The shore was set before him like a bit of scenery on a stage, and he looked at it and understood with his eyes each detail of it.

As the cook passed, much farther to the left, the captain was calling to him, "Turn over on your back, cook! Turn over on your back and use the oar."

"All right, sir." The cook turned on his back, and, paddling with an oar, went ahead as if he were a canoe.

Presently the boat also passed to the left of the correspondent with the captain clinging with one hand to the keel. He would have appeared like a man raising himself to look over a board fence, if it were not for the extraordinary gymnastics of the boat. The correspondent marvelled that the captain could still hold to it.

They passed on, nearer to shore—the oiler, the cook, the captain—and following them went the water-jar, bouncing gayly over the seas.

The correspondent remained in the grip of this strange new enemy—a current. The shore, with its white slope of sand and its green bluff, topped with little silent cottages, was spread like a picture before him. It was very near to him then, but he was impressed as one who in a gallery looks at a scene from Brittany or Holland.

He thought: "I am going to drown? Can it be possible? Can it be possible? Can it be possible?" Perhaps an individual must consider his own death to be the final phenomenon of nature.

But later a wave perhaps whirled him out of this small deadly current, for he found suddenly that he could again make progress toward the shore. Later still, he was aware that the captain, clinging with one hand to the keel of the dingey, had his face turned away from the shore and toward him, and was calling his name. "Come to the boat! Come to the boat!"

In his struggle to reach the captain and the boat, he reflected that when one gets properly wearied, drowning must really be a comfortable arrangement, a cessation of hostilities accompanied by a large degree of relief, and he was glad of it, for the main thing in his mind for some moments had been horror of the temporary agony. He did not wish to be hurt.

Presently he saw a man running along the shore. He was undressing with most remarkable speed. Coat, trousers, shirt, everything flew magically off him.

"Come to the boat," called the captain.

"Allright, Captain." As the correspondent paddled, he saw the captain let himself down to bottom and leave the boat. Then the correspondent performed his one little marvel of the voyage. A large wave caught him and flung him with ease and supreme speed completely over the boat and far beyond it. It struck him even then as an event in gymnastics, and a true miracle of the sea. An overturned boat in the surf is not a plaything to a swimming man.

The correspondent arrived in water that reached only to his waist, but his condition did not enable him to stand for more than a moment. Each wave knocked him into a heap, and the under-tow pulled at him.

Then he saw the man who had been running and undressing, and undressing and running, come bounding into the water. He dragged ashore the cook, and then waded toward the captain, but the captain waved him away, and sent him to the correspondent. He was naked, naked as a tree in winter, but a halo was about his head, and he shone like a saint. He gave a strong pull, and a long drag, and a bully heave at the correspondent's hand. The correspondent, schooled in the minor formulae, said: "Thanks, old man." But suddenly the man cried: "What's that?" He pointed a swift finger. The correspondent said: "Go."

In the shallows, face downward, lay the oiler. His forehead touched sand that was periodically, between each wave, clear of the sea.

The correspondent did not know all that transpired afterward. When he achieved safe ground he fell, striking the sand with each particular part of his body. It was as if he had dropped from a roof, but the thud was grateful to him.

It seems that instantly the beach was populated with men with blankets, clothes, and flasks, and women with coffee-pots and all the remedies sacred to their minds. The welcome of the land to the men from the sea was warm and generous, but a still and dripping shape was carried slowly up the beach, and the land's welcome for it could only be the different and sinister hospitality of the grave.

When it came night, the white waves paced to and fro in the moonlight, and the wind brought the sound of the great sea's voice to the men on shore, and they felt that they could then be interpreters.

The Second Choice

Theodore Dreiser

Shirley Dear:

You don't want the letters. There are only six of them, anyhow, and think, they're all I have of you to cheer me on my travels. What good would they be to you—little bits of notes telling me you're sure to meet me—but me—think of me! If I send them to you, you'll tear them up, whereas if you leave them with me I can dab them with musk and ambergris and keep them in a little silver box, always beside me.[1]

Ah, Shirley dear, you really don't know how sweet I think you are, how dear! There isn't a thing we have ever done together that isn't as clear in my mind as this great big skyscraper over the way here in Pittsburgh, and far more pleasing. In fact, my thoughts of you are the most precious and delicious things I have, Shirley.

But I'm too young to marry now. You know that, Shirley, don't you? I haven't placed myself in any way yet, and I'm so restless that I don't know whether I ever will, really. Only yesterday, old Roxbaum—that's my new employer here—came to me and wanted to know if I would like an assistant overseership on one of his coffee plantations in Java, said there would not be much money in it for a year or two, a bare living, but later there would be more—and I jumped at it. Just the thought of Java and going there did that, although I knew I could make more staving right here.

Can't you see how it is with me. Shirl? I'm too restless and too young. I couldn't take care of you right, and you wouldn't like me after a while if I didn't.

But ah, Shirley sweet. I think the dearest things of you! There isn't an hour, it seems, but some little bit of you comes back—a dear, sweet bit—the night we sat on the grass in Tregore Park and counted the stars through the trees: that first evening at Sparrows Point when we missed the last train and had to walk to Langley. Remember the tree-toads, Shirl? And then that warm April Sunday in Atholby woods! Ah, Shirl, you don't want the six notes! Let me keep them. But think of me, will you, sweet, wherever you go and whatever you do? I'll always think of you, and wish that you had met a better, saner man than me, and that I really could have married you and been all you wanted me to be. By-by, sweet. I may start for Java within the month. If so, and you would want them, I'll send you some cards from there—if they have any.

Your worthless,
ARTHUR.

She sat and turned the letter in her hand, dumb with despair. It was the very last letter she would ever get from him. Of that she was certain. He was gone now, once and for all. She had written him only once, not making an open plea but asking him to return her letters, and then there had come this tender but evasive reply, saying nothing of a possible return but desiring to keep her letters for old times' sake—the happy hours they had spent together.

---

[1] First printed in Cosmopolitan Magazine, February 1918, this story was collected in Free and Other Stories. 1918.

Theodore Dreiser, "The Second Choice," from *Free and Other Stories*, pp. 135–162. Published by Boni & Liveright, Inc., 1918. Copyright in the Public Domain.

The happy hours! Oh, yes, yes, yes—the happy hours!

In her memory now, as she sat here in her home after the day's work, meditating on all that had been in the few short months since he had come and gone, was a world of color and light—a color and a light so transfiguring as to seem celestial, but now, alas, wholly dissipated. It had contained so much of all she had desired—love, romance, amusement, laughter. He had been so gay and thoughtless, or headstrong, so youthfully romantic, and with such a love of play and change and to be saying and doing anything and everything. Arthur could dance in a gay way, whistle, sing after a fashion, play. He could play cards and do tricks, and he had such a superior air, so genial and brisk, with a kind of innate courtesy in it and yet an intolerance for slowness and stodginess or anything dull or dingy, such as characterized—But here her thoughts fled from him. She refused to think of any one but Arthur.

Sitting in her little bedroom now, off the parlor on the ground floor in her home in Bethune Street, and looking out over the Kessels' yard, and beyond that—there being no fences in Bethune Street—over the "yards" or lawns of the Pollards, Bakers, Cryders, and others, she thought of how dull it must all have seemed to him, with his fine imaginative mind and experiences, his love of change and gayety, his atmosphere of something better than she had ever known. How little she had been fitted, perhaps, by beauty or temperament to overcome this—the something—dullness in her work or her home, which possibly had driven him away. For, although many had admired her to date, and she was young and pretty in her simple way and constantly receiving suggestions that her beauty was disturbing to some, still, he had not cared for her—he had gone.

And now, as she meditated, it seemed that this scene, and all that it stood for—her parents, her work, her daily shuttling to and fro between the drug company for which she worked and this street and house—was typical of her life and what she was destined to endure always. Some girls were so much more fortunate. They had fine clothes, fine homes, a world of pleasure and opportunity in which to move. They did not have to scrimp and save and work to pay their own way. And yet she had always been compelled to do it, but had never complained until now—or until he came, and after. Bethune Street, with its common place front yards and houses nearly all alike, and this house, so like the others, room for room and porch for porch, and her parents, too, really like all the others, had seemed good enough, quite satisfactory, indeed, until then. But now, now!

Here, in their kitchen, was her mother, a thin, pale, but kindly woman, peeling potatoes and washing lettuce, and putting a bit of steak or a chop or a piece of liver in a frying-pan day after day, morning and evening, month after month, year after year. And next door was Mrs. Kessel doing the same thing. And next door Mrs. Cryder. And next door Mrs. Pollard. But, until now, she had not thought it so bad. But now—now—oh! And on all the porches or lawns all along this street were the husbands and fathers, mostly middle-aged or old men like her father, reading their papers or cutting the grass before dinner, or smoking and meditating afterward. Her father was out in front now, a stooped, forbearing, meditative soul, who had rarely anything to say—leaving it all to his wife, her mother, but who was fond of her in his dull, quiet way. He was a pattern-maker by trade, and had come into possession of this small, ordinary home via years of toil and saving, her mother helping him. They had no particular religion, as he often said, thinking reasonably human conduct a sufficient passport to heaven, but they had gone occasionally to the Methodist Church over in Nicholas Street, and she had once joined it. But of late she had not gone, weaned away by the other commonplace pleasures of her world.

And then in the midst of it, the dull drift of things, as she now saw them to be, he had come—Arthur—Bristow—young, energetic, good-looking, ambitious, dreamful, and instanter, and with her never knowing quite how, the whole thing had been changed. He had appeared so swiftly—out of nothing, as it were.

Previous to him had been Barton Williams, stout, phlegmatic, good-natured, well-meaning, who was, or had been before Arthur came, asking her to marry him, and whom she allowed to half assume that she would. She had liked him in a feeble, albeit, as she thought, tender way, thinking him the kind, according to the logic of her neighborhood, who would make her a good husband, and, until Arthur appeared on the scene, had really intended to marry him. It was not really a love-match, as she saw now, but she thought it was, which was much the same thing, perhaps. But, as she now recalled, when Arthur came, how the scales fell from her eyes! In a trice, as it were, nearly, there was a new heaven and a new earth. Arthur had arrived, and with him a sense of something different.

Mabel Gove had asked her to come over to her house in Westleigh, the adjoining suburb, for Thanksgiving eve and day, and without a thought of anything, and because Barton was busy handling a part of the work in the despatched office of the Great Eastern and could not see her, she had gone. And then, to her surprise and strange, almost ineffable delight, the moment she had seen him, he was there—Arthur, with his slim, straight figure and dark hair and eyes and clean-cut features, as clean and attractive as those of a coin. And as he had looked at her and smiled and narrated humorous bits of things that had happened to him, something had come over her—a spell—and after dinner they had all gone round to Edith Barringer's to dance, and there as she had danced with him, somehow, without any seeming boldness on his part, he had taken possession of her, as it were, drawn her close, and told her she had beautiful eyes and hair and such a delicately rounded chin, and that he thought she danced gracefully and was sweet. She had nearly fainted with delight.

"Do you like me?" he had asked in one place in the dance, and, in spite of herself, she had looked up into his eyes, and from that moment she was almost mad over him, could think of nothing else but his hair and eyes and his smile and his graceful figure.

Mabel Gove had seen it all, in spite of her determination that no one should, and on their going to bed later, back at Mabel's home, she had whispered:

"Ah, Shirley, I saw. You like Arthur, don't you?"

"I think he's very nice," Shirley recalled replying, for Mabel knew of her affair with Barton and liked him. "but I'm not crazy over him." And for this bit of treason she had sighed in her dreams nearly all night.

And the next day, true to a request and a promise made by him. Arthur had called again at Mabel's to take her and Mabel to a "movie" which was not so far away, and from there they had gone to an ice-cream parlor, and during it all, when Mabel was not looking, he had squeezed her arm and hand and kissed her neck, and she had held her breath, and her heart had seemed to stop.

"And now you're going to let me come out to your place to see you, aren't you?" he had whispered.

And she had replied, "Wednesday evening." and then written the address on a little piece of paper and given it to him.

But now it was all gone, gone!

This house, which now looked so dreary—how romantic it had seemed that first night *he* called—the front room with its commonplace furniture, and later in the spring, the veranda, with its vines just sprouting, and the moon in May. Oh, the moon in May, and June and July, when he was here! How she had lied to Barton to make evenings for Arthur, and occasionally to Arthur to keep him from contact with Barton. She had not even mentioned Barton to Arthur because—because—well, because Arthur was so much better, and somehow (she admitted it to herself now) she had not been sure that Arthur would care for her long, if at all, and then—well, and then, to be quite frank, Barton might be good enough. She did not exactly hate him because she had found Arthur—not at all. She still liked him in a way—he was so kind and faithful, so very dull and straightforward and thoughtful of her, which Arthur was certainly not. Before Arthur had appeared, as she well remembered, Barton had seemed to be plenty good enough—in fact, all that she desired in a pleasant, companionable way, calling for her, taking her places, bringing her flowers and candy, which Arthur rarely did, and for that, if nothing more, she could not help continuing to like him and to feel sorry for him, and besides, as she had admitted to herself before, if Arthur left her—…Weren't his parents better off than hers—and hadn't he a good position for such a man as he—one hundred and fifty dollars a month and the certainty of more later on? A little while before meeting Arthur, she had thought this very good, enough for two to live on at least, and she had thought some of trying it at some time or other—but now—now—

And that first night he had called—how well she remembered it—how it had transfigured the parlor next this in which she was now, filling it with something it had never had before, and the porch outside, too, for that matter, with its gaunt, leafless vine, and this street, too, even—dull, commonplace Bethune Street. There had been a flurry of snow during the afternoon while she was working at the store, and the ground was white with it. All the neighboring homes seemed to look sweeter and happier and more inviting than ever they had as she came past them, with their lights peeping from under curtains and drawn shades. She had hurried into hers and lighted the big red-shaded parlor lamp, her one artistic treasure, as she thought, and put it near the piano, between it and the window, and arranged the chairs, and then bustled to the task of making herself as pleasing as she might. For him she had gotten out her one best filmy house dress and done up her hair in the fashion she thought most becoming—and that he had not seen before—and powdered her cheeks and nose and darkened her eyelashes, as some of the girls at the store did, and put on her new gray satin slippers, and then, being so arrayed, waited nervously, unable to eat anything or to think of anything but him.

And at last, just when she had begun to think he might not be coming, he had appeared with that arch smile and a "Hello! It's here you live, is it? I was wondering. George, but you're twice as sweet as I thought you were, aren't you?" And then, in the little entry way, behind the closed door, he had held her and kissed her on the mouth a dozen times while she pretended to push against his coat and struggle and say that her parents might hear.

And, oh, the room afterward, with him in it in the red glow of the lamp, and with his pale handsome face made handsomer thereby, as she thought! He had made her sit near him and had held her hands and told her about his work and his dreams—all that he expected to do in the future—and then she had found herself wishing intensely to share just such a life—his life—anything that he might wish to do, only, she kept wondering, with a slight pain, whether he would want her to—he was so young, dreamful, ambitious, much younger and more dreamful than herself, although, in reality, he was several years older.

And then followed that glorious period from December to this late September, in which eventhing which was worth happening in love had happened. Oh, those wondrous days the following spring, when, with the first burst of buds and leaves, he had taken her one Sunday to Atholby, where all the great woods were, and they had hunted spring beauties in the grass, and sat on a slope and looked at the river below and watched some boys fixing up a sailboat and setting forth in it quite as she wished she and Arthur might be doing—going somewhere together—far, far away from all commonplace things and life! And then he had slipped his arm about her and kissed her cheek and neck, and tweaked her ear and smoothed her hair—and oh, there on the grass, with the spring flowers about her and a canopy of small green leaves above, the perfection of love had come—love so wonderful that the mere thought of it made her eyes brim now! And then had been days, Saturday afternoons and Sundays, at Atholby and Sparrows Point, where the great beach was, and in lovely Tregore Park, a mile or two from her home, where they could go of an evening and sit in or near the pavilion and have ice-cream and dance or watch the dancers. Oh, the stars, the winds, the summer breath of those days! Ah, me! Ah, me!

Naturally, her parents had wondered from the first about her and Arthur, and her and Barton, since Barton had already assumed a proprietary interest in her and she had seemed to like him. But then she was an only child and a pet, and used to presuming on that, and they could not think of saying anything to her. After all, she was young and pretty and was entitled to change her mind; only, only—she had had to indulge in a career of lying and subterfuge in connection with Barton, since Arthur was headstrong and wanted every evening that he chose—to call for her at the store and keep her down-town to dinner and a show.

Arthur had never been like Barton, shy, phlegmatic, obedient, waiting long and patiently for each little favor, but, instead, masterful and eager, rifling her of kisses and caresses and every delight of love, and teasing and playing with her as a cat would a mouse. She could never resist him. He demanded of her her time and her affection without let or hindrance. He was not exactly selfish or cruel, as some might have been, but gay and unthinking at times, unconsciously so, and yet loving and tender at others—nearly always so. But always he would talk of things in the future as if they really did not include her—and this troubled her greatly—of places he might go, things he might do, which, somehow, he seemed to think or assume that she could not or would not do with him. He was always going to Australia sometime, he thought, in a business way, or to South Africa, or possibly to India. He never seemed to have any fixed clear future for himself in mind.

A dreadful sense of helplessness and of impending disaster came over her at these tunes, of being involved in some predicament over which she had no control, and which would lead her on to some sad end. Arthur, although plainly in love, as she thought, and apparently delighted with her, might not always love her. She began, timidly at first (and always, for that matter), to ask him pretty, seeking questions about himself and her, whether their future was certain to be together, whether he really wanted her—loved her—whether he might not want to marry some one else or just her, and whether she wouldn't look nice in a pearl satin wedding-dress with a long, creamy veil and satin slippers and a bouquet of bridal-wreath. She had been so slowly but surely saving to that end, even before he came, in connection with Barton; only, after *he* came, all thought of the import of it had been transferred to him. But now, also, she was beginning to ask herself sadly, "Would it ever be?" He was so airy so inconsequential, so ready to say: "Yes, yes," and "Sure, sure! That's right! Yes, indeed; you bet! Say, kiddie, but you'll look sweet!" But, somehow, it had always seemed as if this whole thing were a glorious interlude and that it could not last. Arthur was too gay and ethereal and too little settled in his own mind. His ideas of travel and living in different cities, finally winding up in New York or San Francisco, but never with her exactly until she asked him, was too ominous, although he always reassured her gaily: "Of course! Of course!" But somehow she could never believe it really, and it made her intensely sad at times, horribly gloomy. So often she wanted to cry, and she could scarcely tell why.

And then, because of her intense affection for him, she had finally quarreled with Barton, or nearly that, if one could say that one ever really quarreled with him. It had been because of a certain Thursday evening a few weeks before about which she had disappointed him. In a fit of generosity, knowing that Arthur was coming Wednesday, and because Barton had stopped in at the store to see her, she had told him that he might come, having regretted it afterward, so enamored was she of Arthur. And then when Wednesday came, Arthur had changed his mind, telling her he would come Friday instead, but on Thursday evening he had stopped in at the store and asked her to go to Sparrows Point, with the result that she had no time to notify Barton. He had gone to the house and sat with her parents until ten-thirty, and then, a few days later, although she had written him offering an excuse, had called at the store to complain slightly.

"Do you think you did just right, Shirley? You might have sent word, mightn't you? Who was it—the new fellow you won't tell me about?"

Shirley flared on the instant.

"Supposing it was? What's it to you? I don't belong to you yet do I? I told you there wasn't any one, and I wish you'd let me alone about that. I couldn't help it last Thursday—that's all—and I don't want you to be fussing with me—that's all. If you don't want to, you needn't come any more, anyhow."

"Don't say that, Shirley." pleaded Barton. "You don't mean that. I won't bother you, though if you don't want me any more."

And because Shirley sulked not knowing what else to do, he had gone and she had not seen him since.

And then sometime later when she had thus broken with Barton avoiding the railway station where he worked, Arthur had failed to come at his appointed time, sending no word until the next day. when a note came to the store saying that he had been out of town for his firm over Sunday and had not been able to notify her, but that he would call Tuesday. It was an awful blow. At the time, Shirley had a vision of what was to follow. It seemed for the moment as if the whole world had suddenly been reduced to ashes, that there was nothing but black charred cinders anywhere—she felt that about all life. Yet it all came to her clearly then that this was but the beginning of just such days and just such excuses, and that soon, soon, he would come no more. He was beginning to be tired of her and soon he would not even make excuses. She felt it, and it froze and terrified her.

And then, soon after, the indifference which she feared did follow—almost created by her own thoughts, as it were. First, it was a meeting he had to attend somewhere one Wednesday night when he was to have come for her. Then he was going out of town again, over Sunday. Then he was going away for a whole week—it was absolutely unavoidable, he said, his commercial duties were increasing—and once he had casually remarked that nothing could stand in the way where she was concerned—never! She did not think of reproaching him with this; she was too proud. If he was going, he must go. She would not be willing to say to herself that she had never attempted to hold any man. But, just the same, she was agonized by the thought. When he was with her, he seemed tender enough; only, at times, his eyes wandered and he seemed slightly bored. Other girls particularly pretty ones, seemed to interest him as much as she did.

And the agony of the long days when he did not come any more for a week or two at a time! The waiting, the brooding, the wondering, at the store and here in her home—in the former place making mistakes at times because she could not get her mind off him and being reminded of them, and here at her own home at nights, being so absent-minded that her parents remarked on it. She felt sure that her parents must be noticing that Arthur was not coming any more, or as much as he had—for she pretended to be going out with him, going to Mabel Gove's instead—and that Barton had deserted her too, he having been driven off by her indifference, never to come any more, perhaps, unless she sought him out.

And then it was that the thought of saving her own face by taking up with Barton once more occurred to her, of using him and his affections and faithfulness and dulness, if you will, to cover up her own dilemma. Only, this ruse was not to be tried until she had written Arthur this one letter—a pretext merely to see if there was a single ray of hope a letter to be written in a gentle-enough way and asking for the return of the few notes she had written him. She had not seen him now in nearly a month, and the last time she had, he had said he might soon be compelled to leave her awhile—to go to Pittsburgh to work. And it was his reply to this that she now held in her hand—from Pittsburgh! It was frightful! The future without him!

But Barton would never know really what had transpired, if she went back to him. In spite of all her delicious hours with Arthur, she could call him back, she felt sure. She had never really entirely dropped him, and he knew it. He had bored her dreadfully on occasion, arriving on off days when Arthur was not about, with flowers or candy, or both, and sitting on the porch steps and talking of the railroad business and of the whereabouts and doings of some of their old friends. It was shameful, she had thought at times, to see a man so patient, so hopeful, so good-natured as Barton, deceived in this way, and by her, who was so miserable over another. Her parents must see and know, she had thought at these times, but still, what else was she to do?

"I'm a bad girl," she kept telling herself. "I'm all wrong. What right have I to offer Barton what is left?" But still, somehow, she realized that Barton, if she chose to favor him, would only to be too grateful for even the leavings of others where she was concerned, and that even yet, if she but designed to crook a finger, she could have him. He was so simple, so good-natured, so stolid and matter of fact, so different to Arthur whom (she could not help smiling at the thought of it) she was loving now about as Barton loved her—slavishly, hopelessly.

And then, as the days passed and Arthur did not write any more—just this one brief note—she at first grieved horribly, and then in a fit of numb despair attempted, bravely enough from one point of view, to adjust herself to the new situation. Why should she despair? Why die of agony where there were plenty who would still sigh for her—Barton among others? She was young, pretty, very—many told her so. She could, if she chose, achieve a vivacity which she did not feel. Why should she brook this unkindness without a thought of retaliation? Why shouldn't she enter upon a gay and heartless career, indulging in a dozen flirtations at once—dancing and kill all thoughts of Arthur in a round of frivolities? There were many who beckoned to her. She stood at her counter in the drug store on many a day and brooded over this, but at the thought of which one to begin with, she faltered. After her late love, all were so tame, for the present anyhow.

And then—and then—always there was Barton, the humble or faithful to whom she had been so unkind and whom she had used and whom she still really liked. So often self-reproaching thoughts in connection with him crept over her. He must have known, must have seen how badly she was using him all this while, and yet he had not failed to come and come, until she had actually quarreled with him, and any one would have seen that it was literally hopeless. She could not help remembering, especially now in her pain, that he adored her. He was not calling on her now at all—by her indifference she had finally driven him away—but a word, a word—She waited for days, weeks, hoping against hope, and then—

The office of Barton's superior in the Great Eastern terminal had always made him an easy object for her blandishments, coming and going, as she frequently did, via this very station. He was in the office of the assistant train-despatcher on the ground floor, where passing to and from the local, which, at times, was quicker than a street-car, she could easily see him by peering in; only, she had carefully avoided him for nearly a year. If she chose now, and would call for a message-blank at the adjacent telegraph-window which was a part of his room, and raised her voice as she often had in the past, he could scarcely fail to hear, if he did not see her. And if he did, he would rise and come over—of that she was sure, for he never could resist her. It had been a wile of hers in the old days to do this or to make her presence felt by idling outside. After a month of brooding, she felt that she must act—her position as a deserted girl was too much. She could not stand it any longer really—the eyes of her mother, for one.

It was six-fifteen one evening when, coming out of the store in which she worked, she turned her step disconsolately homeward. Her heart was heavy, her face rather pale and drawn. She had stopped in the store's retiring-room before coming out to add to her charms as much as possible by a little powder and rouge and to smooth her hair. It would not take much to reallure her former sweetheart, she felt sure—and yet it might not be so easy after all. Suppose he had found another? But she could not believe that. It had scarcely been long enough since he had last attempted to see her, and he was really so very, very fond of her and so faithful. He was too slow and certain in his choosing—he had been so with her. Still, who knows? With this thought, she went forward in the evening, feeling for the first time the shame and pain that comes or deception, the agony of having to relinquish an ideal and the feeling of despair that comes to those who find themselves in the position of suppliants, stooping to something which in better days and better fortune they would not know. Arthur was the cause of this.

When she reached the station, the crowd that usually filled it at this hour was swarming. There were so many pairs like Arthur and herself laughing and hurrying away or so she felt. First glancing in the small mirror of a weighing scale to see if she were still of her former charm, she stopped thoughtfully at a little flower stand which stood outside, and for a few pennies purchased a tiny bunch of violets. She then went inside and stood near the window, peering first furtively to see if he were present. He was. Bent over his work, a green shade over his eyes, she could see his stolid, genial figure at a table. Stepping back a moment to ponder, she finally went forward and, in a clear voice, asked,

"May I have a blank, please?"

The infatuation of the discarded Barton was such that it brought him instantly to his feet. In his stodgy, stocky way he rose, his eyes glowing with a friendly hope, his mouth wreathed in smiles, and came over. At the sight of her, pale, but pretty—paler and prettier, really, than he had ever seen her—he thrilled dumbly.

"How are you, Shirley?" he asked sweetly, as he drew near, his eyes searching her face hopefully. He had not seen her for so long that he was intensely hungry, and her paler beauty appealed to him more than ever. Why wouldn't she have him? he was asking himself. Why wouldn't his persistent love yet win her? Perhaps it might. "I haven't seen you in a month of Sundays, it seems. How are the folks?"

"They're all right, Bart," she smiled archly, "and so am I. How have you been? It has been a long time since I've seen you. I've been wondering how you were. Have you been all right? I was just going to send a message."

As he had approached, Shirley had pretended at first not to see him, a moment later to affect surprise, although she was really suppressing a heavy sigh. The sight of him, after Arthur, was not reassuring. Could she really interest herself in him any more Could she?

"Sure, sure," he replied genially; "I'm always all right. You couldn't kill me, you know. Not going away, are you, Shirl?" he queried interestedly.

"No; I'm just telegraphing to Mabel. She promised to meet me to-morrow, and I want to be sure she will."

"You don't come past here as often as you did. Shirley," he complained tenderly. "At least. I don't seem to see you so often," he added with a smile. "It isn't anything I have done, is it?" he queried, and then, when she protested quickly, added: "What's the trouble, Shirl? Haven't been sick, have you?"

She affected all her old gaiety and ease, feeling as though she would like to cry.

"Oh, no," she returned; "I've been all right. I've been going through the other door, I suppose, or coming in and going out on the Langdon Avenue car." (This was true, because she had been wanting to avoid him.) "I've been in such a hurry, most nights, that I haven't had time to stop, Bart. You know how late the store keeps us at times."

He remembered, too, that in the old days she had made time to stop or meet him occasionally.

"Yes, I know," he said tactfully. "But you haven't been to any of our old card-parties either of late, have you? At least, I haven't seen you. I've gone to two or three, thinking you might be there."

That was another thing Arthur had done—broken up her interest in these old store and neighborhood parties and a banjo-and-mandolin club to which she had once belonged. They had all seemed so pleasing and amusing in the old days—but now—…In those days Bart had been her usual companion when his work permitted.

"No," she replied evasively, but with a forced air of pleasant remembrance; "I have often thought of how much fun we had at those, though. It was a shame to drop them. You haven't seen Harry Stull or Trina Task recently, have you?" she inquired, more to be saying something than for any interest she felt.

He shook his head negatively, then added:

"Yes, I did, too; here in the waiting-room a few nights ago. They were coming down-town to a theater, I suppose."

His face fell slightly as he recalled how it had been their custom to do this, and what their one quarrel had been about. Shirley noticed it. She felt the least bit sorry for him, but much more for herself, coming back so disconsolately to all this.

"Well, you're looking as pretty as ever, Shirley," he continued, noting that she had not written the telegram and that there was something wistful in her glance. "Prettier, I think," and she smiled sadly. Every word that she tolerated from him was as so much gold to him, so much of dead ashes to her. "You wouldn't like to come down some evening this week and see 'The Mouse-Trap,' would you? We haven't been to a theater together in I don't know when." His eyes sought hers in a hopeful, doglike way.

So—she could have him again—that was the pity of it! To have what she really did not want, did not care for! At the least nod now he would come, and this very devotion made it all but worthless, and so sad. She ought to marry him now for certain, if she began in this way, and could in a month's time if she chose, but oh, oh—could she? For the moment she decided that she could not, would not. If he had only repulsed her—told her to go—ignored her—but no; it was her fate to be loved by him in this moving, pleading way, and hers not to love him as she wished to love—to be loved. Plainly, he needed some one like her, whereas she, she—She turned a little sick, a sense of the sacrilege of gaiety at this time creeping into her voice, and exclaimed:

"No, no!" Then seeing his face change, a heavy sadness come over it, "Not this week, anyhow, I mean" ("Not so soon," she had almost said). "I have several engagements this week and I'm not feeling well. But"—seeing his face change, and the thought of her own state returning—" you might come out to the house some evening instead, and then we can go some other time."

His face brightened intensely. It was wonderful how he longed to be with her, how the least favor from her comforted and lifted him up. She could see also now, however, how little it meant to her, how little it could ever mean, even if to him it was heaven. The old relationship would have to be resumed in toto, once and for all, but did she want it that way now that she was feeling so miserable about this other affair? As she meditated, these various moods racing to and fro in her mind. Barton seemed to notice, and now it occurred to him that perhaps he had not pursued her enough—was too easily put off. She probably did like him yet. This evening, her present visit, seemed to prove it.

"Sure, sure!" he agreed. "I'd like that. I'll come out Sunday, if you say. We can go any time to the play. I'm sorry, Shirley, if you're not feeling well. I've thought of you a lot these days. I'll come out Wednesday, if you don't mind."

She smiled a wan smile. It was all so much easier than she had expected—her triumph—and so ashenlike in consequence, a flavor of dead-sea fruit and defeat about it all, that it was pathetic. How could she, after Arthur? How could he, really?

"Make it Sunday," she pleaded, naming the farthest day off, and then hurried out.

Her faithful lover gazed after her, while she suffered an intense nausea. To think—to think—it should all be coming to this! She had not used her telegraph-blank, and now had forgotten all about it. It was not the simple trickery that discouraged her, but her own future which could find no better outlet than this could not rise above it apparently, or that she had no heart to make it rise above it. Why couldn't she interest herself in some one different to Barton? Why did she have to return to him? Why not wait and meet some other—ignore him as before? But no, no; nothing mattered now—no one—it might as well be Barton really as anyone, and she would at least make him happy and at the same time solve her own problem. She went out into the trainshed and climbed into her train. Slowly, after the usual pushing and jostling of a crowd, it drew out toward Latonia, that suburban region in which her home lay. As she rode, she thought.

"What have I just done? What am I doing?" she kept asking herself as the clacking wheels on the rails fell into a rhythmic dance and the houses of the brown, dry, endless city fled past in a maze, "Severing myself decisively from the past—the happy past—for supposing, once I am married, Arthur should return and want me again—suppose! Suppose!"

Below at one place, under a shed, were some market-gardeners disposing of the last remnants of their day's wares—a sickly, dull life, she thought. Here was Rutgers Avenue, with its line of red streetcars, many wagons and tracks and counter-streams of automobiles—how often had she passed it morning and evening in a shuttle-like way, and how often would, unless she got married! And here, now, was the river flowing smoothly between its banks lined with coal-pockets and wharves—away, away to the huge deep sea which she and Arthur had enjoyed so much. Oh, to be in a small boat and drift out, out into the endless, restless, pathless deep! Somehow the sight of this water, to-night and every night, brought back those evenings in the open with Arthur at Sparrows Point, the long line of dancers in Eckert's Pavilion, the woods at Atholbe, the park, with the dancers in the pavilion—she choked back a sob. Once Arthur had come this way with her on just such an evening as this, pressing her hand and saying how wonderful she was. Oh, Arthur! Arthur! And now Barton was to take his old place again—forever, no doubt. She could not trifle with her life longer in this foolish way, or his. What was the use? But think of it!

Yes, it must be—forever now, she told herself. She must marry. Time would be slipping by and she would become too old. It was her only future—marriage. It was the only future she had ever contemplated really, a home, children, the love of some man whom she could love as she loved Arthur. Ah, what a happy home that would have been for her! But now, now—

But there must be no turning back now, either. There was no other way. If Arthur ever came back—but fear not, he wouldn't! She had risked so much and lost—lost him. Her little venture into true love had been such a failure. Before Arthur had come all had been well enough, Barton, stout and simple and frank and direct, had in some way—how, she could scarcely realize now—offered sufficient of a future. But now, now! He had enough money, she knew, to build a cottage for the two of them. He had told her so. He would do his best always to make her happy, she was sure of that. They could live in about the state her parents were living in or a little better, not much—and would never want. No doubt there would be children, because he craved them—several of them—and that would take up her time, long years of it—the sad, gray years! But then Arthur, whose children she would have thrilled to bear, would be no more, a mere memory—think of that!—and Barton, the dull, the commonplace, would have achieved his finest dream—and why?

Because love was a failure for her—that was why—and in her life there could be no more true love. She would never love any one again as she had Arthur. It could not be, she was sure of it. He was too fascinating, too wonderful. Always, always, wherever she might be, whoever she might marry, he would be coming back, intruding between her and any possible love, receiving any possible kiss. It would be Arthur she would be loving or kissing. She dabbed at her eyes with a tiny handkerchief, turned her face close to the window and stared out, and then as the environs of Latonia came into view, wondered (so deep is romance): What if Arthur should come back at some time—or now! Supposing he should be here at the station now, accidentally or on purpose, to welcome her, to soothe her weary heart. He had met her here before. How she would fly to him, lay her head on his shoulder, forget that Barton ever was, that they had ever separated for an hour. Oh. Arthur! Arthur!

But no, no; here was Latonia—here the viaduct over her train, the long business street and the cars marked "Center" and "Lagdon Avenue" running back into the great city. A few blocks away in tree-shaded Bethune Street, duller and plainer than ever, was her parents' cottage and the routine of that old life which was now. She felt, more fully fastened upon her than ever before—the lawn-mowers, the lawns, the front porches all alike. Now would come the going to and fro of Barton to business as her father and she now went to business, her keeping house, cooking, washing, ironing, sewing for Barton as her mother now did these things for her father and herself. And she would not be in love really, as she wanted to be. Oh, dreadful! She could never escape it really, now that she could endure it less, scarcely for another hour. And yet she must, must, for the sake of—for the sake of—she closed her eyes and dreamed.

She walked up the street under the trees, past the houses and lawns all alike to her own, and found her father on their veranda reading the evening paper. She sighed at the sight.

"Back, daughter?" he called pleasantly.

"Yes."

"Your mother is wondering if you would like steak or liver for dinner. Better tell her."

"Oh, it doesn't matter."

She hurried into her bedroom, threw down her hat and gloves, and herself on the bed to rest silently, and groaned in her soul. To think that it had all come to this!—Never to see him any more!—To see only Barton, and marry him and live in such a street, have four or five children, forget all her youthful companionships—and all to save her face before her parents, and her future. Why must it be? Should it be, really? She choked and stifled. After a little time her mother, hearing her come in, came to the door—thin, practical, affectionate, conventional.

"What's wrong, honey? Aren't you feeling well tonight? Have you a headache? Let me feel,"

Her thin cool fingers crept over her temples and hair. She suggested something to eat or a headache powder right away.

"I'm all right, mother. I'm just not feeling well now. Don't bother. I'll get up soon. Please don't."

"Would you rather have liver or steak to-night, dear?"

"Oh, anything—nothing—please don't bother—steak will do—anything"—if only she could get rid of her and be at rest!

Her mother looked at her and shook her head sympathetically, then retreated quietly, saying no more. Lying so, she thought and thought—grinding, destroying thoughts about the beauty of the past, the darkness of the future—until able to endure them no longer she got up and, looking distractedly out of the window into the yard and the house next door, stared at her future fixedly. What should she do? What should she really do? There was Mrs. Kessel in her kitchen getting her dinner as usual, just as her own mother was now, and Mr. Kessel out on the front porch in his shirt-sleeves reading the evening paper. Beyond was Mr. Pollard in his yard, cutting the grass. All along Bethune Street were such houses and such people—simple, commonplace souls all—clerks, managers, fairly successful craftsmen, like her father and Barton, excellent in their way but not like Arthur the beloved, the lost—and here was she, perforce, or by decision of necessity, soon to be one of them, in some such street, as this no doubt, forever and—. For the moment it choked and stifled her.

She decided that she would not. No, no, no! There must be some other way—many ways. She did not have to do this unless she really wished to—would not—only—. Then going to the mirror she looked at her face and smoothed her hair.

"But what's the use?" she asked of herself wearily and resignedly after a time. "Why should I cry? Why shouldn't I marry Barton? I don't amount to anything, anyhow. Arthur wouldn't have me. I wanted him, and I am compelled to take some one else—or no one—what difference does it really make who? My dreams are too high, that's all. I wanted Arthur, and he wouldn't have me. I don't want Barton, and he crawls at my feet. I'm a failure, that's what's the matter with me."

And then, turning up her sleeves and removing a fichu which stood out too prominently from her breast, she went into the kitchen and, looking about for an apron, observed:

"Can't I help? Where's the tablecloth?" and finding it among the napkins and silverware in a drawer in an adjoining room, proceeded to set the table.

The Metamorphosis

Franz Kafka
Translated by Willa Muir and Edwin Muir

I

As Gregor Samsa awoke one morning from uneasy dreams he found himself transformed in his bed into a gigantic insect. He was lying on his hard, as it were armor-plated, back and when he lifted his head a little he could see his dome-like brown belly divided into stiff arched segments on top of which the bed quilt could hardly keep in position and was about to slide off completely. His numerous legs, which were pitifully thin compared to the rest of his bulk, waved helplessly before his eyes.

What has happened to me? he thought. It was no dream. His room, a regular human bedroom, only rather too small, lay quiet between the four familiar walls. Above the table on which a collection of cloth samples was unpacked and spread out—Samsa was a commercial traveler—hung the picture which he had recently cut out of an illustrated magazine and put into a pretty gilt frame. It showed a lady, with a fur cap on and a fur stole, sitting upright and holding out to the spectator a huge fur muff into which the whole of her forearm had vanished!

Gregor's eyes turned next to the window, and the overcast sky—one could hear rain drops beating on the window gutter—made him quite melancholy. What about sleeping a little longer and forgetting all this nonsense, he thought, but it could not be done, for he was accustomed to sleep on his right side and in his present condition he could not turn himself over. However violently he forced himself towards his right side he always rolled on to his back again. He tried it at least a hundred times, shutting his eyes to keep from seeing his struggling legs, and only desisted when he began to feel in his side a faint dull ache he had never experienced before.

Oh God, he thought, what an exhausting job I've picked on! Traveling about day in, day out. It's much more irritating work than doing the actual business in the office, and on top of that there's the trouble of constant traveling, of worrying about train connections, the bed and irregular meals, casual acquaintances that are always new and never become intimate friends. The devil take it all! He felt a slight itching up on his belly; slowly pushed himself on his back nearer to the top of the bed so that he could lift his head more easily; identified the itching place which was surrounded by many small white spots the nature of which he could not understand and made to touch it with a leg, but drew the leg back immediately, for the contact made a cold shiver run through him.

He slid down again into his former position. This getting up early, he thought, makes one quite stupid. A man needs his sleep. Other commercials live like harem women. For instance, when I come back to the hotel of a morning to write up the orders I've got, these others are only sitting down to breakfast. Let me just try that with my chief; I'd be sacked on the spot. Anyhow, that might be quite a good thing for me, who can tell? If I didn't have to hold my hand because of my parents I'd have given notice long ago, I'd have gone to the chief and told him exactly what I think of him. That would knock him endways from his desk! It's a queer way of doing, too, this sitting

Franz Kafka; Willa Muir & Edwin Muir, trans., "The Metamorphosis," from *The Metamorphosis, In the Penal Colony, and Other Stories.* Published by Schocken Books, 1948. Copyright by Random House, Inc. Permission to reprint granted by the rights holder.

on high at a desk and talking down to employees, especially when they have to come quite near because the chief is hard of hearing. Well, there's still hope; once I've saved enough money to pay back my parents' debts to him—that should take another five or six years—I'll do it without fail. I'll cut myself completely loose then. For the moment, though, I'd better get up, since my train goes at five.

He looked at the alarm clock ticking on the chest. Heavenly Father! he thought. It was half-past six o'clock and the hands were quietly moving on, it was even past the half-hour, it was getting on toward a quarter to seven. Had the alarm clock not gone off? From the bed one could see that it had been properly set for four o'clock; of course it must have gone off. Yes, but was it possible to sleep quietly through that ear-splitting noise? Well, he had not slept quietly, yet apparently all the more soundly for that. But what was he to do now? The next train went at seven o'clock; to catch that he would need to hurry like mad and his samples weren't even packed up, and he himself wasn't feeling particularly fresh and active. And even if he did catch the train he wouldn't avoid a row with the chief, since the firm's porter would have been waiting for the five o'clock train and would have long since reported his failure to turn up. The porter was a creature of the chief's, spineless and stupid. Well, supposing he were to say he was sick? But that would be most unpleasant and would look suspicious, since during his five years' employment he had not been ill once. The chief himself would be sure to come with the sick-insurance doctor, would reproach his parents with their son's laziness and would cut all excuses short by referring to the insurance doctor, who of course regarded all mankind as perfectly healthy malingerers. And would he be so far wrong on this occasion? Gregor really felt quite well, apart from a drowsiness that was utterly superfluous after such a long sleep, and he was even unusually hungry.

As all this was running through his mind at top speed without his being able to decide to leave his bed—the alarm clock had just struck a quarter to seven—there came a cautious tap at the door behind the head of his bed. "Gregor," said a voice—it was his mother's—"it's a quarter to seven. Hadn't you a train to catch?" That gentle voice! Gregor had a shock as he heard his own voice answering hers, unmistakably his own voice, it was true, but with a persistent horrible twittering squeak behind it like an undertone, that left the words in their clear shape only for the first moment and then rose up reverberating round them to destroy their sense, so that one could not be sure one had heard them rightly. Gregor wanted to answer at length and explain everything, but in the circumstances he confined himself to saying: "Yes, yes, thank you, Mother, I'm getting up now." The wooden door between them must have kept the change in his voice from being noticeable outside, for his mother contented herself with this statement and shuffled away. Yet this brief exchange of words had made the other members of the family aware that Gregor was still in the house, as they had not expected, and at one of the side doors his father was already knocking, gently, yet with his fist. "Gregor, Gregor," he called "what's the matter with you?" And after a little while he called again in a deeper voice: "Gregor! Gregor!" At the other side door his sister was saying in a low, plaintive tone: "Gregor? Aren't you well? Are you needing anything?" He answered them both at once: "I'm just ready," and did his best to make his voice sound as normal as possible by enunciating the words very clearly and leaving long pauses between them. So his father went back to his breakfast, but his sister whispered: "Gregor, open the door, do." However, he was not thinking of opening the door, and felt thankful for the prudent habit he had acquired in traveling of locking all doors during the night, even at home.

His immediate intention was to get up quietly without being disturbed to put on his clothes and above all eat his breakfast, and only then to consider what else was to be done, since in bed, he was well aware, his meditations would come to no sensible conclusion. He remembered that often enough in bed he had felt small aches and pains, probably caused by awkward postures, which had proved purely imaginary once he got up, and he looked forward eagerly to seeing this morning's delusions gradually fall away. That the change in his voice was nothing but the precursor of a severe chill, a standing ailment of commercial travelers, he had not the least possible doubt.

To get rid of the quilt was quite easy; he had only to inflate himself a little and it fell off by itself. But the next move was difficult, especially because he was so uncommonly broad. He would have needed arms and hands to hoist himself up; instead he had only the numerous little legs which never stopped waving in all directions and which he could not control in the least. When he tried to bend one of them it was the first to stretch itself straight; and did he succeed at last in making it do what he wanted, all the other legs meanwhile waved the more wildly in a high degree of unpleasant agitation. "But, what's the use of lying idle in bed," said Gregor to himself.

He thought that he might get out of bed with the lower part of his body first, but this lower part, which he had not yet seen and of which he could form no clear conception, proved too difficult to move; it shifted so slowly; and when finally, almost wild with annoyance, he gathered his forces together and thrust out recklessly, he had miscalculated the direction and bumped heavily against the lower end of the bed, and the stinging pain he felt informed him that precisely this lower part of his body was at the moment; probably the most sensitive.

So he tried to get the top part of himself out first, and cautiously moved, his head towards the edge of the bed. That proved easy enough, and despite its breadth and mass the bulk of his body at last slowly followed the movement of his head. Still, when he finally got his head free over the edge of the bed he felt too scared to go on advancing, for after all if he let himself fall in this way it would take a miracle to keep his head from being injured. And at all costs he must not lose consciousness now, precisely now; he would rather stay in bed.

But when after a repetition of the same efforts he lay in his former position again, sighing, and watched his little legs struggling against each other more wildly than ever, if that were possible, and saw no way of bringing any order into this arbitrary confusion, he told himself again that it was impossible to stay in bed and that the most sensible course was to risk everything for the smallest hope of getting away from it. At the same time he did not forget meanwhile to remind himself that cool reflection, the coolest possible, was much better than desperate resolves. In such moments he focused his eyes as sharply as possible on the window, but, unfortunately, the prospect of the morning fog, which muffled even the other side of the narrow street, brought him little encouragement and comfort. "Seven o'clock already," he said to himself when the alarm clock chimed again, "seven o'clock already and still such a thick fog." And for a little while he lay quiet, breathing lightly, as if perhaps expecting such complete repose to restore all things to their real and normal condition.

But then he said to himself: "Before it strikes a quarter past seven I must be quite out of this bed, without fail. Anyhow, by that time someone will have come from the office to ask for me, since it opens before seven." And he set himself to rocking his whole body at once in a regular rhythm, with the idea of swinging it out of the bed. If he tipped himself out in that way he could keep his head from injury by lifting it at an acute angle when he fell. His back seemed to be hard and was not likely to suffer from a fall on the carpet. His biggest worry was the loud crash he would not be able to help making, which would probably cause anxiety, if not terror, behind all the doors. Still, he must take the risk.

When he was already half out of the bed—the new method was more a game than an effort, for he needed only to hitch himself across by rocking to and fro—it struck him how simple it would be if he could get help. Two strong people—he thought of his father and the servant girl—would be am sufficient; they would only have to thrust their arms under his convex back, lever him out of the bed, bend down with their burden and then be patient-enough to let him turn himself right over on to the floor, where it was to be hoped his legs would then find their proper function. Well, ignoring the fact that the doors were all locked, ought he really to call for help? In spite of his misery he could not suppress a smile at the very idea of it.

He had got so far that he could barely keep his equilibrium when he rocked himself strongly, and he would have to nerve himself very soon for the final decision since in five minutes' time it would be a quarter past seven—when the front doorbell rang. "That's someone from the office," he said to himself, and grew almost rigid, while his little legs only jigged about all the faster. For a moment everything stayed quiet. "They're not going to open the door," Said Gregor to himself, catching at some kind of irrational hope. But then of course the servant girl went as usual to the door with her heavy tread and opened it. Gregor needed only to hear the first good morning of the visitor to know immediately who it was—the chief clerk himself. What a fate, to be condemned to work for a firm where the smallest omission at once gave rise to the gravest suspicion! Were all employees in a body nothing but scoundrels, was there not among them one single loyal devoted man who, had he wasted only an hour or so of the firm's time in a morning, was so tormented by conscience as to be driven out of his mind and actually incapable of leaving his bed? Wouldn't it really have been sufficient to send an apprentice to inquire—if any inquiry were necessary at all—did the chief clerk himself have to come and thus indicate to the entire family, an innocent family, that this suspicious circumstance could be investigated by no one less versed in affairs than himself? And more through the agitation caused by these reflections than through any act of will Gregor swung himself out of bed with all his strength. There was a loud thump, but it was not really a crash. His fall was broken to some extent by the carpet, his back, too, was less stiff than he thought, and so there was merely a dull thud, not so very startling. Only he had not lifted his head carefully enough and had hit it; he turned it and rubbed it on the carpet in pain and irritation.

"That was something falling down in there," said the chief clerk in the next room to the left. Gregor tried to suppose to himself that something like what had happened to him today might some day happen to the chief clerks; one really could not deny that it was possible. But as if in brusque reply to this supposition the chief clerk took a couple of firm steps in the next-door room and his patent leather boots creaked. From the right-hand room his sister was whispering to inform him of the situation: "Gregor, the chief clerk's here." "I know," muttered Gregor to himself; but he didn't dare to make his voice loud enough for his sister to hear it.

"Gregor," said his father now from the left-hand room, "the chief clerk has come and wants to know why you didn't catch the early train. We don't know what to say to him. Besides, he wants to talk to you in person. So open the door, please. He will be good enough to excuse the untidiness of your room." "Good morning, Mr. Samsa," the chief clerk was calling amiably meanwhile. "He's not well," said his mother to the visitor, while his father was still speaking through the door, "he's not well, sir, believe me. What else would make him miss a train! The boy thinks about nothing but his work. Its makes me almost cross the way he never goes out in the evenings; he's been here the last eight days and has stayed at home every single evening. He just sits there quietly at the table reading a newspaper or looking through railway timetables. The only amusement he gets is doing fretwork. For instance, he spent two or three evenings cutting out a little picture frame; you would be surprised to see how pretty it is; it's hanging in his room; you'll see it in a minute when Gregor opens the door. I must say I'm glad you've come, sir; we should never have got him to unlock the door by ourselves; he's so obstinate; and I'm sure he's unwell, though he wouldn't have it to be so this morning." "I'm just coming," said Gregor slowly and carefully, not moving an inch for fear of losing one word of the conversation. "I can't think of any other explanation, madam," said the chief clerk, "I hope it's nothing serious. Although on the other hand I must say that we men of business—fortunately or unfortunately—very often simply have to ignore any slight indisposition, since business must be attended to." "Well, can the chief clerk come in now?" asked Gregor's father impatiently, again knocking on the door. "No," said Gregor. In the left-hand room a painful silence followed this refusal, in the right-hand room his sister began to sob.

Why didn't his sister join the others? She was probably newly out of bed and hadn't even begun to put on her clothes yet. Well, why was she crying? Because he wouldn't get up and let the chief clerk in, because he was in danger of losing his job, and because the chief would begin dunning his parents again for the old debts? Surely these were things one didn't need to worry about for the present. Gregor was still at home and not in the least thinking of deserting the family. At the moment, true, he was lying on the carpet and no one who knew the condition he was in could seriously expect him to admit the chief clerk. But for such a small discourtesy, which could plausibly be explained away somehow later on, Gregor could hardly be dismissed on the spot. And it seemed to Gregor that it would be much more sensible to leave him in peace for the present than to trouble him with tears and entreaties. Still, of course, their uncertainty bewildered them all and excused their behavior.

"Mr. Samsa," the chief clerk called now in a louder voice, "what's the matter with you? Here you are, barricading yourself in your room, giving only 'yes' and 'no' for answers, causing your parents a lot of unnecessary trouble and neglecting—I mention this only in passing—neglecting your business duties in an incredible fashion. I am speaking here in the name of your parents and of your chief, and I beg you quite seriously to give me an immediate and precise explanation. You amaze me, you amaze me. I thought you were a quiet, dependable person, and now all at once you seem bent on making a disgraceful exhibition of yourself. The chief did hint to me early this morning a possible explanation for your disappearance—with reference to the cash payments that were entrusted to you recently—but I almost pledged my solemn word of honor that this could not be so. But now that I see how incredibly obstinate you are, I no longer have the slightest desire to take your part at all. And your position in the firm is not so unassailable. I came with the intention of telling you all this in private, but since you are wasting my time so needlessly I don't see why your parents shouldn't hear it too. For some time past your work has been most unsatisfactory; this is not the season of the year for a business boom, of course, we admit that, but a season of the year for doing no business at all, that does not exist, Mr. Samsa, must not exist."

"But, sir," cried Gregor, beside himself and in his agitation forgetting everything else, "I'm just going to open the door this very minute. A slight illness, an attack of giddiness, has kept me from getting up. I'm still lying in bed. But I feel all right again. I'm getting out of bed now. Just give me a moment or two longer! I'm not quite as well as I thought. But I'm all right, really. How a thing like that can suddenly strike one down! Only last night I was quite well, my parents can tell you, or rather I did have a slight presentiment. I must have showed some sign of it. Why didn't I report it at the office! But one always thinks that an indisposition can be got over without staying in the house. Oh sir, do spare my parents! All that you're reproaching me with now has no foundation; no one has ever said a word to me about it. Perhaps you haven't looked at the last orders I sent in. Anyhow, I can still catch the eight o'clock train, I'm much the better for my few hours' rest. Don't let me detain you here, sir; I'll be attending to business very soon, and do be good enough to tell the chief so and to make my excuses to him!"

And while all this was tumbling out pell-mell and Gregor hardly knew what he was saying, he had reached the chest quite easily, perhaps because of the practice he had had in bed, and was now trying to lever himself upright by means of it. He meant actually to open the door, actually to show him and speak to the chief clerk; he was eager to find out what the others, after all their insistence, would say at the sight of him. If they were horrified then the responsibility was no longer his and he could stay quiet. But if they took it calmly, then he had no reason either to be upset, and could really get to the station for the eight o'clock train if he hurried. At first he slipped down a few times from the polished surface of the chest, but at length with a last heave he stood upright; he paid no more attention to the pains in the lower part of his body however they smarted. Then he let himself fall against the back of a near-by chair, and clung with his little legs to the edges of it. That brought him into control of himself again and he stopped speaking, for now he could listen to what the chief clerk was saying.

"Did you understand a word of it?" the chief clerk was asking; "surely he can't be trying to make fools of us?" "Oh dear," cried his mother, in tears; "perhaps he's terribly ill and we're tormenting him. Grete! Grete!" she called out then. "Yes, Mother?"

called his sister from the other side. They were calling to each other across Gregor's room. "You must go this minute for the doctor. Gregor is ill. Go for the doctor, quick. Did you hear how he was speaking?" "That was no human voice," said the chief clerk in a voice noticeably low beside the shrillness of the mother's. "Anna! Anna!" his father was calling through the hall to the kitchen, clapping his hands, "Get a locksmith at once!" And the two girls were already running through the hall with a swish of skirts—how could his sister have got dressed so quickly?—and were tearing the front door open. There was no sound of its closing again; they had evidently left it open, as one does in houses where some great misfortune has happened.

But Gregor was now much calmer. The words he uttered were no longer understandable, apparently, although they seemed clear enough to him, even clearer than before, perhaps because his ear had grown accustomed to the sound of them. Yet at any rate people now believed that something was wrong with him, and were ready to help him. The positive certainty with which these first measures had been taken comforted him. He felt himself drawn once more into the human circle and hoped for great and remarkable results from both the doctor and the locksmith, without really distinguishing precisely between them. To make his voice as clear as possible for the decisive conversation that was now imminent he coughed a little, as quietly as he could, of course, since this noise too might not sound like a human cough for all he was able to judge. In the next room meanwhile there was complete silence. Perhaps his parents were sitting at the table with the chief clerk, whispering, perhaps they were all leaning against the door and listening.

Slowly Gregor pushed the chair towards the door, then let go of it, caught hold of the door for support—the soles at the end of his little legs were somewhat sticky—and rested against it for a moment after his efforts, Then he set himself to turning the key in the lock with his mouth. It seemed, unhappily that he hadn't really any teeth—what could he grip the key with?—but on the other hand his jaws were certainly very strong; with their help he did manage to set the key in motion, heedless of the fact that he was undoubtedly damaging them somewhere, since a brown fluid issued from his mouth, flowed over the key and dripped on the floor. "Just listen to that," said the chief clerk next door; "he's turning the key." That was a great encouragement to Gregor; but they should all have shouted encouragement to him, his father and mother too: "Go on, Gregor," they should have called out, "keep going, hold on to that key!" And in the belief that they were all following his efforts intently, he clenched his jaws recklessly on the key with all the force at his command. As the turning of the key progressed he circled round the lock, holding on now only with his mouth, pushing on the key as required, or pulling it down again with all the weight of his body. The louder click of the finally yielding lock literally quickened Gregor. With a deep breath of relief he said to himself: "So I didn't need the locksmith," and laid his head on the handle to open the door wide.

Since he had to pull the door towards him, he was still invisible when it was really wide open. He had to edge himself slowly round the near half of the double door, and to do it very carefully if he was not to fall plump upon his back just on the threshold. He was still carrying out this difficult manœuvre; with no time to observe anything else, when he heard the chief clerk utter a loud "Oh!"—it sounded like a gust of wind—and now he could see the man, standing as he was nearest to the door, clapping one hand before his open mouth and slowly backing away as if driven by some invisible steady pressure. His mother—in spite of the chief clerk's being there her hair was still undone and sticking up in all directions—first clasped her hands and looked at his father, then took two steps towards Gregor and fell on the floor among her outspread skirts, her face hidden on her breast. His father knotted his first with a fierce expression on his face as if he meant to knock Gregor back into his room, then looked uncertainly round the living room, covered his eyes with his hands and wept till his great chest heaved.

Gregor did not go now into the living room, but leaned against the inside of the firmly shut wing of the door, so that only half his body was visible and his head above it bending sideways to look at the others. The light had meanwhile strengthened; on the other side of the street one could see clearly a section of the endlessly long, dark gray building opposite—it was a hospital—abruptly punctuated by its row of regular windows; the rain was still falling, but only in large singly discernible and literally singly splashing drops. The breakfast dishes were set out on the table lavishly, for breakfast, the most important meal of the day to Gregor's father, who lingered it out for hours over various newspapers. Right opposite Gregor on the wall hung a photograph of himself on military service, as a lieutenant, hand on sword, a carefree smile on his face, inviting one to respect his uniform and military bearing. The door leading to the hall was open, and one could see that the front door stood open too, showing the landing beyond and the beginning of the stairs going down.

"Well," said Gregor, knowing perfectly that he was the only one who had retained any composure, "I'll put my clothes on at once, pack up my samples and start off. Will you only let me go? You see, sir, I'm not obstinate, and I'm willing to work; traveling is a hard life, but I couldn't live without it. Where are you going, sir? To the office? Yes? Will you give a true account of all this? One can be temporarily incapacitated, but that's just the moment for remembering former services and bearing in mind that later on, when the incapacity has been got over, one will certainly work with all the more industry and concentration. I'm loyally bound to serve the chief, you know that very well. Besides, I have to provide for my parents and my sister. I'm in great difficulties, but I'll get out of them again. Don't make things any worse for me than they are. Stand up for me in the firm. Travelers are not popular there, I know. People think they earn sacks of money and just have a good time. A prejudice there's no particular reason for revising. But you, sir, have a more comprehensive view of affairs than the rest of the staff, yes, let me tell you in confidence, a more comprehensive view than the chief himself, who, being the owner, lets his judgment easily be swayed against one of his employees. And you know very well that the traveler, who is never seen in the office almost the whole year round, can so easily fall a victim to gossip and ill luck and unfounded complaints, which he mostly knows nothing about, except when he comes back exhausted from his rounds, and only then suffers in person from their evil consequences, which he can no longer trace back to the original causes. Sir, sir, don't go away without a word to me to show that you think me in the right at least to some extent!"

But at Gregor's very first words the chief clerk had already backed away and only stared at him with parted lips over one twitching shoulder. And while Gregor was speaking he did not stand still one moment but stole away towards the door, without taking his eyes off Gregor, yet only an inch at a time, as if obeying some secret injunction to leave the room. He was already at the hall, and the suddenness with which he took his last step out of the living room would have made one believe he had burned the sole of his foot. Once in the hall he stretched his right arm before him towards the staircase, as if some supernatural power were waiting there to deliver him.

Gregor perceived that the chief clerk must on no account be allowed to go away in this frame of mind if his position in the firm were not to be endangered to the utmost. His parents did not understand this so well; they had convinced themselves in the course of years that Gregor was settled for life in this firm, and besides they were so occupied with their immediate troubles that all foresight had forsaken them. Yet Gregor had this foresight. The chief clerk must be detained, soothed, persuaded and finally won over; the whole future of Gregor and his family depended on it! If only his sister had been there! She was intelligent; she had begun to cry while Gregor was still lying quietly on his back. And no doubt the chief clerk, so partial to ladies, would have been guided by her; she would have shut the door of the flat and in the hall talked him out of his horror. But she was not there, and Gregor would have to handle the situation himself. And without remembering that he was still unaware what powers of movement he possessed, without even remembering that his words in all possibility, indeed in all likelihood, would again be unintelligible, he let go the wing of the door, pushed himself through the opening, started to walk towards the chief clerk, who was already ridiculously clinging with both hands to the railing on the landing; but immediately, as he was feeling for a support, he fell down with a little cry upon all his numerous legs. Hardly was he down when he experienced for the first time this morning a sense of physical comfort; his legs had firm ground under them; they were completely obedient, as he noted with joy; they even strove to carry him forward in whatever direction he chose; and he was inclined to believe that a final relief from all his sufferings was at hand. But in the same moment as he found himself on the floor, rocking with suppressed eagerness to move, not far from his mother, indeed just in front of her, she, who had seemed so completely crushed, sprang all at once to her feet, her arms and fingers outspread, cried: "Help, for God's sake, help!" bent her head down as if to see Gregor better, yet on the contrary kept backing senselessly away; had quite forgotten that the laden table stood behind her; sat upon it hastily, as if in absence of mind, when she bumped into it; and seemed altogether unaware that the big coffee pot beside her was upset and pouring coffee in a flood over the carpet.

"Mother, Mother," said Gregor in a low voice, and looked up at her. The chief clerk, for the moment, had quite slipped from his mind; instead, he could not resist snapping his jaws together at the sight of the streaming coffee. That made his mother screams again, she fled from the table and fell into the arms of his father, who hastened to catch her. But Gregor had now no time to spare for his parents; the chief clerk was already on the stairs; with his chin on the banisters he was taking one last backward look. Gregor made a spring, to be as sure as possible of overtaking him; the chief clerk must have divined his intention, for he leaped down several steps and vanished; he was still yelling "Ugh!" and it echoed through the whole staircase.

Unfortunately, the flight of the chief clerk seemed completely to upset Gregor's father, who had remained relatively calm until now, for instead of running after the man himself, or at least not hindering Gregor in his pursuit, he seized in his right hand the walking stick which the chief clerk had left behind on a chair, together with a hat and greatcoat, snatched in his left hand a large newspaper from the table and began stamping his feet and flourishing the stick and the newspaper to drive Gregor back into his room. No entreaty of Gregor's availed, indeed no entreaty was even understood, however humbly he bent his head his father only stamped on the floor the more loudly. Behind his father his mother had torn open a window, despite the cold weather, and was leaning far out of it with her face in her hands. A strong draught set in from the street to the staircase, the window curtains blew in, the newspapers on the table fluttered, stray pages whisked over the floor. Pitilessly Gregor's father drove him back, hissing and crying "Shoo!" like a savage. But Gregor was quite unpracticed in walking backwards, it really was a slow business. If he only had a chance to turn round he could get back to his room at once, but he was afraid of exasperating his father by the slowness of such a rotation and at any moment the stick in his father's hand might hit him a fatal blow on the back or on the head. In the end, however, nothing else was left for him to do since to his horror he observed that in moving backwards he could not even control the direction he took; and so, keeping an anxious eye on his father all the time over his shoulder, he began to turn round as quickly as he could, which was in reality very slowly. Perhaps his father noted his good intentions, for he did not interfere except every now and then to help him in the manoeuvre from a distance with the point of the stick. If only he would have stopped making that unbearable hissing noise! It made Gregor quite lose his head. He had turned almost completely round when the hissing noise so distracted him that he even turned a little the wrong way again. But when at last his head was fortunately right in front of the doorway, it appeared that his body was too broad simply to get through the opening. His father, of course, in his present mood was far from thinking of such a thing as opening the other half of the door, to let Gregor have enough space. He had merely the fixed idea of driving Gregor back into his room as quickly as possible. He would never have suffered Gregor to make the circumstantial preparations for standing up on end and perhaps slipping his way through the door. Maybe he was now making more noise than ever to urge Gregor forward, as if no obstacle impeded him; to Gregor, anyhow, the noise in his rear sounded no longer like the voice of one single father; this was really no joke, and Gregor thrust himself—come what might—into the doorway. One side of his body rose up, he was tilted at an angle in the doorway, his flank was quite bruised, horrid blotches stained the white door, soon he was stuck fast and, left to himself, could not have moved at all, his legs on one side fluttered trembling to the air, those on the other were crushed painfully to the floor—when from behind his father gave him a strong push which was literally a deliverance and he flew far into the room, bleeding freely. The door was slammed behind him with the stick, and then at last there was silence.

II

Not until it was twilight did Gregor awake out of a deep sleep, more like a swoon than a sleep. He would certainly have waked up of his own accord not much later, for he felt himself sufficiently rested and well-slept, but it seemed to him as if a fleeting step and a cautious shutting of the door leading into the hall had aroused him. The electric lights in the street cast a pale sheen here and there on the ceiling and the upper surfaces of the furniture, but down below, where he lay, it was dark. Slowly, awkwardly trying out his feelers, which he now first learned to appreciate, he pushed his way to the door to see what had been happening there. His left side felt like one single long, unpleasant tense scar, and he had actually to limp on his two rows of legs. One little leg, moreover, had been severely damaged in the course of that morning's events—it was almost a miracle that only one had been damaged—and trailed uselessly behind him.

He had reached the door before he discovered what had really drawn him to it: the smell of food. For there stood a basin filled with fresh milk in which floated little sops of white bread. He could almost have laughed with joy, since he was now still hungrier than in the morning, and he dipped his head almost over the eyes straight into the milk. But soon in disappointment he withdrew it again; not only did he find it difficult to feed because of his tender left side—and he could only feed with the palpitating collaboration of his whole body—he did not like the milk either, although milk had been his favorite drink and that was certainly why his sister had set it there for him, indeed it was almost with repulsion that he turned away from the basin and crawled back to the middle of the room.

He could see through the crack of the door that the gas was turned on in the living room, but while usually at this time his father made a habit of reading the afternoon newspaper in a loud voice to his mother and occasionally to his sister as well, not a sound was now to be heard. Well, perhaps his father had recently given up this habit of reading aloud, which his sister had mentioned so often in conversation and in her letters. But there was the same silence all around, although the flat was certainly not empty of occupants. "What a quiet life our family has been leading," said Gregor to himself, and as he sat there motionless staring into the darkness he felt great pride in the fact that he had been able to provide such a life for his parents and sister in such a fine flat. But what if all the quiet, the comfort, the contentment were now to end in horror? To keep himself from being lost in such thoughts Gregor took refuge in movement and crawled up and down the room.

Once during the long evening one of the side doors was opened a little and quickly shut again, later the other side door too; someone had apparently wanted to come in and then thought better of it. Gregor now stationed himself immediately before the living room door, determined to persuade any hesitating visitor to come in or at least to discover who it might be; but the door was not opened again and he waited in vain. In the early morning, when the doors were locked, they had all wanted to come in, now that he had opened one door and the other had apparently been opened during the day, no one came in and even the keys were on the other side of the doors.

It was late at night before the gas went out in the living room, and Gregor could easily tell that his parents and his sister had all stayed awake until then, for he could clearly hear the three of them stealing away on tiptoe. No one was likely to visit him, not until the morning, that was certain; so he had plenty of time to meditate at his leisure on how he was to arrange his life afresh. But the lofty, empty room in which he had to lie flat on the floor filled him with an apprehension he could not account for, since it had been his very own room for the past five years—and with a half-unconscious action, not without a slight feeling of shame, he scuttled under the sofa, where he felt comfortable at once, although his back was a little cramped and he could not lift his head up, and his only regret was that his body was too broad to get the whole of it under the sofa.

He stayed there all night, spending the time partly in a light slumber, from which his hunger kept waking him up with a start, and partly in worrying and sketching vague hopes, which all led to the same conclusion, that he must lie low for the present and, by exercising patience, and the utmost consideration, help the family to bear the inconvenience he was bound to cause them in his present condition.

Very early in the morning, it was still almost night, Gregor had the chance to test the strength of his new resolutions, for his sister, nearly fully dressed, opened the door from the hall and peered in. She did not see him at once, yet when she caught sight of him under the sofa—well, he had to be *somewhere*, he couldn't have flown away, could he?, she was so startled that without being able to help it she slammed the door shut again. But as if regretting her behavior she opened the door again immediately and came in on tiptoe, as if she were visiting an invalid or even a stranger. Gregor had pushed his head forward to the very edge of the sofa and watched her. Would she notice that he had left the milk standing, and not for lack of hunger and would she bring in some other kind of food more to his taste? If she did not do it of her own accord, he would rather starve than draw her attention to the fact, although he felt a wild impulse to dart out from under the sofa, throw himself at her feet and beg her for something to eat. But his sister at once noticed, with surprise, that the basin was still full, except for a little milk that had been spilt all around it, she lifted it immediately, not with her bare hands, true, but with a cloth and carried it away. Gregor was wildly curious to know what she would bring instead, and made various speculations about it. Yet what she actually did next, in the goodness of her heart, he could never have guessed at. To find out what he liked she brought him a whole selection of food, all set out on an old newspaper. There were old, half-decayed vegetables, bones from last night's supper covered with a white sauce that had thickened; some raisins and almonds; a piece of cheese that Gregor would have called uneatable two days ago; a dry roll of bread, a buttered roll, and a roll both buttered and salted. Besides all that, she set down again the same basin, into which she had poured some water, and which was apparently to be reserved for his exclusive use. And with fine tact, knowing that Gregor would not eat in her presence, she withdrew quickly and even turned the key, to let him understand that he could take his ease as much as he liked. Gregor's legs all whizzed towards the food. His wounds must have healed completely, moreover, for he felt no disability, which amazed him and made him reflect how more than a month ago he had cut one finger a little with a knife and had still suffered pain from the wound only the day before yesterday. Am I less sensitive now? he thought, and sucked greedily at the cheese, which above all the other edibles attracted him at once and strongly One after another and with tears of satisfaction in his eyes he quickly devoured the cheese, the vegetables and the sauce; the fresh food, on the other hand, had no charms for him, he could not even stand the smell of it and actually dragged away to some little distance the things he could eat. He had long finished his meal and was only lying lazily on the same spot when his sister turned the key slowly as a sign for him to retreat. That roused him at once, although he was nearly asleep, and he hurried under the sofa again. But it took considerable self-control for him to stay under the sofa, even for the short time his sister was in the room, since the large meal had swollen his body somewhat and he was so cramped he could hardly breathe. Slight attacks of breathlessness afflicted him and his eyes were starting a little out of his head as he watched his unsuspecting sister sweeping together with a broom not only the remains of what he had eaten but even the things he had not touched, as if these were now of no use to anyone, and hastily shoveling it all into a bucket, which she covered with a wooden lid and carried away. Hardly had she turned her back when Gregor came from under the sofa and stretched and puffed himself out.

In this manner Gregor was fed, once in the early morning while his parents and the servant girl were still asleep, and a second time after they had all had their midday dinner, for then his parents took a short nap and the servant girl could be sent out on some errand or other by his sister. Not that they would have wanted him to starve, of course, but perhaps they could not have borne to know more about his feeding than from hearsay, perhaps too his sister wanted to spare them such little anxieties wherever possible, since they had quite enough to bear as it was.

Under what pretext the doctor and the locksmith had been got rid of on that first morning Gregor could not discover, for since what he had said was not understood by the others it never struck any of them, not even his sister, that he could understand what they said, and so whenever his sister came into his room he had to content himself with hearing her utter only a sigh now and then and an occasional appeal to the saints. Later on, when she had got a little used to the situation—of course she could never get completely used to it—she sometimes threw out a remark which was kindly meant or could be so interpreted. "Well, he liked his dinner today," she would say when Gregor had made a good clearance of his food; and when he had not eaten, which gradually happened more and more often, she would say almost sadly: "Everything's been left standing again."

But although Gregor could get no news directly, he overheard a lot from the neighboring rooms, and as soon as voices were audible, he would run to the door of the room concerned and press his whole body against it. In the first few days especially there was no conversation that did not refer to him somehow, even if only indirectly. For two whole days there were family consultations at every mealtime about what should be done; but also between meals the same subject was discussed, for there were always at least two members of the family at home, since no one wanted to be alone in the flat and to leave it quite empty was unthinkable. And on the very first of these days the household cook—it was not quite clear what and how much she knew of the situation—went down on her knees to his mother and begged leave to go, and when she departed, a quarter of an hour later, gave thanks for her dismissal with tears in her eyes as if for the greatest benefit that could have been conferred on her, and without any prompting swore a solemn oath that she would never say a single word to anyone about what had happened.

Now Gregor's sister had to cook too, helping her mother; true, the cooking did not amount to much, for they ate scarcely anything. Gregor was always hearing one of the family vainly urging another to eat and getting no answer but: "Thanks, I've had all I want," or something similar. Perhaps they drank nothing either. Time and again his sister kept asking his father if he wouldn't like some beer and offered kindly to go and fetch it herself, and when he made no answer suggested that she could ask the concierge to fetch it, so that he need feel no sense of obligation, but then a round "No" came from his father and no more was said about it.

In the course of that very first day Gregor's father explained the family's financial position and prospects to both his mother and his sister.

Now and then he rose from the table to get some voucher or memorandum out of the small safe he had rescued from the collapse of his business five years earlier. One could hear him opening the complicated lock and rustling papers out and shutting it again. This statement made by his father was the first cheerful information Gregor had heard since his imprisonment. He had been of the opinion that nothing at all was left over from his father's business, at least his father had never said anything to the contrary, and of course he had not asked him directly. At the time Gregor's sole desire was to do his utmost to help the family to forget as soon as possible the catastrophe which had overwhelmed the business and thrown them all into a state of complete despair. And so he had set to work with unusual ardor and almost overnight had become a commercial traveler instead of a little clerk, with of course much greater chances of earning money, and his success was immediately translated into good round coin which he could lay on the table for his amazed and happy family. These had been fine times, and they had never recurred, at least not with the same sense of glory, although later on Gregor had earned so much money that he was able to meet the expenses of the whole household and did so. They had simply got used to it, both the family and Gregor; the money was gratefully accepted and gladly given, but there was no special up rush of warm feeling. With his sister alone had he remained intimate, and it was a secret plan of his that she, who loved music, unlike himself, and could play movingly on the violin, should be sent next year to study at the Conservatorium, despite the great expense that would entail, which must be made up in some other way. During his brief visits home the Conservatorium was often mentioned in the talks he had with his sister, but always merely as a beautiful dream which could never come true, and his parents discouraged even these innocent references to it; yet Gregor had made up his mind firmly about it and meant to announce the fact with due solemnity on Christmas Day.

Such were the thoughts, completely futile in his present condition, that went through his head as he stood clinging upright to the door and listening: Sometimes out of sheer weariness he had to give up listening and let his head fall negligently against the door, but he always had to pull himself together again at once, for even the slight sound his head made was audible next door and brought all conversation to a stop. "What can he be doing now?" his father would say after a while, obviously turning towards the door, and only then would the interrupted conversation gradually be set going again.

Gregor was now informed as amply as he could wish—for his father tended to repeat himself in his explanations, partly because it was a long time since he had handled such matters and partly because his mother could not always grasp things at once—that a certain amount of investments, a very small amount it was true, had survived the wreck of their fortunes and had even increased a little because the dividends had not been touched meanwhile. And besides that, the money Gregor brought home every month—he had kept only a few dollars for himself—had never been quite used up and now amounted to a small capital sum. Behind the door Gregor nodded his head eagerly, rejoiced at this evidence of unexpected thrift and foresight. True, he could really have paid off some more of his father's debts to the chief with his extra money, and so brought much nearer the day on which he could quit his job, but doubtless it was better the way his father had arranged it.

Yet this capital was by no means sufficient to let the family live on the interest of it; for one year, perhaps, or at the most two, they could live on the principal, that was all. It was simply a sum that ought not to be touched and should be kept for a rainy day; money for living expenses would have to be earned. Now his father was still hale enough but an old man, and he had done no work for the past five years and could not be expected to do much; during these five years, the first years of leisure in his laborious though unsuccessful life, he had grown rather fat and become sluggish. And Gregor's old mother, how was she to earn a living with her asthma, which troubled her even when she walked through the flat and kept her lying on a sofa every other day panting for breath beside an open window? And was his sister to earn her bread, she who was still a child of seventeen and whose life hitherto had been so pleasant, consisting as it did in dressing herself nicely, sleeping long, helping in the housekeeping, going out to a few modest entertainments and above all playing the violin? At first whenever the need for earning money was mentioned Gregor let go his hold on the door and threw himself down on the cool leather sofa beside it, he felt so hot with shame and grief.

Often he just lay there the long nights through without sleeping at all, scrabbling for hours on the leather. Or he nerved himself to the great effort of pushing an armchair to the window, then crawled up over the window sill and, braced against the chair, leaned against the windowpanes, obviously in some recollection of the sense of freedom that looking out of a window always used to give him. For in reality day by day things that were even a little way off were growing dimmer to his sight; the hospital across the street, which he used to execrate for being all too often before his eyes, was now quite beyond his range of vision, and if he had not known that he lived in Charlotte Street, a quiet street but still a city street, he might have believed that his window gave on a desert waste where gray sky and gray land blended indistinguishably into each other. His quick-witted sister only needed to observe twice that the armchair stood by the window; after that whenever she had tidied the room she always pushed the chair back to the same place at the window and even left the inner casements open.

If he could have spoken to her and thanked her for all she had to do for him, he could have borne her ministrations better; as it was, they oppressed him. She certainly tried to make as light as possible of whatever was disagreeable in her task, and as time went on she succeeded, of course, more and more, but time brought more enlightenment to Gregor too. The very way she came in distressed him. Hardly was she in the room when she rushed to the window, without even taking time to shut the door, careful as she was usually to shield the sight of Gregor's room from the others, and as if she were almost suffocating tore the casements open with hasty fingers, standing then in the open draught for a while even in the bitterest cold and drawing deep breaths. This noisy scurry of hers upset Gregor twice a day; he would crouch trembling under the sofa all the time, knowing quite well that she would certainly have spared him such a disturbance had she found it at all possible to stay in his presence without opening a window.

On one occasion, about a month after Gregor's metamorphosis, when there was surely no reason for her to be still startled at his appearance, she came a little earlier than usual and found him gazing out of the window, quite motionless, and thus well placed to look like a bogey Gregor would not have been surprised had she not come in at all, for she could not immediately open the window while he was there, but not only did she retreat, she jumped back as if in alarm and banged the door shut; a stranger might well have thought that he had been lying in wait for her there meaning to bite her. Of course he hid himself under the sofa at once, but he had to wait until midday before she came again, and she seemed more ill at ease than usual. This made him realize how repulsive the sight of him still was to her, and that it was bound to go on being repulsive, and what an effort it must cost her not to run away even from the sight of the small portion of his body that stuck out from under the sofa. In order to spare her that, therefore, one day he carried a sheet on his back to the sofa—it cost him four hours' labor—and arranged it there in such a way as to hide him completely, so that even if she were to bend down she could not see him. Had she considered the sheet unnecessary, she would certainly have stripped it off the sofa again, for it was clear enough that this curtaining and confining of himself was not likely to conduce Gregor's comfort, but she left it where it was, and Gregor even fancied that he caught a thankful glance from her eye when he lifted the sheet carefully a very little with his head to see how she was taking the new arrangement.

For the first fortnight his parents could not bring themselves to the point of entering his room, and he often heard them expressing their appreciation of his sister's activities, whereas formerly they had frequently scolded her for being as they thought a somewhat useless daughter. But now, both of them often waited outside the door, his father and his mother, while his sister tidied his room, and as soon as she came out she had to tell them exactly how things were in the room, what Gregor had eaten, how he had conducted himself this time and whether there was not perhaps some slight improvement in his condition. His mother, moreover, began relatively soon to want to visit him, but his father and sister dissuaded her at first with arguments which Gregor listened to very attentively and altogether approved. Later, however, she had to be held back by main force, and when she cried out: "Do let me in to Gregor, he is my unfortunate son! Can't you understand that I must go to him?" Gregor thought that it might be well to have her come in, not every day, of course, but perhaps once a week; she understood things, after all, much better than his sister, who was only a child despite the efforts she was making and had perhaps taken on so difficult a task merely out of childish thoughtlessness.

Gregor's desire to see his mother was soon fulfilled. During the daytime he did not want to show himself at the window, out of consideration for his parents, but he could not crawl very far around the few square yards of floor space he had, nor could he bear lying quietly at rest all during the night, while he was fast losing any interest he had ever taken in food, so that for mere recreation he had formed the habit of crawling crisscross over the walls and ceiling. He especially enjoyed hanging suspended from the ceiling; it was much better than lying on the floor; one could breathe more freely; one's body swung and rocked lightly; and in the almost blissful absorption induced by this suspension it could happen to his own surprise that he let go and fell plump on the floor. Yet he now had his body much better under control than formerly, and even such a big fall did him no harm. His sister at once remarked the new distraction Gregor had found for himself—he left traces behind him of the sticky stuff on his soles wherever he crawled—and she got the idea in her head of giving him as wide a field as possible to crawl in and of removing the pieces of furniture that hindered him, above all the chest of drawers and the writing desk. But that was more than she could manage all by herself; she did not dare ask her father to help her; and as for the servant girl, a young creature of sixteen who had had the courage to stay on after the cook's departure, she could not be asked to help, for she had begged as an especial favor that she might keep the kitchen door locked and open it only on a definite summons; so there was nothing left but to apply to her mother at an hour when her father was out. And the old lady did come, with exclamations of joyful eagerness, which, however, died away at the door of Gregor's room. Gregor's sister, of course, went in first, to see that everything was in order before letting her mother enter. In great haste Gregor pulled the sheet lower and rocked it more in folds so that it really looked as if it had been thrown accidentally over the sofa. And this time he did not peer out from under it; he renounced the pleasure of seeing his mother on this occasion and was only glad that she had come at all. "Come in, he's out of sight," said his sister, obviously leading her mother in by the hand. Gregor could now hear the two women struggling to shift the heavy old chest from its place, and his sister claiming the greater part of the labor for herself, without listening to the admonitions of her mother who feared she might overstrain herself. It took a long time. After at least a quarter of an hour's tugging his mother objected that the chest had better be left where it was, for in the first place it was too heavy and could never be got out before his father came home, and standing in the middle of the room like that it would only hamper Gregor's movements, while in the second place it was not at all certain that removing the furniture would be doing a service to Gregor. She was inclined to think to the contrary; the sight of the naked walls made her own heart heavy, and why shouldn't Gregor have the same feeling, considering that he had been used to his furniture for so long and might feel forlorn without it. "And doesn't it look," she concluded in a low voice—in fact she had been almost whispering all the time as if to avoid letting Gregor, whose exact whereabouts she did not know, hear even the tones of her voice, for she was convinced that he could not understand her words—"doesn't it look as if we were showing him, by taking away his furniture, that we have given up hope of his ever getting better and are just leaving him coldly to himself? I think it would be best to keep his room exactly as it has always been, so that when he comes back to us he will find everything unchanged and be able all the more easily to forget what has happened in between."

On hearing these words from his mother Gregor realized that the lack of all direct human speech for the past two months together with the monotony of family life must have confused his mind, otherwise he could not account for the fact that he had quite earnestly looked forward to having his room emptied of furnishing. Did he really want his warm room, so comfortably fitted with old family furniture, to be turned into a naked den in which he would certainly be able to crawl unhampered in all directions but at the price of shedding simultaneously all recollection of his human background? He had indeed been so near the brink of forgetfulness that only the voice of his mother, which he had not heard for so long, had drawn him back from it. Nothing should be taken out of his room; everything must stay as it was; he could not dispense with the good influence of the furniture on his state of mind; and even if the furniture did hamper him in his senseless crawling round and round, that was no drawback but a great advantage.

Unfortunately his sister was of the contrary opinion; she had grown accustomed, and not without reason, to consider herself an expert in Gregor's affairs as against her parents, and so her mother's advice was now enough to make her determined on the removal not only of the chest and the writing desk, which had been her first intention, but of all the furniture except the indispensable sofa. This determination was not, of course, merely the outcome of childish recalcitrance and of the self-confidence she had recently developed so unexpectedly and at such cost; she had in fact perceived that Gregor needed a lot of space to crawl about in, while on the other hand he never used the furniture at all, so far as could be seen. Another factor might have been also the enthusiastic temperament of an adolescent girl, which seeks to indulge itself on every opportunity and which now tempted Grete to exaggerate the horror of her brother's circumstances in order that she might do all the more for him. In a room where Gregor lorded it all alone over empty walls no one save herself was likely ever to set foot.

And so she was not to be moved from her resolve by her mother who seemed moreover to be ill at ease in Gregor's room and therefore unsure of herself, was soon reduced to silence and helped her daughter as best she could to push the chest outside. Now, Gregor could do without the chest, if need be, but the writing desk he must retain. As soon as the two women had got the chest out of his room, groaning as they pushed it, Gregor stuck his head out from under the sofa to see how he might intervene as kindly and cautiously as possible. But as bad luck would have it, his mother was the first to return, leaving Grete clasping the chest in the room next door where she was trying to shift it all by herself, without of course moving it from the spot. His mother however was not accustomed to the sight of him, it might sicken her and so in alarm Gregor backed quickly to the other end of the sofa, yet could not prevent the sheet from swaying a little in front. That was enough to put her on the alert. She paused, stood still for a moment and then went back to Grete.

Although Gregor kept reassuring himself that nothing out of the way was happening, but only a few bits of furniture were being changed round, he soon had to admit that all this trotting to and fro of the two women, their little ejaculations and the scraping of furniture along the floor affected him like a vast disturbance coming from all sides at once, and however much he tucked in his head and legs and cowered to the very floor he was bound to confess that he would not be able to stand it for long. They were clearing his room out; taking away everything he loved; the chest in which he kept his fret saw and other tools was already dragged off; they were now loosening the writing desk which had almost sunk into the floor, the desk at which he had done all his homework when he was at the commercial academy, at the grammar school before that, and, yes, even at the primary school he had no more time to waste in weighing the good intentions of the two women, whose existence he had by now almost forgotten, for they were so exhausted that they were laboring in silence and nothing could be heard but the heavy scuffling of their feet.

And so he rushed out—the women were just leaning against the writing desk in the next room to give themselves a breather—and four times changed his direction, since he really did not know what to rescue first, then on the wall opposite, which was already otherwise cleared, he was struck by the picture of the lady muffled in so much fur and quickly crawled up to it and pressed himself to the glass, which was a good surface to hold on to and comforted his hot belly. This picture at least, which was entirely hidden beneath him, was going to be removed by nobody. He turned his head towards the door of the living room so as to observe the women when they came back.

They had not allowed themselves much of a rest and were already coming; Grete had twined her arm round her mother and was almost supporting her. "Well, what shall we take now?" said Grete, looking round. Her eyes met Gregor's from the wall. She kept her composure, presumably because of her mother, bent her head down to her mother, to keep her from looking up, and said, although in a fluttering, unpremeditated voice: "Come, hadn't we better go back to the living room for a moment?" Her intentions were clear enough to Gregor, she wanted to bestow her mother in safety and then chase him down from the wall. Well, just let her try it! He clung to his picture and would not give it up. He would rather fly in Grete's face.

But Grete's words had succeeded in disquieting her mother, who took a step to one side, caught sight of the huge brown mass on the flowered wallpaper, and before she was really conscious that what she saw was Gregor screamed in a loud, hoarse voice: "Oh God, oh God!" fell with outspread arms over the sofa as if giving up and did not move. "Gregor!" cried his sister, shaking her fist and glaring at him. This was the first time she had directly addressed him since his metamorphosis. She ran into the next room for some aromatic essence with which to rouse her mother from her fainting fit. Gregor wanted to help too—there was still time to rescue the picture—but he was stuck fast to the glass and had to tear himself loose; he then ran after his sister into the next room as if he could advise her, as he used to do; but then had to stand helplessly behind her; she meanwhile searched among various small bottles and when she turned round started in alarm at the sight of him; one bottle fell on the floor and broke; a splinter of glass cut Gregor's face and some kind of corrosive medicine splashed him; without pausing a moment longer Grete gathered up all the bottles she could carry and ran to her mother with them; she banged the door shut with her foot. Gregor was now cut off from his mother, who was perhaps nearly dying because of him; he dared not open the door for fear of frightening away his sister, who had to stay with her mother; there was nothing he could do but wait; and harassed by self-reproach and worry he began now to crawl to and fro, over everything, walls, furniture and ceiling, and finally in his despair, when the whole room seemed to be reeling round him, fell down onto the middle of the big table.

A little while elapsed, Gregor was still lying there feebly and all around was quiet, perhaps that was a good omen. Then the doorbell rang. The servant girl was of course locked in her kitchen, and Grete would have to open the door. It was his father. "What's been happening?" were his first words; Grete's face must have told him everything. Grete answered in a muffled voice, apparently hiding her head on his breast: "Mother has been fainting, but she's better now. Gregor's broken loose." "Just what I expected," said his father, "just what I've been telling you, but you women would never listen." It was clear to Gregor that his father had taken the worst interpretation of Grete's all too brief statement and was assuming that Gregor had been guilty of some violent act. Therefore Gregor must now try to propitiate his father, since he had neither time nor means for an explanation. And so he fled to the door of his own room and crouched against it, to let his father see as soon as he came in from the hall that his son had the good intention of getting back into his room immediately and that it was not necessary to drive him there, but that if only the door were opened he would disappear at once.

Yet his father was not in the mood to perceive such fine distinctions. "Ah!" he cried as soon as he appeared, in a tone which sounded at once angry and exultant. Gregor drew his head back from the door and lifted it to look at his father. Truly, this was not the father he had imagined to himself; admittedly he had been too absorbed of late in his new recreation of crawling over the ceiling to take the same interest as before in what was happening elsewhere in the flat, and he ought really to be prepared for some changes. And yet, and yet, could that be his father? The man who used to lie wearily sunk in bed whenever Gregor set out on a business journey; who welcomed him back of an evening lying in a long chair in a dressing gown; who could not really rise to his feet but only lifted his arms in greeting, and on the rare occasions when he did go out with his family on one or two Sundays a year and on high holidays, walked between Gregor and his mother, who were slow walkers anyhow, even more slowly than they did, muffled in his old greatcoat, shuffling laboriously forward with the help of his crook-handled stick which he set down most cautiously at every step and, whenever he wanted to say anything, nearly always came to a full stop and gathered his escort around him? Now he was standing there in fine shape; dressed in a smart blue uniform with gold buttons, such as bank messengers wear; his strong double chin bulged over the stiff high collar of his jacket; from under his bushy eyebrows his black eyes darted fresh and penetrating glances; his onetime tangled white hair had been combed flat on either side of a shining and carefully exact parting. He pitched his cap, which bore a gold monogram, probably the badge of some bank, in a wide sweep across the whole room on to a sofa and with the tail-ends of his jacket thrown back, his hands in his trouser pockets, advanced with a grim visage towards Gregor. Likely enough he did not himself know what he meant to do; at any rate he lifted his feet uncommonly high, and Gregor was dumbfounded at the enormous size of his shoe soles. But Gregor could not risk standing up to him, aware as he had been from the very first day of his new life that his father believed only the severest measures suitable for dealing with him. And so he ran before his father, stopping when he stopped and scuttling forward again when his father made any kind of move. In this way they circled the room several times without anything decisive happening; indeed the whole operation did not even look like a pursuit because it was carried out so slowly. And so Gregor did not leave the floor, for he feared that his father might take as a piece of peculiar wickedness any excursion of his over the walls or the ceiling. All the same, he could not stay this course much longer, for while his father took one step he had to carry out a whole series of movements. He was already beginning to feel breathless, just as in his former life his lungs had not been very dependable. As he was staggering along, trying to concentrate his energy on running, hardly keeping his eyes open; in his dazed state never even thinking of any other escape than simply going forward; and having almost forgotten that the walls were free to him, which in this room were well provided with finely carved pieces of furniture full of knobs and crevices—suddenly something lightly flung landed close behind him and rolled before him. It was an apple; a second apple followed immediately; Gregor came to a stop in alarm; there was no point in running on, for his father was determined to bombard him. He had filled his pockets with fruit from the dish on the sideboard and was now shying apple after apple, without taking particularly good aim for the moment. The small red apples rolled about the floor as if magnetized and cannoned into each other. An apple thrown without much force grazed Gregor's back and glanced off harmlessly But another following immediately landed right on his back arid sank in; Gregor wanted to drag himself forward, as if this startling, incredible pain could be left behind him: but he felt as if nailed to the spot and flattened himself out in a complete derangement of all his senses. With his last conscious look he saw the door of his room being torn open and his mother rushing out ahead of his screaming sister, in her under bodice, for her daughter had loosened her clothing to let her breathe more freely and recover from her swoon, he saw his mother rushing towards his father, leaving one after another behind her on the floor her loosened petticoats, stumbling over her petticoats straight to his *father* and embracing him, in complete union with him, but here Gregor's sight began to fail—with her hands clasped round his father's neck as she begged for her son's life.

III

The serious injury done to Gregor, which disabled him for more than a month—the apple went on sticking in his body as a visible reminder, since no one ventured to remove it—seemed to have made even his father recollect that Gregor was a member of the family, despite his present unfortunate and repulsive shape, and ought not to be treated as an enemy, that, on the contrary, family duty required the suppression of disgust and the exercise of patience, nothing but patience.

And although his injury had impaired, probably forever, his power of movement, and for the time being it took him long, long minutes to creep across his room like an old invalid—there was no question now of crawling up the wall—yet in his own opinion he was sufficiently compensated for this worsening of his condition by the fact that towards evening the living-room door, which he used to watch intently for an hour or two beforehand, was always thrown open, so that lying in the darkness of his room, invisible to the family, he could see them all at the lamp-lit table and listen to their talk, by general consent as it were, very different from his earlier eavesdropping.

True, their intercourse lacked the lively character of former times, which he had always called to mind with a certain wistfulness in the small hotel bedrooms where he had been wont to throw himself down, tired out, on damp bedding. They were now mostly very silent. Soon after supper his father would fall asleep in his armchair; his mother and sister would admonish each other to be silent; his mother, bending low over the lamp, stitched at fine sewing for an underwear firm; his sister, who had taken a job as a salesgirl, was learning shorthand and French in the evenings on the chance of bettering herself. Sometimes his father woke up, and as if quite unaware that he had been sleeping said to his mother: "What a lot of sewing you're doing today!" and at once fell asleep again, while the two women exchanged a tired smile.

With a kind of mulishness his father persisted in keeping his uniform on even in the house; his dressing gown hung uselessly on its peg and he slept fully dressed where he sat, as if he were ready for service at any moment and even here only at the beck and call of his superior. As a result, his uniform, which was not brand-new to start with, began to look dirty, despite all the loving care of the mother and sister to keep it clean, and Gregor often spent whole evenings gazing at the many greasy spots on the garment, gleaming with gold buttons always in a high state of polish, in which the old man sat sleeping in extreme discomfort and yet quite peacefully.

As soon as the clock struck ten his mother tried to rouse his father with gentle words and to persuade him after that to get into bed, for sitting there he could not have a proper sleep and that was what he needed most, since he had to go to duty at six. But with the mulishness that had obsessed him since he became a bank messenger he always insisted on staying longer at the table, although he regularly fell asleep again and in the end only with the greatest trouble could be got out of his armchair and into his bed. However insistently Gregor's mother and sister kept urging him with gentle reminders, he would go on slowly shaking his head for a quarter of an hour, keeping his eyes shut, and refuse to get to his feet. The mother plucked at his sleeve, whispering endearments in his ear, the sister left her lessons to come to her mother's help, but Gregor's father was not to be caught. He would only sink down deeper in his chair. Not until the two women hoisted him up by the armpits did he open his eyes and look at them both, one after the other, usually with the remark: "This is a life. This is the peace and quiet of my old age." And leaning on the two of them he would heave himself up, with difficulty, as if he were a great burden to himself, suffer them to lead him as far as the door and then wave them off and go on alone, while the mother abandoned her needlework and the sister her pen in order to run after him and help him farther.

Who could find time, in this overworked and tired-out family, to bother about Gregor more than was absolutely needful? The household was reduced more and more; the servant girl was turned off; a gigantic bony charwoman with white hair flying round her head came in morning and evening to do the rough work; everything else was done by Gregor's mother, as well as great piles of sewing. Even various family ornaments, which his mother and sister used to wear with pride at parties and celebrations, had to be sold, as Gregor discovered of an evening from hearing them all discuss the prices obtained. But what they lamented most was the fact that they could not leave the flat which was much too big for their present circumstances, because they could not think of any way to shift Gregor. Yet Gregor saw well enough that consideration for him was not the main difficulty preventing the removal, for they could have easily shifted him in some suitable box with a few air holes in it; what really kept them from moving into another flat was rather their own complete hopelessness and the belief that they had been singled out for a misfortune such as had never happened to any of their relations or acquaintances. They fulfilled to the uttermost all that the world demands of poor people, the father fetched breakfast for the small clerks in the bank, the mother devoted her energy to making underwear for strangers, the sister trotted to and fro behind the counter at the behest of customers, but more than this they had not the strength to do. And the wound in Gregor's back began to nag at him afresh when his mother and sister, after getting his father into bed, came back again, left their work lying, drew close to each other and sat cheek by cheek; when his mother, pointing towards his room, said: "Shut that door now, Grete," and he was left again in darkness, while next door the women mingled their tears or perhaps sat dry-eyed staring at the table.

Gregor hardly slept at all by night or by day. He was often haunted by the idea that next time the door opened he would take the family's affairs in hand again just as he used to do; once more, after this long interval, there appeared in his thoughts the figures of the chief and the chief clerk, the commercial travelers and the apprentices, the porter who was so dull-witted, two or three friends in other firms, a chambermaid in one of the rural hotels, a sweet and fleeting memory, a cashier in a milliner's shop, whom he had wooed earnestly but too slowly—they all appeared, together with strangers or people he had quite forgotten, but instead of helping him and his family they were one and all unapproachable and he was glad when they vanished. At other times he would not be in the mood to bother about his family, he was only filled with rage at the way they were neglecting him, and although he had no clear idea of what he might care to eat he would make plans for getting into the larder to take the food that was after all his due, even if he were not hungry. His sister no longer took thought to bring him what might especially please him, but in the morning and at noon before she went to business hurriedly pushed into his room with her foot any food that was available, and in the evening cleared it out again with one sweep of the broom, heedless of whether it had been merely tasted, or—as most frequently happened—left untouched. The cleaning of his room, which she now did always in the evenings, could not have been more hastily done. Streaks of dirt stretched along the walls, here and there lay balls of dust and filth. At first Gregor used to station himself in some particularly filthy corner when his sister arrived, in order to reproach her with it, so to speak. But he could have sat there for weeks without getting her to make any improvements; she could see the dirt as well as he did, but she had simply made up her mind to leave it alone. And yet, with a touchiness that was new to her, which seemed anyhow to have infected the whole family, she jealously guarded her claim to be the sole caretaker of Gregor's room. His mother once subjected his room to a thorough cleaning, which was achieved only by means of several buckets of water—all this dampness of course upset Gregor too and he lay widespread, sulky and motionless on the sofa—but she was well punished for it. Hardly had his sister noticed the changed aspect of his room than she rushed in high dudgeon into the living room and, despite the imploringly raised hands of her mother, burst into a storm of weeping, while her parents—her father had of course been startled out of his chair—looked on at first in helpless amazement; then they too began to go into action; the father reproached the mother on his right for not having left the cleaning of Gregor's room to his sister; shrieked at the sister on his left that never again was she to be allowed to clean Gregor's room; while the mother tried to pull the father into his bedroom, since he was beyond himself with agitation; the sister, shaken with sobs, then beat upon the table with her small fists; and Gregor hissed loudly with rage because not one of them thought of shutting the door to spare him such a spectacle and so much noise.

Still, even if the sister, exhausted by her daily work, had grown tired of looking after Gregor as she did formerly, there was no need for his mother's intervention or for Gregor's being neglected at all. The charwoman was there. This old widow, whose strong bony frame had enabled her to survive the worst a long life could offer, by no means recoiled from Gregor. Without being in the least curious she had once by chance opened the door of his room and at the sight of Gregor, who, taken by surprise, began to rush to and fro although no one was chasing him, merely stood there with her arms folded. From that time she never failed to open his door a little for a moment, morning and evening, to have a look at him. At first she even used to call him to her, with words which apparently she took to be friendly, such as: "Come along, then, you old dung beetle!" or "Look at the old dung beetle, then!" To such allocutions Gregor made no answer, but stayed motionless where he was, as if the door had never been opened. Instead of being allowed to disturb him so senselessly whenever the whim took her, she should rather have been ordered to clean out his room daily, that charwoman! Once, early in the morning—heavy rain was lashing on the windowpanes, perhaps a sign that spring was on the way—Gregor was so exasperated when she began addressing him again that he ran at her, as if to attack her, although slowly and feebly enough. But the charwoman instead of showing fright merely lifted high a chair that happened to be beside the door, and as she stood there with her mouth wide open it was clear that she meant to shut it only when she brought the chair down on Gregor's back. "So you're not coming any nearer?" she asked, as Gregor turned away again, and quietly put the chair back into the corner.

Gregor was now eating hardly anything. Only when he happened to pass the food laid out for him did he take a bit of something in his mouth as a pastime, kept it there for an hour at a time and usually spat it out again. At first he thought it was chagrin over the state of his room that prevented him from eating, yet he soon got used to the various changes in his room. It had become a habit in the family to push into his room things there was no room for elsewhere, and there were plenty of these now, since one of the rooms had been let to three lodgers. These serious gentlemen—all three of them with full beards, as Gregor once observed through a crack in the door—had a passion for order, not only in their own room but, since they were now members of the household, in all its arrangements, especially in the kitchen. Superfluous, not to say dirty, objects they could not bear. Besides, they had brought with them most of the furnishings they needed. For this reason many things could be dispensed with that it was no use trying to sell but that should not be thrown away either. All of them found their way into Gregor's room. The ash can likewise and the kitchen garbage can. Anything that was not needed for the moment was simply flung into Gregor's room by the charwoman, who did everything in a hurry; fortunately Gregor usually saw only the object, whatever it was, and the hand that held it. Perhaps she intended to take the things away again as time and opportunity offered, or to collect them until she could throw them all out in a heap, but in fact they just lay wherever she happened to throw them, except when Gregor pushed his way through the junk heap and shifted it somewhat, at first out of necessity, because he had not room enough to crawl, but later with increasing enjoyment, although after such excursions, being sad and weary to death, he would lie motionless for hours. And since the lodgers often ate their supper at home in the common living room, the living room door stayed shut many an evening, yet Gregor reconciled himself quite easily to the shutting of the door, for often enough on evenings when it was opened he had disregarded it entirely and lain in the darkest corner of his room, quite unnoticed by the family. But on one occasion the charwoman left the door open a little and it stayed ajar even when the labelers came in for supper and the lamp was lit. They set themselves at the top end of the table where formerly Gregor and his father and mother had eaten their meals, unfolded their napkins and took knife and fork in hand. At once his mother appeared in the other doorway with a dish of meat and close behind her his sister with a dish of potatoes piled high. The food steamed with a thick vapor. The lodgers bent over the food set before them as if to scrutinize it before eating, in fact the man in the middle, who seemed to pass for an authority with the other two, cut a piece of meat as it lay on the dish, obviously to discover if it were tender or should be sent back to the kitchen. He showed satisfaction, and Gregor's mother and sister, who had been watching anxiously, breathed freely and began to smile.

The family itself took its meals in the kitchen. Nonetheless, Gregor's father came into the living room before going in to the kitchen and with one prolonged bow, cap in hand, made a round of the table. The lodgers all stood up and murmured something in their beards. When they were alone again they ate their food in almost complete silence. It seemed remarkable to Gregor that among the various noises coming from the table he could always distinguish the sound of their masticating teeth, as if this were a sign to Gregor that one needed teeth in order to eat, and that with toothless jaws even of the finest make one could do nothing. "I'm hungry enough," said Gregor sadly to himself, "but not for that kind of food. How these lodgers are stuffing themselves, and here am I dying of starvation!"

On that very evening—during the whole of his time there Gregor could not remember ever having heard the violin—the sound of violin-playing came from the kitchen. The lodgers had already finished their supper, the one in the middle had brought out a newspaper and given the other two a page apiece, and now they were leaning back at ease reading and smoking. When the violin began to play they pricked up their ears, got to their feet, and went on tiptoe to the hall door where they stood huddled together. Their movements must have been heard in the kitchen, for Gregor's father called out: "Is the violin-playing disturbing you, gentlemen? It can be stopped at once." "On the contrary," said the middle lodger, "could not Fräulein Samsa come and play in this room, beside us, where it is much more convenient and comfortable?" "Oh certainly," cried Gregor's father, as if he were the violin-player. The lodgers came back into the living room and waited. Presently Gregor's father arrived with the music stand, his mother carrying the music and his sister with the violin. His sister quietly made everything ready to start playing; his parents, who had never let rooms before and so had an exaggerated idea of the courtesy due to lodgers, did not venture to sit down on their own chairs; his father leaned against the door, the right hand thrust between two buttons of his livery coat, which was formally buttoned up; but his mother was offered a chair by one of the lodgers and, since she left the chair just where he had happened to put it, sat down in a corner to one side.

Gregor's sister began to play; the father and mother, from either side, intently watched the movements of her hands. Gregor, attracted by the playing, ventured to move forward a little until his head was actually inside the living room. He felt hardly any surprise at his growing lack of consideration for the others; there had been a time when he prided himself on being considerate. And yet just on this occasion he had more reason than ever to hide himself, since owing to the amount of dust which lay thick in his room and rose into the air at the slightest movement, he too was covered with dust; fluff and hair and remnants of food trailed with him, caught on his back and along his sides; his indifference to everything was much too great for him to turn on his back and scrape himself clean on the carpet, as once he had done several times a day. And in spite of his condition, no shame deterred him from advancing a little over the spotless floor of the living room.

To be sure, no one was aware of him. The family was entirely absorbed in the violin-playing; the lodgers, however, who first of all had stationed themselves, hands in pockets, much too close behind the music stand so that they could all have read the music, which must have bothered his sister, had soon retreated to the window, half-whispering with downbeat heads, and stayed there while his father turned an anxious eye on them. Indeed, they were making it more than obvious that they had been disappointed in their expectation of hearing good or enjoyable violin-playing, that they had had more than enough of the performance and only out of courtesy suffered a continued disturbance of their peace. From the way they all kept blowing the smoke of their cigars high in the air through nose and mouth one could divine their irritation. And yet Gregor's sister was playing so beautifully. Her face leaned sideways, intently and sadly her eyes followed the notes of music. Gregor crawled a little farther forward and lowered his head to the ground so that it might be possible for his eyes to meet hers. Was he an animal, that music had such an effect upon him? He felt as if the way were opening before him to the unknown nourishment he craved. He was determined to push forward till he reached his sister, to pull at her skirt and so let her know that she was to come into his room with her violin, for no one here appreciated her playing as he would appreciate it. He would never let her out of his room, at least, not so long as he lived; his frightful appearance would become, for the first time, useful to him; he would watch all the doors of his room at once and spit at intruders; but his sister should need no constraint, she should stay with him of her own free will; she should sit beside him on the sofa, bend down her ear to him and hear him confide that he had had the firm intention of sending her to the Conservatorium, and that, but for his mishap, last Christmas—surely Christmas was long past?—he would have announced it to everybody without allowing a single objection. After this confession his sister would be so touched that she would burst into tears, and Gregor would then raise himself to her shoulder and kiss her on the neck, which, now that she went to business, she kept free of any ribbon or collar.

"Mr. Samsa!" cried the middle lodger, to Gregor's father, and pointed, without wasting any more words, at Gregor, now working himself slowly forwards. The violin fell silent, the middle lodger first smiled to his friends with a shake of the head and then looked at Gregor again. Instead of driving Gregor out, his father seemed to think it more needful to begin by soothing down the lodgers, although they were not at all agitated and apparently found Gregor more entertaining than the violin-playing. He hurried toward them and, spreading out his arms, tried to urge them back into their own room and at the same time to block their view of Gregor. They now began to be really a little angry, one could not tell whether because of the old man's behavior or because it had just dawned on them that all unwittingly they had such a neighbor as Gregor next door. They demanded explanations of his father, they waved their arms like him, tugged uneasily at their beards, and only with reluctance backed towards their room. Meanwhile Gregor's sister, who stood there as if lost when her playing was so abruptly broken off, came to life again, pulled herself together all at once after standing for a while holding violin and bow in nerveless hanging hands and staring at her music, pushed her violin into the lap of her mother, who was still sitting in her chair fighting asthmatically for breath, and ran into the lodgers' room to which they were now being shepherded by her father rather more quickly than before. One could see the pillows and blankets on the beds flying under her accustomed fingers and being laid in order. Before the lodgers had actually reached their room she had finished making the beds and slipped out.

The old man seemed once more to be so possessed by his mulish self-assertiveness that he was forgetting all the respect he should show to his lodgers. He kept driving them on and driving them on until in the very door of the bedroom the middle lodger stamped his foot loudly on the floor and so brought him to a halt. "I beg to announce," said the lodger, lifting one hand and looking also at Gregor's mother and sister, "that because of the disgusting conditions prevailing in this household and family"—here he spat on the floor with emphatic brevity—"I give you notice on the spot. Naturally I won't pay you a penny for the days I have lived here, on the contrary I shall consider bringing an action for damages against you, based on claims—believe me—that will be easily susceptible of proof." He ceased and stared straight in front of him, as if he expected something. In fact his two friends at once rushed into the breach with these words: "And we too give notice on the spot." On that he seized the door-handle and shut the door with a slam.

Gregor's father, groping with his hands, staggered forward and fell into his chair; it looked as if he were stretching himself there for his ordinary evening nap, but the marked jerking's of his head, which was as if uncontrolled, showed that he was far from asleep. Gregor had simply stayed quietly all the time on the spot where the lodgers had espied him. Disappointment at the failure of his plan, perhaps also the weakness arising from extreme hunger, made it impossible for him to move. He feared, with a fair degree of certainty, that at any moment the general tension would discharge itself in a combined attack upon him, and he lay waiting. He did not react even to the noise made by the violin as it fell off his mother's lap from under her trembling fingers and gave out a resonant note.

"My dear parents," said his sister, slapping her hand on the table by way of introduction, "things can't go on like this. Perhaps you don't realize that, but I do. I won't utter my brother's name in the presence of this creature, and so all I say is: we must try to get rid of it. We've tried to look after it and to put up with it as far as is humanly possible, and I don't think anyone could reproach us in the slightest."

"She is more than right," said Gregor's father to himself. His mother, who was still choking for lack of breath, began to cough hollowly into her hand with a wild look in her eyes.

His sister rushed over to her and held her forehead. His father's thoughts seemed to have lost their vagueness at Grete's words, he sat more upright, fingering his service cap that lay among the plates still lying on the table from the lodgers' supper, and from time to time looked at the still form of Gregor.

"We must try to get rid of it," his sister now said explicitly to her father, since her mother was coughing too much to hear a word, "it will be the death of both of you, I can see that coming. When one has to work as hard as we do, all of us, one can't stand this continual torment at home on top of it. At least I can't stand it any longer." And she burst into such a passion of sobbing that her tears dropped on her mother's face, where she wiped them off mechanically.

"My dear," said the old man sympathetically, and with evident understanding, "but what can we do?"

Gregor's sister merely shrugged her shoulders to indicate the feeling of helplessness that had now overmastered her during her weeping fit, in contrast to her former confidence.

"If he could understand us," said her father, half questioningly; Grete, still sobbing, vehemently waved a hand to show how unthinkable that was.

"If he could understand us," repeated the old man, shutting his eyes to consider his daughter's conviction that understanding was impossible, "then perhaps we might come to some agreement with him. But as it is—"

"He must go," cried Gregor's sister. "That's the only solution, Father. You must just try to get rid of the idea that this is Gregor. The fact that we've believed it for so long is the root of all our trouble. But how can it be Gregor? If this were Gregor, he would have realized long ago that human beings can't live with such a creature, and he'd have gone away on his own accord. Then we wouldn't have any brother, but we'd be able to go on living and keep his memory in honor. As it is, this creature persecutes us, drives away our lodgers, obviously wants the whole apartment to himself and would have us all sleep in the gutter. Just look, Father," she shrieked all at once, "he's at it again!" And in an access of panic that was quite incomprehensible to Gregor she even quitted her mother, literally thrusting the chair from her as if she would rather sacrifice her mother than stay so near to Gregor, and rushed behind her father, who also rose up, being simply upset by her agitation, and half-spread his arms out as if to protect her.

Yet Gregor had not the slightest intention of frightening anyone, far less his sister. He had only begun to turn round in order to crawl back to his room, but it was certainly a startling operation to watch, since because of his disabled condition he could not execute the difficult turning movements except by lifting his head and then bracing it against the floor over and over again. He paused and looked round. His good intentions seemed to have been recognized; the alarm had only been momentary. Now they were all watching him in melancholy silence. His mother lay in her chair, her legs stiffly outstretched and pressed together, her eyes almost closing for sheer weariness; his father and his sister were sitting beside each other, his sister's arm around, the old man's neck.

Perhaps I can go on turning round now, thought Gregor, and began his labors again. He could not stop himself from panting with the effort, and had to pause now and then to take breath. Nor did anyone harass him, he was left entirely to himself. When he had completed the turn-round he began at once to crawl straight back. He was amazed at the distance separating him from his room and could not understand how in his weak state he had managed to accomplish the same journey so recently, almost without remarking it. Intent on crawling as fast as possible, he barely noticed that not a single word, not an ejaculation from his family, interfered with his progress. Only when he was already in the doorway did he turn his head round, not completely, for his neck muscles were getting stiff, but enough to see that nothing had changed behind him except that his sister had risen to her feet. His last glance fell on his mother, who was not quite overcome by sleep.

Hardly was he well inside his room when the door was hastily pushed shut, bolted, and locked. The sudden noise in his rear startled him so much that his little legs gave beneath him. It was his sister who had shown such haste. She had been standing ready waiting and had made a light spring forward, Gregor had not even heard her coming, and she cried "At last!" to her parents as she turned the key in the lock.

"And what now?" said Gregor to himself, looking round in the darkness. Soon he made the discovery that he was now unable to stir a limb. This did not surprise him, rather it seemed unnatural that he should ever actually have been able to move on these feeble little legs. Otherwise he felt relatively comfortable. True, his whole body was aching, but it seemed that the pain was gradually growing less and would finally pass away. The rotting apple in his back and the inflamed area around it, all covered with soft dust, already hardly troubled him. He thought of his family with tenderness and love. The decision that he must disappear was one that he held to even more strongly than his sister, if that were possible. In this state of vacant and peaceful meditation he remained until the tower clock struck three in the morning. The first broadening of light in the world outside the window entered his consciousness once more. Then his head sank to the floor of its own accord and from his nostrils came the last faint flicker of his breath.

When the charwoman arrived early in the morning—what between her strength and her impatience she slammed all the doors so loudly, never mind how often she had been begged not to do so, that no one in the whole apartment could enjoy any quiet sleep after her arrival—she noticed nothing unusual as she took her customary peep into Gregor's room. She thought he was lying motionless on purpose, pretending to be in the sulks; she credited him with every kind of intelligence. Since she happened to have the long-handled broom in her hand she tried to tickle him up with it from the doorway. When that too produced no reaction she felt provoked and poked at him a little harder, and only when she had pushed him along the floor without meeting any resistance was her attention aroused. It did not take her long to establish the truth of the matter, and her eyes widened, she let out a whistle, yet did not waste much time over it but tore open the door of the Samsas' bedroom and yelled into the darkness at the top of her voice: "Just look at this, it's dead; it's lying here dead and done for!"

Mr. and Mrs. Samsa started up in their double bed and before they realized the nature of the charwoman's announcement had some difficulty in overcoming the shock of it. But then they got out of bed quickly, one on either side, Mr. Samsa throwing a blanket over his shoulders, Mrs. Samsa in nothing but her nightgown; in this array they entered Gregor's room. Meanwhile the door of the living room opened, too, where Grete had been sleeping since the advent of the lodgers; she was completely dressed as if she had not been to bed, which seemed to be confirmed also by the paleness of her face. "Dead?" said Mrs. Samsa, looking questioningly at the charwoman, although she could have investigated for herself, and the fact was obvious enough without investigation. "I should say so," said the charwoman, proving her words by pushing Gregor's corpse a long way to one side with her broomstick. Mrs. Samsa made a movement as if to stop her, but checked it. "Well," said Mr. Samsa, "now thanks be to God." He crossed himself, and the three women followed his example. Grete, whose eyes never left the corpse, said: "Just see how thin he was. It's such a long time since he's eaten anything. The food came out again just as it went in." Indeed, Gregor's body was completely flat and dry, as could only now be seen when it was no longer supported by the legs and nothing prevented one from looking closely at it.

"Come in beside us, Grete, for a little while," said Mrs. Samsa with a tremulous smile, and Grete, not without looking back at the corpse, followed her parents into their bedroom. The charwoman shut the door and opened the window wide. Although it was so early in the morning a certain softness was perceptible in the fresh air. After all, it was already the end of March.

The three lodgers emerged from their room and were surprised to see no breakfast; they had been forgotten. "Where's our breakfast?" said the middle lodger peevishly to the charwoman. But she put her finger to her lips and hastily, without a word, indicated by gestures that they should go into Gregor's room. They did so and stood, their hands in the pockets of their somewhat shabby coats, around Gregor's corpse in the room where it was now fully, light.

At that the door of the Samsas' bedroom opened and Mr. Samsa appeared in his uniform, his wife on one arm, his daughter on the other. They all looked a little as if they had been crying; from time to time Grete hid her face on her father's arm.

"Leave my house at once!" said Mr. Samsa, and pointed to the door without disengaging himself from the women. "What do you mean by that?" said, the middle lodger, taken somewhat aback, with a feeble smile. The two others put their hands behind them and kept rubbing them together, as if in gleeful expectation of a fine set-to in which they were bound to come off the winners. "I mean just what I say," answered Mr. Samsa, and advanced in a straight line with his two companions towards the lodger. He stood his ground at first quietly, looking at the floor as if his thoughts were taking a new pattern in his head. "Then let us go, by all means," he said, and looked up at Mr. Samsa as if in a sudden access of humility he were expecting some renewed sanction for this decision. Mr. Samsa merely nodded briefly once or twice with meaning eyes. Upon that the lodger really did go with long strides into the hall, his two friends had been listening and had quite stopped rubbing their hands for some moments and now went scuttling after him as if afraid that Mr. Samsa might get into the hall before them and cut them off from their leader. In the hall they all three took their hats from the rack, their sticks from the umbrella stand, bowed in silence and quitted the apartment. With a suspiciousness which proved quite unfounded Mr. Samsa and the two women followed them out to the landing; leaning over the banister they watched the three figures slowly but surely going down the long stairs, vanishing from sight at a certain turn of the staircase on every floor and corning into view again after a moment or so; the more they dwindled, the more the Samsa family's interest in them dwindled, and when a butcher's boy met them and passed them on the stairs coming up proudly with a tray on his head, Mr. Samsa and the two women soon left the landing and as if a burden had been lifted from them went back into their apartment.

They decided to spend this day in resting and going for a stroll; they had not only deserved such a respite from work but absolutely needed it. And so they sat down at the table and wrote three notes of excuse, Mr. Samsa to his board of management, Mrs. Samsa to her employer and Grete to the head of her firm. While they were writing, the charwoman came in to say that she was going now, since her morning's work was finished. At first they only nodded without looking up, but as she kept hovering there they eyed her irritably. "Well?" said Mr. Samsa. The charwoman stood grinning in the doorway as if she had good news to impart to the family but meant not to say a word unless properly questioned. The small ostrich feather standing upright on her hat, which had annoyed Mr. Samsa ever since she was engaged, was waving gaily in all directions. "Well, what is it then?" asked Mrs. Samsa, who obtained more respect from the charwoman than the others. "Oh," said the charwoman, giggling so amiably that she could not at once continue, "just this, you don't need to bother about how to get rid of the thing next door. It's been seen to already." Mrs. Samsa and Grete bent over their letters again, as if preoccupied; Mr. Samsa, who perceived that she was eager to begin describing it all in detail, stopped her with a decisive hand. But since she was not allowed to tell her story, she remembered the great hurry she was in, being obviously deeply huffed: "Bye, everybody," she said, whirling off violently, and departed with a frightful slamming of doors.

"She'll be given notice tonight," said Mr. Samsa, but neither from his wife nor his daughter did he get any answer, for the charwoman seemed to have shattered again the composure they had barely achieved. They rose, went to the window and stayed there, clasping each other tight. Mr. Samsa turned in his chair to look at them and quietly observed them for a little. Then he called out: "Come along, now, do. Let bygones be bygones. And you might have some consideration for me." The two of them complied at once, hastened to him, caressed him and quickly finished their letters.

Then they all three left the apartment together, which was more than they had done for months, and went by tram into the open country outside the town. The tram, in which they were the only passengers, was filled with warm sunshine. Leaning comfortably back in their seats they canvassed their prospects for the future, and it appeared on closer inspection that these were not at all bad, for the jobs they had got, which so far they had never really discussed with each other, were all three admirable and likely to lead to better things later on. The greatest immediate improvement in their condition would of course arise from moving to another house; they wanted to take a smaller and cheaper but also better situated and more easily run apartment than the one they had, which Gregor had selected. While they were thus conversing, it struck both Mr. and Mrs. Samsa, almost at the same moment, as they became aware of their daughter's increasing vivacity, that in spite of all the sorrow of recent times, which had made her cheeks pale, she had bloomed into a pretty girl with a good figure. They grew quieter and half unconsciously exchanged glances of complete agreement, having come to the conclusion that it would soon be time to find a good husband for her. And it was like a confirmation of their new dreams and excellent intentions that at the end of their journey their daughter sprang to her feet first and stretched her young body.

Odour of Chrysanthemums

D.H. Lawrence

I

The small locomotive engine, Number 4, came clanking, stumbling down from Selston with seven full wagons. It appeared round the corner with loud threats of speed, but the colt that it startled from among the gorse, which still flickered indistinctly in the raw afternoon, out-distanced it at a canter. A woman, walking up the railway line to Underwood, drew back into the hedge, held her basket aside, and watched the footplate[1] of the engine advancing. The trucks thumped heavily past, one by one, with slow inevitable movement, as she stood insignificantly trapped between the jolting black wagons and the hedge; then they curved away towards the coppice where the whithered oak leaves dropped noiselessly, while the birds, pulling at the scarlet hips beside the track, made off into the dusk that had already crept into the spinney. In the open, the smoke from the engine sank and cleaved to the rough grass. The fields were dreary and forsaken, and in the marshy strip that led to the whimsey, a reedy pit-pond, the fowls had already abandoned their run among the alders, to roost in the tarred fowl-house. The pit-bank loomed up beyond the pond, flames like red sores licking its ashy sides, in the afternoon's stagnant light. Just beyond rose the tapering chimneys and the clumsy black headstocks of Brinsley Colliery The two wheels were spinning fast up against the sky, and the winding engine

---

1 Platform on early locomotives for the engineer to stand on.

D. H. Lawrence, "Odour of Chrysanthemums," Copyright in the Public Domain.

rapped out its little spasms. The miners were being turned up.

The engine whistled as it came into the wide bay of railway lines beside the colliery, where rows of trucks stood in harbour.

Miners, single, trailing and in groups, passed like shadows diverging home. At the edge of the ribbed level of sidings squat a low cottage, three steps down from the cinder track. A large bony vine clutched at the house, as if to claw down the tiled roof. Round the bricked yard grew a few wintry primroses. Beyond, the long garden sloped down to a bush-covered brook course. There were some twiggy apple trees, winter-crack trees, and ragged cabbages. Beside the path hung dishevelled pink chrysanthemums, like pink cloths hung on bushes. A woman came stooping out of the felt-covered fowl-house, half-way down the garden. She closed and padlocked the door, then drew herself erect, having brushed some bits from her white apron.

She was a tall woman of imperious mien, handsome, with definite black eyebrows. Her smooth black hair was parted exactly. For a few moments she stood steadily watching the miners as they passed along the railway: then she turned towards the brook course. Her face was calm and set, her mouth was closed with disillusionment. After a moment she called:

"John!" There was no answer. She waited, and then said distinctly:

"Where are you?"

"Here!" replied a child's sulky voice from among the bushes. The woman looked piercingly through the dusk.

"Are you at that brook?" she asked sternly.

For answer the child showed himself before the raspberry-canes that rose like whips. He was a small, sturdy boy of five. He stood quite still, defiantly.

"Oh!" said the mother, conciliated. "I thought you were down at that wet brook—and you remember what I told you—"

The boy did not move or answer.

"Come, come on in," she said more gently, "it's getting dark. There's your grandfather's engine coming down the line!"

The lad advanced slowly, with resentful, taciturn movement. He was dressed in trousers and waistcoat of cloth that was too thick and hard for the size of the garments. They were evidently cut down from a man's clothes.

As they went slowly towards the house he tore at the ragged wisps of chrysanthemums and dropped the petals in handfuls among the path.

"Don't do that—it does look nasty," said his mother. He refrained, and she, suddenly pitiful, broke off a twig with three or four wan flowers and held them against her face. When mother and son reached the yard her hand hesitated, and instead of laying the flower aside, she pushed it in her apron-band. The mother and son stood at the foot of the three steps looking across the bay of lines at the passing home of the miners. The trundle of the small train was imminent. Suddenly the engine loomed past the house and came to a stop opposite the gate.

The engine-driver, a short man with round grey beard, leaned out of the cab high above the woman.

"Have you got a cup of tea?" he said in a cheery, hearty fashion.

It was her father. She went in, saying she would mash. Directly, she returned.

"I didn't come to see you on Sunday," began the little grey-bearded man.

"I didn't expect you," said his daughter.

The engine-driver winced; then, reassuming his cheery, airy manner, he said:

"Oh, have you heard then? Well, and what do you think—?"

"I think it is soon enough," she replied.

At her brief censure the little man made an impatient gesture, and said coaxingly, yet with dangerous coldness:

"Well, what's a man to do? It's no sort of life for a man of my years, to sit at my own hearth like a stranger. And if I'm going to marry again it may as well be soon as late—what does it matter to anybody?"

The woman did not reply, but turned and went into the house. The man in the engine-cab stood assertive, till she returned with a cup of tea and a piece of bread and butter on a plate. She went up the steps and stood near the footplate of the hissing engine.

"You needn't 'a' brought me bread an' butter," said her father. "But a cup of tea"—he sipped appreciatively—"it's very nice." He sipped for a moment or two, then: "I hear as Walter's got another bout on," he said.

"When hasn't he?" said the woman bitterly.

"I heerd tell of him in the 'Lord Nelson' braggin' as he was going to spend that b—afore he went: half a sovereign that was."

"When?" asked the woman.

"A' Sat'day night—I know that's true."

"Very likely," she laughed bitterly. "He gives me twenty-three shillings."

"Aye, it's a nice thing, when a man can do nothing with his money but make a beast of himself!" said the grey-whiskered man. The woman turned her head away. Her father swallowed the last of his tea and handed her the cup.

"Aye," he sighed, wiping his mouth. "It's a settler, it is—"

He put his hand on the lever. The little engine strained and groaned, and the train rumbled towards the crossing. The woman again looked across the metals. Darkness was settling over the spaces of the railway and trucks: the miners, in grey sombre groups, were still passing home. The winding engine pulsed hurriedly, with brief pauses. Elizabeth Bates looked at the dreary flow of men, then she went indoors. Her husband did not come.

The kitchen was small and full of firelight; red coals piled glowing up the chimney mouth. All the life of the room seemed in the white, warm hearth and the steel fender reflecting the red fire. The cloth was laid for tea; cups glinted in the shadows. At the back, where the lowest stairs protruded into the room, the boy sat struggling with a knife and a piece of white wood. He was almost hidden in the shadow. It was half-past four. They had but to await the father's coming to begin tea. As the mother watched her son's sullen little struggle with the woods, she saw herself in his silence and pertinacity; she saw the father in her child's indifference to all but himself. She seemed to be occupied by her husband

He had probably gone past his home, slunk past his own door, to drink before he came in, while his dinner spoiled and wasted in waiting. She glanced at the clock, then took the potatoes to strain them in the yard. The garden and fields beyond the brook were closed in uncertain darkness. When she rose with the saucepan, leaving the drain steaming into the night behind her, she saw the yellow lamps were lit along the high road that went up the hill away beyond the space of the railway lines and the field.

Then again she watched the men trooping home, fewer now and fewer.

Indoors the fire was sinking and the room was dark red. The woman put her saucepan on the hob, and set a batter-pudding near the mouth of the oven. Then she stood unmoving. Directly, gratefully, came quick young steps to the door. Someone hung on the latch a moment, then a little girl entered and began pulling off her outdoor things, dragging a mass of curls, just ripening from gold to brown, over her eyes with her hat.

Her mother chid her for coming late from school, and said she would have to keep her at home the dark winter days.

"Why, mother, it's hardly a bit dark yet. The lamp's not lighted, and my father's not home."

"No, he isn't. But it's a quarter to five! Did you see anything of him?"

The child became serious. She looked at her mother with large, wistful blue eyes.

"No, mother, I've never seen him. Why? Has he come up an' gone past, to Old Brinsley? He hasn't, mother, 'cos I never saw him."

"He'd watch that," said the mother bitterly, "he'd take care as you didn't see him. But you may depend upon it, he's seated in the 'Prince o' Wales.' He wouldn't be this late."

The girl looked at her mother piteously.

"Let's have our teas, mother, should we?" said she.

The mother called John to table. She opened the door once more and looked out across the darkness of the lines. All was deserted: she could not hear the winding-engines.

"Perhaps," she said to herself, "he's stopped to get some ripping done."

They sat down to tea. John, at the end of the table near the door, was almost lost in the darkness. Their faces were hidden from each other. The girl crouched against the fender slowly moving a thick piece of bread before the fire. The lad, his face a dusky mark on the shadow, sat watching her who was transfigured in the red glow.

"I do think it's beautiful to look in the fire," said the child.

"Do you?" said her mother. "Why?"

"It's so red, and full of little caves—and it feels so nice, and you can fair smell it."

"It'll want mending directly," replied her mother, "and then if your father comes he'll carry on and say there never is a fire when a man comes home sweating from the pit. A public house is always warm enough."

There was silence till the boy said complainingly: "Make haste, our Annie."

"Well, I am doing! I can't make the fire do it no faster, can I?"

"She keeps wafflin' it about so's to make 'er slow," grumbled the boy.

"Don't have such an evil imagination, child," replied the mother.

Soon the room was busy in the darkness with the crisp sound of crunching. The mother ate very little. She drank her tea determinedly, and sat thinking. When she rose her anger was evident in the stern unbending of her head. She looked at the pudding in the fender and broke out:

"It is a scandalous thing as a man can't even come home to his dinner! If it's crozzled up to a cinder I don't see why I should care. Past his very door he goes to get to a public-house, and here I sit with his dinner waiting for him—"

She went out. As she dropped piece after piece of coal on the red fire, the shadows fell on the walls, till the room was almost in total darkness.

"I carina see," grumbled the invisible John. In spite of herself, the mother laughed.

"You know the way to your mouth," she said. She set the dust-pan outside the door. When she came again like a shadow on the hearth, the lad repeated, complaining sulkily:

"I canna see."

"Good gracious!" cried the mother irritably, "you're as bad as your father if it's a bit dusk!"

Nevertheless, she took a paper spill from a sheaf on the mantelpiece and proceeded to light the lamp that hung from the ceiling in the middle of the room. As she reached up, her figure displayed itself just rounding with maternity.

"Oh, mother—!" exclaimed the girl.

"What?" said the woman, suspended in the act of putting the lamp-glass over the flame. The copper reflector shone handsomely on her, as she stood with uplifted arm, turning to face her daughter.

"You've got a flower in your apron!" said the child, in a little rapture at this unusual event.

"Goodness me!" exclaimed the woman, relieved. "One would think the house was afire." She replaced the glass and waited a moment before turning up the wick. A pale shadow was seen floating vaguely on the floor.

"Let me smell!" said the child, still rapturously, coming forward and putting her face to her mother's waist.

"Go along, silly!" said the mother, turning up the lamp. The light revealed their suspense so that the woman felt it almost unbearable. Annie was still bending at her waist. Irritably, the mother took the flowers out from her apron-band.

"Oh, mother—don't take them out!" Annie cried, catching her hand and trying to replace the sprig.

"Such nonsense!" said the mother, turning away. The child put the pale chrysanthemums to her lips, murmuring:

"Don't they smell beautiful!"

Her mother gave a short laugh.

"No," she said, "not to me. It was chrysanthemums when I married him, and chrysanthemums when you were born, and the first time they ever brought him home drunk, he'd got brown chrysanthemums in his buttonhole."

She looked at the children. Their eyes and their parted lips were wondering. The mother sat rocking in silence for some time. Then she looked at the clock.

"Twenty minutes to six!" In a tone of fine bitter carelessness she continued: "Eh, he'll not come now till they bring him. There he'll stick! But he needn't come rolling in here in his pit-dirt, for I won't wash him. He can lie on the floor—Eh, what a fool I've been, what a fool! And this is what I came here for, to this dirty hole, rats and all, for him to slink past his very door. Twice last week—he's begun now—"

She silenced herself, and rose to clear the table.

While for an hour or more the children played, subduedly intent, fertile of imagination, united in fear of the mother's wrath, and instead of their father's home-coming, Mrs. Bates sat in her rocking-chair making a "singlet" of thick cream-coloured flannel, which gave a dull wounded sound as she tore off the grey edge. She worked at her sewing with energy, listening to the children, and her anger wearied itself, lay down to rest, opening its eyes from time to time and steadily watching, its ears raised to listen. Sometimes even her anger quailed and shrank, and the mother suspended her sewing, tracing the footsteps that thudded along the sleepers outside: she would lift her head sharply to bid the children "hush" but she recovered herself in time, and the footsteps went past the gate, and the children were not flung out of their play-world.

But at last Annie sighed, and gave in. She glanced at her wagon of slippers, and loathed the game. She turned plaintively to her mother.

"Mother!"—but she was inarticulate.

John crept out like a frog from under the sofa. His mother glanced up.

"Yes," she said, "just look at those shirt-sleeves!"

The boy held them out to survey them, saying nothing. Then somebody called in a hoarse voice away down the line, and suspense bristled in the room, till two people had gone by outside, talking.

"It is time for bed," said the mother.

"My father hasn't come," wailed Annie plaintively. But her mother was primed with courage.

"Never mind. They'll bring him when he does come—like a log." She meant there would be no scene. "And he may sleep on the floor till he wakes himself. I know he'll not go to work to-morrow after this!"

The children had their hands and faces wiped with a flannel. They were very quiet. When they had put on their night-dresses, they said their prayers, the boy mumbling. The mother looked down at them, at the brown silken bush of intertwining curls in the nape of the girl's neck, at the little black head of the lad, and her heart burst with anger at their father, who caused all three such distress. The children hid their faces in her skirts for comfort.

When Mrs. Bates came down, the room was strangely empty, with a tension of expectancy. She took up her sewing and stitched for some time without raising her head. Meantime her anger was tinged with fear.

II

The clock struck eight and she rose suddenly, dropping her sewing on her chair. She went to the stair-foot door, opened it, listening. Then she went out, locking the door behind her.

Something scuffled in the yard, and she started, though she knew it was only the rats with which the place was over-run. The night was very dark. In the great bay of railway lines, bulked with trucks, there was no trace of light, only away back she could see a few yellow lamps at the pit-top, and the red smear of the burning pit-bank on the night. She hurried along the edge of the track, then, crossing the converging lines, came to the stile by the white gates, whence she emerged on the road. Then the fear which had led her shrank. People were walking up to New Brinsley; she saw the lights in the houses; twenty yards farther on were the broad windows of the "Prince of Wales," very warm and bright, and the loud voices of men could be heard distinctly.

What a fool she had been to imagine that anything had happened to him! He was merely drinking over there at the "Prince of Wales." She faltered. She had never yet been to fetch him, and she never would go. So she continued her walk towards the long straggling line of houses, standing back on the highway. She entered a passage between the dwellings.

"Mr. Rigley?—Yes! Did you want him? No, he's not in at this minute."

The raw-boned woman leaned forward from her dark scullery and peered at the other, upon whom fell a dim light through the blind of the kitchen window.

"Is it Mrs. Bates?" she asked in a tone tinged with respect.

"Yes. I wondered if your Master was at home. Mine hasn't come yet."

"'Asn't 'e! Oh, Jack's been 'ome an' 'ad 'is dinner an' gone out. 'E's just gone for 'alf an hour afore bed-time. Did you call at the 'Prince of Wales'? "

"No—"

"No, you didn't like—! It's not very nice." The other woman was indulgent. There was an awkward pause. "Jack never said nothink about—about your Master," she said.

"No!—I expect he's stuck in there!"

Elizabeth Bates said this bitterly, and with recklessness. She knew that the woman across the yard was standing at her door listening, but she did not care. As she turned:

"Stop a minute! Ill just go an' ask Jack if 'e knows anythink," said Mrs. Rigley.

"Oh no—I wouldn't like to put—!"

"Yes, I will, if you'll just step inside an' see as th' childer doesn't come downstairs and set theirselves afire."

Elizabeth Bates, murmuring a remonstrance, stepped inside. The other woman apologised for the state of the room.

The kitchen needed apology. There were little frocks and trousers and childish undergarments on the squab and on the floor, and a litter of playthings everywhere. On the black American cloth of the table were pieces of bread and cake, crusts, slops, and a teapot with cold tea.

"Eh, ours is just as bad," said Elizabeth Bates, looking at the woman, not at the house. Mrs. Rigley put a shawl over her head and hurried out, saying:

"I shanna be a minute."

The other sat, noting with faint disapproval the general untidiness of the room. Then she fell to counting the shoes of various sizes scattered over the floor. There were twelve. She sighed and said to herself: "No wonder!"—glancing at the litter. There came the scratching of two pairs of feet on the yard, and the Rigleys entered. Elizabeth Bates rose. Rigley was a big man, with very large bones. His head looked particularly bony. Across his temple was a blue scar, caused by a wound got in the pit, a wound in which the coal-dust remained blue like tattooing.

"'Asna 'e come whoam yit?" asked the man, without any form of greeting, but with deference and sympathy. "I couldna say wheer he is—'e's non ower theer!"—he jerked his head to signify the "Prince of Wales."

"'E's 'appen gone up to th' 'Yew'" said Mrs. Rigley.

There was another pause. Rigley had evidently something to get off his mind:

"Ah left 'im finishin' a stint" he began. "Loose-all 'ad bin gone about ten minutes when we com'n away, an' I shouted: 'Are ter comin', Walt?' an' 'e said: 'Go on, Ah shanna be but a' ef a minnit,' so we com'n ter th' bottom, me an' Bowers, thinkin' as 'e wor just behint, an' 'ud come up i' th' next bantle—"

He stood perplexed, as if answering a charge of deserting his mate. Elizabeth Bates, now again certain of disaster, hastened to reassure him:

"I expect 'e's gone up to th' 'Yew Tree' as you say. It's not the first time. I've fretted myself into a fever before now. He'll come home when they carry him."

"Ay, isn't it too bad!" deplored the other woman.

"I'll just step up to Dick's an' see if 'e is theer," offered the man, afraid of appearing alarmed, afraid of taking liberties.

"Oh, I wouldn't think of bothering you that far," said Elizabeth Bates, with emphasis, but he knew she was glad of his offer.

As they stumbled up the entry, Elizabeth Bates heard Rigley's wife run across the yard and open her neighbour's door. At this, suddenly all the blood in her body seemed to switch away from her heart.

"Mind!" warned Rigley. "Ah've said many a time as Ah'd fill up them ruts in this entry, sumb'dy'll be breakin' their legs yit."

She recovered herself and walked quickly along with the miner.

"I don't like leaving the children in bed, and nobody in the house," she said.

"No, you dunna!" he replied courteously. They were soon at the gate of the cottage.

"Well, I shanna be many minnits. Dunna you be frettin' now, 'ell be all right," said the butty.[2]

"Thank you very much, Mr. Rigley," she replied.

"You're welcome!" he stammered, moving away. "I shanna be many minnits."

The house was quiet. Elizabeth Bates took off her hat and shawl, and rolled back the rug. When she had finished, she sat down. It was a few minutes past nine. She was startled by the rapid chuff of the winding-engine at the pit, and the sharp whirr of the brakes on the rope as it descended. Again she felt the painful sweep of her blood, and she put her hand to her side, saying aloud: "Good gracious!—it's only the nine o'clock deputy going down," rebuking herself.

She sat still listening. Half an hour of this, and she was wearied out.

"What am I working myself up like this for?" she said pitiably to herself, "I's'll only be doing myself some damage."

She took out her sewing again.

At a quarter to ten there were footsteps. One person! She watched for the door to open. It was an elderly woman, in a black bonnet and a black woollen shawl—his mother. She was about sixty years old, pale, with blue eyes, and her face all wrinkled and lamentable. She shut the door and turned to her daughter-in-law peevishly.

"Eh, Lizzie, whatever shall we do, whatever shall we do!" she cried.

Elizabeth drew back a little, sharply.

"What is it, mother?" she said.

The elder woman seated herself on the sofa.

"I don't know, child, I can't tell you!"—she shook her head slowly. Elizabeth sat watching her, anxious and vexed.

"I don't know," replied the grandmother, sighing very deeply. "There's no end to my troubles, there isn't. The things I've gone through, I'm sure it's enough—!" She wept without wiping her eyes, the tears running.

"But, mother," interrupted Elizabeth, "what do you mean? What is it?"

The grandmother slowly wiped her eyes. The fountains of her tears were stopped by Elizabeth's directness. She wiped her eyes slowly.

"Poor child! Eh, you poor thing!" she moaned. "I don't know what we're going to do, I don't—and you as you are—it's a thing, it is indeed!"

Elizabeth waited.

"Is he dead?" she asked, and at the words her heart swung violently, though she felt a slight flush of shame at the ultimate extravagance of the question. Her words sufficiently frightened the old lady, almost brought her to herself.

"Don't say so, Elizabeth! We'll hope it's not as bad as that; no, may the Lord spare us that, Elizabeth. Jack Rigley came just as I was sittin' down to a glass afore going to bed, an' 'e said: "Appen you'll go down th' line, Mrs. Bates. Walt's had an accident. 'Appen you'll go an' sit wi' 'er till we can get him home.' I hadn't time to ask him a word afore he was gone. An' I put my bonnet on an' come straight down, Lizzie. I thought to myself: 'Eh, that poor blessed child, if anybody should come an' tell her of a sudden, there's no knowin' what'll 'appen to 'er.' You mustn't let it upset you, Lizzie—or you know what to expect. How long is it, six months—or is it five, Lizzie? Ay!"—the old woman shook her head—"time slips on, it slips on! Ay!"

Elizabeth's thoughts were busy elsewhere. If he was killed—would she be able to manage on the little pension and what she could earn?—she counted up rapidly. If he was hurt—they wouldn't take him to the hospital—how tiresome he would be to nurse!—but perhaps she'd be able to get him away from the drink and his hateful ways. She would—while he was ill. The tears offered to come to her eyes at the picture. But what sentimental luxury was this she was beginning? She turned to consider the children. At any rate she was absolutely necessary for them. They were her business.

---

2 A fellow workman in a colliery.

"Ay!" repeated the old woman, "it seems but a week or two since he brought me his first wages. Ay—he was a good lad, Elizabeth, he was, in his way. I don't know why he got to be such a trouble, I don't. He was a happy lad at home, only full of spirits. But there's no mistake he's been a handful of trouble, he has! I hope the Lord'll spare him to mend his ways. I hope so, I hope so. You've had a sight o' trouble with him, Elizabeth, you have indeed. But he was a jolly enough lad wi' me, he was, I can assure you. I don't know how it is…"

The old woman continued to muse aloud, a monotonous irritating sound, while Elizabeth thought concentratedly, startled once, when she heard the winding-engine chuff quickly, and the brakes skirr with a shriek. Then she heard the engine more slowly, and the brakes made no sound. The old woman did not notice. Elizabeth waited in suspense. The mother-in-law talked, with lapses into silence.

"But he wasn't your son, Lizzie, an' it makes a difference. Whatever he was, I remember him when he was little, an' I learned to understand him and to make allowances. You've got to make allowances for them—"

It was half-past ten, and the old woman was saying: "But it's trouble from beginning to end; you're never too old for trouble, never too old for that—" when the gate banged back, and there were heavy feet on the steps.

"I'll go, Lizzie, let me go," cried the old woman, rising. But Elizabeth was at the door. It was a man in pit-clothes.

"They're bringin' 'im, Misses," he said. Elizabeth's heart halted a moment. Then it surged on again, almost suffocating her.

"Is he—is it bad?" she asked.

The man turned away, looking at the darkness:

"The doctor says 'e'd been dead hours. 'E saw 'im i' th' lamp-cabin."

The old woman, who stood just behind Elizabeth, dropped into a chair, and folded her hands, crying: "Oh, my boy, my boy!"

"Hush!" said Elizabeth, with a sharp twitch of a frown. "Be still, mother, don't waken th' children: I wouldn't have them down for anything!"

The old woman moaned softly, rocking herself. The man was drawing away. Elizabeth took a step forward.

"How was it?" she asked.

"Well, I couldn't say for sure," the man replied, very ill at ease. "'E wor finishin' a stint an' th' butties 'ad gone, an' a lot o' stuff come down atop 'n 'im."

"And crushed him?" cried the widow, with a shudder.

"No," said the man, "it fell at th' back of 'im, 'E wor under th' face, an' it niver touched 'im. It shut 'im in. It seems 'e wor smothered."

Elizabeth shrank back. She heard the old woman behind her cry:

"What?—what did 'e say it was?"

The man replied, more loudly: "'E wor smothered!"

Then the old woman wailed aloud, and this relieved Elizabeth.

"Oh, mother," she said, putting her hand on the old woman, "don't waken th' children, don't waken th' children."

She wept a little, unknowing, while the old mother rocked herself and moaned. Elizabeth remembered that they were bringing him home, and she must be ready. "They'll lay him in the parlour," she said to herself, standing a moment pale and perplexed.

Then she lighted a candle and went into the tiny room. The air was cold and damp, but she could not make a fire, there was no fireplace. She set down the candle and looked round. The candlelight glittered on the lustre-glasses, on the two vases that held some of the pink chrysanthemums, and on the dark mahogany. There was a cold, deathly smell of chrysanthemums in the room. Elizabeth stood looking at the flowers. She turned away, and calculated whether there would be room to lay him on the floor, between the couch and the chiffonier. She pushed the chairs aside. There would be room to lay him down and to step round him. Then she fetched the old red tablecloth, and another old cloth, spreading them down to save her bit of carpet. She shivered on leaving the parlour; so, from the dresser drawer she took a clean shirt and put it at the fire to air. All the time her mother-in-law was rocking herself in the chair and moaning.

"You'll have to move from there, mother" said Elizabeth. "They'll be bringing him in. Come in the rocker."

The old mother rose mechanically, and seated herself by the fire, continuing to lament. Elizabeth went into the pantry for another candle, and there, in the little pent-house under the naked tiles, she heard them coming. She stood still in the pantry doorway, listening. She heard them pass the end of the house, and come awkwardly down the three steps, a jumble of shuffling footsteps and muttering voices. The old woman was silent. The men were in the yard.

Then Elizabeth heard Matthews, the manager of the pit, say: "You go in first, Jim. Mind!"

The door came open, and the two women saw a collier backing into the room, holding one end of a stretcher, on which they could see the nailed pit-boots of the dead man. The two carriers halted, the man at the head stooping to the lintel of the door.

"Wheer will you have him?" asked the manager, a short, white-bearded man.

Elizabeth roused herself and came from the pantry carrying the unlighted candle.

"In the parlour," she said.

"In there, Jim!" pointed the manager, and the carriers backed round into the tiny room. The coat with which they had covered the body fell off as they awkwardly turned through the two doorways, and the women saw their man, naked to the waist, lying stripped for work. The old woman began to moan in a low voice of horror.

"Lay th' stretcher at th' side," snapped the manager, "an' put 'im on th' cloths. Mind now, mind! Look you now—!"

One of the men had knocked off a vase of chrysanthemums. He stared awkwardly, then they set down the stretcher. Elizabeth did not look at her husband. As soon as she could get in the room, she went and picked up the broken vase and the flowers.

"Wait a minute!" she said.

The three men waited in silence while she mopped up the water with a duster.

"Eh, what a job, what a job, to be sure!" the manager was saying, rubbing his brow with trouble and perplexity. "Never knew such a thing in my life, never! He'd no business to ha' been left. I never knew such a thing in my life! Fell over him clean as a whistle, an' shut him in. Not four foot of space, there wasn't—yet it scarce bruised him."

He looked down at the dead man, lying prone, half naked, all grimed with coal-dust.

"'Sphyxiated" the doctor said. It is the most terrible job I've ever known. Seems as if it was done o' purpose. Clean over him, an' shut 'im in, like a mouse-trap"—he made a sharp, descending gesture with his hand.

The colliers standing by jerked aside their heads in hopeless comment.

The horror of the thing bristled upon them all.

Then they heard the girl's voice upstairs calling shrilly: "Mother, mother—who is it? Mother, who is it?"

Elizabeth hurried to the foot of the stairs and opened the door:

"Go to sleep!" she commended sharply. "What are you shouting about? Go to sleep at once—there's nothing—"

Then she began to mount the stairs. They could hear her on the boards, and on the plaster floor of the little bedroom. They could hear her distinctly:

"What's the matter now?—what's the matter with you, silly thing?"—her voice was much agitated, with an unreal gentleness.

"I thought it was some men come," said the plaintive voice of the child. "Has he come?"

"Yes, they've brought him. There's nothing to make a fuss about. Go to sleep now, like a good child."

They could hear her voice in the bedroom, they waited whilst she covered the children under the bedclothes.

"Is he drunk?" asked the girl, timidly, faintly.

"No! No—he's not! He—he's asleep."

"Is he asleep downstairs?"

"Yes—and don't make a noise."

There was silence for a moment, then the men heard the frightened child again:

"What's that noise?"

"It's nothing, I tell you, what are you bothering for?"

The noise was the grandmother moaning. She was oblivious of everything, sitting on her chair rocking and moaning. The manager put his hand on her arm and bade her "Sh—sh!!"

The old woman opened her eyes and looked at him. She was shocked by this interruption, and seemed to wonder.

"What time is it?" the plaintive thin voice of the child, sinking back unhappily into sleep, asked this last question.

"Ten o'clock," answered the mother more softly. Then she must have bent down and kissed the children.

Matthews beckoned to the men to come away. They put on their caps and took up the stretcher. Stepping over the body, they tiptoed out of the house. None of them spoke till they were far from the wakeful children.

When Elizabeth came down she found her mother alone on the parlour floor, leaning over the dead man, the tears dropping on him.

"We must lay him out," the wife said. She put on the kettle, then returning knelt at the feet, and began to unfasten the knotted leather laces. The room was clammy and dim with only one candle, so that she had to bend her face almost to the floor. At last she got off the heavy boots and put them away.

"You must help me now," she whispered to the old woman. Together they stripped the man.

When they arose, saw him lying in the naive dignity of death, the women stood arrested in fear and respect. For a few moments they remained still, looking down, the old mother whimpering. Elizabeth felt countermanded. She saw him, how utterly inviolable he lay in himself. She had nothing to do with him. She could not accept it. Stooping, she laid her hand on him, in claim. He was still warm, for the mine was hot where he had died. His mother had his face between her hands, and was murmuring incoherently. The old tears fell in succession as drops from wet leaves; the mother was not weeping, merely her tears flowed. Elizabeth embraced the body of her husband, with cheek and lips. She seemed to be listening, inquiring, trying to get some connection. But she could not. She was driven away. He was impregnable.

She rose, went into the kitchen, where she poured warm water into a bowl, brought soap and flannel and a soft towel.

"I must wash him," she said.

Then the old mother rose stiffly, and watched Elizabeth as she carefully washed his face, carefully brushing the big blond moustache from his mouth with the flannel. She was afraid with a bottomless fear, so she ministered to him. The old woman, jealous, said:

"Let me wipe him!"—and she kneeled on the other side drying slowly as Elizabeth washed, her big black bonnet sometimes brushing the dark head of her daughter-in-law. They worked thus in silence for a long time. They never forgot it was death, and the touch of the man's dead body gave them strange emotions, different in each of the women; a great dread possessed them both, the mother felt the lie was given to her womb, she was denied; the wife felt the utter isolation of the human soul, the child within her was a weight apart from her.

At last it was finished. He was a man of handsome body, and his face showed no traces of drink. He was blond, full-fleshed, with fine limbs. But he was dead.

"Bless him," whispered his mother, looking always at his face, and speaking out of sheer terror. "Dear lad—bless him!" She spoke in a faint, sibilant ectasy of fear and mother love,

Elizabeth sank down again to the floor, and put her face against his neck, and trembled and shuddered. But she had to draw away again. He was dead, and her living flesh had no place against his. A great dread and weariness held her: she was so unavailing. Her life was gone like this.

"White as milk he is, clear as a twelve-month baby, bless him, the darling!" the old mother murmured to herself. "Not a mark on him, clear and clean and white, beautiful as ever a child was made," she murmured with pride. Elizabeth kept her face hidden.

"He went peaceful, Lizzie—peaceful as sleep. Isn't he beautiful, the lamb? Ay—he must ha' made his peace, Lizzie. 'Appen he made it all right, Lizzie, shut in there. He'd have time. He wouldn't look like this if he hadn't made his peace. The lamb, the dear lamb. 'Eh, but he had a hearty laugh. I loved to hear it. He had the heartiest laugh, Lizzie, as a lad—"

Elizabeth looked up. The man's mouth was fallen back, slightly open under the cover of the moustache. The eyes, half shut, did not show glazed in the obscurity. Life with its smoky burning gone from him, had left him apart and utterly alien to her. And she knew what a stranger he was to her. In her womb was ice of fear, because of this separate stranger with whom she had been living as one flesh. Was this what it all meant—utter, intact separateness, obscured by heat of living? In dread she turned her face away. The fact was too deadly. There had been nothing between them, and yet they had come together, exchanging their nakedness repeatedly. Each time he had taken her, they had been two isolated beings, far apart as now. He was no more responsible than she. The child was like ice in her womb. For as she looked at the dead man, her mind, cold and detached, said clearly: "Who am I? What have I been doing? I have been fighting a husband who did not exist. He existed all the time. What wrong have I done? What was that I have been living with? There, lies the reality, this man." And her soul died in her for fear: she knew she had never seen him, he had never seen her, they had met in the dark and had fought in the dark, not knowing whom they met nor whom they fought. And now she saw, and turned silent in seeing. For she had been wrong. She had said he was something he was not; she had felt familiar with him. Whereas he was apart all the while, living as she never lived, feeling as she never felt.

In fear and shame she looked at his naked body, that she had known falsely. And he was the father of her children. Her soul was torn from her body and stood apart. She looked at his naked body and was ashamed, as if she had denied it. After all, it was itself. It seemed awful to her. She looked at his face, and she turned her own face to the wall. For his look was other than hers, his way was not her way. She had denied him what he was—she saw it now. She had refused him as himself. And this had been her life, and his life. She was grateful to death, which restored the truth. And she knew she was not dead.

And all the while her heart was bursting with grief and pity for him. What had he suffered? What stretch of horror for this helpless man! She was rigid with agony. She had not been able to help him. He had been cruelly injured, this naked man, this other being, and she could make no reparation. There were the children—but the children belonged to life. This dead man had nothing to do with them. He and she were only channels through which life had flowed to issue in the children. She was a mother—but how awful she knew it now to have been a wife. And he, dead now, how awful he must have felt it to be a husband. She felt that in the next world he would be a stranger to her. If they met there, in the beyond, they would only be ashamed of what had been before. The children had come, for some mysterious reason, out of both of them. But the children did not unite them. Now he was dead, she knew how eternally he was apart from her, how eternally he had nothing more to do with her. She saw this episode of her life closed. They had denied each other in life. Now he had withdrawn. An anguish came over her. It was finished then: it had become hopeless between them long before he died. Yet he had been her husband. But how little!

"Have you got his shirt, 'Lizabeth?"

Elizabeth turned without answering, though she strove to weep and behave as her mother-in-law expected. But she could not, she was silenced. She went into the kitchen and returned with the garment.

"It is aired," she said, grasping the cotton shirt here and there to try. She was almost ashamed to handle him; what right had she or anyone to lay hands on him; but her touch was humble on his body. It was hard work to clothe him. He was so heavy and inert. A terrible dread gripped her all the while: that he could be so heavy and utterly inert, unresponsive, apart. The horror of the distance between them was almost too much for her—it was so infinite a gap she must look across.

At last it was finished. They covered him with a sheet and left him lying, with his face bound. And she fastened the door of the little parlour, lest the children should see what was lying there. Then, with peace sunk heavy on her heart, she went about making tidy the kitchen. She knew she submitted to life, which was her immediate master. But from death, her ultimate master, she winced with fear and shame.

A Rose for Emily

William Faulkner

I

When Miss Emily Grierson died, our whole town went to her funeral: the men through a sort of respectful affection for a fallen monument, the women mostly out of curiosity to see the inside of her house, which no one save an old manservant—a combined gardener and cook—had seen in at least ten years.

It was a big, squarish frame house that had once been white, decorated with cupolas and spires and scrolled balconies in the heavily lightsome style of the seventies, set on what had once been our most select street. But garages and cotton gins had encroached and obliterated even the august names of that neighborhood; only Miss Emily's house was left, lifting its stubborn and coquettish decay above the cotton wagons and the gasoline pumps—an eyesore among eyesores. And now Miss Emily had gone to join the representatives of those august names where they lay in the cedar-bemused cemetery among the ranked and anonymous graves of Union and Confederate soldiers who fell at the battle of Jefferson.

Alive, Miss Emily had been a tradition, a duty, and a care; a sort of hereditary obligation upon the town, dating from that day in 1894 when Colonel Sartoris, the mayor—he who fathered the edict that no Negro woman should appear on the streets without an apron—remitted her taxes, the dispensation dating from the death of her father on into perpetuity. Not that Miss Emily would have accepted charity. Colonel Sartoris invented an involved tale to the effect that Miss Emily's father had loaned money to the town, which the town, as a matter of business, preferred this way of repaying. Only a man of Colonel Sartoris' generation and thought could have invented it, and only a woman could have believed it.

When the next generation, with its more modern ideas, became mayors and aldermen, this arrangement created some little dissatisfaction. On the first

---

William Faulkner, "A Rose for Emily," Copyright © 1930, 1958 by Estate of William Faulkner. Permission to reprint granted by the publisher.

of the year they mailed her a tax notice. February came, and there was no reply. They wrote her a formal letter, asking her to call at the sheriff's office at her convenience. A week later the mayor wrote her himself, offering to call or to send his car for her, and received in reply a note on paper of an archaic shape, in a thin, flowing calligraphy in faded ink, to the effect that she no longer went out at all. The tax notice was also enclosed, without comment.

They called a special meeting of the Board of Aldermen. A deputation waited upon her, knocked at the door through which no visitor had passed since she ceased giving china-painting lessons eight or ten years earlier. They were admitted by the old Negro into a dim hall from which a stairway mounted into still more shadow. It smelled of dust and disuse—a close, dank smell. The Negro led them into the parlor. It was furnished in heavy, leather-covered furniture. When the Negro opened the blinds of one window, they could see that the leather was cracked; and when they sat down, a faint dust rose sluggishly about their thighs, spinning with slow motes in the single sun-ray. On a tarnished gilt easel before the fireplace stood a crayon portrait of Miss Emily's father.

They rose when she entered—a small, fat woman in black, with a thin gold chain descending to her waist and vanishing into her belt, leaning on an ebony cane with a tarnished gold head. Her skeleton was small and spare; perhaps that was why what would have been merely plumpness in another was obesity in her. She looked bloated, like a body long submerged in motionless water, and of that pallid hue. Her eyes, lost in the fatty ridges of her face, looked like two small pieces of coal pressed into a lump of dough as they moved from one face to another while the visitors stated their errand.

She did not ask them to sit. She just stood in the door and listened quietly until the spokesman came to a stumbling halt. Then they could hear the invisible watch ticking at the end of the gold chain.

Her voice was dry and cold. "I have no taxes in Jefferson. Colonel Sartoris explained it to me. Perhaps one of you can gain access to the city records and satisfy yourselves."

"But we have. We are the city authorities, Miss Emily. Didn't you get a notice from the sheriff, signed by him?"

"I received a paper, yes," Miss Emily said. "Perhaps he considers himself the sheriff…I have no taxes in Jefferson."

"But there is nothing on the books to show that, you see. We must go by the—"

"See Colonel Sartoris. I have no taxes in Jefferson."

"But, Miss Emily—"

"See Colonel Sartoris." (Colonel Sartoris had been dead almost ten years.) "I have no taxes in Jefferson. Tobe!" The Negro appeared. "Show these gentlemen out."

II

So she vanquished them, horse and foot, just as she had vanquished their fathers thirty years before about the smell. That was two years after her father's death and a short time after her sweetheart—the one we believed would marry her—had deserted her. After her father's death she went out very little; after her sweetheart went away, people hardly saw her at all. A few of the ladies had the temerity to call, but were not received, and the only sign of life about the place was the Negro man—a young man then—going in and out with a market basket.

"Just as if a man—any man—could keep a kitchen properly," the ladies said; so they were not surprised when the smell developed. It was another link between the gross, teeming world and the high and mighty Griersons.

A neighbor, a woman, complained to the mayor, Judge Stevens, eighty years old.

"But what will you have me do about it, madam?" he said.

"Why, send her word to stop it," the woman said. "Isn't there a law?"

"I'm sure that won't be necessary," Judge Stevens said. "It's probably just a snake or a rat that nigger of hers killed in the yard. I'll speak to him about it."

The next day he received two more complaints, one from a man who came in diffident deprecation. "We really must do something about it, Judge. I'd be the last one in the world to bother Miss Emily, but we've got to do something." That night the Board of Aldermen met—three graybeards and one younger man, a member of the rising generation.

"It's simple enough," he said. "Send her word to have her place cleaned up. Give her a certain time to do it in, and if she don't…"

"Dammit, sir," Judge Stevens said, "will you accuse a lady to her face of smelling bad?"

So the next night, after midnight, four men crossed Miss Emily's lawn and slunk about the house like burglars, sniffing along the base of the brickwork and at the cellar openings while one of them performed a regular sowing motion with his hand out of a sack slung from his shoulder. They broke open the cellar door and sprinkled lime there, and in all the outbuildings. As they recrossed the lawn, a window that had been dark was lighted and Miss Emily sat in it, the light behind her, and her upright torso motionless as that of an idol. They crept quietly across the lawn and into the shadow of the locusts that lined the street. After a week or two the smell went away.

That was when people had begun to feel really sorry for her. People in our town, remembering how old lady Wyatt, her great-aunt, had gone completely crazy at last, believed that the Griersons held themselves a little too high for what they really were. None of the young men were quite good enough for Miss Emily and such. We had long thought of them as a tableau, Miss Emily a slender figure in white in the background, her father a spraddled silhouette in the foreground, his back to her and clutching a horsewhip, the two of them framed by the backflung front door. So when she got to be thirty and was still single, we were not pleased exactly, but vindicated; even with insanity in the family she wouldn't have turned down all of her chances if they had really materialized.

When her father died, it got about that the house was all that was left to her; and in a way, people were glad. At last they could pity Miss Emily. Being left alone, and a pauper, she had become humanized. Now she too would know the old thrill and the old despair of a penny more or less.

The day after his death all the ladies prepared to call at the house and offer condolence and aid, as is our custom. Miss Emily met them at the door, dressed as usual and with no trace of grief on her face. She told them that her father was not dead. She did that for three days, with the ministers calling on her, and the doctors, trying to persuade her to let them dispose of the body. Just as they were about to resort to law and force, she broke down, and they buried her father quickly.

We did not say she was crazy then. We believed she had to do that. We remembered all the young men her father had driven away, and we knew that with nothing left, she would have to cling to that which had robbed her, as people will.

III

She was sick for a long time. When we saw her again, her hair was cut short, making her look like a girl, with a vague resemblance to those angels in colored church windows—sort of tragic and serene.

The town had just let the contracts for paving the sidewalks, and in the summer after her father's death they began the work. The construction company came with niggers and mules and machinery, and a foreman named Homer Barron, a Yankee—a big, dark, ready man, with a big voice and eyes lighter than his face. The little boys would follow in groups to hear him cuss the niggers, and the niggers singing in time to the rise and fall of picks. Pretty soon he knew everybody in town. Whenever you heard a lot of laughing anywhere about the square, Homer Barron would be in the center of the group. Presently, we began to see him and Miss Emily on Sunday afternoons driving in the yellow-wheeled buggy and the matched team of bays from the livery stable.

At first we were glad that Miss Emily would have an interest, because the ladies all said, "Of course a Grierson would not think seriously of a Northerner, a day laborer." But there were still others, older people, who said that even grief could not cause a real lady to forget *noblesse oblige*—without calling it *noblesse oblige*. They just said, "Poor Emily. Her kinsfolk should come to her." She had some kin in Alabama; but years ago her father had fallen out with them over the estate of old lady Wyatt, the crazy woman, and there was no communication between the two families. They had not even been represented at the funeral.

And as soon as the old people said, "Poor Emily," the whispering began. "Do you suppose it's really so?" they said to one another. "Of course it is. What else could…" This behind their hands; rustling of craned silk and satin behind jalousies closed upon the sun of Sunday afternoon as the thin, swift clop-clop-clop of the matched team passed: "Poor Emily."

She carried her head high enough—even when we believed that she was fallen. It was as if she demanded more than ever, the recognition of her dignity as the last Grierson; as if it had wanted that touch of earthiness to reaffirm her imperviousness. Like when she bought the rat poison, the arsenic. That was over a year after they had begun to say "Poor Emily," and while the two female cousins were visiting her.

"I want some poison," she said to the druggist. She was over thirty then, still a slight woman, though thinner than usual, with cold, haughty black eyes in a face the flesh of which was strained across the temples and about the eye-sockets as you imagine a lighthouse-keeper's face ought to look. "I want some poison," she said.

"Yes, Miss Emily. What kind? For rats and such? I'd recom—"

"I want the best you have. I don't care what kind." The druggist named several. "They'll kill anything up to an elephant.

But what you want is—"

"Arsenic," Miss Emily said. "Is that a good one?"

"Is…arsenic? Yes, ma'am. But what you want—"

"I want arsenic."

The druggist looked down at her. She looked back at him, erect, her face like a strained flag. "Why, of course," the druggist said. "If that's what you want. But the law requires you to tell what you are going to use it for."

Miss Emily just stared at him, her head tilted back in order to look him eye for eye, until he looked away and went and got the arsenic and wrapped it up. The Negro delivery boy brought her the package; the druggist didn't come back. When she opened the package at home there was written on the box, under the skull and bones: "For rats."

IV

So the next day we all said, "She will kill herself"; and we said it would be the best thing. When she had first begun to be seen with Homer Barron, we had said, "She will marry him." Then we said, "She will persuade him yet," because Homer himself had remarked—he liked men, and it was known that he drank with the younger men in the Elks' Club—that he was not a marrying man. Later we said, "Poor Emily" behind the jalousies as they passed on Sunday afternoon in the glittering buggy, Miss Emily with her head high and Homer Barron with his hat cocked and a cigar in his teeth, reins and whip in a yellow glove.

Then some of the ladies began to say that it was a disgrace to the town and a bad example to the young people. The men did not want to interfere, but at last the ladies forced the Baptist minister—Miss Emily's people were Episcopal—to call upon her. He would never divulge what happened during that interview, but he refused to go back again. The next Sunday they again drove about the streets, and the following day the minister's wife wrote to Miss Emily's relations in Alabama.

So she had blood-kin under her roof again and we sat back to watch developments. At first nothing happened. Then we were sure that they were to be married. We learned that Miss Emily had been to the jeweler's and ordered a man's toilet set in silver, with the letters H.B. on each piece. Two days later we learned that she had bought a complete outfit of men's clothing, including a nightshirt, and we said, "They are married." We were really glad. We were glad because the two female cousins were even more Grierson than Miss Emily had ever been.

So we were not surprised when Homer Barron—the streets had been finished some time since—was gone. We were a little disappointed that there was not a public blowing-off, but we believed that he had gone on to prepare for Miss Emily's coming, or to give her a chance to get rid of the cousins. (By that time it was a cabal, and we were all Miss Emily's allies to help circumvent the cousins.) Sure enough, after another week they departed. And, as we had expected all along, within three days Homer Barron was back in town. A neighbor saw the Negro man admit him at the kitchen door at dusk one evening.

And that was the last we saw of Homer Barron. And of Miss Emily for some time. The Negro man went in and out with the market basket, but the front door remained closed. Now and then we would see her at the window for a moment, as the men did that night when they sprinkled the lime, but for almost six months she did not appear on the streets. Then we knew that this was to be expected too; as if that quality of her father which had thwarted her woman's life so many times had been too virulent and too furious to die.

When we next saw Miss Emily, she had grown fat and her hair was turning gray. During the next few years it grew grayer and grayer until it attained an even pepper-and-salt iron-gray, when it ceased turning. Up to the day of her death at seventy-four it was still that vigorous iron-gray, like the hair of an active man.

From that time on her front door remained closed, save during a period of six or seven years, when she was about forty, during which she gave lessons in china-painting. She fitted up a studio in one of the downstairs rooms, where the daughters and granddaughters of Colonel Sartoris' contemporaries were sent to her with the same regularity and in the same spirit that they were sent to church on Sundays with a twenty-five-cent piece for the collection plate. Meanwhile her taxes had been remitted.

Then the newer generation became the backbone and the spirit of the town, and the painting pupils grew up and fell away and did not send their children to her with boxes of color and tedious brushes and pictures cut from the ladies' magazines. The front door closed upon the last one and remained closed for good. When the town got free postal delivery, Miss Emily alone refused to let them fasten the metal numbers above her door and attach a mailbox to it. She would not listen to them.

Daily, monthly, yearly we watched the Negro grow grayer and more stooped, going in and out with the market basket. Each December we sent her a tax notice, which would be returned by the post office a week later, unclaimed. Now and then we would see her in one of the downstairs windows—she had evidently shut up the top floor of the house—like the carven torso of an idol in a niche, looking or not looking at us, we could never tell which. Thus she passed from generation to generation—dear, inescapable, impervious, tranquil, and perverse.

And so she died. Fell ill in the house filled with dust and shadows, with only a doddering Negro man to wait on her. We did not even know she was sick; we had long since given up trying to get any information from the Negro. He talked to no one, probably not even to her, for his voice had grown harsh and rusty, as if from disuse.

She died in one of the downstairs rooms, in a heavy walnut bed with a curtain, her gray head propped on a pillow yellow and moldy with age and lack of sunlight.

V

The Negro met the first of the ladies at the front door and let them in, with their hushed, sibilant voices and their quick, curious glances, and then he disappeared. He walked right through the house and out the back and was not seen again.

The two female cousins came at once. They held the funeral on the second day, with the town coming to look at Miss Emily beneath a mass of bought flowers, with the crayon face of her father musing profoundly above the bier and the ladies sibilant and macabre; and the very old men—some in their brushed Confederate uniforms—on the porch and the lawn, talking of Miss Emily as if she had been a contemporary of theirs, believing that they had danced with her and courted her perhaps, confusing time with its mathematical progression, as the old do, to whom all the past is not a diminishing road but, instead, a huge meadow which no winter ever quite touches, divided from them now by the narrow bottleneck of the most recent decade of years.

Already we knew that there was one room in that region above stairs which no one had seen in forty years, and which would have to be forced. They waited until Miss Emily was decently in the ground before they opened it.

The violence of breaking down the door seemed to fill this room with pervading dust. A thin, acrid pall as of the tomb seemed to lie everywhere upon this room decked and furnished as for a bridal: upon the valance curtains of faded rose color, upon the rose-shaded lights, upon the dressing table, upon the delicate array of crystal and the man's toilet things backed with tarnished silver, silver so tarnished that the monogram was obscured. Among them lay a collar and tie, as if they had just been removed, which, lifted, left upon the surface a pale crescent in the dust. Upon a chair hung the suit, carefully folded; beneath it the two mute shoes and the discarded socks.

The man himself lay in the bed.

For a long while we just stood there, looking down at the profound and fleshless grin. The body had apparently once lain in the attitude of an embrace, but now the long sleep that outlasts love, that conquers even the grimace of love, had cuckolded him. What was left of him, rotted beneath what was left of the nightshirt, had become inextricable from the bed in which he lay; and upon him and upon the pillow beside him lay that even coating of the patient and biding dust.

Then we noticed that in the second pillow was the indentation of a head. One of us lifted something from it, and leaning forward, that faint and invisible dust dry and acrid in the nostrils, we saw a long strand of iron-gray hair.

1931

The Dead

James Joyce

Lily, the caretaker's daughter, was literally run off her feet. Hardly had she brought one gentleman into the little pantry behind the office on the ground floor and helped him off with his overcoat than the wheezy hall-door bell clanged again and she had to scamper along the bare hallway to let in another guest. It was well for her she had not to attend to the ladies also. But Miss Kate and Miss Julia had thought of that and had converted the bathroom upstairs into a ladies' dressing-room. Miss Kate and Miss Julia were there, gossiping and laughing and fussing, walking after each other to the head of the stairs, peering down over the banisters and calling down to Lily to ask her who had come.

It was always a great affair, the Misses Morkan's annual dance. Everybody who knew them came to it, members of the family, old friends of the family, the members of Julia's choir, any of Kate's pupils that were grown up enough and even some of Mary Jane's pupils too. Never once had it fallen flat. For years and years it had gone off in splendid style as long as anyone could remember; ever since Kate and

---

James Joyce, "The Dead," from *Dubliners*. Published by Grant Richards Ltd., 1914. Copyright in the Public Domain.

Julia, after the death of their brother Pat, had left the house in Stoney Batter and taken Mary Jane, their only niece, to live with them in the dark gaunt house on Usher's Island, the upper part of which they had rented from Mr Fulham, the corn-factor on the ground floor. That was a good thirty years ago if it was a day. Mary Jane, who was then a little girl in short clothes, was now the main prop of the household for she had the organ in Haddington Road. She had been through the Academy and gave a pupils' concert every year in the upper room of the Antient Concert Rooms. Many of her pupils belonged to better-class families on the Kingstown and Dalkey line. Old as they were, her aunts also did their share. Julia, though she was quite grey, was still the leading soprano in Adam and Eve's, and Kate, being too feeble to go about much, gave music lessons to beginners on the old square piano in the back room. Lily, the caretaker's daughter, did housemaid's work for them. Though their life was modest they believed in eating well; the best of everything: diamond-bone sirloins, three-shilling tea and the best bottled stout. But Lily seldom made a mistake in the orders so that she got on well with her three mistresses. They were fussy, that was all. But the only thing they would not stand was back answers.

Of course they had good reason to be fussy on such a night. And then it was long after ten o'clock and yet there was no sign of Gabriel and his wife. Besides they were dreadfully afraid that Freddy Malins might turn up screwed. They would not wish for worlds that any of Mary Jane's pupils should see him under the influence; and when he was like that it was sometimes very hard to manage him. Freddy Malins always came late but they wondered what could be keeping Gabriel: and that was what brought them every two minutes to the banisters to ask Lily had Gabriel or Freddy come.

—O, Mr Conroy, said Lily to Gabriel when she opened the door for him, Miss Kate and Miss Julia thought you were never coming. Good-night, Mrs Conroy.

—I'll engage they did, said Gabriel, but they forget that my wife here takes three mortal hours to dress herself.

He stood on the mat, scraping the snow from his goloshes, while Lily led his wife to the foot of the stairs and called out:

—Miss Kate, here's Mrs Conroy.

Kate and Julia came toddling down the dark stairs at once. Both of them kissed Gabriel's wife, said she must be perished alive and asked was Gabriel with her.

—Here I am as right as the mail, Aunt Kate! Go on up. I'll follow, called out Gabriel from the dark.

He continued scraping his feet vigorously while the three women went upstairs, laughing, to the ladies' dressing-room. A light fringe of snow lay like a cape on the shoulders of his overcoat and like toecaps on the toes of his goloshes; and, as the buttons of his overcoat slipped with a squeaking noise through the snow-stiffened frieze, a cold fragrant air from out-of-doors escaped from crevices and folds.

—Is it snowing again, Mr Conroy? asked Lily. She had preceded him into the pantry to help him off with his overcoat. Gabriel smiled at the three syllables she had given his surname and glanced at her. She was a slim, growing girl, pale in complexion and with hay-coloured hair. The gas in the pantry made her look still paler. Gabriel had known her when she was a child and used to sit on the lowest step nursing a rag doll.

—Yes, Lily, he answered, and I think we're in for a night of it.

He looked up at the pantry ceiling, which was shaking with the stamping and shuffling of feet on the floor above, listened for a moment to the piano and then glanced at the girl, who was folding his overcoat carefully at the end of a shelf.

—Tell me, Lily, he said in a friendly tone, do you still go to school?

—O no, sir, she answered. I'm done schooling this year and more.

—O, then, said Gabriel gaily, I suppose we'll be going to your wedding one of these fine days with your young man, eh?

The girl glanced back at him over her shoulder and said with great bitterness:

—The men that is now is only all palaver and what they can get out of you.

Gabriel coloured as if he felt he had made a mistake and, without looking at her, kicked off his goloshes and flicked actively with his muffler at his patent-leather shoes.

He was a stout tallish young man. The high colour of his cheeks pushed upwards even to his forehead where it scattered itself in a few formless patches of pale red; and on his hairless face there scintillated restlessly the polished lenses and the bright gilt rims of the glasses which screened his delicate and restless eyes. His glossy black hair was parted in the middle and brushed in a long curve behind his ears where it curled slightly beneath the groove left by his hat.

When he had flicked lustre into his shoes he stood up and pulled his waistcoat down more tightly on his plump body. Then he took a coin rapidly from his pocket.

—O Lily, he said, thrusting it into her hands, it's Christmastime, isn't it? Just…here's a little….

He walked rapidly towards the door.

—O no, sir! cried the girl, following him. Really, sir, I wouldn't take it.

—Christmastime! Christmastime! said Gabriel, almost trotting to the stairs and waving his hand to her in deprecation.

The girl, seeing that he had gained the stairs, called out after him:

—Well, thank you, sir.

He waited outside the drawing-room door until the waltz should finish, listening to the skirts that swept against it and to the shuffling of feet. He was still discomposed by the girl's bitter and sudden retort. It had cast a gloom over him which he tried to dispel by arranging his cuffs and the bows of his tie. Then he took from his waistcoat pocket a little paper and glanced at the headings he had made for his speech. He was undecided about the lines from Robert Browning for he feared they would be above the heads of his hearers. Some quotation that they could recognise from Shakespeare or from the Melodies would be better. The indelicate clacking of the men's heels and the shuffling of their soles reminded him that their grade of culture differed from his. He would only make himself ridiculous by quoting poetry to them which they could not understand. They would think that he was airing his superior education. He would fail with them just as he had failed with the girl in the pantry. He had taken up a wrong tone. His whole speech was a mistake from first to last, an utter failure.

Just then his aunts and his wife came out of the ladies' dressing-room. His aunts were two small plainly dressed old women. Aunt Julia was an inch or so the taller. Her hair, drawn low over the tops of her ears, was grey; and grey also, with darker shadows, was her large flaccid face. Though she was stout in build and stood erect her slow eyes and parted lips gave her the appearance of a woman who did not know where she was or where she was going. Aunt Kate was more vivacious. Her face, healthier than her sister's, was all puckers and creases, like a shrivelled red apple, and her hair, braided in the same old-fashioned way, had not lost its ripe nut colour.

They both kissed Gabriel frankly. He was their favourite nephew, the son of their dead elder sister, Ellen, who had married T. J. Conroy of the Port and Docks.

—Gretta tells me you're not going to take a cab back to Monkstown to-night, Gabriel, said Aunt Kate.

—No, said Gabriel, turning to his wife, we had quite enough of that last year, hadn't we? Don't you remember, Aunt Kate, what a cold Gretta got out of it? Cab windows rattling all the way, and the east wind blowing in after we passed Merrion. Very jolly it was. Gretta caught a dreadful cold.

Aunt Kate frowned severely and nodded her head at every word.

—Quite right, Gabriel, quite right, she said. You can't be too careful.

—But as for Gretta there, said Gabriel, she'd walk home in the snow if she were let.

Mrs Conroy laughed.

—Don't mind him, Aunt Kate, she said. He's really an awful bother, what with green shades for Tom's eyes at night and making him do the dumb-bells, and forcing Eva to eat the stirabout. The poor child! And she simply hates the sight of it!…O, but you'll never guess what he makes me wear now!

She broke out into a peal of laughter and glanced at her husband, whose admiring and happy eyes had been wandering from her dress to her face and hair. The two aunts laughed heartily too, for Gabriel's solicitude was a standing joke with them.

—Goloshes! said Mrs Conroy. That's the latest. Whenever it's wet underfoot I must put on my goloshes. Tonight even he wanted me to put them on, but I wouldn't. The next thing he'll buy me will be a diving suit.

Gabriel laughed nervously and patted his tie reassuringly while Aunt Kate nearly doubled herself, so heartily did she enjoy the joke. The smile soon faded from Aunt Julia's face and her mirthless eyes were directed towards her nephew's face. After a pause she asked:

—And what are goloshes, Gabriel?

—Goloshes, Julia! exclaimed her sister. Goodness me, don't you know what goloshes are? You wear them over your…over your boots, Gretta, isn't it?

—Yes, said Mrs Conroy. Guttapercha things. We both have a pair now. Gabriel says everyone wears them on the continent.

—O, on the continent, murmured Aunt Julia, nodding her head slowly.

Gabriel knitted his brows and said, as if he were slightly angered:

—It's nothing very wonderful but Gretta thinks it very funny because she says the word reminds her of Christy Minstrels.

—But tell me, Gabriel, said Aunt Kate, with brisk tact. Of course, you've seen about the room. Gretta was saying…

—O, the room is all right, replied Gabriel. I've taken one in the Gresham.

—To be sure, said Aunt Kate, by far the best thing to do. And the children, Gretta, you're not anxious about them?

—O, for one night, said Mrs Conroy. Besides, Bessie will look after them.

—To be sure, said Aunt Kate again. What a comfort it is to have a girl like that, one you can depend on! There's that Lily, I'm sure I don't know what has come over her lately. She's not the girl she was at all.

Gabriel was about to ask his aunt some questions on this point but she broke off suddenly to gaze after her sister who had wandered down the stairs and was craning her neck over the banisters.

—Now, I ask you, she said, almost testily, where is Julia going? Julia! Julia! Where are you going?

Julia, who had gone halfway down one flight, came back and announced blandly:

—Here's Freddy.

At the same moment a clapping of hands and a final flourish of the pianist told that the waltz had ended. The drawing-room door was opened from within and some couples came out. Aunt Kate drew Gabriel aside hurriedly and whispered into his ear:

—Slip down, Gabriel, like a good fellow and see if he's all right, and don't let him up if he's screwed. I'm sure he's screwed. I'm sure he is.

Gabriel went to the stairs and listened over the banisters. He could hear two persons talking in the pantry. Then he recognised Freddy Malins' laugh. He went down the stairs noisily.

—It's such a relief, said Aunt Kate to Mrs Conroy, that Gabriel is here. I always feel easier in my mind when he's here…Julia, there's Miss Daly and Miss Power will take some refreshment. Thanks for your beautiful waltz, Miss Daly. It made lovely time.

A tall wizen-faced man, with a stiff grizzled moustache and swarthy skin, who was passing out with his partner said:

—And may we have some refreshment, too, Miss Morkan?

—Julia, said Aunt Kate summarily, and here's Mr Browne and Miss Furlong. Take them in, Julia, with Miss Daly and Miss Power.

—I'm the man for the ladies, said Mr Browne, pursing his lips until his moustache bristled and smiling in all his wrinkles. You know, Miss Morkan, the reason they are so fond of me is—

He did not finish his sentence, but, seeing that Aunt Kate was out of earshot, at once led the three young ladies into the back room. The middle of the room was occupied by two square tables placed end to end, and on these Aunt Julia and the caretaker were straightening and smoothing a large cloth. On the sideboard were arrayed dishes and plates, and glasses and bundles of knives and forks and spoons. The top of the closed square piano served also as a sideboard for viands and sweets. At a smaller sideboard in one corner two young men were standing, drinking hop-bitters.

Mr Browne led his charges thither and invited them all, in jest, to some ladies' punch, hot, strong and sweet. As they said they never took anything strong he opened three bottles of lemonade for them. Then he asked one of the young men to move aside, and, taking hold of the decanter, filled out for himself a goodly measure of whisky. The young men eyed him respectfully while he took a trial sip.

—God help me, he said, smiling, it's the doctor's orders.

His wizened face broke into a broader smile, and the three young ladies laughed in musical echo to his pleasantry, swaying their bodies to and fro, with nervous jerks of their shoulders. The boldest said:

—O, now, Mr Browne, I'm sure the doctor never ordered anything of the kind.

Mr Browne took another sip of his whisky and said, with sidling mimicry:

—Well, you see, I'm like the famous Mrs Cassidy, who is reported to have said: *Now, Mary Grimes, if I don't take it, make me take it, for I feel I want it.*

His hot face had leaned forward a little too confidentially and he had assumed a very low Dublin accent so that the young ladies, with one instinct, received his speech in silence. Miss Furlong, who was one of Mary Jane's pupils, asked Miss Daly what was the name of the pretty waltz she had played; and Mr Browne, seeing that he was ignored, turned promptly to the two young men who were more appreciative.

A red-faced young woman, dressed in pansy, came into the room, excitedly clapping her hands and crying:

—Quadrilles! Quadrilles!

Close on her heels came Aunt Kate, crying:

—Two gentlemen and three ladies, Mary Jane!

—O, here's Mr Bergin and Mr Kerrigan, said Mary Jane. Mr Kerrigan, will you take Miss Power? Miss Furlong, may I get you a partner, Mr Bergin. O, that'll just do now.

—Three ladies, Mary Jane, said Aunt Kate.

The two young gentlemen asked the ladies if they might have the pleasure, and Mary Jane turned to Miss Daly.

—O, Miss Daly, you're really awfully good, after playing for the last two dances, but really we're so short of ladies to-night.

—I don't mind in the least, Miss Morkan.

—But I've a nice partner for you, Mr Bartell D'Arcy, the tenor. I'll get him to sing later on. All Dublin is raving about him.

—Lovely voice, lovely voice! said Aunt Kate.

As the piano had twice begun the prelude to the first figure Mary Jane led her recruits quickly from the room. They had hardly gone when Aunt Julia wandered slowly into the room, looking behind her at something.

—What is the matter, Julia? asked Aunt Kate anxiously. Who is it?

Julia, who was carrying in a column of table-napkins, turned to her sister and said, simply, as if the question had surprised her:

—It's only Freddy, Kate, and Gabriel with him.

In fact right behind her Gabriel could be seen piloting Freddy Malins across the landing. The latter, a young man of about forty, was of Gabriel's size and build, with very round shoulders. His face was fleshy and pallid, touched with colour only at the thick hanging lobes of his ears and at the wide wings of his nose. He had coarse features, a blunt nose, a convex and receding brow, tumid and protruded lips. His heavy-lidded eyes and the disorder of his scanty hair made him look sleepy. He was laughing heartily in a high key at a story which he had been telling Gabriel on the stairs and at the same time rubbing the knuckles of his left fist backwards and forwards into his left eye.

—Good-evening, Freddy, said Aunt Julia.

Freddy Malins bade the Misses Morkan good-evening in what seemed an offhand fashion by reason of the habitual catch in his voice and then, seeing that Mr Browne was grinning at him from the sideboard, crossed the room on rather shaky legs and began to repeat in an undertone the story he had just told to Gabriel.

—He's not so bad, is he? said Aunt Kate to Gabriel.

Gabriel's brows were dark but he raised them quickly and answered:

—O no, hardly noticeable.

—Now, isn't he a terrible fellow! she said. And his poor mother made him take the pledge on New Year's Eve. But come on, Gabriel, into the drawing-room.

Before leaving the room with Gabriel she signalled to Mr Browne by frowning and shaking her forefinger in warning to and fro. Mr Browne nodded in answer and, when she had gone, said to Freddy Malins:

—Now, then, Teddy, I'm going to fill you out a good glass of lemonade just to buck you up.

Freddy Malins, who was nearing the climax of his story, waved the offer aside impatiently but Mr Browne, having first called Freddy Malins' attention to a disarray in his dress, filled out and handed him a full glass of lemonade. Freddy Malins' left hand accepted the glass mechanically, his right hand being engaged in the mechanical readjustment of his dress. Mr Browne, whose face was once more wrinkling with mirth, poured out for himself a glass of whisky while Freddy Malins exploded, before he had well reached the climax of his story, in a kink of high-pitched bronchitic laughter and, setting down his untasted and overflowing glass, began to rub the knuckles of his left fist backwards and forwards into his left eye, repeating words of his last phrase as well as his fit of laughter would allow him.

·　·　·　·　·

Gabriel could not listen while Mary Jane was playing her Academy piece, full of runs and difficult passages, to the hushed drawing-room. He liked music but the piece she was playing had no melody for him and he doubted whether it had any melody for the other listeners, though they had begged Mary Jane to play something. Four young men, who had come from the refreshment-room to stand in the doorway at the sound of the piano, had gone away quietly in couples after a few minutes. The only persons who seemed to follow the music were Mary Jane herself, her hands racing along the key-board or lifted from it at the pauses like those of a priestess in momentary imprecation, and Aunt Kate standing at her elbow to turn the page.

Gabriel's eyes, irritated by the floor, which glittered with beeswax under the heavy chandelier, wandered to the wall above the piano. A picture of the balcony scene in Romeo and Juliet hung there and beside it was a picture of the two murdered princes in the Tower which Aunt Julia had worked in red, blue and brown wools when she was a girl. Probably in the school they had gone to as girls that kind of work had been taught, for one year his mother had worked for him as a birthday present a waistcoat of purple tabinet, with little foxes' heads upon it, lined with brown satin and having round mulberry buttons. It was strange that his mother had had no musical talent though Aunt Kate used to call her the brains carrier of the Morkan family. Both she and Julia had always seemed a little proud of their serious and matronly sister. Her photograph stood before the pierglass. She held an open book on her knees and was pointing out something in it to Constantine who, dressed in a man-o'-war suit, lay at her feet. It was she who had chosen the names for her sons for she was very sensible of the dignity of family life. Thanks to her, Constantine was now senior curate in Balbriggan and, thanks to her, Gabriel himself had taken his degree in the Royal University. A shadow passed over his face as he remembered her sullen opposition to his marriage. Some slighting phrases she had used still rankled in his memory; she had once spoken of Gretta as being country cute and that was not true of Gretta at all. It was Gretta who had nursed her during all her last long illness in their house at Monkstown.

He knew that Mary Jane must be near the end of her piece for she was playing again the opening melody with runs of scales after every bar and while he waited for the end the resentment died down in his heart. The piece ended with a trill of octaves in the treble and a final deep octave in the bass. Great applause greeted Mary Jane as, blushing and rolling up her music nervously, she escaped from the room. The most vigorous clapping came from the four young men in the doorway who had gone away to the refreshment-room at the beginning of the piece but had come back when the piano had stopped.

Lancers were arranged. Gabriel found himself partnered with Miss Ivors. She was a frank-mannered talkative young lady, with a freckled face and prominent brown eyes. She did not wear a low-cut bodice and the large brooch which was fixed in the front of her collar bore on it an Irish device.

When they had taken their places she said abruptly:

—I have a crow to pluck with you.

—With me? said Gabriel.

She nodded her head gravely.

—What is it? asked Gabriel, smiling at her solemn manner.

—Who is G. C.? answered Miss Ivors, turning her eyes upon him.

Gabriel coloured and was about to knit his brows, as if he did not understand, when she said bluntly:

—O, innocent Amy! I have found out that you write for *The Daily Express*. Now, aren't you ashamed of yourself?

—Why should I be ashamed of myself? asked Gabriel, blinking his eyes and trying to smile.

—Well, I'm ashamed of you, said Miss Ivors frankly. To say you'd write for a rag like that. I didn't think you were a West Briton.

A look of perplexity appeared on Gabriel's face. It was true that he wrote a literary column every Wednesday in *The Daily Express*, for which he was paid fifteen shillings. But that did not make him a West Briton surely. The books he received for review were almost more welcome than the paltry cheque. He loved to feel the covers and turn over the pages of newly printed books. Nearly every day when his teaching in the college was ended he used to wander down the quays to the second-hand booksellers, to Hickey's on Bachelor's Walk, to Webb's or Massey's on Aston's Quay, or to O'Clohissey's in the by-street. He did not know how to meet her charge. He wanted to say that literature was above politics. But they were friends of many years' standing and their careers had been parallel, first at the University and then as teachers: he could not risk a grandiose phrase with her. He continued blinking his eyes and trying to smile and murmured lamely that he saw nothing political in writing reviews of books.

When their turn to cross had come he was still perplexed and inattentive. Miss Ivors promptly took his hand in a warm grasp and said in a soft friendly tone:

—Of course, I was only joking. Come, we cross now.

When they were together again she spoke of the University question and Gabriel felt more at ease. A friend of hers had shown her his review of Browning's poems. That was how she had found out the secret: but she liked the review immensely. Then she said suddenly:

—O, Mr Conroy, will you come for an excursion to the Aran Isles this summer? We're going to stay there a whole month. It will be splendid out in the Atlantic. You ought to come. Mr Clancy is coming, and Mr Kilkelly and Kathleen Kearney. It would be splendid for Gretta too if she'd come. She's from Connacht, isn't she?

—Her people are, said Gabriel shortly.

—But you will come, won't you? said Miss Ivors, laying her warm hand eagerly on his arm.

—The fact is, said Gabriel, I have already arranged to go—

—Go where? asked Miss Ivors.

—Well, you know every year I go for a cycling tour with some fellows and so—

—But where? asked Miss Ivors.

—Well, we usually go to France or Belgium or perhaps Germany, said Gabriel awkwardly.

—And why do you go to France and Belgium, said Miss Ivors, instead of visiting your own land?

—Well, said Gabriel, it's partly to keep in touch with the languages and partly for a change.

—And haven't you your own language to keep in touch with—Irish? asked Miss Ivors.

—Well, said Gabriel, if it comes to that, you know, Irish is not my language.

Their neighbours had turned to listen to the cross-examination. Gabriel glanced right and left nervously and tried to keep his good humour under the ordeal which was making a blush invade his forehead.

—And haven't you your own land to visit, continued Miss Ivors, that you know nothing of, your own people, and your own country?

—O, to tell you the truth, retorted Gabriel suddenly, I'm sick of my own country, sick of it!

—Why? asked Miss Ivors.

Gabriel did not answer for his retort had heated him.

—Why? repeated Miss Ivors.

They had to go visiting together and, as he had not answered her, Miss Ivors said warmly:

—Of course, you've no answer.

Gabriel tried to cover his agitation by taking part in the dance with great energy. He avoided her eyes for he had seen a sour expression on her face. But when they met in the long chain he was surprised to feel his hand firmly pressed. She looked at him from under her brows for a moment quizzically until he smiled. Then, just as the chain was about to start again, she stood on tiptoe and whispered into his ear:

—West Briton!

When the lancers were over Gabriel went away to a remote corner of the room where Freddy Malins' mother was sitting. She was a stout feeble old woman with white hair. Her voice had a catch in it like her son's and she stuttered slightly. She had been told that Freddy had come and that he was nearly all right. Gabriel asked her whether she had had a good crossing. She lived with her married daughter in Glasgow and came to Dublin on a visit once a year. She answered placidly that she had had a beautiful crossing and that the captain had been most attentive to her. She spoke also of the beautiful house her daughter kept in Glasgow, and of all the nice friends they had there. While her tongue rambled on Gabriel tried to banish from his mind all memory of the unpleasant incident with Miss Ivors. Of course the girl or woman, or whatever she was, was an enthusiast but there was a time for all things. Perhaps he ought not to have answered her like that. But she had no right to call him a West Briton before people, even in joke. She had tried to make him ridiculous before people, heckling him and staring at him with her rabbit's eyes.

He saw his wife making her way towards him through the waltzing couples. When she reached him she said into his ear:

—Gabriel, Aunt Kate wants to know won't you carve the goose as usual. Miss Daly will carve the ham and I'll do the pudding.

—All right, said Gabriel.

—She's sending in the younger ones first as soon as this waltz is over so that we'll have the table to ourselves.

—Were you dancing? asked Gabriel.

—Of course I was. Didn't you see me? What words had you with Molly Ivors?

—No words. Why? Did she say so?

—Something like that. I'm trying to get that Mr D'Arcy to sing. He's full of conceit, I think.

—There were no words, said Gabriel moodily, only she wanted me to go for a trip to the west of Ireland and I said I wouldn't.

His wife clasped her hands excitedly and gave a little jump.

—O, do go, Gabriel, she cried. I'd love to see Galway again.

—You can go if you like, said Gabriel coldly.

She looked at him for a moment, then turned to Mrs Malins and said:

—There's a nice husband for you, Mrs Malins.

While she was threading her way back across the room Mrs Malins, without adverting to the interruption, went on to tell Gabriel what beautiful places there were in Scotland and beautiful scenery. Her son-in-law brought them every year to the lakes and they used to go fishing. Her son-in-law was a splendid fisher. One day he caught a fish, a beautiful big big fish, and the man in the hotel boiled it for their dinner.

Gabriel hardly heard what she said. Now that supper was coming near he began to think again about his speech and about the quotation. When he saw Freddy Malins coming across the room to visit his mother Gabriel left the chair free for him and retired into the embrasure of the window. The room had already cleared and from the back room came the clatter of plates and knives. Those who still remained in the drawing-room seemed tired of dancing and were conversing quietly in little groups. Gabriel's warm trembling fingers tapped the cold pane of the window. How cool it must be outside! How pleasant it would be to walk out alone, first along by the river and then through the park! The snow would be lying on the branches of the trees and forming a bright cap on the top of the Wellington Monument. How much more pleasant it would be there than at the supper-table!

He ran over the headings of his speech: Irish hospitality, sad memories, the Three Graces, Paris, the quotation from Browning. He repeated to himself a phrase he had written in his review: *One feels that one is listening to a thought-tormented music.* Miss Ivors had praised the review. Was she sincere? Had she really any life of her own behind all her propagandism? There had never been any ill-feeling between them until that night. It unnerved him to think that she would be at the supper-table, looking up at him while he spoke with her critical quizzing eyes. Perhaps she would not be sorry to see him fail in his speech. An idea came into his mind and gave him courage. He would say, alluding to Aunt Kate and Aunt Julia: *Ladies and Gentlemen, the generation which is now on the wane among us may have had its faults but for my part I think it had certain qualities of hospitality, of humour, of humanity, which the new and very serious and hypereducated generation that is growing up around us seems to me to lack.* Very good: that was one for Miss Ivors. What did he care that his aunts were only two ignorant old women?

A murmur in the room attracted his attention. Mr Browne was advancing from the door, gallantly escorting Aunt Julia, who leaned upon his arm, smiling and hanging her head. An irregular musketry of applause escorted her also as far as the piano and then, as Mary Jane seated herself on the stool, and Aunt Julia, no longer smiling, half turned so as to pitch her voice fairly into the room, gradually ceased. Gabriel recognised the prelude. It was that of an old song of Aunt Julia's—*Arrayed for the Bridal*. Her voice, strong and clear in tone, attacked with great spirit the runs which embellish the air and though she sang very rapidly she did not miss even the smallest of the grace notes. To follow the voice, without looking at the singer's face, was to feel and share the excitement of swift and secure flight. Gabriel applauded loudly with all the others at the close of the song and loud applause was borne in from the invisible supper-table. It sounded so genuine that a little colour struggled into Aunt Julia's face as she bent to replace in the music-stand the old leather-bound song-book that had her initials on the cover. Freddy Malins, who had listened with his head perched sideways to hear her better, was still applauding when everyone else had ceased and talking animatedly to his mother who nodded her head gravely and slowly in acquiescence. At last, when he could clap no more, he stood up suddenly and hurried across the room to Aunt Julia whose hand he seized and held in both his hands, shaking it when words failed him or the catch in his voice proved too much for him.

—I was just telling my mother, he said, I never heard you sing so well, never. No, I never heard your voice so good as it is to-night. Now! Would you believe that now? That's the truth. Upon my word and honour that's the truth. I never heard your voice sound so fresh and so…so clear and fresh, never.

Aunt Julia smiled broadly and murmured something about compliments as she released her hand from his grasp. Mr Browne extended his open hand towards her and said to those who were near him in the manner of a showman introducing a prodigy to an audience:

—Miss Julia Morkan, my latest discovery!

He was laughing very heartily at this himself when Freddy Malins turned to him and said:

—Well, Browne, if you're serious you might make a worse discovery. All I can say is I never heard her sing half so well as long as I am coming here. And that's the honest truth.

—Neither did I, said Mr Browne. I think her voice has greatly improved.

Aunt Julia shrugged her shoulders and said with meek pride:

—Thirty years ago I hadn't a bad voice as voices go.

—I often told Julia, said Aunt Kate emphatically, that she was simply thrown away in that choir. But she never would be said by me.

She turned as if to appeal to the good sense of the others against a refractory child while Aunt Julia gazed in front of her, a vague smile of reminiscence playing on her face.

—No, continued Aunt Kate, she wouldn't be said or led by anyone, slaving there in that choir night and day, night and day. Six o'clock on Christmas morning! And all for what?

—Well, isn't it for the honour of God, Aunt Kate? asked Mary Jane, twisting round on the piano-stool and smiling.

Aunt Kate turned fiercely on her niece and said:

—I know all about the honour of God, Mary Jane, but I think it's not at all honourable for the pope to turn out the women out of the choirs that have slaved there all their lives and put little whipper-snappers of boys over their heads. I suppose it is for the good of the Church if the pope does it. But it's not just, Mary Jane, and it's not right.

She had worked herself into a passion and would have continued in defence of her sister for it was a sore subject with her but Mary Jane, seeing that all the dancers had come back, intervened pacifically:

—Now, Aunt Kate, you're giving scandal to Mr Browne who is of the other persuasion.

Aunt Kate turned to Mr Browne, who was grinning at this allusion to his religion, and said hastily:

—O, I don't question the pope's being right. I'm only a stupid old woman and I wouldn't presume to do such a thing. But there's such a thing as common everyday politeness and gratitude. And if I were in Julia's place I'd tell that Father Healy straight up to his face…

—And besides, Aunt Kate, said Mary Jane, we really are all hungry and when we are hungry we are all very quarrelsome.

—And when we are thirsty we are also quarrelsome, added Mr Browne.

—So that we had better go to supper, said Mary Jane, and finish the discussion afterwards.

On the landing outside the drawing-room Gabriel found his wife and Mary Jane trying to persuade Miss Ivors to stay for supper. But Miss Ivors, who had put on her hat and was buttoning her cloak, would not stay. She did not feel in the least hungry and she had already overstayed her time.

—But only for ten minutes, Molly, said Mrs Conroy. That won't delay you.

—To take a pick itself, said Mary Jane, after all your dancing.

—I really couldn't, said Miss Ivors.

—I am afraid you didn't enjoy yourself at all, said Mary Jane hopelessly.

—Ever so much, I assure you, said Miss Ivors, but you really must let me run off now.

—But how can you get home? asked Mrs Conroy.

—O, it's only two steps up the quay.

Gabriel hesitated a moment and said:

—If you will allow me, Miss Ivors, I'll see you home if you really are obliged to go.

But Miss Ivors broke away from them.

—I won't hear of it, she cried. For goodness sake go in to your suppers and don't mind me. I'm quite well able to take care of myself.

—Well, you're the comical girl, Molly, said Mrs Conroy frankly.

—*Beannacht libh*, cried Miss Ivors, with a laugh, as she ran down the staircase.

Mary Jane gazed after her, a moody puzzled expression on her face, while Mrs Conroy leaned over the banisters to listen for the hall-door. Gabriel asked himself was he the cause of her abrupt departure. But she did not seem to be in ill humour: she had gone away laughing. He stared blankly down the staircase.

At that moment Aunt Kate came toddling out of the supper-room, almost wringing her hands in despair.

—Where is Gabriel? she cried. Where on earth is Gabriel? There's everyone waiting in there, stage to let, and nobody to carve the goose!

—Here I am, Aunt Kate! cried Gabriel, with sudden animation, ready to carve a flock of geese, if necessary.

A fat brown goose lay at one end of the table and at the other end, on a bed of creased paper strewn with sprigs of parsley, lay a great ham, stripped of its outer skin and peppered over with crust crumbs, a neat paper frill round its shin and beside this was a round of spiced beef. Between these rival ends ran parallel lines of side-dishes: two little minsters of jelly, red and yellow; a shallow dish full of blocks of blancmange and red jam, a large green leaf-shaped dish with a stalk-shaped handle, on which lay bunches of purple raisins and peeled almonds, a companion dish on which lay a solid rectangle of Smyrna figs, a dish of custard topped with grated nutmeg, a small bowl full of chocolates and sweets wrapped in gold and silver papers and a glass vase in which stood some tall celery stalks. In the centre of the table there stood, as sentries to a fruit-stand which upheld a pyramid of oranges and American apples, two squat old-fashioned decanters of cut glass, one containing port and the other dark sherry. On the closed square piano a pudding in a huge yellow dish lay in waiting and behind it were three squads of bottles of stout and ale and minerals, drawn up according to the colours of their uniforms, the first two black, with brown and red labels, the third and smallest squad white, with transverse green sashes.

Gabriel took his seat boldly at the head of the table and, having looked to the edge of the carver, plunged his fork firmly into the goose. He felt quite at ease now for he was an expert carver and liked nothing better than to find himself at the head of a well-laden table.

—Miss Furlong, what shall I send you? he asked. A wing or a slice of the breast?

—Just a small slice of the breast.

—Miss Higgins, what for you?

—O, anything at all, Mr Conroy.

While Gabriel and Miss Daly exchanged plates of goose and plates of ham and spiced beef Lily went from guest to guest with a dish of hot floury potatoes wrapped in a white napkin. This was Mary Jane's idea and she had also suggested apple sauce for the goose but Aunt Kate had said that plain roast goose without apple sauce had always been good enough for her and she hoped she might never eat worse. Mary Jane waited on her pupils and saw that they got the best slices and Aunt Kate and Aunt Julia opened and carried across from the piano bottles of stout and ale for the gentlemen and bottles of minerals for the ladies. There was a great deal of confusion and laughter and noise, the noise of orders and counter-orders, of knives and forks, of corks and glass-stoppers. Gabriel began to carve second helpings as soon as he had finished the first round without serving himself. Everyone protested loudly so that he compromised by taking a long draught of stout for he had found the carving hot work. Mary Jane settled down quietly to her supper but Aunt Kate and Aunt Julia were still toddling round the table, walking on each other's heels, getting in each other's way and giving each other unheeded orders. Mr Browne begged of them to sit down and eat their suppers and so did Gabriel but they said there was time enough so that, at last, Freddy Malins stood up and, capturing Aunt Kate, plumped her down on her chair amid general laughter.

When everyone had been well served Gabriel said, smiling:

—Now, if anyone wants a little more of what vulgar people call stuffing let him or her speak.

A chorus of voices invited him to begin his own supper and Lily came forward with three potatoes which she had reserved for him.

—Very well, said Gabriel amiably, as he took another preparatory draught, kindly forget my existence, ladies and gentlemen, for a few minutes.

He set to his supper and took no part in the conversation with which the table covered Lily's removal of the plates. The subject of talk was the opera company which was then at the Theatre Royal. Mr Bartell D'Arcy, the tenor, a dark-complexioned young man with a smart moustache, praised very highly the leading contralto of the company but Miss Furlong thought she had a rather vulgar style of production. Freddy Malins said there was a negro chieftain singing in the second part of the Gaiety pantomime who had one of the finest tenor voices he had ever heard.

—Have you heard him? he asked Mr Bartell D'Arcy across the table.

—No, answered Mr Bartell D'Arcy carelessly.

—Because, Freddy Malins explained, now I'd be curious to hear your opinion of him. I think he has a grand voice.

—It takes Teddy to find out the really good things, said Mr Browne familiarly to the table.

—And why couldn't he have a voice too? asked Freddy Malins sharply. Is it because he's only a black?

Nobody answered this question and Mary Jane led the table back to the legitimate opera. One of her pupils had given her a pass for *Mignon*. Of course it was very fine, she said, but it made her think of poor Georgina Burns. Mr Browne could go back farther still, to the old Italian companies that used to come to Dublin—Tietjens, Ilma de Murzka, Campanini, the great Trebelli, Giuglini, Ravelli, Aramburo. Those were the days, he said, when there was something like singing to be heard in Dublin. He told too of how the top gallery of the old Royal used to be packed night after night, of how one night an Italian tenor had sung five encores to *Let Me Like a Soldier Fall*, introducing a high C every time, and of how the gallery boys would sometimes in their enthusiasm unyoke the horses from the carriage of some great prima donna and pull her themselves through the streets to her hotel. Why did they never play the grand old operas now, he asked, *Dinorah, Lucrezia Borgia*? Because they could not get the voices to sing them: that was why.

—O, well, said Mr Bartell D'Arcy, I presume there are as good singers to-day as there were then.

—Where are they? asked Mr Browne defiantly.

—In London, Paris, Milan, said Mr Bartell D'Arcy warmly. I suppose Caruso, for example, is quite as good, if not better than any of the men you have mentioned.

—Maybe so, said Mr Browne. But I may tell you I doubt it strongly.

—O, I'd give anything to hear Caruso sing, said Mary Jane.

—For me, said Aunt Kate, who had been picking a bone, there was only one tenor. To please me, I mean. But I suppose none of you ever heard of him.

—Who was he, Miss Morkan? asked Mr Bartell D'Arcy politely.

—His name, said Aunt Kate, was Parkinson. I heard him when he was in his prime and I think he had then the purest tenor voice that was ever put into a man's throat.

—Strange, said Mr Bartell D'Arcy. I never even heard of him.

—Yes, yes, Miss Morkan is right, said Mr Browne. I remember hearing of old Parkinson but he's too far back for me.

—A beautiful pure sweet mellow English tenor, said Aunt Kate with enthusiasm.

Gabriel having finished, the huge pudding was transferred to the table. The clatter of forks and spoons began again. Gabriel's wife served out spoonfuls of the pudding and passed the plates down the table. Midway down they were held up by Mary Jane, who replenished them with raspberry or orange jelly or with blancmange and jam. The pudding was of Aunt Julia's making and she received praises for it from all quarters. She herself said that it was not quite brown enough.

—Well, I hope, Miss Morkan, said Mr Browne, that I'm brown enough for you because, you know, I'm all brown.

All the gentlemen, except Gabriel, ate some of the pudding out of compliment to Aunt Julia. As Gabriel never ate sweets the celery had been left for him. Freddy Malins also took a stalk of celery and ate it with his pudding. He had been told that celery was a capital thing for the blood and he was just then under doctor's care. Mrs Malins, who had been silent all through the supper, said that her son was going down to Mount Melleray in a week or so. The table then spoke of Mount Melleray, how bracing the air was down there, how hospitable the monks were and how they never asked for a penny-piece from their guests.

—And do you mean to say, asked Mr Browne incredulously, that a chap can go down there and put up there as if it were a hotel and live on the fat of the land and then come away without paying a farthing?

—O, most people give some donation to the monastery when they leave, said Mary Jane.

—I wish we had an institution like that in our Church, said Mr Browne candidly.

He was astonished to hear that the monks never spoke, got up at two in the morning and slept in their coffins. He asked what they did it for.

—That's the rule of the order, said Aunt Kate firmly.

—Yes, but why? asked Mr Browne.

Aunt Kate repeated that it was the rule, that was all. Mr Browne still seemed not to understand. Freddy Malins explained to him, as best he could, that the monks were trying to make up for the sins committed by all the sinners in the outside world. The explanation was not very clear for Mr Browne grinned and said:

—I like that idea very much but wouldn't a comfortable spring bed do them as well as a coffin?

—The coffin, said Mary Jane, is to remind them of their last end.

As the subject had grown lugubrious it was buried in a silence of the table during which Mrs Malins could be heard saying to her neighbour in an indistinct undertone:

—They are very good men, the monks, very pious men.

The raisins and almonds and figs and apples and oranges and chocolates and sweets were now passed about the table and Aunt Julia invited all the guests to have either port or sherry. At first Mr Bartell D'Arcy refused to take either but one of his neighbours nudged him and whispered something to him upon which he allowed his glass to be filled. Gradually as the last glasses were being filled the conversation ceased. A pause followed, broken only by the noise of the wine and by unsettlings of chairs. The Misses Morkan, all three, looked down at the tablecloth. Someone coughed once or twice and then a few gentlemen patted the table gently as a signal for silence. The silence came and Gabriel pushed back his chair and stood up.

The patting at once grew louder in encouragement and then ceased altogether. Gabriel leaned his ten trembling fingers on the tablecloth and smiled nervously at the company. Meeting a row of upturned faces he raised his eyes to the chandelier. The piano was playing a waltz tune and he could hear the skirts sweeping against the drawing-room door. People, perhaps, were standing in the snow on the quay outside, gazing up at the lighted windows and listening to the waltz music. The air was pure there. In the distance lay the park where the trees were weighted with snow. The Wellington Monument wore a gleaming cap of snow that flashed westward over the white field of Fifteen Acres.

He began:

—Ladies and Gentlemen.

—It has fallen to my lot this evening, as in years past, to perform a very pleasing task but a task for which I am afraid my poor powers as a speaker are all too inadequate.

—No, no! said Mr Browne.

—But, however that may be, I can only ask you tonight to take the will for the deed and to lend me your attention for a few moments while I endeavour to express to you in words what my feelings are on this occasion.

—Ladies and Gentlemen. It is not the first time that we have gathered together under this hospitable roof, around this hospitable board. It is not the first time that we have been the recipients—or perhaps, I had better say, the victims—of the hospitality of certain good ladies.

He made a circle in the air with his arm and paused. Everyone laughed or smiled at Aunt Kate and Aunt Julia and Mary Jane who all turned crimson with pleasure. Gabriel went on more boldly:

—I feel more strongly with every recurring year that our country has no tradition which does it so much honour and which it should guard so jealously as that of its hospitality. It is a tradition that is unique as far as my experience goes (and I have visited not a few places abroad) among the modern nations. Some would say, perhaps, that with us it is rather a failing than anything to be boasted of. But granted even that, it is, to my mind, a princely failing, and one that I trust will long be cultivated among us. Of one thing, at least, I am sure. As long as this one roof shelters the good ladies aforesaid—and I wish from my heart it may do so for many and many a long year to come—the tradition of genuine warm-hearted courteous Irish hospitality, which our forefathers have handed down to us and which we in turn must hand down to our descendants, is still alive among us.

A hearty murmur of assent ran round the table. It shot through Gabriel's mind that Miss Ivors was not there and that she had gone away discourteously: and he said with confidence in himself:

—Ladies and Gentlemen.

—A new generation is growing up in our midst, a generation actuated by new ideas and new principles. It is serious and enthusiastic for these new ideas and its enthusiasm, even when it is misdirected, is, I believe, in the main sincere. But we are living in a sceptical and, if I may use the phrase, a thought-tormented age: and sometimes I fear that this new generation, educated or hypereducated as it is, will lack those qualities of humanity, of hospitality, of kindly humour which belonged to an older day. Listening to-night to the names of all those great singers of the past it seemed to me, I must confess, that we were living in a less spacious age. Those days might, without exaggeration, be called spacious days: and if they are gone beyond recall let us hope, at least, that in gatherings such as this we shall still speak of them with pride and affection, still cherish in our hearts the memory of those dead and gone great ones whose fame the world will not willingly let die.

—Hear, hear! said Mr Browne loudly.

—But yet, continued Gabriel, his voice falling into a softer inflection, there are always in gatherings such as this sadder thoughts that will recur to our minds: thoughts of the past, of youth, of changes, of absent faces that we miss here tonight. Our path through life is strewn with many such sad memories: and were we to brood upon them always we could not find the heart to go on bravely with our work among the living. We have all of us living duties and living affections which claim, and rightly claim, our strenuous endeavours.

—Therefore, I will not linger on the past. I will not let any gloomy moralising intrude upon us here to-night. Here we are gathered together for a brief moment from the bustle and rush of our everyday routine. We are met here as friends, in the spirit of good-fellowship, as colleagues, also to a certain extent, in the true spirit of *camaraderie*, and as the guests of—what shall I call them?—the Three Graces of the Dublin musical world.

The table burst into applause and laughter at this sally. Aunt Julia vainly asked each of her neighbours in turn to tell her what Gabriel had said.

—He says we are the Three Graces, Aunt Julia, said Mary Jane.

Aunt Julia did not understand but she looked up, smiling, at Gabriel, who continued in the same vein:

—Ladies and Gentlemen.

—I will not attempt to play to-night the part that Paris played on another occasion. I will not attempt to choose between them. The task would be an invidious one and one beyond my poor powers. For when I view them in turn, whether it be our chief hostess herself, whose good heart, whose too good heart, has become a byword with all who know her, or her sister, who seems to be gifted with perennial youth and whose singing must have been a surprise and a revelation to us all to-night, or, last but not least, when I consider our youngest hostess, talented, cheerful, hard-working and the best of nieces, I confess, Ladies and Gentlemen, that I do not know to which of them I should award the prize.

Gabriel glanced down at his aunts and, seeing the large smile on Aunt Julia's face and the tears which had risen to Aunt Kate's eyes, hastened to his close. He raised his glass of port gallantly, while every member of the company fingered a glass expectantly, and said loudly:

—Let us toast them all three together. Let us drink to their health, wealth, long life, happiness and prosperity and may they long continue to hold the proud and self-won position which they hold in their profession and the position of honour and affection which they hold in our hearts.

All the guests stood up, glass in hand, and, turning towards the three seated ladies, sang in unison, with Mr Browne as leader:

For they are jolly gay fellows,
For they are jolly gay fellows,
For they are jolly gay fellows,
Which nobody can deny.

Aunt Kate was making frank use of her handkerchief and even Aunt Julia seemed moved. Freddy Malins beat time with his pudding-fork and the singers turned towards one another, as if in melodious conference, while they sang, with emphasis:

Unless he tells a lie,
Unless he tells a lie.

Then, turning once more towards their hostesses, they sang:

For they are jolly gay fellows,
For they are jolly gay fellows,
For they are jolly gay fellows,
Which nobody can deny.

The acclamation which followed was taken up beyond the door of the supper-room by many of the other guests and renewed time after time, Freddy Malins acting as officer with his fork on high.

. . . . .

The piercing morning air came into the hall where they were standing so that Aunt Kate said:

—Close the door, somebody. Mrs Malins will get her death of cold.

—Browne is out there, Aunt Kate, said Mary Jane.

—Browne is everywhere, said Aunt Kate, lowering her voice.

Mary Jane laughed at her tone.

—Really, she said archly, he is very attentive.

—He has been laid on here like the gas, said Aunt Kate in the same tone, all during the Christmas.

She laughed herself this time good-humouredly and then added quickly:

—But tell him to come in, Mary Jane, and close the door. I hope to goodness he didn't hear me.

At that moment the hall-door was opened and Mr Browne came in from the doorstep, laughing as if his heart would break. He was dressed in a long green overcoat with mock astrakhan cuffs and collar and wore on his head an oval fur cap. He pointed down the snow-covered quay from where the sound of shrill prolonged whistling was borne in.

—Teddy will have all the cabs in Dublin out, he said. Gabriel advanced from the little pantry behind the office, struggling into his overcoat and, looking round the hall, said:

—Gretta not down yet?

—She's getting on her things, Gabriel, said Aunt Kate.

—Who's playing up there? asked Gabriel.

—Nobody. They're all gone.

—O no, Aunt Kate, said Mary Jane. Bartell D'Arcy and Miss O'Callaghan aren't gone yet.

—Someone is strumming at the piano, anyhow, said Gabriel.

Mary Jane glanced at Gabriel and Mr Browne and said with a shiver:

—It makes me feel cold to look at you two gentlemen muffled up like that. I wouldn't like to face your journey home at this hour.

—I'd like nothing better this minute, said Mr Browne stoutly, than a rattling fine walk in the country or a fast drive with a good spanking goer between the shafts.

—We used to have a very good horse and trap at home, said Aunt Julia sadly.

—The never-to-be-forgotten Johnny, said Mary Jane, laughing.

Aunt Kate and Gabriel laughed too.

—Why, what was wonderful about Johnny? asked Mr Browne.

—The late lamented Patrick Morkan, our grandfather, that is, explained Gabriel, commonly known in his later years as the old gentleman, was a glue-boiler.

—O, now, Gabriel, said Aunt Kate, laughing, he had a starch mill.

—Well, glue or starch, said Gabriel, the old gentleman had a horse by the name of Johnny. And Johnny used to work in the old gentleman's mill, walking round and round in order to drive the mill. That was all very well; but now comes the tragic part about Johnny. One fine day the old gentleman thought he'd like to drive out with the quality to a military review in the park.

—The Lord have mercy on his soul, said Aunt Kate compassionately.

—Amen, said Gabriel. So the old gentleman, as I said, harnessed Johnny and put on his very best tall hat and his very best stock collar and drove out in grand style from his ancestral mansion somewhere near Back Lane, I think.

Everyone laughed, even Mrs Malins, at Gabriel's manner and Aunt Kate said:

—O now, Gabriel, he didn't live in Back Lane, really. Only the mill was there.

—Out from the mansion of his forefathers, continued Gabriel, he drove with Johnny. And everything went on beautifully until Johnny came in sight of King Billy's statue: and whether he fell in love with the horse King Billy sits on or whether he thought he was back again in the mill, anyhow he began to walk round the statue.

Gabriel paced in a circle round the hall in his goloshes amid the laughter of the others.

—Round and round he went, said Gabriel, and the old gentleman, who was a very pompous old gentleman, was highly indignant. *Go on, sir! What do you mean, sir? Johnny! Johnny! Most extraordinary conduct! Can't understand the horse!*

The peals of laughter which followed Gabriel's imitation of the incident were interrupted by a resounding knock at the hall-door. Mary Jane ran to open it and let in Freddy Malins. Freddy Malins, with his hat well back on his head and his shoulders humped with cold, was puffing and steaming after his exertions.

—I could only get one cab, he said.

—O, we'll find another along the quay, said Gabriel.

—Yes, said Aunt Kate. Better not keep Mrs Malins standing in the draught.

Mrs Malins was helped down the front steps by her son and Mr Browne and, after many manœuvres, hoisted into the cab. Freddy Malins clambered in after her and spent a long time settling her on the seat, Mr Browne helping him with advice. At last she was settled comfortably and Freddy Malins invited Mr Browne into the cab. There was a good deal of confused talk, and then Mr Browne got into the cab. The cabman settled his rug over his knees, and bent down for the address. The confusion grew greater and the cabman was directed differently by Freddy Malins and Mr Browne, each of whom had his head out through a window of the cab. The difficulty was to know where to drop Mr Browne along the route and Aunt Kate, Aunt Julia and Mary Jane helped the discussion from the doorstep with cross-directions and contradictions and abundance of laughter. As for Freddy Malins he was speechless with laughter. He popped his head in and out of the window every moment, to the great danger of his hat, and told his mother how the discussion was progressing till at last Mr Browne shouted to the bewildered cabman above the din of everybody's laughter:

—Do you know Trinity College?

—Yes, sir, said the cabman.

—Well, drive bang up against Trinity College gates, said Mr Browne, and then we'll tell you where to go. You understand now?

—Yes, sir, said the cabman.

—Make like a bird for Trinity College.

—Right, sir, cried the cabman.

The horse was whipped up and the cab rattled off along the quay amid a chorus of laughter and adieus.

Gabriel had not gone to the door with the others. He was in a dark part of the hall gazing up the staircase. A woman was standing near the top of the first flight, in the shadow also. He could not see her face but he could see the terracotta and salmonpink panels of her skirt which the shadow made appear black and white. It was his wife. She was leaning on the banisters, listening to something. Gabriel was surprised at her stillness and strained his ear to listen also. But he could hear little save the noise of laughter and dispute on the front steps, a few chords struck on the piano and a few notes of a man's voice singing.

He stood still in the gloom of the hall, trying to catch the air that the voice was singing and gazing up at his wife. There was grace and mystery in her attitude as if she were a symbol of something. He asked himself what is a woman standing on the stairs in the shadow, listening to distant music, a symbol of. If he were a painter he would paint her in that attitude. Her blue felt hat would show off the bronze of her hair against the darkness and the dark panels of her skirt would show off the light ones. Distant Music he would call the picture if he were a painter.

The hall-door was closed; and Aunt Kate, Aunt Julia and Mary Jane came down the hall, still laughing.

—Well, isn't Freddy terrible? said Mary Jane. He's really terrible.

Gabriel said nothing but pointed up the stairs towards where his wife was standing. Now that the hall-door was closed the voice and the piano could be heard more clearly. Gabriel held up his hand for them to be silent. The song seemed to be in the old Irish tonality and the singer seemed uncertain both of his words and of his voice. The voice, made plaintive by distance and by the singer's hoarseness, faintly illuminated the cadence of the air with words expressing grief:

*O, the rain falls on my heavy locks
And the dew wets my skin,
My babe lies cold…*

—O, exclaimed Mary Jane. It's Bartell D'Arcy singing and he wouldn't sing all the night. O, I'll get him to sing a song before he goes.

—O do, Mary Jane, said Aunt Kate.

Mary Jane brushed past the others and ran to the staircase but before she reached it the singing stopped and the piano was closed abruptly.

—O, what a pity! she cried. Is he coming down, Gretta? Gabriel heard his wife answer yes and saw her come down towards them. A few steps behind her were Mr Bartell D'Arcy and Miss O'Callaghan.

—O, Mr D'Arcy, cried Mary Jane, it's downright mean of you to break off like that when we were all in raptures listening to you.

—I have been at him all the evening, said Miss O'Callaghan, and Mrs Conroy too and he told us he had a dreadful cold and couldn't sing.

—O, Mr D'Arcy, said Aunt Kate, now that was a great fib to tell.

—Can't you see that I'm as hoarse as a crow? said Mr D'Arcy roughly.

He went into the pantry hastily and put on his overcoat. The others, taken aback by his rude speech, could find nothing to say. Aunt Kate wrinkled her brows and made signs to the others to drop the subject. Mr D'Arcy stood swathing his neck carefully and frowning.

—It's the weather, said Aunt Julia, after a pause.

—Yes, everybody has colds, said Aunt Kate readily, everybody.

—They say, said Mary Jane, we haven't had snow like it for thirty years; and I read this morning in the newspapers that the snow is general all over Ireland.

—I love the look of snow, said Aunt Julia sadly.

—So do I, said Miss O'Callaghan. I think Christmas is never really Christmas unless we have the snow on the ground.

—But poor Mr D'Arcy doesn't like the snow, said Aunt Kate, smiling.

Mr D'Arcy came from the pantry, fully swathed and buttoned, and in a repentant tone told them the history of his cold. Everyone gave him advice and said it was a great pity and urged him to be very careful of his throat in the night air. Gabriel watched his wife who did not join in the conversation. She was standing right under the dusty fanlight and the flame of the gas lit up the rich bronze of her hair which he had seen her drying at the fire a few days before. She was in the same attitude and seemed unaware of the talk about her. At last she turned towards them and Gabriel saw that there was colour on her cheeks and that her eyes were shining. A sudden tide of joy went leaping out of his heart.

—Mr D'Arcy, she said, what is the name of that song you were singing?

—It's called *The Lass of Aughrim*, said Mr D'Arcy, but I couldn't remember it properly. Why? Do you know it?

—*The Lass of Aughrim*, she repeated. I couldn't think of the name.

—It's a very nice air, said Mary Jane. I'm sorry you were not in voice to-night.

—Now, Mary Jane, said Aunt Kate, don't annoy Mr D'Arcy. I won't have him annoyed.

Seeing that all were ready to start she shepherded them to the door where good-night was said:

—Well, good-night, Aunt Kate, and thanks for the pleasant evening.

—Good-night, Gabriel. Good-night, Gretta!

—Good-night, Aunt Kate, and thanks ever so much. Good-night, Aunt Julia.

—O, good-night, Gretta, I didn't see you.

—Good-night, Mr D'Arcy. Good-night, Miss O'Callaghan.

—Good-night, Miss Morkan.

—Good-night, again.

—Good-night, all. Safe home.

—Good-night. Good-night.

The morning was still dark. A dull yellow light brooded over the houses and the river; and the sky seemed to be descending. It was slushy underfoot; and only streaks and patches of snow lay on the roofs, on the parapets of the quay and on the area railings. The lamps were still burning redly in the murky air and, across the river, the palace of the Four Courts stood out menacingly against the heavy sky.

She was walking on before him with Mr Bartell D'Arcy, her shoes in a brown parcel tucked under one arm and her hands holding her skirt up from the slush. She had no longer any grace of attitude but Gabriel's eyes were still bright with happiness. The blood went bounding along his veins; and the thoughts went rioting through his brain, proud, joyful, tender, valorous.

She was walking on before him so lightly and so erect that he longed to run after her noiselessly, catch her by the shoulders and say something foolish and affectionate into her ear. She seemed to him so frail that he longed to defend her against something and then to be alone with her. Moments of their secret life together burst like stars upon his memory. A heliotrope envelope was lying beside his breakfast-cup and he was caressing it with his hand. Birds were twittering in the ivy and the sunny web of the curtain was shimmering along the floor: he could not eat for happiness. They were standing on the crowded platform and he was placing a ticket inside the warm palm of her glove. He was standing with her in the cold, looking in through a grated window at a man making bottles in a roaring furnace. It was very cold. Her face, fragrant in the cold air, was quite close to his; and suddenly she called out to the man at the furnace:

—Is the fire hot, sir?

But the man could not hear her with the noise of the furnace. It was just as well. He might have answered rudely.

A wave of yet more tender joy escaped from his heart and went coursing in warm flood along his arteries. Like the tender fires of stars moments of their life together, that no one knew of or would ever know of, broke upon and illumined his memory. He longed to recall to her those moments, to make her forget the years of their dull existence together and remember only their moments of ecstasy. For the years, he felt, had not quenched his soul or hers. Their children, his writing, her household cares had not quenched all their souls' tender fire. In one letter that he had written to her then he had said: *Why is it that words like these seem to me so dull and cold? Is it because there is no word tender enough to be your name?*

Like distant music these words that he had written years before were borne towards him from the past. He longed to be alone with her. When the others had gone away, when he and she were in their room in the hotel, then they would be alone together. He would call her softly:

—Gretta!

Perhaps she would not hear at once: she would be undressing. Then something in his voice would strike her. She would turn and look at him...

At the corner of Winetavern Street they met a cab. He was glad of its rattling noise as it saved him from conversation. She was looking out of the window and seemed tired. The others spoke only a few words, pointing out some building or street. The horse galloped along wearily under the murky morning sky, dragging his old rattling box after his heels, and Gabriel was again in a cab with her, galloping to catch the boat, galloping to their honeymoon.

As the cab drove across O'Connell Bridge Miss O'Callaghan said:

—They say you never cross O'Connell Bridge without seeing a white horse.

—I see a white man this time, said Gabriel.

Where? asked Mr Bartell D'Arcy.

Gabriel pointed to the statue, on which lay patches of snow. Then he nodded familiarly to it and waved his hand.

—Good-night, Dan, he said gaily.

When the cab drew up before the hotel Gabriel jumped out and, in spite of Mr Bartell D'Arcy's protest, paid the driver. He gave the man a shilling over his fare. The man saluted and said:

—A prosperous New Year to you, sir.

—The same to you, said Gabriel cordially.

She leaned for a moment on his arm in getting out of the cab and while standing at the curbstone, bidding the others good-night. She leaned lightly on his arm, as lightly as when she had danced with him a few hours before. He had felt proud and happy then, happy that she was his, proud of her grace and wifely carriage. But now, after the kindling again of so many memories, the first touch of her body, musical and strange and perfumed, sent through him a keen pang of lust. Under cover of her silence he pressed her arm closely to his side; and, as they stood at the hotel door, he felt that they had escaped from their lives and duties, escaped from home and friends and run away together with wild and radiant hearts to a new adventure.

An old man was dozing in a great hooded chair in the hall. He lit a candle in the office and went before them to the stairs. They followed him in silence, their feet falling in soft thuds on the thickly carpeted stairs. She mounted the stairs behind the porter, her head bowed in the ascent, her frail shoulders curved as with a burden, her skirt girt tightly about her. He could have flung his arms about her hips and held her still for his arms were trembling with desire to seize her and only the stress of his nails against the palms of his hands held the wild impulse of his body in check. The porter halted on the stairs to settle his guttering candle. They halted too on the steps below him. In the silence Gabriel could hear the falling of the molten wax into the tray and the thumping of his own heart against his ribs.

The porter led them along a corridor and opened a door. Then he set his unstable candle down on a toilet-table and asked at what hour they were to be called in the morning.

—Eight, said Gabriel.

The porter pointed to the tap of the electric-light and began a muttered apology but Gabriel cut him short.

—We don't want any light. We have light enough from the street. And I say, he added, pointing to the candle, you might remove that handsome article, like a good man.

The porter took up his candle again, but slowly for he was surprised by such a novel idea. Then he mumbled good-night and went out. Gabriel shot the lock to.

A ghostly light from the street lamp lay in a long shaft from one window to the door. Gabriel threw his overcoat and hat on a couch and crossed the room towards the window. He looked down into the street in order that his emotion might calm a little. Then he turned and leaned against a chest of drawers with his back to the light. She had taken off her hat and cloak and was standing before a large swinging mirror, unhooking her waist. Gabriel paused for a few moments, watching her, and then said:

—Gretta!

She turned away from the mirror slowly and walked along the shaft of light towards him. Her face looked so serious and weary that the words would not pass Gabriel's lips. No, it was not the moment yet.

—You looked tired, he said.

—I am a little, she answered.

—You don't feel ill or weak?

—No, tired: that's all.

She went on to the window and stood there, looking out. Gabriel waited again and then, fearing that diffidence was about to conquer him, he said abruptly:

—By the way, Gretta!

—What is it?

—You know that poor fellow Malins? he said quickly.

—Yes. What about him?

—Well, poor fellow, he's a decent sort of chap after all, continued Gabriel in a false voice. He gave me back that sovereign I lent him and I didn't expect it really. It's a pity he wouldn't keep away from that Browne, because he's not a bad fellow at heart.

He was trembling now with annoyance. Why did she seem so abstracted? He did not know how he could begin. Was she annoyed, too, about something? If she would only turn to him or come to him of her own accord! To take her as she was would be brutal. No, he must see some ardour in her eyes first. He longed to be master of her strange mood.

—When did you lend him the pound? she asked, after a pause.

Gabriel strove to restrain himself from breaking out into brutal language about the sottish Malins and his pound. He longed to cry to her from his soul, to crush her body against his, to overmaster her. But he said:

—O, at Christmas, when he opened that little Christmas-card shop in Henry Street.

He was in such a fever of rage and desire that he did not hear her come from the window. She stood before him for an instant, looking at him strangely. Then, suddenly raising herself on tiptoe and resting her hands lightly on his shoulders, she kissed him.

—You are a very generous person, Gabriel, she said.

Gabriel, trembling with delight at her sudden kiss and at the quaintness of her phrase, put his hands on her hair and began smoothing it back, scarcely touching it with his fingers. The washing had made it fine and brilliant. His heart was brimming over with happiness. Just when he was wishing for it she had come to him of her own accord. Perhaps her thoughts had been running with his. Perhaps she had felt the impetuous desire that was in him and then the yielding mood had come upon her. Now that she had fallen to him so easily he wondered why he had been so diffident.

He stood, holding her head between his hands. Then, slipping one arm swiftly about her body and drawing her towards him, he said softly:

—Gretta dear, what are you thinking about?

She did not answer nor yield wholly to his arm. He said again, softly:

—Tell me what it is, Gretta. I think I know what is the matter. Do I know?

She did not answer at once. Then she said in an outburst of tears:

—O, I am thinking about that song, *The Lass of Aughrim.*

She broke loose from him and ran to the bed and, throwing her arms across the bed-rail, hid her face. Gabriel stood stock-still for a moment in astonishment and then followed her. As he passed in the way of the cheval-glass he caught sight of himself in full length, his broad, well-filled shirt-front, the face whose expression always puzzled him when he saw it in a mirror and his glimmering gilt-rimmed eyeglasses. He halted a few paces from her and said:

—What about the song? Why does that make you cry?

She raised her head from her arms and dried her eyes with the back of her hand like a child. A kinder note than he had intended went into his voice.

—Why, Gretta? he asked.

—I am thinking about a person long ago who used to sing that song.

—And who was the person long ago? asked Gabriel, smiling.

—It was a person I used to know in Galway when I was living with my grandmother, she said.

The smile passed away from Gabriel's face. A dull anger began to gather again at the back of his mind and the dull fires of his lust began to glow angrily in his veins.

—Someone you were in love with? he asked ironically.

—It was a young boy I used to know, she answered, named Michael Furey. He used to sing that song, *The Lass of Aughrim*. He was very delicate.

Gabriel was silent. He did not wish her to think that he was interested in this delicate boy.

—I can see him so plainly, she said after a moment. Such eyes as he had: big dark eyes! And such an expression in them—an expression!

—O then, you were in love with him? said Gabriel.

—I used to go out walking with him, she said, when I was in Galway.

A thought flew across Gabriel's mind.

—Perhaps that was why you wanted to go to Galway with that Ivors girl? he said coldly.

She looked at him and asked in surprise:

—What for?

Her eyes made Gabriel feel awkward. He shrugged his shoulders and said:

—How do I know? To see him perhaps.

She looked away from him along the shaft of light towards the window in silence.

—He is dead, she said at length. He died when he was only seventeen. Isn't it a terrible thing to die so young as that?

—What was he? asked Gabriel, still ironically.

—He was in the gasworks, she said.

Gabriel felt humiliated by the failure of his irony and by the evocation of this figure from the dead, a boy in the gasworks. While he had been full of memories of their secret life together, full of tenderness and joy and desire, she had been comparing him in her mind with another. A shameful consciousness of his own person assailed him. He saw himself as a ludicrous figure, acting as a pennyboy for his aunts, a nervous well-meaning sentimentalist, orating to vulgarians and idealising his own clownish lusts, the pitiable fatuous fellow he had caught a glimpse of in the mirror. Instinctively he turned his back more to the light lest she might see the shame that burned upon his forehead.

He tried to keep up his tone of cold interrogation but his voice when he spoke was humble and indifferent.

—I suppose you were in love with this Michael Furey, Gretta, he said.

—I was great with him at that time, she said.

Her voice was veiled and sad. Gabriel, feeling now how vain it would be to try to lead her whither he had purposed, caressed one of her hands and said, also sadly:

—And what did he die of so young, Gretta? Consumption, was it?

—I think he died for me, she answered.

A vague terror seized Gabriel at this answer as if, at that hour when he had hoped to triumph, some impalpable and vindictive being was coming against him, gathering forces against him in its vague world. But he shook himself free of it with an effort of reason and continued to caress her hand. He did not question her again for he felt that she would tell him of herself. Her hand was warm and moist: it did not respond to his touch but he continued to caress it just as he had caressed her first letter to him that spring morning.

—It was in the winter, she said, about the beginning of the winter when I was going to leave my grandmother's and come up here to the convent. And he was ill at the time in his lodgings in Galway and wouldn't be let out and his people in Oughterard were written to. He was in decline, they said, or something like that. I never knew rightly.

She paused for a moment and sighed.

—Poor fellow, she said. He was very fond of me and he was such a gentle boy. We used to go out together, walking, you know, Gabriel, like the way they do in the country. He was going to study singing only for his health. He had a very good voice, poor Michael Furey.

—Well; and then? asked Gabriel.

—And then when it came to the time for me to leave Galway and come up to the convent he was much worse and I wouldn't be let see him so I wrote a letter saying I was going up to Dublin and would be back in the summer and hoping he would be better then.

She paused for a moment to get her voice under control and then went on:

—Then the night before I left I was in my grandmother's house in Nuns' Island, packing up, and I heard gravel thrown up against the window. The window was so wet I couldn't see so I ran downstairs as I was and slipped out the back into the garden and there was the poor fellow at the end of the garden, shivering.

—And did you not tell him to go back? asked Gabriel.

—I implored of him to go home at once and told him he would get his death in the rain. But he said he did not want to live. I can see his eyes as well as well! He was standing at the end of the wall where there was a tree.

—And did he go home? asked Gabriel.

—Yes, he went home. And when I was only a week in the convent he died and he was buried in Oughterard where his people came from. O, the day I heard that, that he was dead!

She stopped, choking with sobs, and, overcome by emotion, flung herself face downward on the bed, sobbing in the quilt. Gabriel held her hand for a moment longer, irresolutely, and then, shy of intruding on her grief, let it fall gently and walked quietly to the window.

She was fast asleep.

Gabriel, leaning on his elbow, looked for a few moments unresentfully on her tangled hair and half-open mouth, listening to her deep-drawn breath. So she had had that romance in her life: a man had died for her sake. It hardly pained him now to think how poor a part he, her husband, had played in her life. He watched her while she slept as though he and she had never lived together as man and wife. His curious eyes rested long upon her face and on her hair: and, as he thought of what she must have been then, in that time of her first girlish beauty, a strange friendly pity for her entered his soul. He did not like to say even to himself that her face was no longer beautiful but he knew that it was no longer the face for which Michael Furey had braved death.

Perhaps she had not told him all the story. His eyes moved to the chair over which she had thrown some of her clothes. A petticoat string dangled to the floor. One boot stood upright, its limp upper fallen down: the fellow of it lay upon its side. He wondered at his riot of emotions of an hour before. From what had it proceeded? From his aunt's supper, from his own foolish speech, from the wine and dancing, the merry-making when saying good-night in the hall, the pleasure of the walk along the river in the snow. Poor Aunt Julia! She, too, would soon be a shade with the shade of Patrick Morkan and his horse. He had caught that haggard look upon her face for a moment when she was singing Arrayed for the Bridal. Soon, perhaps, he would be sitting in that same drawing-room, dressed in black, his silk hat on his knees. The blinds would be drawn down and Aunt Kate would be sitting beside him, crying and blowing her nose and telling him how Julia had died. He would cast about in his mind for some words that might console her, and would find only lame and useless ones. Yes, yes: that would happen very soon.

The air of the room chilled his shoulders. He stretched himself cautiously along under the sheets and lay down beside his wife. One by one they were all becoming shades. Better pass boldly into that other world, in the full glory of some passion, than fade and wither dismally with age. He thought of how she who lay beside him had locked in her heart for so many years that image of her lover's eyes when he had told her that he did not wish to live.

Generous tears filled Gabriel's eyes. He had never felt like that himself towards any woman but he knew that such a feeling must be love. The tears gathered more thickly in his eyes and in the partial darkness he imagined he saw the form of a young man standing under a dripping tree. Other forms were near. His soul had approached that region where dwell the vast hosts of the dead. He was conscious of, but could not apprehend, their wayward and flickering existence. His own identity was fading out into a grey impalpable world: the solid world itself which these dead had one time reared and lived in was dissolving and dwindling.

A few light taps upon the pane made him turn to the window. It had begun to snow again. He watched sleepily the flakes, silver and dark, falling obliquely against the lamplight. The time had come for him to set out on his journey westward. Yes, the newspapers were right: snow was general all over Ireland. It was falling on every part of the dark central plain, on the treeless hills, falling softly upon the Bog of

Allen and, farther westward, softly falling into the dark mutinous Shannon waves. It was falling, too, upon every part of the lonely churchyard on the hill where Michael Furey lay buried. It lay thickly drifted on the crooked crosses and headstones, on the spears of the little gate, on the barren thorns. His soul swooned slowly as he heard the snow falling faintly through the universe and faintly falling, like the descent of their last end, upon all the living and the dead.

Araby

James Joyce

North Richmond Street, being blind, was a quiet street except at the hour when the Christian Brothers' School set the boys free. An uninhabited house of two storeys stood at the blind end, detached from its neighbours in a square ground. The other houses of the street, conscious of decent lives within them, gazed at one another with brown imperturbable faces.

The former tenant of our house, a priest, had died in the back drawing-room. Air, musty from having been long enclosed, hung in all the rooms, and the waste room behind the kitchen was littered with old useless papers. Among these I found a few paper-covered books, the pages of which were curled and damp: *The Abbot*, by Walter Scott, *The Devout Communicant*, and *The Memoirs of Vidocq*. I liked the last best because its leaves were yellow. The wild garden behind the house contained a central apple-tree and a few straggling bushes, under one of which I found the late tenant's rusty bicycle-pump. He had been a very charitable priest; in his will he had left all his money to institutions and the furniture of his house to his sister.

When the short days of winter came, dusk fell before we had well eaten our dinners. When we met in the street the houses had grown sombre. The space of sky above us was the colour of ever-changing violet and towards it the lamps of the street lifted their feeble lanterns. The cold air stung us and we played till our bodies glowed. Our shouts echoed in the silent street. The career of our play brought us through the dark muddy lanes behind the houses, where we ran the gantlet of the rough tribes from the cottages, to the back doors of the dark dripping gardens where odours arose from the ashpits, to the dark odorous stables where a coachman smoothed and combed the horse or shook music from the buckled harness. When we returned to the street, light from the kitchen windows had filled the areas. If my uncle was seen turning the corner, we hid in the shadow until we had seen him safely housed. Or if Mangan's sister came out on the doorstep to call her brother in to his tea, we watched her from our shadow peer up and down the street. We waited to see whether she would remain or go in and, if she remained, we left our shadow and walked up to Mangan's steps resignedly. She was waiting for us, her figure defined by the light from the half-opened door. Her brother always teased her before he obeyed, and I stood by the railings looking at her. Her dress swung as she moved her body, and the soft rope of her hair tossed from side to side.

James Joyce, "Araby," from *Dubliners*. Published by Grant Richards Ltd., 1914. Copyright in the Public Domain.

Every morning I lay on the floor in the front parlour watching her door. The blind was pulled down to within an inch of the sash so that I could not be seen. When she came out on the doorstep my heart leaped. I ran to the hall, seized my books and followed her. I kept her brown figure always in my eye and, when we came near the point at which our ways diverged, I quickened my pace and passed her. This happened morning after morning. I had never spoken to her, except for a few casual words, and yet her name was like a summons to all my foolish blood.

Her image accompanied me even in places the most hostile to romance. On Saturday evenings when my aunt went marketing I had to go to carry some of the parcels. We walked through the flaring streets, jostled by drunken men and bargaining women, amid the curses of labourers, the shrill litanies of shop-boys who stood on guard by the barrels of pigs' cheeks, the nasal chanting of street-singers, who sang a come-all-you about O'Donovan Rossa, or a ballad about the troubles in our native land. These noises converged in a single sensation of life for me: I imagined that I bore my chalice safely through a throng of foes. Her name sprang to my lips at moments in strange prayers and praises which I myself did not understand. My eyes were often full of tears (I could not tell why) and at times a flood from my heart seemed to pour itself out into my bosom. I thought little of the future. I did not know whether I would ever speak to her or not or, if I spoke to her, how I could tell her of my confused adoration. But my body was like a harp and her words and gestures were like fingers running upon the wires.

One evening I went into the back drawing-room in which the priest had died. It was a dark rainy evening and there was no sound in the house. Through one of the broken panes I heard the rain impinge upon the earth, the fine incessant needles of water playing in the sodden beds. Some distant lamp or lighted window gleamed below me. I was thankful that I could see so little. All my senses seemed to desire to veil themselves and, feeling that I was about to slip from them, I pressed the palms of my hands together until they trembled, murmuring: O love! O love! many times.

At last she spoke to me. When she addressed the first words to me I was so confused that I did not know what to answer. She asked me was I going to Araby. I forgot whether I answered yes or no. It would be a splendid bazaar; she said she would love to go.

—And why can't you? I asked.

While she spoke she turned a silver bracelet round and round her wrist. She could not go, she said, because there would be a retreat that week in her convent. Her brother and two other boys were fighting for their caps, and I was alone at the railings. She held one of the spikes, bowing her head towards me. The light from the lamp opposite our door caught the white curve of her neck, lit up her hair that rested there and, falling, lit up the hand upon the railing. At fell over one side of her dress and caught the white border of a petticoat, just visible as she stood at ease.

—It's well for you, she said.

—If I go, I said, I will bring you something.

What innumerable follies laid waste my waking and sleeping thoughts after that evening! I wished to annihilate the tedious intervening days. I chafed against the work of school. At night in my bedroom and by day in the classroom her image came between me and the page I strove to read. The syllables of the word Araby were called to me through the silence in which my soul luxuriated and cast an Eastern enchantment over me. I asked for leave to go to the bazaar on Saturday night. My aunt was surprised, and hoped it was not some Freemason's affair. I answered few questions in class. I watched my master's face pass from amiability to sternness; he hoped I was not beginning to idle. I could not call my wandering thoughts together. I had hardly any patience with the serious work of life which, now that it stood between me and my desire, seemed to me child's play, ugly monotonous child's play.

On Saturday morning I reminded my uncle that I wished to go to the bazaar in the evening. He was fussing at the hallstand, looking for the hat-brush, and answered me curtly:

—Yes, boy, I know.

As he was in the hall I could not go into the front parlour and lie at the window. I left the house in bad humour and walked slowly towards the school. The air was pitilessly raw and already my heart misgave me.

When I came home to dinner my uncle had not yet been home. Still it was early. I sat staring at the clock for some time and, when its ticking began to irritate me, I left the room. I mounted the staircase and gained the upper part of the house. The high, cold, empty, gloomy rooms liberated me and I went from room to room singing. From the front window I saw my companions playing below in the street. Their cries reached me weakened and indistinct and, leaning my forehead against the cool glass, I looked over at the dark house where she lived. I may have stood there for an hour, seeing nothing but the brown-clad figure cast by my imagination, touched discreetly by the lamplight at the curved neck, at the hand upon the railings and at the border below the dress.

When I came downstairs again I found Mrs Mercer sitting at the fire. She was an old, garrulous woman, a pawnbroker's widow, who collected used stamps for some pious purpose. I had to endure the gossip of the tea-table. The meal was prolonged beyond an hour and still my uncle did not come. Mrs Mercer stood up to go: she was sorry she couldn't wait any longer, but it was after eight o'clock and she did not like to be out late, as the night air was bad for her. When she had gone I began to walk up and down the room, clenching my fists. My aunt said:

—I'm afraid you may put off your bazaar for this night of Our Lord.

At nine o'clock I heard my uncle's latchkey in the hall door. I heard him talking to himself and heard the hallstand rocking when it had received the weight of his overcoat. I could interpret these signs. When he was midway through his dinner I asked him to give me the money to go to the bazaar. He had forgotten.

—The people are in bed and after their first sleep now, he said.

I did not smile. My aunt said to him energetically:

—Can't you give him the money and let him go? You've kept him late enough as it is.

My uncle said he was very sorry he had forgotten. He said he believed in the old saying: All work and no play makes Jack a dull boy. He asked me where I was going and, when I told him a second time, he asked me did I know The Arab's Farewell to his Steed. When I left the kitchen he was about to recite the opening lines of the piece to my aunt.

I held a florin tightly in my hand as I strode down Buckingham Street towards the station. The sight of the streets thronged with buyers and glaring with gas recalled to me the purpose of my journey. I took my seat in a third-class carriage of a deserted train. After an intolerable delay the train moved out of the station slowly. It crept onward among ruinous houses and over the twinkling river. At Westland Row Station a crowd of people pressed to the carriage doors; but the porters moved them back, saying that it was a special train for the bazaar. I remained alone in the bare carriage. In a few minutes the train drew up beside an improvised wooden platform. I passed out on to the road and saw by the lighted dial of a clock that it was ten minutes to ten. In front of me was a large building which displayed the magical name.

I could not find any sixpenny entrance and, fearing that the bazaar would be closed, I passed in quickly through a turnstile, handing a shilling to a weary-looking man. I found myself in a big hall girded at half its height by a gallery. Nearly all the stalls were closed and the greater part of the hall was in darkness. I recognized a silence like that which pervades a church after a service. I walked into the centre of the bazaar timidly. A few people were gathered about the stalls which were still open. Before a curtain, over which the words Café Chantant were written in coloured lamps, two men were counting money on a salver. I listened to the fall of the coins.

Remembering with difficulty why I had come, I went over to one of the stalls and examined porcelain vases and flowered tea-sets. At the door of the stall a young lady was talking and laughing with two young gentlemen. I remarked their English accents and listened vaguely to their conversation.

—O, I never said such a thing!

—O, but you did!

—O, but I didn't!

—Didn't she say that?

—Yes. I heard her.

—O, there's a…fib!

Observing me, the young lady came over and asked me did I wish to buy anything. The tone of her voice was not encouraging; she seemed to have spoken to me out of a sense of duty. I looked humbly at the great jars that stood like eastern guards at either side of the dark entrance to the stall and murmured:

—No, thank you.

The young lady changed the position of one of the vases and went back to the two young men. They began to talk of the same subject. Once or twice the young lady glanced at me over her shoulder.

I lingered before her stall, though I knew my stay was useless, to make my interest in her wares seem the more real. Then I turned away slowly and walked down the middle of the bazaar. I allowed the two pennies to fall against the sixpence in my pocket. I heard a voice call from one end of the gallery that the light was out. The upper part of the hall was now completely dark.

Gazing up into the darkness I saw myself as a creature driven and derided by vanity; and my eyes burned with anguish and anger.

A Painful Case

James Joyce

Mr. James Duffy lived in Chapelizod because he wished to live as far as possible from the city of which he was a citizen and because he found all the other suburbs of Dublin mean, modern and pretentious. He lived in an old sombre house and from his windows he could look into the disused distillery or upwards along the shallow river on which Dublin is built. The lofty walls of his uncarpeted room were free from pictures. He had himself bought every article of furniture in the room: a black iron bedstead, an iron washstand, four cane chairs, a clothes-rack, a coal-scuttle, a fender and irons and a square table on which lay a double desk. A bookcase had been made in an alcove by means of shelves of white wood. The bed was clothed with white bedclothes and a black and scarlet rug covered the foot. A little hand-mirror hung above the washstand and during the day a white-shaded lamp stood as the sole ornament of the mantelpiece. The books on the white wooden shelves were arranged from below upwards according to bulk. A complete Wordsworth stood at one end of the lowest shelf and a copy of the *Maynooth Catechism*, sewn into the cloth cover of a notebook, stood at one end of the top shelf. Writing materials were always on the desk. In the desk lay a manuscript translation of Hauptmann's *Michael Kramer*, the stage directions of which were written in purple ink, and a little sheaf of papers held together by a brass pin. In these sheets a sentence was inscribed from time to time and, in an ironical moment, the headline of an advertisement for *Bile Beans* had

James Joyce, "A Painful Case," from *Dubliners*. Published by Grant Richards Ltd., 1914. Copyright in the Public Domain.

been pasted on to the first sheet. On lifting the lid of the desk a faint fragrance escaped—the fragrance of new cedarwood pencils or of a bottle of gum or of an overripe apple which might have been left there and forgotten.

Mr. Duffy abhorred anything which betokened physical or mental disorder. A mediaeval doctor would have called him saturnine. His face, which carried the entire tale of his years, was of the brown tint of Dublin streets. On his long and rather large head grew dry black hair and a tawny moustache did not quite cover an unamiable mouth. His cheekbones also gave his face a harsh character; but there was no harshness in the eyes which, looking at the world from under their tawny eyebrows, gave the impression of a man ever alert to greet a redeeming instinct in others but often disappointed. He lived at a little distance from his body, regarding his own acts with doubtful side-glasses. He had an odd autobiographical habit which led him to compose in his mind from time to time a short sentence about himself containing a subject in the third person and a predicate in the past tense. He never gave alms to beggars and walked firmly, carrying a stout hazel.

He had been for many years cashier of a private bank in Baggot Street. Every morning he came in from Chapelizod by tram. At midday he went to Dan Burke's and took his lunch—a bottle of lager beer and a small trayful of arrowroot biscuits. At four o'clock he was set free. He dined in an eating-house in George's Street where he felt himself safe from the society of Dublin's gilded youth and where there was a certain plain honesty in the bill of fare. His evenings were spent either before his landlady's piano or roaming about the outskirts of the city. His liking for Mozart's music brought him sometimes to an opera or a concert: these were the only dissipations of his life.

He had neither companions nor friends, church nor creed. He lived his spiritual life without any communion with others, visiting his relatives at Christmas and escorting them to the cemetery when they died. He performed these two social duties for old dignity's sake but conceded nothing further to the conventions which regulate the civic life. He allowed himself to think that in certain circumstances he would rob his bank but, as these circumstances never arose, his life rolled out evenly—an adventureless tale.

One evening he found himself sitting beside two ladies in the Rotunda. The house, thinly peopled and silent, gave distressing prophecy of failure. The lady who sat next him looked round at the deserted house once or twice and then said:

—What a pity there is such a poor house tonight! It's so hard on people to have to sing to empty benches.

He took the remark as an invitation to talk. He was surprised that she seemed so little awkward. While they talked he tried to fix her permanently in his memory. When he learned that the young girl beside her was her daughter he judged her to be a year or so younger than himself. Her face, which must have been handsome, had remained intelligent. It was an oval face with strongly marked features. The eyes were very dark blue and steady. Their gaze began with a defiant note but was confused by what seemed a deliberate swoon of the pupil into the iris, revealing for an instant a temperament of great sensibility. The pupil reasserted itself quickly, this half-disclosed nature fell again under the reign of prudence, and her astrakhan jacket, moulding a bosom of a certain fullness, struck the note of defiance more definitely.

He met her again a few weeks afterwards at a concert in Earlsfort Terrace and seized the moments when her daughter's attention was diverted to become intimate. She alluded once or twice to her husband but her tone was not such as to make the allusion a warning. Her name was Mrs. Sinico. Her husband's great-great-grandfather had come from Leghorn. Her husband was captain of a mercantile boat plying between Dublin and Holland; and they had one child.

Meeting her a third time by accident he found courage to make an appointment. She came. This was the first of many meetings; they met always in the evening and chose the most quiet quarters for their walks together. Mr. Duffy, however, had a distaste for underhand ways and, finding that they were compelled to meet stealthily, he forced her to ask him to her house. Captain Sinico encouraged his visits, thinking that his daughter's hand was in question. He had dismissed his wife so sincerely from his gallery of pleasures that he did not suspect that anyone else would take an interest in her. As the husband was often away and the daughter out giving music lessons Mr. Duffy had many opportunities of enjoying the lady's society. Neither he nor she had had any such adventure before and neither was conscious of any incongruity. Little by little he entangled his thoughts with hers. He lent her books, provided her with ideas, shared his intellectual life with her. She listened to all.

Sometimes in return for his theories she gave out some fact of her own life. With almost maternal solicitude she urged him to let his nature open to the full; she became his confessor. He told her that for some time he had assisted at the meetings of an Irish Socialist Party where he had felt himself a unique figure amidst a score of sober workmen in a garret lit by an inefficient oil-lamp. When the party had divided into three sections, each under its own leader and in its own garret, he had discontinued his attendances. The workmen's discussions, he said, were too timorous; the interest they took in the question of wages was inordinate. He felt that they were hard-featured realists and that they resented an exactitude which was the produce of a leisure not within their reach. No social revolution, he told her, would be likely to strike Dublin for some centuries.

She asked him why did he not write out his thoughts. For what, he asked her, with careful scorn. To compete with phrasemongers, incapable of thinking consecutively for sixty seconds? To submit himself to the criticisms of an obtuse middle class which entrusted its morality to policemen and its fine arts to impresarios?

He went often to her little cottage outside Dublin; often they spent their evenings alone. Little by little, as their thoughts entangled, they spoke of subjects less remote. Her companionship was like a warm soil about an exotic. Many times she allowed the dark to fall upon them, refraining from lighting the lamp. The dark discreet room, their isolation, the music that still vibrated in their ears united them. This union exalted him, wore away the rough edges of his character, emotionalised his mental life. Sometimes he caught himself listening to the sound of his own voice. He thought that in her eyes he would ascend to an angelical stature; and, as he attached the fervent nature of his companion more and more closely to him, he heard the strange impersonal voice which he recognised as his own, insisting on the soul's incurable loneliness. We cannot give ourselves, it said: we are our own. The end of these discourses was that one night during which she had shown every sign of unusual excitement, Mrs. Sinico caught up his hand passionately and pressed it to her cheek.

Mr. Duffy was very much surprised. Her interpretation of his words disillusioned him. He did not visit her for a week, then he wrote to her asking her to meet him. As he did not wish their last interview to be troubled by the influence of their ruined confessional they meet in a little cakeshop near the Parkgate. It was cold autumn weather but in spite of the cold they wandered up and down the roads of the Park for nearly three hours. They agreed to break off their intercourse: every bond, he said, is a bond to sorrow. When they came out of the Park they walked in silence towards the tram; but here she began to tremble so violently that, fearing another collapse on her part, he bade her good-bye quickly and left her. A few days later he received a parcel containing his books and music.

Four years passed. Mr. Duffy returned to his even way of life. His room still bore witness of the orderliness of his mind. Some new pieces of music encumbered the music-stand in the lower room and on his shelves stood two volumes by Nietzsche: *Thus Spake Zarathustra* and *The Gay Science*. He wrote seldom in the sheaf of papers which lay in his desk. One of his sentences, written two months after his last interview with Mrs. Sinico, read: Love between man and man is impossible because there must not be sexual intercourse and friendship between man and woman is impossible because there must be sexual intercourse. He kept away from concerts lest he should meet her. His father died; the junior partner of the bank retired. And still every morning he went into the city by tram and every evening walked home from the city after having dined moderately in George's Street and read the evening paper for dessert.

One evening as he was about to put a morsel of corned beef and cabbage into his mouth his hand stopped. His eyes fixed themselves on a paragraph in the evening paper which he had propped against the water-carafe. He replaced the morsel of food on his plate and read the paragraph attentively. Then he drank a glass of water, pushed his plate to one side, doubled the paper down before him between his elbows and read the paragraph over and over again. The cabbage began to deposit a cold white grease on his plate. The girl came over to him to ask was his dinner not properly cooked. He said it was very good and ate a few mouthfuls of it with difficulty. Then he paid his bill and went out.

He walked along quickly through the November twilight, his stout hazel stick striking the ground regularly, the fringe of the buff *Mail* peeping out of a side-pocket of his tight reefer overcoat. On the lonely road which leads from the Parkgate to Chapelizod he slackened his pace. His stick struck the ground less emphatically and his breath, issuing irregularly, almost with a sighing sound, condensed in the wintry air. When he reached his house he went up at once to his bedroom and, taking the paper from his pocket, read the paragraph again by the failing light of the window. He read it not aloud, but moving his lips as a priest does when he reads the prayers *Secreto*. This was the paragraph:

Death Of A Lady At Sydney Parade
A Painful Case

Today at the City of Dublin Hospital the Deputy Coroner (in the absence of Mr. Leverett) held an inquest on the body of Mrs. Emily Sinico, aged forty-three years, who was killed at Sydney Parade Station yesterday evening. The evidence showed that the deceased lady, while attempting to cross the line, was knocked down by the engine of the ten o' clock slow train from Kingstown, thereby sustaining injuries of the head and right side which led to her death.

James Lennon, driver of the engine, stated that he had been in the employment of the railway company for fifteen years. On hearing the guard's whistle he set the train in motion and a second or two afterwards brought it to rest in response to loud cries. The train was going slowly.

P. Dunne, railway porter, stated that as the train was about to start he observed a woman attempting to cross the lines. He ran towards her and shouted, but, before he could reach her, she was caught by the buffer of the engine and fell to the ground.

A juror—You saw the lady fall?
Witness—Yes.

Police Sergeant Croly deposed that when he arrived he found the deceased lying on the platform apparently dead. He had the body taken to the waiting-room pending the arrival of the ambulance.

Constable 57E corroborated.

Dr. Halpin, assistant house surgeon of the City of Dublin Hospital, stated that the deceased had two lower ribs fractured and had sustained severe contusions of the right shoulder. The right side of the head had been injured in the fall. The injuries were not sufficient to have caused death in a normal person. Death, in his opinion, had been probably due to shock and sudden failure of the heart's action.

Mr. H. B. Patterson Finlay, on behalf of the railway company, expressed his deep regret at the accident. The company had always taken every precaution to prevent people crossing the lines except by the bridges, both by placing notices in every station and by the use of patent spring gates at level crossings. The deceased had been in the habit of crossing the lines late at night from platform to platform and, in view of certain other circumstances of the case, he did not think the railway officials were to blame.

Captain Sinico, of Leoville, Sydney Parade, husband of the deceased, also gave evidence. He stated that the deceased was his wife. He was not in Dublin at the time of the accident as he had arrived only that morning from Rotterdam. They had been married for twenty-two years and had lived happily until about two years ago when his wife began to be rather intemperate in her habits.

Miss Mary Sinico said that of late her mother had been in the habit of going out at night to buy spirits. She, witness, had often tried to reason with her mother and had induced her to join a league. She was not at home until an hour after the accident. The jury returned a verdict in accordance with the medical evidence and exonerated Lennon from all blame.

The Deputy Coroner said it was a most painful case, and expressed great sympathy with Captain Sinico and his daughter. He urged on the railway company to take strong measures to prevent the possibility of similar accidents in the future. No blame attached to anyone.

Mr. Duffy raised his eyes from the paper and gazed out of his window on the cheerless evening landscape. The river lay quiet beside the empty distillery and from time to time a light appeared in some house on the Lucan road. What an end! The whole narrative of her death revolted him and it revolted him to think that he had ever spoken to her of what he held sacred. The threadbare phrases, the inane expressions of sympathy, the cautious words of a reporter won over to conceal the details of a commonplace vulgar death attacked his stomach. Not merely had she degraded herself; she had degraded him. He saw the squalid tract of her vice, miserable and malodorous. His soul's companion! He thought of the hobbling wretches whom he had seen carrying cans and bottles to be filled by the barman. Just God, what an end! Evidently she had been unfit to live, without any strength of purpose, an easy prey to habits, one of the wrecks on which civilisation has been reared. But that she could have sunk so low! Was it possible he had deceived himself so utterly about her? He remembered her outburst of that night and interpreted it in a harsher sense than he had ever done. He had no difficulty now in approving of the course he had taken.

As the light failed and his memory began to wander he thought her hand touched his. The shock which had first attacked his stomach was now attacking his nerves. He put on his overcoat and hat quickly and went out. The cold air met him on the threshold; it crept into the sleeves of his coat. When he came to the public-house at Chapelizod Bridge he went in and ordered a hot punch.

The proprietor served him obsequiously but did not venture to talk. There were five or six working-men in the shop discussing the value of a gentleman's estate in County Kildare. They drank at intervals from their huge pint tumblers and smoked, spitting often on the floor and sometimes dragging the sawdust over their spits with their heavy boots. Mr. Duffy sat on his stool and gazed at them, without seeing or hearing them. After a while they went out and he called for another punch. He sat a long time over it. The shop was very quiet. The proprietor sprawled on the counter reading the *Herald* and yawning. Now and again a tram was heard swishing along the lonely road outside.

As he sat there, living over his life with her and evoking alternately the two images in which he now conceived her, he realised that she was dead, that she had ceased to exist, that she had become a memory. He began to feel ill at ease. He asked himself what else could he have done. He could not have carried on a comedy of deception with her; he could not have lived with her openly. He had done what seemed to him best. How was he to blame? Now that she was gone he understood how lonely her life must have been, sitting night after night alone in that room. His life would be lonely too until he, too, died, ceased to exist, became a memory—if anyone remembered him.

It was after nine o' clock when he left the shop. The night was cold and gloomy. He entered the Park by the first gate and walked along under the gaunt trees. He walked through the bleak alleys where they had walked four years before. She seemed to be near him in the darkness. At moments he seemed to feel her voice touch his ear, her hand touch his. He stood still to listen. Why had he withheld life from her? Why had he sentenced her to death? He felt his moral nature falling to pieces.

When he gained the crest of the Magazine Hill he halted and looked along the river towards Dublin, the lights of which burned redly and hospitably in the cold night. He looked down the slope and, at the base, in the shadow of the wall of the Park, he saw some human figures lying. Those venal and furtive loves filled him with despair. He gnawed the rectitude of his life; he felt that he had been outcast from life's feast. One human being had seemed to love him and he had denied her life and happiness: he had sentenced her to ignominy, a death of shame. He knew that the prostrate creatures down by the wall were watching him and wished him gone. No one wanted him; he was outcast from life's feast. He turned his eyes to the grey gleaming river, winding along towards Dublin. Beyond the river he saw a goods train winding out of Kingsbridge Station, like a worm with a fiery head winding through the darkness, obstinately and laboriously. It passed slowly out of sight; but still he heard in his ears the laborious drone of the engine reiterating the syllables of her name.

He turned back the way he had come, the rhythm of the engine pounding in his ears. He began to doubt the reality of what memory told him. He halted under a tree and allowed the rhythm to die away. He could not feel her near him in the darkness nor her voice touch his ear. He waited for some minutes listening. He could hear nothing: the night was perfectly silent. He listened again: perfectly silent. He felt that he was alone.

The Lottery

Shirley Jackson

The morning of June 27th was clear and sunny, with the fresh warmth of a full-summer day; the flowers were blossoming profusely and the grass was richly green. The people of the village began to gather in the square, between the post office and the bank, around ten o' clock; in some towns there were so many people that the lottery took two days and had to be started on June 26th, but in this village, where there were only about three hundred people, the whole lottery took less than two hours, so it could begin at ten o' clock in the morning and still be through in time to allow the villagers to get home for noon dinner.

The children assembled first, of course. School was recently over for the summer, and the feeling of liberty sat uneasily on most of them; they tended to gather together quietly for a while before they broke into boisterous play, and their talk was still of the classroom and the teacher, of books and reprimands. Bobby Martin had already stuffed his pockets full of stones, and the other boys soon followed his example, selecting the smoothest and roundest stones;

Shirley Jackson, The Lottery, from *The New Yorker*, pp. 25–28. Copyright © 1948 by Conde Nast Publications, Inc. Permission to reprint granted by the publisher.

Bobby and Harry Jones and Dickie Delacroix—the villagers pronounced this name "Dellacroy"—eventually made a great pile of stones in one corner of the square and guarded it against the raids of the other boys. The girls stood aside, talking among themselves, looking over their shoulders at the boys, and the very small children rolled in the dust or clung to the hands of their older brothers or sisters.

Soon the men began to gather, surveying their own children, speaking of planting and rain, tractors and taxes. They stood together, away from the pile of stones in the corner, and their jokes were quiet and they smiled rather than laughed. The women, wearing faded house dresses and sweaters, came shortly after their menfolk. They greeted one another and exchanged bits of gossip as they went to join their husbands. Soon the women, standing by their husbands, began to call to their children, and the children came reluctantly, having to be called four or five times. Bobby Martin ducked under his mother's grasping hand and ran, laughing, back to the pile of stones. His father spoke up sharply, and Bobby came quickly and took his place between his father and his oldest brother.

The lottery was conducted—as were the square dances, the teenage club, the Halloween program—by Mr. Summers, who had time and energy to devote to civic activities. He was a round-faced, jovial man and he ran the coal business, and people were sorry for him, because he had no children and his wife was a scold. When he arrived in the square, carrying the black wooden box, there was a murmur of conversation among the villagers, and he waved and called, "Little late today, folks." The postmaster, Mr. Graves, followed him, carrying a three-legged stool, and the stool was put in the center of the square and Mr. Summers set the black box down on it. The villagers kept their distance, leaving a space between themselves and the stool, and when Mr. Summers said, "Some of you fellows want to give me a hand?" there was a hesitation before two men. Mr. Martin and his oldest son, Baxter, came forward to hold the box steady on the stool while Mr. Summers stirred up the papers inside it.

The original paraphernalia for the lottery had been lost long ago, and the black box now resting on the stool had been put into use even before Old Man Warner, the oldest man in town, was born. Mr. Summers spoke frequently to the villagers about making a new box, but no one liked to upset even as much tradition as was represented by the black box. There was a story that the present box had been made with some pieces of the box that had preceded it, the one that had been constructed when the first people settled down to make a village here. Every year, after the lottery, Mr. Summers began talking again about a new box, but every year the subject was allowed to fade off without anything's being done. The black box grew shabbier each year; by now it was no longer completely black but splintered badly along one side to show the original wood color, and in some places faded or stained.

Mr. Martin and his oldest son, Baxter, held the black box securely on the stool until Mr. Summers had stirred the papers thoroughly with his hand. Because so much of the ritual had been forgotten or discarded, Mr. Summers had been successful in having slips of paper substituted for the chips of wood that had been used for generations. Chips of wood, Mr. Summers had argued, had been all very well when the village was tiny, but now that the population was more than three hundred and likely to keep on growing, it was necessary to use something that would fit more easily into he black box. The night before the lottery, Mr. Summers and Mr. Graves made up the slips of paper and put them in the box, and it was then taken to the safe of Mr. Summers's coal company and locked up until Mr. Summers was ready to take it to the square next morning. The rest of the year, the box was put way, sometimes one place, sometimes another; it had spent one year in Mr. Graves's barn and another year underfoot in the post office, and sometimes it was set on a shelf in the Martin grocery and left there.

There was a great deal of fussing to be done before Mr. Summers declared the lottery open. There were the lists to make up—of heads of families, heads of households in each family, members of each household in each family. There was the proper swearing-in of Mr. Summers by the postmaster, as the official of the lottery; at one time, some people remembered, there had been a recital of some sort, performed by the official of the lottery, a perfunctory, tuneless chant that had been rattled off duly each year; some people believed that the official of the lottery used to stand just so when he said or sang it, others believed that he was supposed to walk among the people, but years and years ago this part of the ritual had been allowed to lapse. There had been, also, a ritual salute, which the official of the lottery had had to use in addressing each person who came up to draw from the box, but this also had changed with time, until now it was felt necessary only for the official to speak to each person approaching. Mr. Summers was very good at all this; in his clean white shirt and blue jeans, with one hand resting carelessly on the black box, he seemed very proper and important as he talked interminably to Mr. Graves and the Martins.

Just as Mr. Summers finally left off talking and turned to the assembled villagers, Mrs. Hutchinson came hurriedly along the path to the square, her sweater thrown over her shoulders, and slid into place in the back of the crowd. "Clean forgot what day it was," she said to Mrs. Delacroix, who stood next to her, and they both laughed softly. "Thought my old man was out back stacking wood," Mrs. Hutchinson went on, "and then I looked out the window and the kids was gone, and then I remembered it was the twenty-seventh and came a-running." She dried her hands on her apron, and Mrs. Delacroix said, "You're in time, though. They're still talking away up there."

Mrs. Hutchinson craned her neck to see through the crowd and found her husband and children standing near the front. She tapped Mrs. Delacroix on the arm as a farewell and began to make her way through the crowd. The people separated good-humoredly to let her through; two or three people said, in voices just loud enough to be heard across the crowd, "Here comes your, Missus, Hutchinson," and "Bill, she made it after all." Mrs. Hutchinson reached her husband, and Mr. Summers, who had been waiting, said cheerfully. "Thought we were going to have to get on without you, Tessie." Mrs. Hutchinson said, grinning, "Wouldn't have me leave m' dishes in the sink, now, would you. Joe?" and soft laughter ran through the crowd as the people stirred back into position after Mrs. Hutchinson's arrival.

"Well, now." Mr. Summers said soberly, "guess we better get started, get this over with, so's we can go back to work. Anybody ain't here?"

"Dunbar," several people said. "Dunbar, Dunbar."

Mr. Summers consulted his list. "Clyde Dunbar," he said. "That's right. He's broke his leg, hasn't he? Who's drawing for him?"

"Me. I guess," a woman said, and Mr. Summers turned to look at her. "Wife draws for her husband," Mr. Summers said. "Don't you have a grown boy to do it for you, Janey?" Although Mr. Summers and everyone else in the village knew the answer perfectly well, it was the business of the official of the lottery to ask such questions formally. Mr. Summers waited with an expression of polite interest while Mrs. Dunbar answered.

"Horace's not but sixteen yet," Mrs. Dunbar said regretfully. "Guess I gotta fill in for the old man this year."

"Right," Mr. Summers said. He made a note on the list he was holding. Then he asked, "Watson boy drawing this year?"

A tall boy in the crowd raised his hand. "Here," he said. "I'm drawing for my mother and me." He blinked his eyes nervously and ducked his head as several, voices in the crowd said things like "Good fellow, lack," and "Glad to see your mother's got a man to do it."

"Well," Mr. Summers said, "guess that's everyone. Old Man Warner make it?"

"Here," a voice said, and Mr. Summers nodded.

A sudden hush fell on the crowd as Mr. Summers cleared his throat and looked at the list. "All ready?" he called. "Now, I'll read the names—heads of families first—and the men come up and take a paper out of the box. Keep the paper folded in your hand without looking at it until everyone has had a turn. Everything clear?"

The people had done it so many times that they only half listened to the directions; most of them were quiet, wetting their lips, not looking around. Then Mr. Summers raised one hand high and said, "Adams." A man disengaged himself from the crowd and came forward. "Hi, Steve," Mr. Summers said, and Mr. Adams said. "Hi, Joe," They grinned at one another humorlessly and nervously. Then Mr. Adams reached into the black box and took out a folded paper. He held it firmly by one corner as he turned and went hastily back to his place in the crowd, where he stood a little apart from his family, not looking down at his hand.

"Allen," Mr. Summers said. "Anderson…Bentham."

"Seems like there's no time at all between lotteries any more." Mrs. Delacroix said to Mrs. Graves in the back row.

"Seems like we got through with the last one only last week."

"Time sure goes fast," Mrs. Graves said.

"Clark…Delacroix"

"There goes my old man," Mrs. Delacroix said. She held her breath while her husband went forward.

"Dunbar," Mr. Summers said, and Mrs. Dunbar went steadily to the box while one of the women said, "Go on, Janey," and another said, "There she goes."

"We're next," Mrs. Graves said. She watched while Mr. Graves came around from the side of the box, greeted Mr. Summers gravely and selected a slip of paper from the box. By now, all through the crowd there were men holding the small folded papers in their large hand, turning them over and over nervously. Mrs. Dunbar and her two sons stood together, Mrs. Dunbar holding the slip of paper.

"Harburt…Hutchinson."

"Get up there, Bill," Mrs. Hutchinson said, and the people near her laughed.

"Jones."

"They do say," Mr. Adams said to Old Man Warner, who stood next to him, "that over in the north village they're talking of giving up the lottery."

Old Man Warner snorted. "Pack of crazy fools," he said. "Listening to the young folks, nothing's good enough for *them*. Next thing you know, they'll be wanting to go back to living in caves, nobody work any more, live *that* way for a while. Used to be a saying about 'Lottery in June, corn be heavy soon.' First thing you know, we'd all be eating stewed chickweed and acorns. There's *always* been a lottery," he added petulantly. "Bad enough to see young Joe Summers up there joking with everybody."

"Some places have already quit lotteries." Mrs. Adams said.

"Nothing but trouble in *that*," Old Man Warner said stoutly. "Pack of young fools."

"Martin." And Bobby Martin watched his father go forward. "Overdyke…Percy."

"I wish they'd hurry," Mrs. Dunbar said to her older son. "I wish they'd hurry."

"They're almost through," her son said.

"You get ready to run tell Dad," Mrs. Dunbar said.

Mr. Summers called his own name and then stepped forward precisely and selected a slip from the box. Then he called, "Warner."

"Seventy-seventh year I been in the lottery," Old Man Warner said as he went through the crowd. "Seventy-seventh time."

"Watson" The tall boy came awkwardly through the crowd. Someone said, "Don't be nervous, Jack," and Mr. Summers said, "Take your time, son."

"Zanini."

After that, there was a long pause, a breathless pause, until Mr. Summers, holding his slip of paper in the air, said, "All right, fellows." For a minute, no one moved, and then all the slips of paper were opened. Suddenly, all the women began to speak at once, saying. "Who is it?, "Who's got it?" "Is it the Dunbars?" "Is it the Watsons?" Then the voices began to say, "It's Hutchinson. It's Bill," "Bill Hutchinson's got it."

"Go tell your father," Mrs. Dunbar said to her older son.

People began to look around to see the Hutchinsons. Bill Hutchinson was standing quiet, staring down at the paper in his hand. Suddenly. Tessie Hutchinson shouted to Mr. Summers. "You didn't give him time enough to take any paper he wanted. I saw you. It wasn't fair!"

"Be a good sport, Tessie, Mrs. Delacroix called, and Mrs. Graves said, "All of us took the same chance."

"Shut up, Tessie," Bill Hutchinson said.

"Well, everyone," Mr. Summers said, "that was done pretty fast, and now we've got to be hurrying a little more to get done in time." He consulted his next list. "Bill," he said, "you draw for the Hutchinson family. You got any other households in the Hutchinsons?"

"There's Don and Eva," Mrs. Hutchinson yelled. "Make them take their chance!"

"Daughters draw with their husbands' families, Tessie," Mr. Summers said gently. "You know that as well as anyone else."

"It wasn't *fair*," Tessie said.

"I guess not, Joe." Bill Hutchinson said regretfully. "My daughter draws with her husband's family, that's only fair. And I've got no other family except the kids."

"Then, as far as drawing for families is concerned, it's you," Mr. Summers said in explanation, "and as far as drawing for households is concerned, that's you, too. Right?"

"Right," Bill Hutchinson said.

"How many kids, Bill?" Mr. Summers asked formally.

"Three," Bill Hutchinson said.

"There's Bill, Jr., and Nancy, and little Dave. And Tessie and me."

"All right, then," Mr. Summers said. "Harry, you got their tickets back?"

Mr. Graves nodded and held up the slips of paper. "Put them in the box, then," Mr. Summers directed. "Take Bill's and put it in."

"I think we ought to start over," Mrs. Hutchinson said, as quietly as she could. "I tell you it wasn't fair. You didn't give him time enough to choose. Everybody saw that."

Mr. Graves had selected the five slips and put them in the box, and he dropped all the papers but those onto the ground, where the breeze caught them and lifted them off.

"Listen, everybody," Mrs. Hutchinson was saying to the people around her.

"Ready, Bill?" Mr. Summers asked, and Bill Hutchinson, with one quick glance around at his wife and children, nodded.

"Remember," Mr. Summers said. "take the slips and keep them folded until each person has taken one, Harry, you help little Dave." Mr. Graves took the hand of the little boy, who came willingly with him up to the box. "Take a paper out of the box, Davy." Mr. Summers said. Davy put his hand into the box and laughed. "Take just *one* paper," Mr. Summers said. "Harry, you hold it for him." Mr. Graves took the child's hand and removed the folded paper from the tight fist and held it while little Dave stood next to him and looked up at him wonderingly.

"Nancy next," Mr. Summers said. Nancy was twelve, and her school friends breathed heavily as she went forward switching her skirt, and took a slip daintily from the box. "Bill, Jr.," Mr. Summers said, and Billy, his face red and his feet overlarge, near knocked the box over as he got a paper out. "Tessie," Mr. Summers said. She hesitated for a minute, looking around defiantly, and then set her lips and went up to the box. She snatched a paper out and held it behind her.

"Bill," Mr. Summers said, and Bill Hutchinson reached into the box and felt around, bringing his hand out at last with the slip of paper in it.

The crowd was quiet. A girl whispered, "I hope it's not Nancy," and the sound of the whisper reached the edges of the crowd.

"It's not the way it used to be," Old Man Warner said clearly. "People ain't the way they used to be."

"All right," Mr. Summers said. "Open the papers. Harry, you open little Dave's."

Mr. Graves opened the slip of paper and there was a general sigh through the crowd as he held it up and everyone could see that it was blank. Nancy and Bill. Jr., opened theirs at the same time, and both beamed and laughed, turning around to the crowd and holding their slips of paper above their heads.

"Tessie," Mr. Summers said. There was a pause, and then Mr. Summers looked at Bill Hutchinson, and Bill unfolded his paper and showed it. It was blank.

"It's Tessie," Mr. Summers said, and his voice was hushed. "Show us her paper. Bill."

Bill Hutchinson went over to his wife and forced the slip of paper out of her hand. It had a black spot on it, the black spot Mr. Summers had made the night before with the heavy pencil in the coal company office. Bill Hutchinson held it up, and there was a stir in the crowd.

"All right, folks," Mr. Summers said. "Let's finish quickly."

Although the villagers had forgotten the ritual and lost the original black box, they still remembered to use stones. The pile of stones the boys had made earlier was ready; there were stones on the ground with the blowing scraps of paper that had come out of the box Delacroix selected a stone so large she had to pick it up with both hands and turned to Mrs. Dunbar. "Come on," she said. "Hurry up."

Mr. Dunbar had small stones in both hands, and she said, gasping for breath. "I can't run at all. You'll have to go ahead and I'll catch up with you."

The children had stones already. And someone gave little Davy Hutchinson few pebbles.

Tessie Hutchinson was in the center of a cleared space by now, and she held her hands out desperately as the villagers moved in on her. "It isn't fair," she said. A stone hit her on the side of the head. Old Man Warner was saying, "Come on, come on, everyone." Steve Adams was in the front of the crowd of villagers, with Mrs. Graves beside him.

"It isn't fair, it isn't right," Mrs. Hutchinson screamed, and then they were upon her.

A Conversation With My Father

Grace Paley

My father is eighty-six years old and in bed. His heart, that bloody motor, is equally old and will not do certain jobs any more. It still floods his head with brainy light. But it won't let his legs carry the weight of his body around the house. Despite my metaphors, this muscle failure is not due to his old heart, he says, but to a potassium shortage. Sitting on one pillow, leaning on three, he offers last-minute advice and makes a request.

"I would like you to write a simple story just once more" he says, "the kind de Maupassant wrote, or Chekhov, the kind you used to write. Just recognizable people and then write down what happened to them next."

I say, "Yes, why not? That's possible." I want to please him, though I don't remember writing that way. I *would* like to try to tell such a story, if he means the kind that begins: "There was a woman…" followed by plot, the absolute line between two points which I've always despised. Not for literary reasons, but because it takes all hope away. Everyone, real or invented, deserves the open destiny of life.

Finally I thought of a story that had been happening for a couple of years right across the street. I wrote it down, then read it aloud. "Pa," I said, "how about this? Do you mean something like this?"

> Once in my time there was a woman and she had a son. They lived nicely, in a

Grace Paley, "A Conversation With My Father," *The Collected Stories*, pp. 232-237. Copyright © 1994 by Grace Paley. Reprinted with permission by Farrar, Straus and Giroux.

small apartment in Manhattan. This boy at about fifteen became a junkie, which is not unusual in our neighborhood. In order to maintain her close friendship with him, she became a junkie too. She said it was part of the youth culture, with which she felt very much at home. After a while, for a number of reasons, the boy gave it all up and left the city and his mother in disgust. Hopeless and alone, she grieved. We all visit her.

"O.K., Pa, that's it," I said, "an unadorned and miserable tale." "But that's not what I mean," my father said. "You misunderstood me on purpose. You know there's a lot more to it. You know that. You left everything out. Turgenev wouldn't do that. Chekhov wouldn't do that. There are in fact Russian writers you never heard of, you don't have an inkling of, as good as anyone, who can write a plain ordinary story who would not leave out what you have left out. I object not to facts but to people sitting in trees talking senselessly, voices from who knows where…"

"Forget that one, Pa, what have I left out now? In this one?"

"Her looks, for instance."

"Oh. Quite handsome, I think. Yes."

"Her hair?"

"Dark, with heavy braids, as though she were a girl or a foreigner" "What were her parents like, her stock? That she became such a person. It's interesting, you know."

"From out of town. Professional people. The first to be divorced in their county. How's that? Enough?" I asked.

"With you, it's all a joke," he said. "What about the boy's father? Why didn't you mention him? Who was he? Or was the boy born out of wedlock?" "Yes," I said. "He was born out of wedlock."

"For Godsakes, doesn't anyone in your stories get married? Doesn't anyone have the time to run down to City Hall before they jump into bed?" "No," I said. "In real life, yes. But in my stories, no." "Why do you answer me like that?"

"Oh, Pa, this is a simple story about a smart woman who came to N.Y.C. full of interest love trust excitement very up to date, and about her son, what a hard time she had in this world. Married or not, it's of small consequence." "It is of great consequence," he said. "O.K.," I said.

"O.K. O.K, yourself," he said, "but listen. I believe you that she's good-looking, but I don't think she was so smart."

"That's true," I said. "Actually that's the trouble with stories. People start out fantastic. You think they're extraordinary, but it turns out as the work goes along, they're just average with a good education. Sometimes the other way around, the person's a kind of dumb innocent, but he outwits you and you can't even think of an ending good enough."

"What do you do then?" he asked. He had been a doctor for a couple of decades and then an artist for a couple of decades and he's still interested in details, craft, technique.

"Well, you just have to let the story lie around till some agreement can be reached between you and the stubborn hero."

"Aren't you talking silly now?" he asked. "Start again," he said. "It so happens I'm not going out this evening. Tell the story again. See what you can do this time."

"O.K.," I said. "But it's not a five-minute job." Second attempt:

Once, across the street from us, there was a fine handsome woman, our neighbor. She had a son whom she loved because she'd known him since birth (in helpless chubby infancy, and in the wrestling, hugging ages, seven to ten, as well as earlier and later). This boy, when he fell into the fist of adolescence, became a junkie. He was not a hopeless one. He was in fact hopeful, an ideologue and successful converter. With his busy brilliance, he wrote persuasive articles for his high-school newspaper. Seeking a wider audience, using important connections, he drummed into Lower Manhattan newsstand distribution a periodical called *Oh! Golden Horse!*

In order to keep him from feeling guilty (because guilt is the stony heart of nine tenths of all clinically diagnosed cancers in America today, she said), and because she had always believed in giving bad habits room at home where one could keep an eye on them, she too became a junkie. Her kitchen was famous for a while—a center for intellectual addicts who knew what they were doing. A few felt artistic like Coleridge[1] and others were scientific and revolutionary like Leary.[2] Although she was often high herself, certain good mothering reflexes remained, and she saw to it that there was lots of orange juice around and honey and milk and vitamin pills. However, she never cooked anything but chili, and that no more than once a week. She explained, when we talked to her, seriously, with neighborly concern, that it was her part in the youth culture and she would rather be with the young, it was an honor, than with her own generation.

One week, while nodding through an Antonioni film, this boy was severely jabbed by the elbow of a stern and proselytizing girl, sitting beside him. She offered immediate apricots and nuts for his sugar level, spoke to him sharply, and took him home.

She had heard of him and his work and she herself published, edited, and wrote a competitive journal called *Man Does Live by Bread Alone*. In the organic heat of her continuous presence he could not help but become interested once more in his muscles, his arteries, and nerve connections. In fact he began to love them, treasure them, praise them with funny little songs in *Man Does Live*...

the fingers of my flesh transcend
my transcendental soul
the tightness in my shoulders end
my teeth have made me whole

To the mouth of his head (that glory of will and determination) he brought hard apples, nuts, wheat germ, and soybean oil. He said to his old friends, From now on, I guess I'll keep my wits about me. I'm going on the natch. He said he was about to begin a spiritual deep-breathing journey. How about you too, Mom? he asked kindly.

His conversion was so radiant, splendid, that neighborhood kids his age began to say that he had never been a real addict at all, only a journalist along for the smell of the story. The mother tried several times to give up what had become without her son and his friends a lonely habit. This effort only brought it to supportable levels. The boy and his girl took their electronic mimeograph and moved to the bushy edge of another borough. They were very strict. They said they would not see her again until she had been off drugs for sixty days.

At home alone in the evening, weeping, the mother read and reread the seven issues of *Oh! Golden Horse!* They seemed to her as truthful as ever. We often crossed the street to visit and console. But if we mentioned any of our children who were at college or in the hospital or dropouts at home, she would cry out, My baby! My baby! and burst into terrible, face-scarring, time-consuming tears. The End.

First my father was silent, then he said, "Number One: You have a nice sense of humor. Number Two: I see you can't tell a plain story. So don't waste

---

1 Coleridge: Samuel Taylor Coleridge (1772-1834), the English Romantic poet, was an opium addict.
2 Leary: Timothy Leary (1920-1996) was a former Harvard professor of psychology and early advocate of the use of LSD.

time." Then he said sadly, "Number Three: I suppose that means she was alone, she was left like that, his mother. Alone. Probably sick?"

I said, "Yes."

"Poor woman. Poor girl, to be born in a time of fools, to live among fools. The end. The end. You were right to put that down. The end."

I didn't want to argue, but I had to say, "Well, it is not necessarily the end, Pa."

"Yes," he said, "what a tragedy. The end of a person."

"No, Pa," I begged him. "It doesn't have to be. She's only about forty. She could be a hundred different things in this world as time goes on. A teacher or a social worker. An ex-junkie! Sometimes it's better than having a master's in education."

"Jokes," he said. "As a writer that's your main trouble. You don't want to recognize it. Tragedy! Plain tragedy! Historical tragedy! No hope. The end."

"Oh, Pa," I said. "She could change."

"In your own life, too, you have to look it in the face." He took a couple of nitroglycerin. "Turn to five," he said, pointing to the dial on the oxygen tank. He inserted the tubes into his nostrils and breathed deep. He closed his eyes and said, "No."

I had promised the family to always let him have the last word when arguing, but in this case I had a different responsibility. That woman lives across the street. She's my knowledge and my invention. I'm sorry for her. I'm not going to leave her there in that house crying. (Actually neither would Life, which unlike me has no pity.)

Therefore: She did change. Of course her son never came home again. But right now, she's the receptionist in a storefront community clinic in the East Village. Most of the customers are young people, some old friends. The head doctor has said to her, "If we only had three people in this clinic with your experiences…"

"The doctor said that?" My father took the oxygen tubes out of his nostrils and said, "Jokes. Jokes again."

"No, Pa, it could really happen that way, it's a funny world nowadays."

"No," he said. "Truth first. She will slide back. A person must have character. She does not."

"No, Pa," I said. "That's it. She's got a job. Forget it. She's in that storefront working."

"How long will it be?" he asked. "Tragedy! You too. When will you look it in the face?"

Lost in the Funhouse

John Barth

For whom is the funhouse fun? Perhaps for lovers. For Ambrose it is a *place of fear and confusion.* He has come to the seashore with his family for the holiday, *the occasion of their visit is Independence Day, the most important secular holiday of the United States of America. A single straight underline is the manuscript mark for italic type, which in turn is the printed equivalent to* oral emphasis of words and phrases as well as the customary type for titles of complete works, not to mention. Italics are also employed, in fiction stories especially, for "outside," intrusive, or artificial voices, such as radio announcements, the texts of telegrams and newspaper articles, et cetera. They

John Barth, "Lost in the Funhouse," from *Lost in the Funhouse*, pp. 72–97. Published by Doubleday Publishing, 1968. Copyright by Random House, Inc. Permission to reprint granted by the rights holder.

should be used *sparingly*. If passages originally in roman type are italicized by someone repeating them, it's customary to acknowledge the fact. *Italics mine.*

Ambrose was "at that awkward age." His voice came out high-pitched as a child's if he let himself get carried away; to be on the safe side, therefore, he moved and spoke with *deliberate calm* and *adult gravity*. Talking soberly of unimportant or irrelevant matters and listening consciously to the sound of your own voice are useful habits for maintaining control in this difficult interval. *En route* to Ocean City he sat in the back seat of the family car with his brother Peter, age fifteen, and Magda G—, age fourteen, a pretty girl and exquisite young lady, who lived not far from them on B—Street in the town of D—, Maryland. Initials, blanks, or both were often substituted for proper names in nineteenth-century fiction to enhance the illusion of reality. It is as if the author felt it necessary to delete the names for reasons of tact or legal liability. Interestingly, as with other aspects of realism, it is an *illusion* that is being enhanced, by purely artificial means. Is it likely, does it violate the principle of verisimilitude, that a thirteen-year-old boy could make such a sophisticated observation? A girl of fourteen is *the psychological coeval* of a boy of fifteen or sixteen; a thirteen-year-old boy, therefore, even one precocious in some other respects, might be three years *her emotional junior*.

Thrice a year—on Memorial, Independence, and Labor Days—the family visits Ocean City for the afternoon and evening. When Ambrose and Peter's father was their age, the excursion was made by train, as mentioned in the novel *The 42nd Parallel* by John Dos Passos. Many families from the same neighborhood used to travel together, with dependent relatives and often with Negro servants; schoolfuls of children swarmed through the railway cars; everyone shared everyone else's Maryland fried chicken, Virginia ham, deviled eggs, potato salad, beaten biscuits, iced tea. Nowadays (that is, in 19—, the year of our story) the journey is made by automobile—more comfortably and quickly though without the extra fun though without the *camaraderie* of a general excursion. It's all part of the deterioration of American life, their father declares; Uncle Karl supposes that when the boys take *their* families to Ocean City for the holidays they'll fly in Autogiros. Their mother, sitting in the middle of the front seat like Magda in the second, only with her arms on the seat-back behind the men's shoulders, wouldn't want the good old days back again, the steaming trains and stuffy long dresses; on the other hand she can do without Autogiros, too, if she has to become a grandmother to fly in them.

Description of physical appearance and mannerisms is one of several standard methods of characterization used by writers of fiction. It is also important to "keep the senses operating"; when a detail from one of the five senses, say visual, is "crossed" with a detail from another, say auditory, the reader's imagination is oriented to the scene, perhaps unconsciously. This procedure may he compared to the way surveyors and navigators determine their positions by two or more compass bearings, a process known as triangulation. The brown hair on Ambrose's mother's forearms gleamed in the sun like. Though right-handed, she took her left arm from the seat back to press the dashboard cigar lighter for Uncle Karl. When the glass bead in its handle glowed red, the lighter was ready for use. The smell of Uncle Karl's cigar smoke reminded one of. The fragrance of the ocean came strong to the picnic ground where they always stopped for lunch, two miles inland from Ocean City. Having to pause for a full hour almost within sound of the breakers was difficult for Peter and Ambrose when they were younger; even at their present age it was not easy to keep their anticipation, *stimulated by the briny spume,* from turning into short temper. The Irish author James Joyce, in his unusual novel entitled *Ulysses,* now available in this country uses the adjectives *snot-green* and *scrotum-tightening* to describe the sea. Visual, auditory tactile, olfactory, gustatory Peter and Ambrose's father, while steering their black 1936 LaSalle sedan with one hand, could with the other remove the first cigarette from a white pack of Lucky Strikes and, more remarkably, light it with a match forefmgered from its book and thumbed against the flint paper without being detached. The matchbook cover merely advertised U.S.

War Bonds and Stamps. A fine metaphor, simile, or other figure of speech, in addition to its obvious "first-order" relevance to the thing it describes, will be seen upon reflection to have a second order of significance: it may be drawn from the *milieu* of the action, for example, or be particularly appropriate to the sensibility of the narrator, even hinting to the reader things of which the narrator is unaware; or it may cast further and subtler lights upon the things it describes, sometimes ironically qualifying the more evident sense of the comparison.

To say that Ambrose's and Peter's mother was *pretty* is to accomplish nothing; the reader may acknowledge the proposition, but his imagination is not engaged. Besides, Magda was also pretty, yet in an altogether different way. Although she lived on B—Street she had very good manners and did better than average in school. Her figure was very well developed for her age. Her right hand lay casually on the plush upholstery of the seat, very near Ambrose's left leg, on which his own hand rested. The space between their legs, between her right and his left leg, was out of the line of sight of anyone sitting on the other side of Magda, as well as anyone glancing into the rear-view mirror. Uncle Karl's face resembled Peter's—rather, vice versa. Both had dark hair and eyes, short husky statures, deep voices. Magda's left hand was probably in a similar position on her left side. The boys' father is difficult to describe; no particular feature of his appearance or manner stood out. He wore glasses and was principal of a T-County grade school. Uncle Karl was a masonry contractor.

Although Peter must have known as well as Ambrose that the latter, because of his position in the car, would be first to see the electrical towers of the power plant at V—, the halfway point of their trip, he leaned forward and slightly toward the center of the car and pretended to be looking for them through the flat pinewoods and tuckahoe creeks along the highway. For as long as the boys could remember, "Looking for the Towers" had been a feature of the first half of their excursions to Ocean City, "looking for the standpipe" of the second. Though the game was childish, their mother preserved the tradition of rewarding the first to see the Towers with a candy-bar or piece of fruit. She insisted now that Magda play the game; the prize, she said, was "something hard to get nowadays." Ambrose decided not to join in; he sat far back in his seat. Magda, like Peter, leaned forward. Two sets of straps were discernible through the shoulders of her sun dress; the inside right one, a brassiere-strap, was fastened or shortened with a small safety pin. The right armpit of her dress, presumably the left as well, was damp with perspiration. The simple strategy for being first to espy the Towers, which Ambrose had understood by the age of four, was to sit on the right-hand side of the car. Whoever sat there, however, had also to put up with the worst of the sun, and so Ambrose, without mentioning the matter, chose sometimes the one and sometimes the other. Not impossibly Peter had never caught on to the trick, or thought that his brother hadn't simply because Ambrose on occasion preferred shade to a Baby Ruth or tangerine.

The shade-sun situation didn't apply to the front seat, owing to the windshield; if anything the driver got more sun, since the person on the passenger side not only was shadowed below by the door and dashboard but might swing down his sun visor all the way too.

"Is that them?" Magda asked. Ambrose's mother teased the boys for letting Magda win, insinuating that "somebody [had] a girlfriend." Peter and Ambrose's father reached a long thin arm across their mother to butt his cigarette in the dashboard ashtray, under the lighter. The prize this time for seeing the Towers first was a banana. Their mother bestowed it after chiding their father for wasting a half-smoked cigarette when everything was so scarce. Magda, to take the prize, moved her hand from so near Ambrose's that he could have touched it as though accidentally. She offered to share the prize, things like that were so hard to find; but everyone insisted it was hers alone. Ambrose's mother sang an iambic trimeter couplet from a popular song, femininely rhymed:

"What's good is in the Army;
What's left will never harm me."

Uncle Karl tapped his cigar ash out the ventilator window; some particles were sucked by the slipstream back into the car through the rear window on the passenger side. Magda demonstrated her ability to hold a banana in one hand and peel it with her teeth. She still sat forward; Ambrose pushed his glasses back onto the bridge of his nose with his left hand, which he then negligently let fall to the seat cushion immediately behind her. He even permitted the single hair, gold, on the second joint of his thumb to brush the fabric of her skirt. Should she have sat back at that instant, his hand would have been caught under her.

Plush upholstery prickles uncomfortably through gabardine slacks in the July sun. The function of the *beginning* of a story is to introduce the principal characters, establish their initial relationships, set the scene for the main action, expose the background of the situation if necessary, plant motifs and foreshadowings where appropriate, and initiate the first complication or whatever of the "rising action." Actually, if one imagines a story called "The Funhouse," or "Lost in the Funhouse," the details of the drive to Ocean City don't seem especially relevant. The *beginning* should recount the events between Ambrose's first sight of the funhouse early in the afternoon and his entering it with Magda and Peter in the evening. The *middle* would narrate all relevant events from the time he goes in to the time he loses his way; middles have the double and contradictory function of delaying the climax while at the same time preparing the reader for it and fetching him to it. Then the *ending* would tell what Ambrose does while he's lost, how he finally finds his way out, and what everybody makes of the experience. So far there's been no real dialogue, very little sensory detail, and nothing in the way of a *theme*. And a long time has gone by already without anything happening; it makes a person wonder. We haven't even reached Ocean City yet: we will never get out of the funhouse.

The more closely an author identifies with the narrator, literally or metaphorically, the less advisable it is, as a rule, to use the first-person narrative viewpoint. Once three years previously the young people *aforementioned* played Niggers and Masters in the backyard; when it was Ambrose's turn to be Master and theirs to be Niggers Peter had to go serve his evening papers; Ambrose was afraid to punish Magda alone, but she led him to the whitewashed Torture Chamber between the woodshed and the privy in the Slaves Quarters; there she knelt sweating among bamboo rakes and dusty Mason jars, pleadingly embraced his knees, and while bees droned in the lattice as if on an ordinary summer afternoon, purchased clemency at a surprising price set by herself. Doubtless she remembered nothing of this event; Ambrose on the other hand seemed unable to forget the least detail of his life. He even recalled how, standing beside himself with awed impersonality in the reeky heat, he'd stared the while at an empty cigar box in which Uncle Karl kept stonecutting chisels: beneath the words *El Producto,* a laureled, loose-toga'd lady regarded the sea from a marble bench; beside her, forgotten, or not yet turned to, was a five-stringed lyre. Her chin reposed on the back of her right hand; her left depended negligently from the bench-arm. The lower half of scene and lady was peeled away; the words EXAMINED BY—were inked there into the wood. Nowadays cigar boxes are made of pasteboard. Ambrose wondered what Magda would have done, Ambrose wondered what Magda would do when she sat back on his hand as he resolved she should. Be angry Make a teasing joke of it. Give no sign at all. For a long time she leaned forward, playing cowpoker with Peter against Uncle Karl and Mother and watching for the first sign of Ocean City. At nearly the same instant, picnic ground and Ocean City standpipe hove into view; an Amoco filling station on their side of the road cost Mother and Uncle Karl fifty cows and the game; Magda bounced back, clapping her right hand on Mother's right arm; Ambrose moved clear "in the nick of time."

At this rate our hero, at this rate our protagonist will remain in the funhouse forever. Narrative ordinarily consists of alternating dramatization and summarization. One symptom of nervous tension, paradoxically, is repeated and violent yawning; neither Peter nor Magda nor Uncle Karl nor Mother reacted in this manner. Although they were no longer small children, Peter and Ambrose were each given a dollar to spend on boardwalk amusements in addition to what money of their own they'd brought along. Magda too, though she protested she had ample spending money. The boys' mother made a little scene out of distributing the bills; she pretended that her sons and Magda were small children and cautioned them not to spend the sum too quickly or in one place. Magda promised with a merry laugh and, having both hands free, took the bill with her left. Peter laughed also and pledged in a falsetto to be a good boy. His imitation of a child was not clever. The boys' father was tall and thin, balding, fair-complexioned. Assertions of that sort are not effective; the reader may acknowledge the proposition, but. We should be much farther along than we are; something has gone wrong; not much of the preliminary rambling seems relevant. Yet everyone begins in the same place; how is it that most go along without difficulty but a few lose their way?

"Stay out from under the boardwalk," Uncle Karl growled from the side of his mouth. The boys' mother pushed his shoulder *in mock annoyance.* They were all standing before Fat May the Laughing Lady who advertised the funhouse. Larger than life, Fat May mechanically shook, rocked on her heels, slapped her thighs while recorded laughter—uproarious, female—came amplified from a hidden loudspeaker. It chuckled, wheezed, wept; tried in vain to catch its breath; tittered, groaned, exploded raucous and anew. You couldn't hear it without laughing yourself, no matter how you felt. Father came back from talking to a Coast-Guardsman on duty and reported that the surf was spoiled with crude oil from tankers recently torpedoed offshore. Lumps of it, difficult to remove, made tarry tidelines on the beach and stuck on swimmers. Many bathed in the surf nevertheless and came out speckled; others paid to use a municipal pool and only sunbathed on the beach. We would do the latter. We would do the latter. We would do the latter.

Under the boardwalk, matchbook covers, grainy other things. What is the story's theme? Ambrose is ill. He perspires in the dark passages, candied apples-on-a-stick, delicious-looking, disappointing to eat. Funhouses need men's and ladies' rooms at intervals. Others perhaps have also vomited in corners and corridors; may even have had bowel movements liable to be stepped in in the dark. The word *fuck* suggests suction and/or and/or flatulence. Mother and Father; grandmothers and grandfathers on both sides; great-grandmothers and great-grandfathers on four sides, et cetera. Count a generation as thirty years: in approximately the year when Lord Baltimore was granted charter to the province of Maryland by Charles I, five hundred twelve women—English, Welsh, Bavarian, Swiss—of every class and character, received into themselves the penises the intromittent organs of five hundred twelve men, ditto, in every circumstance and posture, to conceive the five hundred twelve ancestors and the two hundred fifty-six ancestors of the et cetera et cetera et cetera et cetera et cetera et cetera et cetera et cetera of the author, of the narrator, of this story, *Lost in the Funhouse.* In alleyways, ditches, canopy beds, pinewoods, bridal suites, ship's cabins, coach-and-fours, coaches, and four sultry toolsheds; on the cold sand under boardwalks, littered with *El Producto* cigar butts, treasured with Lucky Strike cigarette stubs, Coca-Cola caps, gritty turds, cardboard lollipop sticks, matchbook covers warning that A Slip of the Lip Can Sink a Ship. The shluppish whisper, continuous as seawash round the globe, tidelike falls and rises with the circuit of dawn and dusk.

Magda's teeth. She *was* left-handed. Perspiration. They've gone all the way, through, Magda and Peter, they've been waiting for hours with Mother and Uncle Karl while Father searches for his lost son; they draw french-fried potatoes from a paper cup and shake their heads. They've named the children they'll one day have and bring to Ocean City on holidays. Can spermatozoa properly be thought of as male animalcules when there are no female spermatozoa? They grope through hot, dark windings, past Love's Tunnel's fearsome obstacles. Some perhaps lose their way.

Peter suggested then and there that they do the funhouse; he had been through it before, so had Magda, Ambrose hadn't and suggested, his voice cracking on account of Fat May's laughter, that they swim first. All were chuckling, couldn't help it; Ambrose's father, Ambrose's and Peter's father came up grinning like a lunatic with two boxes of syrup-coated popcorn, one for Mother, one for Magda; the men were to help themselves. Ambrose walked on Magda's right; being by nature left-handed, she carried the box in her left hand. Up front the situation was reversed.

"What are you limping for?" Magda inquired of Ambrose. He supposed in a husky tone that his foot had gone to sleep in the car. Her teeth flashed. "Pins and needles?" It was the honeysuckle on the lattice of the former privy that drew the bees. Imagine being stung there. How long is this going to take?

The adults decided to forgo the pool; but Uncle Karl insisted they change into swimsuits and do the beach. "He wants to watch the pretty girls," Peter teased, and ducked behind Magda from Uncle Karl's pretended wrath. "You've got all the pretty girls you need right here," Magda declared, and Mother said: "Now that's the gospel truth." Magda scolded Peter, who reached over her shoulder to sneak some popcorn. "Your brother and father aren't getting any" Uncle Karl wondered if they were going to have fireworks that night, what with the shortages. It wasn't the shortages, Mr. M—replied; Ocean City had fireworks from pre-war. But it was too risky on account of the enemy submarines, some people thought.

"Don't seem like Fourth of July without fireworks," said Uncle Karl. The inverted tag in dialogue writing is still considered permissible with proper names or epithets, but sounds old-fashioned with personal pronouns. "We'll have 'em again soon enough," predicted the boys' father. Their mother declared she could do without fireworks: they reminded her too much of the real thing. Their father said all the more reason to shoot off a few now and again. Uncle Karl asked *rhetorically* who needed reminding, just look at people's hair and skin.

"The oil, yes," said Mrs. M.

Ambrose had a pain in his stomach and so didn't swim but enjoyed watching the others. He and his father burned red easily Magda's figure was exceedingly well developed for her age. The too declined to swim, and got mad, and became angry when Peter attempted to drag her into the pool. She always swam, he insisted; what did she mean not swim? Why did a person come to Ocean City?

"Maybe I want to lay here with Ambrose," Magda teased.

Nobody likes a pedant.

"Aha," said Mother. Peter grabbed Magda by one ankle and ordered Ambrose to grab the other. She squealed and rolled over on the beach blanket. Ambrose pretended to help hold her back. Her tan was darker than even Mother's and Peter's. "Help out, Uncle Karl!" Peter cried. Uncle Karl went to seize the other ankle. Inside the top of her swimsuit, however, you could see the line where the sunburn ended and, when she hunched her shoulders and squealed again, one nipple's auburn edge. Mother made them behave themselves. "*You* should certainly know," she said to Uncle Karl. Archly "That when a lady says she doesn't feel like swimming, a gentleman doesn't ask questions." Uncle Karl said excuse *him;* Mother winked at Magda; Ambrose blushed; stupid Peter kept saying "Phooey on *feel like!*" and tugging at Magda's ankle; then even he got the point, and cannonballed with a holler into the pool.

"I swear," Magda said, in mock *in feigned* exasperation.

The diving would make a suitable literary symbol. To go off the high board you had to wait in a line along the poolside and up the ladder. Fellows tickled girls and goosed one another and shouted to the ones at the top to hurry up, or razzed them for bellyfloppers. Once on the springboard some took a great while posing or clowning or deciding on a dive or getting up their nerve; others ran right off. Especially among the younger fellows the idea was to strike the funniest pose or do the craziest stunt as you fell, a thing that got harder to do as you kept on and kept on. But whether you hollered *Geronimo!* or *Sieg heil!*, held your nose or "rode a bicycle," pretended to be shot or did a perfect jackknife or changed your mind halfway down and ended up with nothing, it was over in two seconds, after all that wait. Spring, pose, splash. Spring, neat-o, splash, Spring, aw fooey, splash.

The grown-ups had gone on; Ambrose wanted to converse with Magda; she was remarkably well developed for her age; it was said that that came from rubbing with a turkish towel, and there were other theories. Ambrose could think of nothing to say except how good a diver Peter was, who was showing off for her benefit. You could pretty well tell by looking at their bathing suits and arm muscles how far along the different fellows were. Ambrose was glad he hadn't gone in swimming, the cold water shrank you up so. Magda pretended to be uninterested in the diving; she probably weighed as much as he did. If you knew your way around in the funhouse like your own bedroom, you could wait until a girl came along and then slip away without ever getting caught, even if her boyfriend right with her. She'd think *he* did it! It would be better to be the boyfriend, and act outraged, and tear the funhouse apart.

Not act; *be*.

"He's a master diver," Ambrose said. In feigned admiration. "You really have to slave away at it to get that good." What would it matter anyhow if he asked her right out whether she remembered, even teased her with it as Peter would have?

There's no point in going farther; this isn't getting anybody anywhere; they haven't even come to the funhouse yet. Ambrose is off the track, in some new or old part of the place that's not supposed to be used; he strayed into it by some one-in-a-million chance, like the time the roller-coaster car left the tracks in the nineteen-teens against all the laws of physics and sailed over the boardwalk in the dark. And they can't locate him because they don't know where to look. Even the designer and operator have forgotten this other part, that winds around on itself like a whelk shell. That winds around the right part like the snakes on Mercury's caduceus. Some people, perhaps, don't "hit their stride" until their twenties, when the growing-up business is over and women appreciate other things besides wisecracks and teasing and strutting. Peter didn't have one-tenth the imagination *he* had, not one-tenth. Peter did this naming-their-children thing as a joke, making up names like Aloysius and Murgatroyd, but Ambrose knew *exactly* how it would feel to be married and have children of your own, and be a loving husband and father, and go comfortably to work in the mornings and to bed with your wife at night, and wake up with her there. With a breeze coming through the sash and birds and mockingbirds singing in the Chinese-cigar trees. His eyes watered, there aren't enough ways to say that. He would be quite famous in his line of work. Whether Magda was his wife or not, one evening when he was wise-lined and gray at the temples he'd smile gravely, at a fashionable dinner party and remind her of his youthful passion. The time they went with his family to Ocean City; the *erotic fantasies* he used to have about her. How long ago it seemed, and childish! Yet tender, too, *n 'est-ce pas?* Would she have imagined that the world-famous whatever remembered how many strings were on the lyre on the bench beside the girl on the label of the cigar box he'd stared at in the tool shed at age ten while, she, age eleven. Even then he had felt *wise beyond his years;* he'd stroked her hair and said in his deepest voice and correctest English, as to a dear child: "I shall never forget this moment."

But though he had breathed heavily, groaned as if ecstatic, what he'd really felt throughout was an odd detachment, as though someone else were Master. Strive as he might to be transported, he heard his mind take notes upon the scene: *This is what they call* passion. *I am experiencing it.* Many of the digger machines were out of order in the penny arcades and could not be repaired or replaced for the duration. Moreover the prizes, made now in USA, were less interesting than formerly, pasteboard items for the most part, and some of the machines wouldn't work on white pennies. The gypsy fortuneteller machine might have provided a foreshadowing of the climax of this story if Ambrose had operated it. It was even dilapidateder than most: the silver coating was worn off the brown metal handles, the glass windows around the dummy were cracked and taped, her kerchiefs and silks long faded. If a man lived by himself, he could take a department-store mannequin with flexible joints and modify her in certain ways. *However:* by the time he was that old he'd have a real woman. There was a machine that stamped your name around a white-metal coin with a star in the middle: A . His son would be the second, and when the lad reached thirteen or so he would put a strong arm around his shoulder and tell him calmly: "It is perfectly normal. We have all been through it. It will not last forever." Nobody knew how to be what they were right. He'd smoke a pipe, teach his son how to fish and softcrab, assure him he needn't worry about himself. Magda would certainly give, Magda would certainly yield a great deal of milk, although guilty of occasional solecisms. It don't taste so bad. Suppose the lights came on now!

The day wore on. You think you're yourself, but there are other persons in you. Ambrose gets hard when Ambrose doesn't want to, *and obversely.* Ambrose watches them disagree; Ambrose watches him watch. In the fun-house mirror room you can't see yourself go on forever, because no matter how you stand, your head gets in the way. Even if you had a glass periscope, the image of your eye would cover up the thing you really wanted to see. The police will come; there'll be a story in the papers. That must be where it happened. Unless he can find a surprise exit, an unofficial backdoor or escape hatch opening on an alley, say, and then stroll up to the family in front of the funhouse and ask where everybody's been; *he's* been out of the place for ages. That's just where it happened, in that last lighted room: Peter and Magda found the right exit; he found one that you weren't supposed to find and strayed off into the works somewhere. In a perfect funhouse you'd be able to go only one way, like the divers off the high board; getting lost would be impossible; the doors and halls would work like minnow traps on the valves in veins.

On account of German U-boats, Ocean City was "browned out": streetlights were shaded on the seaward side; shop-windows and boardwalk amusement places were kept dim, not to silhouette tankers and Liberty ships for torpedoing. In a short story about Ocean City, Maryland, during World War II, the author could make use of the image of sailors on leave in the penny arcades and shooting galleries, sighting through the crosshairs of toy machine guns at swastika'd subs, while out in the black Atlantic a U-boat skipper squints through his periscope at real ships outlined by the glow of penny arcades. After dinner the family strolled back to the amusement end of the boardwalk. The boys' father had burnt red as always and was masked with Noxzema, a minstrel in reverse. The grownups stood at the end of the boardwalk where the Hurricane of '33 had cut an inlet from the ocean to Assawoman Bay.

"Pronounced with a long *o,* " Uncle Karl reminded Magda with a wink. His shirt sleeves were rolled up; Mother punched his brown biceps with the arrowed heart on it and said his mind was naughty. Fat May's laugh came suddenly from the funhouse, as if she'd just got the joke; the family laughed too at the coincidence. Ambrose went under the boardwalk to search for out-of-town matchbook covers with the aid of his pocket flashlight; he looked out from the edge of the North American continent and wondered how far their laughter carried over the water. Spies in rubber rafts; survivors in lifeboats. If the joke had been beyond his understanding, he could have said:

"The laughter was over his head." And let the reader see the serious wordplay on second reading.

He turned the flashlight on and then off at once even before the woman whooped. He sprang away, heart athud, dropping the light. What had the man grunted? Perspiration drenched and chilled him by the time he scrambled up to the family. "See anything?" his father asked. His voice wouldn't come; he shrugged and violently brushed sand from his pants legs.

"Let's ride the old flying horses!" Magda cried. I'll never be an author. It's been forever already, everybody's gone home, Ocean City's deserted, the ghost-crabs are tickling across the beach and down the littered cold streets. And the empty halls of clapboard hotels and abandoned funhouses. A tidal wave; an enemy air raid; a monster-crab swelling like an island from the sea. *The inhabitants fled in terror.* Magda clung to his trouser leg; he alone knew the maze's secret. "He gave his life that we might live," said Uncle Karl with a scowl of pain, as he. The fellow's hands had been tattooed; the woman's legs, the woman's fat white legs had. *An astonishing coincidence.* He yearned to tell Peter. He wanted to throw up for excitement. They hadn't even chased him. He wished he were dead.

One possible ending would be to have Ambrose come across another lost person in the dark. They'd match their wits together against the funhouse, struggle like Ulysses past obstacle after obstacle, help and encourage each other. Or a girl. By the time they found the exit they'd be closest friends, sweethearts if it were a girl; they'd know each other's inmost souls, be bound together *by the cement of shared adventure;* then they'd emerge into the light and it would turn out that his friend was a Negro. A blind girl. President Roosevelt's son. Ambrose's former archenemy

Shortly after the mirror room he'd groped along a musty corridor, his heart already misgiving him at the absence of phosphorescent arrows and other signs. He'd found a crack of light—not a door, it turned out, but a seam between the ply board wall panels—and squinting up to it, espied a small old man, *in appearance not unlike* the photographs at home of Ambrose's late grandfather, nodding upon a stool beneath a bare, speckled bulb. A crude panel of toggle-and knife-switches hung beside the open fuse box near his head; elsewhere in the little room were wooden levers and ropes belayed to boat cleats. At the time, Ambrose wasn't lost enough to rap or call; later he couldn't find that crack. Now it seemed to him that he'd possibly dozed off for a few minutes somewhere along the way; certainly he was exhausted from the afternoon's sunshine and the evening's problems; he couldn't be sure he hadn't dreamed part or all of the sight. Had an old black wall fan droned like bees and shimmied two flypaper streamers? Had the funhouse operator—gentle, somewhat sad and tired-appearing, in expression not unlike the photographs at home of Ambrose's late Uncle Konrad—murmured in his sleep? Is there really such a person as Ambrose, or is he a figment of the author's imagination? Was it Assawoman Bay or Sinepuxent? Are there other errors of fact in this fiction? Was there another sound besides the little slap slap of thigh on ham, like water sucking at the chine-boards of a skiff?

When you're lost, the smartest thing to do is stay put till you're found hollering if necessary. But to holler guarantees humiliation as well as rescue; keeping silent permits some saving of face—you can act surprised at the fuss when your rescuers find you and swear you weren't lost, if they do. What's more you might find your own way yet, *however belatedly.*

"Don't tell me your foot's still asleep!" Magda exclaimed as the three young people walked from the inlet to the area set aside for ferris wheels, carrousels, and other carnival rides, they having decided in favor of the vast and ancient merry-go-round instead of the funhouse. What a sentence, everything was wrong from the outset. People don't know what to make of him, he doesn't know what to make of himself, he's only thirteen, *athletically and socially inept,* not astonishingly bright, but there are antennae; he has…some sort of receivers in his head; things speak to him, he understands more than he should, the world winks at him through its objects, grabs grinning at his coat. Everybody else is in on some secret he doesn't know; they've forgotten to tell him. Through simple *procrastination* his mother put off his baptism until this year. Everyone else had it done as a baby; he'd assumed the same of himself, as had his mother, so she claimed, until it was time for him to join Grace Methodist-Protestant and the oversight came out. He was mortified, but pitched sleepless through his private catechizing, intimidated by the ancient mysteries, a thirteen year old would never say that, resolved to experience conversion like St. Augustine. When the water touched his brow and Adam's sin left him, he contrived by a strain like defecation to bring tears into his eyes—but felt nothing. There was some simple, radical difference about him; he hoped it was genius, feared it was madness, devoted himself to amiability and inconspicuousness. Alone on the seawall near his house he was seized by the terrifying transports he'd thought to find in tool shed, in Communion-cup. The grass was alive! The town, the river, himself, were not imaginary; time roared in his ears like wind; the world was *going on!* This part ought to be dramatized. The Irish author James Joyce once wrote. Ambrose M—is going to scream.

There is no *texture of rendered sensory detail,* for one thing. The faded distorting mirrors beside Fat May; the impossibility of choosing a mount when one had but a single ride on the great carrousel; the *vertigo attendant on his recognition* that Ocean City was worn out, the place of fathers and grandfathers, straw-boatered men and parasoled ladies survived by their amusements. Money spent, the three paused at Peter's insistence beside Fat May to watch the girls get their skirts blown up. The object was to tease Magda, who said: "I swear, Peter M—, you've got a one-track mind! Amby and me aren't *interested* in such things." In the tumbling-barrel, too, just inside the Devil's mouth enhance to the funhouse, the girls were upended and their boyfriends and others could see up their dresses if they cared to. Which was the whole point, Ambrose realized. Of the entire funhouse! If you looked around, you noticed that almost all the people on the boardwalk were paired off into couples except the small children; in a way, that was the whole point of Ocean City! If you had X-ray eyes and could see everything going on at that instant under the boardwalk and in all the hotel rooms and cars and alleyways, you'd realize that all that normally *showed*, like restaurants and dance halls and clothing and test-your-strength machines, was merely preparation and intermission. Fat May screamed.

Because he watched the going-ons from the corner of his eye, it was Ambrose who spied the half-dollar on the boardwalk near the tumbling-barrel. Losers weepers. The first time he'd heard some people moving through a corridor not far away, just after he'd lost sight of the crack of light, he'd decided not to call to them, for fear they'd guess he was scared and poke fun; it sounded like roughnecks; he'd hoped they'd come by and he could follow in the dark without their knowing. Another time he'd heard just one person, unless he imagined it, bumping along as if on the other side of the plywood; perhaps Peter coming back for him, or Father, or Magda lost too. Or the owner and operator of the funhouse. He'd called out once, as though merrily:

"Anybody know where the heck we are?" But the query was too stiff, his voice cracked, when the sounds stopped he was terrified: maybe it was a queer who waited for fellows to get lost, or a longhaired filthy monster that lived in some cranny of the funhouse. He stood rigid for hours it seemed like, scarcely respiring. His future was shockingly clear, in outline. He tried holding his breath to the point of unconsciousness. There ought to be a button you could push to end your life absolutely without pain; disappear in a flick, like turning out a light. He would push it instantly! He despised Uncle Karl. But he despised his father too, for not being what he was supposed to be. Perhaps his father hated *his* father, and so on, and his son would hate him, and so on. Instantly!

Naturally he didn't have nerve enough to ask Magda to go through the funhouse with him. With incredible nerve and to everyone's surprise he invited Magda, quietly and politely, to go through the funhouse with him. "I warn you, I've never been through it before," he added, *laughing easily;* "but I reckon we can manage somehow. The important thing to remember, after all, is that it's meant to be a funhouse; that is, a place of amusement. If people really got lost or injured or too badly frightened in it, the owner'd go out of business. There'd even be lawsuits. No character in a work of fiction can make a speech this long without interruption or acknowledgment from the other characters."

Mother teased Uncle Karl: "Three's a crowd, I always heard." But actually Ambrose was relieved that Peter now had a quarter too. Nothing was what it looked like. Every instant, under the surface of the Atlantic Ocean, millions of living animals devoured one another. Pilots were falling in flames over Europe; women were being forcibly raped in the South Pacific. His father should have taken him aside and said: "There is a simple secret to getting through the funhouse, as simple as being first to see the Towers. Here it is. Peter does not know it; neither does your Uncle Karl. You and I are different. Not surprisingly, you've often wished you weren't. Don't think I haven't noticed how unhappy your childhood has been! But you'll understand, when I tell you, why it had to be kept secret until now. And you won't regret not being like your brother and your uncle. *On the contrary!"* If you knew all the stories behind all the people on the boardwalk, you'd see that *nothing* was what it looked like. Husbands and wives often hated each other; parents didn't necessarily love their children; et cetera. A child took things for granted because he had nothing to compare his life to and everybody acted as if things were as they should be. Therefore each saw himself as the hero of the story, when the truth might turn out to be that he's the villain, or the coward. And there wasn't one thing you could do about it!

Hunchbacks, fat ladies, fools—that no one chose what he was was unbearable. In the movies he'd meet a beautiful young girl in the funhouse; they'd have hairs-breadth escapes from real dangers; he'd do and say the right things; she also; in the end they'd be lovers; their dialogue lines would match up; he'd be perfectly at ease; she'd not only like him well enough, she'd think he was *marvelous;* she'd lie awake thinking about *him,* instead of vice versa—the way *his* face looked in different lights and how he stood and exactly what he'd said—and yet that would be only one small episode in his wonderful life, among many many others. Not a *turning point* at all. What had happened in the tool shed was nothing. He hated, he loathed his parents! One reason for not writing a lost-in-the-funhouse story is that either everybody's felt what Ambrose feels, in which case it goes without saying, or else no normal person feels such things, in which case Ambrose is a freak. "Is anything more tiresome, in fiction, than the problems of sensitive adolescents?" And it's all too long and rambling, as if the author. For all a person knows the first time through, the end could be just around any corner; perhaps, *not impossibly* it's been within reach any number of times. On the other hand he may be scarcely past the start, with everything yet to get through, an intolerable idea.

Fill in: His father's raised eyebrows when he announced his decision to do the funhouse with Magda. Ambrose understands now, but didn't then, that his father was wondering whether he knew what the funhouse was *for*—especially since he didn't object, as he should have, when Peter decided to come along too. The ticket-woman, witchlike, mortifying him when inadvertently he gave her his name-coin instead of the half-dollar, then unkindly calling Magda's attention to the birthmark on his temple: "Watch out for him, girlie, he's a marked man!" She wasn't even cruel, he understood, only vulgar and insensitive. Somewhere in the world there was a young woman with such splendid understanding that she'd see him entire, like a poem or story, and find his words so valuable after all that when he confessed his apprehensions she would explain why they were in fact the very things that made him precious to her...and to Western Civilization! There was no such girl, the simple truth being. Violent yawns as they approached the mouth. Whispered advice from an old-timer on a bench near the barrel: "Go crab wise and ye'll get an eyeful without upsetting!" Composure vanished at the first pitch: Peter hollered joyously, Magda tumbled, shrieked, clutched her skirt; Ambrose scrambled crab wise, tight-lipped with terror, was soon out, watched his dropped name-coin slide among the couples. Shame-faced he saw that to get through expeditiously was not the point; Peter feigned assistance in order to trip Magda up, shouted "I see Christmas!" when her legs went flying. The old man, his latest betrayer, cackled approval. A dim hail then of black-thread cobwebs and recorded gibber: he took Magda's elbow to steady her against revolving discs set in the slanted floor to throw your feet out from under, and explained to her in a calm, deep voice his theory that each phase of the funhouse was triggered either automatically, by a series of photoelectric devices, or else manually by operators stationed at peepholes. But he lost his voice thrice as the discs unbalanced him; Magda was anyhow squealing; but at one point she clutched him about the waist to keep from falling, and her right cheek pressed for a moment against his belt-buckle. Heroically he drew her up, it was his chance to clutch her close as if for support and say: "I love you." He even put an arm lightly about the small of her back before a sailor-and-girl pitched into them from behind, sorely treading his left big toe and knocking Magda asprawl with them. The sailor's girl was a string-haired hussy with a loud laugh and light blue drawers; Ambrose realized that he wouldn't have said "I love you" anyhow, and was smitten with self-contempt. How much better it would be to be that common sailor! A wiry little Seaman 3rd, the fellow squeezed a girl to each side and stumbled hilarious into the mirror room, closer to Magda in thirty seconds than Ambrose had got in thirteen years. She giggled at something the fellow said to Peter; she drew her hair from her eyes with a movement so womanly it struck Ambrose's heart; Peter's smacking her backside then seemed particularly coarse. But Magda made a pleased indignant face and cried, "All right for *you,* mister!" and pursued Peter into the maze without a backward glance. The sailor followed after, leisurely, drawing his girl against his hip; Ambrose understood not only that they were all so relieved to be rid of his burdensome company that they didn't even notice his absence, but that he himself shared their relief. Stepping from the treacherous passage at last into the mirror-maze, he saw once again, more clearly than ever, how readily he deceived himself into supposing he was a person. He even foresaw, wincing at his dreadful self-knowledge, that he would repeat the deception, at ever-rarer intervals, all his wretched life, so fearful were the alternatives. Fame, madness, suicide; perhaps all three. It's not believable that so young a boy could articulate that reflection, and in fiction the merely true must always yield to the plausible. Moreover, the symbolism is in places heavy-footed. Yet Ambrose M—understood, as few adults do, that the famous loneliness of the great was no popular myth but a general truth—furthermore, that it was as much cause as effect.

All the preceding except the last few sentences is exposition that should've been done earlier or interspersed with the present action instead of lumped together. No reader would put up with so much with such *prolixity*. It's interesting that Ambrose's father, though presumably an intelligent man (as indicated by his role as grade-school principal), neither encouraged nor discouraged his sons at all in any way—as if he either didn't care about them or cared all right but didn't know how to act. If this fact should contribute to one of them's becoming a celebrated but wretchedly unhappy scientist, was it a good thing or not? He too might someday face the question; it would be useful to know whether it had tortured his father for years, for example, or never once crossed his mind.

In the maze two important things happened. First, our hero found a name-coin someone else had lost or discarded: AMBROSE, suggestive of the famous lightship and of his late grandfather's favorite dessert, which his mother used to prepare on special occasions out of coconut, oranges, grapes, and what else. Second, as he wondered at the endless replication of his image in the mirrors, second, as he *lost himself in the reflection* that the necessity for an observer makes perfect observation impossible, better make him eighteen at least, yet that would render other things unlikely, he heard Peter and Magda chuckling somewhere together in the maze. "Here!" "No, here!" they shouted to each other; Peter said, "Where's Amby?" Magda murmured "Amb?" Peter called. In a pleased, friendly voice. He didn't reply. The truth was, his brother was a *happy-go-lucky youngster* who'd've been better off with a regular brother of his own, but who seldom complained of his lot and was generally cordial. Ambrose's throat ached; there aren't enough different ways to say that. He stood quietly while the two young people giggled and thumped through the glittering maze, hurrah'd their discovery of its exit, cried out in joyful alarm at what next beset them. Then he set his mouth and followed after, as he supposed, took a wrong turn, strayed into the pass *wherein he lingers yet*.

The action of conventional dramatic narrative may be represented by a diagram called Freitag's Triangle:

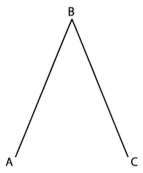

or more accurately by a variant of that diagram:

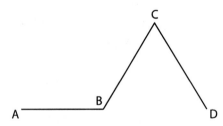

in which *AB* represents the exposition, *B* the introduction of conflict, *BC* the "rising action," complication, or development of the conflict, *C* the climax, or turn of the action, *CD* the denouement, or resolution of the conflict. While there is no reason to regard this pattern as an absolute necessity, like many other conventions it became conventional because great numbers of people over many years learned by trial and error that it was effective; one ought not to forsake it, therefore, unless one wishes to forsake as well the effect of drama or has clear cause to feel that deliberate violation of the "normal" pattern can better can better effect that effect. This can't go on much longer; it can go on forever. He died telling stories to himself in the dark; years later, when that vast unsuspected area of the funhouse came to light, the first expedition found his skeleton in one of its labyrinthine corridors and mistook it for part of the entertainment. He died of starvation telling himself stories in the dark; but unbeknownst unbeknownst to him, an assistant operator of the funhouse, happening to overhear him, crouched just behind the ply board partition and wrote down his every word. The operator's daughter, an exquisite young woman with a figure unusually well developed for her age, crouched just behind the partition and transcribed his every word. Though she had never laid eyes on him, she recognized that here was one of Western Culture's truly great imaginations, the eloquence of whose suffering would be an inspiration to unnumbered. And her heart was torn between her love for the misfortunate young man (yes, she loved him, though she had never laid though she knew him only—but how well!—through his words, and the deep, calm voice in which he spoke them) between her love et cetera and her womanly intuition that only in suffering and isolation could he give voice et cetera. Lone dark dying. Quietly she kissed the rough ply board, and a tear fell upon the page. Where she had written in shorthand *Where she had written in shorthand* Where she had written in shorthand *Where she* et cetera. A long time ago we should have passed the apex of Freitag's Triangle and made brief work of the *denouement;* the plot doesn't rise by meaningful steps but winds upon itself, digresses, retreats, hesitates, sighs, collapses, expires, The climax of the story must be its protagonist's discovery of a way to get through the funhouse. But he had found none, may have ceased to search.

What relevance does the war have to the story? Should there be fireworks outside or not?

Ambrose wandered, languished, dozed. Now and then he fell into his habit of rehearsing to himself the unadventurous story of his life, narrated from the third-person point of view, from his earliest memory parenthesis of maple leaves stirring in the summer breath of tidewater Maryland end of parenthesis to the present moment. Its principal events, on this telling, would appear to have been *A, B, C,* and *D*.

He imagined himself years hence, successful, married, at ease in the world, the trials of his adolescence far behind him. He has come to the seashore with his family for the holiday: how Ocean City has changed! But at one seldom at one ill-frequented end of the boardwalk a few derelict, amusements survive from times gone by: the great carrousel from the turn of the century, with its monstrous griffins and mechanical concert band; the roller coaster rumored since 1916 to have been condemned; the mechanical shooting gallery in which only the image of our enemies changed: His own son laughs with Fat May and wants to know what a funhouse is; Ambrose hugs the sturdy lad close and smiles around his pipe stem at his wife.

The family's going home. Mother sits between Father and Uncle Karl, who teases him good-naturedly who chuckles over the fact that the comrade with whom he'd fought his way shoulder to shoulder through the funhouse had turned out to be a blind Negro girl—to their mutual discomfort, as they'd opened their souls. But such are the walls of custom, which even. Whose arm is where? How must it feel. He dreams of a funhouse vaster by far than any yet constructed; but by then they may be out of fashion, like steamboats and excursion trains. Already quaint and seedy: the draperied ladies on the frieze of the carrousel are his father's father's mooncheeked dreams; if he thinks of it more he will vomit his apple-on-a-stick.

He wonders: will he become a regular person? Something has gone wrong; his vaccination didn't take; at the Boy-Scout initiation campfire he only pretended to be deeply moved, as he pretends to this hour that it is not so bad after all in the funhouse, and that he has a little limp. How long will it last? He envisions a truly astonishing funhouse, incredibly complex yet utterly controlled from a great central switchboard like the console of a pipe organ. Nobody had enough imagination. He could design such a place himself, wiring and all, and he's only thirteen years old. He would be its operator: panel lights would show what was up in every cranny of its cunning of its multivarious vastness; a switch-flick would ease this fellow's way, complicate that's, to balance things out; if anyone seemed lost or frightened, all the operator had to do was.

He wishes he had never entered the funhouse. But he has. Then he wishes he were dead. But he's not. Therefore he will construct funhouses for others and be their secret operator—though he would rather be among the lovers for whom funhouses are designed.

1968

The Kugelmass Episode

Woody Allen

Kugelmass, a professor of humanities at City College, was unhappily married for the second time. Daphne Kugelmass was an oaf. He also had two dull sons by his first wife, Flo, and was up to his neck in alimony and child support.

"Did I know it would turn out so badly?" Kugelmass whined to his analyst one day. "Daphne had promised. Who suspected she'd let herself go and swell up like a beach ball? Plus she had a few bucks, which is not in itself a healthy reason to marry a person, but it doesn't hurt, with the kind of operating nut I have. You see my point?"

Kugelmass was bald and as hairy as a bear, but he had soul.

"I need to meet a new woman," he went on. "I need to have an affair. I may not look the part, but I'm a man who needs romance. I need softness, I need flirtation. I'm not getting younger, so before it's too late I want to make love in Venice, trade quips at "21"[1] and exchange coy glances over red wine and candlelight. You see what I'm saying?"

Dr. Mandel shifted in his chair and said, "An affair will solve nothing. You're so unrealistic. Your problems run much deeper."

"And also this affair must be discreet," Kugelmass continued. "I can't afford a second divorce. Daphne would really sock it to me."

"Mr. Kugelmass—"

"But it can't be anyone at City College, because Daphne also works there. Not that anyone on the faculty at C.C.N.Y. is any great shakes, but some of those coeds..."

"Mr. Kugelmass—"

"Help me. I had a dream last night. I was skipping through a meadow holding a picnic basket and the basket was marked 'Options.' And then I saw there was a hole in the basket."

"Mr. Kugelmass, the worst thing you could do is act out. You must simply express your feelings here, and together we'll analyze them. You have been in treatment long enough to know there is no overnight cure. After all, I'm an analyst, not a magician."

"Then perhaps what I need is a magician," Kugelmass said, rising from his chair. And with that he terminated his therapy.

---
1 A famous restaurant in New York City.

Woody Allen, "The Kugelmass Episode," *The New Yorker*, May, 2, 1977. Copyright © 1977 by Conde Nast Publications. Reprinted with permission.

A couple of weeks later, while Kugelmass and Daphne were moping around in their apartment one night like two pieces of old furniture, the phone rang.

"I'll get it," Kugelmass said. "Hello."

"Kugelmass?" a voice said. "Kugelmass, this is Persky."

"Who?"

"Persky Or should I say The Great Persky?"

"Pardon me?"

"I hear you're looking all over town for a magician to bring a little exotica into your life? Yes or no?"

"Sh-h-h," Kugelmass whispered. "Don't hang up. Where are you calling from, Persky?"

Early the following afternoon, Kugelmass climbed three flights of stairs in a broken-down apartment house in the Bushwick section of Brooklyn. Peering through the darkness of the hall, he found the door he was looking for and pressed the bell. I'm going to regret this, he thought to himself.

Seconds later, he was greeted by a short, thin, waxy-looking man.

"You're Persky the Great?" Kugelmass said.

"The Great Persky. You want a tea?"

"No, I want romance. I want music, I want love and beauty."

"But not tea, eh? Amazing. O.K., sit down."

Persky went to the back room, and Kugelmass heard the sounds of boxes and furniture being moved around. Persky reappeared, pushing before him a large object on squeaky roller-skate wheels. He removed some old silk handkerchiefs that were lying on its top and blew away a bit of dust. It was a cheap-looking Chinese cabinet, badly lacquered.

"Persky," Kugelmass said, "what's your scam?"

"Pay attention," Persky said. "This is some beautiful effect. I developed it for a Knights of Pythias date last year, but the booking fell through. Get into the cabinet."

"Why, so you can stick it full of swords or something?"

"You see any swords?"

Kugelmass made a face and, grunting, climbed into the cabinet. He couldn't help noticing a couple of ugly rhinestones glued onto the raw plywood just in front of his face. "If this is a joke," he said.

"Some joke. Now, here's the point. If I throw any novel into this cabinet with you, shut the doors, and tap it three times, you will find yourself projected into that book."

Kugelmass made a grimace of disbelief.

"It's the emess,"[2] Persky said. "My hand to God. Not just a novel, either. A short story, a play, a poem. You can meet any of the women created by the world's best writers. Whoever you dreamed of. You could carry on all you like with a real winner. Then when you've had enough you give a yell, and I'll see you're back here in a split second."

"Persky, are you some kind of outpatient?"

"I'm telling you it's on the level," Persky said.

Kugelmass remained skeptical. "What are you telling me—that this cheesy homemade box can take me on a ride like you're describing?"

"For a double sawbuck."[3]

Kugelmass reached for his wallet. "I'll believe this when I see it" he said.

Persky tucked the bills in his pants pocket and turned toward his bookcase. "So who do you want to meet? Sister Carrie? Hester Prynne? Ophelia? Maybe someone by Saul Bellow? Hey, what about Temple Drake?[4] Although for a man your age she'd be a workout."

"French, I want to have an affair with a French lover."

"Nana?"[5]

"I don't want to have to pay for it."

"What about Natasha in 'War and Peace'?"

"I said French. I know! What about Emma Bovary?[6] That sounds to me perfect."

---

2 The truth.

3 $20.

4 Carrie Meeber is the heroine of Theodore Dreiser's novel Sister Carrie (1900); Hester Prynne is in Nathaniel Hawthorne's novel The Scarlet Letter (1850); Ophelia is in Hamlet (c. 1600); and Temple Drake is a character in William Faulkner's novel Sanctuary (1931).

5 Nana is in Emile Zola's Nana (1880).

6 Emma Bovary is the heroine of Gustave Flaubert's novel Madame Bovary (1865).

"You got it, Kugelmass. Give me a holler when you've had enough." Persky tossed in a paperback copy of Flaubert's novel.

"You sure this is safe?" Kugelmass asked as Persky began shutting the cabinet doors.

"Safe. Is anything safe in this crazy world?" Persky rapped three times on the cabinet and then flung open the doors.

Kugelmass was gone. At the same moment, he appeared in the bedroom of Charles and Emma Bovary's house at Yonville. Before him was a beautiful woman standing alone with her back turned to him as she folded some linen. I can't believe this, thought Kugelmass, staring at the doctor's ravishing wife. This is uncanny. I'm here. It's her.

Emma turned in surprise. "Goodness, you startled me," she said. "Who are you?" She spoke in the same fine English translation as the paperback.

It's simply devastating, he thought. Then, realizing that it was he whom she had addressed, he said, "Excuse me, I'm Sidney Kugelmass. I'm from City College. A professor of humanities. C.C.N.Y.? Uptown. I—oh, boy!"

Emma Bovary smiled flirtatiously and said, "Would you like a drink? A glass of wine, perhaps?"

She is beautiful, Kugelmass thought. What a contrast with the troglodyte who shared his bed! He felt a sudden impulse to take this vision into his arms and tell her she was the kind of woman he had dreamed of all his life.

"Yes, some wine," he said hoarsely. "White. No, red. No, white. Make it white."

"Charles is out for the day," Emma said, her voice full of playful implication.

After the wine, they went for a stroll in the lovely French countryside. "I've always dreamed that some mysterious stranger would appear and rescue me from the monotony of this crass rural existence" Emma said, clasping his hand. They passed a small church. "I love what you have on" she murmured. "I've never seen anything like it around here. It's so…so modern."

"It's called a leisure suit," he said romantically. "It was marked down." Suddenly he kissed her. For the next hour they reclined under a tree and whispered together and told each other deeply meaningful things with their eyes. Then Kugelmass sat up. He had just remembered he had to meet Daphne at Bloomingdale's. "I must go," he told her. "But don't worry. I'll be back."

"I hope so," Emma said.

He embraced her passionately, and the two walked back to the house. He held Emma's face cupped in his palms, kissed her again, and yelled, "O.K., Persky! I got to be at Bloomingdale's by three-thirty."

There was an audible pop, and Kugelmass was back in Brooklyn.

"So? Did I lie?" Persky asked triumphantly.

"Look, Persky, I'm right now late to meet the ball and chain at Lexington Avenue, but when can I go again? Tomorrow?"

"My pleasure. Just bring a twenty. And don't mention this to anybody."

"Yeah. I'm going to call Rupert Murdoch."[7]

Kugelmass hailed a cab and sped off to the city. His heart danced on point. I am in love, he thought, I am the possessor of a wonderful secret. What he didn't realize was that at this very moment students in various classrooms across the country were saying to their teachers, "Who is this character on page 100? A bald Jew is kissing Madame Bovary?" A teacher in Sioux Falls, South Dakota, sighed and thought, Jesus, these kids, with their pot and acid. What goes through their minds!

Daphne Kugelmass was in the bathroom-accessories department at Bloomingdale's when Kugelmass arrived breathlessly. "Where've you been?" she snapped. "It's four-thirty."

"I got held up in traffic" Kugelmass said.

Kugelmass visited Persky the next day, and in a few minutes was again passed magically to Yonville. Emma couldn't hide her excitement at seeing him. The two spent hours together, laughing and talking about their different backgrounds. Before Kugelmass left, they made love. "My God, I'm doing it with Madame Bovary!" Kugelmass whispered to himself. "Me, who failed freshman English,"

---

[7] Rupert Murdoch (b. 1931) is an Australian newspaper tycoon.

As the months passed, Kugelmass saw Persky many times and developed a close and passionate relationship with Emma Bovary. "Make sure and always get me into the book before page 120," Kugelmass said to the magician one day. "I always have to meet her before she hooks up with this Rodolphe character."

"Why?" Persky asked. "You can't beat his time?"

"Beat his time. He's landed gentry. Those guys have nothing better to do than flirt and ride horses. To me, he's one of those faces you see in the pages of Women's Wear Daily. With the Helmut Berger hairdo. But to her he's hot stuff."

"And her husband suspects nothing?"

"He's out of his depth. He's a lack-lustre little paramedic who's thrown in his lot with a jitterbug. He's ready to go to sleep by ten, and she's putting on her dancing shoes. Oh, well… See you later."

And once again Kugelmass entered the cabinet and passed instantly to the Bovary estate at Yonville. "How you doing, cupcake?" he said to Emma.

"Oh, Kugelmass," Emma sighed. "What I have to put up with. Last night at dinner, Mr. Personality dropped off to sleep in the middle of the dessert course. I'm pouring my heart out about Maxim's and the ballet, and out of the blue I hear snoring."

"It's O.K., darling, I'm here now," Kugelmass said, embracing her. I've earned this, he thought, smelling Emma's French perfume and burying his nose in her hair. I've suffered enough. I've paid enough analysts. I've searched till I'm weary. She's young and nubile, and I'm here a few pages after Leon and just before Rodolphe. By showing up during the correct chapters, I've got the situation knocked.

Emma, to be sure, was just as happy as Kugelmass. She had been starved for excitement, and his tales of Broadway night life, of fast cars and Hollywood and TV stars, enthralled the young French beauty

"Tell me again about O. J. Simpson," she implored that evening, as she and Kugelmass strolled past Abbe Bournisien's church.

"What can I say? The man is great. He sets all kinds of rushing records. Such moves. They can't touch him."

"And the Academy Awards?" Emma said wistfully. "I'd give anything to win one."

"First you've got to be nominated."

"I know. You explained it. But I'm convinced I can act. Of course, I'd want to take a class or two. With Strasberg maybe. Then, if I had the right agent—"

"We'll see, we'll see. I'll speak to Persky."

That night, safely returned to Persky's flat, Kugelmass brought up the idea of having Emma visit him in the big city.

"Let me think about it," Persky said. "Maybe I could work it. Stranger things have happened." Of course, neither of them could think of one.

"Where the hell do you go all the time?" Daphne Kugelmass barked at her husband as he returned home late that evening. "You got a chippie stashed somewhere?"

"Yeah, sure, I'm just the type," Kugelmass said wearily. "I was with Leonard Popkin. We were discussing Socialist agriculture in Poland. You know Popkin. He's a freak on the subject."

"Well; you've been very odd lately," Daphne said. "Distant. Just don't forget about my father's birthday. On Saturday?"

"Oh, sure, sure," Kugelmass said, heading for the bathroom.

"My whole family will be there. We can see the twins. And Cousin Hamish. You should be more polite to Cousin Hamish—he likes you."

"Right, the twins," Kugelmass said, closing the bathroom door and shutting out the sound of his wife's voice. He leaned against it and took a deep breath. In a few hours, he told himself, he would be back in Yonville again, back with his beloved. And this time, if all went well, he would bring Emma back with him.

At three-fifteen the following afternoon, Persky worked his wizardry again. Kugelmass appeared before Emma, smiling and eager. The two spent a few hours at Yonville with Binet and then remounted the Bovary carriage. Following Persky's instructions, they held each other tightly, closed their eyes, and counted to ten. When they opened them, the carriage was just drawing up at the side door of the

Plaza Hotel, where Kugelmass had optimistically reserved a suite earlier in the day.

"I love it! It's everything I dreamed it would be" Emma said as she whirled joyously around the bedroom, surveying the city from their window. "There's F.A.O. Schwarz. And there's Central Park, and the Sherry is which one? Oh, there—I see. It's too divine."

On the bed there were boxes from Halston and Saint Laurent. Emma unwrapped a package and held up a pair of black velvet pants against her perfect body.

"The slacks suit is by Ralph Lauren," Kugelmass said. "You'll look like a million bucks in it. Come on, sugar, give us a kiss."

"I've never been so happy!" Emma squealed as she stood before the mirror. "Let's go out on the town. I want to see Chorus Line and the Guggenheim and this Jack Nicholson character you always talk about. Are any of his flicks showing?"

"I cannot get my mind around this," a Stanford professor said. "First a strange character named Kugelmass, and now she's gone from the book. Well, I guess the mark of a classic is that you can reread it a thousand times and always find something new."

The lovers passed a blissful weekend. Kugelmass had told Daphne he would be away at a symposium in Boston, and would return Monday. Savoring each moment, he and Emma went to the movies, had dinner in Chinatown, passed two hours at a discotheque, and went to bed with a TV movie. They slept till noon on Sunday, visited SoHo, and ogled celebrities at Elaine's. They had caviar and champagne in their suite on Sunday night and talked until dawn. That morning; in the cab taking them to Persky's apartment, Kugelmass thought, It was hectic, but worth it. I can't bring her here too often, but now and then it will be a charming contrast with Yonville.

At Persky's, Emma climbed into the cabinet, arranged her new boxes of clothes neatly around her, and kissed Kugelmass fondly. "My place next time," she said with a wink. Persky rapped three times on the cabinet. Nothing happened.

"Hmm," Persky said, scratching his head. He rapped again, but still no magic. "Something must be wrong," he mumbled.

"Persky, you're joking!" Kugelmass cried. "How can it not work?"

"Relax, relax. Are you still in the box, Emma?"

"Yes."

Persky rapped again—harder this time.

"I'm still here, Persky."

"I know, darling. Sit tight."

"Persky, we have to get her back," Kugelmass whispered. "I'm a married man, and I have a class in three hours. I'm not prepared for anything more than a cautious affair at this point."

"I can't understand it," Persky muttered. "It's such a reliable little trick."

But he could do nothing. "It's going to take a little while," he said to Kugelmass. "I'm going to have to strip it down. I'll call you later."

Kugelmass bundled Emma into a cab and took her back to the Plaza. He barely made it to his class on time. He was on the phone all day, to Persky and to his mistress. The magician told him it might be several days before he got to the bottom of the trouble.

"How was the symposium?" Daphne asked him that night.

"Fine, fine," he said, lighting the filter end of a cigarette.

"What's wrong? You're as tense as a cat."

"Me? Ha, that's a laugh. I'm as calm as a summer night. I'm just going to take a walk." He eased out the door, hailed a cab, and flew to the Plaza.

"This is no good," Emma said. "Charles will miss me."

"Bear with me, sugar," Kugelmass said. He was pale and sweaty. He kissed her again, raced to the elevators, yelled at Persky over a pay phone in the Plaza lobby, and just made it home before midnight.

"According to Popkin, barley prices in Krakow have not been this stable since 1971," he said to Daphne, and smiled wanly as he climbed into bed.

The whole week went by like that. On Friday night, Kugelmass told Daphne there was another symposium he had to catch, this one in Syracuse. He hurried back to the Plaza, but the second weekend there was nothing like the first. "Get me back into the novel or marry me," Emma told Kugelmass. "Meanwhile, I want to get a job or go to class, because watching TV all day is the pits."

"Fine. We can use the money," Kugelmass said. "You consume twice your weight in room service."

"I met an Off Broadway producer in Central Park yesterday, and he said I might be right for a project he's doing," Emma said.

"Who is this clown?" Kugelmass asked.

"He's not a clown. He's sensitive and kind and cute. His name's Jeff Something-or-Other, and he's up for a Tony."

Later that afternoon, Kugelmass showed up at Persky's drunk.

"Relax," Persky told him. "You'll get a coronary."

"Relax. The man says relax. I've got a fictional character stashed in a hotel room, and I think my wife is having me tailed by a private shamus."[8]

"O.K., O.K. We know there's a problem." Persky crawled under the cabinet and started banging on something with a large wrench.

"I'm like a wild animal," Kugelmass went on. "I'm sneaking around town, and Emma and I have had it up to here with each other. Not to mention a hotel tab that reads like the defense budget."

"So what should I do? This is the world of magic," Persky said. "It's all nuance."

"Nuance, my foot. I'm pouring Dom Perignon and black eggs into this little mouse, plus her wardrobe, plus she's enrolled at the Neighborhood Playhouse and suddenly needs professional photos. Also, Persky, Professor Fivish Kopkind, who teaches Comp Lit and who has always been jealous of me, has identified me as the sporadically appearing character in the Flaubert book. He's threatened to go to Daphne. I see ruin and alimony; jail. For adultery with Madame Bovary, my wife will reduce me to beggary."

"What do you want me to say? I'm working on it night and day. As far as your personal anxiety goes, that I can't help you with. I'm a magician, not an analyst."

---

8 Detective.

By Sunday afternoon, Emma had locked herself in the bathroom and refused to respond to Kugelmass's entreaties. Kugelmass stared out the window at the Wollman Rink and contemplated suicide. Too bad this is a low floor, he thought, or I'd do it right now. Maybe if I ran away to Europe and started life over… Maybe I could sell the International Herald Tribune, like those young girls used to.

The phone rang. Kugelmass lifted it to his ear mechanically.

"Bring her over," Persky said. "I think I got the bugs out of it."

Kugelmass's heart leaped. "You're serious?" he said. "You got it licked?"

"It was something in the transmission. Go figure."

"Persky, you're a genius. We'll be there in a minute. Less than a minute."

Again the lovers hurried to the magician's apartment, and again Emma Bovary climbed into the cabinet with her boxes. This time there was no kiss. Persky shut the doors, took a deep breath, and tapped the box three times. There was the reassuring popping noise, and when Persky peered inside, the box was empty. Madame Bovary was back in her novel. Kugelmass heaved a great sigh of relief and pumped the magician's hand.

"It's over," he said. "I learned my lesson. I'll never cheat again, I swear it." He pumped Persky's hand again and made a mental note to send him a necktie.

Three weeks later, at the end of a beautiful spring afternoon, Persky answered his doorbell. It was Kugelmass, with a sheepish expression on his face.

"O.K., Kugelmass," the magician said. "Where to this time?"

"It's just this once," Kugelmass said. "The weather is so lovely, and I'm not getting any younger. Listen, you've read Portnoy's Complaint? Remember The Monkey?"[9]

"The price is now twenty-five dollars, because the cost of living is up, but I'll start you off with one freebie, due to all the trouble I caused you."

---

9 The Monkey is the sexually liberated heroine of Philip Roth's novel Portnoy's Complaint (1969).

"You're good people," Kugelmass said, combing his few remaining hairs as he climbed into the cabinet again. "This'll work all right?"

"I hope. But I haven't tried it much since all that unpleasantness."

"Sex and romance," Kugelmass said from inside the box. "What we go through for a pretty face."

Persky tossed in a copy of Portnoy's Complaint and rapped three times on the box. This time, instead of a popping noise there was a dull explosion, followed by a series of crackling noises and a shower of sparks. Persky leaped back, was seized by a heart attack, and dropped dead. The cabinet burst into flames, and eventually the entire house burned down.

Kugelmass, unaware of this catastrophe, had his own problems. He had not been thrust into Portnoy's Complaint, or into any other novel, for that matter. He had been projected into an old textbook, Remedial Spanish, and was running for his life over a barren, rocky terrain as the word tener ("to have") a large and hairy irregular verb—raced after him on its spindly legs.

What We Talk About When We Talk About Love

Raymond Carver

My friend Mel McGinnis was talking. Mel McGinnis is a cardiologist, and sometimes that gives him the right.

The four of us were sitting around his kitchen table drinking gin. Sunlight filled the kitchen from the big window behind the sink. There were Mel and me and his second wife, Teresa—Terri, we called her—and my wife, Laura. We lived in Albuquerque then. But we were all from somewhere else.

There was an ice bucket on the table. The gin and the tonic water kept going around, and we somehow got on the subject of love. Mel thought real love was nothing less than spiritual love. He said he'd spent five years in a seminary before quitting to go to medical school. He said he still looked back on those years in the seminary as the most important years in his life.

Terri said the man she lived with before she lived with Mel loved her so much he tried to kill her. Then Terri said, "He beat me up one night. He dragged me around the living room by my ankles. He kept saying, 'I love you, I love you, you bitch.' He went on dragging me around the living room. My head kept knocking on things." Terri looked around the table. "What do you do with love like that?"

She was a bone-thin woman with a pretty face, dark eyes, and brown hair that hung down her back. She liked necklaces made of turquoise, and long pendant earrings.

Raymond Carver, *What We Talk About When We Talk About Love,* from What We Talk About When We Talk About Love: Stories. Published by Knopf Publishing Group, 1989. Copyright by Random House, Inc. Permission to reprint granted by the rights holder.

"My God, don't be silly. That's not love, and you know it," Mel said. "I don't know what you'd call it, but I sure know you wouldn't call it love."

"Say what you want to, but I know it was," Terri said. "It may sound crazy to you, but it's true just the same. People are different, Mel. Sure, sometimes he may have acted crazy. Okay. But he loved me. In his own way maybe, but he loved me. There was love there, Mel. Don't say there wasn't."

Mel let out his breath. He held his glass and turned to Laura and me. "The man threatened to kill me," Mel said. He finished his drink and reached for the gin bottle. "Terri's a romantic. Terri's of the kick-me-so-I'll-know-you-love-me school. Terri, hon, don't look that way." Mel reached across the table and touched Terri's cheek with his fingers. He grinned at her.

"Now he wants to make up," Terri said.

"Make up what?" Mel said. "What is there to make up? I know what I know. That's all."

"How'd we get started on this subject, anyway?" Terri said. She raised her glass and drank from it. "Mel always has love on his mind," she said. "Don't you, honey?" She smiled, and I thought that was the last of it.

"I just wouldn't call Ed's behavior love. That's all I'm saying, honey," Mel said. "What about you guys?" Mel said to Laura and me. "Does that sound like love to you?"

"I'm the wrong person to ask," I said. "I didn't even know the man. I've only heard his name mentioned in passing. I wouldn't know. You'd have to know the particulars. But I think what you're saying is that love is an absolute."

Mel said, "The kind of love I'm talking about is. The kind of love I'm talking about, you don't try to kill people."

Laura said, "I don't know anything about Ed, or anything about the situation. But who can judge anyone else's situation?"

I touched the back of Laura's hand. She gave me a quick smile. I picked up Laura's hand. It was warm, the nails polished, perfectly manicured. I encircled the broad wrist with my fingers, and I held her.

"When I left, he drank rat poison," Terri said. She clasped her arms with her hands. "They took him to the hospital in Sante Fe. That's where we lived then, about ten miles out. They saved his life. But his gums went crazy from it. I mean they pulled away from his teeth. After that, his teeth stood out like fangs. My God," Terri said. She waited a minute, then let go of her arms and picked up her glass.

"What people won't do!" Laura said.

"He's out of the action now," Mel said. "He's dead."

Mel handed me the saucer of limes. I took a section, squeezed it over my drink, and stirred the ice cubes with my finger.

"It gets worse," Terri said. "He shot himself in the mouth. But he bungled that too. Poor Ed," she said. Terri shook her head.

"Poor Ed nothing," Mel said. "He was dangerous."

Mel was forty-five years old. He was tall and rangy with curly soft hair. His face and arms were brown from the tennis he played. When he was sober, his gestures, all his movements, were precise, very careful.

"He did love me though, Mel. Grant me that," Terri said. "That's all I'm asking. He didn't love me the way you love me. I'm not saying that. But he loved me. You can grant me that, can't you?"

"What do you mean, he bungled it?" I said.

Laura leaned forward with her glass. She put her elbows on the table and held her glass in both hands. She glanced from Mel to Terri and waited with a look of bewilderment on her open face, as if amazed that such things happened to people you were friendly with.

"How'd he bungle it when he killed himself?" I said.

"I'll tell you what happened," Mel said. "He took this twenty-two pistol he'd bought to threaten Terri and me with. Oh, I'm serious, the man was always threatening. You should have seen the way we lived in those days. Like fugitives. I even bought a gun myself. Can you believe it? A guy like me? But I did. I bought one for self-defense and carried it in the glove compartment. Sometimes I'd have to leave the apartment in the middle of the night. To go to the hospital, you know? Terri and I weren't married then, and my first wife had the house and kids, the dog, everything, and Terri and I were living in this apartment here. Sometimes, as I say, I'd get a call in the middle of the night and have to go in to the hospital at two or three in the morning. It'd be dark out there in the parking lot, and I'd break into a sweat before I could even get to my car. I never knew if he was going to come up out of the shrubbery or from behind a car and start shooting. I mean, the man was crazy. He was capable of wiring a bomb, anything. He used to call my service at all hours and say he needed to talk to the doctor, and when I'd return the call, he'd say, 'Son of a bitch, your days are numbered.' Little things like that. It was scary, I'm telling you."

"I still feel sorry for him," Terri said.

"It sounds like a nightmare," Laura said. "But what exactly happened after he shot himself?"

Laura is a legal secretary. We'd met in a professional capacity. Before we knew it, it was a courtship. She's thirty-five, three years younger than I am. In addition to being in love, we like each other and enjoy one another's company She's easy to be with.

"What happened?" Laura said.

Mel said, "He shot himself in the mouth in his room. Someone heard the shot and told the manager. They came in with a passkey, saw what had happened, and called an ambulance. I happened to be there when they brought him in, alive but past recall. The man lived for three days. His head swelled up to twice the size of a normal head. I'd never seen anything like it, and I hope I never do again. Terri wanted to go in and sit with him when she found out about it. We had a fight over it. I didn't think she should see him like that. I didn't think she should see him, and I still don't."

"Who won the fight?" Laura said.

"I was in the room with him when he died," Terri said. "He never came up out of it. But I sat with him. He didn't have anyone else."

"He was dangerous," Mel said. "If you call that love, you can have it."

"It was love," Terri said. "Sure, it's abnormal in most people's eyes. But he was willing to die for it. He did die for it."

"I sure as hell wouldn't call it love," Mel said. "I mean, no one knows what he did it for. I've seen a lot of suicides, and I couldn't say anyone ever knew what they did it for."

Mel put his hands behind his neck and tilted his chair back. "I'm not interested in that kind of love," he said. "If that's love, you can have it."

Terri said, "We were afraid. Mel even made a will out and wrote to his brother in California who used to be a Green Beret. Mel told him who to look for if something happened to him."

Terri drank from her glass. She said, "But Mel's right—we lived like fugitives. We were afraid. Mel was, weren't you, honey? I even called the police at one point, but they were no help. They said they couldn't do anything until Ed actually did something. Isn't that a laugh?" Terri said.

She poured the last of the gin into her glass and waggled the bottle. Mel got up from the table and went to the cupboard. He took down another bottle.

"Well, Nick and I know what love is," Laura said. "For us, I mean," Laura said. She bumped my knee with her knee. "You're supposed to say something now," Laura said, and turned her smile on me.

For an answer, I took Laura's hand and raised it to my lips. I made a big production out of kissing her hand. Everyone was amused.

"We're lucky," I said.

"You guys," Terri said. "Stop that now. You're making me sick. You're still on the honeymoon, for God's sake. You're still gaga, for crying out loud. Just wait. How long have you been together now? How long has it been? A year? Longer than a year?"

"Going on a year and a half," Laura said, flushed and smiling.

"Oh, now," Terri said. "Wait awhile."

She held her drink and gazed at Laura.

"I'm only kidding," Terri said.

Mel opened the gin and went around the table with the bottle. "Here, you guys," he said. "Let's have a toast. I want to propose a toast. A toast to love. To true love," Mel said.

We touched glasses.

"To love," we said.

Outside in the backyard, one of the dogs began to bark. The leaves of the aspen that leaned past the window ticked against the glass. The afternoon sun was like a presence in this room, the spacious light of ease and generosity. We could have been anywhere, somewhere enchanted. We raised our glasses again and grinned at each other like children who had agreed on something forbidden.

"I'll tell you what real love is," Mel said. "I mean, I'll give you a good example. And then you can draw your own conclusions." He poured more gin into his glass. He added an ice cube and a sliver of lime. We waited and sipped our drinks. Laura and I touched knees again. I put a hand on her warm thigh and left it there.

"What do any of us really know about love?" Mel said. "It seems to me we're just beginners at love. We say we love each other and we do, I don't doubt it. I love Terri and Terri loves me, and you guys love each other too. You know the kind of love I'm talking about now. Physical love, that impulse that drives you to someone special, as well as love of the other person's being, his or her essence, as it were. Carnal love and, well, call it sentimental love, the day-to-day caring about the other person. But sometimes I have a hard time accounting for the fact that I must have loved my first wife too. But I did, I know I did. So I suppose I am like Terri in that regard. Terri and Ed." He thought about it and then he went on. "There was a time when I thought I loved my first wife more than life itself. But now I hate her guts. I do. How do you explain that? What happened to that love? What happened to it, is what I'd like to know. I wish someone could tell me. Then there's Ed. Okay, we're back to Ed. He loves Terri so much he tries to kill her and he winds up killing himself." Mel stopped talking and swallowed from his glass. "You guys have been together eighteen months and you love each other. It shows all over you. You glow with it. But you both loved other people before you met each other. You've both been married before, just like us. And you probably loved other people before that too, even. Terri and I have been together five years, been married for four. And the terrible thing, the terrible thing is, but the good thing too, the saving grace, you might say, is that if something happened to one of us—excuse me for saying this—but if something happened to one of us tomorrow I think the other one, the other person, would grieve for a while, you know, but then the surviving party would go out and love again, have someone else soon enough. All this, all of this love we're talking about, it would just be a memory. Maybe not even a memory. Am I wrong? Am I way off base? Because I want you to set me straight if you think I'm wrong. I want to know. I mean, I don't know anything, and I'm the first one to admit it."

"Mel, for God's sake," Terri said. She reached out and took hold of his wrist. "Are you getting drunk? Honey? Are you drunk?"

"Honey, I'm just talking," Mel said. "All right? I don't have to be drunk to say what I think. I mean, we're all just talking, right?" Mel said. He fixed his eyes on her.

"Sweetie, I'm not criticizing," Terri said.

She picked up her glass.

"I'm not on call today," Mel said. "Let me remind you of that. I am not on call," he said.

"Mel, we love you," Laura said.

Mel looked at Laura. He looked at her as if he could not place her, as if she was not the woman she was.

"Love you too, Laura," Mel said. "And you, Nick, love you too. You know something?" Mel said. "You guys are our pals," Mel said.

He picked up his glass.

Mel said, "I was going to tell you about something. I mean, I was going to prove a point. You see, this happened a few months ago, but it's still going on right now, and it ought to make us feel ashamed when we talk like we know what we're talking about when we talk above love."

"Come on now," Terri said. "Don't talk like you're drunk if you're not drunk."

"Just shut up for once in your life," Mel said very quietly. "Will you do me a favor and do that for a minute? So as I was saying, there's this old couple who had this car wreck out on the interstate. A kid hit them and they were all torn to shit and nobody was giving them much chance to pull through."

Terri looked at us and then back at Mel. She seemed anxious, or maybe that's too strong a word.

Mel was handing the bottle around the table.

"I was on call that night," Mel said. "It was May or maybe it was June. Terri and I had just sat down to dinner when the hospital called. There'd been this thing out on the interstate. Drunk kid, teenager, plowed his dad's pickup into this camper with this old couple in it. They were up in their mid-seventies, that couple. The kid—eighteen, nineteen, something—he was DOA. Taken the steering wheel through his sternum. The old couple, they were alive, you understand. I mean, just barely. But they had everything. Multiple fractures, internal injuries, hemorrhaging, contusions, lacerations, the works, and they each of them had themselves concussions. They were in a bad way, believe me. And, of course, their age was two strikes against them. I'd say she was worse off than he was. Ruptured spleen along with everything else. Both kneecaps broken. But they'd been wearing their seatbelts and, God knows, that's what saved them for the time being."

"Folks, this is an advertisement for the National Safety Council," Terri said. "This is your spokesman, Dr. Melvin R. McGinnis, talking." Terri laughed. "Mel," she said, "sometimes you're just too much. But I love you, hon," she said.

"Honey, I love you," Mel said.

He leaned across the table. Terri met him halfway. They kissed.

"Terri's right," Mel said as he settled himself again. "Get those seatbelts on. But seriously, they were in some shape, those oldsters. By the time I got down there, the kid was dead, as I said. He was off in a corner, laid out on a gurney. I took one look at the old couple and told the ER nurse to get me a neurologist and an orthopedic man and a couple of surgeons down there right away."

He drank from his glass. "I'll try to keep this short," he said. "So we took the two of them up to the OR and worked like fuck on them most of the night. They had these incredible reserves, those two. You see that once in a while. So we did everything that could be done, and toward morning we're giving them a fifty-fifty chance, maybe less than that for her. So here they are, still alive the next morning. So, okay, we move them into the ICU, which is where they both kept plugging away at it for two weeks, hitting it better and better on all the scopes. So we transfer them out to their own room."

Mel stopped talking. "Here," he said, "let's drink this cheapo gin the hell up. Then we're going to dinner, right? Terri and I know a new place. That's where we'll go, to this new place we know about. But we're not going until we finish up this cut-rate, lousy gin."

Terri said, "We haven't actually eaten there yet. But it looks good. From the outside, you know."

"I like food," Mel said. "If I had it to do all over again, I'd be a chef, you know? Right, Terri?" Mel said.

He laughed. He fingered the ice in his glass.

"Terri knows," he said. "Terri can tell you. But let me say this. If I could come back again in a different life, a different time and all, you know what? I'd like to come back as a knight. You were pretty safe wearing all that armor. It was all right being a knight until gunpowder and muskets and pistols came along."

"Mel would like to ride a horse and carry a lance," Terri said.

"Carry a woman's scarf with you everywhere," Laura said.

"Or just a woman," Mel said.

"Shame on you," Laura said.

Terri said, "Suppose you came back as a serf. The serfs didn't have it so good in those days," Terri said.

"The serfs never had it good," Mel said. "But I guess even the knights were vessels to someone. Isn't that the way it worked? But then everyone is always a vessel to someone. Isn't that right? Terri? But what I liked about knights, besides their ladies, was that they had that suit of armor, you know, and they couldn't get hurt very easy. No cars in those days, you know? No drunk teenagers to tear into your ass."

"Vassals," Terri said.

"What?" Mel said.

"Vassals," Terri said. "They were called vassals, not vessels."

"Vassals, vessels," Mel said, "what the fuck's the difference? You knew what I meant anyway. All right," Mel said. "So I'm not educated. I learned my stuff. I'm a heart surgeon, sure, but I'm just a mechanic. I go in and I fuck around and I fix things. Shit," Mel said.

"Modesty doesn't become you," Terri said.

"He's just a humble sawbones," I said. "But sometimes they suffocated in all that armor, Mel. They'd even have heart attacks if it got too hot and they were too tired and worn out. I read somewhere that they'd fall off their horses and not be able to get up because they were too tired to stand with all that armor on them. They got trampled by their own horses sometimes."

"That's terrible," Mel said. "That's a terrible thing, Nicky. I guess they'd just lay there and wait until somebody came along and made a shish kebab out of them."

"Some other vessel," Terri said.

"That's right," Mel said. "Some vassal would come along and spear the bastard in the name of love. Or whatever the fuck it was they fought over in those days."

"Same things we fight over these days," Terri said.

Laura said, "Nothing's changed."

The color was still high in Laura's cheeks. Her eyes were bright. She brought her glass to her lips.

Mel poured himself another drink. He looked at the label closely as if studying a long row of numbers. Then he slowly put the bottle down on the table and slowly reached for the tonic water.

"What about the old couple?" Laura said. "You didn't finish that story you started."

Laura was having a hard time lighting her cigarette. Her matches kept going out.

The sunshine inside the room was different now, changing, getting thinner. But the leaves outside the window were still shimmering, and I stared at the pattern they made on the panes and on the Formica counter. They weren't the same patterns, of course.

"What about the old couple?" I said.

"Older but wiser," Terri said.

Mel stared at her.

Terri said, "Go on with your story, hon. I was only kidding. Then what happened?"

"Terri, sometimes," Mel said.

"Please, Mel," Terri said. "Don't always be so serious, sweetie. Can't you take a joke?"

"Where's the joke?" Mel said.

He held his glass and gazed steadily at his wife.

"What happened?" Laura said.

Mel fastened his eyes on Laura. He said, "Laura, if I didn't have Terri and if I didn't love her so much, and if Nick wasn't my best friend, I'd fall in love with you, I'd carry you off, honey," he said.

"Tell your story," Terri said. "Then we'll go to that new place, okay?"

"Okay," Mel said. "Where was I?" he said. He stared at the table and then he began again.

"I dropped in to see each of them every day, sometimes twice a day if I was up doing other calls anyway. Casts and bandages, head to foot, the both of them. You know, you've seen it in the movies. That's just the way they looked, just like in the movies. Little eye-holes and nose-holes and mouth-holes. And she had to have her legs slung up on top of it. Well, the husband was very depressed for the longest while. Even after he found out that his wife was going to pull through, he was still very depressed. Not about the accident, though. I mean, the accident was one thing, but it wasn't everything. I'd get up to his mouth-hole, you know, and he'd say no, it wasn't the accident exactly but it was because he couldn't see her through his eye-holes. He said that was what was making him feel so bad. Can you imagine? I'm telling you, the man's heart was breaking because he couldn't turn his goddamn head and *see* his goddamn wife."

Mel looked around the table and shook his head at what he was going to say.

"I mean, it was killing the old fart just because he couldn't *look* at the fucking woman."

We all looked at Mel.

"Do you see what I'm saying?" he said.

Maybe we were a little drunk by then. I know it was hard keeping things in focus. The light was draining out of the room, going back through the window where it had come from. Yet nobody made a move to get up from the table to turn on the overhead light.

"Listen," Mel said. "Let's finish this fucking gin. There's about enough left here for one shooter all around. Then let's go eat. Let's go to the new place."

"He's depressed," Terri said. "Mel, why don't you take a pill?"

Mel shook his head. "I've taken everything there is."

"We all need a pill now and then," I said.

"Some people are born needing them," Terri said.

She was using her finger to rub at something on the table. Then she stopped rubbing.

"I think I want to call my kids," Mel said. "Is that all right with everybody? I'll call my kids," he said.

Terri said, "What if Marjorie answers the phone? You guys, you've heard us on the subject of Marjorie? Honey, you know you don't want to talk to Marjorie. It'll make you feel even worse."

"I don't want to talk to Marjorie," Mel said. "But I want to talk to my kids."

"There isn't a day goes by that Mel doesn't say he wishes she'd get married again. Or else die," Terri said. "For one thing," Terri said, "she's bankrupting us. Mel says it's just to spite him that she won't get married again. She has a boyfriend who lives with her and the kids, so Mel is supporting the boyfriend too."

"She's allergic to bees," Mel said. "If I'm not praying she'll get married again, I'm praying she'll get herself stung to death by a swarm of fucking bees."

"Shame on you," Laura said.

"Bzzzzzzz," Mel said, turning his fingers into bees and buzzing them at Terri's throat. Then he let his hands drop all the way to his sides.

"She's vicious," Mel said. "Sometimes I think I'll go up there dressed like a beekeeper. You know, that hat that's like a helmet with the plate that comes down over your face, the big gloves, and the padded coat? I'll knock on the door and let loose a hive of bees in the house. But first I'd make sure the kids were out, of course."

He crossed one leg over the other. It seemed to take him a lot of time to do it. Then he put both feet on the floor and leaned forward, elbows on the table, his chin cupped in his hands.

"Maybe I won't call the kids, after all. Maybe it isn't such a hot idea. Maybe we'll just go eat. How does that sound?"

"Sounds fine to me," I said. "Eat or not eat. Or keep drinking. I could head right on out into the sunset."

"What does that mean, honey?" Laura said.

"It just means what I said," I said. "It means I could just keep going. That's all it means."

"I could eat something myself," Laura said. "I don't think I've ever been so hungry in my life. Is there something to nibble on?"

"I'll put out some cheese and crackers," Terri said.

But Terri just sat there. She did not get up to get anything.

Mel turned his glass over. He spilled it out on the table.

"Gin's gone," Mel said.

Terri said, "Now what?"

I could hear my heart beating. I could hear everyone's heart. I could hear the human noise we sat there making, not one of us moving, not even when the room went dark.

1981

Happy Endings

Margaret Atwood

John and Mary meet.
What happens next?
If you want a happy ending, try A.

A

John and Mary fall in love and get married. They both have worthwhile and remunerative jobs which they find stimulating and challenging. They buy a charming house. Real estate values go up. Eventually, when they can afford live-in help, they have two children, to whom they are devoted. The children turn out well. John and Mary have a stimulating and challenging sex life and worthwhile friends. They go on fun vacations together. They retire. They both have hobbies which they find stimulating and challenging. Eventually they die. This is the end of the story.

B

Mary falls in love with John but John doesn't fall in love with Mary. He merely uses her body for selfish pleasure and ego gratification of a tepid kind. He comes to her apartment twice a week and she cooks him dinner, you'll notice that he doesn't even consider her worth the price of a dinner out, and after he's eaten the dinner he fucks her and after that he falls asleep, while she does the dishes so he won't think she's untidy, having all those dirty dishes lying around, and puts on fresh lipstick so she'll look good when he wakes up, but when he wakes up he doesn't even notice, he puts on his socks and his shorts and his pants and his shirt and his tie and his shoes, the reverse order from the one in which he took them off. He doesn't take off Mary's clothes, she takes them off herself, she acts as if she's dying for it every time, not because she likes sex exactly, she doesn't, but she wants John to think she does because if they do it often enough surely he'll get used to her, he'll come to depend on her and they will get married, but John goes out the door with hardly so much as a good-night and three days later he turns up at six o'clock and they do the whole thing over again.

Mary gets run-down. Crying is bad for your face, everyone knows that and so does Mary but she can't stop. People at work notice. Her friends tell her John is a rat, a pig, a dog, he isn't good enough for her, but she can't believe it. Inside John, she thinks, is another John, who is much nicer. This other John will emerge like a butterfly from a cocoon, a Jack from a box, a pit from a prune, if the first John is only squeezed enough.

One evening John complains about the food. He has never complained about the food before. Mary is hurt.

Her friends tell her they've seen him in a restaurant with another woman, whose name is Madge. It's not even Madge that finally gets to Mary: it's the restaurant. John has never taken Mary to a restaurant. Mary collects all the sleeping pills and aspirins she can find, and takes them and a half a bottle of sherry. You can see what kind of a woman she is by the fact that it's not even whiskey. She leaves a note for John. She hopes he'll discover her and get her to

Margaret Atwood, "Happy Endings," from *Murder in the Dark: Short Fictions and Prose Poems*. Published by Jonathan Cape Ltd., 1984. Copyright by The Random House Group Limited. Permission to reprint granted by the rights holder.

the hospital in time and repent and then they can get married, but this fails to happen and she dies.

John marries Madge and everything continues as in A.

C

John, who is an older man, falls in love with Mary, and Mary, who is only twenty-two, feels sorry for him because he's worried about his hair falling out. She sleeps with him even though she's not in love with him. She met him at work. She's in love with someone called James, who is twenty-two also and not yet ready to settle down.

John on the contrary settled down long ago: this is what is bothering him. John has a steady, respectable job and is getting ahead in his field, but Mary isn't impressed by him, she's impressed by James, who has a motorcycle and a fabulous record collection. But James is often away on his motorcycle, being free. Freedom isn't the same for girls, so in the meantime Mary spends Thursday evenings with John. Thursdays are the only days John can get away.

John is married to a woman called Madge and they have two children, a charming house which they bought just before the real estate values went up, and hobbies which they find stimulating and challenging, when they have the time. John tells Mary how important she is to him, but of course he can't leave his wife because a commitment is a commitment. He goes on about this more than is necessary and Mary finds it boring, but older men can keep it up longer so on the whole she has a fairly good time.

One day James breezes in on his motorcycle with some top-grade California hybrid and James and Mary get higher than you'd believe possible and they climb into bed. Everything becomes very underwater, but along comes John, who has a key to Mary's apartment. He finds them stoned and entwined. He's hardly in any position to be jealous, considering Madge, but nevertheless he's overcome with despair. Finally he's middle-aged, in two years he'll be bald as an egg and he can't stand it. He purchases a handgun, saying he needs it for target practice—this is the thin part of the plot, but it can be dealt with later—and shoots the two of them and himself.

Madge, after a suitable period of mourning, marries an understanding man called Fred and everything continues as in A, but under different names.

D

Fred and Madge have no problems. They get along exceptionally well and are good at working out any little difficulties that may arise. But their charming house is by the seashore and one day a giant tidal wave approaches. Real estate values go down. The rest of the story is about what caused the tidal wave and how they escape from it. They do, though thousands drown, but Fred and Madge are virtuous and lucky. Finally on high ground they clasp each other, wet and dripping and grateful, and continue as in A.

E

Yes, but Fred has a bad heart. The rest of the story is about how kind and understanding they both are until Fred dies. Then Madge devotes herself to charity work until the end of A. If you like, it can be "Madge", "cancer", "guilty and confused," and "bird watching."

F

If you think this is all too bourgeois, make John a revolutionary and Mary a counterespionage agent and see how far that gets you. Remember, this is Canada. You'll still end up with A, though in between you may get a lustful brawling saga of passionate involvement, a chronicle of our times, sort of.

You'll have to face it, the endings are the same however you slice it. Don't be deluded by any other endings, they're all fake, either deliberately fake, with malicious intent to deceive, or just motivated by excessive optimism if not by downright sentimentality.

The only authentic ending is the one provided here:

John and Mary die. John and Mary die. John and Mary die.

So much for endings. Beginnings are always more fun. True connoisseurs, however, are known to favor the stretch in between, since it's the hardest to do anything with.

That's about all that can be said for plots, which anyway are just one thing after another, a what and a what and a what.

Now try How and Why.

1983

Rape Fantasies

Margaret Atwood

The way they're going on about it in the magazines you'd think it was just invented, and not only that but it's something terrific, like a vaccine for cancer. They put it in capital letters on the front cover, and inside they have these questionnaires like the ones they used to have about whether you were a good enough wife or an endomorph or an ectomorph, remember that? with the scoring upside down on page 73, and then these numbered do-it-yourself dealies, you know? RAPE, TEN THINGS TO DO ABOUT IT, like it was ten new hairdos or something. I mean, what's so new about it?

So at work they all have to talk about it because no matter what magazine you open, there it is, staring you right between the eyes, and they're beginning to have it on the television, too. Personally I'd prefer a June Allyson[1] movie anytime but they don't make them any more and they don't even have them that much on the Late Show. For instance, day before yesterday, that would be Wednesday, thank god it's Friday as they say, we were sitting around in the women's lunch room—the lunch room, I mean you'd think you could get some peace and quiet in there—and Chrissy closes up the magazine she's been reading and says, "How about it, girls, do you have rape fantasies?"

The four of us were having our game of bridge the way we always do, and I had a bare twelve points counting the singleton with hot that much of a bid in anything. So I said one club, hoping Sondra would remember about the one club convention, because the time before when I used that she thought I really meant clubs and she bid us up to three, and all I had was four little ones with nothing higher than a six, and we went down two and on top of that we were vulnerable. She is not the world's best bridge player. I mean, neither am I but there's a limit.

Darlene passed but the damage was done, Sondra's head went round like it was on ball bearings and she said, "What fantasies?"

---

[1] June Allyson: actress (b. 1917) known for her bright smile and scratchy voice. She specialized in "sweet" movie and musical roles, 1943–1959, and still appears regularly in TV commercials.

Margaret Atwood, "Rape Fantasies," *Dancing Girls and Other Stories*. Copyright © 1977 by O.W. Toad Ltd. Reprinted with permission by McClelland & Stewart Ltd.

"Rape fantasies," Chrissy said. She's a receptionist and she looks like one; she's pretty but cool as a cucumber, like she's been painted all over with nail polish, if you know what I mean. Varnished. "It says here all women have rape fantasies."

"For Chrissake, I'm eating an egg sandwich," I said, "and I bid one club and Darlene passed."

"You mean, like some guy jumping you in an alley or something," Sondra said. She was eating her lunch, we all eat our lunches during the game, and she bit into a piece of that celery she always brings and started to chew away on it with this thoughtful expression in her eyes and I knew we might as well pack it in as far as the game was concerned.

"Yeah, sort of like that," Chrissy said. She was blushing a little, you could see it even under her makeup.

"I don't think you should go out alone at night," Darlene said, "you put yourself in a position," and I may have been mistaken but she was looking at me. She's the oldest, she's forty-one though you wouldn't know it and neither does she, but I looked it up in the employees' file. I like to guess a person's age and then look it up to see if I'm right. I let myself have an extra pack of cigarettes if I am, though I'm trying to cut down. I figure it's harmless as long as you don't tell. I mean, not everyone has access to that file, it's more or less confidential. But it's all right if I tell you, I don't expect you'll ever meet her, though you never know, it's a small world. Anyway.

"For heaven's sake, it's only Toronto," Greta said. She worked in Detroit for three years and she never lets you forget it, it's like she thinks she's a war hero or something, we should all admire her just for the fact that she's still walking this earth, though she was really living in Windsor the whole time, she just worked in Detroit. Which for me doesn't really count. It's where you sleep, right?

"Well, do you?" Chrissy said. She was obviously trying to tell us about hers but she wasn't about to go first, she's cautious, that one.

"I certainly don't," Darlene said, and she wrinkled up her nose, like this, and I had to laugh. "I think it's disgusting." She's divorced, I read that in the file too, she never talks about it. It must've been years ago anyway. She got up and went over to the coffee machine and turned her back on us as though she wasn't going to have anything more to do with it.

"Well," Greta said. I could see it was going to be between her and Chrissy. They're both blondes, I don't mean that in a bitchy way but they do try to outdress each other. Greta would like to get out of Filing, she'd like to be a receptionist too so she could meet more people. You don't meet much of anyone in Filing except other people in Filing. Me, I don't mind it so much, I have outside interests.

"Well," Greta said, "I sometimes think about, you know my apartment? It's got this little balcony, I like to sit out there in the summer and I have a few plants out there. I never bother that much about locking the door to the balcony, it's one of those sliding glass ones, I'm on the eighteenth floor for heaven's sake, I've got a good view of the lake and the CN Tower and all. But I'm sitting around one night in my housecoat, watching TV with my shoes off, you know how you do, and I see this guy's feet, coming down past the window, and the next thing you know he's standing on the balcony, he's let himself down by a rope with a hook on the end of it from the floor above, that's the nineteenth, and before I can even get up off the chesterfield he's inside the apartment. He's all dressed in black with black gloves on"—I knew right away what show she got the black gloves off because I saw the same one—" and then he, well, you know."

"You know what?" Chrissy said, but Greta said, "And afterwards he tells me 15 that he goes all over the outside of the apartment building like that, from one floor to another, with his rope and his hook... and then he goes out to the balcony and tosses his rope, and he climbs up it and disappears."

"Just like Tarzan," I said, but nobody laughed.

"Is that all?" Chrissy said. "Don't you ever think about, well, I think about being in the bathtub, with no clothes on..."

"So who takes a bath in their clothes?" I said, you have to admit it's stupid when you come to think of it, but she just went on, "... with lots of bubbles, what I use is Vitabath, it's more expensive but it's so relaxing, and my hair pinned up, and the door opens and this fellow's standing there...."

"How'd he get in?" Greta said.

"Oh, I don't know, through a window or something. Well, I can't very well 20 get out of the bathtub, the bathroom's too small and besides he's blocking the doorway, so I just lie there, and he starts to very slowly take his own clothes off, and then he gets into the bathtub with me."

"Don't you scream or anything?" said Darlene. She'd come back with her cup of coffee, she was getting really interested. "I'd scream like bloody murder."

"Who'd hear me?" Chrissy said. "Besides, all the articles say it's better not to resist, that way you don't get hurt."

"Anyway you might get bubbles up your nose," I said, "from the deep breathing," and I swear all four of them looked at me like I was in bad taste, like I'd insulted the Virgin Mary or something. I mean, I don't see what's wrong with a little joke now and then. Life's too short, right?

"Listen," I said, "those aren't rape fantasies. I mean, you aren't getting raped, it's just some guy you haven't met formally who happens to be more attractive than Derek Cummins"—he's the Assistant Manager, he wears elevator shoes or at any rate they have these thick soles and he has this funny way of talking, we call him Derek Duck—" and you have a good time. Rape is when they've got a knife or something and you don't want to."

"So what about you, Estelle," Chrissy said, she was miffed because I laughed at her fantasy, she thought I was putting her down. Sondra was miffed too, by this time she'd finished her celery and she wanted to tell about hers, but she hadn't got in fast enough.

"All right, let me tell you one," I said. "I'm walking down this dark street at night and this fellow comes up and grabs my arm. Now it so happens that I have a plastic lemon in my purse, you know how it always says you should carry a plastic lemon in your purse? I don't really do it, I tried it once but the darn thing leaked all over my chequebook, but in this fantasy I have one, and I say to him, "You're intending to rape me, right?" and he nods, so I open my purse to get the plastic lemon, and I can't find it! My purse is full of all this junk, Kleenex and cigarettes and my change purse and my lipstick and my driver's licence, you know the kind of stuff: so I ask him to hold out his hands, like this, and I pile all this junk into them and down at the bottom there's the plastic lemon, and I can't get the top off. So I hand it to him and he's very obliging, he twists the top off and hands it back to me, and I squirt him in the eye."

I hope you don't think that's too vicious. Come to think of it, it is a bit mean, especially when he was so polite and all.

"That's your rape fantasy?" Chrissy says, "I don't believe it."

"She's a card," Darlene says, she and I are the ones that've been here the longest and she never will forget the time I got drunk at the office party and insisted I was going to dance under the table instead of on top of it, I did a sort of Cossack number[2] but then I hit my head on the bottom of the table—actually it was a desk—when I went to get up, and I knocked myself out cold. She's decided that's the mark of an original mind and she tells everyone new about it and I'm not sure that's fair. Though I did do it.

"I'm being totally honest," I say. I always am and they know it. There's no point in being anything else, is the way Hook at it, and sooner or later the truth will out so you might as well not waste the time, right? "You should hear the one about the Easy-Off Cleaner."

But that was the end of the lunch hour, with one bridge game shot to hell, and the next day we spent most of the time arguing over whether to start a new game or play out the hands we had left over from the day before, so Sondra never did get a chance to tell about her rape fantasy.

It started me thinking though, about my own rape fantasies. Maybe I'm abnormal or something, I mean I have fantasies about handsome strangers coming in through the window too, like Mr. Clean, I wish one would, please god somebody without flat feet and big sweat marks on his shirt, and over five

---

[2] Cossack number: a Ukrainian folk dance movement performed in a squatting position, with much hand clapping.

feet five, believe me being tall is a handicap though it's getting better, tall guys are starting to like someone whose nose reaches higher than their belly button. But if you're being totally honest you can't count those as rape fantasies. In a real rape fantasy, what you should feel is this anxiety, like when you think about your apartment building catching on fire and whether you should use the elevator or the stairs or maybe stick your head under a wet towel, and you try to remember everything you've read about what to do but you can't decide.

For instance, I'm walking along this dark street at night and this short, ugly fellow conies up and grabs my arm, and not only is he ugly, you know, with a sort of puffy nothing face, like those fellows you have to talk to in the bank when your account's overdrawn—of course I don't mean they're all like that—but he's absolutely covered in pimples. So he gets me pinned against the wall, he's short but he's heavy, and he starts to undo himself and the zipper gets stuck. I mean, one of the most significant moments in a girl's life, it's almost like-getting married or having a baby or something, and he sticks the zipper.

So I say, kind of disgusted, "Oh for Chrissake," and he starts to cry. He tells me he's never been able to get anything right in his entire life, and this is the last straw, he's going to go jump off a bridge.

"Look," I say, I feel so sorry for him, in my rape fantasies I always end up feeling sorry for the guy, I mean there has to be something wrong with them, if it was Clint Eastwood[3] it'd be different but worse luck it never is. I was the kind of little girl who buried dead robins, know what I mean? It used to drive my mother nuts, she didn't like me touching them, because of the germs I guess. So I say, "Listen, I know how you feel. You really should do something about those pimples, if you got rid of them you'd be quite good looking, honest; then you wouldn't have to go around doing stuff like this. I had them myself once," I say, to comfort him, but in fact I did, and it ends up I give him the name of my old dermatologist, the one I had in high school, that was back in Leamington,[4] except I used to go to St. Catharine's for the dermatologist. I'm telling you, I was really lonely when I first came here; I thought it was going to be such a big adventure and all, but it's a lot harder to meet people in a city. But I guess it's different for a guy.

Or I'm lying in bed with this terrible cold, my face is all swollen up, my eyes are red and my nose is dripping like a leaky tap, and this fellow comes in through the window and he has a terrible cold too, it's a new kind of flu that's been going around. So he says, "I'b goig do rabe you"—I hope you don't mind me holding my nose like this but that's the way I imagine it—and he lets out this terrific sneeze, which slows him down a bit, also I'm no object of beauty myself, you'd have to be some kind of pervert to want to rape someone with a cold like mine, it'd be like raping a bottle of LePages mucilage the way my nose is running. He's looking wildly around the room, and I realize it's because he doesn't have a piece of Kleenex! "Id's ride here," I say, and I pass him the Kleenex, god knows why he even bothered to get out of bed, you'd think if you were going to go around climbing in windows you'd wait till you were healthier, right? I mean, that takes a certain amount of energy. So I ask him why doesn't he let me fix him a NeoCitran and scotch, that's what I always take, you still have the cold but you don't feel it, so I do and we end up watching the Late Show together. I mean, they aren't all sex maniacs, the rest of the time they must lead a normal life. I figure they enjoy watching the Late Show just like anybody else.

I do have a scarier one though…where the fellow says he's hearing angel voices that're telling him he's got to kill me, you know, you read about things like that all the time in the papers. In this one I'm not in the apartment where I live now, I'm back in my mother's house in Leamington and the fellow's been hiding in the cellar, he grabs my arm when I go downstairs to get ajar of jam and he's got hold of the axe too, out of the garage, that one is really scary. I mean, what do you say to a nut like that?

---

3 Clint Eastwood: born 1930, star of many tough-guy detective and western movies; most famous as "Dirty Harry" (1971).

4 Leamington: in Ontario on the north shore of Lake Erie, southeast of Windsor.

So I start to shake but after a minute I get control of myself and I say, is he sure the angel voices have got the right person, because I hear the same angel voices and they've been telling me for some time that I'm going to give birth to the reincarnation of St. Anne who in turn has the Virgin Mary and right after that comes Jesus Christ and the end of the world, and he wouldn't want to interfere with that, would he? So he gets confused and listens some more, and then he asks for a sign and I show him my vaccination mark, you can see it's sort of an odd-shaped one, it got infected because I scratched the top off, and that does it, he apologizes and climbs out the coal chute[5] again, which is how he got in in the first place, and I say to myself there's some advantage in having been brought up a Catholic even though I haven't been to church since they changed the service into English,[6] it just isn't the same, you might as well be a Protestant. I must write to Mother and tell her to nail up that coal chute, it always has bothered me. Funny, I couldn't tell you at all what this man looks like but I know exactly what kind of shoes he's wearing, because that's the last I see of him, his shoes going up the coal chute, and they're the old-fashioned kind that lace up the ankles, even though he's a young fellow. That's strange, isn't it?

Let me tell you though I really sweat until I see him safely out of there and I go upstairs right away and make myself a cup of tea. I don't think about that one much. My mother always said you shouldn't dwell on unpleasant things and I generally agree with that, I mean, dwelling on them doesn't make them go away. Though not dwelling on them doesn't make them go away either, when you come to think of it.

Sometimes I have these short ones where the fellow grabs my arm but I'm really a Kung-Fu[7] expert, can you believe it, in real life I'm sure it would just be a conk on the head and that's that, like getting your tonsils out, you'd wake up and it would be all over except for the sore places, and you'd be lucky if your neck wasn't broken or something, I could never even hit the volleyball in gym and a volleyball is fairly large, you know?—and I just go zap with my fingers into his eyes and that's it, he falls over, or I flip him against a wall or something. But I could never really stick my fingers in anyone's eyes, could you? It would feel like hot jello and I don't even like cold jello, just thinking about it gives me the creeps. I feel a bit guilty about that one, I mean how would you like walking around knowing someone's been blinded for life because of you?

But maybe it's different for a guy.

The most touching one I have is when the fellow grabs my arm and I say, sad and kind of dignified, "You'd be raping a corpse." That pulls him up short and I explain that I've just found out I have leukaemia and the doctors have only given me a few months to live. That's why I'm out pacing the streets alone at night, I need to think, you know, come to terms with myself. I don't really have leukaemia but in the fantasy I do, I guess I chose that particular disease because a girl in my grade four class died of it, the whole class sent her flowers when she was in the hospital. I didn't understand then that she was going to die and I wanted to have leukaemia too so I could get flowers. Kids are funny, aren't they? Well, it turns out that he has leukaemia himself, and he only has a few months to live, that's why he's going around raping people, he's very bitter because he's so young and his life is being taken from him before he's really lived it. So we walk along gently under the street lights, it's spring and sort of misty, and we end up going for coffee, we're happy we've found the only other person in the world who can understand what we're going through, it's almost like fate, and after a while we just sort of look at each other and our hands touch, and he comes back with me and moves into my apartment and we spend our last months together before we die, we just sort of don't wake up in the morning, though I've never decided which one of us gets to die first. If it's him I have to go on

---

5 coal chute: trough for delivering coal from a truck into a basement coal bin. Estelle's remark indicates that the chute was not fastened over the opening to the bin, thus permitting an illegal entry.

6 into English: In accord with the Second Vatican Council (1962–1965), the Latin Mass was replaced by vernacular languages in the late 1960s.

7 Kung-Fu: elaborate self-defense system developed in China, similar to Karate.

and fantasize about the funeral, if it's me I don't have to worry about that, so it just about depends on how tired I am at the time. You may not believe this but sometimes I even start crying. I cry at the end of movies, even the ones that aren't all that sad, so I guess it's the same thing. My mother's like that too.

The funny thing about these fantasies is that the man is always someone I don't know, and the statistics in the magazines, well, most of them anyway, they say it's often someone you do know, at least a little bit, like your boss or something—I mean, it wouldn't be my boss, he's over sixty and I'm sure he couldn't rape his way out of a paper bag, poor old thing, but it might be someone like Derek Duck, in his elevator shoes, perish the thought—or someone you just met, who invites you up for a drink, it's getting so you can hardly be sociable any more, and how are you supposed to meet people if you can't trust them even that basic amount? You can't spend your whole life in the Filing Department or cooped up in your own apartment with all the doors and windows locked and the shades down. I'm not what you would call a drinker but I like to go out now and then for a drink or two in a nice place, even if I am by myself, I'm with Women's Lib on that even though I can't agree with a lot of the other things they say. Like here for instance, the waiters all know me and if anyone, you know, bothers me…I don't know why I'm telling you all this, except I think it helps you get to know a person, especially at first, hearing some of the things they think about. At work they call me the office worry wart, but it isn't so much like worrying, it's more like figuring out what you should do in an emergency, like I said before.

Anyway, another thing about it is that there's a lot of conversation, in fact I spend most of my time, in the fantasy that is, wondering what I'm going to say and what he's going to say, I think it would be better if you could get a conversation going. Like, how could a fellow do that to a person he's just had a long conversation with, once you let them know you're human, you have a life too, I don't see how they could go ahead with it, right? I mean, I know it happens but I just don't understand it, that's the part I really don't understand.

The Crevasse

Bernardo Atxaga

THE SHADOW of death passed over Camp One, when Sherpa Tamng arrived with the news that Philippe Auguste Bloy had fallen down a crevasse. The usual bustle and laughter of supper ceased abruptly and cups of tea, still steaming, were left forgotten in the snow. Not one of the expedition members dared ask f details, no one said anything. Fearing they had not understood him, the Sherpa repeated the news. The ice had swallowed up Philippe Auguste, the crevasse seemed very d e e p.

At last the man who was leading the expedition asked: 'Couldn't you have got him out, Tamng?' The man's name was Mathias Reimz, a native of Geneva, a man who merited an entry into every encyclopaedia on mountaineering for his ascent of Dhaugaliri.

The sherpa shook his head.

Bernardo Atxaga, "The Crevasse," *Obabakoak: Stories from a Village*. Copyright © 1992 by Random House UK. Reprinted with permission.

'*Chiiso*, Mister Reimz. Almost night,' he said.

It was a weighty enough reason As soon as night fell, the cold—*chiiso*—was intense, the temperature around Lhotse could drop to forty below zero, a temperature that could in itself prove fatal to a climber but which also destabilised the great slabs of ice on the mountain. At night new crevasses opened up whilst other older ones closed over for ever. Rescue was almost impossible.

'What did you leave as a marker, Tamng?'

Turning round, the sherpa showed his back. The missing rucksack in red nylon was the marker, securely fixed at the top of the crevasse with pitons.

'Was he alive?'

'Don't know, Mister Reimz.'

Everyone assumed that the sole aim of these questions was to begin preparations for the rescue party that would leave at first light the following day. To their surprise, Mathias Reimz began clipping on his crampons and calling for a torch and some ropes. The man from Geneva intended setting out immediately.

'*Lemu mindu!*' shouted the old sherpa making gestures of surprise. He did not approve of that decision, which seemed to him suicidal.

'The moon will help me, Gyalzen,' replied Reimz looking up at the sky. The moon was nearly full. Its light illuminated the newly fallen snow, making it seem even paler.

Then, addressing his companions, he declared that he would not accept anyone's help. **He** would go completely alone. He was the one who should risk his life, it.was his duty.

Mathias Reimz and Philippe Auguste Bloy worked together at the ski resorts around Geneva and that was how the Europeans on the expedition understood the decision, as the result of the close ties formed, during their long acquaintance. Less well-informed, the sherpas attributed it to his position as leader, as the man responsible for the group.

When the orange shadow of Reimz's anorak disappeared into the snow and the night, a murmur of admiration arose in Camp One. It was an admirable thing to do, to put one's own life at risk to save that of another. Some spoke of the power of friendship and the heart, others, of the spirit shown by mountaineers, their daring and their sense of solidarity. Old Gyalzen waved his white prayer shawl in the air: may good fortune go with him, may great Vishnu protect him.

No one suspected the truth. It occurred to no one that the decision might have its roots in hatred.

Philippe Auguste Bloy's broken leg ached as did the deep cut he had sustained in one side. But even so he was falling asleep; the drowsiness brought on by the cold in the crevasse was stronger than pain, stronger thajn his will. He couldn't keep his eyes open. He could already feel the warmth that always precedes the gentle death of mountaineers.

He was lying down on the ice, absorbed in his private struggle, trying to distinguish the darkness of the crevasse from the darkness of sleep, and so he failed to notice the ropes thrown from above when they landed on his boots. Nor did he see the man who, having lowered himself down on them, was now kneeling beside him.

When the man shone the torch on him, Philippe Auguste Bloy sat up with a shout. The light had startled him.

Then he exclaimed: 'Don't shine the torch in my face, Tamng!' and smiled at his reaction. He felt safe.

He heard someone say: 'It's me, Mathias.' The voice sounded threatening.

Philippe Auguste tilted his head to one side to avoid the glare of the torch. But the beam followed his movement and continued to dazzle him.

'Why have you come?' he asked at last.

The deep voice of Mathias Reimz echoed **round** the crevasse. He spoke very slowly, like a man who is very tired.

'I want to talk to you as a friend, Phil. And what I have to tell you may seem ridiculous. But don't laugh. Consider that before you is a man who has suffered greatly.'

Philippe Auguste put himself on guard. Behind that statement he heard the hiss of the serpent.

'Vera and I first met when we were very young,' Mathias went on. 'We must have been about fifteen; in fact, she was fifteen and I was sixteen. And she wasn't a pretty girl then. She was even rather ugly.

Too tall for her age and very bony. But despite that I fell in love with her the moment I saw her. I remember I felt like crying and for a moment everything seemed bathed in violet light. That will seem odd to you, but it's true, I saw everything that colour. The sky was violet, the mountains were violet, and the rain was violet too. I don't know, maybe falling in love changes the sensitivity of the eyes. And now it's almost the same. The feelings I had when I was sixteen are still there. They didn't even disappear when we got married and you know what they say about marriage putting an end to love. Well, not in my case. I'm still in love with her, I carry her always in my heart. And that's how I managed to climb Dhaugaliri, because I was thinking about her, that's the only reason.'

The silence that followed his words emphasised the solitude of the crevasse.

'We've never been to bed together, Math!' Philippe Auguste shouted suddenly. His words resounded round the four frozen walls.

Mathias gave a short laugh.

'I almost went crazy when they showed me your photos, Phil. Vera and you holding hands at the Ambassador Hotel in Munich on the sixteenth and seventeenth of March. Or at the Tivoli in Zurich on the tenth and eleventh of April. Or in Apartments Trummer in Geneva itself on the twelfth, thirteenth and fourteenth of May. And at Lake Villiers in Lausanne, for a whole week, just when I was preparing for this expedition.'

Philippe Auguste's mouth went dry. The muscles in his face, grown stiff with cold, twitched.

'Math!' he cried, 'you're making too much out of things that have no importance whatsoever.'

But no one heard him. The single eye of the torah was staring pitilessly at him.

'I've had many doubts, Phil. I'm not a murderer. I felt really bad every time I thought about killing you. I was on the point of trying it in Kathmandu. And when we landed in Lukla. But those places are sacred to me, Phil, and I didn't want to stain them with your blood. Now, though, the Mountain has judged you for me, and that's why you're here, because it has handed down its own sentence to you.

Whether it will take away your life, I don't know. You may live until morning and the rest of the group will rescue you. But I don't think so, Phil. I have the feeling you're going to stay in this crevasse for ever. That's why I came, so that you wouldn't leave this world without knowing how much I hate you.'

'Get me out of here, Math!' Philippe Auguste's bottom lip was trembling.

'It's not up to me, Phil. As I said, the Mountain will decide.'

Philippe Auguste breathed deeply. He had to accept his fate.

His voice filled with scorn.

'You think you're better than everyone else, Math. An exemplary mountaineer, an exemplary husband, an exemplary friend. But you're nothing but a pathetic clown. No one who really knows you can stand you!'

Too late. Mathias Reimz was already pulling himself up on the ropes.

'Vera will cry for me! She wouldn't for you!' shouted Philippe Auguste as loudly as he could.

The crevasse was plunged into darkness once more.

The excitement of the visit roused Philippe Auguste's body. His heart beat strongly now and the blood that had been about to freeze in his veins flowed easily into his muscles. Suddenly, perhaps because his brain was also working better, he remembered that mountaineers never take with them the ropes they use to descend into crevasses. They were a dead weight, an unnecessary burden on the journey back to camp.

'What if Mathias …,' he thought. He was gripped by hope. He got up and felt around in the dark. It was only a moment but **so** intense that it made him laugh out loud with joy. There were the three ropes which, by force of habit, Mathias Reimz had left behind him.

Philippe Auguste's wounds made him groan with pain, but he knew that **a** greater suffering, the worst of all, awaited him at the bottom of the crevasse. Tightening his lips against the pain, Philippe Auguste took hold of the ropes and began to climb, slowly, trying not to bump against the frozen walls.

He used the narrower places to rest, forming a bridge with his back and his good leg. An hour later, he had managed to climb the first ten yards.

When he had climbed some eighteen yards, an avalanche of snow threw him off balance crushing him against a hard lump on the wall. Philippe Auguste felt the blow on the same side he had the cut and the pain filled his eyes with tears. For a moment he thought of the gentle death awaiting him at the bottom of the crevasse. But hope was still there in his heart and it whispered a 'perhaps' to him that he could not ignore. After all, he was lucky. Fate had given him a chance. He had no right to doubt it. Besides, the fall of snow indicated that the mouth of the crevasse must be very near.

Half an hour later, the walls of the crevasse became first grey then white. Philippe Auguste considered that, in throwing him against the wall, Fate had wanted to put him to the test, and that this, at last, was his reward.

'The sky!' he gasped. And it was indeed the rosy sky of dawn. A new day was breaking over **Nepal.**

The sun was shining on the snow. Ahead of him, towards the north, rose **the** mighty form of Lhotse. To his right, across the frozen valley, **was** the zigzagging path down to Camp One.

Philippe Auguste felt his lungs revive as he breathed in the clean air of morning. He opened his arms to the vastness and, raising his eyes to the blue sky, mumbled a few **words** of thanks to the Mountain.

He was still in that position when a strange feeling troubled him. It seemed to him that the arms he had stretched out had bent again, against **his** will, and were embracing him. But who was embracing him?

He looked down to see what was happening and a grimace of terror contorted his face. Mathias Reimz stood in front o fhim. He was smiling mockingly.

'It's not nice to cheat, Phil,' **he** heard him say just before he felt the shove. And, for an instant, as he fell towards the bottom of the crevasse, Philippe Auguste Bloy thought he understood the meaning of those last hours of his life.

Everything—the visit, leaving behind the ropes—had been a premeditated plan of torture: Mathias Reimz had not even wanted to spare him the pain of unfounded hope.